D0530866

THEORIES OF EDUCATION
STUDIES OF SIGNIFICANT INNOVATION IN WESTERN EDUCATIONAL ∘THOUGHT∘

SECOND EDITION

JAMES BOWEN
University of New England

PETER R. HOBSON
University of New England

CLARE COUNTY LIBRARY
WITHDRAWN FROM STOCK

John Wiley & Sons
BRISBANE   NEW YORK   CHICHESTER
TORONTO   SINGAPORE   WEINHEIM

First published 1974 by
JACARANDA WILEY LTD
33 Park Road, Milton, Qld 4064

Offices also in Sydney and Melbourne

Typeset in 10/11 pt Baskerville

Second edition 1987

© Jacaranda Wiley Ltd 1974, 1987

National Library of Australia
Cataloguing-in-Publication data

Bowen, James, 1928–
    Theories of education.

    2nd ed.
    Bibliography.
    ISBN 0 471 33420 0.

    1. Education — Philosophy. 2. Education. I. Hobson,
Peter R. (Peter Ross). II. Title.

370'.1

All rights reserved. No part of this publication
may be reproduced, stored in a retrieval system,
or transmitted in any form or by any means,
electronic, mechanical, photocopying, recording,
or otherwise, without the prior permission of
the publisher.

Printed in Singapore

10 9 8 7 6

Contents

PART II VARIATIONS ON THE DEBATE

SOME RECENT INNOVATIONS

PART III THE DEBATE CONTINUES

PROSPECTS FOR THE FUTURE

Preface to the First Edition

This book aims to provide an introduction to philosophy of education and to educational theory in general for the beginning student who has had no previous training in philosophy. Such students often have trouble in coming to grips with courses in educational theory which rely purely on a philosophical treatment of the issues, either through the examination of systematic philosophical theories and their relevance (if any) for education, or through the application of the techniques of contemporary philosophical analysis to educational questions. For those students who are taking philosophy of education as only one component in their educational studies, there is generally not sufficient time to acquire the necessary expertise in philosophical thinking to enable them to gain the full benefit of such courses.

We try to avoid this problem by making educational *thought* rather than educational *philosophy* the focus of attention, while at the same time covering the major philosophical viewpoints concerning education. Under the heading "educational thought" we include all general and systematic approaches to the aims, methods and content of education, whether these come from philosophers, psychologists, sociologists or actual practising teachers. "Education" itself we take in its broadest sense, covering all deliberate attempts to shape or transform man and society.

From our experience with teaching large numbers of students in introductory courses in philosophy and theory of education over the past few years, we have found one very useful way to simplify and systematise the vast body of thought about education. This is to present it in terms of a continuing historical debate. Such an approach enables us to highlight the fact that educational theory is never static, that it is constantly evolving and changing in response to our efforts to understand the process itself and to adequately meet the problems it presents. This in turn obliges us to take into account the continuity of education and the fact that, at any particular moment, current practices and beliefs are often carried forward from the past.

To further simplify this complex field we have introduced the concept of "significant innovation". The rationale behind this is set out in the Introduction which follows, but we may briefly point out here that this book presents what we regard as nine major significant innovations in Western educational thought, structured according to their position in the fundamental educational debate between traditionalists and progressives. Part I gives the four classic figures covering both sides of the debate up to the twentieth century. Part II provides five modern variations and reactions to the two basic positions. At this stage in the continuing development of educational thought we cannot say which of these five thinkers will become classics in the same way as those in Part I. Only time will tell, but in the meantime their theories are presented here as some of the most significant innovations in Western educational thought produced since the publication of John Dewey's *Democracy and Education* in 1916.

We recognise that our concept of significant innovation itself may create a degree of controversy; certainly some will disagree over the choice of the particular thinkers selected. It is of course possible to make out quite strong cases for the inclusion of other thinkers. For example, Augustine and Aquinas in the Christian millennium were very important educational thinkers, but in terms of the basic educational debate between traditionalists and progressives, we believe that their innovations were not as significant as those of the particular theorists selected in Part I. Similarly, contemporary radical viewpoints on education could have been represented by Paul Goodman or Paulo Freire, but we consider that the idea of deschooling society is the most significant contemporary radical contribution to educational thought in the broad sense considered here, and that Illich has been the most explicit and influential exponent of this viewpoint. Nonetheless, if the discussion of the adequacy of the criterion of significant innovation develops, and the thinkers illustrated here are compared against others, some of the purposes of this text will already have been met. For we hope that students of education will come to see that its philosophy is an essential element which must constantly be examined, debated and assessed if we wish to understand and continue to improve the practice of education itself.

As this book is written for beginning students in the subject, we have included along with each set of readings a stimulative and explanatory commentary, sufficiently detailed, we believe, to lead the student into an interested and informed reading of the thinker represented. These commentaries also aim to highlight the contemporary relevance of each thinker's ideas and to raise questions designed to provoke the student's own thinking on the basic educational issues facing the world today. A detailed index has been provided so that the reader will be able to locate easily the various discussions of fundamental educational problems as they occur throughout the book.

This work has been a conjoint venture throughout and both authors have shared responsibility, although at the same time each has brought his own particular emphases to bear: James Bowen is primarily an historian of educational ideas; Peter Hobson is primarily an analytic philosopher of education. For the reader who is concerned to distinguish the individual contributions, James Bowen did the major part of the writing of the Introduction and wrote the commentaries on Plato, Dewey, Makarenko, Neill and Illich; Peter Hobson did the bulk of the work in selecting the readings and organising the overall structure of the book, and wrote the commentaries on Aristotle, Rousseau, Peters and Skinner.

Finally, we would expressly like to thank the publishers for their support and encouragement, particularly William Douglas and Carol Buck, and for the invaluable assistance of our wives, respectively, Margarita and Roswitha.

University of New England   J.B.
Armidale, New South Wales   P.R.H.
January, 1974

Preface to the Second Edition

It is now twelve years since the first edition of this book appeared in 1974. That was a time of considerable ferment in education which had been going on for a decade against the background of the Vietnam War and student protest movements, the violence of the Cultural Revolution in China, heightened tensions resulting from international confrontation and the arms race, the rapid increase in world population, pressures on resources and threats to the safety of the environment. In education it was a time of rapidly growing school, college and university enrolments, of rising expectations by all of the population, accompanied by an urgent need to improve the quality of public education.

The past decade, however, has seen major changes in the world scene which have exercised a profound influence upon education. In 1974–75 came a profound downturn in the world economy leading to a widespread, and continuing economic recession. This was accompanied, in Western industrial nations, by a new political and economic conservatism, and, given the rapidly falling infant populations, a reduced demand for teachers. At the same time there came a demand for higher quality in the teaching profession. So arose the question: does this text have continuing relevance? Information from students and lecturers, and a sustained demand for new printings has convinced us that it continues to meet an important need. Yet we have not felt justified in offering simply another reprinting; careful revision is obviously required. We remain convinced that the original format of the study of major educational theorists, in terms of the concept of significant innovation, is sound, and we see no reason to change the nine persons selected. Regardless of current events, Plato and Aristotle are still the twin foundations on which the traditional model of education has been built; Rousseau and Dewey remain the two great historical innovators of progressive thinking in education. The theories of Makarenko, Skinner, Neill, Peters and Illich, although giving rise to a good deal of controversy, continue to be distinctive and significant contributions to the debate about the nature and aims of education.

There have been developments, however, in the thinking of two of these theorists since 1974. R. S. Peters was the most articulate and widely-known representative of the liberal-analytic approach to philosophy of education, which exercised a profound influence in the period of the mid-sixties to the late seventies, and no other like-minded theorist has really surpassed him. He has continued to refine his thought and to moderate it to accommodate changing social developments as well as to respond to criticisms from other theorists. Ivan Illich has lessened his specific demands for "deschooling" but has developed a broader range of social criticisms, still reflecting a similar anti-institutional, anti-authoritarian viewpoint. Meanwhile the thought of his one-time colleague, Paulo Freire, has become more educationally conspicuous. Illich's educational position, none the less, remains stimulating and highly distinctive, and continues to provide a provocative challenge to our conception of the role of school in society.

The nine thinkers originally covered thus continue to provide a firm basis for grappling with the educational issues of the 1980s and beyond. We have, however, attempted to deal with the new trends in education and society by modifying the original text with careful editing, and by the addition of a new final chapter, which appears as Part III of the present edition. In that new section, we present an outline of major developments in Western educational thought over the past decade, taking account of the social context in which such developments occurred; Peters and Illich are brought up-to-date, and the new significance of Freire is discussed. We examine, moreover, the current position of traditional theory in its various manifestations, as well as emerging theories advanced by challenging radicals, Marxists, and Humanistic thinkers. We maintain the term "Western" in the title of the book, using it in its wider cultural sense, rather than its more narrow political sense, as pointed out in the Introduction.

In preparing this new edition we have attempted to revise the commentaries in non-sexist language wherever possible. In order to avoid fatuous periphrasis we have kept "man" as a generic term and the associated pronouns when used in the same context, of "he", "him" and "his", since it sometimes distorts meaning to resort to plurals or passives. At the same time, there are places where we have kept the sexist language which the theorists under discussion employed as giving a more faithful reflection of their style of thought. This has been particularly so in the case of Aristotle, Rousseau, Makarenko, Skinner and Peters.

A valuable feature of this edition will be found in the completely revised, extensive and up-to-date bibliographies of all the thinkers previously covered, which includes relevant new works written by them (included in the Select Bibliographies at the end of the appropriate chapter) as well as new material written about them (included in the new General Bibliography at the end of Part II). There is also a detailed bibliography attached to the new chapter covering the various positions and thinkers discussed there.

As in all such enterprises, many persons have assisted us in our work, and we are particularly grateful to colleagues in other institutions as well as to our students over the past twelve years, for many helpful comments and suggestions. It is a pleasure to acknowledge the assistance of Max Lawson and Anthony Welch in our own Centre for Social & Cultural Studies in Education, and of John Barrie of the Northern Rivers C.A.E., Lismore, in commenting upon the final chapter. In particular we have benefited considerably from the thorough knowledge of Tom Moore in the area of developments in Humanistic and psychologically-grounded educational theory, and to him we extend our deep appreciation. We also owe a considerable debt of gratitude to Dianne Hill who has been unfailingly supportive and exact in the preparation of this script. We welcome, moreover, continuing suggestions from our many colleagues and students.

University of New England   J.B.
Armidale, New South Wales   P.R.H.
January, 1986

Introduction

The Concept of Education

The concept of education is difficult to define since the word "education" is used in so many ways. In its most common use it is synonymous with schooling, and brings to mind the whole range of activities that takes place in kindergartens, schools, colleges, institutes and universities. Its meaning in this sense is very loose, for it can designate learnings of almost every kind, from those of specific instrumental skills, usually linked with the attainment of vocational competency, through to the most abstract and symbolic forms of knowledge, which have little apparent practical application and are acquired for their own intrinsic value. Again, in this context, education can also refer to the actual behaviour of the students in the school quite apart from the content of instruction; we can talk of education being the acquisition of attitudes, beliefs and values learned by participation in the general social life of the school.

Yet this is only part of the concept. We also speak of life itself as being educational, and in this sense we usually have in mind the idea that if schoolroom activities are educational, then there are many similar ones taking place outside the school that have the same kind of influence on us. Again, however, the same sorts of ideas are present; life in the wider social environment outside the school has a "hidden" curriculum of knowledge, attitudes and skills to be learned, and there is usually pressure upon us to acquire them so that we are able to participate effectively in the social life of the community. Education in this sense, then, designates the broader process whereby we come to accept the goals and values of our society. And for this reason, we can talk of education being a lifelong process. We do not care to restrict the term to the activities of school-type institutions, and indeed to make a distinction here we often refer to the process of schooling as "formal" education, and to that in the wider community as "informal". This latter designation has been applied because the influence of the wider community usually comes through direct encounters with specific situations that occur more or less randomly, and not in a fixed, planned sequence as schooling usually does. Yet these two areas are not mutually exclusive and it is also true that socialisation proceeds within the school as well as outside it.

So far, then, we can say that the term "education" designates that basic social process whereby individuals acquire the culture of their society; we call this the process of socialisation. Now all societies do this, but they set about it in different ways, and it is this that is largely responsible for variations in culture. Some societies rest content at the point, so that education is more or less limited to the process of socialisation acquired through both formal and informal means. Yet this does not exhaust the meaning of the term, for if education is equivalent to socialisation it is a wholly conservative activity. In the intellectual history of our own society (known generically as the West because of its origins in western Europe following the fall of the Roman Empire), this conception has always been criticised because of its narrowness, and attacked because it provides no wider goals for man. Indeed, Western civilisation has developed a third level of meaning for the term education that accepts the processes of formal and informal education just outlined as two necessary aspects but goes on to suggest a higher and more ideal kind of attainment.

No society can be absolutely conservative and maintain education as a purely socialising activity; some degree of adaptability to varying circumstances must occur if it is to survive. So we can distinguish two necessary aspects to any culture: conservation and creativity. When we speak of a static or primitive society we mean one in which conservative practices predominate, while creative ones are kept at a minimum and are adopted only with difficulty. By contrast, one of the important characteristics of advanced societies is a concern to provide for creativity and change and the recognition of the ideal of humanity in itself and of human potential for excellence, independent of social pressures. Western society, in particular, has always taken pride in its concern with creativity and its particular intellectual history is one of continued searching for challenges and of attempts to conquer them. This has given rise to the ideal of the life of intellectual adventure, and our civilisation places a very high value on people who are able to produce new ideas, new conceptions, innovations of every kind. If these can be translated into practical applications which appear to benefit society, so much the better. Not, of course, that all individuals in Western civilisation have been involved in this process of creative endeavour. On the contrary, it has been maintained by a small minority, and the majority has had no significant participation. So we come to the concept of education as one of heightened awareness and intellectual curiosity concerning everything that takes place on earth, and the quest to satisfy this curiosity. Through education in this sense, man can get beyond the limitations of conservative practices to creative thought and action; the concept of education is enlarged from one of socialisation to one that includes the idea of transcendence. By this we mean that education in its most ideal sense provides us with a wider vision, one that transcends the restrictive boundaries of our own particular society. This process is really independent of institutions, yet it has always been regarded as the highest goal of the school, in the generic sense, and in fact from the time of the ancient Greeks to the present day efforts have been made to attain this goal through the formal process of education.

Now although there has always been a general agreement on education as encompassing a range of activities from simple skills to the highest forms of intellectual vision, there has not been agreement on how these activities should be pursued. On the contrary, in the history of Western education there has been constant argument about the content of education, about who should be educated, and about how this education should be conducted. Throughout most of this history, education has been pursued in this threefold way: the majority of the people have been illiterate and unschooled and their education has been of the informal, direct, community-learning kind; a minority has had superimposed upon this some degree of formal schooling; and a miniscule number has achieved the highest flights of the intellect. Quite a literature has been written to justify all of this, chiefly on the grounds that it accords with the purposes of nature. But it has not been universally accepted and in recent times, because the advent of industrial democracy has made it possible, the school has been extended to ever-increasing proportions of the population.

At present we have reached the point where in most Western societies education in the sense of schooling has been in the ascendant and from an early age children are enrolled in schools — whether they like it or not — and attempts made to stimulate their minds. They are taught to read, write and reckon, they are given some kinds of vocational training and, if they are judged sufficiently able, their mental boundaries are enlarged through an introduction to the human experience in literature and history, the current ongoing range of human activities via such social studies as geography and economics, and to man's efforts to change present conditions through the experimental method of the laboratory sciences.

At the same time, there has been a tremendous movement to formalise and institutionalise many kinds of learning that previously occurred in community contexts. Consider, for example, the way in which, by public demand, we are currently developing formal programmes that run the entire spectrum of a person's life: infant care, preschooling, outdoor activities, driver training, sports training, sex instruction, drug counselling, pregnancy and mothercraft courses, marriage guidance, adult education and continuing right through to the worthy use of geriatric leisure. And this is not restricted to the able; the infirm and handicapped suffering from nearly every kind of disability are increasingly being involved in various programmes of "special" education. We are relentlessly institutionalising most of the learnings required of us in life.

Crisis in Education: Historical Background

This world-wide movement towards a mass, public, institutionalised education is now creating a virtual crisis situation, and as a first step towards understanding this crisis it is necessary to look briefly at the main historical features of its development. We begin with the striking fact that Western civilisation up to the time of Rousseau in the eighteenth century had developed only one fundamental conception of the process of education, although there were inner variations. This conception was first set out by the Greeks, gained almost total acceptance in the ancient world and, despite the opposed theories of Rousseau, Dewey and other progressives from the eighteenth century onwards, has remained the pre-eminent model of educational practice right down to the present day.

It was the ancient Greeks who developed the notion that the only activities worthy of the name of education are those that enable us to transcend the limitations of time and space imposed by our finiteness; the limitations, that is, of a biological basis that tie us to a particular moment and place in which to live our lives. Man, conceived in the generic sense, has the capacity to make this transcendence through a properly organised set of experiences, and the Greek position was that these should be concerned firstly with heightening sensitivity to, and facility in, language (both speech and writing); and, secondly, through this instrumentality, with exploring the realm of the timeless and placeless; that is, the realm of ideas. Following the persuasive arguments of Pythagoras, and then Plato, these experiences were generally believed to be best expressed in mathematical form, and it is significant to note that the early Greek word for knowledge, *mathesis,* later became restricted to mathematics alone. Because they were held to be the means by which we can be liberated from our limitations, these studies, based on language and mathematics, were therefore called the liberal arts, and this distinguished them from the "illiberal" crafts, which were the customary activities of menial workers.

In the early Christian centuries this approach to education lent itself admirably to a religious view of life because the whole purpose of transcendence into the realm of ideas is to reach their ultimate form in a single overarching unity, a concept that already existed in Greek philosophy as the *"arché"* and that Christians very readily identified with their own concept of God. Not that this composite philosophy was quickly or simply achieved; on the contrary, the way in which the accommodation between the Greek and Christian views became worked out had a complex and tortuous history. However it remains true that down through the past two thousand years some version or other of this original Greek view has constituted the dominant theme of acceptable education. It has of course had periods of changing emphasis; but whether it be that intended by Charlemagne in the late eighth century (to make Europe a reborn empire of Christ), or that of both Erasmus and Luther in the sixteenth century (to make education, through the study of pious literature, the vehicle for reaching God), the view has always been evident. So, as late as the nineteenth century, the study of the classical liberal arts through the sequence of elementary or preparatory school, grammar school, and the arts faculty of the university remained dominant, and any other approach to education struggled for existence, much less for acceptance.

This attitude is easily illustrated by contrasting it with that towards vocational preparation, at whatever level. We are never deeply troubled about what "being educated" means in a practical context; one is educated if one is fit to meet the needs of daily life. So, in ordinary speech we have no difficulty in understanding what is meant by "physical education", "sex education", "driver education", "technical education", "vocational education", "education for leisure" and the like. And we are never under any illusions that our meaning is global; on the contrary, our understanding accepts implicitly the limitations of the relevant range of operations.

Our difficulties come from the nagging awareness that these are limited goals that fall short of a grander and nobler ideal of education. The Greek notion that genuine education is wholly disinterested and autonomous, for example, survives fully in our concept of the truly educated person. Implanted firmly in us all is the belief that each of us has an unfulfilled "potential" and that only "genuine" or "true" education will ever develop this. Although we may try to ignore the intuition, we suspect that inside each of us is the void of unrealised excellence. We always set the simpler descriptive definitions of education against a wider frame of reference; we are aware that these operational definitions are partial, transitory and derive from a greater concept that is ultimate and universal. "Of course he's a clever engineer (or doctor, or whatever), but he's certainly not an educated person". How often have we heard or used such a phrase to refer, not only to engineers or doctors, but to any occupation or activity we care to consider?

At the same time the West has only really developed one institutional model for education, the school with a corresponding rather narrow range of teaching procedures or "methods". To the ancient Greeks, the word "school" (*scholé*) meant leisure or recreation, and was used by them to describe those groups of leisured thinkers who gathered to pursue their "mathematical" (the term was later supplanted by the Pythagorean coinage of "philosophical") enquiries into the nature of universal ideas. But schools very quickly came to be formalised and conducted according to rigid routines, and down through the centuries we can trace this process in relentless operation. The early Greeks sat the pupil on a bench with tablet on lap and writing stylus in hand; the Hellenistic Greeks formalised the chanting of multiplication tables and paradigms of verbs; the Romans added the method of question-and-answer teaching by recital. By the fifteenth century paper notebooks and the necessary correlative of the desk appeared; a century later, with the invention of printing, came the uniform textbook for the pupil's own use and, because of it, stricter grading could be employed. So Jacob Sturm in Strassburg developed the nine-grade sequence of instruction and later on in the sixteenth century the Jesuits, who became known as the "school-masters of Europe", extended this theory and practice of education not only throughout the Catholic regions of Europe but carried it later into much of the New World.

The seventeenth, eighteenth, and nineteenth centuries saw a great upsurge of educational improvement, implemented by a tremendous number of enthusiastic reformers of whom Comenius, Rousseau, Pestalozzi, Herbart and Froebel are the outstanding names. In general, however, virtually all of the activity of these centuries continued within the established traditional framework: most of the reformers, with the obvious exception of Rousseau, sought to modify, improve and upgrade existing practices. This reforming period was itself stimulated by the increasing industrialisation and urbanisation of Europe, which required the improvement of the instrumental skills of ever-growing numbers of the population, and it was only natural for the notion of education to be evoked as the relevant process. At first this proved to be adequate, especially since, as transmitted through the ages, it always rested upon a preliminary basis in the elements of literacy: reading, writing and reckoning. So education began to be provided for an increasing percentage of the population and to meet this need the number of "schools" multiplied proportionately. But with this increase, the situation became more complex for, as new needs arose, they were usually rationalised in such a way that they could be met in terms of an organised curriculum taught in conventional schoolrooms. Although the ideology of education as a "liberalising" activity remained dominant, it was misunderstood and often ignored, and as increasing numbers of teachers were trained at minimal expense in the rapidly established, primitive teachers' colleges (often called "normal" schools) to teach the burgeoning school populations, the dissonance between theory and practice became correspondingly greater. By the middle of the twentieth century, more than a quarter of the total populations of advanced societies attended school, and in many ways this institution is still little changed from that which had evolved centuries before, for quite different purposes.

Crisis in Education: The Rhetoric of Concern

The advent of mass education has, at the same time, been responsible for creating a much wider public awareness of the process, and throughout the recent decades of this century there has been a growing public concern that is being expressed increasingly in a need, and a demand, for ever-better provisions. Interest in education in all of its senses has ceased to be an affair of the schoolroom and reflection and writing upon it is no longer restricted to a minority of scholars within the vocation. Particularly over the last decade or so, education has become a world-wide public preoccupation, not only in the advanced technologies but also in the under-developed and developing countries.

Such universal attention has been promoted by a number of factors, all arising from wider provisions of education, and stemming generally from an earlier and almost universal belief in the power of education to advance man's welfare. This belief too has a long history, but it first began to become increasingly evident in the early nineteenth century. Since then it has progressively accelerated to the extent that by the middle of the twentieth century all of the advanced technological societies were enthusiastically engaged in programmes to extend education as widely as possible, while many of the less developed societies (often under the guidance of international agencies) were seeking to introduce such programmes, hoping thereby to reap the same kinds of benefits.

At the same time, this movement has been accompanied by a growing public dissatisfaction — even disenchantment. For it now seems that the promise of universal education is not being fulfilled, and that somehow education as we now have it is quite unsatisfactory. Indeed, the belief is being generated, and is taking hold quite strongly, that the conceptions of education that were held in the nineteenth century, and that many have continued to cling to in the twentieth (and which teachers find themselves involved in mediating) have proved incapable, at least in their traditional forms, of providing an adequate basis for the future. We are now witnessing the appearance of a rhetoric of dissent which argues that the present educational upsurge has been considerable hampered — perhaps even fatally flawed — by the forms of implementation that have been employed; that, paradoxically, as we increase our efforts the educational position becomes correspondingly worsened. We are now challenged to make sense of, and find constructive solutions to, a situation which deteriorates the more we try to improve it.

It is quite obvious that in an increasingly interdependent world in which actions can have very far-reaching consequences, and in which education is being employed in an influential role, the evaluation of educational theories and practices is a mandatory task. And it is becoming all the more pressing because discussion is so often based on a lack of understanding of the issues involved; the literature of education is expanding beyond the realm of informed theory into a highly emotional rhetoric which often contains a great deal of uninformed nonsense. This is a very dangerous situation, for the new rhetoric of radicalism is being taken up uncritically in places as a substitute for serious thinking. In its analysis of the problems of modern education, this new rhetoric argues that it now needs to be secured by new conceptions, transmitted by new practices and implemented in new ways and by new institutions. It calls for a virtual renaissance in all educational thought and practice.

The problem, however, is not seen in precisely this way by all educational thinkers. Its existence is not doubted, it is the method of working towards a solution that is controversial. Granted the world educational crisis, there is a continued belief that it is not to be solved by a wholesale dismantling of the historical structures and procedures, even if that were technically feasible. Solutions can best be achieved by augmenting our theories and practices, not by dramatically, and perhaps rather flamboyantly, discarding them. For, indeed, over the past hundred years or so there has been a responsible and profound recognition of the many problems that the movement to mass education would inevitably generate. Rational investigation is a necessary prior step that must be taken if constructive and creative solutions are to be developed.

The challenge today is to assess the controversy between the conservative, liberal and radical viewpoints: to establish the extent to which education stands in need of change. For we live in an age in which unthinking habit, especially in education, is totally inadequate. At the same time, it is also very important to be aware that it is impossible to teach independently of theory. Even unthinking habit has at least an implicit theoretical basis: each one of us operates according to some assumptions and beliefs, no matter how personally ignorant of them we may be. The task in this critical era of rapid social, intellectual and technological change is to become aware of the bases on which we proceed; to make our own educational thought as explicit as possible, and to expand this into a wider social dialogue.

Role of the Teacher in Modern Education

Centrally involved in all of this are teachers, for upon them devolves the task of implementing whatever form of education we seek to cultivate. Teachers in the modern climate can no longer be unquestioning functionaries; in many ways their task is becoming increasingly difficult. For both the theory and the general literature of education are being added to continually, at an accelerating rate, and we are now confronted with the difficult situation that the more we learn about the process the more demanding becomes the task of assessment and evaluation of competing alternatives. This entails serious consequences. In the first place, it means that the study of education as a fundamental social process is developing into an extremely sophisticated activity, particularly since education is becoming increasingly institutionalised and formalised. And this in turn means that all who participate in the process of education, and particularly those who are responsible for providing leadership — chiefly the teachers, in the wider sense of the word — must attain a high degree of awareness and understanding of the issues involved.

In this context, it is necessary to point out what this wider sense of the teacher is. We usually think of a teacher as a person who stands in front of a class of students, in the formal process, and instructs from a position of social and intellectual authority. This, of course, is only part of the concept, and in this age of rapid transformation of society and the increasing extension and formalisation of the process of education, we would do well to realise that there are a number of ways in which a person can act as a teacher; that is to say, there are many different ways in which teaching, and its correlative of learning, takes place, from the consciously deliberate and formal through to the unintentional and informal. Whenever architects, for example, set out to advise us of the environmental consequences of a given building, and urge us to act in a particular way, then they are acting as teachers. As our society becomes more complex and independent, the vocation of teaching, in whatever style and for whatever purposes, will become more important; and because the narrow model of the classroom instructor is becoming increasingly challenged, and supplanted, it is important for us to be aware of this wider and fuller sense of the term.

Whereas in earlier times it was quite feasible and, indeed, generally common, for teachers simply to teach their pupils what they themselves had been taught and in much the same manner, with little or no awareness of the existence of a wider theoretical framework, this approach is now clearly inappropriate. It is, of course, quite possible to continue to teach in a customary, minimally informed way, but to do so must henceforth indicate a conscious, even wilful, indifference; it is simply not possible for teachers to be unaware that the practices of their vocation are guided by a large body of complex theory. On the contrary, contemporary teachers need much more than the acquisition of a number of techniques along with some body of relevant knowledge. They stand in need of a personal point of view on their function as teachers and the rationale underlying this function. Because of the current questioning of all traditions, beliefs and authorities, today's teachers are obliged to work out for themselves what is important in education and what role it should play in society. Such an exercise is also necessary if teachers are to become more independent and take a greater share in policy decisions about curriculum, methods of teaching, administration of the institution in which they work, and so on. They are, moreover, increasingly being called upon by students, parents, and the wider public to state and defend their basic aims and methods in educating, and to do this adequately they will need to have thought their ideas, beliefs and practices through to their basic philosophical premises. This means, in effect, that today's teachers need to develop their own theory of education.

The Academic Study of Education

In our modern society, teachers themselves certainly have to become highly educated, both with respect to their own personal development and their competence to teach. Their education with respect to the latter is usually undertaken in colleges and universities in the academic study of Education. So we come to yet a fourth meaning of the word "education": when spelled with a capital letter it designates a field of academic enquiry concerned with the study of education in all of the senses already discussed. We usually refer to Education by the metaphor of a "field" in order to make it clear that it is not a discipline in itself but an area of investigation in which other, distinct disciplines converge, of which history, sociology, psychology and measurement are, at present, among the most prominent. Each of these disciplines studies the process of education from its own particular point of view and each has generated a large literature of findings that provide, in effect, special and limited theories of education. But before any kind of intelligent action can proceed, these theories must be brought together into some coherent whole; they must be unified into what we might call a general theory of education. The drawing together of particular theories into a general theory, the assessment of the adequacy of this theory, the evaluation of competing and conflicting views, and the consequent suggestion of the best possible courses of action are the province of the philosophy of education.

It is at this point that the contribution of philosophy to education becomes immediately relevant. For intelligent action issues from disciplined thought, which also must precede any meaningful engagement with the rhetoric of radicalism. This raises an important question: how can the philosophy of education be most fruitfully studied? There is, of course, no single answer, no one correct approach. We must look at individual circumstances. Obviously, each person must make a beginning somewhere, and for most students of education this comes either in academic courses in Education or in teacher preparation programmes.

It is to this class of students that this text is directed: those who come to educational philosophy without any prior acquaintance with philosophy or the history of ideas; that is, without any kind of cognate studies. As explained in the preface, we feel that the best way for such students to begin the study of philosophy of education is by considering some concrete ideas about the aims, content and methods of education, structured in terms of the historical dialectic that has determined the development of educational thought. This gives students some basic material with which to come to grips and which to use as a guide to their own theorising about education. While this approach may perhaps lack some of the philosophical advantages of the analytic method of direct assessment of the concepts and arguments used in philosophising about education, it does seem to serve as a stronger means of arousing interest on the part of the beginning students in the basic educational ideas presented in this book.

At the same time, however, another approach to the further study of these issues would be to explore in more detail the philosophical schools of thought — idealism, realism, pragmatism, logical analysis, for example — underlying these various educational innovations. This could also lead on to the comparison and assessment of these philosophies against other philosophies and the educational theories derived from them.

In a first course in educational philosophy of the type represented in this book it is clearly impossible to examine the entire philosophical tradition: criteria of importance and selection have to be established as a basis from which to proceed. In this text the criteria are contained in the subtitle: Studies of Significant Innovation in Western Educational Thought.

Significant Innovation: An Approach to Educational Theory

In explaining the rationale behind these criteria it is necessary to make clear at the outset the cultural context from which the studies have been selected. Obviously, everything we do on the face of the earth can have some relevance, but, within the constraints of reality, limits have to be set. The studies presented here are drawn exclusively from Western civilisation: the term "West" is used to designate the civilisation of Western Europe, which began with the Athenian Empire of the fourth century B.C., became successively enlarged into the Hellenistic Empire of Alexander and the Roman Empire, and took its final shape in the millennium from the sixth to the sixteenth century A.D. with its political centre in Western Europe. Since then the West has expanded to many regions on the fringes of Europe, including Russia, as well as outside; first into the colonial settlements of the New World and subsequently into the conquered regions of the Third World. In the process of this vigorous — some would say virulent — expansion during the past four hundred years, the West has imposed its forms of education, whether willingly or under compulsion. While there is obviously much that we can and should learn from the cultures of the world's other great historical civilisations, it is considered that a beginning can be best effected through a study of our own culture first. Moreover, to study Western educational thought because of its historical ascendence throughout the world does not imply that we must accept it as necessarily superior; it is simply historical fact that it has been the world's most dominant form. If there has to be a radical reassessment of the continuing efficacy and validity of Western education for the emerging nations — as in the West itself — it can only be done by first examining the problem in its proper historical and cultural context.

A great deal of Western educational thought is not philosophical in the strictest sense of the term; that is, if we take philosophy to refer to a systematic, consistently articulated theory incorporating a metaphysics (theory of the nature of existence), an epistemology (theory of what knowledge is, and how we come to know) and an axiology (theory of what is valuable and good, which is known as ethics when it deals with human behaviour, and aesthetics when it is concerned with the creative arts). Nor is a lot of this thought philosophical according to the criteria of the school of modern philosophical analysis. Indeed, the history of Western education shows that there have been very few fully developed philosophies of education; perhaps only three: those of Plato, Aristotle and Dewey. Rousseau, it is necessary to point out, did not produce an educational philosophy of the same comprehensiveness or complexity as these three, although his ideas were extremely influential. Limited or unsystematic ideas, in fact are often valuable and many important contributions to the corpus of educational theory have been made in this fashion. To appreciate the full range and variety of Western educational theory, therefore, it is necessary to go beyond the few fully developed philosophies to the study of these limited and incomplete ideas. For this reason, the coverage of this text is broader than that of "educational philosophy" strictly defined, and the term "educational thought" is a more apt description of its subject matter.

With these considerations in mind, the task becomes one of establishing further criteria by which Western educational thought can be presented. Again, recognising the need to present and interpret this to students with no necessary background in philosophy or history of ideas, only the most important and influential theories have been selected for this book. Concern with fine detail, with the shades of difference among similar positions and developments of positions, is a more subtle procedure and should properly come later, after the essential features have been apprehended.

Western educational thought had its first definitive statement in the writings of Plato and his sometime student, Aristotle, in the fourth century B.C. Between them they developed the two main alternative versions of the first fundamental theory of Western education; they established its philosophical "position" for which the Greek word is *thesis*. So they represent the focus of the Western educational tradition and it is again a matter of historical fact that for more than two thousand years — in effect down to the eighteenth century — all educational thought consisted of variations and developments of their educational ideas. The first direct challenge, which we can term an *antithesis,* appeared in the writings of Jean-Jacques Rousseau. The second challenge, which brings new meanings to that antithesis, came in the work of John Dewey, early in the twentieth century. Since then the pace of creativity has increased and in recent times there are a number of new interpretations of these historical models, along with various original reactions to them. What appear to be the five most significant of these theories are given in the second part of this book. These are the positions put forward by A. S. Makarenko, B. F. Skinner, A. S. Neill, R. S. Peters and Ivan Illich.

All of these theorists, from Plato and Aristotle right down to the contemporary thinkers, have contributed what we call a "significant innovation" in Western educational thought. By its nature, this concept cannot be defined in precise terms, but a reasonably clear idea of its meaning can be gained from the notion of "significance" being used to designate the intrinsic merit of the idea, the attention that it aroused and its persistence in the intellectual tradition; and "innovation" to designate some form of genuine originality and not merely a restatement of existing ideas.

Obviously there can, and doubtless will, be endless argument about whether these thinkers exhaust all of the possible significant innovations in education. There are many important figures in the development of educational thought that are worthy of deep study (and some of these will be referred to in the commentaries), and other theories of education that perhaps may in themselves be more logically coherent or more comprehensive than some of those presented here. For example, the Christian development of Plato's theories by Augustine, and of Aristotle's by Thomas Aquinas, are of major importance. Likewise the nineteenth-century theories of Herbart, building on a Kantian and Hegelian basis, of Pestalozzi and of Froebel deserve close scrutiny. But the list then becomes large and unmanageable — and again the task becomes one of studying finer distinctions. In indicating the major topography of Western educational thought it is a matter of appeal to the historical record that the thinkers selected here are pre-eminent in terms of significant innovation.

So far as is possible, these theories are presented in chronological order, and for the first four, Plato, Aristotle, Rousseau and Dewey, this poses no problem. The remaining five, all of whom produced their writings in the present century, are arranged in a kind of spectrum according to their theoretical positions. At this point it is necessary to emphasise that this presentation is not meant as a continuous history of educational ideas, valuable as this is in assisting philosophical enquiry. The chronological structure is used to put the ideas of the various thinkers into the most simple of all mental contexts — temporal sequence — and also, more importantly, to show how there has been a dialectic of education in operation through the centuries; to show that educational thought can be seen as emerging from the interplay between thesis and antithesis, and that any assessment of the modern position and planning for the future can be better made through an awareness of this dialectical structure. So, a continuous historical treatment is not of primary concern here, the major aim is to provide a set of studies of the main lines of the development of Western educational thought that will provide students with a sound basis for thinking philosophically about present problems in education, including those in which they are involved. Furthermore, since education raises most general philosophical questions in a practical way, the student will find a wider range of application to society in general from a study of the issues discussed here.

Organisation of Commentaries and Selections

Bearing in mind that philosophical ideas, and particularly those concerning education, arise not from a vacuum but occur as responses to real human issues in historical situations, we have organised the studies presented here in terms of the way in which these responses have appeared. The student can thus gain a greater degree of empathy with the human needs and problems involved, and appreciate how the particular solutions were arrived at. So, in the first place, these studies are presented in two parts, designated respectively as Part I: "The Great Debate", and Part II: "Variations on the Debate". The notion of debate in Part I is intended to heighten the contrast between the basic "positions" or *theses* set out by Plato and Aristotle in classical times (which produced the traditional view that had two thousand years of acceptance), and the first significantly, and deliberately, opposed viewpoints or *antitheses* of Rousseau and Dewey, which are usually designated as progressive.

Although they differ on many fundamental philosophical points, both Plato and Aristotle assert the priority of intellect in man, and put forward the notion of education as transcendence gained by an intellectual elite, with the masses maintained in a sufficiently comfortable physical and material state, but one of mental vassalage.

Rousseau, in the mid-eighteenth century, was the first person to reject the rigorous programme of lifelong discipline in linguistic and philosophical study that these classical views entailed. He argued for the complete abolition of formal book learning in childhood and advocated that the child be allowed to learn through the internal processes of his own growth and development, at his own pace, and in a practical, not a verbal environment. Dewey went further: he rejected the whole dualism of body and mind (and so the system of slaves and aristocrats) and emphasised education as being the intelligent solution of current problems, again in a practical environment, but by the method of scientific, and reflective, thinking.

It is, of course, appreciated that these two groups of theorists (that is, the traditionalists and the progressives) were not necessarily opposed in everything they said and that there are educational beliefs common to both. This is not surprising, either, when one considers the very high value all these philosophers placed upon what education can do for man and society. Overall, however, the two groups do present strongly contrasting theories of education and have inspired widely differing educational policies, and it is the main features of these that are our special concern.

These contrasting theories and policies may be summarised in terms of two distinct models of what the educational process is and how it should operate. As has been indicated, the first of these, the traditional model, is based largely on the philosophies of Plato and Aristotle, although it also includes other elements that historically have become associated with it. In this model, the authority of the teacher is stressed and the teacher's role is seen as one of instilling in pupils a required body of set subject matter. Little attention is paid to individual differences or children's interests; children are expected to remain quiet and passive and, to this end, coercive techniques are common. The school is cut off from outside life and what goes on within is seen primarily as a preparation for the future rather than an enrichment of the present. The basic stress is on the knowledge to be acquired and it is this that determines the aims; notions such as development of potentialities or self-realisation being largely ignored. Utilitarian and practical knowledge is seen as fit only for the less able, who are to receive a minimum education, the full programme being open only to the intellectually gifted. Not all these features were necessarily present at any single time or place, but were in themselves typical of the traditional model of education that dominated educational thought at least until the time of Rousseau and which is still influential today.

The second, and strongly contrasted, model of the educational process, which has been influenced profoundly by the ideas of Rousseau and Dewey, is the progressive model. Here, the child's interests and needs are regarded as the main factor in deciding what should be taught, and instrumental and practical knowledge is given a place in the curriculum. Activity methods and learning by discovery replace formal instruction as the dominant educative process, and examinations and testing are given less stress. The teacher's role is seen as one of encouraging the development of individual potentialities rather than moulding children according to some preconceived pattern, becoming a guide more than an external authority figure and thus coercive' techniques are used only as a last resort, if at all. Life in the school is related wherever possible to life outside the school, and education is seen as an enrichment of the present at least as much as a preparation for the future.

Once again, not all these features have necessarily been present in any particular school, but they are all typical of the progressive approach to education. Further details and explanation of both these models will become apparent as one reads through the various theorists represented in this book.

Since the first decades of the twentieth century, when Dewey was most active and influential, all subsequent writers on the theory of education up to the present day have been forced to react in one way or another to these two dominant models. But what new alternatives might there be? What scope remains for further innovations in educational thought? Three possible approaches exist: there could be a new and original way of interpreting or implementing one of these two basic models of the traditional and progressive position; there could be an attempt at a synthesis or compromise between the two positions; or there could be a totally new, radical way of looking at the process of education. All of these possibilities are represented in Part II. It is suggested that Makarenko in Soviet Russia and Skinner in the contemporary United States offer new ways of interpreting and implementing the traditional approach, while Neill in the United Kingdom does the same for the progressive position. A synthesis of the two basic positions has been attempted by Peters. The radical rethinking of education, which has a large, and growing number of modern exponents, is represented by Illich. Obviously, this classification of the five writers raises some questions, and qualifications need to be made; regardless, we believe that the student who is beginning studies in the philosophy of education will find this an illuminating way of understanding these modern theories.

Given these arguments, the final question remains: how can the nine thinkers represented here best be understood? To help students read them with the maximum profit, four major problem areas in educational discussion have been chosen and, as far as possible, readings that provide for some encounter with these areas have been selected. It is hoped that students can thereby trace the various contrasting viewpoints on each of these problems, and use them as a prelude to their own attempts to formulate decisions about them, and perhaps to reach satisfactory — even if tentative — conclusions. Having done this, students will be taking the steps towards working out their own educational theory, which although it may contain elements similar to some of those existing in the nine theorists studied here, might also have aspects distinctive to themselves.

The four problem areas, and some of the main issues that they raise, are as follows:

1. The nature of education and the curriculum: what knowledge is most valuable? Is education valuable in itself, or is it only a means to some further end? How, then, should the curriculum be organised to achieve the desired result?

2. Teacher-pupil relationship: what is the role of the teacher? What in fact, is a teacher, and so what is teaching? What then is learning, and so what is a pupil? Is there a valid distinction between the concepts of authority

and authoritarianism? Is freedom in education a meaningful concept? How then can discipline be viewed, and what is the role of punishment?

3. Morality and education: can the curriculum and the teaching-learning situation remain neutral, or are values involved? If so, how? What moral values are relevant to education? Should children themselves be expected to acquire moral values by virtue of their schooling, and if so, how should this take place?

4. The state and education: what role does the state have in providing education? Should education be aimed primarily at developing the individual, or members of society? Is education in a democracy necessarily superior to that in a totalitarian society? Does the state ever have the right to introduce censorship and indoctrination into education?

Finding solutions to these questions is the responsibility of the reader, for it is this kind of competence that the study of educational philosophy seeks to promote. Some guidance to the reader in this regard is provided in the commentaries attached to each of the nine sets of primary readings. The basic aim of all these commentaries is to explain and stimulate, rather than provide a detailed scholarly analysis. That is, they are intended to lead you into an informed and interested reading of the theorists themselves and the questions they raise, rather than pre-empt your judgement on the issues that lie ahead. For this reason we have also, in a number of places in these commentaries, raised questions and left the reader to work out his or her own answers from the readings.

One final word: these readings have been chosen so as to provide, within the necessary limitations of space, as representative a coverage as possible of the basic educational ideas of each theorist on the one hand, and some treatment of each of the four major problem areas on the other. Since the text is dealing with the most significant innovations in the history of Western educational thought, it should be realised that the thinkers included have generally developed their theories at length in a considerable body of writing; the excerpts given here can only sketch in the general features. But a full understanding of any writer can only come from a study of his complete works, and to help the student go beyond the first stages presented here, a select bibliography has been included in the commentary on each theorist. Also, we have listed at the end of Part II some of the major critical studies on the various theorists, together with a number of general histories of educational thought, which may be consulted for a deeper insight into the ideas and issues that follow.

PART I
The Great Debate

Thesis:
The Traditional View

1

PLATO

Commentary

Biography

Plato (428–348/7 B.C.) was born into an aristocratic Athenian family; his parents, Ariston and Perictione, were both descended from distinguished families. As a boy he received the usual education of the privileged class in the elements of literacy — reading, writing and reckoning — and in the great mythopoeic traditions of the Greeks, which were transmitted in the epic literature composed by Homer and Hesiod.

The formal process of education was not well developed in the late fifth century B.C., and generally the privileged boy (for girls were not given any schooling) studied with private tutors. In late childhood and early adolescence, with the elements of literacy already mastered, studies were of two major kinds: physical and literary. The former had as their object the development of physical fitness, mainly because it promoted good bodily health, but also because it was a necessary element of military training. Every free-born boy had to undergo a period of military service and swear an oath of loyalty to the state; indeed, it was a precondition of citizenship. Literary studies were promoted because they served a number of functions. In the first place, the Greeks had no concept of race as it exists today: a Greek was a person who spoke Greek and subscribed to the traditional Greek values as embodied in the *Iliad* and *Odyssey* of Homer and the similar compositions of Hesiod, *Theogony, Shield of Heracles* and *Works and Days*. So literature in the broad sense, often sung to the accompaniment of the lyre, promoted the Greek identity. At the same time, the word *barbarian* was Greek for mumbler; citizens obviously had to speak clearly, correctly and effectively. Theirs was, of course, a largely face-to-face society and the art of speech (their word was *rhetoriké*, which has come down to us in the Latin form of rhetoric) was of paramount importance. For example, there was no legal profession and each person had to plead his own case in the courts. Moreover citizenship, which carried membership in the assembly (or *ekklesia*), could only be exercised properly if the citizen could speak well on his feet. The art of oratory was a very powerful acquisition.

Plato followed, then, this customary path, but in his early adult years he became attracted to the new study of philosophy which was gaining some following in opposition to rhetoric. Because rhetoric had attracted a number of disreputable practitioners, and lent itself as much to dishonest persuasion as to honest, it had become the object of some suspicion on the part of those who, calling themselves philosophers, sought ultimate absolute values, independently of any verbal persuasion. The most outstanding of these was Socrates (469–399 B.C.), and Plato became his student and admirer. But Socrates' career was a thorny one and in 399 B.C. he was indicted for offences against the state, including criticisms of democracy. The record of the trial, admittedly partisan, survives in Plato's dialogue the *Apology*, and gives a picture of the subversion of justice in the interests of gaining a conviction. Socrates was found guilty and sentenced to death. Plato thereupon left Athens in disgust and wandered the Mediterranean for some ten years, visiting various scholars and philosophers. In this time, with Socrates' treatment ever in his mind, he became preoccupied with the search for absolute justice, one higher than the public will and beyond human manipulation. He seems to have returned to Athens around 389 B.C., and some time after that he founded a school of philosophy dedicated to this search for the absolute nature of all things. This school was established in a grove near the gymnasium, known as the Academy after the early hero Academus. In time, the school too came to be known as the Academy, and here Plato taught his famous doctrines and composed his great corpus of writings, the twenty-five dialogues, which became the first great philosophical system in the world. Although these works purport to be the teachings of Socrates, it is generally agreed that most of them are the products of Plato's own development of Socratic ideas. Plato's school attracted a group of followers who were interested in pursuing philosophy, and of these the one who became most renowned was Aristotle. After Plato's death the Academy continued in operation, and for more than nine hundred years it was a major intellectual centre of the ancient world, until it was closed by the Emperor Justinian in A.D. 529. The doctrines of Plato, however, continued to be taught, chiefly in a Christianised version known as Neoplatonism, and have experienced continuing waves of popularity right down to the present day. Platonism still stands as a major — many would say pre-eminent — intellectual force in our lives. It certainly continues to influence educational thinking profoundly.

Main Features of Plato's Educational Thought

What, then, was Plato's significant innovation in education? This is easily stated: he was the first person in the history of civilisation to develop a systematic theory of education based upon a comprehensive philosophy, and this was done with the flair and competence of genius. In a real sense, he established the ground rules from which all educational and philosophical thought has developed. How is it, we may ask further, that Plato's education theory continues to exert an influence on us to this day? To answer this question, and indeed, to thereby come to an understanding of so many factors that have moulded modern educational thought and practice, it is necessary first to look at the forces that shaped Plato's ideas, and then at his philosophy in general, in broad outline.

We begin with the activities in the sixth century B.C. of small groups of leisured thinkers in various places throughout the Mediterranean. The Greek word for leisure is *scholé*, and so the idea of "schools" came into existence, concerned, in the first instance, with speculation. Among these early schools, one which acquired a great reputation was that of Pythagoras (?580/70– c. 500 B.C.). A native of the island of Samos, he migrated to Croton in southern Italy, which was a Greek territory at the time, where he established a colony of people — both men and women, interestingly enough — who were concerned with the search for knowledge in itself, free of any practical application. There already was at that time a growing concern among some Greek thinkers to find the ultimate basis of matter and existence. It is a fascinating and complex story but the general outline of their argument is this. The world is obviously in a process of continual change: season follows season: organic life has its never-ending cycle of birth, growth to maturity, death. Some cycles are fairly rapid and man can observe them easily; others, like the weathering of the earth, are slower but still evident. Yet this activity is constantly self-restoring and self-renewing; in the midst of instability and change there is balance and continuity. What, then, are the principles that govern the appearances (the Greek plural is *phenomena*) of existence? Are there principles of timelessness, permanency, eternality that bind phenomena together into some kind of order, or *kosmos*? Thinkers posited the hypothesis that indeed there is some eternal principle; since then, men have found it difficult to think easily or comfortably without it. The conceptions of this principle varied, but generally they suggested such ideas as the "boundless", the "infinite", the "primeval void and atoms"; generically they were called simply the "first principle", the *arché*.

Pythagoras sought to take these investigations further: what, he wondered, did the *arché* itself consist of? Obviously, it had to be outside physical existence, which depends upon corruptible matter. Now physical objects are not just randomly made; they have an architecture, a deliberate design. The veins in leaves, the whorl of petals on a flower, the progression of waves breaking on the seashore, the proportions of limbs in trees, animals and man all show some orderly arrangement. Eventually Pythagoras came to see a mathematical structure and as his studies progressed — particularly as he studied the behaviour of vibrating strings on monochords (primitive one-stringed guitars) — he came to discard the actual objects and to explore the world of numerical relationships. So the Greeks came to investigate the nature of the earth and the universe, the nature of man, even the nature of "nature", for which their word was *physis*, giving us a term for the physical world.

Although their thought became increasingly abstract, it is important to remember that initially the Greeks studied only the kinds of "nature" that revealed themselves in the craft technologies; the word *sophos* originally meant craft, and technology comes from the root *tech*, which had a similar meaning.

As they accumulated their knowledge of mathematics, they came to be concerned to formulate it easily and in its simplest conceptual terms. So mathematics became very much an abstract affair and shorthand notations were used; it became a world of symbolic operations, organised into four sub-studies, three of whose names, significantly, reveal their origins in a real world: *geometry* came from the measurement of the earth (*ge*, the earth; *metros*, a measure); *astronomy* was concerned with celestial movements (*aster*, a star; *nomos*, a law); *harmonics* investigated the nature of the vibrating string (*harmonia*, concord or agreement, and originally referring to the craft of ship-building, in which the various wooden members came together in a fitting concord, to produce a unity out of many). Only *arithmetic* was a "pure" study. It took its name from the word for number, meaning a digit or integer. So Pythagoras was responsible for the introduction of the idea that mathematics is the best and purest form of knowledge; indeed he restricted the usual word for knowledge, *mathesis*, to this concept. Mathematics, of course, is a vast world of autonomous knowledge, and its practitioners came to feel that it is the ultimate cement of the universe: the study of mathematics can take us beyond the appearances, the *phenomena*, to the ultimate elements of pure intellection, or *noumena*. In attaining this, we gain the highest experience life can offer: vision of the Infinite. And to this pursuit Pythagoras gave the name "philosophy": literally, the love of wisdom.

Plato built onto this basis, and the central element of his theory of the nature of existence (it is technically termed metaphysics) is the belief that *noumena*, or ideas, are more than mental constructions — they have a real and timeless existence. This is known as his celebrated theory of Forms. Put very briefly, this theory was derived from the two sources of logical induction and mathematical analogy. Firstly, the *phenomena* must be stripped of their physical and accidental properties, for these hinder our ability to see ultimate reality. This is best illustrated in mathematics. We recognise that the mathematical figures we draw — circles, triangles, squares and so on — are only temporary imperfect versions of perfect figures and that these must somehow have a permanent, and hence timeless, existence. All circles, for example, share in the form of circularity and so, by induction, we can see that from a number of instances, there is a common element in which all participate but which is at the same time apart from them. In this example, it is the Form of the Circle. Plato extended this theory to all phenomena. Individual men, for example, vary enormously, yet all share in a common element that he supposed to be the Form of Man. So too, can political states have forms culminating in the Form of the Just State. All of the forms themselves, he argued further, are elements of the total design of the cosmos, they are parts of one great form — the *arché* — which is the Form of the Good. In making this assertion, Plato drew upon the Greek philosophical tradition that behind the universe is a principle of balance or harmony that maintains continuity in the face of change and diversity, and since it promotes the general well-being of the cosmos, must be itself the ultimate Good.

Man, of course, as a conscious and self-motivating agent, becomes involved in the operations of the world, and Plato's philosophy gives a great deal of attention to this. One of the important questions to answer properly is: how, and what, do we know? This field of study is still designated by its Greek term of epistemology (from *episteme*, another word for "knowledge") and Plato was responsible for giving the world a very distinctive kind of epistemological theory. Following his metaphysical theories, Plato asserted that since phenomena are in constant process of change, nothing can be said about them with certainty. They are themselves only individual and hence imperfect instances of ultimate forms; therefore they are merely appearances and about them we can only have opinions, even though, because of the way language operates, we might seem to be making valid statements. Knowledge can only be of what *is*, and what *is* must be timeless and absolute. Therefore we have knowledge only of the forms themselves, and this, said Plato, arises somehow from within us. We really can't say how we come by our awareness and understanding of deep truths and he suggested that we are born with them; that pre-existent knowledge is somehow implanted in us. So he argued that knowing is really becoming aware of, or "recollecting", what we already have latently within us.

This led to a very significant view of learning and teaching for, according to Plato, although we may have knowledge implanted within us, we do not easily apprehend it. True, vague stirrings take place in our minds and tantalising glimpses of truth may occasionally come into focus, but most frequently they slip back again and are lost. Yet we also know that talking about things helps raise them to consciousness, and that by the verbal arts we can facilitate the development of ideas and heighten our awareness. This was part of the claims of the teachers of rhetoric, known as sophists, but Plato sought to get beyond rhetoric, which is essentially persuasive, to philosophical truth, which he wanted to make demonstrably conclusive. To do this, he sought a method of conducting verbal enquiries properly and to this end he developed the method of dialectic. Essentially, this is the process of ordered debate, discussion and argument by which we can most properly establish satisfactory statements; it has an even deeper meaning as the process whereby we come to know conclusively. In Plato's day, we remember, the processes of syllogistic reasoning known as logic were not yet highly developed; that was part of Aristotle's contribution.

To illustrate how dialectic itself works Plato used the analogy of childbirth, which was an apposite one in the Mediterranean world where so much of life was tied to the rhythms of nature, and fertility was a continued preoccupation. The first use of the idea came from Socrates, and Plato records this in two dialogues in particular: *Theaetetus** and *Meno*. Just as the uterus has pre-existent seeds that become fertilised and, following a period of gestation, come to birth (which may or may not be successful), so too does the

---

*A relevant extract from this dialogue has been included in the selections from Plato that follow.

mind contain seeds of knowledge (the Greek term is *spermatikoi logoi*) that somehow follow a similar course. In a world of primitive hygiene and imperfect medical knowledge, miscarriages, abortions and deformed births were common and so this lent greater credence to the theory of how the mind too has difficulty in bringing forth thoughts successfully. The pregnant woman must finally manage her own labour and the best that outsiders can do is to assist her delivery by the ancillary art of midwifery. So too, the labouring mind can draw only on its own inner resources, and the quality of its thinking depends on the pre-existent nature of the individual mind. Others can help, and it was Socrates who suggested that teaching is really the practice of psychic midwifery; the teacher is there to ask questions, to stimulate the learner to so order his ideas as to produce a sound result. From the Greek word for childbirth, *maieutiké*, comes the name for the practice of dialectical assistance, *maieutic*. To this day we find ourselves using physical metaphors to explain what are still obscure mental processes: our mind conceives, we get fertile thoughts; in universities we deliberately call some kinds of classes "seminars".

This idea of knowledge being pre-existent in the mind enabled Plato to explain how individuals vary in their intellectual quality: he appealed to the overall design of nature. Following the usual Greek custom of ascribing this design to the gods — as many still do — he suggested that each one of us has a mixture of qualities, which Plato referred to by analogy with gold, silver and bronze. It is simply a fact of nature that we are, like everything else in the world, composed of elements in varying proportions. For Plato this also provided a rationalisation for the existing social order in which slaves and workers supported a small aristocracy.

The Greeks' philosophical concern with the nature of existence and the search for some ultimate *arché* also led them to ask yet another question: what is the point or purpose of existence? This is a disturbing kind of question because, once raised, it is difficult, probably impossible, to ignore. Again Plato followed the general trends of Greek thought by seeking purpose within the processes of nature itself; and so the purpose of human existence, which was the question at the centre of this philosophical enquiry, came to be answered in terms of man's nature: we should become what we already latently are. Bronze people, he asserted, by an appeal to the evidence, are dominated by appetitive processes, so they must necessarily follow the path of maintaining equilibrium with the tasks of production — agriculture, artisanship, and so on — that provide this. Silver and gold people have a greater "endowment" (the concept remains with us yet) in terms of intellect, and so their life, while it certainly requires the meeting of daily needs, should not rest there. They should go on to the cultivation of intellect for two reasons: in the first place, because it fulfils this teleological function built into us; in the second place because these people are natural leaders, and as they develop their intellect they become better fitted to govern. And since the gold are the highest, they should become philosopher rulers while the silver ones become the "auxiliaries", or military class, that protect society.

In Plato the Greek philosophical notion of an underlying order or design to the universe, or "cosmos" as the term itself implies, receives an explicit expression.

So, in the thought of Plato, the three traditional aspects of philosophy are thoroughly worked out: his metaphysics is one of the ultimate reality of pure forms, culminating in the Form of the Good; his epistemology presents man as being endowed, according to a ratio of nature, with pre-existent knowledge that, if properly activated, enables him to come to an understanding of the world; his value system, or axiology, is based upon the absolute nature of the Good which man must seek to grasp by means of a heightened vision. This provided his theory with its moral, or ethical, elements. Following the belief that we vary in endowment, Plato suggested that the gold and silver ones can come to an understanding of the good by intellection; the bronze must gain theirs, which can only be partial, by habit-uation. And as this kind of argument indicates, Plato's philosophy lent itself very easily to the elaboration of an educational theory. In fact, in traversing the main features of Plato's philosophy, the reader finds that his educational views have already been implicitly set out. And this, incidentally, illustrates how a complete educational theory rests upon a fully systematic philosophical basis.

Plato's educational theory is thoroughly interwoven into all of his writings, which were exclusively in dialogue form, usually — but not always — with Socrates as the chief interlocutor. This is partly because the dialogues them-selves are records of dialectical quests for knowledge, but also because Plato's view was that the highest form of existence for man is this quest for knowledge; that is, education — the means of transcendence. Yet some of his dialogues deal with education specifically; these are the *Republic* and the *Laws*, and of these, the former has exercised a tremendous influence on Western educational thought to the present day.

Education for Plato is tied to the philosophical assumption of the total interrelatedness of the cosmos and the operation in nature of harmony and balance, themselves basic Pythagorean concepts. Man, being part of nature, should therefore follow it and strive to utilise its principles. So the fun-damental concern in society should be to maintain this principle of harmony or balance, which in its human equivalent is justice; on this the state should be built, and individuals should devote their energies to securing and main-taining it. Following the natural distribution of intellect, people contribute to society in different ways, but it is self-evident that leadership should come from those most fit to provide it. Plato says very little of education at the levels of socialisation and the earlier stages of schooling. His preoccupation is with education for transcendence and how this might be assisted through a formal programme of instruction.

There is, by definition, Plato says, little that can be done for the lower levels of society beyond seeing that their lives are reasonably comfortable and secure. Lacking the capacity for high-level intellectual life, the labouring masses should be protected from disturbing ideas by having their myths and legends maintained; indeed, they should be shielded from intellectual challenges because, lacking the ability to solve them, they can only become disturbed and frightened, and perhaps liable to stampede. Social disorder is the most likely outcome. Of course they should be helped to pursue their daily activities by being provided with vocational skills, but these are best learned by community involvement and the traditional method of direct apprenticeship. If their calling demands it, they should learn to read, write and reckon, but this must perforce remain for them a local and instrumental skill.

True education should be given only to those who can benefit from it and should be primarily a responsibility of the state. By the state, Plato of course meant the city-state of his own time, with a total population of anything from fifty thousand to two hundred thousand. The Greeks used the terms *polis* or *politeia* for this, which are the roots of modern words like "politics" and "political". In fact the title of Plato's *Republic* in Greek is *Politeia*, and the Latin term "republic" is not at all a felicitous translation. The concern of the state is mandatory because only by the exercising of firm control over the activities of all citizens can the fundamental value of justice be secured and maintained. The state then exercises the responsibility of deciding who are to be given a full education to fit them to be the guardians of the state — these are the children of silver and gold, who are selected by the usual tests. That is, all children are assessed by adults and judgments made on their intellectual capacities; the fittest proceed and the less fit fall by the wayside.

Precise details of the operation of the process are given in the *Republic*, and this can be studied in the abridgement which follows. Granting the priority of the state and the need to provide leadership of the highest quality by selecting the most intellectually capable, Plato argues that education must be the process of producing this heightened awareness of the order of all things, the vision of the Good. So instruction must be concerned with assisting the chosen individuals to get beyond appearances to the realm of forms, or, as Plato says to get from the visible to the intelligible world. The curriculum is then specially designed to promote this; it is based on mathematics because the study of mathematics frees the mind from particulars and allows it to concentrate upon universals. The study of mathematics, then, enables the mind to think abstractly; the next and final stage of education, reached only by those of gold, is that of dispensing even with the forms of mathematics and exercising pure thought — dialectic — on the forms themselves, reaching up to the Form of the Good. To provide a clear indication of this, Plato gives two of his very famous illustrations, the analogy of the divided line and the allegory of the cave, both of which occur in the following abridgement of the *Republic*.

The whole process of education, then, is intended to serve the state, and we must remember that in Plato's day individuality was not given as high a value as public participation in civic life: active citizenship was the great value. The *Republic*, of course, is an idealised version of how society should be organised and how education can serve the ends of justice, and it is doubtful that Plato really expected it to be implemented in precise detail. Rather it seems to have been put up as an ideal to remind us that we should strive to find the best in society and in ourselves that we can, and to serve as a constant example to encourage us to seek always the highest values possible.

A theory as thoroughly elaborated and as distinctive as Plato's must generate considerable debate, and this it has done throughout the course of history. The recent great mathematician-philosopher Alfred North Whitehead has gone so far as to say that man's philosophical history consists of nothing more than a set of footnotes to Plato. Just what does this mean? How many practices and beliefs of contemporary education are to be found in Plato? In attempting to evaluate his theory there are questions that can be raised at every point, and obviously this can be an exhausting and perhaps difficult business. To organise your thoughts, it is probably easiest to make a critical examination of each aspect of Plato's philosophy, centring on:

- his distinction between a real world of pure forms and our everyday world of appearances;
- his inference that we should therefore become concerned with attaining intellective knowledge as our highest end;
- his assumption that people vary in ability and aptitude and that serious education — the search for ideas — should only be given to a few;
- his desire to develop a state in which justice obtains as a result of complete human concord.

The number of questions that can be, and have been asked is endless, but there are perhaps two that are especially pertinent to modern times. Consider Plato's attitude to the masses, especially his belief that they should not be disturbed from their unthinking mode of life. Then consider the condition of modern mass society in which the bulk of occupations are relatively mindless daily rounds, and in which such consumer satisfactions as the tabloid press, banal television, spectator sports and the production of drugs, tobacco and alcohol are all vast enterprises that appear to be absolutely vital to human existence. It there any essential departure in our modern mass life from Plato's recommendations? Can you imagine the consequences of getting people to abandon these pursuits and seek instead for the cultivation of their own inner excellence?

The second question concerns the following point. It is often alleged, rather smugly, that the big objection to the *Republic* is that it is a blueprint for totalitarianism and promotes an elitist educational system. But how different are we today in our educational practices? Consider, for example, how we grade children according to ability and performance, a small proportion going on to higher education, from which most of the future leaders of society are chosen.

SELECT BIBLIOGRAPHY

Plato's own works consist of twenty-five authentic dialogues. In addition there is a number of spurious ones, and a collection of pseudepigraphic letters, although one of these, the *Seventh Letter*, is regarded as possibly genuine. There is a number of editions of the complete works, both in Greek and in translation. English-speaking scholars usually take the Oxford Classical Text as the definitive Greek edition and translations are generally made from this, as is the case with the Penguin edition by H.D.P. Lee used here. The bibliographic citation is

PLATO, *Opera* (5 Vols), Clarendon Press, Oxford, 1953-56.

The Complete corpus was translated into English by Benjamin Jowett in the nineteenth century and published by the Oxford University Press. With revisions, it is still available.

Plato's major works on education are *Republic* and *Laws*, while specialised aspects of education are developed in *Protagoras, Theaetetus* and *Meno*. All are available in various English-language translations.

There is a very large literature on Plato, and a guide to that available on his educational thought is given in the general bibliography at the end of this book.

Selections

Two selections from Plato are given here, from Theaetetus *and the* Republic. *The brief extract from* Theaetetus *is used to illustrate succinctly the art of maieutic whereby teaching is seen as the task of assisting the mind to develop its own ideas. The longer selection from the* Republic *is a virtual abridgement of the whole of the educational argument of the dialogue and it sets out what is the first systematic educational theory ever developed in Western civilisation.*

Plato's great corpus of writing can be separated into three broad categories, known as the early, middle and late dialogues. The early group are generally called the "Socratic" dialogues because they give an exposition of Socrates' methods and ideas. These reveal a concern with the pursuit of meaning and an insistence on the classification of terms, intended in large part to uncover ill-conceived or unsecured beliefs. The middle group illustrates Plato's mature period (even though he retains Socrates as the interlocutor) in which his concern was to move beyond the rather negative phase of exposing ignorance, prejudice and opinion to a more positive one of building up a systematic theory. The Republic *belongs to this middle period. In the late dialogues, Plato deals more thoroughly with issues that had arisen in earlier dialogues and which he wanted to develop further. To this last group belong his celebrated cosmogony,* Timaeus, *and his other major and more practical treatise on education,* Laws.

The Republic *is organised into ten sections, technically called "books" which do not correspond exactly with the logic of the argument. The discussion is conducted, as was generally the case, between Socrates and a group of Plato's leisured companions in some kind of informal situation — in this case at a dinner party in the home of Polemarchus. In addition to the host there are a number of others present, all Polemarchus' relatives and friends, along with Socrates, and Plato's elder brothers, Adeimantus and Glaucon. Although the dialogue begins as a general conversation, by the time it gets to the central issue of education it is conducted among these last three.*

The evening's discussion begins with the notion of justice and how this might be properly distributed so that all people receive their due. In the opening book, the common Socratic technique of the elenchus is illustrated, in which a speaker advances a position, and Socrates, by careful cross-questioning, is able either to bring him to an impasse or else to show him to be in self-contradiction, from either of which no further argument is possible. By means of this elenctic method Socrates disposes of the two positions that justice is either conventional morality or simply plain self-interest. So is raised the third viewpoint that justice is independent of man's manipulations. In order to study this idea of justice more thoroughly, Socrates suggests that the discussants look at its opera-tions on a larger scale, in the political arena itself, and that a useful way of making such a study would be to construct, in theory, an ideal state.

In doing this there must be some guiding principles, and these are set out in Book II of the Republic. *The primary principles of social organisations are said to be mutual need and the division of labour based upon aptitude, and this leads Socrates to consider the general question of government and the ruling group of the state. So the dialogue develops the notion that if aptitude is to be a criterion of the division of labour then those who govern should possess attributes of leadership. There must, then, be a selec-tion and training of persons whose aptitude marks them out for such a position.*

*These leaders are called guardians, and the special attributes which endow them with
the capability of maintaining the just state are set out by Socrates as being a philosophic
disposition, high spirits, speed and strength. At the end of Book II where the extracts
from the* Republic *begin, Socrates picks up the question of how these guardians are
to be educated.*

The selections from Plato now follow, beginning with a short extract from Theaetetus.

Theaetetus

SOCRATES. My art of midwifery is in general like [that of the midwives];
the only difference is that my patients are men, not women, and my concern is not with the body but with the soul that is in travail of birth. And
the highest point of my art is the power to prove by every test whether the
offspring of a young man's thought is a false phantom or instinct with life
and truth. I am so far like the midwife, that I cannot myself give birth to
wisdom; and the common reproach is true, that, though I question others,
I can myself bring nothing to light because there is no wisdom in me. The
reason is this: heaven constrains me to serve as a midwife, but has debarred
me from giving birth. So of myself I have no sort of wisdom, nor has any
discovery ever been born to me as the child of my soul. Those who frequent
my company at first appear, some of them, quite unintelligent; but, as we
go further with our discussions, all who are favoured by heaven make
progress at a rate that seems surprising to others as well as to themselves,
although it is clear that they have never learned anything from me; the many
admirable truths they bring to birth have been discovered by themselves
from within. But the delivery is heaven's work and mine.

The proof of this is that many who have not been conscious of my
assistance but have made light of me, thinking it was all their own doing,
have left me sooner than they should whether under others' influence or of
their own motion, and thence forward suffered miscarriage of their thoughts
through falling into bad company; and they have lost the children of whom
I had delivered them by bringing them up badly, caring more for false
phantoms than for the true; and so at last their lack of understanding has
become apparent to themselves and to everyone else. Such a one was
Aristides, son of Lysimachus, and there have been many more. When they
come back and beg for a renewal of our intercourse with extravagant pro-
testations, sometimes the divine warning that comes to me forbids it; with
others it is permitted, and these begin again to make progress. In yet another
way, those who seek my company have the same experience as a woman
with child: they suffer the pains of labour and by night and day, are full
of distress far greater than a woman's; and my art has power to bring on
these pangs or to allay them. So it fares with these; but there are some,

From *Plato's Theory of Knowledge*, translated by F. M. Cornford, Routledge and Kegan Paul,
London, 1935. Reprinted by permission of the publishers and Humanities Press Inc., New York.

Theaetetus, whose minds, as I judge, have never conceived at all. I see that they have no need of me and with all goodwill I seek a match for them. Without boasting unduly, I can guess pretty well whose society will profit them. I have arranged many of these matches with Prodicus, and with other men of inspired sagacity.

And now for the upshot of this long discourse of mine. I suspect that, as you yourself believe, your mind is in labour with some thought it has conceived. Accept, then, the ministration of a midwife's son who himself practises his mother's art, and do the best you can to answer the questions I ask. Perhaps when I examine your statements I may judge one or another of them to be an unreal phantom.If I then take the abortion from you and cast it away, do not be savage with me like a woman robbed of her first child. People have often felt like that towards me and been positively ready to bite me for taking away some foolish notion they have conceived. They do not see that I am doing them a kindness. They have not learned that no divinity is ever ill-disposed towards man, nor is such action on my part due to unkindness; it is only that I am not permitted to acquiesce in false-hood and suppress the truth.

[150B–151D]

Republic
Early Education of the Guardians

In the discussion that follows, Socrates argues that since character is formed at an early age, the education of guardians must begin in their earliest years. The children selected for this training should therefore be exposed only to the good, which should first appear in simplified and censored form, all directed towards the aim of producing harmonious personalities; persons, that is, possessed neither of an unintelligent philistinism with an animal addiction to settling everything by brute force, nor weak bookworms, mentally gutless and feeble at fighting. In the character of the guardians, energy and initiative should be in balance with reason. To cultivate these qualities, it is suggested that the customary studies of the Athenians should be used: music, literature and physical training.

Book II

"We may assume then that our guardians need these qualities. But how are they to be brought up and educated? If we try to answer this question, I wonder whether it will help us at all in our main enquiry into the origin of justice and injustice? We do not want to leave out anything relevant, but we don't want to embark on a long digression."

To which Adeimantus replied, "I expect it will help us all right."

From PLATO, *The Republic*, translated by H. D. P. Lee, Penguin Classics, 1955. Copyright ©H. D. P. Lee, 1955. Reprinted by permission of the publisher.

"Then my dear Adeimantus, we must certainly pursue the question," I [Socrates] rejoined, "even though it proves a long business. So let us set about educating our guardians as if we had as much time on our hands as the traditional story-teller."

"Let us by all means."

"What kind of education shall we give them then? We shall find it difficult to improve on the time-honoured distinction between the training we give to the body and the training we give to the mind and character."

"True."

"And we shall begin with the mind and character, shall we not?"

"Of course."

"In this type of education you would include stories would you not?"

"Yes."

"These are of two kinds, true stories and fiction. Our education must use both, and start with fiction."

"I don't understand you."

"But you know that we begin by telling children stories. These are, in general, fiction, though they contain some truth. And we tell children stories before we start them on physical training."

"That is so."

"That is what I meant by saying that we start to train the mind before the body. And the first step, as you know, is always what matters most, particularly when we are dealing with those who are young and tender. That is the time when they are taking shape and when any impression we choose to make leaves a permanent mark."

"That is certainly true."

"Shall we therefore allow our children to listen to any stories written by anyone, and to form opinions the opposite of those we think they should have when they grow up?"

"We shall certainly not."

"Then it seems that our first business is to supervise the production of stories, and choose only those we think suitable, and reject the rest. We shall persuade mothers and nurses to tell our chosen stories to their children and so mould their minds and characters rather than their bodies. The greater part of the stories current today we shall have to reject."

"Which are you thinking of?"

"We can take some of the major legends as typical. For all are cast in the same mould and have the same effect. Do you agree?"

"Yes: but I'm not sure which you refer to as major."

"The stories in Homer and Hesiod and the poets. For it is the poets who have always made up stories to tell to men."

"Which stories do you mean and what fault do you find in them?"

"The worst fault possible," I replied, "especially if the story is an ugly one."

"And what is that?"

"Misrepresenting gods and heroes, like a portrait painter who fails to catch a likeness. . . ."

Book III

"Good literature, therefore, and good music and beauty of form generally all depend on goodness of character; I don't mean that lack of awareness of the world which we politely call "goodness", but a character of real judgment and principle."

"I quite agree."

"And are not these things which our young men must try to acquire, if they are to perform their function in life properly?"

"They must."

"And they are to be seen in painting and similar arts, in weaving and embroidery, in architecture and furniture, and in living things, animals and plants. For in all of these we find beauty and ugliness. And ugliness of form and disharmony are akin to bad art and bad character, and their opposites are akin to and represent good character and discipline."

"That is perfectly true."

"It is not only to the poets therefore that we must issue orders requiring them to represent good character in their poems or not to write at all; we must issue similar orders to all artists and prevent them portraying bad character, ill-discipline, meanness, or ugliness in painting, sculpture, architecture, or any work of art, and if they are unable to comply they must be forbidden to practise their art. We shall thus prevent our guardians being brought up among representations of what is evil, and so day by day and little by little, by feeding as it were in an unhealthy pasture, insensibly doing themselves grave psychological damage. Our artists and craftsmen must be capable of perceiving the real nature of what is beautiful, and then our young men, living as it were in a good climate will benefit because all the works of art they see and hear influence them for good, like the breezes from some healthy country, insensibly moulding them into sympathy and conformity with what is rational and right."

"That would indeed be the best way to bring them up."

"And that, my dear Glaucon," I said, "is why this stage of education is crucial. For rhythm and harmony penetrate deeply into the mind and have a most powerful effect on it, and if education is good, bring balance and fairness, if it is bad, the reverse. And moreover the proper training we propose to give will make a man quick to perceive the shortcomings of works of art or nature, whose ugliness he will rightly dislike; anything beautiful he will welcome, and will accept and assimilate it for his own good, anything ugly he will rightly condemn and dislike, even when he is still young and cannot understand the reason for so doing, while when reason comes he will recognise and welcome her as a familiar friend because of his education."

"In my view," he said, "that is the purpose of this stage of education."

"Well then," I went on, "when we were learning to read we were not satisfied until we could recognise the letters of the alphabet wherever they occurred; we did not think them beneath our notice in large words or small, but tried to recognise them everywhere on the grounds that we should not have learned to read till we could."

"That is true."

"And we can't recognise reflections of the letters in water or in a mirror till we know the letters themselves. The same process of learning gives us skill to recognise both."

"Yes, it does."

"Then I must surely be right in saying that we shall not be properly educated ourselves, nor will the guardians whom we are training, until we can recognise the qualities of discipline, courage, generosity, greatness of mind, and others akin to them, as well as their opposites, in all their many manifestations. We must be able to perceive both the qualities themselves and representations of them wherever they occur, and must not despise instances great or small, but reckon that the same process of learning gives us skill to recognise both." . . .

"The next stage in the training of our young men will be physical education. And here again they must be carefully trained from childhood onwards. I have my own opinions about it: let me see if you agree. In my view physical excellence does not of itself produce good character: on the other hand, excellency of mind and character *will* make the best of the physique it is given. What do you think?"

"I agree.". . .

". . .the purpose of the two established types of education (literary and physical) is not, as some suppose, to deal one with the mind and the other with the body."

"What is it then?" he asked.

"I think that perhaps in the main both aim at training the mind."

"And how do they do that?"

"Have you noticed," I asked, "how a lifelong devotion to physical exercise, to the exclusion of anything else, produces a certain type of mind? Just as a neglect of it produces another type? One type tends to be tough and uncivilised, the other soft and oversensitive, and. . . ."

"Yes, I have noticed that," he broke in; "excessive emphasis on athletics produces a pretty uncivilised type, while a purely literary and academic training leaves a man with less backbone than is decent."

"It is the energy and initiative in their nature that may make them uncivilised," I said; "if you treat it properly it should make them brave, but if you overstrain it it turns them tough and uncouth, as you would expect."

"I agree," he said.

"The philosophic temperament, on the other hand, is gentle; too much relaxation may produce an excessive softness, but if it is treated properly the result should be civilised and humane."

"That is so."

"Now we agreed that our guardians must have both these elements in their nature, did we not?"

"Yes."

"And must not the two elements be combined to produce a mind that is civilised and brave, as opposed to cowardly and uncivilised?"

"That is so.". . .

"What I should say therefore is that these two methods of education seem to have been given by god to men to train our initiative and our reason. They are not intended, one to train body, the other mind, except incidentally, but to ensure a proper harmony between energy and initiative on the one hand and reason on the other, by tuning each to the right pitch. And so we may venture to assert that anyone who can produce the best blend of the physical and intellectual sides of education and apply them to the training of character, is producing harmony in a far more important sense than any mere musician."

"A very reasonable assertion."

"We must therefore ensure, my dear Glaucon," I said, "that there is always someone like this in charge of education in our state, if its constitution is to be preserved."

"We most certainly must."

Selection of the Guardians: Metaphor of the Three Metals

The discussion now turns to the selection of the future guardians of this ideal state, and the primary criterion advanced is that such persons must possess a devotion to the common good which overrides any personal feelings. Such a quality, and other specified ones, is not found in everyone in the same degree; people vary in their make-up and to explain this Plato uses the famous metaphor of the three metals, in which he argues that individual differences are due to god mixing in our souls, in varying proportions, the psychic equivalents of the metals of gold, silver, and bronze. It is those in whom gold predominates who are most fit to rule; that is, those who have within them the qualities of concern for justice and the public good.

"That, then, is an outline of the way in which we should educate and bring up our guardians. For we need not go into detail about their dramatic performances, field sports of various kinds, and athletic competitions on foot or horseback. The details follow naturally from what we have said, and should give no particular difficulty."

"Yes, I dare say they won't be particularly difficult," he agreed.

"Well," I continued, "what comes next? We shall have to decide, I suppose, which of our guardians are to govern, and which to be governed."

"I suppose so."

"Well, it is obvious that the elder must have authority over the younger."

"That is obvious."

"And again that those who govern must be the best."

"That's equally obvious."

"And the best farmers are those who have the greatest skill at farming, are they not?"

"Yes."

"And so if we want to pick the best guardians, we must pick those who have the greatest skill in watching over the interests of the community."

"Yes."

"For that shan't we need men who, besides being intelligent and capable, really care for those interests?"

"True."

"But we care most for what we love."

"Inevitable."

"And the deepest affection is based on community of interest, when we feel that our own good and ill fortune is completely bound up with that of someone else."

"That is so."

"So we must choose from among our guardians those who appear to us, when we scrutinise their whole career, to be most completely devoted to what they judge to be the interests of the community, and never prepared to act against them."

"They are the men for our purpose."

"A close watch must be kept on them, then, at all ages, to see if they stick to this principle, and do not forget or throw overboard, under the influence of force or propaganda, the conviction that they must always do what is best for the community."

"What do you mean by throwing overboard?" he said.

"I will explain," I said. "It seems to me that when any belief leaves us, the loss is either voluntary or involuntary. Voluntary when the belief is false and we learn better, involuntary whenever the belief is true."

"I understand what you mean by a voluntary loss, but I don't see how it happens involuntarily."

"But why? Surely you agree that men are always unwilling to lose a good thing, but willing enough to be rid of a bad one. And isn't it a bad thing to be deceived about the truth, and a good thing to know what the truth is? For I assume that by knowing the truth you mean knowing things as they really are."

"Yes, you are quite right," he conceded, "and I agree that men are unwilling to lose a belief that is true."

"So when it happens it must be due to theft or propaganda or force."

"Now I don't understand again," he said.

"I'm afraid I'm talking too theatrically," I answered. "By 'theft' I simply mean the insensible process by which we are argued out of our beliefs, or else simply forget them in course of time. Now perhaps you understand."

"Yes."

"By 'force' I mean what happens when we change our beliefs under the influence of pain or suffering."

"This too I understand," he said.

"And I think that you too would call it 'propaganda' when people are enticed into a change of opinion by promises of pleasure, or terrified into it by threats."

"Yes, propaganda and deceit always go together."

"To go back to what I was saying, then," I continued, "we must look for the guardians who will stick most firmly to the principle that they must always do what they think best for the community. We must watch them closely from their earliest years, and set them tasks in doing which they are most likely to forget or be led astray from this principle; and we must choose only those who don't forget and are not easily misled. Do you agree?"

"Yes."

"And with the same end in view we must see how they stand up to pain and suffering."

"We must."

"We must also watch their reactions to the third kind of test, propaganda. If we want to find out if a colt is nervous we expose him to alarming noises: so we must introduce our guardians when they are young to fear and, by contrast, give them opportunities for pleasure, proving them far more rigorously than we prove gold in the furnace. If they bear themselves well and are not easily bamboozled, if they show themselves self-reliant and maintain in all circumstances the principles of balance and harmony they learned in their education, then they may be expected to be of the greatest service to the community as well as to themselves. And any guardian who survives these continuous trials in childhood, youth, and manhood unscathed, shall be given authority in our state: he shall be honoured during his lifetime and when he is dead shall have the tribute of a public funeral and appropriate memorial.

"That in brief, and without going into details," I concluded, "is the way in which I would select the guardians who are to be given authority as rulers."

"And that's the way I think it should be done," he replied.

" Strictly speaking, then, it is for them that we should reserve the term guardian in its fullest sense, their function being to see that friends at home shall not wish, nor foes abroad be able, to harm our state: while the young men whom we have been describing as guardians should more strictly be called auxiliaries, their function being to assist the rulers in the execution of their decisions."

"I agree," he said.

"Now I wonder if we could contrive one of those convenient stories we were talking about a few minutes ago," I asked. "Some magnificent myth that would in itself carry conviction to our whole community, including, if possible, the guardians themselves?"

"What sort of story?"

"Nothing new — a fairy story like those the poets tell about the sort of thing that often happened 'once upon a time', but never does now: indeed, if it did, I doubt if people would believe it without a lot of persuasion, though they believed the poets."

"You seem to be hesitating to tell us more," he said.

"And when I do you will understand my hesitation," I assured him.

"Never mind," he replied, "tell us".

"I will," I said, "though I don't know how I'm to find the courage or the words to do so. I shall try to persuade first the rulers and soldiers, and then the rest of the community that the upbringing and education we have given them was all something that happened only in a dream. In reality they were fashioned and reared, and their arms and equipment manufactured, in the depths of the earth, and Earth herself, their mother, brought them up, when they were complete, into the light of day; so now they must think of the land in which they live as their mother and protect her if she is attacked, while their fellow citizens they must regard as brothers born of the same mother earth."

"No wonder you were ashamed to tell your story," he commented. I agreed that it was indeed no wonder, but asked him to listen to the rest of the story.

"We shall," I said, "address our citizens as follows:

'You are, all of you in this land, brothers. But when god fashioned you, he added gold in the composition of those of you who are qualified to be rulers (which is why their prestige is greatest); he put silver in the auxiliaries, and iron and bronze in the farmers and the rest. Now since you are all of the same stock, though children will commonly resemble their parents, occasionally a silver child will be born of golden parents, or a golden child of silver parents, and so on. Therefore the first and most important of god's commandments to the rulers is that they must exercise their function as guardians with particular care in watching the mixture of metals in the characters of the children. If one of their own children has bronze or iron in its make-up, they must harden their hearts, and degrade it to the ranks of the industrial and agricultural class where it properly belongs: similarly, if a child of this class is born with gold or silver in its nature, they will promote it appropriately to be a guardian or an auxiliary. For they know that there is a prophecy that the state will be ruined when it has guardians of silver or bronze.'

"That is the story. Do you think there is any way of making them believe it?"

"Not in the first generation," he said, "but you might succeed with the second and later generations."

"Even so it should serve to increase their loyalty to the state and to each other, for I think that's what you mean.". . .

Book IV

"But seriously, Adeimantus," I said, "there's nothing very much in all these things we are asking them to do, provided they take care of the main feature, or rather the sufficient condition of the whole system."

"And what is that?"

"The educational system. If they are well brought up, and become reasonable men, they can easily see to all we have asked them to, and indeed a good many things we have omitted, such as the position of women, marriage, and the production of children, all of which ought so far as possible to be dealt with on the proverbial basis of 'all things in common between friends'."

"Yes, they can deal with all these problems."

"And once we have given our community a good start," I pointed out, "the process will be cumulative. By maintaining a sound system of education you produce citizens of good character, and citizens of sound character, with the advantage of a good education, produce in turn children better than themselves and better able to produce still better children in their turn, as can be seen with animals."

"That is likely enough."

"In a word, therefore, those in charge of our state must stick to the system of education and see that no deterioration creeps in; they must maintain it as a first priority and avoid at all costs any innovation in the established physical or literary curriculum. When they hear someone saying 'it is always the latest song men care for most', they must be afraid that people will think that the poet means not new songs, but a new *kind* of song, and that that is what he is recommending. But such innovation should not be recommended, nor should the poet be so understood. You should hesitate to change the style of your literature, because you risk everything if you do; the music and literature of a country cannot be altered without major political changes — we have Damon's word for it and I believe him."

"And you can count on my agreement too," said Adeimantus.

"And so it is here, in education, that our guardians must build their strong point."

"It is in education that bad discipline can most easily creep in unobserved," he replied.

"Yes," I agreed, "because people don't treat it seriously there, and think no harm can come of it."

"It only does harm," he said, "because it makes itself at home and gradually undermines morals and manners; from them it invades business dealings generally, and then spreads into the laws and constitution without any restraint, until it has made complete havoc of private and public life."

"Is it really as bad as that?" I said.

"Yes, I think it is."

"Then doesn't it follow, as we said to begin with, that our children's amusements must be more strictly controlled; because once they and the children lose their discipline, it becomes impossible to produce good orderly citizens?"

"Yes, it follows."

"But if children play on the right lines from the beginning and learn orderly habits from their education, it produces quite the opposite results and corrects any previous flaws there may have been in the society?"

"True enough."

"And people so brought up discover rules which seem quite trivial but which their predecessors had entirely neglected."

"What sorts of rules?"

"Things like when to be silent in the presence of your elders, when to sit down and stand up, and one's duty to look after one's parents; besides the whole business of one's dress and bearing, keeping one's hair and clothes and shoes tidy, and so on. Do you agree?"

"Yes."

"But I think it would be silly to try and legislate for such things. Laws and regulations won't either produce them or maintain them."

"No, they won't."

"No, Adeimantus," I said; "for it's the bent given by education that is likely to determine all that follows — birds of a feather, you know."

"Yes, of course."

"And the final consequence is a grand result that is good or bad accordingly."

"Inevitably," he agreed.

"And that," I concluded, "is why I should not try to legislate for such minor matters. ". . .

Justice in the State

Having considered the principles by which future guardians should be selected, the dialogue then deals with general matters of social organisation and distinguishes those that should be the subject of legislation from those that should not. Then the four virtues of the ideal state are listed: wisdom, courage, discipline and justice. Wisdom is the distinguishing quality of the guardians, courage of the auxiliaries and discipline exists generally throughout society because each of the classes accepts its particular role in the overall scheme and all accept the right of the guardians to be the rulers. Socrates then goes on to consider how the fourth virtue, justice, is present.

"Good," said I; "it looks as if we had spotted three of the qualities we are looking for in our state. What about the fourth element in its goodness? It must obviously be justice."

"Obviously."

"Then we must stand like hunters round a covert and make sure that justice does not escape us and disappear from view. It must be somewhere about. Try and see if you can catch sight of it before I can, and tell me where it is."

"I wish I could," he said, "It's about as much as I can manage to follow your lead and see things when you point them out."

"Then follow me and hope for the best."

"I will," he said; "lead on."

"It looks to me," I said, "as if we were in a pretty difficult and obscure spot; it's dark and I can't see my way through it. But we must push on all the same."

"Yes, we must," he agreed.

I cast about a bit and then cried, "Tally ho, Glaucon! I think we are on the track, and our quarry won't altogether escape us."

"That's good news."

"In what way?"

"Our quarry is right under our noses all the time, and we haven't seen it but have been making perfect fools of ourselves. We are like people looking for something they have in their hands all the time; we're looking in all directions except at the thing we want, which is probably why we haven't found it."

"How do you mean?"

"I mean that it seems to me that we have failed to understand that we have in a sort of a way been talking about it all through our discussion."

"You are a long time leading up to what you've got to say; I'm getting impatient."

"Well, then listen, and see if you think I'm talking sense. I believe justice is the principle we laid down at the beginning and have consistently followed in founding our state, or else some variant of it. We laid down, if you remember, and have often repeated, that in our state one man was to do one job, the job he was naturally most suited for."

"Yes, we did."

"And further, we have often heard and often said that justice consists in minding your own business and not interfering with other people."

"Yes."

"So perhaps justice is, in a certain sense, just this minding one's own business. Do you know why I think so?"

"No, why?"

"Because I think that the virtue left over, now that we have discussed discipline, courage and wisdom, must be what makes their existence possible and preserves them by its presence. And we agreed that it would be justice that was left over if we found the other three."

"It must be."

"Now, if we were asked to judge which of these virtues by its presence contributed most to the goodness of our state, we should find it a difficult decision to make. Is it the agreement between rulers and subjects? Is it the retention by our soldiers of a proper judgment about what is and is not dangerous? Is it the guardians' ability to govern wisely? Or is it the ability of the individual — child or woman, slave, free man or artisan, ruler or subject — to get on with his own job and not interfere with other people?"

"A difficult decision, I agree."

"At any rate, wisdom, discipline, courage, and the ability to mind one's own business are all comparable in this respect: and we can regard justice as making a contribution to the goodness of our city comparable with that of the rest."

"Yes, certainly."

"Look at it again this way. I assume that you will make it the duty of our rulers to administer justice?"

"Of course."

"And won't they try to follow the principle that men should not take other people's belongings or be deprived of their own?"

"Yes, they're bound to."

"Their reason presumably being that it is *just*."

"Yes."

"So we reach again by another route the conclusion that justice is keeping to what belongs to one and doing one's own job."

"That is true."

"There's another point on which I should like your agreement. Suppose a builder and a shoemaker tried to exchange jobs, each taking on the tools and the prestige of the other's trade, or suppose alternatively the same man tried to do both jobs, would this and other exchanges of the kind do great harm to the state?"

"Not much."

"But if someone who belongs by nature to the class of artisans and businessmen is puffed up by wealth or popular support or physical strength or any similar quality, and tries to do an auxiliary's job; or if an auxiliary who is not up to it tries to take on the functions and decisions of a ruler and exchange tools and prestige with him; or if a single individual tries to do all these jobs at the same time — well, I think you'll agree that this sort of mutual interchange and interference spells destruction to our state."

"Certainly."

"Interference by the three classes with each other's jobs, and interchange of jobs between them, therefore, does the greatest harm to our state, and we are entirely justified in calling it the worst of evils."

"Absolutely justified."

"But will you not agree that the worst of evils for a state is injustice?"

"Of course."

"Then that gives us a definition of injustice. And conversely, when each of our three classes (businessmen, auxiliaries, and guardians) does its own job and minds its own business, that, by contrast, is justice and makes our city just."

"I entirely agree with what you say," he said.

"Don't let's be too emphatic about it yet," I replied. "If we find that the same definition of justice applies to the individual, we can finally agree to it — there will be nothing to prevent us; if not, we shall have to think again. For the moment let us finish our investigation." . . .

Justice as a Human Quality

The argument so far has established that the good state is the balanced state in which all persons do their own job, and, according to the principle of the division of labour, good rulers are those most fitted by nature to be so. Socrates now goes on to argue that justice in the individual is analogous to justice in the state. The individual is wise because of reason, brave because of spirit, disciplined when appetite (that is, instinctive desires) and spirit are under the control of reason. The individual is just when each of these faculties performs its own proper job and does not encroach on the function of others.

"Well, it's been a rough passage, but we've got there all right and are pretty well agreed that there are the same three elements in the individual as in the state."

"True."

"Must it not follow, then, that the individual is wise in the same way and with the same part of himself as the state? And similarly with courage and with all the other virtues?"

"It must."

"And so, my dear Glaucon," I went on, "we shall also say that the individual man is just in the same way that the state is just."

"That must follow too."

"And I suppose we have not forgotten that the state was just when the three elements within it each minded their own business."

"No, I don't think we've forgotten that."

"Then we must remember that each of us will be just, and do his duty, only if each part of him is performing its proper function."

"Yes, we must certainly remember that."

"So the reason ought to rule, having the ability and foresight to act for the whole, and the spirit ought to obey and support it. And this concord between them is effected, as we said, by a combination of intellectual and physical training, which tunes up the reason by intellectual training and tones down the crudeness of natural high spirits by harmony and rhythm."

"Certainly."

"When these two elements have been brought up and trained to their proper function, they must be put in charge of appetite, which forms the greater part of each man's make-up and is naturally insatiable. They must prevent it taking its fill of the so-called physical pleasures, for otherwise it will get too large and strong to mind its own business and will try to subject and control the other elements, which it has no right to do, and so wreck life entirely."

"True."

"At the same time," I went on, "won't these two elements be the best defence that mind and body have against external enemies? One of them will do the thinking, the other will fight under the orders of its superior and provide the courage to carry its decisions into effect."

"Yes, I agree."

"And we call an individual brave, I think, when he has the spirit to obey reason in danger, in spite of pleasure and pain?"

"That is quite right."

"And we call him wise in virtue of that small part of him which is in control and issues the orders, knowing as it does what is best for each of the three elements and for the whole."

"Yes, I agree."

"Then don't we call him self-controlled when all these three elements are in harmonious agreement, when reason and its subordinates are all agreed that reason should rule and there is no dissension?"

"That is exactly what we mean by self-control or discipline in a city or in an individual."

"And a man will be just in virtue of the principle we have referred to so often."

"That must be so."

"Well, then," I said, "is our picture in any way indistinct? Does it look as if justice in the individual were different from what we found it to be in the state?"

"I can't see any difference," he answered.

"If there are still any doubts in anyone's mind," I said, "a few elementary examples should finally convince them."

"What sort of examples?"

"Well, suppose for instance we were asked whether our state or a man of corresponding nature and training would embezzle money. Do you think we should reckon him more likely to do it than other people?"

"He would be the last person to do such a thing."

"And wouldn't it be out of the question for him to commit sacrilege or theft, or to betray his friends or his country?"

"Out of the question."

"And he would never break any promise or agreement, and be most unlikely to commit adultery, dishonour his parents or be irreligious."

"Most unlikely."

"And is not the reason for all this that each element within him is performing its proper function, whether it is giving or obeying orders?"

"Yes, that is the reason."

"Are you now convinced, then, that justice is the quality that produces men and states of this character?"

"Yes, I am quite convinced," he said.

"So our dream has come true, and, as we guessed, we have been lucky enough to run across an elementary type of justice right at the beginning of the foundation of our state."

"Yes, we have."

"In fact the provision that the man naturally fitted to be a shoemaker, or carpenter, or anything else, should stick to his own trade has turned out to be a kind of image of justice — hence its usefulness."

"So it seems."

"Justice, therefore, we may say, is a principle of this kind; but its real concern is not with external actions, but with a man's inward self. The just man will not allow the three elements which make up his inward self to trespass on each other's functions or interfere with each other, but, by keeping all three in tune, like the notes of a scale (high, middle, and low, or whatever they be), will in the truest sense set his house in order, and be his own lord and master and at peace with himself. When he has bound these elements into a single controlled and orderly whole and so unified himself, he will be ready for action of any kind, whether personal, financial, political or commercial; and whenever he calls any course of action just and fair, he will mean that it contributes to and helps to maintain this disposition of mind, and will call the knowledge which controls such action wisdom. Similarly, by injustice he will mean any action destructive of this disposition, and by ignorance the ideas which control such action."

"That is all absolutely true, Socrates."

"Good," I said. "So we shan't be very far wrong if we claim to have discerned what the just man and the just state are, and in what their justice consists."

"Certainly not."

"Shall we make the claim, then?"

"Yes."

"So much for that," I said. "And next, I suppose, we ought to consider injustice."

"Obviously."

"It must be some kind of internal quarrel between these same three elements, when they interfere with each other and trespass on each other's functions, or when one of them sets itself up to control the whole when it has no business to do so, because its natural role is one of subordination to the control of its superior. This sort of situation, when the elements of the mind are in confusion, is what produces injustice, indiscipline, cowardice, ignorance and vice of all kinds."

"Yes, that's so."

"And if we know what injustice and justice are, it's clear enough, isn't it, what is meant by acting unjustly and doing wrong or, again, by acting justly?"

"How do you mean?"

"Well," I said, "there is an analogy here with physical health and sickness."

"How?"

"Healthy activities produce health, and unhealthy activities produce sickness."

"True."

"Well, then, don't just actions produce justice, and unjust actions injustice?"

"They must."

"And as health is produced by establishing a natural order of control and subordination among the constituents of the body, disease by the opposite process, so justice is produced by establishing in the mind a similar order of control and subordination among its constituents, and injustice by the opposite process."

"Certainly."

"It seems, then, that virtue is a kind of mental health or beauty or fitness, and vice a kind of illness or deformity or weakness."

"That is so."

"And virtue and vice are in turn the result of one's practice, good or bad."

"They must be."

"We are left, then, I suppose, with the question whether it pays to act justly and do right and be just irrespective of appearances, or to do wrong and be unjust provided you escape punishment and consequent improvement."

"I think we have already shown the question to be an absurd one, Socrates," he replied. "Men don't reckon that life is worth living when their physical health breaks down, even though they have all the food and drink and wealth and power in the world. So we can hardly reckon it worth living when the principle of life itself breaks down in confusion, and a man wilfully avoids the one thing that will rid him of vice and crime, the acquisition of justice and virtue in the sense which we have shown them to bear." . . .

The Philosopher Ruler

Following the discussion of justice, the argument then makes the revolutionary sugges-tion (for the times) that the family should be abolished, that women should be admitted to full equality with men, and that children should be raised communally. Socrates then goes on to make the point that justice will never obtain until rulers become philosophers, and philosophers become rulers. Knowing that this would sound too naive to most persons, he shows in the example of the quarrelling crew on a storm-tossed ship, that simply because the common people do not appreciate the degree of skill and knowledge required for the exercise of a profession, this does not mean that such skill and knowledge is unneces-sary. So, by analogy, because philosophy is presently undervalued and most people can not see the relevance of philosophical training or its body of expertise, this does not negate the value of philosophy. Indeed, it is argued here that public opinion is formed by the disreputable sophists (usually itinerant teachers) who misuse education and create a false impression of it. If a truly just state is to be developed, then it must come from a new start, and this leads to a discussion of the education of the genuine philosopher who has a knowledge of the Good.

Book V

"But it seems to me Socrates, that if we let you go on like this you will forget all about your promise to prove that the state we have described is a prac-tical possibility, and if so how; all you've been saying has merely been put-ting the question off. I'll admit that your state would be ideal if it existed, and I'll fill in the gaps in your description myself. I know that the mutual loyalty the citizens would feel because they know they can call each other brothers, fathers, and sons, would make them most formidable enemies; and that the presence of their women on campaign, whether they fought with them or acted as a reserve, would make them altogether invincible, because of the panic it would cause in their enemies and the support it would give in case of need; and I can see how many domestic advantages they would have. I grant all this, and a thousand other things too, *if* our state existed, and I don't want to hear any more details. Let us now concentrate on the job of proving *that* it can exist and *how* it can exist."

"This a very sudden attack," I countered, "and you've no sympathy with my delays. I've just escaped two waves; but the third, which you are trying to bring on me now, is the biggest and the most difficult of the three, though you may not know it. When you have seen and heard it, you will forgive me for the very natural hesitation which made me afraid to put forward and examine such a paradoxical theory."

"The more of these excuses we hear," he replied, "the less likely we are to let you off explaining how our state can be realised. Get on and don't waste time."

"Well," I said, "perhaps I ought to remind you first of all that we started our discussion by trying to find a definition of justice and injustice."

"Yes—what of it?" he asked.

"I was only going to ask whether, when we find out what justice is, we shall require the just man to answer the description exactly, without any modification? Or shall we be content if he approximates to it pretty closely and has more of it about him than other men?"

"That will content us."

"Then we were looking for an ideal when we tried to define justice and injustice, and to describe what the perfectly just or perfectly unjust man would be like if he ever existed. By looking at these perfect patterns and the measure of happiness or unhappiness they would enjoy, we force ourselves to admit that the nearer we approximate to them the more nearly we share their lot. That was our purpose, rather than to show that they could be realised in practice, was it not?"

"That is quite true."

"If a painter, then, draws an idealised picture of a man, complete to the last detail, is he any the worse painter because he cannot point to a real original?"

"No, certainly not."

"But haven't we been painting a word picture of an ideal state?"

"True."

"Is our picture any the worse drawn, then, because we can't show how it can be realised in fact?"

"No."

"That, then, is the truth of the matter. But if I'm to go on, to oblige you, and show how and under what conditions we can get nearest our ideal, you must admit that the same principles apply."

"What principles?"

"Does practice ever square with theory? Is it not in the nature of things that, whatever people think, practice should fall short of the precision of theory? What do you think?"

"I agree."

"Then don't insist on my showing that every detail of our description can be realised in practice, but grant that we shall have met your demand that the ideal should be realised, if we are able to find the conditions under which a state can approximate most clearly to it. Will you be content with that? I would."

"And so will I."

"The next thing, I suppose, is to try to show what fault it is in the constitutions of existing states that prevents them from being run like ours, and what is the least change that would bring them into conformity with it — a single change if possible, failing that two, or as few and as small as may be."

"Certainly."

"I think we can show that the necessary transformation can be effected by a single change," I said, "but it's hardly a small or easy one, though it is possible."

"Tell us what it is."

"I'm now facing what we called the biggest wave," I replied. "I'll tell you what it is, even if it swamps me in a surge of laughter and I'm drowned in ridicule; so listen to what I'm going to say."

"Go on."

"The society we have described can never grow into a reality or see the light of day, and there will be no end to the troubles of states, or indeed, my dear Glaucon, of humanity itself, till philosophers become kings in this world, or till those we now call kings and rulers really and truly become philosophers, and political power and philosophy thus come into the same hands, while the many natures now content to follow either to the exclusion of the other are forcibly debarred from doing so. This is what I have hesitated to say so long, knowing what a paradox it would sound; for it is not easy to see that there is no other road to happiness, either for society or the individual."

Glaucon's reply to this was to exclaim, "My dear Socrates, if you produce theories of that sort, you can't be surprised if most decent people take their coats off, pick up the nearest weapon, and come after you in their shirt-sleeves to do something terrible to you. If you can't find an argument to hold them off and escape, you'll learn to your cost what it is to be laughed at."

"But it's all your doing," said I.

"And I've done very well too," he retorted. "But I won't desert you, and will give you what help I can, though it won't amount to more than encouragement, and perhaps a willingness to answer your questions more reasonably than others would. So you must try to convince the sceptics with that amount of help."

"You're such a powerful ally that I will go ahead," I replied. . . .

Book VI

Here Adeimantus interrupted. "Of course no one can deny what you have said, Socrates. But whenever people hear you talking like this they have an uneasy feeling that because they're not very experienced in this pro cedure of question and answer, you lead them on with your questions bit by bit, until at the end of the argument all their admissions are added up and they are badly caught out and shown to have contradicted themselves; they feel your arguments are like a kind of verbal chess in which the unskilled player is always in the end checkmated and reduced to silence by the expert, though he's really in the right none the less. Look at our present discussion. It might well be said that it was impossible to contradict you at any point of the argument, but yet that it was perfectly plain that people who study philosophy too long, and don't treat it simply as part of their early educa tion and then drop it, become, most of them, very odd birds, not to say thoroughly vicious; while even the best of them are reduced by this study you praise so highly to complete uselessness as members of society."

When he had finished, I asked him whether he thought these charges untrue, to which he replied, "I don't know; I'd like to hear what you think." I answered that they seemed to me perfectly true. "Then how," he asked, "can you possibly say that society's troubles will never cease until it is ruled by philosophers, if you agree that they're useless members of society?"

"To answer that question," I said, "I must give you an illustration."

"A thing which, of course, you never normally do!"

"There you go," I said, "pulling my leg when you've landed me with such a difficult point to prove. But just you listen to my illustration, and you'll see what a jam I'm in. For there's really no single thing one can use to illus trate the plight of the better type of philosopher in contemporary society; one must draw on several sources for one's illustrations in defence of him, like a painter combining two or more animals in one.

"Suppose the following to be the state of affairs on board a ship or ships. The captain is larger and stronger than any of the crew, but a bit deaf and short-sighted, and doesn't know much about navigation. The crew are all quarrelling with each other about how to navigate the ship, each thinking he ought to be at the helm; they know no navigation and cannot say that anyone ever taught it to them, or that they spent any time studying it; indeed they say it can't be taught and are ready to murder anyone, who says it can. They spend all their time milling round the captain and trying to get him to give them the wheel. If one faction is more successful than another, their rivals may kill them and throw them overboard, lay out the honest captain with drugs or drink, take control of the ship, help themselves to what's on board, and behave as if they were on a drunken pleasure cruise. Finally, they reserve their admiration for the man who knows how to lend a hand in controlling the captain by force or fraud; they praise his seaman ship and navigation and knowledge of the sea and condemn everyone else as useless. They have no idea that the true navigator must study the seasons of the year, the sky, the stars, the winds and other professional subjects, if he is to be really fit to control a ship; and they think that it's quite impossible to acquire professional skill in navigation (quite apart from whether they want it exercised) and that there's no such thing as an art of navigation. In these circumstances aren't the sailors on any such ship bound to regard the true navigator as a gossip and a star-gazer, of no use to them at all?"

"Yes, they are," Adeimantus agreed.

"I think you probably understand, without any explanation, that my illustration is intended to show the present attitude of society towards the true philosopher."

"Yes, I understand."

"Then you must tell it to anyone who is surprised that society does not value its philosophers, and try, first, to convince him that it would be far more surprising if it did."

"I will," he said.

"And tell him it's quite true that the best of the philosophers are of no use to their fellows; but that he should blame, not the philosophers, but those who fail to make use of them. For it is not natural for the master to request the crew to be guided by him or for the wise to wait on the rich (the author of that epigram was wrong); the true and natural order is for the sick man, whether rich or poor, to wait on the doctor, and for those in want of guidance to wait on him who can give it, if he's really any use, and not for him to wait on them. And you won't be far wrong if you compare the politicians who at present rule us to the sailors in our illustration, and those whom they call useless visionaries to the true navigators."

"That is very true."

"These are the reasons and conditions which make it difficult for the best of all pursuits to get a good reputation from men whose practice runs contrary to it. But far the most damaging reproach to philosophy is brought on it by those who pretend to practise it, and whom your critic has in mind when he says that most people who practise it are vicious, and the best of them useless — a criticism with which I agreed, did I not?"

"Yes."

"Well, we have explained the reason for the uselessness of the best of them."

"Yes, we have." . . .

"Well, then, that part of our job is done — and it's not been easy; we must now go on to the next, and ask about the position and training of these saviours of our society. What are they to learn and at what age are they to learn it?"

"Yes, that's our next question."

"I didn't really gain anything," I said, "by being clever and putting off the difficulties about the possession of women, the production of children and the establishment of rulers till later. I knew that my true society would give offence and be difficult to realise; but I have had to describe it all the same. I've dealt with the business about women and children, and now I've got to start again on the rulers. You will remember that we said they must love their country, and be tested both in pleasure and pain, to ensure that their loyalty remained unshaken by pain or fear or any other misfortune; those who failed the test were to be rejected, but those who emerged unscathed, like gold tried in the fire, were to be established as rulers and given honours and rewards both in life and after death. This is roughly what we said, but we were afraid of stirring up the problems we are now facing, and our argument evaded the issue and tried to get by without being seen, as it were."

"Yes, I remember," he said.

"You know, I hesitated before to say the rash things I've said," I replied; "but now let me be brave and say that our guardians, in the fullest sense, must be philosophers."

"So be it."

"Think how few of them there are likely to be. The elements in the character which we have insisted they must have don't usually combine into a whole, but are normally found separately."

"What do you mean?"

"Readiness to learn and remember, quickness and keenness of mind and the qualities that go with them, and enterprise and breadth of vision, aren't usually combined with steadiness, discipline, and willingness to lead a quiet life, such keen temperaments are very unstable and quite devoid of steadiness."

"True."

"And again steady, trustworthy, reliable characters, who are unmoved by fear in war, are equally unmoved by instruction. Their immobility amounts indeed to numbness and, faced with anything that demands intellectual effort, they yawn and sink into slumber."

"That's all quite true."

"But we demand a fair share of both sets of qualities from anyone who is to be given the highest form of education and any share of office or authority."

"And rightly."

"So the character we want will be a rare occurrence."

"It will."

"And we must not only test it in the pains and fears and pleasures we have already described, but also try it out in a series of intellectual studies which we omitted before, to see if it has the endurance to pusue the highest forms of knowledge, without flinching as others flinch in physical trials." . . .

". . .the highest form of knowledge is knowledge of the essential nature of goodness, from which things that are just and so on derive their usefulness and value. You know pretty well that that's what I have to say, and that I'm going to add that our knowledge of it is inadequate, and that because we are ignorant of it the rest of our knowledge, however perfect, can be of no benefit to us, just as it's no use possessing anything if you can't get any good out of it. Or do you think there's any point in possessing anything if it's no good? Is there any point in having all other forms of knowledge, if you don't know what is right and good?"

"I certainly don't think there is."

"And you know of course that most people think that pleasure is the Good, while the more sophisticated think it is knowledge."

"Yes."

"But those who hold this last view can't tell us what knowledge they mean, but are compelled in the end to say they mean knowledge of the Good."

"Which is quite absurd."

"An absurdity they can't avoid, if, after criticising us for *not* knowing the Good, they then turn round and talk to us as if we *did* know it; for they say it is 'knowledge of the Good' as if we understood what they meant when they use the word 'good'."

"That's perfectly true."

"Then what about those who define Good as pleasure? Is their confusion any less? Aren't they compelled to admit that there are bad pleasures?"

"Of course they are."

"And they thus find themselves admitting that the same things are both good and bad, don't they?"

"Yes."

"So it's obvious that the subject is full of obscurities."

"It is indeed."

"Well, then, isn't it obvious too that when it's a matter of justice or fairness many people prefer the appearance to the reality, and are glad to appear to have these qualities even when they haven't; but that no one is satisfied with something that only *appears* good for him, but wants something that *really* is, and has no use here for appearances?"

"Absolutely true."

"Good, then, is the end of all endeavour, the object on which every heart is set, whose existence it divines, though it finds it difficult to say just what is it; and because it can't grasp it with the same assurance as other things it misses any value those other things have. Can we possibly agree that the best of our citizens, to whom we are going to entrust everything, should be in the dark about so important a subject?"

"It's the last thing we can admit."

"At any rate a man will not be a very useful guardian of what is right and fair if he does not know in what their goodness consists; and I suspect that until he knows this no one can understand them."

"Your suspicions are well founded."

"So our society will not be properly regulated unless it is in charge of a guardian who has this knowledge."

"That must be so," he said. "But what about you? Do you think that the Good is knowledge or pleasure? Or do you think it's something else?" . . .

The Form of the Good

To define the Good is crucial to the argument and Plato does this through his theory of Forms, which is presented in an extended metaphor. In the physical world, he explains, the eye is able to see objects because they are illuminated by the sun as a source of light; so, in the intelligible world the mind's eye is able to "see" intelligible objects because they are illuminated by the Form of the Good as the source of intellectual light. To make his point another way Plato uses the famous illustration of the divided line in which he asks us to draw a line and then to divide it into two parts, corresponding to the visible and intelligible realms. The visible we can subdivide into two more parts, the class of images and that of objects. These, since they are phenomenal, and therefore subject to change, can only provide us with opinion and belief. Now in like fashion, the intelligible part of the line can be subdivided, by analogy, into two classes, that of (mathematical) figures and that of pure Forms. These two classes, because they are noumenal, and therefore timeless, are the sources of knowledge. To make his point even more secure, Plato goes on to his equally famous allegory of the cave. In this he argues that most people see only the shadows of reality, and knowing nothing else, mistake these shadows for that reality.

Herein lies his essential educational argument: only some people have the ability to "see" in the intelligible world and so to reach the Form of the Good. These are people who have a "capacity innate in their mind" [. . . τὴν ἐνοῦσαν ἑκάστου δύναμιν ἐν τῇ ψυχῇ]. It follows that the state, therefore, should be ruled by these persons, and, since they already themselves contain justice in their composition, they will recognise their obligation to give the state the benefit of their wisdom.

"We distinguish between the many particular things which we call beautiful or good, and absolute beauty and goodness. Similarly with all other collections of things, we say there is corresponding to each set a single, unique Form which we call an 'absolute' reality."

"That is so."

"And we say that the particulars are objects of sight but not of intelligence, while the Forms are the objects of intelligence but not of sight."

"Certainly."

"And with what part of ourselves do we see what we see?"

"With our eyes."

"And we hear with our ears, and so on with the other senses and their objects."

"Of course."

"Then have you noticed," I asked, "how extremely lavish the designer of our senses was when he gave us the faculty of sight and made objects visible?"

"I can't say I have."

"Then look. Do hearing and speech need something else in addition to themselves to enable the ear to hear and the sound to be heard — some third element without which the one cannot hear or the other be heard?"

"No."

"And the same is true of most, indeed all, the other senses. Or can you think of any that needs such an element?"

"No, I can't."

"But haven't you noticed that sight and its objects do need one?"

"How?"

"If your eyes have the power of sight and you try to use them, and if objects have colour, yet you will see nothing and the colours will remain invisible unless a third element is present which is specially constituted for the purpose."

"What is that?" he asked.

"What you call light," I answered.

"True."

"Then the sense of sight and the visibility of objects are connected by something that is by a long way the most valuable of all links — that is, if light is a thing of value."

"Which it most certainly is."

"Which, then, of the heavenly bodies do you regard as responsible for it? Whose light would you say it is that makes our eyes see and objects be seen most perfectly?"

"I should say the same as you or anyone else: you mean the sun, of course."

"Then is the relation of sun and sight such that the sun is identical neither with sight itself nor with the eye in which sight resides, though the eye is the sense organ most similar to the sun?"

"Yes."

"So the eye's power of sight is a kind of effusion dispensed to it by the sun."

"Yes."

"Then, moreover, though the sun is not itself sight, it is the cause of sight and is seen by the sight it causes."

"That is so."

"Well, this is the child of the Good, of which I spoke," I said. "The Good has begotten it in its own likeness, and it bears the same relation to sight and visibility in the visible world that the Good bears to intelligence and intelligibility in the intelligible world."

"Will you explain that a bit further?" he asked.

"You know that when we turn our eyes to objects whose colours are no longer illuminated by daylight, but only by moonlight or starlight, they see dimly and appear to be almost blind, as if they had no clear vision."

"Yes."

"But when we turn them on things on which the sun is shining, then they see clearly and their power of vision is restored."

"Certainly."

"Apply the analogy to the mind. When the mind's eyes rests on objects illuminated by truth and reality, it understands and comprehends them, and functions intelligently; but when it turns to the twilight world of change and decay, it can only form opinions, its vision is confused and its beliefs shifting, and it seems to lack intelligence."

"That is true."

"Then what gives the objects of knowledge their truth and the mind the power of knowing is the Form of the Good. It is the cause of knowledge and truth, and you will be right to think of it as being something other than, and even higher than, knowledge and truth. And just as it was right to think of light and sight as being like the sun, but wrong to think of them as being the sun itself, so here again it is right to think of knowledge and truth as being like the Good, but wrong to think of either of them as being the Good, which must be given a still higher place of honour."

"You are making it something remarkably exalted, if it is the source of knowledge and truth, and yet itself higher than they are. For I suppose you can't mean it to be pleasure?" he asked.

"A monstrous suggestion," I replied. "Let us pursue our analogy further."

"Go on."

"The sun, I think you will agree, not only makes the things we see visible, but causes the processes of generation, growth and nourishment, without itself being such a process."

"True."

"The Good therefore may be said to be the source not only of the intelligibility of the objects of knowledge, but also of their existence and reality; yet it is not itself identical with reality, but is beyond reality, and superior to it in dignity and power."

"It really must be devilish superior," remarked Glaucon with a grin.

"Now, don't blame me," I protested; "it was you who made me say what I thought about it."

"Yes, and please go on. At any rate finish off the analogy with the sun, if you haven't finished it."

"I've not nearly finished it."

"Then go on and don't leave anything out."

"I'm afraid I must leave a lot out," I said. "But I'll do my best to get in everything I can at the moment."

"Yes, please do."

"You must suppose, then," I went on, "that there are these two powers of which I have spoken, and that one of them is supreme over everything in the intelligible world, the other over everything in the visible world — I won't say in the physical universe or you will think I'm playing with words. At any rate you understand there are these two orders of things, the visible and the intelligible?"

"Yes I understand."

"Well, take a line divided into two unequal parts, corresponding to the visible and the intelligible worlds, and then divide the two parts again in the same ratio, to represent degrees of clarity and obscurity. In the visible world one section stands for images: by 'images' I mean first shadows, then reflections in water and other close-grained, polished surfaces, and all that sort of thing if you understand me."

"I understand."

"Let the other section stand for the objects which are the originals of the images — animals, plants and manufactured objects of all kinds."

"Very good."

"Would you be prepared to admit that these sections differ in their degree of truth, and that the relation of image to original is the same as that of opinion to knowledge?"

"I would."

"Then consider next how the intelligible part of the line is to be divided. In one section the mind uses the originals of the visible world in their turn as images, and has to base its enquiries on assumptions and proceed from them to its conclusions instead of going back to first principles: in the other it proceeds from assumption back to self-sufficient first principles, making no use of the images employed in the other section, but pursuing its enquiry solely by means of Forms."

"I don't quite understand."

"I will try again; and what I have just said will help you to understand. I think you know that students of geometry and similar forms of reasoning begin by taking for granted odd and even numbers, geometrical figures and the three kinds of angle, and other kindred data in their various subjects; these they regard as known, and treat as basic assumptions which it is quite unnecessary to explain to themselves or anyone else because they are self-evident. Starting from them, they proceed through a series of consistent steps to the propositions which they set out to examine."

"Yes, I know that."

"You know too that they make use of and reason about visible figures, though they are not really thinking about them at all, but about the originals which they resemble; they are arguing not about the square or diagonal which they have drawn but about the absolute square or diagonal, or whatever the figure may be. The figures they draw or model, which again have their shadows and reflections in water, they treat as illustrations only, the real subjects of their investigation being invisible except to the eye of the mind."

"That is quite true."

"This sort of reality I described as intelligible, but said that the mind was forced to use assumptions in investigating it, and because it was unable to ascend from these assumptions to a first principle, used as illustrations objects which in turn have their images on a lower plane, in comparison with which they are themselves thought to have a superior clarity and value."

"I understand," he said. "You are referring to what happens in geometry and kindred sciences."

"Then when I speak of the other section of the intelligible part of the line you will understand that I mean that which reason apprehends directly by the power of pure thought; it treats assumptions not as principles, but as assumptions in the true sense, that is, as starting points and steps in the ascent to the universal, self-sufficient first principle; when it has reached that principle it can again descend by keeping to the consequences that follow from it, to a final conclusion. The whole procedure involves nothing in the sensible world, but deals throughout with Forms and finishes with Forms."

"I understand," he said; "though not entirely, because what you describe sounds like a long job. But you want to distinguish the section of intelligible reality which is studied by the activity of pure thought, as having greater clarity and certainty than the section studied by the mathematical sciences; in these sciences assumptions serve as principles and their subject matter must be reasoned about and not directly perceived, and because they proceed *from* assumptions and not *to* first principles they can never finally understand their subject matter, even though it can be understood with the help of a first principle. And I think that you call the state of mind of geometers and the like reason but not intelligence, meaning by reason something midway between opinion and intelligence."

"You have understood me well enough," I said. "And you may assume that there are, corresponding to the four sections of the line, four states of mind: to the top section Intelligence, to the second Reason, to the third Opinion, and to the fourth Illusion. And you may arrange them in a scale, and assume that they have degrees of clarity corresponding to the degree of truth and reality possessed by their subject matter."

"I understand," he replied, "and agree with your proposed arrangement."

Book VII

"I want you to go on to picture the enlightenment or ignorance of our human conditions somewhat as follows. Imagine an underground chamber, like a cave with an entrance open to the daylight and running a long way underground. In this chamber are men who have been prisoners there since they were children, their legs and necks being so fastened that they can only look straight ahead of them and cannot turn their heads. Behind them and above them a fire is burning, and between the fire and the prisoners runs a road, in front of which a curtain-wall has been built, like the screen at puppet shows between the operators and their audience, above which they show their puppets."

"I see."

"Imagine further that there are men carrying all sorts of gear along behind the curtain-wall, including figures of men and animals made of wood and stone and other materials, and that some of these men, as is natural, are talking and some not."

"An odd picture and an odd sort of prisoner."

"They are drawn from life," I replied. "For, tell me, do you think our prisoners could see anything of themselves or their fellows except the shadows thrown by the fire on the wall of the cave opposite them?"

"How could they see anything else if they were prevented from moving their heads all their lives?"

"And would they see anything more of the objects carried along the road?"

"Of course not."

"Then if they were able to talk to each other, would they not assume that the shadows they saw were real things?"

"Inevitably."

"And if the wall of their prison opposite them reflected sound, don't you think that they would suppose, whenever one of the passers-by on the road spoke, that the voice belonged to the shadow passing before them?"

"They would be bound to think so."

"And so they would believe that the shadows of the objects we mentioned were in all respects real."

"Yes, inevitably."

"Then think what would naturally happen to them if they were released from their bonds and cured of their delusions. Suppose one of them were let loose, and suddenly compelled to stand up and turn his head and look and walk towards the fire; all these actions would be painful and he would be too dazzled to see properly the objects of which he used to see the shadows. So if he was told that what he used to see was mere illusion and that he was now nearer reality and seeing more correctly, because he was turned towards objects that were more real, and if on top of that he were compelled to say what each of the passing objects was when it was pointed out to him, don't you think he would be at a loss, and think that what he used to see was more real than the objects now being pointed out to him?"

"Much more real."

"And if he were made to look directly at the light of the fire, it would hurt his eyes and he would turn back and take refuge in the things which he could see, which he would think really far clearer than the things being shown him."

"Yes."

"And if," I went on, "he were forcibly dragged up the steep and rocky ascent and not let go till he had been dragged out into the sunlight, the process would be a painful one, to which he would much object, and when he emerged into the light his eyes would be so overwhelmed by the brightness of it that he wouldn't be able to see a single one of the things he was now told were real."

"Certainly not at first," he agreed.

"Because he would need to grow accustomed to the light before he could see things in the world outside the cave. First he would find it easiest to look at shadows, next at the reflections of men and other objects in water, and later on at the objects themselves. After that he would find it easier to observe the heavenly bodies and the sky at night than by day, and to look at the light of the moon and stars, rather than at the sun and its light."

"Of course."

"The thing he would be able to do last would be to look directly at the sun, and observe its nature without using reflections in water or any other medium, but just as it is."

"That must come last."

"Later on he would come to the conclusion that it is the sun that produces the changing seasons and years and controls everything in the visible world, and is in a sense responsible for everything that he and his fellow prisoners used to see."

"That is the conclusion which he would obviously reach."

"And when he thought of his first home and what passed for wisdom there, and of his fellow prisoners, don't you think he would congratulate himself on his good fortune and be sorry for them?"

"Very much so."

"There was probably a certain amount of honour and glory to be won among the prisoners, and prizes for keen-sightedness for anyone who could remember the order of sequence among the passing shadows and so be best able to predict their future appearances. Will our released prisoner hanker after these prizes or envy this power or honour? Won't he be more likely to feel, as Homer says, that he would far rather be 'a serf in the house of some landless man', or indeed anything else in the world, than live and think as they do?"

"Yes," he replied, "he would prefer anything to a life like theirs."

"Then what do you think would happen," I asked, "if he went back to sit in his old seat in the cave? Wouldn't his eyes be blinded by the darkness, because he had come in suddenly out of the daylight?"

"Certainly."

"And if he had to discriminate between the shadows, in competition with the other prisoners, while he was still blinded and before his eyes got used to the darkness — a process that might take some time — wouldn't he be likely to make a fool of himself? And they would say that his visit to the upper world had ruined his sight, and that the ascent was not worth even attempting. And if anyone tried to release them and lead them up, they would kill him if they could lay hands on him."

"They certainly would."

"Now, my dear Glaucon," I went on, "this simile must be connected, throughout, with what preceded it. The visible realm corresponds to the prison, and the light of the fire in the prison to the power of the sun. And you won't go wrong if you connect the ascent into the upper world and the sight of the objects there with the upward progress of the mind into the intelligible realm — that's my guess, which is what you are anxious to hear. The truth of the matter is, after all, known only to God. But in my opinion, for what it is worth, the final thing to be perceived in the intelligible realm, and perceived only with difficulty, is the absolute form of Good; once seen, it is inferred to be responsible for everything right and good, producing in the visible realm light and the source of light, and being, in the intelligible realm itself, the controlling source of reality and intelligence. And anyone who is going to act rationally either in public or private must perceive it."

"I agree," he said, "so far as I am able to understand you."

"Then you will perhaps also agree with me that it won't be surprising if those who get so far are unwilling to return to mundane affairs, and if their minds long to remain among higher things. That's what we should expect if our simile is to be trusted."

"Yes, that's to be expected."

"Nor will you think it strange that anyone who descends from contemplation of the divine to the imperfections of human life should blunder and make a fool of himself, if, while still blinded and unaccustomed to the surrounding darkness, he's forcibly put on trial in the law courts or elsewhere about the images of justice or their shadows, and made to dispute about the conceptions of justice held by men who have never seen absolute justice."

"There's nothing strange in that."

"But anyone with any sense," I said, "will remember that the eyes may be unsighted in two ways, by a transition either from light to darkness or from darkness to light, and that the same distinction applies to the mind. So when he sees a mind confused and unable to see clearly he will not laugh without thinking, but will ask himself whether it has come from a clearer world and is confused by the unaccustomed darkness, or whether it is dazzled by the stronger light of the clearer world to which it has escaped from its previous ignorance. The first state is a reason for congratulation, the second for sympathy, though if one wants to laugh at it one can do so with less absurdity than at the mind that has descended from the daylight of the upper world."

"You put it very reasonably."

"If this is true," I continued, "We must reject the conception of education professed by those who say that they can put into the mind knowledge that was not there before — rather as if they could put sight into blind eyes."

"It is a claim that is certainly made," he said.

"But our argument indicates that this is a capacity which is innate in each man's mind, and that the faculty by which he learns is like an eye which cannot be turned from darkness to light unless the whole body is turned; in the same way the mind as a whole must be turned away from the world of change until its eye can bear to look straight at reality, and at the brightest of all realities which is what we call the Good. Isn't that so?"

"Yes."

"Then this business of turning the mind round might be made a subject of professional skill, which would effect the conversion as easily and effectively as possible. It would not be concerned to implant sight, but to ensure that someone who had it already was turned in the right direction and looking the right way."

"That may well be so."

"The rest, therefore, of what are commonly called qualities of the mind perhaps resemble those of the body, in that they are not innate, but are implanted by training and practice; but the power of knowing, it seems, belongs to some diviner faculty, which never loses its power, but whose effects are good or bad according to the direction in which it is turned. Have you never noticed how shrewd is the glance of the type of men commonly called bad but clever? Their intelligence is limited, but their sight is sharp enough in matters that concern them; it's not that their sight is weak, but that they put it to bad use, so that the keener it is the worse its effects."

"That's true."

"But suppose," I said, "that such natures were cut loose, when they were still children, from the dead weight of worldliness, fastened on them by sensual indulgences like gluttony, which distorts their mind's vision to lower things, and suppose that when so freed they were turned towards the truth, then the same faculty in them would have as keen a vision of truth as it has of the objects on which it is at present turned."

"Very likely."

"And is it not also likely, and indeed a necessary consequence of what we have said, that society will never be properly governed either by the uneducated, who have no knowledge of the truth, or by those who are allowed to spend all their lives in purely intellectual pursuits? The uneducated have no single aim in life to which all their actions, public and private, are directed; the intellectuals will take no practical action of their own accord, fancying themselves to be no longer of this world."

"True."

"Then our job as lawgivers is to compel the best minds to attain what we have called the highest form of knowledge, and to ascend to the vision of Good as we have described, and when they have achieved this and seen enough, prevent them behaving as they now do."

"What do you mean by that?"

"Remaining in the upper world, and refusing to return again to the prisoners in the cave below and share their labours and rewards, whether they are worth having or not."

"But surely," he protested, "that will not be fair. We shall be compelling them to live a poorer life than they might live."

"The object of our legislation," I reminded him again, "is not the welfare of any particular class, but of the whole community. It uses persuasion or force to unite all citizens and make them share together the benefits which each individually can confer on the community; and its purpose in fostering this attitude is not to enable everyone to please himself, but to make each man a link in the unity of the whole."

"You are right; I had forgotten," he said.

"You see, then, Glaucon," I went on, "we shan't be unfair to our philosophers, but shall be quite justified in compelling them to have some care and responsibility for others. We shall tell them that philosophers in other states can reasonably refuse to take part in the hard work of politics; for society produces them quite involuntarily and unintentionally, and it is only just that anything that grows up on its own should feel it has nothing to repay for an upbringing which it owes to no one. 'But you,' we shall say, 'have been bred to rule to your own advantage and that of the whole community, like king bees in a hive; you are better educated than the rest and better qualified to combine the practice of philosophy and politics. You must therefore each descend in turn and live with your fellows in the cave and get used to seeing in the dark; once you get used to it you will see a thousand times better than they do and will recognise the various shadows, and know what they are shadows of, because you have seen the truth about things right and just and good. And so our state and yours will be really awake, and not merely dreaming like most societies today, with their shadow battles and their stuggles for political power, which they treat as some great prize. The truth is quite different: the state whose rulers come to their duties with least enthusiasm is bound to have the best and most tranquil government, and the state whose rulers are eager to rule the worst.'"

"I quite agree."

"Then will our pupils, when they hear what we say, refuse to take their share of the hard work of government, though spending the greater part of their time together in the pure air of philosophy?"

"They cannot refuse, for we are making a just demand of just men. But of course, unlike present rulers, they will approach the business of government as an unavoidable necessity."

"Yes, of course," I agreed. "The truth is that if you want a well-governed state you must find for your future rulers some career they like better than government; for only then will you have government by the truly rich, those, that is, whose riches consist not of money, but of the happiness of a right and rational life. If you get, in public affairs, men who are so morally impoverished that they have nothing they can contribute themselves, but who hope to snatch some compensation for their own inadequacy from a political career, there can never be good government. They start fighting for power, and the consequent internal and domestic conflicts ruin both them and society."

"True indeed."

"Is there any other life except that of true philosophy which looks down on political power?"

"None that I know of."

"And yet the only men to get power should be men who do not love it, otherwise we shall have rivals' quarrels."

"That is certain."

"Who else, then, are we to compel to undertake the responsibilities of ruling, if it is not to be those who know most about good government and who yet value other things more highly than politics and its rewards?"

"There is no one else."

Programme of Studies for the Education of the Guardian

The discussion now turns to the programme of studies for the guardian-designate. Building on the foundation of prior studies in music, literature and physical training, which customarily went on in ancient Greece till about mid-adolescence, when the youths then did their period of military service, the following section considers the studies to be provided in the years of early adulthood. A ten-year programme of mathematics is proposed —

arithmetic, geometry (plane and solid), astronomy and harmonics — to be followed by a five-year period of dialectic. The latter, because it is concerned with a "definition of the essential nature of things" must necessarily be the terminus of intellectual attainment, and so should be the "coping-stone" of the programme of education for the guardian.

Then would you like us to consider how men of this kind are to be produced, and how they are to be led up to the light, like the men in stories who are said to have risen from the underworld to heaven?"

"I should like it very much."

"It's not a thing we can settle by spinning a coin," I said. "What is at issue is the conversion of the mind from the twilight of error to the truth, that climb up into the real world which we shall call true philosophy."

"Yes, of course."

"So we must try to find out what sort of studies have this effect."

"Yes."

"Well, Glaucon," I asked, "what should men study if their minds are to be drawn from the world of change to reality? Now it occurs to me that we said our rulers must be trained for war when they were young."

"We did."

"Then the subject we're looking for must be relevant in war too."

"How do you mean?"

"It mustn't be useless to soldiers."

"Not if we can avoid it."

"Well, we've already arranged for their physical training and their education in literature and music. And of these two physical training is concerned with the world of change and decay, for the body, which it looks after, grows and declines."

"Yes, clearly."

"So it won't be the study we are looking for."

"No."

"Then what about the literary education which we described earlier on?"

"That," he reminded me, "was the complement of their physical education. It gave them a moral training, and used music and rhythm to produce a certain harmony and balance of character rather than knowledge; and its literature, whether fabulous or factual, had a similar ethical content. There was nothing in it to produce the effect you are seeking."

"Your memory's quite correct," I said, "we shan't find what we want there. But where shall we find it, Glaucon? The more practical forms of skill don't seem very elevating —"

"Certainly not. But if we exclude them, as well as physical and literary education, what else is there left?"

"Well, if we can't think of anything outside them, we must find some feature they all share."

"What do you mean?"

"For example, there is one thing that all occupations, practical, intellectual, or scientific, make use of — one of the first things we must all learn."

"What?"

"Something quite ordinary — to tell the difference between one, two and three; in a word, to count and calculate. Must not every practical or scientific activity be able to do that?"

"Yes, it must," he agreed.

"And war as much as any other?"

"Very much so."

"I wonder if you have noticed what a silly sort of general Agamemnon is made to look on the stage when Palamedes claims to have invented number, and so organised the army at Troy and counted the ships and everything else. It implies that nothing had been counted before and that Agamemnon, apparently, did not know how many feet he had, if he couldn't count. He must have been a funny sort of general!"

"He must indeed," he said, "if it's really true."

"So soldiers must learn, as well as other things, how to calculate and count."

"Yes, of course, if they're to be able to organise an army, indeed if they are to be human at all."

"I wonder, then," I asked, "if you would agree with me that this is probably one of the subjects we are looking for, which naturally stimulates thought, though no one makes proper use of its power to draw men to the truth."

"How do you mean?"

"I'll try to explain what I have in mind," I said, "and show you how I distinguish in my own mind between things that have the effect I mean and things that have not. If you will tell me where you agree and disagree, we can then see more clearly whether I have the right idea."

"Explain."

"Right," I said. "You see, there are some perceptions which don't call for any further exercise of thought, because sensation can judge them adequately, but others which demand the exercise of thought because sensation cannot give a sure result."

"You obviously mean things seen at a distance, or drawn in perspective."

"No, you haven't quite got my meaning," I replied.

"Then what do you mean?" he asked.

"By perceptions that don't call for thought I mean those that don't lead to contradiction; those that do call for thought are those that lead to contradiction in the sense that in them sensation is ambiguous between two contraries, irrespective of distance. But you will understand more clearly if I put it as follows. Here, we say, are three fingers, the middle, third and little one."

"Yes."

"And you've got what I call a close view of them. But there's a further point."

"What is it?"

"Each of them looks as much a finger as any other, and it makes no difference whether it's in the middle or at either end, whether it's white or black, fat or thin, and so on. There is nothing here to force the mind of the ordinary man to stop and think what a finger is; for at no stage has sight presented the finger to it as being also the opposite of a finger."

"No, it hasn't."

"So there's nothing in this sort of perception likely to call for or stimulate thought."

"No."

"But what about the size of the fingers? Can sight distinguish their differences of size properly? Does it matter which one is in the middle or at the end? And can touch distinguish differences of thickness or degrees of hardness and softness? Aren't all the senses in fact deficient in their perception of such qualities? Don't they operate as follows — touch, for example, which is concerned with hardness must also be concerned with softness, and reports to the mind that the same object is both hard and soft."

"Yes."

"Then must not the mind find it difficult in such cases to understand what this sense means by hard, if it says the same thing is soft as well? Or again, what light and heavy mean, if the sense concerned indicates that what is heavy is light and what is light is heavy?"

"Yes; this sort of message puzzles the mind and needs investigation."

"It's probably in this sort of case, then," I said, "that the mind calls in reason and thought, and tries to investigate whether one object has been reported to it or two."

"I suppose so."

"And if the answer is two, each of the pair is a separate entity."

"Yes."

"And if each is a separate entity, and between them they make up two, then the mind will perceive two separate entities; for if they weren't separate it wouldn't perceive two but one."

"That is correct."

"But sight, we said, perceives large and small as qualities which are not distinct but run into each other."

"Yes, so we said."

"And to clear the matter up thought must adopt the opposite approach and look at large and small as distinct and separate qualities. And from that there follows the question, what is meant by large and small?"

"That's perfectly true."

"And that is how we came to distinguish the intelligible and the visible."

"Correct."

"This was what I was trying to say just now, when I said that we are called on to think when our senses receive opposite impressions, but that otherwise thought remains dormant."

"Yes, I understand now," he said, "and agree with you."

"Then in which category do you think the unit and number fall?"

"I don't know."

"You can work it out from what we have said," I told him. "If our perception of the unit, by sight or any other sense, is quite unambiguous, then it provides no more stimulus to seek for truth than did our perception of a finger. But if it is always combined with the perception of its opposite, and seems to involve plurality as much as unity, then it calls for the exercise of judgment and forces the mind into a quandary in which it must stir itself to think, and ask what unity in its absolute sense means; and if that is so, the study of the unit is among those that provoke the mind and turn it to the vision of reality."

"Well, the perception of unity by sight most certainly has these characteristics; for we see the same thing both as a unit and as an unlimited plurality."

"And if that's true of the unit," I said, "it must be true of number as a whole."

"It must."

"And number is the medium of counting and calculation."

"Of course."

"So both will lead the mind on to search for truth."

"Yes, they are extraordinarily effective for the purpose."

"And so they should be included among the studies we are looking for. Soldiers must study them so that they can organise their armies, and philosophers because they cannot escape from this transient world to ultimate reality unless they can reason. And our guardians are both soldiers and philosophers."

"That is true."

"We can, then, properly lay it down that arithmetic shall be a subject for study by those who are to hold positions of responsibility in our state; and we shall ask them not to be amateurish in their approach to it, but to pursue it till they come to understand, by pure thought, the nature of numbers — they aren't concerned with its usefulness for mere commercial calculation, but for war and for the easier conversion of the soul from the world of becoming to that of reality and truth."

"Excellent."

"You know," I said, "now that we have mentioned arithmetic, it occurs to me what a subtle and useful instrument it is for our purpose, if one studies it for the sake of knowledge and not for commercial ends."

"How is that?" he asked.

"As we have just said, it draws the mind upwards and forces it to argue about pure numbers, and will not be put off by attempts to confine the argument to collections of visible or tangible objects. You must know how the experts in the subject, if one tries to argue that the unit is divisible, won't have it, but make you look absurd by multiplying it if you try to divide it, to make sure that their unit is never shown to contain a multiplicity of parts."

"Yes, that's quite true."

"What do you think they would say, Glaucon, if one were to say to them, 'This is very extraordinary — what are these numbers you are arguing about, in which you claim that every unit is exactly equal to every other, and at the same time not divisible into parts?' What do you think their answer would be to that?"

"I suppose they would say that the numbers they mean can be apprehended by thought, but that there is no other way of grasping them."

"You see therefore," I pointed out to him, "that this study looks as if it were really necessary to us, since it so obviously compels the mind to think in order to get at the truth."

"It certainly does have that effect," he agreed.

"Another point — have you noticed how those who are naturally good at calculation are nearly always quick at learning anything else, and how the slow-witted, if trained and practised in calculation, always improve in speed even if they get no other benefit? Yet I suppose there's hardly any form of study which comes harder to those who learn or practise it."

"That is true."

"For all these reasons, then, we must retain this subject and use it to train our ablest citizens."

"I agree."

"That's one subject settled, then. Next let us see if the one that follows it is of any use to us."

"Do you mean geometry?" he asked.

"Exactly."

"It's obviously useful in war," he said. "If a man knows geometry it will make all the difference to him when it comes to pitching camp or taking up a position, or concentrating or deploying an army, or any other military manoeuvre in battle or on the march."

"For that sort of purpose," I replied, "the amount of geometry or calculation needed is small. What we want to find out is whether the subject is on the whole one which, when taken further, has the effect of making it easier to see the Form of the Good. And that, we say, is the tendency of everything which compels the mind to turn to the blessedness of the ultimate reality which it must somehow contrive to see."

"I agree," he said.

"So if it compels us to contemplate reality, it will be useful, but otherwise not."

"That's our view."

"Well, then, no one with even an elementary knowledge of geometry will dispute that it's a science quite the reverse of what is implied by the terms its practitioners use."

"Explain."

"The terms are quite absurd, but they are hard put to it to find others. They talk about 'squaring' and 'applying' and 'adding' and so on, as if they were *doing* something and their reasoning had a practical end, and the subject were not, in fact, pursued for the sake of knowledge."

"Yes, that's true."

"And what is more, it must, I think, be admitted that the objects of that knowledge are eternal and not liable to change and decay."

"Yes, there's no question of that: the objects of geometrical knowledge are eternal."

"Then it will tend to draw the mind to the truth and direct the philosophers' thoughts upwards, instead of to our present mundane affairs."

"It is sure to."

"Then you must be sure to require the citizens of your ideal state not to neglect geometry. It has considerable incidental advantages too."

"What are they?" he asked.

"Its usefulness for war, which you have already mentioned," I replied; "and there is a certain facility for learning all other subjects in which we know that those who have studied geometry lead the field."

"They are miles ahead," he agreed.

"So shall we make this the second subject our young men must study?"

"Yes."

"And the third should be astronomy. Or don't you agree?"

"Yes, I certainly agree. A degree of skill in telling the seasons, months and years is useful not only to the farmer and sailor but also to the soldier."

"You amuse me," I said, "with your obvious fear that the public will disapprove if the subjects you prescribe aren't thought useful. But it is in fact very difficult for people to believe that there is a faculty in the mind of each of us which these studies purify and rekindle after it has been ruined and blinded by other pursuits, though it is more worth preserving than any eye since it is the only organ by which we perceive the truth. Those who agree will think your proposals admirable; but those who have never realised it will probably think you are talking nonsense, as they won't see what other benefit is to be expected from such studies. Make up your mind which party you are going to argue with — or will you ignore both and pursue the argument for your own satisfaction, though without grudging anyone else any benefit he may get from it?"

"That's what I'll do," he replied; "I'll go on with the discussion chiefly for my own satisfaction."

"Then you must go back a bit," I said, "as we made a wrong choice of subject to put next to geometry."

"How was that?"

"We proceeded straight from plane geometry to solid bodies in motion without considering solid bodies first on their own. The right thing is to proceed from second dimension to third, which brings us to cubes and other three-dimensional figures."

"That's true enough," he agreed, "but the subject is one which doesn't seem to have been much investigated yet, Socrates."

"For two reasons," I replied. "There is no state which sets any value on it, and so, being difficult, it is not pursued with energy; and research is not likely to progress without a director, who is difficult to find and, even if found, is unlikely to be obeyed in the present intolerant mood of those who study the subject. But under the general direction of a state that set a value on it, their obedience would be assured, and research pressed forward continuously and energetically till the problems were solved. Even now, with all the neglect and inadequate treatment it has suffered from students who do not understand its real uses, the subject is so attractive that it makes progress in spite of all handicaps, and it would not be surprising if its problems were solved."

"Yes, it has very great attractions," he said. "But explain more clearly what you said just now. You said geometry dealt with plane surfaces."

"Yes."

"Then you first said astronomy came next, but subsequently went back on what you had said."

"More haste less speed," I said. "In my hurry I overlooked solid geometry, because it's so absurdly undeveloped, and put astronomy, which is concerned with solids in motion, after plane geometry."

"Yes that's what you did," he agreed.

"Then let us put astronomy fourth, and assume that the neglect of solid geometry would be made good under state encouragement."

"That is fair enough," he said. "And since you have just been attacking me for approving of astronomy for low motives, let me approve of it now on your principles; for it must be obvious to everyone that it, of all subjects, compels the mind to look upwards and leads it from earth to heaven."

"Perhaps I'm an exception," I said, "for I don't agree. I think that, as it's at present handled by those who use it as an introduction to philosophy, it makes us look down, not up."

"What do you mean?" he asked.

"I think you've a really splendid idea of the study of 'higher things'," I replied. "Perhaps you think that anyone who puts his head back and studies a painted ceiling is using his mind and not his eyes. You may be right, and I may be just simple-minded, but I can't believe that the mind is made to look upwards except by studying the ultimate unseen reality. If anyone tries to learn anything about the world of sense whether by gaping upwards or blinking downwards, I don't reckon that the result is *knowledge* — there is no knowledge to be had of such things — nor do I reckon his mind is directed upwards, even if he's lying on his back or floating on the sea."

"I'm guilty," he said, "and deserve to be scolded. But how else do you mean that astronomy ought to be studied if it's to serve our purpose?"

"Like this," I said. "The stars in the sky, though we rightly regard them as the finest and most perfect of visible things, are far inferior, just because they are visible, to the true realities; that is, to the movements and bodies in movement whose true relative speeds are to be found in terms of pure numbers and perfect figures, and which are perceptible to reason and thought but not visible to the eye. Do you agree?"

"Yes."

"Well, then," I went on, "we ought to treat the visible splendours of the sky as illustrations to our study of the true realities, just as one might treat a wonderful and carefully drawn design by Daedalus or any other artist or draughtsman. Anyone who knew anything about geometry, and saw such a design, would admire the skill with which it was done, but would think it absurd to study it in the serious hope of learning the truth about proportions such as double or half."

"I would be absurd to hope for that," he agreed.

"Isn't the true astronomer in the same position when he watches the movements of the stars?" I asked. "He will think that the sky and the heavenly bodies have been put together by their maker as well as such things can be; but he will also think it absurd to suppose that there is anything constant or invariable about the relation of day to night, or of day and night to month, or month to year, or, again, of the periods of the other stars to them and to each other. They are all visible and material, and it's absurd to look for exact truth in them."

"I agree now you put it like that," he said.

"We shall therefore treat astronomy, like geometry, as setting us problems for solution," I said, "and ignore the visible heavens, if we want to make a genuine study of the subject and use it to put the mind's native wit to a useful purpose."

"You are demanding a lot more work than astronomy at present involves," he said.

"We shall make other demands like it, I think, if we are to be any use as lawgivers. But," I asked, "can you think of any other suitable study?"

"Not at the moment."

"All the same, there are several species of motion," I said, "I suppose that an expert could enumerate them all; but even I can distinguish two of them."

"What are they?"

"The one we've been talking about and its counterpart."

"What's that?"

"I think we may say that, just as our eyes are made for astronomy, so our ears are made for harmony, and that the two are, as the Pythagoreans say, and as we should agree, sister sciences. Isn't that so?"

"Yes."

"And as the work involved is considerable we will consult them on the subject, and perhaps on others too. But all through we must maintain the principle we laid down when dealing with astronomy, that our pupils must not leave their studies incomplete or stop short of the final objective. They can do this just as much in harmonics as they could in astronomy, by wasting their time on measuring audible concords and notes."

"Lord, yes and pretty silly they look," he said. "They talk about 'intervals' of sound, and listen as carefully as if they were trying to hear a conversation next door. And some say they can distinguish a note between two others, which gives them a minimum unit of measurement, while others maintain that there's no difference between the notes in question. They are all using their ears instead of their minds."

"You mean those people who torment catgut, and try to wring the truth out of it by twisting it on pegs. I might continue the metaphor and talk about strokes of the bow, and accusations against the strings and their shameless denials — but I'll drop it, because I'm not thinking so much of these people as of the Pythagoreans, who we said would tell us about harmonics. For they do just what the astronomers do; they look for numerical relationships in audible concords, and never get as far as formulating problems and asking which numerical relations are concordant and why."

"But that would be a fearsome job," he protested

"A useful one, none the less," I said, "when the object is to discover what is right and good; though not otherwise."

"That may well be."

"Yes," I said, "for it's only if we can pursue all these studies until we see their kinship and common ground, and can work out their relationship, that they contribute to our purpose and are worth the trouble we spend on them."

"So I should imagine. But it means a great deal of work."

"And you don't suppose it's more than a beginning, do you?" I asked.

"The subjects we've described are only a prelude to our main theme. For you don't think that people who are good at them are trained philosophers, do you?"

"Heavens, no, with very few exceptions."

"And can they ever acquire the knowledge we regard as essential if they can't argue logically?"

"No, they can't."

"But isn't this just the note which dialectic must strike? It is an intellectual process, but is paralleled in the visible world, as we said, by the progress of sight from shadows to real creatures, and then to the stars, and finally to the sun itself. So when one tries to reach ultimate realities by the exercise of pure reason, without any aid from the senses, and refuses to give up until the mind has grasped what the Good is, one is at the end of an intellectual progress parallel to the visual progress we described."

"That's perfectly true."

"And isn't this progress what we call 'dialectic'?"

"Yes."

"The prisoners in our cave," I went on, "were released and turned round from the shadows to the images which cast them and to the fire, and then climbed up into the sunlight; there they were unable to look at animals and plants and at the light of the sun, but turned to reflections in water and shadows of things (real things, that is, and not mere images throwing shadows in the light of a fire itself derivative compared with the sun). Well, the whole study of the subjects we have described has the effect of leading the best element in the mind up towards the vision of the highest reality, just as the body's most perceptive organ was led to see the brightest of all things in the material and visible world."

"I quite agree with all you've said myself," said Glaucon; "I think it's very difficult to accept in some ways, but as hard to deny in others. However, as this isn't the only occasion on which we shall hear about it and there will be plenty of opportunities to return to it in the future, let us suppose it is so for the present and go on to deal with the main course as thoroughly as we have dealt with the prelude. Tell us what sort of power dialectic has, and how many kinds of it there are and how they are pursued; for they seem to lead to our destination, where we shall get some rest at the end of our journey."

"My dear Glaucon," I said, "you won't be able to follow me further, not because of any unwillingness on my part, but because what you'd see would no longer be an image but truth itself, that is, so far as I can see it; I wouldn't like to be sure my vision is true, but I'm quite sure there is something for us to see, aren't you?"

"Of course."

"And you agree that dialectic ability can only be acquired after the course of study we have described, and in no other way?"

"I'm quite sure of that."

"And it can't be denied that it's the only activity which systematically sets about the definition of the essential nature of things. Of other activities some are concerned with human opinions or desires, or with growing or making things and looking after them when they are grown or made; others, geometry and the like, though, as we have said, concerned with reality, can only see it in a kind of dream, and never clearly, so long as they leave their assumptions unquestioned and cannot account for them. For how can any chain of reasoning result in knowledge if it starts from a premise it does not really know and proceeds to a conclusion and through steps which it does not know either?"

"It can't possibly."

"Dialectic, in fact, is the only activity whose method is to challenge its own assumptions so that it may rest firmly on first principles. When the eye of the mind gets really bogged down in a morass of ignorance, dialectic gently pulls it out and leads it up, using the studies we have described to convert and help it. These studies we have often, through force of habit, referred to as branches of *knowledge*, but we really need another term, to indicate a greater degree of clarity than opinion but a lesser degree than knowledge — we called it reasoning earlier on. But I don't think we shall quarrel about a word, the subject of our enquiry is too important for that."

"It is indeed."

"So we shall be content to use any term that will indicate clearly the faculty we mean."

"Yes."

"Then let us be content with the terms we used earlier on for the four divisions of our line — knowledge, reason, belief, and illusion. The last two we class together as opinion, the first two as intelligence, opinion being concerned with the world of becoming, knowledge with the world of reality.

Knowledge stands to opinion as the world of reality does to that of becoming, and intelligence stands to belief and reason to illusion as knowledge stands to opinion. The relation of the realities corresponding to intelligence and opinion and the twofold divisions into which they fall we had better omit if we're not to land ourselves in an argument even longer than we've already had."

"Yes," said Glaucon; "I agree about all that, so far as I can follow you."

"So you agree in calling the ability to give an account of the essential nature of each particular thing dialectic; and in saying that anyone who is unable to give such an account of things either to himself or to other people has to that extent failed to understand them."

"I can hardly do otherwise."

"Then doesn't the same apply to the Good? If a man can't define the Form of the Good and distinguish it clearly from everything else, and then defend it against all comers, not merely as a matter of opinion but in strict logic, and come through with his argument unshaken, you wouldn't say he knew what Absolute Good was, or indeed any other good. Any notion such a man has is based on opinion rather than knowledge, and he's living in a dream from which he's unlikely to awake this side of the grave, where he will finally sleep for ever."

"With all that I agree emphatically."

"Well, then, if you ever really had the job of bringing up and educating these imaginary children of yours, you would not, I imagine, let them reach positions of high responsibility in society without having their ideas put in order?"

"No."

"So you will lay it down that their powers of argument must be developed by an appropriate education."

"With your help I will."

"Then we can regard dialectic as the coping-stone of our educational system, which completes the course of studies and needs no further addition."

"Yes."

Summary of the Argument

The argument is summarised in this final section. Plato here sets out again his belief that justice comes from the rule of the morally and intellectually fit; those in whom both the necessary aptitude and capacity coexist. These persons should have a long period of training, although their studies in philosophy should be delayed until they have reached years of sufficient maturity. Plato wanted to avoid the denigration of philosophic enquiry into mere verbal quarrelling, or eristic as the Greeks called it. The early introduction of philosophy would simply teach the young students to behave like argumentative puppies. For those who are selected, after a ten-year study of mathematics (from their twentieth to their thirtieth year) and a further five-year study of dialectics, the first exercise of authority should be given in their thirty-fifth year, and this should consist of minor responsibilities such as the command of army units. Following about fifteen years of such tasks, the guardians, aged now about fifty, should have reached the point of intellectual and moral development sufficent for them to be entrusted with the ruling of the state. In this way, Plato argues, justice will come to prevail.

"All you have to do now, then," I went on, "is to decide who should study these subjects and how."

"Yes, that's all."

"Do you remember the kind of people we picked when you were choosing our rulers?"

"Of course I do."

"In most respects we should pick them again — we should prefer the steadiest and bravest and, so far as possible, the best-looking. But we shall also look not only for moral integrity and toughness, but for natural aptitude for this kind of education."

"And how would you define that?"

"Well, my dear chap," I said, "they need intellectual eagerness, and must learn easily. For the mind shirks mental effort more than physical, in which it can share the hard work with the body."

"True."

"They must have good memories, determination and a fondness for hard work. How, otherwise, will they be ready to go through with such an elaborate course of study on top of their physical training?"

"They won't unless they have every natural advantage."

"Which explains what is wrong with philosophy today and why it has a bad reputation; as we said before, it isn't taken seriously enough, and the people who take it up aren't genuine about it as they should be."

"How do you mean?" he asked.

"First of all," I said, "anyone who takes it up must have no inhibitions about hard work. He mustn't be only half inclined to work, and half not — for instance, a man who is very fond of hunting and athletics and all kinds of physical exercise, but has no inclination to learn and dislikes intellectual effort of any kind. And there are people just as one-sided in the opposite way"

"That's very true."

"We shall regard as equally crippled for the pursuit of truth a mind which, while it detests deliberate lying, and will not abide it in itself and is indignant to find it in others, cheerfully acquiesces in conventional misrepresentations and feels no indignation when its own ignorance is shown up, but wallows in it like a pig in a sty."

"I entirely agree."

"We must be careful to distinguish genuine and bogus in dealing with all the virtues — discipline, courage, broadmindedness and the rest. Failure to make the distinction on the part of an inividual or a community merely leads to the unwitting employment of people who are unsound and bogus in some way whether as friends or rulers."

"That is very true."

"We must avoid these mistakes," I went on. "If we pick those who are sound in body and mind and then put them through our long course of instruction and training, Justice herself can't blame us and we shall preserve the constitution of our society; if we make any other choice the effect will be precisely the opposite, and we shall plunge philosophy even deeper in ridicule than it is at present."

"Which would be a shameful thing to do."

"It would," I agreed. "But I'm not sure I'm not being slightly ridiculous at the moment myself."

"How?"

"I was forgetting that we are amusing ourselves with an imaginary sketch, and got too worked up. I had in mind as I spoke the unjust criticisms that are made of philosophy, which annoyed me, and my anger at the critics made me speak more seriously than I should."

"Oh, come!" he said, "I didn't think you were too serious."

"Well, I felt I was. However, don't let's forget that when we were making our earlier choice, we chose elderly men; but that won't do now. We mustn't let Solon persuade us that as one grows old one's capacity for learning increases, any more than one's ability to run; the time for all serious effort is when we are young."

"Undoubtedly."

"Arithmetic and geometry and the other studies leading to dialectic should be introduced in childhood, though we mustn't exercise any form of compulsion."

"Why?" he asked.

"Because a free man ought not to learn anything under duress. Compulsory physical exercise does no harm to the body, but compusory learning never sticks in the mind."

"True."

"Then, don't use compulsion," I said to him, "but let your children's lessons take the form of play. You will learn more about their natural abilities that way."

"There's something in what you say,"

"Do you remember," I reminded him, "that we said that our children ought to be taken on horseback to watch fighting, and, if it was safe, taken close up and given their taste of blood, like your hounds?"

"Yes, I remember."

"Well, we must enrol in a select number those who show themselves most at home in all these exercises and studies and dangers."

"At what age?" he asked.

"As soon as their necessary physical training is over. During that time, whether it be two or three years, they won't be able to do anything else; physical fatigue and sleep are unfavourable to study. And one of the most important tests is to see how they show up in their physical training."

"True."

"After that time, then, at the age of twenty, some of them will be selected for promotion, and will have to bring together the disconnected subjects they studied in childhood and take a comprehensive view of their relationship with each other and with reality."

"That is the only way to make knowledge permanent."

"And also the best test of aptitude for dialectic, which is the ability to take the comprehensive view."

"I agree."

"You will have to keep all this in view and make a further choice among your selected candidates when they pass the age of thirty. Those who show the required perseverance in their studies, in war, and in their other duties, will be promoted to higher privileges, and their ability to follow truth into the realm of pure reality, without the use of sight or any other sense, tested by means of dialectic. And here, my friend, you will have to go to work very carefully."

"Why particularly?"

"Haven't you noticed the appalling harm done by dialectic at present?"

"What harm?"

"It fills people with indiscipline."

"Oh, yes, I've noticed that."

"And does it surprise you?" I asked. "Aren't you sorry for the victims?"

"Why should I be?"

"Well, imagine a child who has been brought up in a large, rich, and powerful family, with many hangers-on; when he grows up he discovers that he is not the child of his so-called parents, but can't discover who his real parents are. Can you imagine how he will feel towards the hangers-on and his supposed parents, first while he still doesn't know they aren't his real parents, and then when he does? Shall I tell you what I should expect?"

"Yes, do."

"Well, I should expect that, so long as he didn't know they weren't his real parents, he would respect his mother and father and supposed relations more than the hangers-on, be more concerned with their needs, and less inclined to do or say anything outrageous to them, or to disobey them in matters of importance."

"Very likely."

"But when he discovered the truth, I should expect him to give up respecting them seriously and devote himself to the hangers-on; their influence with him would increase, he'd associate with them openly and live by their standards, and, unless his natural instincts were particularly decent, he'd pay no more attention to his reputed parents and relations."

"That's all very likely. But," he asked, "what bearing has the illustration on philosophic discussions?"

"This. There are certain opinions about what is right and fair in which we are brought up from childhood, and whose authority we respect like that of our parents."

"True."

"And there are certain habits of an opposite kind, which have a deceitful attraction because of the pleasures they offer, but which no one of any decency gives in to, because he respects the authority of tradition."

"True again."

"Yes," I said, "but what happens when he is confronted with the question, 'What do you mean by "fair"?' When he gives the answer tradition has taught him, he is refuted in argument, and when that has happened many times and on many different grounds, he is driven to think that there's no difference between fair and foul, and so on with all the other moral values, like right and good, that he used to revere. What sort of respect for their authority do you think he'll feel at the end of it all?"

"He's bound to feel quite differently."

"Then when he's lost any respect or feeling for his former beliefs but not yet found the truth, where is he likely to turn? Won't it be to the deceitful attractions of pleasure?"

"Yes, it will."

"And so we see indiscipline supplanting traditon."

"Inevitably."

"Yet all this is a natural consequence of starting on philosophic discussions in this way, and, as I've just said, there's every reason for us to excuse it."

"Yes, and be sorry about it," he agreed.

"Then if you want to avoid being sorry for your thirty-year-olders, you must be very careful how you introduce them to such discussions."

"Very careful,"

"And there's one great precaution you can take, which is to stop their getting a taste of them too young. You must have noticed how young men, after their first taste of argument, are always contradicting people just for the fun of it; someone proves them wrong, and they follow his lead and argue that other people are wrong, like puppies who love to pull and tear anyone within reach."

"They like nothing better," he said.

"So when they've proved a lot of people wrong and been proved wrong often themselves, they soon slip into the belief that nothing they believed before was true; with the result that they discredit themselves and the whole business of philosophy in the eyes of the world."

"That's perfectly true," he said.

"But someone who's a bit older," I went on, "will refuse to have anything to do with this sort of idiocy; he won't contradict just for the fun of the thing but will be more likely to follow the lead of someone whose arguments are aimed at finding the truth. He's a more reasonable person and will get philosophy a better reputation."

"True."

"In fact all we've been saying has been said in the attempt to ensure that only men of steady and disciplined character shall be admitted to philosophic discussions, and not anyone, however unqualified, as happens at present,"

"I entirely agree."

"Then suppose twice as long is spent on a continuous and intensive study of philosophy as we proposed should be spent on physical training, will that be enough?"

"Do you mean six years or four?"

"It doesn't matter," said I; "make it five. After that they must be sent down again into the cave we spoke of, and compelled to hold any military or other office suitable for the young, so that they may have as much practical experience as their fellows. And here again they must be tested to see if they stand up to the temptations of all kinds or give way to them."

"And how long do you allow for this stage?"

"Fifteen years. And when they are fifty, those who have come through all our practical and intellectual tests with success must be brought to their final trial, and made to lift their mind's eye to look at the source of all light, and see the Good itself, which they can take as a pattern for ordering their own life as well as that of society and the individual. For the rest of their lives they will spend most of their time in philosophy, but when their turn comes they will turn to the weary business of politics and do their duty as rulers not for the honour they get by it but as a matter of necessity. And so, when they have brought up successors like themselves, they will depart this life, and the state will set up a public memorial to them and sacrifice to them, if the Pythian Oracle approves, as divinities, or at any rate as saints."

"It's a fine picture you have drawn of our rulers, Socrates."

"And some of them will be women," I reminded him. "All I have said about men applies equally to women, if they have the necessary qualifications."

"Of course," he agreed, "if they are to share equally in everything with the men, as we described."

"Well, then, do you agree that the society and constitution we have sketched is not merely an idle dream, difficult though its realisation may be? The indispensable condition is that political power should be in the hands of one or more true philosophers. They would despise all present honours as mean and worthless, and care most for doing right and any rewards it may bring; and — most important and essential of all — they would, throughout their reorganisation of society, serve and forward the interests of justice."

"How would they proceed?"

"They would begin by sending away into the country all citizens over the age of ten; having thus removed the children from the influence of their parents' present way of life, they would bring them up on their own methods and rules, which we have described. This is the best and quickest way to establish our society and constitution, and for it to succeed and bring its benefits to any people among which it is established."

"Yes, that's much the best way; and I think, Socrates," he added, "that you have explained very well how such a society would come into existence, if ever it did."

"Then haven't we said enough about this state of ours and the corresponding type of man? For it's surely obvious what type we shall want."

"Perfectly obvious," he agreed. "And I agree with you that there's no more to be said."

2

ARISTOTLE

Commentary

Biography

Aristotle (385/4–322 B.C.) was born at Stagira, a town in northern Greece. His father, Nicomachus, was court physician to Amyntas II, the king of Macedonia, and so Aristotle spent part of his early life in the Macedonian capital of Pella. When he was aged about eighteen, he travelled down to Athens to complete his education and studied at the Academy, but it is uncertain whether Plato was present at that time. Aristotle was certainly strongly influenced by Plato's ideas, but as we shall see, later came to reject quite a few of them. When Plato died in 347 B.C., Aristotle left the Academy and travelled first to Assos in Asia Minor and then to Mytilene on the island of Lesbos, where he continued his studies, especially in biology and marine life.

He achieved fame about the year 343 B.C. when he was invited by Philip, king of Macedonia, to act as tutor to his thirteen-year-old son Alexander, the future conqueror of the Persian Empire. Here was the opportunity to put into practice Plato's greatest ideal, that of the philosopher king, an ideal Aristotle to a large extent shared. But as it turned out, Aristotle's influence on Alexander in this direction does not seem to have been very marked. Alexander became king when he was only twenty, after his father's assassination in 336 B.C., and after that had no more time for philosophical studies. Moreover his later political policies seem to have little in common with Aristotle's own political ideals.

Soon after Philip's death Aristotle returned once more to Athens, where he established a school of his own known as the Lyceum, where he taught for twelve years. The subjects of instruction covered a broader spectrum than those at Plato's Academy and as far as we know included physics, biology, ethics, politics and rhetoric. The Lyceum became known as the Peripatetic School of Philosophy (from Greek *peripatein*, to walk about) due to Aristotle's habit of teaching his students while they strolled together in the gardens attached to the school.

Aristotle was unfortunately forced to leave Athens in 323 B.C. (the year of Alexander's death) and though after his departure the Lyceum continued to function, it does not seem to have retained its influence to the same extent that Plato's Academy did. The reason for Aristotle's departure was the growing Athenian hostility towards Macedonia, which had led to a short-lived revolt against Macedonian rule after Alexander's death. Aristotle's obvious links with Alexander and Macedonia meant that his continued presence in Athens was not safe and so he left to settle in Chalcis, the mother city of his native Stagira, where he died the following year, in 322 B.C.

Main Features of Aristotle's Educational Thought

Aristotle's work has exerted a tremendous influence on Western thought, although it was not until the thirteenth century that the main corpus of his writing was rediscovered in Western Europe. However after that time, and especially since the fifteenth century when the bulk of his writings became known, his work achieved great fame and was accepted as authoritative on a large number of intellectual questions. Indeed, for many centuries anyone who wished to propound a new philosophical or scientific theory generally felt obliged to indicate where and why it differed from that of Aristotle.

Unfortunately, though, not all of Aristotle's works have come down to us and what we do have are mainly copies of what are believed to be his lecture notes (or in some cases students' notes of his lectures). This partly explains two differences from Plato's work that soon become apparent. In the first place Aristotle's style of writing is not as smooth, and is repetitive in some parts and incomplete in others. Secondly, his ideas on education have to be pieced together from a number of his books — we have no one complete educational treatise comparable to Plato' *Republic*.

The bibliography at the end of this section gives a list of Aristotle's main works and the subjects they cover. Those most relevant to his educational ideas are the *Nicomachean Ethics* and the *Politics*, which are the major sources for his moral and political philosophy. These two books contain the bulk of his explicit writings on education as well as much else that has direct relevance to his overall educational philosophy.

Before discussing these works we will note briefly some of the main features of Aristotle's thought in general and see where it diverges from Plato's. It has been said (originally by Samuel Taylor Coleridge) that everyone is born either a Platonist or an Aristotelian and it does seem to be true that, between them, these two cover most of the main standpoints that can be taken on philosophical questions. This is not to say they were opposed on all issues; they do share quite a few ideas, including many about education.

The basic philosophical difference between the two was that while Plato was an idealist, Aristotle was a realist. It was crucial to all Plato's philosophy that there existed two worlds of reality, the real or sensible world and the ideal or intelligible world; for Aristotle, no such clear-cut divisions existed. For him all our knowledge is of the real world (the world we perceive through the senses) and the forms that Plato considers separate entities in the ideal world, Aristotle sees as belonging to material objects. That is, every object is composed of both matter and form and we have no need to posit another order of reality to explain the one we perceive directly in everyday experience.

This fundamental philosophical difference is also reflected in what the two philosophers regarded as the prime method of reasoning. Because Plato believed that all our knowledge is derived from the basic forms or ideas that are somehow present in us at birth, the main process of thought is one of deduction from general principles (universals) to particular facts. This is of course the method of reasoning used in mathematics, the subject on which Plato placed so much stress.

Aristotle, on the other hand, believing that our knowledge is built up by extracting the form or essence of an object by experiencing particular instances of it, favoured the inductive method of reasoning, which starts with particular facts and works up to generalisations based on these. However, because we can rarely experience *all* the particular instances of any general principle, Aristotle says a final intuitive jump is needed to reach the appropriate conclusion (that is, by what he calls the act of "intuitive reason" we see that all the other instances must be like the ones we have experienced and that therefore the generalisation is true). One of the fundamental tasks of the teacher, then, is to provide the child with the concrete expriences necessary to make this final reflective judgment, which leads to definite knowledge. When a child is born, its mind is like a blank tablet on which sense experiences are received and then, by the action of the reasoning powers latent in the mind, general principles or knowledge as we know it, are built up. This model of how the mind acquires knowledge has been very influential as a guide to the nature of the teaching — learning process right down to modern times and has given much support to the traditional concept of the teacher as one whose task it is to feed the necessary items of knowledge into the developing mind.*

Of course, Aristotle also realised that deductive reasoning is possible and had much to say on the nature of the syllogism (the basic form of deductive argument), but overall he stressed the inductive method as the prime method of learning and teaching. It is also, by and large, the method of reasoning used in science, and it is therefore not surprising that Aristotle (unlike Plato) gave an important place to the empirical sciences among the subjects taught at the Lyceum.

In general then, whereas Plato's philosophical beliefs inclined him to look beyond the world of commonsense experience for the basic answers to human problems, Aristotle's beliefs led him to examine our commonsense experience in minute detail in order to find the answers from it. Thus one could say that Plato is likely to appeal more to the mystic, Aristotle to the practical-minded man, but in fact each of their philosophies contains enough richness and variety to interest all types of people.

---

*In the first reading for Aristotle, which is a short passage from his *Posterior Analytics*, he deals with the nature of inductive reasoning as here outlined.

Before turning directly to Aristotle's educational ideas it is necessary to know something of his view of the nature of man. (The main source for this is his book *On the Soul*.) Aristotle held that man possesses a soul, which gives form to the body, which is matter. This should not be confused with the Christian idea of the soul; Aristotle's conception does not necessarily imply any supernatural connection. He says the soul may be divided into two parts: the rational and the irrational (strictly, "non-rational"). These two aspects provide the means for the operation of the three basic functions of man — the intellective (reason), the appetitive (instinctive desires) and the vegetative (biological processes). The intellective function is controlled by the rational soul, the vegetative by the non-rational and the appetitive comes under the control of both. What this means basically is that the desires and instincts are not in themselves rational but may be regulated in varying degrees by the power of reason.

Man is the only living thing with all three functions. Plants have only the vegetative, animals only the vegetative and appetitive functions. Man is therefore distinguished by his intellectual capacities, hence Aristotle's famous definition of man as "a rational animal". Like Plato, Aristotle gives supreme importance to man's ability to reason, and the implications of this for his educational philosophy will be indicated later.

Let us look now at the *Ethics*, where Aristotle's educational ideas become explicit. His argument here may be briefly summarised in the following way. He begins in Book I by maintaining the teleological view that all our actions are done for a purpose. He then asks what can be this general purpose underlying the actions of man, and answers "the seeking of happiness". This is the only self-sufficient end. In other words, happiness is the only thing of which it makes no sense to ask: "Why do you want that?" But happiness can only be achieved, says Aristotle, if we are virtuous. What then is virtue? Remember that Plato also tried to answer this question and found that true virtue and goodness can only be achieved by a small minority. The Form of the Good which is the essence of all virtue can only be apprehended by pure thought alone: only by that small group of people who are able to reach the pinnacle of Plato's educational system. Aristotle was not satisfied with this answer, and to try to solve the problem, made an important distinction between moral and intellectual virtue. The former corresponded to the appetitive and the latter to the intellective function of the human soul. Intellective virtue is roughly equivalent to what we would call intelligence.

We should add here that the Greek word we translate as "virtue", *areté*, has a much wider connotation than our present day concept of virtue. It means, roughly, "inner excellence" or "fitness or purpose". Bearing this in mind, it is easier to see why Aristotle regards virtue as essential to happiness. If virtue is lacking, we are not functioning as we should, we are not fulfilling our purposes efficiently and therefore it is impossible for us to achieve happiness. This is not to say that Aristotle is not talking about moral qualities as we know them; obviously he is doing so as many of his examples (courage, honesty and so forth) indicate. However, he is also including under the same heading, intelligence and all other qualities that will assist man to achieve his purpose in life, namely happiness.

However, it is moral virtue with which Aristotle is specifically concerned in the *Ethics*, and in Book II he proceeds to examine its precise nature. He describes it as a disposition to choose between two extremes of conduct. For example, the virtue of courage is a mean between the extremes of cowardice and foolhardiness. This idea of the virtuous action as being a mid-point between two extremes has been popular with moralists ever since, coming to be known as the doctrine of the "Golden Mean."

Aristotle's argument that virtue is necessary for happiness may seem to take a merely expedient attitude to virtue: we should only follow it because it will bring us happiness. But here again, the meaning we give to happiness is not the same as that given by Aristotle. *Eudaimonia*, the Greek word we translate as "happiness", does not just mean a feeling of personal pleasure (see for instance what Aristotle says about it in Book X). It means living the good life, doing well in addition to faring well, and it involves basing one's behaviour on reason and morality. Moreover it is not something that comes and goes but something that should last right through our life. As Aristotle says in Book I, "One swallow does not make a summer; neither does one fine day. And one day, or indeed any brief period of felicity, does not make a man entirely and perfectly happy."

All the above has obvious implications for moral education and Aristotle goes on to treat directly the question of how virtue (or this disposition to choose the mean) can be acquired. He has already said at the beginning of Book II that whereas intellective virtue is achieved primarily through teaching, moral virtue is acquired mainly by habit. Aristotle's answer, therefore, is very different to Plato's. In line with his more commonsense, empirical approach to philosophy, he believes that morality develops through experience, through the repeated performance of good acts until they become part of our character. Hence the great importance of correct guidance by parents and teachers; it is essential that they accustom us to performing the right sort of acts from an early age.

Then Aristotle poses the following objection to his own account: how can we do moral acts if we are not already moral? Consider carefully the answer he gives, noting in particular the distinction he draws between acts in accordance with morality and moral acts proper. Now consider whether he correctly describes the way young children's moral education ought to begin and how the transition to full moral awareness should take place. Does Aristotle say enough about such a transition and would the early habit training he recommends in any way inhibit this?*

---

*This question will arise again in later chapters of this book, especially the one dealing with the contemporary analytical philosopher, R. S. Peters, who takes a somewhat similar approach to Aristotle on the acquisition of moral virtue.

An important problem arising from the discussion is that of discovering in what activity man's virtue is best exhibited (or in what activity the highest type of virtue is achieved), this being the activity that will therefore bring him the most happiness. His answer (given in Book X) is contemplation — this is where man's distinctive function of intellection is most exemplified. As we have seen, Aristotle stresses the fact that of all living things only man has the capacity to reason and to attempt to understand and explain the nature of the world in which he lives. It is interesting to note that Aristotle here comes very close to Plato, who placed great stress on pure thought and dialectic as the highest activity of man. (However you will by now be aware that what they regarded as the most appropriate objects of this power of reasoning and contemplation differ considerably.) It is also interesting to note the similarity between Plato's and Aristotle's conclusions here and that of certain Eastern mystics and others who place great stress on meditation. Once again however, the objects of this meditation may be rather different from those of the two Greek philosophers, although there may well be some similarities, at least in the case of Plato.

Thus Aristotle's basic educational goal, like Plato's, is that of producing philosophers, or at least people who have the time, inclination and capacity to devote themselves to the life of reason and contemplation. What this and the rest of his educational recommendations require in the way of political arrangements we will now examine by turning to his *Politics*.

In this work Aristotle relates the moral conclusions reached in the *Ethics* to society in general and outlines the type of education needed to produce both the ideal state and the virtuous and happy person who manifests the contemplative way of life. Like Plato, Aristotle divides the state into rulers, warriors and workers. (Slaves were not counted as members of the state). Only the first two groups are capable of true virtue, but this is nonetheless an enlargement on Plato's view that only the rulers are capable of really understanding the nature of virtue (that is, apprehending the Form of the Good). Aristotle's view, that full moral virtue is more widely distributed in the population that Plato allows, is mainly due to his broader conception of the way in which virtue is acquired.

A large part of the *Politics* is devoted to the analysis of the three different forms of government: monarchy, aristocracy and polity, and what Aristotle calls their corresponding perversions: despotism, oligarchy and democracy. He favoured polity, in which all full citizens have a right to participate. Polity is thus more broadly based than aristocracy (which was really what Plato favoured) but not as broad as democracy, which he saw as being uninformed and working mainly for the benefit of the unenlightened and poor.

As will be seen from his remarks at the beginning of Book VIII Aristotle believed quite firmly that the state should have complete control of education, that education should be the same for all (that is, for all citizens; workers and slaves are not deemed worthy of education as such, but only of the minimal training necessary to perform their functions), and that the process of education should be one of moulding children into the desired citizen types required by the state. All of this is a very important feature of the traditional model of education and one against which progressive philosophers like Rousseau and Dewey reacted strongly.

Aristotle never outlines in detail his ideas on how the curriculum should be constructed, though from various remarks he makes (mainly in Books VII and VIII of the *Politics*) it is possible to piece together some idea of the general educational programme he envisaged. He would divide children's educational development into five stages. Firstly, infancy, which is the period of nurture and the beginning of habit training. The main learning here is of bodily movements. Aristotle recommends accustoming children to the cold from their earliest years, which he says greatly conduces to health and hardens them for military service.

The second stage lasts up to the age of five. As yet there should be no study lessons or compulsory tasks. Physical skills and games are important at this stage. Like Plato, Aristotle recommends that the experiences of the young child should be carefully controlled so that it does not learn anything harmful. This of course is consonant with Aristotle's belief that moral virtue can only be acquired by developing morally good habits, which depend on the right sorts of examples and guidance being provided. Therefore any stories or music that the child hears must be carefully censored to make sure that they present a morally beneficial experience.

The third stage is only a brief one from about age five to age seven in which Aristotle says children continue their previous education and begin to watch and to copy older children.

The fourth and fifth stages occupy the years from seven to puberty (the actual age of which is unspecified) and from puberty to twenty-one respectively. This should be the period of public, state-controlled education in which children are given the basic skills and knowledge necessary for the continued good functioning of the state. Aristotle does not set out in any detail the actual subjects that should be taught or when they should be introduced and completed. (However it is certain that gymnastics, reading, writing, music and drawing would be among the subjects studied). Nothing should be pursued in excess, however, because this, he says, only leads to vulgarisation.

Apart from their utilitarian value these subjects are also designed to prepare the citizen for the sixth and final period of education, which is to last for the rest of life and extends beyond the confines of the school. This is the period of liberal education; liberal both in the sense that it frees the mind from ignorance and also that it is appropriate for free men. It includes the sort of studies that we believe were taught at the Lyceum (which were also many of the subjects dealt with in Aristotle's own writings): chiefly mathematics, logic, metaphysics, ethics, politics, aesthetics, music, poetry, rhetoric, physics and biology.

It is this final period that obviously interested Aristotle the most and the one that he saw as being worthwhile in itself or of intrinsic value. This is where the ideal of leisured contemplation becomes realised. Remember that only a minority of the whole population could ever reach this stage and the fact that they could devote their lives to such an ideal was only made possible by a slave-based society. However there are important implications for today's society in this idea of how leisure time should be used. Because the majority of the population now has much more free time than it had in the past (due largely to the advent of the machine, which has taken the place of the slave in Greek society), the question of what should be done with this time is a crucial social issue. If people could be persuaded to devote a significant proportion of it to liberal education, as Aristotle suggests, it would surely be of immense value both to society and themselves. This is not to say that ordinary entertainment and recreation should be excluded, but that at least some of people's non-working hours should be devoted to enlarging their intellectual and cultural life. As Aristotle says, this must obviously result in a richer and more complete conception of what it means to be human. Of course, if such a state of affairs were to be achieved it would require a great expansion of educational facilities, particularly at the levels of recurrent and adult education.

One of the subjects that Aristotle saw as performing an important role in liberal education is music, and as will be seen in the *Politics*, he has quite a lot to say about its educative value. Aristotle believed music performs basically three different functions in education: (a) it helps with character formation in the early years; (b) it is an important part of liberal education; and (c) it provides for emotional purification or catharsis. Consult the later sections of Book VIII to ascertain how he sees each of these functions being performed. Consider also whether some of his ideas about the role of music are applicable today. For example, does modern popular music perform a cathartic function? Should music appreciation be an essential part of liberal education now? Should music be used more systematically in the early character training of children?

To conclude this commentary on Aristotle it may now be indicated how his work stands as a significant innovation in Western educational thought. It has already been noted how he diverges from Plato on a number of basic philosophical issues and in doing this has provided us with some new and very influential philosophical theories, theories that have attracted many followers right down to the present day. In the area of educational thought in particular, some of the significant innovations his work presents are the following:

1. The inductive model of how the mind acquires knowledge and the implications of this for the teaching–learning process.
2. The division of virtue into two kinds; intellectual and moral, the former acquired mainly by instruction, the latter mainly by habit training.
3. The idea that happiness, virtue and contemplation are all interdependent and together provide a model of the way of life it is the function of education to produce.
4. The idea of liberal education as a leisure time activity and as an end in itself (not necessarily tied to producing future leaders for the state as

in Plato). This provided the basis for one very important strand of educational thought that occurs repeatedly to the present day — the view that the essential meaning of education lies in its intrinsic and non-utilitarian values.

SELECT BIBLIOGRAPHY

What has survived of Aristotle's work covers a large number of areas of thought. For education, the most important works are the *Nicomachean Ethics* and the *Politics*, both available in the Penguin Classics series.

His other important works can be grouped under the following subject headings:

Logic: the works collectively known as *Organon*, of which the most important are *Categories, On Interpretation, Prior Analytics* and *Posterior Analytics.*

Philosophy of Nature and Metaphysics: *Physics, Metaphysics.*

Philosophy of Man and Psychology: *On the Soul, On Sense, Perception, On Memory and Recollection.*

Biology: *The History of Animals, On the Parts of Animals, On the Generation of Animals.*

Aesthetics: *Poetics* and *Rhetorics.*

All of Aristotle's major works (translated by various authors) are included in *The Basic Works of Aristotle,* R. McKeon (Ed.), Random House, New York, 1941.

Selections

Three selections from Aristotle follow, taken from Posterior Analytics, Nicomachean Ethics *and* Politics. *The contents of each have been discussed in the preceding commentary. They provide, respectively, an insight into Aristotle's ideas on learning, morality and politics. In each case the particular extracts chosen are those most relevant to his overall educational philosophy.*

Posterior Analytics

It is clearly a characteristic of all living beings that they possess an innate faculty of discrimination, known as sense perception. But although sense perception belongs to all living beings, some retain their sense impressions, while others do not. When impressions do not persist, there is no knowledge at all extending beyond the moment of sense perception. When perceptions do persist after the moment of perception, the living being retains them in his soul. When this occurs frequently, a clear distinction is evident between those living beings who are able systematically to organise the impressions that persist and those who cannot do this.

Thus memory has its roots in sense perception, while experience arises from frequently repeated memories of the same occurrence; the memories are multiple but constitute one single experience. Furthermore experience, that is, the universal idea which has taken up its position in the soul, the universal which is the one corresponding to the many, the unity which exists identically the same within each single memory, provides the starting point of the arts and scientific knowledge, the arts being concerned with production, scientific knowledge with what already exists. Thus these mental capacities neither exist in clearly determined form from birth nor are derived from other higher capacities. In fact they originate in sense perception. The procedure is something like this: imagine that a rout has taken place on a field of battle; then one man makes a stand followed by another and another until the original formation is restored. The soul is so constituted that it behaves in a similar kind of way.

Let us then repeat what we said a little earlier but with insufficient clarity. When one particular has "made its stand", this is the first beginning of a universal idea within the soul; for, although it is the particular thing that is perceived, nevertheless perception includes the universal idea. To take an example: we perceive "man" in general and not merely a particular man, say Callias. Further stands are made among these rudimentary universals until the indivisible concepts, that is the true universals, are established, as for example when a particular species of animal leads on to the general idea of animal and so to ideas of wider generality. Obviously then it must

---

From ARISTOTLE, *Posterior Analytics*, taken from George Howie's translation. By kind permission of Collier-Macmillan Publishers, London.

be by induction that we come to know the first principles, for this is the method by which sense perception produces the universal idea within us.

Now of the thought processes by which we reach truth some are unfailingly reliable, while others are open to error. Scientific knowledge and intuitive reason are reliable, while opinion and calculation, for example, are not. No other kind of knowing is more accurate than scientific knowledge with the exception of intuitive reason. Also first principles are more knowable than demonstrative proofs, and all scientific knowledge depends on reason. Accordingly there can be no scientific knowledge of the first principles, and since nothing except intuitive reason can be more truthful than scientific knowledge, it is by intuitive reason that first principles are known. This conclusion also follows from the fact that the starting point of demonstration is not itself demonstration, nor in consequence of this is scientific knowledge itself the starting point of scientific knowledge. Therefore, if we have no other kind of knowing than scientific knowledge, intuitive reason must be the starting point of scientific knowledge.

[From Book II, Ch. 19]

Nicomachean Ethics

Book I

It is thought that every activity, artistic or scientific, in fact every deliberate action or pursuit, has for its object the attainment of some good. We may therefore assent to the view which has been expressed that "the good" is "that at which all things aim". Since modes of action involving the practised hand and the instructed brain are numerous, the number of their ends is proportionately large. For instance, the end of medical science is health; of military science, victory; of economic science, wealth. All skills of that kind which come under a single "faculty" — a skill in making bridles or any other part of a horse's gear comes under the faculty or art of horsemanship, while horsemanship itself and every branch of military practice comes under the art of war, and in like manner other arts and techniques are subordinate to yet others — in all these the ends of the master arts are to be preferred to those of the subordinate skills, for it is the former that provide the motive for pursuing the latter.

Now if there is an end which we as moral agents seek for its own sake, and which is the cause of our seeking all the other ends — if we are not to go on choosing one act for the sake of another, thus landing ourselves in an infinite progression with the result that desire will be frustrated and ineffectual — it is clear that this must be the good, that is the absolutely good. May we not then argue from this that a knowledge of the good is

From *The Ethics of Aristotle*, translated by J. A. K. Thomson, Allen and Unwin, London, 1953. Reprinted by permission of the publisher.

a great advantage to us in the conduct of our lives? Are we not more likely to hit the mark if we have a target? If this be true, we must do our best to get at least a rough idea of what the good really is, and which of the sciences, pure or applied, is concerned with the business of achieving it.

Now most people would regard the good as the end pursued by that study which has most authority and control over the rest. Need I say that this is the science of politics? It is political science that prescribes what subjects are to be taught in states, which of these the different sections of the population are to learn, and up to what point. We see also that the faculties which obtain most regard come under this science: for example, the art of war, the management of property, the ability to state a case. Since, therefore, politics makes use of the other practical sciences and lays them down besides what we must do and what we must not do, its end must include theirs. And that end, in politics as well as in ethics, can only be the good for man. For even if the good of the community coincides with that of the individual, the good of the community is clearly a greater and more perfect good both to get and to keep. This is not to deny that the good of the individual is worth while. But what is good for a nation or a city has a higher, a diviner, quality.

Such being the matters we seek to investigate, the investigation may fairly be represented as the study of politics. . . .

In our actions we aim at more ends than one — that seems to be certain but, since we choose some (wealth, for example, or flutes and tools or instruments generally) as means to something else, it is clear that not all of them are ends in the full sense of the word, whereas the good, that is the supreme good, is surely such an end. Assuming then that there is some one thing which alone is an end beyond which there are no further ends, we call *that* the good of which we are in search. If there be more than one such final end, the good will be that end which has the highest degree of finality. An object pursued for its own sake possesses a higher degree of finality than one pursued with an eye to something else. A corollary to that is that a thing which is never chosen as a means to some remoter object has a higher degree of finality than things which are chosen both as ends in themselves and as means to such ends. We may conclude, then, that something which is always chosen for its own sake and never for the sake of something else is without qualification a final end.

Now happiness more than anything else appears to be just such an end, for we always choose if for its own sake and never for the sake of some other thing. It is different with honour, pleasure, intelligence and good qualities generally. We choose them indeed for their own sake in the sense that we should be glad to have them irrespective of any advantage which might accrue from them. But we also choose them for the sake of our happiness in the belief that they will be instrumental in promoting that. On the other hand, nobody chooses happiness as a means of achieving them or anything else whatsoever than just happiness. . . .

Happiness then, the end to which all our conscious acts are directed, is found to be something final and self-sufficient. But no doubt people will say, "To call happiness the highest good is a truism. We want a more distinct account of what it is." We might arrive at this if we could grasp what is meant by the "function" of a human being. If we take a flautist or a sculptor or any craftsman — in fact any class of men at all who have some special job or profession — we find that his special talent and excellence comes out in that job, and this is his function. The same thing will be true of man — that is of course if "man" does have a function. But is it likely that joiners and shoemakers have certain functions or specialised activities, while man as such has none but has been left by nature a functionless being? Seeing that eye and hand and foot and every one of our members has some obvious function, must we not believe that in like manner a human being has a function over and above these particular functions? Then what exactly is it? The mere act of living is not peculiar to man — we find it even in the vegetable kingdom — and what we are looking for is something peculiar to him. We must therefore exclude from our definition the life that manifests itself in mere nurture and growth. A step higher should come the life that is confined to experiencing sensations. But that we see is shared by horses, cows, and the brute creation as a whole. We are left, then, with a life concerning which we can make two statements. First, it belongs to the rational part of man. Secondly, it finds expression in actions. The rational part may be either active or passive: passive in so far as it follows the dictates of reason, active in so far as it possesses and exercises the power of reasoning. A similar distinction can be drawn within the rational life; that is to say, the reasonable element in it may be active or passive. Let us take it that what we are concerned with here is the reasoning power in action, for it will be generally allowed that when we speak of "reasoning" we really mean *exercising* our reasoning faculties. (This seems the more correct use of the word.) Now let us assume for the moment the truth of the following propositions. (a) The function of a man is the exercise of his non-corporeal faculties or "soul" in accordance with, or at least not divorced from, a rational principle. (b) The function of an individual and of a *good* individual in the same class — a harp player, for example, and a good harp player, and so through the classes — is generically the same, except that we must add superiority in accomplishment to the function, the function of the harp player being merely to play on the harp, while the function of the good harp player is to play on it well. (c) The function of man is a certain form of life, namely an activity of the soul exercised in combination with a rational principle or reasonable ground of action. (d) The function of a good man is to exert such activity well. (e) A function is performed well when performed in accordance with the excellence proper to it. If these assumptions are granted, we conclude that the good for man is "an activity of soul in accordance with goodness" or (on the supposition that there may be more than one form of goodness) "in accordance with the best and most complete form of goodness."

There is another condition of happiness: it cannot be achieved in less than a complete lifetime. One swallow does not make a summer; neither does one fine day. And one day, or indeed any brief period of felicity, does not make a man entirely and perfectly happy. . . .

Happiness, then, being an activity of the soul in conformity with perfect goodness, it follows that we must examine the nature of goodness. When we have done this we should be in a better position to investigate the nature of happiness. There is this, too. The genuine statesman is thought of as a man who has taken peculiar pains to master this problem, desiring as he does to make his fellow citizens good men obedient to the laws. Now, if the study of moral goodness is a part of political science, our enquiry into its nature will clearly follow the lines laid down in our preliminary observations.

Well, the goodness we have to consider is human goodness. This — I mean human goodness or (if you prefer to put it that way) human happiness — was what we set out to find. By human goodness is meant not fineness of physique but a right condition of the soul, and by happiness a condition of the soul. That being so, it is evident that the statesman ought to have some inkling of psychology, just as the doctor who is to specialise in diseases of the eye must have a general knowledge of physiology. Indeed, such a general background is even more necessary for the statesman in view of the fact that his science is of a higher order than the doctor's. Now the best kind of doctor takes a good deal of trouble to acquire a knowledge of the human body as a whole. Therefore the statesman should also be a psychologist and study the soul with an eye to his profession. Yet he will do so only as far as his own problems make it necessary; to go into greater detail on the subject would hardly be worth the labour spent on it.

Psychology has been studied elsewhere and some of the doctrines stated there may be accepted as adequate for our present purpose and used by us here. The soul is represented as consisting of two parts, a rational and an irrational. As regards the irrational part there is one subdivision of it which appears to be common to all living things, and this we may designate as having a "vegetative" nature, by which I mean that it is the cause of nutrition and growth, since one must assume the existence of some such vital force in all things that assimilate food. Now the excellence peculiar to this power is evidently common to the whole of animated nature and not confined to man. This view is supported by the admitted fact that the vegetative part of us is particularly active in sleep, when the good and the bad are hardest to distinguish. Such a phenomenon would be only natural, for sleep is a cessation of that function on the operation of which depends the goodness or badness of the soul. But enough of this, let us say no more about the nutritive part of the soul since it forms no portion of goodness in the specifically *human* character.

But there would seem to be another constituent of the soul which, while irrational, contains an element of rationality. It may be observed in the types of men we call "continent" and "incontinent". They have a principle — a rational element in their souls — which we commend, because it encourages them to perform the best actions in the right way. But such natures appear at the same time to contain an irrational element in active opposition to the rational. In paralytic cases it often happens that when the patient wills to move his limbs to the right they swing instead to the left. Exactly the same thing may happen to the soul; the impulses of the incontinent man carry him in the opposite direction from that towards which he was aiming. The only difference is that, where the body is concerned, we see the uncontrolled limb, while the erratic impulse we do not see. Yet this should not prevent us from believing that besides the rational an irrational principle exists running opposite and counter to the other. Yet, as I said, it is not altogether irrational; at all events it submits to direction in the continent man, and may be assumed to be still more amenable to reason in the "temperate" and in the brave man, in whose moral make-up there is nothing which is at variance with reason.

We have, then, this clear result. The irrational part of the soul, like the soul itself, consists of two parts. The first of these is the vegetative, which has nothing rational about it at all. The second is that from which spring the appetites and desire in general; and this does in a way participate in reason, seeing that it is submissive and obedient to it. . . . That the rational element in us need not be heedless of the irrational is proved by the fact that we find admonition, indeed every form of censure and exhortation, not ineffective. It may be, however, that we ought to speak of the appetitive part of the soul as rational, too. In that event it will rather be the rational part that is divided in two, one division rational in the proper sense of the word and in its nature, the other in the derivative sense in which we speak of a child as "listening to reason" in the person of its father.

These distinctions within the soul supply us with a classification of the virtues. Some are called "intellectual", as wisdom, intelligence, prudence. Others are "moral", as liberality and temperance. When we are speaking of a man's *character* we do not describe him as wise or intelligent but as gentle or temperate. Yet we praise a wise man, too, on the ground of his "disposition" or settled habit of acting wisely. The dispositions so praised are what we mean by "virtues".

Book II

Virtue, then, is of two kinds, intellectual and moral. Of these the intellectual is in the main indebted to teaching for its production and growth, and this calls for time and experience. Moral goodness, on the other hand, is the child of habit, from which it has got its very name, ethics being derived from *ethos*, "habit", by a slight alteration in the quantity of the *e*. This is an indication that none of the moral virtues is implanted in us by nature, since nothing that nature creates can be taught by habit to change the direction of its development. For instance a stone, the natural tendency of which is to fall down, could never, however often you threw it up in the air, be trained to go in that direction. No more can you train fire to burn downwards. Nothing in fact, if the law of its being is to behave in one way, can be habituated to behave in another. The moral virtues, then, are produced in us neither *by* nature nor *against* nature. Nature, indeed, prepares in us the ground for their reception, but their complete formation is the product of habit.

Consider again these powers or faculties with which nature endows us. We acquire the ability to use them before we do use them. The senses provide us with a good illustration of this truth. We have not acquired the sense of sight from repeated acts of seeing, or the sense of hearing from repeated acts of hearing. It is the other way round. We had these senses before we used them, we did not acquire them as a result of using them. But the moral virtues we do acquire by first exercising them. The same is true of the arts and crafts in general. The craftsman has to learn how to make things, but he learns in the process of making them. So men become builders by building, harp players by playing the harp. By a similar process we become just by performing just actions, temperate by performing temperate actions, brave by performing brave actions. Look at what happens in political societies — it confirms our view. We find legislators seeking to make good men of their fellows by making good behaviour habitual with them. That is the aim of every lawgiver, and when he is unable to carry it out effectively, he is a failure; nay, success or failure in this is what makes the difference between a good constitution and a bad.

Again, the creation and the destruction of any virtue are effected by identical causes and identical means; and this may be said, too, of every art. It is as a result of playing the harp that harpists become good or bad in their art. The same is true of builders and all other craftsmen. Men will become good builders as a result of building well, and bad builders as a result of building badly. Otherwise what would be the use of having anyone to teach a trade? Craftsmen would all be born either good or bad. Now this holds also of the virtues. It is in the course of our dealings with our fellow men that we become just or unjust. It is our behaviour in a crisis and our habitual reactions to danger that make us brave or cowardly, as it may be. So with our desires and passions. Some men are made temperate and gentle, others profligate and passionate, the former by conducting themselves in one way, the latter by conducting themselves in another, in situations in which their feelings are involved. We may sum it all up in the generalisation, "Like activities produce like dispositions." This makes it our duty to see that our activities have the right character, since the differences of quality in them are repeated in the dispositions that follow in their train. So it is a matter of real importance whether our early education confirms us in one set of habits or another. It would be nearer the truth to say that it makes a very great difference indeed, in fact all the difference in the world.

Since the branch of philosophy on which we are at present engaged differs from the others in not being a subject of merely intellectual interest —

I mean we are not concerned to know what goodness essentially is, but how we are to become good men, for this alone gives the study its practical value — we must apply our minds to the solution of the problems of conduct. For, as I remarked, it is our actions that determine our dispositions.

Now that when we act we should do so according to the right principle is common ground, and I propose to take it as a basis of discussion. But we must begin with the admission that any theory of conduct must be content with an outline without much precision in details. We noted this when I said at the beginning of our discussion of this part of our subject that the measure of exactness of statement in any field of study must be determined by the nature of the matter studied. Now matters of conduct and considerations of what is to our advantage have no fixity about them any more than matters affecting our health. And if this be true of moral philosophy as a whole, it is still more true that the discussion of particular problems in ethics, admits of no exactitude. For they do not fall under any science or professional tradition, but those who are following some line of conduct are forced in every collocation of circumstances to think out for themselves what is suited to these circumstances, just as doctors and navigators have to do in their different *métiers*. We can do no more than give our arguments, inexact as they necessarily are, such support as is available.

Let us begin with the following observation. It is in the nature of moral qualities that they can be destroyed by deficiency on the one hand and excess on the other. We can see this in the instances of bodily health and strength. Physical strength is destroyed by too much and also by too little exercise. Similarly health is ruined by eating and drinking either too much or too little, while it is produced, increased, and preserved by taking the right quantity of drink and victuals. Well, it is the same with temperance, courage, and the other virtues. The man who shuns and fears everything and can stand up to nothing becomes a coward. The man who is afraid of nothing at all, but marches up to every danger, becomes foolhardy. In the same way the man who indulges in every pleasure without refraining from a single one becomes incontinent. If, on the other hand, a man behaves like the boor in comedy and turns his back on every pleasure, he will find his sensibilities becoming blunted. So also temperance and courage are destroyed both by excess and deficiency, and they are kept alive by observance of the mean.

Let us go back to our statement that the virtues are produced and fostered as a result, and by the agency, of actions of the same quality as effect their destruction. It is also true that after the virtues have been formed they find expression in actions of that kind. We may see this in a concrete instance — bodily strength. It results from taking plenty of nourishment and going in for hard training, and it is the strong man who is best fitted to cope with such conditions. So with the virtues. It is by refraining from pleasures that we become temperate, and it is when we have become temperate that we are most able to abstain from pleasures. Or take courage. It is by habituating ourselves to make light of alarming situations and to confront them that we become brave, and it is when we have become brave that we shall be most able to face an alarming situation.

We may use the pleasure (or pain) that accompanies the exercise of our dispositions as an index of how far they have established themselves. A man is temperate who abstaining from bodily pleasures finds this abstinence pleasant; if he finds it irksome, he is intemperate. Again, it is the man who encounters danger gladly, or at least without painful sensations, who is brave; the man who has these sensations is a coward. In a word, moral virtue has to do with pains and pleasures. There are a number of reasons for believing this. (a) Pleasure has a way of making us do what is disgraceful; pain deters us from doing what is right and fine. Hence the importance — I quote Plato — of having been brought up to find pleasure and pain in the right things. True education is just such a training. (b) The virtues operate with actions and emotions, each of which is accompanied by pleasure or pain. This is only another way of saying that virtue has to do with pleasures and pains. (c) Pain is used as an instrument of punishment. For in her remedies nature works by opposites, and pain can be remedial. (d) When any disposition finds its complete expression it is, as we noted, in dealing with just those things by which it is its nature to be made better or worse, and which constitute the sphere of its operations. Now when men become bad it is under the influence of pleasures and pains when they seek the wrong ones among them, or seek them at the wrong time, or in the wrong manner, or in any of the wrong forms which such offences may take; and in seeking the wrong pleasures and pains they shun the right. This has led some thinkers to identify the moral virtues with conditions of the soul in which passion is eliminated or reduced to a minimum. But this is to make too absolute a statement — it needs to be qualified by adding that such a condition must be attained "in the right manner and at the right time" together with the other modifying circumstances.

So far, then, we have got this result. Moral goodness is a quality disposing us to act in the best way when we are dealing with pleasures and pains, while vice is one which leads us to act in the worst way when we deal with them.

(e) The point may be brought out more clearly by some other considerations. There are three kinds of things that determine our choice in all our actions — the morally fine, the expedient, the pleasant; and three that we shun — the base, the harmful, the painful. Now in his dealings with all of these it is the good man who is most likely to go right, and the bad man who tends to go wrong, and that most notably in the matter of pleasure. The sensation of pleasure is felt by us in common with all animals, accompanying everything we choose for even the fine and the expedient have a pleasurable effect upon us. (f) The capacity for experiencing pleasure has grown in us from infancy as part of our general development, and human life, being dyed in the grain with it, receives therefrom a colour hard to scrape off. (g) Pleasure and pain are also the standards by which with greater or less strictness we regulate our considered actions. Since to feel pleasure and pain rightly or wrongly is an important factor in human behaviour, it follows that we are primarily concerned with these sensations. (h) Heraclitus says it is hard to fight against anger, but it is harder still to fight against pleasure. Yet to grapple with the harder has always been the business, as of art, so of goodness, success in a task being proportionate to its difficulty. This gives us another reason for believing that morality and statesmanship must concentrate on pleasures and pains, seeing it is the man who deals rightly with them who will be good, and the man who deals with them wrongly who will be bad.

Here, then, are our conclusions. (a) Virtue is concerned with pains and pleasures. (b) The actions which produce virtue are identical in character with those which increase it. (c) These actions differently performed destroy it. (d) The actions which produced it are identical with those in which it finds expression.

A difficulty, however, may be raised as to what we mean when we say that we must perform just actions if we are to become just, and temperate actions if we are to be temperate. It may be argued that, if I do what is just and temperate, I am just and temperate already, exactly as, if I spell words or play music correctly, I must already be literate or musical. This I take to be a false analogy, even in the arts. It is possible to spell a word right by accident or because somebody tips you the answer. But you will be a scholar only if your spelling is done as a scholar does it, that is thanks to the scholarship in your own mind. Nor will the suggested analogy with the arts bear scrutiny. A work of art is good or bad in itself — let it possess a certain quality, and that is all we ask of it. But virtuous actions are not done in a virtuous — a just or temperate — way merely because *they* have the appropriate quality. The *doer* must be in a certain frame of mind when he does them. Three conditions are involved. (a) The agent must act in full consciousness of what he is doing. (b) He must "will" his action, and will it for its own sake. (c) The act must proceed from a fixed and unchangeable disposition. Now these requirements, if we except mere knowledge, are not counted among the necessary qualifications of an artist. For the acquisition of virtue, on the other hand, knowledge is of little or no value, but the other requirements are of immense, of sovereign, importance, since it is the repeated performance of just and temperate actions that produces virtue. Actions, to be sure, are *called* just and temperate when they are such as a just or temperate man would do. But the doer is just or temperate not because he does such things but when he does them in the way of just and temperate persons. It is therefore quite fair to say that a man becomes just by the performance of just, and temperate by the performance of temperate, actions; nor is there the smallest likelihood of a man's becoming good by any other course of conduct. It is not, however, a popular line to take, most men preferring theory to practice under the impression that arguing about morals proves them to be philosophers, and that in this way they will turn out to be fine characters. Herein they resemble invalids, who listen carefully to all the doctor says but do not carry out a single one of his orders. The bodies of such people will never respond to treatment — nor will the souls of such "philosophers".

We now come to the formal definition of virtue. Note first, however, that the human soul is conditioned in three ways. It may have (a) feelings, (b) capacities, (c) dispositions; so virtue must be one of these three. By "feelings" I mean desire, anger, fear, daring, envy, gratification, friendliness, hatred, longing, jealousy, pity and in general all states of mind that are attended by pleasure or pain. By "capacities" I mean those faculties in virtue of which we may be described as capable of the feelings in question — anger, for instance, or pain or pity. By "dispositions" I mean states of mind in virtue of which we are well — or ill — disposed in respect of the feelings concerned. We have, for instance, a bad disposition where angry feelings are concerned if we are disposed to become excessively or insufficiently angry, and a good disposition in this respect if we consistently feel the due amount of anger, which comes between these extremes. So with the other feelings.

Now, neither the virtues nor the vices are feelings. We are not spoken of as good or bad in respect of our feelings but of our virtues and vices. Neither are we praised or blamed for the way we feel. A man is not praised for being frightened or angry, nor is he blamed just for being angry; it is for being angry in a particular way. But we *are* praised and blamed for our virtues and vices. Again, feeling angry or frightened is something we can't help, but our virtues are in a manner expressions of our will; at any rate there is an element of will in their formation. Finally, we are said to be "moved" when our feelings are affected, but when it is a question of moral goodness or badness we are not said to be "moved" but to be "disposed" in a particular way. A similar line of reasoning will prove that the virtues and vices are not capacities either. We are not spoken of as good or bad, nor are we praised or blamed, merely because we are *capable* of feeling. Again, what capacities we have, we have by nature; but it is not nature that makes us good or bad. . . . So, if the virtues are neither feelings nor capacities, it remains that they must be dispositions. . . .

We may now define virtue as a disposition of the soul in which, when it has to choose among actions and feelings, it observes the mean relative to us, this being determined by such a rule or principle as would take shape in the mind of a man of sense or practical wisdom. We call it a mean condition as lying between two forms of badness, one being excess and the other deficiency; and also for this reason, that, whereas badness either falls short of or exceeds the right measure in feelings and actions, virtue discovers the mean and deliberately chooses it. Thus, looked at from the point of view of its essence as embodied in its definition, virtue no doubt is a mean; judged by the standard of what is right and best, it is an extreme.

But choice of a mean is not possible in every action or every feeling. The very names of some have an immediate connotation of evil. Such are malice, shamelessness, envy among feelings, and among actions adultery, theft, murder. All these and more like them have a bad name as being evil in themselves; it is not merely the excess or deficiency of them that we censure. In their case, then, it is impossible to act rightly; whatever we do is wrong. Nor do circumstances make any difference in the rightness or wrongness of them. When a man commits adultery there is no point in asking whether it is with the right woman or at the right time or in the right way, for to do anything like that is simply wrong. It would amount to claiming that there is a mean and excess and defect in unjust or cowardly or intemperate actions. If such a thing were possible, we should find ourselves with a mean quantity of excess, a mean of deficiency, an excess of excess and a deficiency of deficiency. But just as in temperance and justice there can be no mean or excess or deficiency, because the mean in a sense *is* an extreme, so there can be no mean or excess or deficiency in those vicious actions — however done, they are wrong. Putting the matter into general language, we may say that there is no mean in the extremes, and no extreme in the mean, to be observed by anybody. . . .

I have said enough to show that moral excellence is a mean, and I have shown in what sense it is so. It is, namely, a mean between two forms of badness, one of excess and the other of defect, and is so described because it aims at hitting the mean point in feelings and in actions. This makes virtue hard of achievement, because finding the middle point is never easy. It is not everybody, for instance, who can find the centre of a circle — that calls for a geometrician. Thus, too, it is easy to fly into a passion — anybody can do that — but to be angry with the right person and to the right extent and at the right time and with the right object and in the right way — that is not easy, and it is not everyone who can do it. This is equally true of giving or spending money. Hence we infer that to do these things properly is rare, laudable and fine.

In view of this we shall find it useful when aiming at the mean to observe these rules. (a) *Keep away from that extreme which is the more opposed to the mean.* It is Calypso's advice: "Swing round the ship clear of this surf and surge."

For one of the extremes is always a more dangerous error than the other; and — since it is hard to hit the bull's-eye — we must take the next best course and choose the least of the evils. And it will be easiest for us to do this if we follow the rule I have suggested. (b) *Note the errors into which we personally are most liable to fall.* (Each of us has his natural bias in one direction or another.) We shall find out what ours are by noting what gives us pleasure and pain. After that we must drag ourselves in the opposite direction. For our best way of reaching the middle is by giving a wide berth to our darling sin. It is the method used by a carpenter when he is straightening a warped board. (c) *Always be particularly on your guard against pleasure and pleasant things.* When pleasure is at the bar the jury is not impartial. So it will be best for us if we feel towards her as the Trojan elders felt towards Helen, and regularly apply their words to her. If we are for packing her off, as they were with Helen, we shall be the less likely to go wrong.

To sum up. These are the rules by observation of which we have the best chance of hitting the mean. But of course difficulties spring up, especially when we are confronted with an exceptional case. For example, it is not easy to say precisely what is the right way to be angry and with whom and on what grounds and for how long. In fact we are inconsistent on this point, sometimes praising people who are deficient in the capacity for anger and calling them "gentle", sometimes praising the choleric and calling them "stout fellows". To be sure we are not hard on a man who goes off the straight path in the direction of too much or too little, if he goes off only a little way. We reserve our censure for the man who swerves widely from the course, because then we are bound to notice it. Yet it is not easy to find a formula by which we may determine how far and up to what point a man may go wrong before he incurs blame. But this difficulty of definition is inherent in every object of perception; such questions of degree are bound up with the circumstances of the individual case, where our only criterion *is* the perception.

So much, then, has become clear. In all our conduct it is the mean state that is to be praised. But one should lean sometimes in the direction of the more, sometimes in that of the less, because that is the readiest way of attaining to goodness and the mean. . . .

Book X

Having finished our discussion of the different forms of goodness, friendship and pleasure, it remains for us to produce a sketch of happiness; for happiness we regard as the end to be sought in human life. We may, however, shorten the discussion by recapitulating what was said before. We stated then that happiness is not a condition — not a state of mind or disposition of character. If it were, it might belong to a man whose whole existence was passed in sleep, while he lived the life of a vegetable, or to the victim of some appalling misfortune. So if we cannot accept this but feel that we must rather insist that happiness is some form of activity; if, moreover, activities may be classified into those which are necessary to some end desirable for the sake of something beyond themselves, and those that are desirable in and for themselves, clearly happiness must be classed among activities desirable in themselves, and not among those desirable as a means to something else. For happiness is not in need of anything — it is self-sufficient. As for activities, they are desirable in themselves when all that is asked of them is their own exercise. Actions which are in conformity with goodness evidently have this character, for the performance of morally good and beautiful actions is desirable on its own account.

But amusements also are desirable on their own account. We do not go in for them for the sake of something else — in fact they tend to do us more harm than good by leading us to neglect our health and our finances. Yet such pleasures are the great resource of those whom the public regards as happy, and it explains why those who have a ready talent for these pastimes are popular in the most exalted circles. They make themselves agreeable by providing the sort of amusement that their patrons like, and so they are always in request. Hence these amusements are thought to be necessary to happiness, because the occupants of thrones devote their leisure to them. But what persons of that kind do proves little or nothing. Good morals and sound sense are not inevitable concomitants of power, and it is good morals and sound sense that prompt our best activities. If these persons, who have never tasted pure and liberal pleasure, have recourse to carnal delights, that is no reason why we should think them the most desirable. Children are sure that the things they prize most highly are the best, and so it is natural that, as children and adults have different notions of what is valuable, so should good men and bad. To repeat what I have said more than once, it is the things that are valuable and pleasant in the eyes of the good man that are really such. Everyone considers the activity most natural to his own disposition to be the most desirable. So the good man considers activity in the way of goodness to be most desirable. It is not in amusements that happiness is to be found. Certainly it would be strange if the end of life were amusement, and we are to labour and endure hardness all our days merely for the fun of it. Almost every objective we choose is chosen for an ulterior purpose. But not happiness; happiness is an end in itself. To make a serious business of amusement and spend laborious days upon it is the height of folly and childishness. The maxim of Anacharsis, "Play so that you may be serious", may be taken as pointing in the right direction. For amusement is a form of rest or relaxation, and rest we need because we cannot always be working. Rest then is not an end but a means to future activity. Also we believe that it is the life lived in accordance with goodness that is the happy life; and such cannot be divorced from seriousness or spent in amusing oneself. We maintain, too, that serious things are intrinsically better than funny or amusing things, and that the activity of a man, or of some organ or faculty of his, is more serious in proportion as it possesses a higher excellence. Such an activity then is itself superior and therefore more conducive to happiness. We may add another argument. Anybody can enjoy fleshly pleasures — a slave no less than a Socrates. But nobody is prepared to give a slave a life of his own; that is, nobody is prepared to give him a measure of happiness. So — once more — happiness does not consist in pastimes and amusements but in virtuous activities.

But if happiness is an activity in accordance with virtue, it is reasonable to assume that it will be in accordance with the highest virtue; and this can only be the virtue of the best part of us. Whether this be the intellect or something else — whatever it is that is held to have a natural right to govern and guide us, and to have an insight into what is noble and divine, either as being itself also divine or more divine than any other part of us — it is the activity of this part of accordance with the virtue proper to it that will be perfect happiness. Now we have seen already that this activity has a speculative or contemplative character. This is a conclusion which may be accepted as in harmony with our earlier arguments and with the truth.

For "contemplation" is the highest form of activity, since the intellect is the highest thing in us and the objects which come within its range are the highest that can be known. But it is also the most continuous activity, for we can think about intellectual problems more continuously than we can keep up any sort of physical action. Again, we feel sure that a modicum of pleasure must be one of the ingredients of happiness. Now it is admitted that activity along the lines of "wisdom" is the pleasantest of all the good activities. At all events it is thought that philosophy ("the pursuit of wisdom") has pleasures marvellous in purity and duration, and it stands to reason that those who have knowledge pass their time more pleasantly than those who are engaged in its pursuit. Again, self-sufficiency will be found to belong in an exceptional degree to the exercise of the speculative intellect. The wise man, as much as the just man and everyone else, must have the necessaries of life. But, given an adequate supply of these, the just man also needs people with and towards whom he can put his justice into operation: and we can use similar language about the temperate man, the brave man, and so on. But the wise man can do more. He can speculate all by himself, and the wiser he is the better he can do it. Doubtless it helps to have fellow workers, but for all that he is the most self-sufficing of men. Finally it may well be thought that the activity of contemplation is the only one that is praised on its own account, because nothing comes of it beyond the act of contemplation, whereas from practical activities we count on gaining something more or less over and above the mere action. Again, it is commonly believed that, to have happiness, one must have leisure; we occupy ourselves in order that we may have leisure, just as we make war for the sake of peace. Now the practical virtues find opportunity for their exercise in politics and in war, but these are occupations which are supposed to leave no room for leisure. Certainly it is true of the trade of war, for no one deliberately chooses to make war for the sake of making it or tries to bring about a war. A man would be regarded as a bloodthirsty monster if he were to make war on a friendly state just to produce battles and slaughter. The business of the politician also makes leisure impossible. Besides the activity itself, politics aims at securing positions of power and honour or the happiness of the politician himself or his fellow citizens — a happiness obviously distinct from that which we are seeking.

We are now in a position to suggest the truth of the following statements. (a) Political and military activities, while pre-eminent among good activities in beauty and grandeur, are incompatible with leisure, and are not chosen for their own sake but with a view to some remoter end, whereas the activity of the intellect is felt to excel in the serious use of leisure, taking as it does the form of contemplation, and not to aim at any end beyond itself, and to own a pleasure peculiar to itself, thereby enhancing its activity. (b) In this activity we easily recognise self-sufficiency, the possibility of leisure and such freedom from fatigue as is humanly possible, together with all the other blessings of pure happiness. Now if these statements are received as true, it will follow that it is this intellectual activity which forms perfect happiness for a man — provided of course that it ensures a complete span of life, for nothing incomplete can be an element in happiness.

Yes, but such a life will be too high for *human* attainment. It will not be lived by us in our merely human capacity but in virtue of something divine within us, and so far as this divine particle is superior to man's composite nature, to that extent will its activity be superior to that of the other forms of excellence. If the intellect is divine compared with man, the life of the intellect must be divine compared with the life of a human creature. And we ought not to listen to those who counsel us *O man, think as man should* and *O mortal, remember your mortality.* Rather ought we, so far as in us lies, to put on immortality and to leave nothing unattempted in the effort to live in conformity with the highest thing within us. Small in bulk it may be, yet in power and preciousness it transcends all the rest. We may in fact believe that this is the true self of the individual, being the sovereign and better part of him. It would be strange, then, if a man should choose to live not his own life but another's. Moreover, the rule, as I stated it a little before, will apply here — the rule that what is best and pleasantest for each creature is that which intimately belongs to it. Applying it, we shall conclude that the life of the intellect is the best and pleasantest for man, because the intellect more than anything else *is* the man. Thus it will be the happiest life as well. . . .

Assuming then that we have adequately discussed, at least in outline, the subjects of happiness and the different forms of goodness together with friendship and pleasure, may we consider the task we set before us as now complete? Or would it not be better to say that in the science of conduct the end, as we have so often had occasion to say, is not to obtain a theoretical acquaintance with the different points at issue, but rather to put our theories into practice? If that be true, it is not enough to *know* about goodness; we must endeavour to possess and use it, and in some way to see to it that we become good. Now if discourses on the theory of ethics were enough in themselves to make men good, "Many and great the rewards they would win," as Theognis has it. And they would deserve them, and all we should have to do would be to provide ourselves with such discourse. But the plain truth is that, while theories may very powerfully stimulate and encourage generous youth, and may inspire a character naturally noble and sincerely loving the beauty of goodness with a passion of virtue, they are unable to push the many in the direction of lofty principles. For it is the nature of the many to yield to the suggestions of fear rather than honour, and to abstain from evil not because of the disgrace but the penalties entailed by not abstaining. Living under the dictates of passion, they chase the pleasures fit for such natures and the means of gratifying them, and they shun the pains which are the opposite of these pleasures. But the honourable and the truly delightful — of that they have no conception, having never tasted genuine pleasure. What theory, what homily can ever reform people like that? To uproot by argument habits long embedded in the character is a difficult, perhaps an impossible, task. We may, I take it, regard ourselves as fortunate if we can get some portion of goodness by acquiring for ourselves all the recognised means of becoming good.

Now some thinkers hold that goodness comes by nature, others that we acquire it by habit, others that we are made good by teaching. The bounty of nature is clearly beyond our control; it is bestowed by some divine dispensation on those who are in the true sense of the word "fortunate". As for arguments and teaching, it is to be feared they are not efficacious in all instances. Like a piece of land, which has to be prepared for seed that is to grow there, the mind of the pupil has to be prepared for the inculcation of good habits, if it is to like and dislike the things it ought. The man who is passion's slave will not listen to or understand the logic of anyone who tries to dissuade him from going on as he is doing. When a man is in that state, what chance have you of changing his mind by argumentation? In fact one may venture on the broad statement that passion is not amenable to reason but only to force. We must then have a character to work upon which has a natural bias towards virtue, loving the noble and hating the base.

Yet it is far from easy to obtain a right training in goodness from youth upwards, unless one has been brought up under right laws. To live a hard and sober life is not an attractive prospect for most, especially when they are young. For this reason the nurture and the pursuits of young persons should be regulated by law, for hard conditions and sober living will cease to be painful when they have become habitual. Of course, it is not enough to receive the right nurture and supervision in youth. We must also practise what we have learned and make a habit of it when we are grown up. So we shall need laws for the regulation of adult behaviour as well, for the whole indeed of our lives, for people are by and large readier to submit to punishment and compulsion than moved by arguments and ideals. Hence some believe that, while lawgivers are under an obligation to encourage and inspire the citizens in the pursuit of virtue for its beauty, not doubting that those who have been well brought up will respond, they are also bound to inflict chastisement and penalties on the disobedient and ill-conditioned, and to depart the hopeless cases altogether. They take the line that, while the good man no doubt, living as he does with some kind of moral standard, will listen to reason, the degraded, who are all for pleasure, must be chastised by pain, like beasts of burden. This is also the reason they give for maintaining that the punishment for transgressors should take the form of those pains which come nearest to being the opposite of their darling pleasures.

Be that as it may, I repeat that, if a man is to turn out well, he must have been properly educated and trained, and must therefore persevere in good habits of life and do no wrong either with or against his will. This result can be produced only by submitting one's life to the guidance of intelligence in some form and a right system with truth in it. Now a father has not got the power to enforce obedience to his authority, nor indeed, broadly speaking, has any individual, unless he happens to be a king or something equivalent. But law, emanating as a rule from a certain wisdom and intelligence, does have the power of compulsion. We dislike people who thwart our inclinations, even if they are entirely justified in doing so, but we do not grumble at the law when it orders what is right. Yet Sparta, with perhaps one or two other places, is the only state in which the lawgiver seems to have been at pains to regulate the nurture and day-to-day life of the community. In the majority of states the problem has not been faced, and every man does as he likes with his life in the manner of the Cyclops in Homer, "laying down the law for children and wife".

The best that could happen would be the institution of a sound system of public supervision of these matters. But, if they are entirely neglected by the state, it is the plain duty of the private citizen, to help his own children and friends to become good men or, if that is beyond him, at least to make it his ambition. But what has been said suggests that his success in this will be greater, if he acquires the art of legislation. So much is clear — if you are to have state supervision, it must be exercised through the laws and, if it is to be good, the laws must be good. But whether they are written or unwritten, whether they are to direct the education of one person or more, would seem to be questions of no greater importance than they are for music or physical training or any other form of education. Paternal advice and domestic habits have their influence in the family, just as law and custom command obedience in the state. And they have it in even greater measure because of the blood relationship and the benefits flowing from that which unites the father and the family, whose natural affection and obedience are original assets in his favour. One may go even farther. Private education, like individual treatment in medicine, is superior to public. It is a general rule in medicine that rest and fasting are beneficial in fever cases. But it may be the wrong treatment in a particular case. We may take it, too, that a professor of boxing does not make all his pupils adopt the same style. It would appear then that individual attention permits of greater accuracy in dealing with particular cases, for then the individual has a better chance of getting the treatment that suits him. For all that, the best treatment of a particular case will be given by a doctor (or trainer or whoever the instructor may be) who has a general knowledge of what is good for all, or for all of a particular class. For, as their names imply, the sciences are sciences of the universal. This is not to deny that in a special case it is perfectly possible that treatment may be successfully applied by someone who has not had a professional training but has an empirical knowledge derived from detailed observation of the results of particular treatments. Thus some people appear to be their own best physicians, although they would be quite incapable of doing anyone else good. Still there can surely be no question that anybody who wants to be fully qualified in the art and science of a subject like education must proceed to the study of general or universal principles and familiarise himself with these in the only way possible. For science, as I said, deals with the universal. This surely permits us to assume that anyone who aspires to make people (few or many; it makes no difference) better by supervision must do his best to acquire the art of legislation, if he accepts, as no doubt he will, the principle that we can be made good by laws. We need such a legislator, because predisposing to virtue the first man that comes along is not a task for everybody. It can only be done by one (supposing him available) who has the scientific knowledge to do it. That is just as true of legislation as it is of medicine and the other professions which call for a technique and practical good sense. . . .

The Politics

Book VII

The period following birth must be regarded as the time when the nourishment given to a child has the greatest effect on the development of the body. It is clear from an examination, both of other animals and of those nations that make a point of rearing their young to be fighting fit, that abundant milk diet is very suitable for their young bodies, but a diet that includes wine is likely to upset them. Next, it is good for them to make all the bodily movements that they are capable of at that age. To prevent the still soft limbs from becoming bent some peoples still make use of mechanical devices for keeping them straight. From infancy too they ought to be used to cold; to be thus habituated is most useful for future health and for the activities of warfare. Hence among certain non Greek peoples it is the custom to dip newly born infants in cold river water; others, for example the Kelts, put on them very little clothing. It is a good thing to start very young in accustoming children to such things as it is possible to accustom them to, but the process must be gradual; the warmth of the young body gives it a condition well suited for training to resist cold. In these and similar ways the training of children in infancy should proceed.

The next stage is up to five years of age. During this period it is not a good plan to try and teach them anything or make them do tasks that would interfere with their development. At the same time they must have exercise, not a state of passivity. They will get exercise in many ways but most of all in play. Their games, like everything else, should be worthy of free men and neither laborious nor unsystematic. The officials known as inspectors of children's welfare ought also to pay attention to deciding what kind of literature and stories children of this age are to hear; for all that they hear now is to be regarded as preparation for the schooling that is to follow. Hence their games ought largely to consist in playing at or rehearsing what they will later be doing in earnest. It is wrong to try and prohibit small children from crying and dilating the lungs, as is suggested in the *Laws*; it is in fact an exercise of the lungs which is beneficial for the growth of the body. In addition to regulating the time spent on play and on exercise and the rest, those in charge should particularly see that very little time is

From ARISTOTLE, *The Politics*, translated by T. A. Sinclair, Penguin Classics, 1962. Copyright © the estate of T. A. Sinclair, 1962. Reprinted by permission of the publisher.

spent in the company of slaves. Children of this age and up to seven must inevitably live at home, and even as young as that they are liable to pick up by eye or by ear "ungentlemanliness".

In general, the legislator ought to banish from the state, as he would any other evil, all unseemly talk; the indecent remark lightly dropped results in conduct of a like kind. Especially therefore it must be kept away from youth; let them not hear or see anything of that kind. If any is found doing or saying any of the forbidden things, he shall, if he is of gentle birth but not yet old enough to be allowed to eat at the common tables, be punished by whipping, while a youth who is rather older shall be punished by loss of privileges of the freeborn, just because his conduct has been that of a slave. And since we exclude all unseemly talk, we must also forbid looking at pictures or literature of the same kind. Let it therefore be a duty of the rulers to see that there shall be nothing at all, statue or painting, that is a representation of unseemly actions, except those that are in the shrines of those gods to whom the law concedes the privilege of indecency. The law further allows men who have reached a certain age to pay honour to these gods on behalf of their wives, their children, and themselves. But it should be laid down that younger persons shall not be spectators at comedies or recitals of scurrilous iambics, not, that is to say, until they have reached the age at which they become entitled to recline at banquets, and share in the drinking; by this time their upbringing will have rendered them immune to any harm that might come from such spectacles. What we have just been saying has been said only incidentally; we must later go into the question in greater detail and decide whether or not they ought to attend, and, if so, under what conditions. We have only said as much as would serve the present occasion. Theodorus the tragic actor made, I think, a very apt remark in this connection when he refused to allow any other actor, even quite an inferior one, to appear on the stage before him, because, he said, an audience always takes kindly to the first voice that meets their ears. I think something of the same kind is true in men's relations with each other and the things they see and hear. We tend to love at first sight. Therefore we must keep all that is of inferior quality far away from the young, particularly these things that contain repulsive evil.

When they have passed their fifth birthday they should for the next two years learn, simply by observation, whatever they may be required to learn. Education after that may be divided into two stages — from the seventh year to puberty and from puberty to the completion of twenty-one years. Thus those who divide life into periods of seven years are not far wrong, and we ought to keep to the divisions that nature makes. For all training and education aim at filling the gaps that nature leaves. It therefore becomes our business to enquire whether we ought to lay down a system for the education of boys, then whether it is advisable to have a public authority in charge of it, or leave it in private hands, as is the usual practice in cities at the present time, and thirdly to discuss what the system of education should be.

Book VIII

No one would dispute the fact that it is a lawgiver's prime duty to arrange for the education of the young. There is no doubt that where this is not done the quality of the constitution suffers every time. Education must be related to the particular constitution in each case, for the character of the constitution is just that which makes it specifically what it is. Its own character made it at the start and continues to maintain it, the democratic character preserves a democracy, the oligarchic an oligarchy. And in all circumstances the best character produces the best constitution. There must also be the preparatory training for all the various crafts and professions and a process of habituation to the various jobs; so it is obvious that there must also be training for the activities of virtue. But since there is but one aim for the entire city, it follows that education must be one and the same for all and that the oversight of education must be a public concern, not the private affair which is now is, each man separately bringing up his own children and teaching them just what he thinks they ought to learn. In all matters that belong to the whole community the learning to do them must also be the concern of the community as a whole. And it is not right either that any of the citizens should think that he belongs just to himself; all citizens belong to the state, for each is a part of the state; and the care bestowed on each part naturally looks also towards the care of the whole. In this respect the Lacedaemonians earn our approval; the greatest possible attention is given to youth in Sparta and all on a national basis.

It is clear then that there should be laws laid down about education and that education itself must be made a national concern. But we must not forget the question of what that education is to be, and how it is to be brought into operation. For in modern times there are opposing views about the practice of education. There is no general agreement about what the young should learn either in relation to virtue or in relation to the best life; nor is it clear whether their education ought to be directed more towards the intellect than towards the character of the soul. The problem has been complicated by what we see happening before our eyes, and it is not certain whether training should be directed at things useful in life, or at those conducive to virtue, or at non-essentials. (All these answers have been given.) And there is no agreement as to what in fact does tend towards virtue. Men do not all prize most highly the same virtue, so naturally they differ also about the proper training for it.

Then as to useful things — there are obviously certain essentials which the young must learn, but they do not have to learn all useful things, since we distinguish those that are proper for a free man and those that are not. The citizen must take part in only those useful occupations which do not degrade the doer. Among degrading activities and vulgar pursuits we must reckon all those which render the body or soul or intellect of free men unserviceable for the demands and activities of virtue. We therefore call degrading those occupations which have a deleterious effect on the body's condition and all work that is paid for. For these make the mind preoccupied and unable to rise above menial things. Even in the liberal subjects there is a limit beyond which their study becomes illiberal. Too great concentration on them, too much mastering of detail — these are liable to cause the same degradation of spirit that we have been speaking of. In this connection a most important criterion is the purpose for which the action or the study is undertaken. It is proper for a free man to do something for himself or for his friends or on account of its value in itself, but he that does the same action on others' account may on occasion be regarded as doing something paid for or servile.

The subjects nowadays regularly studied serve both virtue and utility, as we have already noted. About four are generally taught to children, (1) reading and writing, (2) physical training, (3) music, and (4) not always included, drawing. Reading and writing and drawing are useful in daily life in a variety of ways, gymnastic because it aims to make men strong and brave. But about music there is a real question. Most men nowadays take part in music for the sake of the pleasure it gives; but some lay it down that music is fundamental in education on the ground that nature herself, as has often been said, aims at producing men not merely able to work properly but fit also for the life of cultivated leisure. And this latter, we repeat, is the basis of the whole business. It is true that we need both; but if not-working is preferable to, and is the end sought by, working, we must ask ourselves what are the proper activities of leisure.

Obviously not play; for that would be to make play the object of living, our end in life, which is unthinkable. Play has its uses, but they belong rather to the sphere of work; for he who works hard needs rest, and play is a way of resting, while work is inseparable from stress and strain. We must therefore for therapeutic reasons admit the necessity of games, while keeping them to their proper times and proper uses; taking exercise in this way is both a relaxation of the mind and, just because we enjoy it, a recreation. But the way of leisure that we are speaking of here is something positive, in itself a pleasant happy existence which the life of work and business cannot be. For he that is working is working for some hitherto unattained end, and happiness is an end, happiness which is universally regarded as concomitant not with toil but with enjoyment. Admittedly men do not agree as to what that enjoyment is; each man decides for himself following his own character and disposition, the finest character choosing the highest kind of enjoyment on the loftiest plane. Thus it becomes clear that preparation for spending time at leisure requires a great deal of learning and education. The educational processes and the subjects studied must have their own intrinsic merit, as distinct from those necessary professional subjects which are studied for reasons outside themselves. Hence, in the past, men laid down music as part of the curriculum of education not as being necessary, for it is not in that category, nor yet as being useful in the way that a knowledge of reading and writing is useful for business or administration, for study and for many citizens' activities, nor as a knowledge of drawing is useful for the better judging of artists' works, nor again as gymnastic is useful for health and strength; for we do not see either of these accruing as a result of playing music. There remains one purpose — to provide an occupation for leisure; and that is clearly the reason why they did introduce music into education, regarding it as an occupation of free men. Thus Homer wrote "to summon him alone to the rich banquet" and after these words he introduces certain others "who summon the bard whose singing shall delight them all". And elsewhere he speaks of Odysseus saying that the best recreation is when men get together and "sit in rows up and down the hall feasting and listening to the singer".

Clearly then there is a form of education which we must provide for our sons, not as being useful or essential but elevated and gentlemanly. We must on a later occasion discuss whether this education is one or many, what subjects it includes and how they are to be taught. But as it turns out, we have made some progress in that direction; music at least must be included. We have the evidence of the ancients derived from the subjects laid down by them.

The case of music makes that clear, but it does not stand alone; there are other subjects which the young must learn, for example their letters, not only because they are useful but because these are often the means to learning yet further subjects. Similarly drawing and a knowledge of design are useful not merely for the avoidance of mistakes in one's private purchases or that one may not be taken in when buying and selling furniture, but rather more especially because it teaches us to be observant of beauty in any physical object. But to be constantly asking "What is the use of ?" is unbecoming to those of superior mentality and free birth.

Since it is obvious that education by habit-forming must precede education by reasoned instruction (as that of the body precedes that of the mind), it is clear that we must subject our children to gymnastics and to training in wrestling and fighting; the former produces the condition of the body, the latter its actions.

In our own day those cities which have the greatest reputation for looking after their youth either aim at producing an athlete's condition, to the detriment of both the appearance and the development of the child's body, or else like the Spartans who have avoided that particular error, by severity of treatment they render them like animals, under the impression that this is conducive to courage.But, as has often been pointed out, the care of the young must be directed not to producing one quality only and not that more than the rest. And if courage is their aim, they do not even manage to secure it. For neither among animals nor among less civilised peoples do we find courage to be a characteristic of the most fierce, but rather (among animals) of the gentler and feline species; and among human beings there are many tribes that enjoy slaughter and the consumption of human flesh, in Pontus Achaeans and Heniochi and some of the mainland tribes, some better, some worse; raiders they may be, but they are not endowed with courage. And of the Lacedaemonians themselves too we know that so long as they applied themselves to strenuous training, they were superior to the rest, but nowadays they fall short of others both in war and athletics. For their former superiority was not due to their particular way of training the young but merely to the fact that they trained, and their opponents did not. The prime object therefore must be not any animal quality but nobility of character. One cannot struggle because it is the right thing to do; but that is what a brave man will do. Those who put their young to excessive military training, neglecting their education in essentials, are in sober fact rendering them vulgar and uneducated, making them useful for one part only of citizen life and even for that, as our argument shows, less useful than others. We should judge the Spartans by their present-day performance, not by what they used to be like. They now have rivals in the field of education, which formerly they did not have.

There is to be sure a place for gymnastics in education and there is general agreement as to what that place should be: up to puberty the exercises should be light and easy; nothing should be done that would interfere with the body's growth, no heavy dieting or strenuous forced hardships; for these are liable to have just that ill effect, as is shown by the fact that it is rare for the same men to be successful in the Olympic games both as boys and as men; their severe gymnastic training as boys has caused them to lose their strength. But when for the three years after puberty they have been engaged in learning other things, then the subsequent period may very properly be devoted to strenuous exercise and compulsory heavy dieting. Vigorous exercise of mind and body must not be combined; each naturally works in the opposite direction from the other, bodily toil interfering with the mind, mental with the body.

We have already discussed some of the questions that arose about music, but it would be well to resume the subject and carry it further, because I think that what I have to say will provide a key to any future discussions about music. To begin with, it is not easy to define either what the effect of music is or what our object is in learning it. Is it for our amusement and refreshment, like taking a nap or having a drink? I hardly think so, because these things are not in themselves of prime importance, though they are pleasant and help us to forget our worries, as Euripides says. Must we not rather regard music as a stimulus to goodness, capable of having an effect on the character, in just the same way as gymnastic training produces a body of a certain type, and so capable of forming men who have the habit of right critical appreciation? Thirdly, it surely has a contribution to make to the intelligent and cultivated pastimes.

It is clear then that we are not to educate the young with a view to amusement. Learning is hard work; while children are learning they are not playing. They are as yet too young for the cultivation of the intellect by means of music as an occupation; the complete life does not belong to the incomplete body. Still one might perhaps say that serious study in childhood may have for its aim the amusement of the complete and adult man.

But if this is so, what need is there for themselves to learn music? Why not do as kings of Persians and Medes do, have others to make music for them, so that they may listen and enjoy? For surely those who have perfected their skill in the making and production of music will give better performances than those who have devoted to learning music only such times as will enable them to listen intelligently. If we reject that and say that we must ourselves work hard at producing music, does it follow that we must also learn to produce good meals? Certainly not.

The same questions arises when we ask whether music has the power to improve the character. Why learn music oneself and not rather do as the Lacedaemonians do — acquire the art of right judgment and good taste by listening to others? They claim that without learning music they are capable of correctly distinguishing good music from bad. The same argument applies also when we ask whether music ought to be used as a means to making pleasant and cultivated pastimes for gentle folk. Why must they learn to perform themselves instead of simply enjoying the fruits of others' study? We may in this connection refer to our conception of the gods; the poets do not depict Zeus as playing and singing in person. In fact we regard professional performers as belonging to the lower classes, though a man may play and sing for his own amusement or at a party when he has had a good deal to drink.

Perhaps this question should be postponed till later; our chief enquiry now is whether or not music is to be put into education and what music can do. Is it an education or an amusement or a pastime? It is reasonable to reply that it is directed towards and participates in all three. Amusement is for the purpose of relaxation and relaxation must necessarily be pleasant, since it is a kind of cure for the ills we suffer in working hard. As to the pastimes of a cultivated life, there must, as is universally agreed, be present an element of pleasure as well as of nobility, for the happiness which belongs to that life consists of both these. We all agree that music is among the most delightful and pleasant things, whether instrumental or accompanied by singing, so that one might from that fact alone infer that the young should be taught it. For things that are pleasant and harmless belong rightly not only to the end in view but also to relaxation by the way. But since it rarely happens that men attain and keep their goal, and they frequently rest and amuse themselves with no other thought than the pleasure of it, there is surely a useful purpose in the pleasure derived from music.

On the other hand, men have been known to make amusement an end in itself. No doubt there is something pleasant about one's own chosen end but it is a very special kind of pleasure, and men in seeking pleasure mistake the one kind for the other. For there is indeed a resemblance; the end is not pursued for the sake of anything that may accrue thereafter but always for its own sake; similarly these recreation-pleasures are not for future but for present benefits; their pleasure arises from what is past — labour and pain finished. This would seem to be a reasonable explanation of why men try to get happiness through these pleasures. But it is certainly not for this reason alone that men take up music; the main reason, it seems, is that it provides relaxation.

Nevertheless we must ask whether, though this is commonly the case, the true nature of music be not something of greater value than filling the need for relaxation. Music certainly has a pleasure of its own; all ages and all types like and enjoy it. But we must do more than merely share in the general pleasure which all men find in it; we must consider whether music has any effect on the character and the mind. We could answer this question if we could say that we become of such and such a disposition through music. And surely it is obvious from many examples that music does indeed have such an effect, not least from the tunes composed by Olympus. These are well known to affect the personality, making men wildly excited — a frenzied excitement which is both a mental and a moral condition. Again, when listening to theatrical performances all men are affected in a manner in keeping with the performance, even apart from the tunes and rhythms employed. Since music belongs to the class of things pleasant, and since it is virtue therein to enjoy rightly, to like and dislike the right things, clearly there are no more important lessons to be learned or habits to be formed than those of taking pleasure in good morals and noble actions.

Now in rhythms and in tunes there is a close resemblance to reality — the realities of anger and gentleness, also of courage and moderation, and of the opposites of these, indeed of all moral qualities; and the fact that music heard does indeed cause an emotional change in us is an indication of this. To have the habit of feeling pleasure (or pain) in things that are like to reality is very near to having the same disposition towards reality. I mean if a man enjoys looking at a statue of someone for no other reason than that he likes the look of it, then inevitably he will enjoy looking at the original, whose likeness he is at the moment contemplating. Now it is true that objects perceived by the senses, touched or tasted, do not present any similarity to moral qualities, but in music moral qualities are present, represented in the very tunes we hear. This is obvious, for to begin with there is the natural distinction between the modes or harmonies, which cause different reactions in the hearers, who are not all moved in the same way. For example, men are inclined to be mournful or tense when they listen to that which is called Mixo-Lydian, they are more relaxed when they listen to the looser harmonies. An equable feeling, midway between these, is produced, I think, only by the Dorian mode, while the Phrygian makes men greatly excited. These are the results of some excellent work which has been done on this aspect of education; the investigators have made practical tests and based their conclusions on them. The same is true also of the different types of rhythm; some have a steadying effect, others an unsettling, and of these latter some give rise to vulgar movements, some to more gentlemanly.

It follows from all this that music has indeed the power to induce certain conditions of mind, and if it can do that, clearly it must be applied to education and the young must be educated in and by it. And the teaching of music is particularly apt for the young; for they because of their youth do not willingly tolerate anything that is not made pleasant for them, and music is one of those things that are by nature made to give pleasure. Moreover there is a certain affinity between us and music's harmonies and rhythms; so that many experts say that the soul is a harmony, others that it has harmony.

We must now return to a question raised earlier — must they learn to sing themselves and play instruments with their own hands? Clearly actual participation in performing is going to make a big difference to the quality of the person that will be produced; it is impossible, or at any rate very difficult, to produce good judges of musical performance from among those who have never themselves performed. And all that we have been saying makes it clear that musical education must include actual performing; and it is not difficult to decide what is appropriate and what is not for different ages, or to find an answer to those who assert that learning to perform is vulgar and degrading. First, since as we have have seen, actual performance is needed to make a good critic, they should while young do much playing and singing, and then, when they are older, give up performing; they will then, thanks to what they have learned in their youth, be able to enjoy music aright and give good judgments. As for the objection, brought by some, that musical performance is degrading to a gentleman, this can easily be answered if we consider to what extent boys, who are being educated to discharge the highest functions in the state, ought to take part in music, what tunes and what rhythms they are to perform, and on what instruments they are to learn to play, for that too will make a difference. In the answers to these quesions will be found the answer to the objection; and an answer must be found, for it is very likely that certain kinds of music do have the effect mentioned.

It is clear therefore that learning music must not be allowed to have any adverse effect on later activities, or make the body banausic and ill-fitted for the training of citizen or soldier, the practice in youth, the theory in later years. What is needed is that the pupil shall not struggle to acquire the degree of skill that is needed for professional competitions, or to master those peculiar and sensational pieces of music which have begun to penetrate the competitions and have even affected education. Musical exercises, even if not of this kind, should be pursued only up to the point at which the pupil becomes capable of appreciating good melodies and rhythms, and not just the popular music such as appeals to slaves, children, and even some animals. . . .

We must investigate a little this matter of harmonies and rhythms and its relation to education. Are we to make use of all the harmonies and rhythms or should we not make distinctions? And will the same basis of classification serve also those who are concerned with education, or must we lay down a third? Certainly music is, as we know, divided into melody-making and rhythm, and we must not omit to consider what bearing each of these has on education, and whether we are to rate higher music with a good tune or music with a good rhythm. I believe that these topics are very well dealt with both by some modern musicians and by others whose approach is philosophical but who have actual experience of music in relation to education. I would advise those who want detailed treatment of the several questions to seek advice in that quarter. Here let me give a conventional account and simply refer to the usual typology.

We accept the classification of melodies as given by some educationalists — ethical, active, and emotional — and regard the harmonies as being appropriate, one here and another there in that scheme. But we say that music ought to be used not as conferring one benefit only but many; for example, for education and cathartic purposes, as an intellectual pastime, as relaxation and for relief after tension. While then we must make use of all the harmonies, we are not to use them all in the same manner, but for education use those which improve the character, for listening to others performing use both the activating and the emotion-stirring or enthusiastic. Any feeling which comes strongly to some exists in all others to a greater or lesser degree, pity and fear, for example, but also this "enthusiasm". This is a kind of excitement which affects some people very strongly. It may arise out of religious music, and it is noticeable that when they have been listening to melodies that have an orgiastic effect they are, as it were, set on their feet, as if they had undergone a curative and purifying treatment. And those who feel pity or fear or other emotions must be affected in just the same way to the extent that the emotion comes upon each. To them all comes a pleasant feeling of purgation and relief. In the same way cathartic music brings men an elation which is not at all harmful. Hence these are the harmonies and melodies that ought to receive particular attention from those who are concerned with contests in theatrical music. . . .

Antithesis:
The Progressive View

3

ROUSSEAU

Commentary

Historical Link: Aristotle to Rousseau

Because there is such a large time gap between the death of Aristotle in 322 B.C. and the birth of Rousseau in A.D. 1712, a short summary of the main educational developments throughout this period may be helpful to the student as a prelude to a consideration of Rousseau's work.

The educational thought of Plato and Aristotle was not developed into any specific programme outside of the Academy and Lyceum. Instead, their work laid a basis or a programme in general education that was to have wide influence.

Alexander unified the Greek world in the late fourth century B.C. and the period from about 300 B.C. was known as the Hellenistic Era. The Greeks developed a concept and practice of what they called *enkyklios paideia*, literally translated as "general education". This was based on the seven liberal arts, comprising the four areas of the content of knowledge which came to be known as the *quadrivium* — arithmetic, geometry, astronomy and harmonics — and the three methods of organising and treating this content — dialectic (or logic), rhetoric and grammar, together known as the *trivium*. Along with exercises in the gymnasium this was the content of "all round" education. Of course it was served by a preliminary sequence of mythopoeic literature and the three Rs: reading, writing and reckoning.

The Romans occupied as conquerors all of the Mediterranean by the end of the first century B.C., in the meantime having already been largely Hellenised in their own programme of education. The chief educational result of their military hegemony was thus the consolidation of the Greek approach to education, and its further extension to Roman colonies in Europe, particularly Gaul, Iberia and Britain. Yet the Romans did not accept all of the seven liberal arts equally. They found most of the four mathematics of the *quadrivium* too abstruse and speculative; dialectic too, held little real interest for them. Grammar and rhetoric, however, proved very appealing and these received an exceptionally strong emphasis, particularly since they appealed to the Romans' pride in being practical minded and to their need for the instrumental skill of rhetoric in the oratorical activities of politics. With the decline of the Roman Empire and its interpenetration by the barbarians — collectively the various northern tribes of *Germani* — much of the educational achievement was lost and schools declined from the fifth century A.D. until the tenth. Meanwhile Christianity had spread and it required only a minimal acquaintance with literacy, sufficient to read the Bible and the Patristic corpus: chiefly Augustine, Ambrose and Jerome. During these five centuries, known as the Dark Ages, a tenuous educational tradition of antiquity was maintained in Europe, chiefly by monks and priests.

Meanwhile the classical education system was sustained relatively intact — but atrophied — in the regions of Greek Christianity, known as Byzantium. From the tenth century onward the Latin West of Europe developed stronger links with the Greek East of Byzantium, from which it had been formally separated by the emperor Diocletian in A.D. 285, and the classical form of education, admittedly with a Christian emphasis, gained ground.

From the tenth to the twelfth centuries there was a rapid increase of European acquaintance with the classical tradition, stimulated by the need for a more educated clergy in a climate of growing trade and commerce. Education became centred more and more in cathedral schools and monasteries and as the classical corpus became translated from Greek to Latin, often through Arabic versions which came in through Spain, the curriculum more closely followed classical lines. The main educational activities of Europe from the eleventh to the fourteenth centuries were in recovering the classical corpus and transmitting this to a larger body of scholars. In the process, of course, a great deal of controversial material (from a Christian point of view) was received and this caused lengthy and bitter debate, one of the consequences of which was to strengthen the autonomy of the cathedral schools (the Latin term is *universitates*) that were set up to handle this vast accession of knowledge. So the institution of the university was developed. Throughout the thirteenth century the universities became the intellectual centres of Europe, and increased in numbers quite rapidly. From their concern with the close study of the classical past a new enthusiasm for cultural history ensued. In the fourteenth century the lead in this was taken by Italy, and Dante, Petrarch and Boccaccio were the important figures in the movement. This resulted in a vigorous attempt to see classical civilisation reborn in Europe — and so the phenomenon of the Renaissance took place. But the aim was clearly the recovery and imitation of the classical past, not the implementation of any new cultural or educational ideals. Indeed the Renaissance continued into the fifteenth and sixteenth centuries where it became annexed into specific religious plans resulting from the Lutheran schism. Northern Germany and the other Protestant regions saw classical education as capable of strengthening Bible studies in schools; the Catholic south of Europe felt that the same studies would confirm the title of Rome to ecclesiastical hegemony of the West.

Education in the seventeenth century saw a continued strengthening of the ideal of recovering the classical past, and the work of Comenius (1592–1670) is a superb testimony to the continued enthusiasm for this. His grand scheme of a sequence of a school of infancy, primary school, grammar school and university providing a means for the transmission of the classical heritage was the apogee of the movement. Behind it was the classical ideal of *enkyklios paideia*, but now crowned with the attainment of Christian vision. In itself it did not eventuate, but limited versions were carried throughout Catholic Europe and its colonies by the Jesuits, and throughout Protestant Europe by individual schoolmasters.

Yet Europe's cultural revival was being challenged by new developments in trade, technology and science and the seventeenth century saw the floodgates burst open with a torrent of new ideas (we can only list the names: Bacon, Descartes, Locke, Harvey, Boyle, Huygens, Leewenhoek, among others) and the consequences of this flood carried over into the eighteenth century into the movement of the Enlightenment. But the schools and educational thought and practice had not kept pace with the development of man's philosophy, science and technology. Education was still fixed at the level of providing a grammar-school education — and university for a tiny minority — to help the study of the classical and Christian literature.

This then was the educational tradition that Rousseau inherited. Let us now examine his reaction to it.

Biography

Jean-Jacques Rousseau (1712-78) was born in the Swiss city of Geneva. His mother died very soon after his birth and Rousseau was brought up by his father, who was responsible for his early education. At the age of ten his education was placed in the hands of a tutor, a pastor in the village of Bossey, who taught Rousseau for about two years. That was the only formal education he ever received and soon afterwards he was given training in a notary's office and then apprenticed to an engraver, not remaining long in either position. He then left Geneva and lived, according to his *Confessions*, as a vagabond for a number of years, travelling through France and Italy.

He tried various occupations which included servant duties, studying for the priesthood, a career in music (he put a lot of effort into trying to publicise a new system of musical notation), acting as a secretary and then, for a brief period, as a tutor. None of these led to anything and it was not until 1749 that he finally achieved some success. In that year the Academy of Dijon, reflecting the concern that was beginning to be felt about some of the consequences of the Age of Enlightenment, offered a prize for the best essay on the subject, "Has the progress of the arts and sciences contributed to the corruption or to the purification of morals?" The posing of such a question appealed to Rousseau who, on the advice of Diderot, the famous French philosopher, presented an essay to the Academy in which he argued that the arts and sciences had led to the corruption of morals. For this he was awarded the prize and he achieved his first taste of public fame, which evidently meant a lot to him and stimulated him to become more involved in these growing social concerns.

Three years later, in 1752, he presented another essay, the "Discourse

Upon Inequality", to the Dijon Academy and although this time he failed to win a prize, the essay received considerable public attention when Rousseau had it published in 1755. Having now found a vocation, Rousseau continued to write whenever he could. In 1755 he contributed the article on "Political Economy" to Diderot's *Encyclopédie* and the time from then until 1762 constituted his most fertile literary period. His novel *Julie ou La Nouvelle Héloïse*, appeared in 1761, *The Social Contract* and *Emile* in 1762.

Emile immediately aroused the hostility of the Catholic church, primarily because of the section known as "The Creed of the Savoyard Priest", which criticises a number of Catholic doctrines. The book was also attacked as immoral and revolutionary and was condemned by the *Parlement* of Paris. In danger of arrest, Rousseau fled to Switzerland, but when the Council of Geneva also condemned the book Rousseau renounced his Genevan citizenship and spent the next few years on the move, largely still inside Switzerland, finally deciding to seek refuge from persecution in England. He was befriended there by David Hume, the great Scottish empiricist philosopher. By this time Rousseau's personality had grown very unstable and he had become almost paranoic. This caused bitter quarrels with Hume and other friends in Britain and in 1770 he returned to Paris.

He then completed his autobiography, the *Confessions*, which he had begun in England, and some minor works, including *Considerations on the Government of Poland*. Poverty-stricken and with his health now beginning to fail, he moved to the country in 1778 but died soon after in July of that year.

Main Features of Rousseau's Educational Thought

It seems clear that many of the attitudes Rousseau developed to both education and life in general were strongly influenced by his own unsettled life and especially his early unsuccessful attempts to find vocation. He appears to have suffered throughout from a sense of frustration and unfulfilment and remained strongly antipathetic to most of the societies in which he lived. The lack of a settled home life and of a proper education are sure to have played a large part in determining both his initial interest in education and the revolutionary viewpoint he took towards it.

His radical views first became apparent in the prize-winning essay for the Academy of Dijon and this work foreshadows some of the ideas expressed later in *Emile*. The second essay, the "Discourse on Inequality", develops further his view that man is naturally good and only made bad by society. The inequalities between men, he says, are not natural but due to social arrangement.

The next important work, *La Nouvelle Héloïse*, expresses in novelistic form many of the ideas that he was later to argue in *Emile*. It contains an illustration of domestic education in which the young children are educated at home, away from the corrupting influences of society, and are thus able to preserve their natural goodness.

The Social Contract was originally planned to come after *Emile* and to form a sequence of thought with it, but due to a last-minute change in publishers, *Emile* was delayed and *The Social Contract* appeared first. The notion of a social contract was first expressed by Thomas Hobbes in *On the Citizen* and then developed further by John Locke, paricularly in his *Second Treatise on Government*. Rousseau's work on this subject begins with the well-known words:

> Man is born free; and everywhere he is in chains. One thinks himself the master of others, and still remains a greater slave than they. How did this come about? I do not know. What can make it legitimate? That question I think I can answer.

Rousseau's answer is that government is based upon a contract implicitly made between the citizens and the rulers to the effect that the citizens will surrender some of their individual rights for the sake of the protection of a central authority. The government therefore represents the general will of the community and cannot be justified in enforcing any law which goes against this general will. This book had a great influence on revolutionary opinion in France and was a significant factor in the development of events leading to the French Revolution, providing as it did a model of government radically opposed to that of absolute monarchy.

These then were the major developments in Rousseau's thought up to the publication of *Emile* and it is clear that he had by this time developed the basis of a general social and moral philosophy that could be fruitfully applied to education. In so doing he produced an educational philosophy that constituted the first significant challenge to the philosophy of education derived from Plato and Aristotle, that had provided the dominant educational doctrine right up to the eighteenth century.

The revolutionary change suggested by Rousseau is that instead of education being centred on *what* is taught (the subject matter), it should be centred on *who* is taught, that is, the child. Education, he argued, should be adapted to meet the child's needs, not arranged according to the criterion of the subject matter it is thought should be learnt. This then is a radical shifting of emphasis in the educational process, because coupled with the dethroning of subject matter as the basic element in the educational process, it also leads to a dethroning of the teacher as the figure of authority whose function it is to convey this subject matter to the learner.

A further consequence of placing the child at the centre of education is that it becomes necessary to treat its needs and interests as paramount. And it is an historical fact that nearly all who take the child-centred approach combine it with a view that the child contains within itself the potentialities for desirable educational development and that it is the teacher's task to let these develop according to their own laws rather than to try to impose some external pattern. But Rousseau went even further than this; he claimed that the child's nature is intrinsically good and that contrary to the Christian doctrine of original sin, there is no evil present in the newborn child. As the opening lines of *Emile* proclaim: "Everything is good as it comes from the hands of the Maker of the world but degenerates once it gets into the hands of man."

Natural development, then, is the ideal and any interferences with it are to be avoided. Education in the old style is deleterious on this count for it tries to make the child into a good citizen; this involves educating people for others rather than for themselves. So public education is ruled out in *Emile* as unnatural, and individual education is to take its place. This individual education will shield the child from the harmful effects of corrupt society and allow innate goodness to develop as it should. Once this has been achieved it is safe for the child, uncorrupted as it is, to enter society being now impervious to its harmful influences.

But how can the child be shielded from society and still receive a proper education? *Emile* is Rousseau's attempt to answer this question. One of the main tasks Rousseau sets himself in this work is to describe the child's nature and how it should be allowed to develop according to its own inner laws. This then will provide a clear model for all those who follow Rousseau and take the individualist approach to education. To present his ideas to the reader Rousseau takes an imaginary pupil, an orphan called Emile, whom Rousseau has been given the job of rearing. In his description of how he would do this, Rousseau is able to express all his fundamental ideas about the new type of education.

His expression of these ideas is generally very forceful and he makes much use of rhetoric and exaggeration, sometimes at the expense of logical consistency. Indeed it is best to view *Emile* as the manifesto of a revolutionary new educational programme rather than a carefully argued intellectual exercise. Rousseau realised quite rightly that this would be a more effective way of communicating his ideas to the general public. If we therefore read the book in this light, not expecting it to be either a practical programme that can be implemented in all details or a tight and logically coherent set of philosophical arguments, we are likely to benefit more from it. This is not to say that it should not be criticised where it is impractical, inconsistent or misguided (and some of the main weaknesses here will be mentioned later), but that these criticisms should be balanced against its undoubted worth as a clear statement of many valuable new educational ideas, ideas that have exerted an immense influence ever since.

Emile is divided into five books, each one dealing with a separate stage in the child's development. The main features of the first four stages and the educational provisions that are appropriate in each case are set out in the following extracts which comprise the reading for Rousseau.* Some of the main points the reader should notice in each book are the following.

Book I, after some general remarks about education according to nature, covers the first stage of a child's development, that of infancy, which Rousseau places from birth to about the age of two. He stresses the importance

---

*Due to limitations of space, extracts from the fifth book, dealing with the period after the age of twenty and Emile's marriage, are not included.

of the child being brought up by his own mother and not handed over to a nurse as was common among the well-to-do in the eighteenth century. At this stage the main role of the tutor is to ensure that the child's opportunities for as many different experiences as possible are not restricted unless he is likely to suffer harm. Do not allow the child to contract any habits, says Rousseau, because these create new needs that are not due to nature. (In Rousseau's day, "habit" had the connotation of being something unnatural or artificial. He would presumably not be opposed to the development of what we would today call "natural" or "necessary" habits in a child's upbringing, such as the habits involved in learning to walk or talk.)

The next stage of development is boyhood, which, according to Rousseau, lasts from two to twelve. This is covered in Book II. Here he introduces the concept of negative education, which means shielding the child from harmful influences rather than teaching him things for which he is not ready. Education at this stage, he says, "consists not in teaching virtue and truth, but in preserving the heart from vice and the mind from error".

What the young child does learn is based on sensory and practical experience rather than ideas or reasoning. He is not ready for purely mental activity yet and any attempt to introduce it will be an unnatural interference with his development. Learning experiences that are appropriate now are drawing, measuring, speaking and singing. Subjects that require verbal or symbolic knowledge such as geography, history, languages and literature are for the future. He illustrates the common errors of teaching subjects like geography at too early an age and in the wrong way, as in his example of the young child who has learned the names of numerous places on the map but cannot find the way from Paris to St Denis. It is the latter type of knowledge that should come first.

Negative education is also the model in the sphere of morality. Rousseau recommends that when the child does wrong he should not be punished but instead should be left to suffer the consequences of his own misbehaviour, as in his example of the child breaking the window of his bedroom. This policy has come to be known as the doctrine of natural consequences. It is however open to question whether such a doctrine is a fully adequate approach to the control of the young child's behaviour; is it true, for instance, that children will always suffer in some way as a result of their wrong doing if there is no outside interference? And even if they do, will this always be sufficient to teach them the appropriate lesson?

Rousseau further maintains that the ideas of duty and obedience are unnecessary and harmful. Once again these are unnatural limitations on behaviour. The law of necessity is the only law to which the child should be subject; in other words, he should be dependent on things rather than men. The child at this stage cannot understand moral or social rules and any attempt to teach them would be wasted. "Childhood," says Rousseau, "has ways of seeing, thinking and feeling peculiar to itself: nothing can be more foolish than to seek to substitute our ways for them."

It is only natural that at this stage the child's dominant motive should be self-love, or concern with personal pleasures and pains. This is not necessarily to imply selfishness, which suggests that one is concerned with one's own desires at the expense of other people's. Rather it means that the young child is not yet able to put itself in the place of other people and see things from their point of view.

By the end of this stage of development, Emile has maintained his natural goodness and freedom, and is ready to approach adolescence without any misgivings. As Rousseau states: "He has acquired all the reason possible for his age, and in doing so has been as free and as happy as his nature allowed him to be."

The next period of his life is treated in Book III and covers the years from twelve to fifteen, the period of early adolescence in Rousseau's scheme. By this time the child's innate curiosity is much more developed and, because his natural interest about the world has not been dampened by premature attempts at teaching verbal and abstract knowledge, he is keen and ready to explore the environment in which he lives. The basic technique of learning that Rousseau advocates is the problem-solving or discovery method, by which the child himself finds answers to the questions that interest him. Thus all learning should still come from his own observations and experience, not from that of his tutor or from books.

The only book he would be allowed to read in this period is *Robinson Crusoe* and it is easy to see why Rousseau chooses this one. It is the story of a man living in a wholly natural environment, uncorrupted by society and using his native intelligence and abilities in order to solve the practical problems that arise on his island. It is the perfect model of the sort of life that Rousseau sees as appropriate at this stage.

Emile is still not ready for the formal subjects of the traditional school, but he can begin to learn some elementary science, not from his tutor but from his own experience of the natural world. He can, as well, learn a practical craft such as carpentry, which will also serve to give him some idea of the vocations of man. (This would have been a rather radical proposal for children of the aristocracy in eighteenth-century France.)

At age fifteen, Emile, says Rousseau:

> . . .is ready to cease being a child and to enter on an individual life . . . We have made him an efficient thinking being and nothing further remains for us in the production of the complete man but to make him a loving, sensitive being: in fact, to perfect reason through sentiment.

This is the turning point in his education, and in the fourth stage, that of adolescence, Emile's educational programme undergoes marked changes. This is the period from ages fifteen to twenty, treated in Book IV. Emile is at last ready for social and intellectual activities and the type of education he receives now is not very different to normal eighteenth-century practice. The important point for Rousseau is that it has been postponed until the child is ready, and in this way he comes to it fresh and unsullied and so gains the maximum benefit.

The curriculum will contain history, literature, art, languages, social studies and politics. On this topic Rousseau has some interesting remarks to make about the problems inherent in the study of history, and, in regard to literature, clearly prefers the classics. To broaden his education, Emile will go on the traditional "Grand Tour" of Europe, undertaken by most young aristocrats of the time to complete their education. His entry into society is safe now because he is equipped to meet its dangers. He will see the selfishness and deceit common among men and he will learn to avoid these in himself. Self-love (*amour de soi*) will develop into self-esteem (*amour propre*), which has its dangers, but Emile will withstand them. He will acquire good taste (upon which Rousseau places much stress) through the study of literature and drama, through taking part in polite society and through travel.

Rather surprisingly, then, the final model of the educated man that Rousseau presents is not very different to the current eighteenth-century ideal of the liberally educated man with the subjects of instruction including the usual literary and linguistic studies of the traditional *studia humanitatis* curriculum. What is new in Rousseau is that this type of education is delayed until the child is fifteen and the methods used to convey it are child centred and stress the child's active involvement in the learning process.

It is also interesting to note that Rousseau now echoes Aristotle in saying that "it is by doing good that we become good". The difference is that Aristotle would begin such moral habit training much earlier — and this raises the question whether Rousseau has delayed it until too late. In any event, Emile will be subject to new passions surging within him and the awakening of the sex drives will lead to the need for careful guidance by the tutor in the spheres of morality and the emotions. Rousseau here takes a common sense, practical approach to these questions and avoids the extremes of either a rigid puritanism or an unbridled libertinism.

Emile is also given religious guidance by means of hearing an account of the confessions of a Savoyard priest.* The main burden of it is an appeal to a basic, natural form of religion, in which the individual's own inner faith is central and the rituals and dogma of the institutionalised church are regarded as peripheral. This is the section of the book that caused Rousseau so much difficulty with the church. Today it is difficult to see why it should have created so much furore; this is a clear indication of the differing intellectual climates of his age and our own.

The final chapter of *Emile* comes as something of an anticlimax from the educational point of view. It deals with Emile's marriage to Sophie, who has received a very different education to that of Emile. In fact, Rousseau's ideas on women's education are distinctly reactionary and would certainly

---

*This account takes up a large section of Book IV and is too long to include in the readings for this text.

attract little support from contemporary feminist movements. The whole basis of the education of Sophie, who represents the ideal woman, is to make her a pleasing and useful partner to man and this was by and large the conventional eighteenth-century view on women's education. Her education will therefore consist mainly of learning how to perform household duties, acquiring social accomplishments (such as learning how to play a musical instrument) and the methods of making herself charming to men. In addition she should be given a simple form of religion only, which she will learn from her mother.

The book ends with their marriage, followed by the birth of a son whom Emile undertakes to educate. So while the device of the tutor was a useful way for Rousseau to present his educational ideas, in real life he maintains that the parents, especially the father, should look after the child's education. An outsider could not really be expected to devote his whole life to the bringing up of a young child as in the case of Emile's tutor. It is rather ironical at this point to note (if what Rousseau says in his *Confessions* is true) that he himself had five children by his housekeeper Thérèse (whom he only eventually married two years before his death), and placed them all in a foundling hospital at birth.

After *Emile*, Rousseau produced only one other work with important bearings on education. This was *Considerations on the Government of Poland*, written in 1771 in response to a request from a Polish nobleman for advice concerning the reform of the Polish government. This was at a particularly difficult period in Polish history, when Poland was threatened by powerful neighbours on all sides and was in fact, subjected to partition in the year that Rousseau wrote his work.

Rousseau's educational advice in the *Considerations* is strongly at variance with what he proclaims in *Emile*, for he now strongly advocates a national system of education, stating that "It is the national institutions that form the genius, the character, the tastes, and the morals of a people and render it different from every other people."[1] Polish strength and unity could only be achieved by a public system of education controlled by high-ranking magistrates whose aim is to produce patriotic and useful citizens. Plato's *Republic* immediately springs to mind as the model, and indeed Rousseau here comes very close to recommending what is basically the Platonic educational system. As in the *Republic*, the education of young Poles would include the knowledge necessary to fit them for their future roles in society, and gymnastic exercises and games to render them physically fit and to promote the spirit of co-operation.

How can one reconcile all this with the educational theories of *Emile*? It would not seem that this represents a change of mind by Rousseau after he wrote that book because he puts forward a very similar argument in an earlier work, his article for the *Encyclopédie*, entitled "Political Economy", which was written in 1755, seven years before *Emile*. In that essay he states:

> It cannot be left to individual man to be sole judge as to his duties. Still less should children's education be left to the ignorance and prejudice of their fathers . . . Public education, regulated by the state, under magistrates appointed by the supreme authority, is an essential condition of popular government.[2]

The only possible aswer to this apparent paradox in Rousseau's thought is that in *Emile* he was dealing with education in the context of eighteenth-century France (prior to the revolution), which Rousseau saw as clearly a corrupt society. In his recommendations for the Polish government and in the article on "Political Economy", on the other hand, he is looking at education in the context of political reform, and in an ideal state of the type he is discussing, education is an integral part of the political system. That is, under ideal social and political conditions, the corrupting influences of society will be eradicated and the needs and interests of the child will be best met in a public form of education. Nonetheless the whole tone of the two sets of writings is in marked contrast and it is hard to see how the great stress placed on personal guidance and the individual needs of the child in *Emile* could ever be met in a state system of education.

Regardless of these apparent inconsistencies, it is the ideas of *Emile* that constitute Rousseau's significant innovation, and it is the individual child-centred approach to education represented there that has had such a profound influence on all subsequent educational thought. To assist the reader in making a final assessment of the adequacy of Rousseau's ideas some questions and problems will now be raised that point to possible weaknesses in *Emile*.

In the first place, consider Rousseau's great stress on nature as intrinsically good and as the guide to all educational development. What exactly does the word "nature" mean (the French word itself is *nature*)? As G. H. Bantock points out,[3] Rousseau seems to use it in at least three different ways in *Emile*; as that which is the opposite of *nurture* or the training given by other men; as that which is in accord with the behaviour of primitive, precivilised, and therefore uncorrupted, man; and thirdly as the phenomenal world apart from man, in particular the world of plants and animals. Nor does Rousseau tell us which of these is central and which is the one that is most relevant to education.

Apart from the confusion of meanings here, there is also a basic philosophical problem in using nature as a model for education. For why should we base education on what we conceive nature to be? This assumes the basic value judgment that whatever is natural is best and should be followed — something for which Rousseau offers little argument. Are there not aspects of nature that may be harmful to follow? And might there not be something to say for the opposite point of view: that it is what distinguishes man from the rest of nature, that is, his reason, which is of supreme value? (This, it may be recalled, was the view of Plato and Aristotle.)

Secondly, does not Rousseau's account of child growth and development depend too much on a rigid faculty psychology: sensations in infancy, sense-judgment in childhood, practical thought in pre-adolescence and finally, abstract reasoning in adolescence? In actual fact children's psychological development seems much more flexible than this, with more overlapping between the various stages, and with the capacity to reason and to understand moral and social relations being possible earlier than he allows.

Nevertheless, it may be added on Rousseau's behalf that this was a step in the right direction, at least he had shown the need to study and understand the facts of children's development and to relate what is taught to the child's present capacities. Moreover, bearing in mind the limited psychological knowledge of his time, his account is in many ways remarkably perceptive.

Thirdly, because of Rousseau's stress on learning from experience, without being taught by someone else, does not he undervalue the need in education for a sound training in the fundamental disciplines of knowledge? Children are not likely to go very far in science, for example, without being given some basic instruction in the facts and methods of science. (This is, of course, even more necessary today than it was in the eighteenth century.) The idea of the child exploring the world around him and learning science just by observation of nature and its processes does not really work beyond a very simple level, unless he already knows what to look for and is able to sort out what is important from what is merely incidental. If, for instance, it was true that Sir Isaac Newton was prompted to work out the law of gravity because of the apple falling on his head, it was only because he had the necessary scientific background and training to be able to recognise this as an instance of general scientific law.

In general, Rousseau seems to play down too much the importance of acquiring a basic grounding in the various modes or forms of thought. Even if the child does not realise at the time that it is in his interest to acquire such knowledge, the teacher may be justified in requiring him to learn it. Contrary to what Rousseau says, it is not always obvious to the child what is in his own interest and often it is not until he has been taught a certain subject that the child will appreciate its value (either in its own right or as leading on to something else that he values). Indeed, this is one of the main reasons why we have teachers — if the child always knew what was in his interest and how to learn it, what need would there be for a teacher?

Finally, we may pose the question of just how much Emile is in fact developing freely and naturally if his tutor is always in the background ensuring that he has the sorts of experiences that fit a preconceived model of how a child should develop. For instance, is it always "natural" to refrain from interfering when a child misbehaves? Is it "natural" to isolate a child from society for a long period of his childhood, and can such a child develop a proper moral outlook in isolation from social contacts? And what if Emile wants to do something at an earlier stage than Rousseau thinks appropriate, to read a book other than *Robinson Crusoe*, for instance? Prohibition here may be just as harmful as introducing book learning too early. In all these instances Rousseau is in danger of manipulating or indoctrinating the child just as surely as the child in the conventional school is manipulated, the only difference being the kind of goals, toward which this is directed.

In considering these criticisms of Rousseau's ideas, however, it is important to bear in mind the remarks made earlier in this commentary to the effect that we should regard *Emile* more as a set of educational ideals expressed in terms of the story of the bringing up of a young child by his tutor, rather than a systematic philosophical treatise on education. It represents the manifesto of a revolutionary new approach to education and as with most such attempts to convert to a wholly new way of thinking the case is stated very strongly, which possibly leads in places to over-reaction against past practices. The important thing about *Emile* is its radical new perspective on education and while his expression of this new point of view contains weaknesses, many of these were not necessary features of it and later progressive thinkers such as Dewey, were able to build on and extend the initial insights which he presented. Rousseau has, in fact, done educational thought a permanent service by switching the emphasis to the child as the centre of the educational process. Some of the new trends in educational theory (many of which have become accepted by educational thinkers of virtually all shades of opinion) that flow from this shift of emphasis and which clearly establish Rousseau's significant innovation in educational thought are the following:

1. appreciating the value of discovery learning and problem-solving as educational techniques;
2. confining the child's early learning to things that are within his own experience and therefore have meaning for him;
3. stressing the rights of each child to individual consideration, freedom and happiness;
4. realising the need to understand the child's nature and the way this develops through childhood and adolescence, and using the knowledge of this in determining what he should learn at each stage of his development; and
5. treating the child as a being in his own right, not just a miniature adult, and therefore stressing the enrichment of his present experience rather than preparing him for some distant future.

NOTES AND REFERENCES

1. *The Minor Educational Writings of Jean-Jacques Rousseau*, selected and translated by W. Boyd, Blackie, London, 1910. Reprinted by the Bureau of Publications, Teachers College, Columbia University, New York, 1962, p. 96.
2. Ibid., p. 41.
3. G. H. Bantock, "Emile Reconsidered", in *Education and Values*, Faber, London, 1965, pp. 67–69.

SELECT BIBLIOGRAPHY

All of Rousseau's important works that have direct or indirect bearing on his educational thought have been mentiond above. In order of publication they are:

"Discourse on the Arts and Sciences", 1750
"Discourse upon Inequality", 1755

The Encyclopédie article, "Political Economy", 1755
Julie ou La Nouvelle Heloïse, 1761
The Social Contract, 1762
Emile, 1762
Considerations on the Government of Poland, 1773
Confessions, 1781

The selections from *Emile* for this text have been taken from W. Boyd's translation in his *Emile for Today*, Heinemann, London 1956. The same translator's *Minor Educational Writings of Jean-Jacques Rousseau*, Blackie, London, 1910 (reprinted by Bureau of Publications, Teachers College, Columbia University, New York, 1962) contains extracts from Rousseau's *Encyclopédie* article, *Julie ou La Nouvelle Héloïse, Considerations on the Government of Poland* and the *Confessions*.

Selections

The selections from Rousseau are all taken from Emile *and cover the first four books, which comprise the periods of infancy (age 0–2), boyhood (2–12), early adolescence (12–15) and adolescence (15–20). The full version of* Emile *is quite lengthy (over 600 pages in the standard French Garnier edition) and the extracts given here have been chosen to bring out, as far as possible, Rousseau's essential educational views, and in particular to highlight his ideas on individualistic and natural education.*

Emile

Book I

Everything is good as it comes from the hands of the Maker of the world but degenerates once it gets into the hands of man. Man makes one land yield the products of another, disregards differences of climates, elements and seasons, mutilates his dogs, and horses, perverts and disfigures everything. Not content to leave anything as nature has made it, he must needs shape man himself to his notions, as he does the trees in his garden.

But under present conditions, human beings would be even worse than they are without this fashioning. A man left entirely to himself from birth would be the most misshapen of creatures. Prejudices, authority, necessity, example, the social institutions in which we are immersed, would crush out nature in him without putting anything in its place. He would fare like a shrub that has grown up by chance in the middle of a road, and got trampled under foot by the passers-by.

Plants are fashioned by cultivation, men by education. We are born feeble and need strength; possessing nothing, we need assistance; beginning without intelligence, we need judgment. All that we lack at birth and need when grown up is given us by education. This education comes to us from nature, from men, or from things. The internal development of our faculties and organs is the education of nature. The use we learn to make of this development is the education of men. What comes to us from our experience of the things that affect us is the education of things. Each of us therefore is fashioned by three kinds of teachers. When their lessons are at variance the pupil is badly educated, and is never at peace with himself. When they coincide and lead to a common goal he goes straight to his mark and lives single-minded. Now, of these three educations the one due to nature is independent of us, and the one from things only depends on us to a limited extent. The education that comes from men is the only one within our control, and even that is doubtful. Who can hope to have the entire direction of the words and deeds of all the people around a child?

From *Emile for Today*, translated by W. Boyd, Heinemann Educational Books, London, 1956. Reprinted by permission of the publisher.

It is only by luck that the goal can be reached. What is this goal? It is nature's goal. Since the three educations must work together for a perfect result, the one that cannot be modified determines the course of the other two. But perhaps "nature" is too vague a word. We must try to fix its meaning. Nature, it has been said, is only habit. Is that really so? Are there not habits which are formed under pressure, leaving the original nature unchanged? One example is the habit of plants which have been forced away from the upright direction. When set free, the plant retains the bent forced upon it; but the sap has not changed its first direction and any new growth the plant makes returns to the vertical. It is the same with human inclinations. So long as there is no change in conditions the inclinations due to habits, however unnatural, remain unchanged, but immediately the restraint is removed the habit vanishes and nature reasserts itself.

We are born capable of sensation and from birth are affected in diverse ways by the objects around us. As soon as we become conscious of our sensations we are inclined to seek or to avoid the objects which produce them: at first, because they are agreeable or disagreeable to us, later because we discover that they suit or do not suit us, and ultimately because of the judgments we pass on them by reference to the idea of happiness or perfection we get from reason. These inclinations extend and strengthen with the growth of sensibility and intelligence, but under the pressure of habit they are changed to some extent with our opinions. The inclinations before this change are what I call our nature. In my view everything ought to be in conformity with these original inclinations.

There would be no difficulty if our three educations were merely different. But what is to be done when they are at cross purposes? Consistency is plainly impossible when we seek to educate a man for others, instead of for himself. If we have to combat either nature or society, we must choose between making a man or making a citizen. We cannot make both. There is an inevitable conflict of aims, from which come two opposing forms of education: the one communal and public, the other individual and domestic.

To get a good idea of communal education, read Plato's *Republic*. It is not a political treatise, as those who merely judge books by their titles think. It is the finest treatise on education ever written. Communal education in this sense, however, does not and can not now exist. There are no longer any real fatherlands and therefore no real citizens. The words "fatherland" and "citizen" should be expunged from modern languages.

I do not regard the instruction given in those ridiculous establishments called colleges as "public", any more than the ordinary kind of education. This education makes for two opposite goals and reaches neither. The men it turns out are double-minded, seemingly concerned for others, but really only concerned for themselves. From this contradiction comes the conflict we never cease to experience in ourselves. We are drawn in different directions by nature and by man, and take a midway path that leads us nowhere. In this state of confusion we go through life and end up with our contradictions unsolved, never having been any good to ourselves or to other people.

There remains then domestic education, the education of nature. But how will a man who has been educated entirely for himself get on with other people? If there were any way of combining in a single person the twofold aim, and removing the contradictions of life, a great obstacle to happiness would be removed. But before passing judgment on this kind of man it would be necessary to follow his development and see him fully formed. It would be necessary, in a word, to make the acquaintance of the natural man. This is the subject of our quest in this book.

What can be done to produce this very exceptional person? In point of fact all we have to do is to prevent anything being done. When it is only a matter of sailing against the wind it is enough to tack, but when the sea runs high and you want to stay where you are, you must throw out the anchor.

In the social order where all stations in life are fixed, everyone needs to be brought up for his own station. The individual who leaves the place for which he has been trained is useless in any other. In Egypt, where the son was obliged to follow in his father's footsteps, education had at least an assured aim: in our country where social ranks are fixed, but the men in them are constantly changing, nobody knows whether he is doing his son a good or a bad turn when he educates him for his own rank.

In the natural order where all men are equal, manhood is the common vocation. One who is well educated for that will not do badly in the duties that pertain to it. The fact that my pupil is intended for the army, the church or the bar, does not greatly concern me. Before the vocation determined by his parents comes the call of nature to the life of human kind. Life is the business I would have him learn. When he leaves my hands, I admit he will not be a magistrate, or a soldier, or a priest. First and foremost, he will be a man. All that a man must be he will be when the need arises, as well as anyone else. Whatever the changes of fortune he will always be able to find a place for himself. . . .

A man of high rank once suggested that I should be his son's tutor. But having had experience already I knew myself unfit and I refused. Instead of the difficult task of educating a child, I now undertake the easier task of writing about it. To provide details and examples in illustration of my views and to avoid wandering off into airy speculations, I propose to set forth the education of Emile, an imaginary pupil, from birth to manhood. I take for granted that I am the right man for the duties in respect of age, health, knowledge and talents.

A tutor is not bound to his charge by the ties of nature as the father is, and so is entitled to choose his pupil, especially when as in this case he is providing a model for the education of other children. I assume that Emile is no genius, but a boy of ordinary ability; that he is the inhabitant of some temperate climate, since it is only in temperate climates that human beings develop completely; that he is rich, since it is only the rich who have need of the natural education that would fit them to live under all conditions;

that he is to all intents and purposes an orphan, whose tutor having undertaken the parents' duties will also have their right to control all the circumstances of his upbringing; and, finally, that he is a vigorous, healthy, well-built child. . . .

We are born with a capacity for learning, but know nothing and distinguish nothing. The mind is cramped by imperfect half-formed organs and has not even the consciousness of its own existence. The movements and cries of the newborn child are purely mechanical, quite devoid of understanding and will.

Children's first sensations are wholly in the realm of feeling. They are only aware of pleasure and pain. With walking and grasp undeveloped, it takes a long time for them to construct the representative sensations which acquaint them with external objects; but even before these objects reach up to and depart from their eyes, if one may put it so, the recurrence of the sensations begins to subject them to the bondage of habit. You see their eyes always turning to the light and unconsciously taking the direction from which the light comes, so that you have to be careful to keep them facing the light in order to prevent them acquiring a squint or becoming cross-eyed. Similarly, they have to be accustomed quite early to darkness, or soon they will wail and cry if they find themselves in the dark. Food and sleep, if too precisely organised, come to be necessary at definite intervals, and soon the desire for them is due not to need but to habit. Or rather, habit adds a new need to that of nature. That is something to be avoided.

The only habit the child should be allowed to acquire is to contract none. He should not be carried on one arm more than the other or allowed to make use of one hand more than the other, or to want to eat, sleep or do things at definite hours; and he should be able to remain alone by night or day. Prepare in good time for the reign of freedom and the exercise of his powers, by allowing his body its natural habits and accustoming him always to be his own master and follow the dictates of his will as soon as he has a will of his own.

When the child begins to distinguish objects, careful choice must be made of those to be brought to his notice. Everything new is naturally interesting. Man feels himself so feeble that he dreads anything unfamiliar. The habit of seeing new things without emotion destroys this dread. Children brought up in well-kept houses where spiders are not tolerated are afraid of spiders, and the fear often lasts when they grow up. I have never seen a peasant, man, woman or child, afraid of spiders. . . .

At the beginning of life when memory and imagination are still inactive the child attends only to what actually affects his senses. Since his sensations are the primary material of knowledge, the presentation of them in proper order prepares the memory for delivering them in the same order to the understanding later on. But as the child only attends to his sensations, it is sufficient in the first instance to show him very distinctly the connection of these sensations with the objects which cause them. He wants to touch and handle everything. Put no obstacle in the way of his restless movements. He learns to feel heat, cold, hardness, softness, weight, and comes to judge of the size and shape of bodies and all their sensory qualities, by looking at them, fingering them, listening to them, above all by comparing sight and touch. . . .

Book II

Your first duty is to be humane. Love childhood. Look with friendly eyes on its games, its pleasures, its amiable dispositions. Which of you does not sometimes look back regretfully on the age when laughter was ever on the lips and the heart free of care? Why steal from the little innocents the enjoyment of a time that passes all too quickly?

Already I hear the clamour of the false wisdom that regards the present as of no account and is forever chasing a future which flees as we advance. This is the time to correct the evil inclinations of mankind, you reply. Suffering should be increased in childhood when it is least felt, to reduce it at the age of reason. But how do you know that all the fine lessons with which you oppress the feeble mind of the child will not do more harm than good? Can you prove that these bad tendencies you profess to be correcting are not due to your own misguided efforts rather than to nature?

If we are to keep in touch with reality we must never forget what befits our condition. Humanity has its place in the scheme of things. Childhood has its place in the scheme of human life. We must view the man as a man, and the child as a child. The best way to ensure human well-beings is to give each person his place in life and keep him there, regulating the passions in accordance with the individual constitution. The rest depends on external factors without our control.

We can never know absolute good or evil. Everything in this life is mixed. We never experience a pure sentiment, or remain in the same state for two successive moments. Weal and woe are common to us all, but in differing measure. The happiest man is the one who suffers least; the most miserable the one who has least pleasure. Always the sufferings outweigh the enjoyments. The felicity of man here below is therefore a negative state, to be measured by the fewness of his ills. Every feeling of pain is inseparable from the desire to escape from it; every idea of pleasure inseparable from the desire for its enjoyment. Privation is implicit in desire, and all privations are painful. Consequently unhappiness consists in the excess of desire over power. A conscious being whose powers equalled his desires would be absolutely happy.

In what then does the human wisdom that leads to true happiness consist? Not simply in the diminution of desires, for if they fell below our power to achieve, part of our faculties would be unemployed and our entire being would not be satisfied. Neither does it consist in the extension of our faculties, for a disproportionate increase in our desires would only make us more miserable. True happiness comes with equality of power and will. The only man who gets his own way is the one who does not need another's help to get it: from which it follows that the supreme good is not authority, but freedom. The true free man wants only what he can get, and does only what pleases him. This is my fundamental maxim. Apply it to childhood and all the rules of education follow.

There are two kinds of dependence: dependence on things, which is natural, and dependence on men, which is social. Dependence on things, being non-moral, is not prejudicial to freedom and engenders no vices; dependence on men, being capricious, engenders them all. The only cure for this evil in society would be put the law in place of the individual, and to arm the general will with a real power that made it superior to every individual will.

Keep the child in sole dependence on things and you will follow the natural order in the course of his education. Put only physical obstacles in the way of indiscreet wishes and let his punishments spring from his own actions. Without forbidding wrongdoing, be content to prevent it. Experience or impotence apart from anything else should take the place of law for him. Satisfy his desires, not because of his demands but because of his needs. He should have no consciousness of obedience when he acts, nor of mastery when someone acts for him. Let him experience liberty equally in his actions and in yours.

Be specially careful not to give the child empty formulas of politeness, to serve as magic words for subjecting his surroundings to his will and getting him what he wants at once. For my part I am less afraid of rudeness than of arrogance in Emile, and would rather have him say "Do this" as a request than "Please" as a command. I am not concerned with the words he uses, but with what they imply.

Excessive severity and excessive indulgence are equally to be avoided. If you let children suffer you endanger health and life. If you are over-careful in shielding them from trouble of every kind you are laying up much unhappiness for the future; you are withdrawing them from the common lot of man, to which they must one day become subject in spite of you.

You will tell me that I am making the same mistake as those bad fathers whom I blamed for sacrificing their children's happiness for the sake of a distant time that may never come. This is not so, for the liberty I allow my pupil amply compensates for the slight hardships I let him experience. I see little scamps playing in the snow, blue and stiff with cold and scarcely able to move a finger. There is nothing to hinder them warming themselves, but they don't. If they were forced to come indoors they would feel the rigours of constraint a hundred times more than the cold. What then is there to complain about? Am I making the child unhappy by exposing him to hardships which he is quite willing to endure? I am doing him good at the present moment by leaving him free. I am doing him good in the future by arming him against inevitable evils. If he had to choose between being my pupil or yours, do you think he would hesitate for an instant?

The surest way to make your child unhappy is to accustom him to get everything he wants. With desire constantly increasing through easy satisfaction, lack of power will sooner or later force you to a refusal in spite of yourself, and the unwonted refusal will cause him deeper annoyance than the mere lack of what he desires. First he will want the stick in your hand, then the bird that flies past, then the star that shines above him. Everything he sees he will want: and unless you were God you could never hope to satisfy him. How could such a child possibly be happy? Happy! He is a despot, at once the meanest of slaves and the most wretched of creatures. Let us get back to the primitive way. Nature made children to be loved and helped, not to be obeyed and feared. Is there in the world a being more feeble and unhappy, more at the mercy of his environment, more in need of pity and protection than a child? Surely then there is nothing more offensive or more unseemly than the sight of a dictatorial headstrong child, issuing orders to those around him and assuming the tone of a master to people without whom he would perish.

On the other hand, it should be obvious that with the many restrictions imposed on children by their own weakness it is barbarous for us to add subjection to our caprices to the natural subjection, and take from them such limited liberty as they possess. Social servitude will come with the age of reason. Why anticipate it by a domestic servitude? Let one moment of life be free from this yoke which nature has not imposed, and leave the child to the enjoyment of his natural liberty.

I come back to practice. I have already said that what your child gets he should get because he needs it, not because he asks for it, and that he should never act from obedience but only from necessity. For this reason, the words "obey" and "command" must be banished from his vocabulary, still more the words "duty" and "obligation"; but "force", "necessity", "weakness" and "constraint" should be emphasised. It is impossible to form any idea of moral facts or social relations before the age of reason. Consequently the use of terms which express such ideas should as far as possible be avoided, for fear the child comes to attach to these words false ideas which cannot or will not be eradicated at a later time.

"Reason with children" was Locke's chief maxim. It is the one most popular today, but it does not seem to me justified by success. For my part I do not see any children more stupid than those who have been much reasoned with. Of all the human faculties, reason, which may be said to be compounded of all the rest develops most slowly and with greatest difficulty. Yet it is reason that people want to use in the development of the first faculties. A reasonable man is the masterwork of a good education: and we actually pretend to be educating children by means of reason! That is beginning at the end. If children appreciated reason they would not need to be educated.

Instead of appealing to reason, say to the child: "You must not do that!" "Why not?" "Because it is wrong." "Why is it wrong?" "Because it is forbidden." "Why is it forbidden?" "Because it is wrong." That is the inevitable circle.

To distinguish right from wrong and appreciate the re
of man is beyond a child's powers.

Nature wants children to be children before they ar
ately depart from this order we shall get premature fru
ripe nor well flavoured and which soon decay. We sha
and grown-up children. Childhood has ways of seeing
peculiar to itself: nothing can be more foolish than to seek to
ways for them. I should as soon expect a child of ten to be five feet in height
as to be possessed of judgment.

Treat your pupil according to his age. Begin by putting him in his place
and keep him in it so firmly that he will not think of leaving it. Then he
will practise the most important lesson of wisdom before he knows what
wisdom is. Give him absolutely no orders of any kind. Do not even let him
imagine that you claim any authority over him. Let him only know that
he is weak and you are strong, and that therefore he is at your mercy. Quite
early let him feel the heavy yoke which nature imposes on man, the yoke
of the necessity in things as opposed to human caprice. If there is anything
he should not do, do not forbid him, but prevent him without explanation
or reasoning. Whatever you give, give at the first word without prayers or
entreaty, and above all without conditions. Give with pleasure, refuse with
regret, but let your refusals be irrevocable. Your "No" once uttered must
be a wall of brass which the child will stop trying to batter down once he
has exhausted his strength on it five or six times.

It is strange that all the time people have been bringing up children nobody
has thought of any instruments for their direction but emulation, jealousy,
envy, vanity, greed or base fear; most dangerous passions all of them, sure
to corrupt the soul. Foolish teachers think they are working wonders when
they are simply making the children wicked in the attempt to teach them
about goodness. Then they announce gravely: such is man. Yes, such is
the man you have made. All the instruments have been tried but one, and
that as it happens is the only one that can succeed: well-regulated liberty.

Avoid verbal lessons with your pupil. The only kind of lesson he should
get is that of experience. Never inflict any punishment, for he does not know
what it is to be at fault. Being devoid of all morality in his actions he can
do nothing morally wrong, nothing that deserves either punishment or
reprimand.

Let us lay it down as an incontestable principle that the first impulses
of nature are always right. There is no original perversity in the human
heart. Of every vice we can say how it entered and whence it came. The
only passion natural to man is self-love, or self-esteem in a broad sense.
This self-esteem has no necessary reference to other people. In so far as it
relates to ourselves it is good and useful. It only becomes good or bad in
the social application we make of it. Until reason, which is the guide of self-
esteem, makes its appearance, the child should not do anything because he
is seen or heard by other people, but only do what nature demands of him.
Then he will do nothing but what is right.

not mean to say that he will never do any mischief; that he will never ⟨hurt⟩ himself, for example, or break a valuable bit of furniture. He might ⟨do⟩ a great deal that was bad without being bad, because the wrong action depends on harmful intention and that he will never have. When children are left free to blunder it is better to remove everything that would make blundering costly, and not leave anything fragile and precious within reach. Their room should be furnished with plain solid furniture, without mirrors, china or ornaments. My Emile whom I am bringing up in the country will have nothing in his room to distinguish it from that of a peasant. If in spite of your precautions the child manages to upset things and break some useful articles, do not punish or scold him for your own negligence. Do not even let him guess that he has annoyed you. Behave as if the furniture had got broken of itself. Consider you have done very well if you can avoid saying anything.

May I set forth at this point the most important and the most useful rule in all education? It is not to save time but to waste it. The most dangerous period in human life is that between birth and the age of twelve. This is the age when errors and vices sprout, before there is any instrument for their destruction. When the instrument is available the roots have gone too deep to be extracted. The mind should remain inactive till it has all its faculties.

It follows from this that the first education should be purely negative. It consists not in teaching virtue and truth, but in preserving the heart from vice and the mind from error. If you could do nothing and let nothing be done, so that your pupil came to the age of twelve strong and healthy but unable to distinguish his right hand from his left, the eyes of his understanding would be open to reason from your very first lessons. In the absence of both prejudices and habits there would be nothing in him to oppose the effects of your teaching and care.

Do the opposite of what is usually done and you will almost always be right. Fathers and teachers, anxious to make a learned doctor instead of a child, correct, reprove, flatter, instruct, reason. There is a better way. Be reasonable and do not reason with your pupil. It is a mistake to try to get him to approve of things he dislikes. To bring reason into what is disagreeable at this stage ill only discredit it. Exercise body, senses, powers, but keep the mind inactive as long as possible. Let childhood ripen in children. . . .

My plan is not to go into details, but only to set forth general principles and give examples in difficult cases. I do not think it is possible to bring up a child to the age of twelve in society without giving him some idea of the relations of man to man and the moral aspects of human conduct. The best one can do is to postpone these necessary notions as long as possible, and when they can be no longer postponed to limit them to the immediate requirement.

Our first duties are to ourselves. Self is the centre of the primitive sentiments. The natural impulses all relate in the first instance to our preservation and well-being. Hence the first sentiment of justice does not come to us from what we owe others, but from what others owe us. It is another of the blunders of the ordinary education to talk to children about their duties, and say nothing about their rights. This takes them beyond their comprehension and their interest.

The first idea a child should have given him is not that of liberty, but of property. To get that he must possess something of his own. To tell him that he owns his clothes, his furniture, his toys, means nothing to him. Though he uses them he does not know why or how they are his. He must be taken back to the origin of property.

The easiest way for him to learn about property is through the work he does in the garden in imitation of the gardener. He plants beans and when they come up they "belong" to him. To explain what that term means I make him feel that he has put his time, his work, his effort, himself into them. Then one day he finds his beans dug up by Robert the gardener. The ground "belongs" to the gardener and he must come to an arrangement with the man before he can raise beans again. The destructive child has to learn his lesson in another way. He breaks the windows of his room — let the wind blow on him night and day and do not worry about him catching cold. It is better for him to catch cold than to be a fool. If he goes on breaking windows shut him up in a dark room without windows. The time will come when he has learned what property means and he is willing to respect other people's belongings.

We are now in the moral world and the door is open to vice. With conventions and duties come deceit and lying. As soon as we can do what we ought not to do, we seek to hide our misdeeds. With the failure to prevent evildoing the question of punishment arises. In fact there is never any need to inflict punishment as such on children. It should always come to them as the natural consequence of their bad conduct. In the case of lying, for example, you need not punish them because they have lied, but so arrange that if they lie they will not be believed even when they speak the truth, and will be accused of bad things they have not done.

Actually children's lies are all the work of their teachers. They try to teach them to tell the truth and in doing so teach them to lie. As for those of us who only give our pupils lessons of a practical kind and prefer them to be good rather than clever, we never demand the truth from them for fear they should hide it, and we never exact any promise lest they be tempted to break it. If something wrong has been done in my absence and I do not know the culprit, I take care not to accuse Emile or to ask: "Was it you?" Nothing could be more indiscreet than such a question, especially if the child is guilty. If he thinks you know he has done wrong you will seem to be trying to trap him and the idea will turn him against you. If he thinks you do not know he will ask: "Why should I reveal my fault?" and the imprudent question will be a temptation to lying.

What has been said about lying applies in many respects to all the other duties prescribed for children. To make them pious you take them to church where they are bored. You make them gabble prayers till they look forward to the happy time when they no longer pray to God. You make them give alms to inspire charity, as if alms-giving were a matter for children only. Drop these pretences, teachers. Be virtuous and good yourselves, and the examples you set will impress themselves on your pupils' memories, and in due season will enter their hearts.

The apparent ease with which children learn is their misfortune. It is not seen that this very facility proves that they are learning nothing. Their smooth polished brain is like a mirror which throws back the objects presented to it. Nothing gets in, nothing remains behind. They remember words but ideas are reflected off. Those who listen to them understand what the words mean but they themselves do not.

Though memory and reasoning are essentially different faculties they depend on each other in their development. Before the age of reason the child receives images but not ideas. The difference between them is that images are simply the exact pictures of sense-given objects, whereas ideas are notions of the objects determined by their relations. An image may exist by itself in the imagining mind, but every idea presupposes other ideas. Imagination is just seeing, but conception implies comparison. Our sensations are purely passive, different from our perceptions or ideas which are the outcome of an active principle of judgment.

That is why I say that children being incapable of judgment have no true memory. They retain sounds, shapes, sensations, but rarely ideas, and still more rarely their relations. It may be objected that they learn some of the elements of geometry, but really that only shows that so far from being able to reason for themselves they cannot even recollect the reasoning of others. For if you follow these little geometricians in their lesson you will find that all they have recollected is the exact picture of the figure and the words of the demonstration. The least new question upsets them and so does any change of figure. Their knowledge is all in sensation; nothing has got through to the understanding. Their memory itself is scarcely any more perfect than the other faculties since they nearly always have to relearn the things whose names they learned in childhood when they grow up. Nevertheless I am far from thinking that children have no kind of reasoning. On the contrary, I notice that they think very well on everything which bears on their present and obvious interest. Where people go wrong is in regard to the things they actually know. They credit them with knowledge they do not possess, and make them reason about things beyond their comprehension.

The professional pedagogues speak differently, but it is evident from their own performance that they think exactly as I do. For what in fact do they teach? Nothing but words. Among the various sciences they boast of teaching their pupils, they take good care not to include those which are really useful, because these would be the sciences dealing with facts, in which the children's failure would be evident. They choose subjects like heraldry, geography, chronology and the language in which acquaintance with terms gives the appearance of knowledge — studies so remote from men and especially from children that it would be surprising if ever they came to be of use even once in a lifetime.

Languages

It may seem strange that I reckon the study of languages among the futilities of education, but it must be remembered that I am only speaking now about the studies of the early years; and whatever may be said I do not believe that, apart from prodigies, any child under twelve or fifteen has ever really learned two languages. I agree that if the study of language was merely one of words it would be quite proper for children, but with the change in symbols the ideas represented are also modified. It is only the thought that is common; the spirit in each language has its own distinctive form. Of these different forms the child has only the one he uses, and he is limited to it till the age of reason. To have two languages he would have to be able to compare ideas, and how can he compare ideas he can barely conceive? He can then learn only a single language. But, you will tell me, some pupils learn several languages. I deny that. I have seen little prodigies who were supposed to speak five or six languages. I have heard them speak German, then use Latin, French and Italian in succession. Actually they made use of five or six different vocabularies, but in every case it was German they were speaking. The words were changed, but not the language.

To conceal their own incapacity teachers prefer the dead languages in which there are no longer any judges to call them in question. The familiar use of these languages has been lost a long time ago and we have to be content to imitate the language found in books. That is what is called "speaking the language". If the teachers' Latin and Greek are like that, judge what the children's are like.

Geography

In any study whatever, the representing symbols mean nothing apart from the idea of the things represented. But children are always limited to symbols. The teacher thinks he is giving them a description of the earth in geography, but actually he is only giving them a knowledge of maps. He tells them the names of towns, countries, rivers, but the children have no notion that they exist anywhere but on the paper shown to them. I remember seeing somewhere a geography which began: "What is the world? It is a cardboard globe." There you have the child's geography. I maintain in fact that after two years of the sphere and cosmography, there is not a ten-year-old child who could find his way from Paris to St Denis by the rules he has been taught. These are the learned doctors who know just where Pekin, Ispahan, Mexico and all the countries of the world are.

History

It is still more ridiculous to set children to study history. History is supposed to be a collection of facts within their comprehension. But what is meant by "facts"? Is it credible that the relations determining historical facts should be so easy to grasp that the ideas of them should readily take shape in children's minds? Or that there can be a real knowledge of events without knowledge of their causes and their effects? If history is no more than an account of human actions in purely physical terms there is absolutely nothing to be learned from it. Try to make children appreciate these actions in terms of moral relations and you will see then whether they are old enough to learn history.

It is easy to put into their mouths words like "king", "empire", "war", "conquest", "revolution", "law", but when it comes to a question of attaching precise ideas to such words, the explanations will be very different from those Emile got in his dealings with Robert the gardener.

Even if there is no book study the kind of memory the child has does not remain idle. All that he sees and hears makes its impression on him and he remembers it. He keeps a record in himself of the deeds and words of people. The world around him is the book in which without knowing it he is continually adding to the stores of memory, against the time when his judgment can profit by them. It is in the choice of these objects and in the constant care taken to put before him the things he can know and hide from him the things he ought not to know that the art of memory training consists. This is what must be done to form a storehouse of the knowledge which is to serve for his education in youth and for his conduct all through life.

Fables

Emile will never learn anything by heart, not even fables like those of La Fontaine, simple and charming though they be; for the words of fables are no more fables than the words of history are history. How can people be so blind as to call fables the ethics of childhood and not realise that the moral which amuses also misleads? Fables may instruct men, but it is necessary to speak the naked truth to children. My contention is that the child does not understand the fables he is taught, for whatever you do to make them simple the instruction you want to draw from them implies ideas beyond his grasp.

In all La Fontaine's book of fables there are only five or six of childlike simplicity. The first and best of these is *"The Crow and the Fox"*. Analyse it line by line and it will be evident how very unsuitable it is for children. *"Mr Crow, on a tree perched."* Have the children seen a crow? Do they know what a crow is? Why "Mr"? The usual order of words would be: "perched on a tree". Why the inversion? *"Held in his beak a cheese"*. What kind of a cheese? Could a crow hold a cheese in its beak? There are difficulties in every line, not merely of understanding, but of morals. The fox flatters and lies to get the crow to drop the cheese. What conclusion will the child draw? Watch children learning their fables and you will see that the morals they draw are just the opposite of what they were intended to draw. They laugh at the crow but are fond of the fox.

Reading

When I get rid of all the usual tasks of children in this way I also get rid of the books which are the chief cause of unhappiness to them. Reading is the greatest plague of childhood. Emile at the age of twelve will scarcely know what a book is. But at least, I will be told, he must be able to read. I agree. He must be able to read when he needs to read. Before that it will only be a bother to him.

If nothing is to be exacted from children by way of obedience it follows that they will only learn what they feel to be of actual and present advantage, either because they like it, or because it is of use to them. Otherwise, what motive would they have for learning? The art of speaking to absent people and hearing from them, of communicating personally our sentiments and our wishes, is an art whose usefulness can be made obvious to people of all ages; but by some strange perversity it has become a torment for childhood. Why should this be? Because the children have been compelled to learn it against their will, and made to put it to purposes which mean nothing for them.

Great stress is laid on finding better methods of teaching children to read. Reading cases and cards have been invented, and the child's room has been turned into a printer's shop. Locke suggested the use of dice. Fancy all this elaborate contrivance! A surer way that nobody thinks of is to create the desire to read. Give the child this desire and have done with gadgets and any method will be good.

Present interest: that is the great motive impulse, the only one that leads sure and far. Emile sometimes receives from his father or his friends letters inviting him to a dinner, a walk, a boating party, or some public entertainment. These notes are short, clear, precise and well written. He must find some one to read them for him. This person is either not to be found at the right moment or is no more disposed to be helpful to the boy than the boy was to him the night before. In this way the chance is lost. By the time the note is read the time is past. If only he could read himself! He receives more letters and does his best to read them; and finally deciphers half a letter, something about going out tomorrow to eat cream. But where? And with whom? How hard he tries to read the rest! I do not think Emile will have any need of reading devices. Shall I go on now to speak about writing? Oh no. I am ashamed to amuse myself with such trifles in an educational treatise. . . .

Assuming that my method is that of nature and that I have not made any mistakes in putting it into practice, I have now brought my pupil through the land of the sensations right up to the bounds of childish reason. The first step beyond this should take him towards manhood. But before entering on this new stage let us cast our eyes backward for a moment on perfection, its own distinctive maturity. People sometimes speak about a complete man. Let us think rather of a complete child. This vision will be new for us and perhaps not less agreeable.

When I picture to myself a boy of ten or twelve, healthy, strong and well built for his age, only pleasant thoughts arise in me, whether for his present or for his future. I see him bright, eager, vigorous, carefree, completely absorbed in the present, rejoicing in abounding vitality. I see him in the years ahead using senses, mind and power as they develop from day to day. I view him as a child and he pleases me. I think of him as a man and he pleases me still more. His warm blood seems to heat my own. I feel as if I were living in his life and am rejuvenated by his vivacity.

The clock strikes and all is changed. In an instant his eye grows dull and his merriment disappears. No more mirth, no more games! A severe, hard-faced man takes him by the hand, says gravely, "Come away, sir," and leads him off. In the room they enter I get a glimpse of books. Books! What a cheerless equipment for his age. As he is dragged away in silence, he casts a regretful look around him. His eyes are swollen with tears he dare not shed, his heart heavy with sighs he dare not utter.

Come, my happy pupil, and console us for the departure of the wretched boy. Here comes Emile, and at his approach I have a thrill of joy in which I see he shares. It is his friend and comrade, the companion of his games to whom he comes. His person, his bearing, his countenance reveal assurance and contentment. Health glows in his face. His firm step gives him an air of vigour. His complexion is refined without being effeminate; sun and wind have put on it the honourable imprint of his sex. His eyes are still unlighted by the fires of sentiment and have all their native serenity. His manner is open and free without the least insolence or vanity.

His ideas are limited but precise. If he knows nothing by heart, he knows a great deal by experience. If he is not as good a reader in books as other children, he reads better in the book of nature. His mind is not in his tongue but in his head. He has less memory but more judgment. He only knows one language, but he understands what he says; and if he does not talk as well as other children he can do things better than they can.

Habit, routine and custom mean nothing to him. What he did yesterday has no effect on what he does today. He never follows a fixed rule and never accepts authority or example. He only does or says what seems good to himself. For this reason you must not expect stock speeches or studied manners from him but just the faithful expression of his ideas and the conduct that comes from his inclinations.

You will find in him a few moral notions relating to his own situation, but not being an active member of society he has none relating to manhood. Talk to him about liberty, property and even convention, and he may understand you thus far. But speak to him about duty and obedience, and he will not know what you mean. Command him to do something, and he will pay no heed. But say to him: "If you will do me this favour, I will do the same for you another time"; and immediately he will hasten to oblige.

For his part, if he needs any help he will ask the first person he meets as a matter of course. If you grant his request he will not thank you, but will feel that he has contracted a debt. If you refuse, he will neither complain nor insist. He will only say: "It could not be done." He does not rebel against necessity once he recognises it.

Work and play are all the same to him. His games are his occupations: he is not aware of any difference. He goes into everything he does with a pleasing interest and freedom. It is indeed a charming spectacle to see a nice boy of this age with open smiling countenance, doing the most serious things in his play or profoundly occupied with the most frivolous amusements.

Emile has lived a child's life and has arrived at the maturity of childhood, without any sacrifice of happiness in the achievement of his own perfection. He has acquired all the reason possible for his age, and in doing so has been as free and as happy as his nature allowed him to be. If by chance the fatal scythe were to cut down the flower of our hopes we would not have to bewail at the same time his life and his death, nor add to our griefs the memory of those we caused him. We would say that at any rate he had enjoyed his childhood and that nothing we had done had deprived him of what nature gave. . . .

Book III

The whole course of life up to adolescence is a time of weakness, but there is one point during this first age of man at which strength exceeds the demands made on it by needs, and the growing creature though still absolutely weak becomes relatively strong. With needs incompletely developed, his powers more than suffice. As a man he would be very feeble: as a child he is very strong. This is the third stage of early life which for lack of a better word I continue to call childhood. It is not yet the age of puberty, but adolescence draw near.

At twelve or thirteen the child's powers develop much more rapidly than his needs. The sex passions, the most violent and terrible of all, have not yet awakened. He is indifferent to the rigours of weather and seasons, and braves them light-heartedly. His growing body heat takes the place of clothing. Appetite is his sauce, and everything nourishing tastes good. When he is tired he stretches himself out on the ground and goes to sleep. He is not troubled by imaginary wants. What people think does not trouble him. Not only is he self-sufficient but his strength goes beyond his requirements. It is the most precious time in life, and it comes but once. Being very short, it is all the more important for him to make good use of it. It is the time for labour, for instruction, for studies. That is what nature herself indicates. . . .

Make your pupil attend to the phenomena of nature, and you will soon arouse his curiosity. But to nourish this curiosity, be in no hurry to satisfy it. Suggest problems but leave the solving of them to him. Whatever he knows, he should know not because you have told him, but because he has grasped it himself. Do not teach him science; let him discover it. If ever you substitute authority for reason in his mind, he will stop reasoning, and become the victim of other people's opinions.

To teach this child geography you set out to look for globes, spheres and maps. Why all these contrivances? Instead of these representations, begin by showing him the real thing, and let him know at least what you are talking about. . . .

His two starting points will be his home town and his father's country house: then will come the places between the two and the nearby rivers; and finally the observation of the sun's position, to enable him to get his directions. This last is where the different facts meet. He should make a map of it all for himself: a very simple map, with only two objects marked on it to begin with, to which he will gradually add the others as he comes to know them and determine their position and their distance. You can see already the advantage we have gained by putting a compass in his eyes.

Nevertheless, it will probably be necessary to give him a little guidance. But let it be very little, and avoid the appearance of it. If he goes wrong, do not correct his errors. Say nothing till he sees them and corrects them himself; or at most, arrange some practical situation which will make him realise things personally. If he never made mistakes he would never learn properly. In any case, the important thing is not that he should know the topography of the country, but that he should be able to get his information for himself. It does not matter greatly whether he has maps in his head, provided he knows what they represent and has a clear idea of the art of construction.

The essential principle in my method is not to teach the child a great many things but to allow him to form only clear, exact ideas. It would not matter greatly if he knew nothing so long as he did not go wrong in his thinking. I only put truths into his head to save him from the errors he might learn instead. Reason and judgment are slow to come, but prejudices crowd in; and it is necessary to protect him from them.

During the first period of life time was plentiful. We only sought to have it occupied in any way at all to prevent it being put to bad use. Now it is just the opposite, and we have not enough time to get all done that is useful. Bear in mind that the passions are near at hand, and that as soon as they knock at the door your pupil will no longer attend to anything else. The quiet period of intellect passes so rapidly and has so many other necessary occupations that it is folly to try to make the child a scholar within its span. It is not a question of teaching him the sciences, but of giving him a taste for them, and methods of acquiring them when this taste is better developed. This is most certainly a fundamental principle in all good education. . . .

With the child's advance in intelligence other considerations compel greater care in the choice of his occupations. As soon as he comes to know himself well enough to understand what constitutes happiness for him and can judge what is fitting and what is not, he is in a position to appreciate the difference between work and play, and to regard play as relaxation from work. Thereafter matters of real utility may enter into his studies and lead him to apply himself more diligently than he did to mere amusements. The law of necessity, always operative, soon teaches man to do what he does not like, in order to avoid evils he would like still less. Such is the practice of foresight; and from foresight, well or ill directed, comes all the wisdom or all the unhappiness of mankind.

When children foresee their needs their intelligence has made real progress. They begin to know the value of time. For this reason, it is important to accustom them to employ their time on objects of an obvious utility that are within their understanding. All that pertains to the moral order and to social usage should not be put before them yet, because it does not mean anything for them. Why do you want to set a child to the studies of an age he may never reach, to the detriment of studies suited for the present? But you will ask: "Will there be time for him to learn what he ought to know when the occasion for its use arises?" That I do not know. What I do know is that it is impossible for him to learn it sooner. Our real teachers are experience and feeling, and no one ever appreciates what is proper to manhood till he enters into its situations. A child knows that he is destined to become a man. Such of the ideas of adult life as are within his comprehension are occasions of instruction for him, but he ought to be kept in absolute ignorance of all the rest. This whole book is one long demonstration of this educational principle. . . .

I hate books. They only teach us to talk about what we do not know. It is said that Hermes engraved the elements of science on pillars for fear his discoveries might perish in a deluge. If he had impressed them firmly on the human brain, they would have been kept safe there by tradition.

Is there no way of bringing together all the lessons scattered through a multitude of books and grouping them together round some common object which, even at this age, might be easy to see, interesting to follow and thought provoking? If it were possible to invent a situation in which all the natural needs of mankind were made obvious to the mind of a child, and the ways of providing for these made equally clear, the simple lifelike picture of this condition of things would give the child's imagination its first training.

Eager philosopher, I see your own imagination lighting up. Do not trouble yourself. This situation has been found, and with all respect to you has been described better than you could do it, at any rate with greater truth and simplicity. Since it is essential that there should be books, there happens to be one book which in my opinion furnishes the most satisfactory treatise on natural education. This is the first book my Emile will read. For a long time it will constitute his entire library, and will always occupy an honoured place it it. It will be the text on which all our talks on the natural sciences will form a commentary. It will serve as a touchstone for our judgment as we progress, and so long as our taste remains unspoiled, it will continue to give us pleasure. What is this marvellous book? Is it Aristotle? Or Pliny? Or Buffon? Oh no, it is *Robinson Crusoe*.

Robinson Crusoe alone on his island, without the help of his fellows and the tools of the various arts, yet managing to procure food and safety, and even a measure of well-being: here is something of interest for every age, capable of being made attractive to children in a thousand ways. This condition, I admit, is not that of social man, and probably is not to be that of Emile, but he should use it in the evaluation of all other conditions. The surest way for him to rise above prejudices and to bring his own judgments into line with the true relations of things is to put himself at the point of view of solitary man, and to judge everything as this man would with reference to its real utility. . . .

The practice of the natural arts for which a single man is sufficient leads to the pursuit of the industrial arts which call for the co-operation of many hands. The former can be practised by solitaries and savages, but the latter can only come into being in the society which they make necessary. So long as there is only physical need each man is self-sufficient. It is the introduction of luxuries that makes the sharing and differentiation of labour essential.

Your main endeavour should be to keep away from your pupil all the notions of social relations which are beyond his comprehension; but when the interrrelation of knowledge forces you to show him the mutual dependence of men, avoid the moral aspects and direct his attention to industry and the mechanical arts which make them useful to each other. As you take him from one workshop to another, never let him see any kind of work without putting his hand to it, and never let him leave till he knows perfectly the reason for all that he has observed. With that in view, set him an example by working yourself in the different occupations. To make him a master become an apprentice. You can be sure that he will learn more from an hour's work than he would remember after a day's explanations.

The value popularly attached to the different arts is in inverse ratio to their usefulness. The most useful arts are the worst paid, because the work necessary for everybody must be kept at a price within the reach of the poor. On the other hand, those important people who are called not artisans but artists work for the idle rich and put an arbitrary price on their baubles. My opinion is that in all cases the art which is most generally useful and most indispensable is the one which should be most highly regarded. The art which needs least help from the other arts is more entitled to esteem than those dependent on others. The first and most honourable of all the arts is agriculture. The forge comes second, carpentry third and the rest after. That is precisely how the child who has not been seduced by vulgar prejudices will judge them. Our Emile, thinking about the furnishing of his island, will draw important conclusions in these matters from his Robinson.

Reader, do not give too much thought to the bodily activity and the skill of hand of our pupil. Consider rather the direction we are giving to his childish curiosities. Consider his senses, his inventive mind, his foresight. Consider the good head he will have. He will want to know all about everything he sees and does, and will take nothing for granted. He will refuse to learn anything until he acquires the knowledge that is implied in it. When he sees a spring made he will want to know how the steel was got from the mine. If he sees the pieces of a box put together, he will want to know how the tree was cut. When he is using a tool himself he will not fail to say of the tool he uses: "If I did not have this tool, how would I make one like it, or manage without it?"

At the beginning of this period of life we have taken advantage of the fact that our strength greatly exceeds our needs, to get away beyond ourselves. We have soared into the heavens and have surveyed the earth. We have studied the laws of nature. In a word, we have traversed the whole of our island. Now we come back gradually to our own dwelling. What is there for us to do when we have completed the study of our surroundings? We must convert them as much as we can to our own purposes. Up to this point, we have provided ourselves with all kinds of instruments without knowing which of them we will need. It may be that those which are of no use to us may be of service to other people and that we in turn may need theirs. In this way we will all find ourselves gaining by these exchanges. For this we must know the mutual needs of men; what each of us has to give and to get. Suppose there are ten men, each with ten kinds of needs, each applying himself to ten different kinds of work to provide for the necessities of life. The ten, because of differences of gift and talent, are likely to be less apt at some tasks than others, and all will be badly served when each does everything. But make a society of these ten, and let each man apply himself for his own benefit and that of the other nine to the kind of work that suits him best. Each one will profit by the talents of the others as if he personally had them all, and at the same time grow more perfect in his own line of work by constant practice. So it will come that the whole ten are perfectly provided for and will still have something left for others. This is the obvious basis of all our social institutions.

In this way the ideas of social relations take shape in the child's mind little by little, even before he becomes an active member of society himself. Emile sees that in order to have things for his own use he must have some he can exchange with other people. It is easy to lead him to feel the need for such exchanges and put himself in a position to profit by them.

As soon as he knows what life is, my first concern will be to teach him to preserve it. Up to this point I have ignored differences of station, rank or fortune, and I shall say little more about them in what follows, because man is the same in all stations. The rich man's stomach is no bigger than the poor man's, and his digestion no better. The master's arms are no longer and no stronger than the slave's. A "great" man is no greater than a man of the people. Natural needs being everywhere alike, the means of satisfying them should likewise be equal. Fit man's education to what man really is. Do you not see that if you try to fit him exclusively for one way of life you make him useless for every other? You put your trust in the existing social order and do not take into account the fact that that order is subject to inevitable revolutions, and that you can neither forsee nor prevent the revolution that may affect your children. We are approaching a state of crisis and an age of revolution. It is impossible that the great monarchies of Europe should endure much longer. Who can tell what will happen then? What man has made, man can destroy. The only indestructible characters are those with nature's imprint, and nature makes neither princes, nor men of wealth, nor grand lords. . . .

Here is our child, ready to cease being a child and to enter on an individual life. More than ever he feels the necessity which binds him to things. After training his body and his senses, we have trained his mind and his judgment. In short, we have combined the use of his limbs with that of his faculties. We have made him an efficient thinking being and nothing further remains for us in the production of a complete man but to make him a loving, sensitive being; in fact, to perfect reason through sentiment. But before entering on this new order of things let us look back over the one we are leaving, and see where we have reached.

To begin with, our pupil had only sensations, now he has ideas: he had only feelings, now he judges; for from the comparison of several sensations, whether successive or simultaneous, and the judgment passed on them, there comes a sort of mixed or complex sensation which I call an idea. It is the particular way of forming ideas that gives its character to the human mind. A solid mind forms its ideas on real relations: a superficial one is content with appearances. Greater or less aptitude in the comparison of ideas and the discovery of relations is what makes the difference in the mental capacity of different people.

In sensation, judgment is purely passive — we feel what we feel: in perception or idea, it is active — it connects, compares, determines relations. It is never the sensation that is wrong but the judgment passed on it. The child says about the ice cream that it burns. That is a right sensation but a wrong judgment. So with the experiences of those who see a mirror for the first time, or enter a cellar at different times of the year, or dip a warm or cold hand into lukewarm water, or see the clouds passing over the moon as if they were stationary, or think the stick immersed in water is broken. All our mistakes in these cases come from judgment. Unfortunately social man is dependent on a great many things about which he has to judge. He must therefore be taught to reason correctly.

I will be told that in training the child to judge, I am departing from nature. I do not think so. Nature chooses her instruments, and makes use of them not according to opinion but according to necessity. There is a great difference between natural man living in nature and natural man living in the social state. Emile is not a savage to be banished to the deserts; he is a savage made to live in a town. He must know how to get a living in towns, and how to get on with their inhabitants, and to live with them, if not to live like them.

The best way of learning to judge correctly is to simplify our sense experiences as much as possible. To do this we must learn to check the reports of each sense by itself, over and above the check from the other senses. Then each sensation will become an idea, and this idea will always conform to the truth. This is the kind of acquirement I have tried to secure in this third stage of childhood.

Emile, who has been compelled to learn for himself and use his reason, has a limited knowledge, but the knowledge he has is his own, none of it half-known. Among the small number of things he really knows the most important is that there is much he does not know which he may one day come to know, much more that other people know that he will never know, and an infinity of things that nobody will ever know. He has a universal mind, not because of what he knows but from his faculty for acquiring knowledge; a mind open, intelligent, responsive, and (as Montaigne says) if not instructed, capable of being instructed. I am content if he knows the "wherefore" of all he does, and the "why" of all he believes.

The only knowledge Emile has at this stage is in the sphere of natural and physical facts. He does not even know the name of history, nor what metaphysics and ethics are. He knows the essential relations between man and things, but none of the moral relations between man and man. He has little ability to form general ideas or abstractions. He sees the qualities common to certain bodies without reasoning about the qualities in themselves. He knows abstract space by means of geometrical figures, and abstract quantity by means of algebraic symbols. These figures and signs are the basis of the abstractions, on which his senses rest. He does not seek to know things in themselves, but through the relations which interest him. He only judges external facts by their relation to himself, but this judgment of his is sound. Nothing fantastic or conventional enters into it. He sets most store on what is useful for him, and as he never departs from this method of evaluation, he is not swayed by accepted opinion.

Emile is hard working, temperate, patient, stable and courageous. His imagination, still unstimulated, does not exaggerate dangers. Few evils affect him and he can endure suffering calmly because he has learned not to fight against fate. As for death, he does not yet know what it is, but being accustomed to submit unresistingly to the laws of nature, he will die if he must without a struggle. To live a free man and hold human affairs lightly is the best way to prepare for death. In a word, Emile has every personal virtue. To add the social virtues he only needs to know the relations which call them into being. That knowledge his mind is now quite ready to receive.

He still thinks of himself without regard to others and is quite satisfied that others should give no thought to him. He asks nothing from other people and does not believe that he owes anything to them. Thus far he stands alone in human society. He is self-dependent and is better entitled to be so than any other person, since he is all that a child could be at his age.

He has no mistaken ideas and no vices, other than those that nobody can avoid. He has a healthy body, agile limbs, a true mind free from prejudice, a free heart devoid of passion. Self-esteem, the first and most natural of all the passions, has still to awaken in him. Without disturbing anybody's peace he has lived happy, contented and free within the bounds of nature. Do you think that a child who has reached his fifteenth year like this has wasted his childhood? . . .

Book IV

We are born twice over: the first time for existence, the second for life; once as human beings and later as men or as women. Up to puberty, children of the two sexes have nothing obvious to distinguish them. They are similar in features, in complexion, in voice. Girls are children, boys are children. The same name suffices for beings so much alike.

But man is not meant to remain a child for ever. At the time prescribed by nature he passes out of his childhood. As the fretting of the sea precedes the distant storm, this disturbing change is announced by the murmur of nascent passions. A change of mood, frequent tantrums, a constant unease of mind make the child hard to manage. He no longer listens to his master's voice. He is a lion in a fever. He mistrusts his guide and is averse to control.

With the moral signs of changing mood go patent physical changes. His countenance develops and takes on the imprint of a definite character. The soft slight down on his cheeks grows darker and firmer. His voice breaks, or rather, gets lost. He is neither child nor man, and he speaks like neither. His eyes, organs of the soul, which have hitherto said nothing, find language and expression as they light up with a new fire. He is becoming conscious that they can tell too much and he is learning to lower them and blush. He is disturbed for no reason whatever.

This is the second birth of which I spoke. Now is the time that man really enters into life and finds nothing alien to him. So far his guardian's responsibility has been child's play: it is only now that his task comes to have real importance. This stage at which ordinary educations end is just that when ours should begin.

The passions are the chief instruments for our preservation. The child's first sentiment is self-love, the only passion that is born with man. The second, which is derived from it, is the love he has for the people he sees ready to help him, and from this develops a kindly feeling for mankind. But with fresh needs and growing dependence on others comes the consciousness of social relations and with it the sense of duties and preferences. It is at this point that the child may become domineering, jealous, deceitful, vindictive. Self-love, being concerned only with ourselves, is content when our real needs are satisfied; but self-esteem, which involves comparisons with other people, never can be content because it makes the impossible demand that others should prefer us to themselves. That is how it comes that the gentle kindly passions issue from self-love, while hate and anger spring from self-esteem. Great care and skill are required to prevent the human heart being depraved by the new needs of social life.

The proper study of man is that of his relationships. So long as he is aware of himself only as a physical being he should study himself in his relations with things. That is the task of childhood. When he comes to consciousness of himself as a moral being he should study himself in his relations with his fellows. This is the occupation of his whole life, beginning at the point we have now reached. . . .

So long as a child's feelings are confined to himself, his actions have no moral character. It is only when they begin to take him beyond himself that he first forms the sentiments, and later the ideas of good and evil which make him truly man and an integral part of humanity. It is on this point that we must fix attention in the first place. To do so we must reject the example of those sophisticated children who are men in thought long before they are really men, and look for those in whom the successive developments follow the course of nature. . . .

Teachers complain that the impetuosity of this age makes youth insubordinate, and I see it myself. But is it not their own fault? Do they not realise that once they have allowed this ardour to find expression through the senses, no other way is possible? So far from this adolescent fire being an obstacle to education, it is by means of it that education is brought to completion. It gives the guardian a hold on the heart of the young man when he ceases to be the stronger. The youth's first affections are the reins by which all his movements can be directed once he is free. So long as he loved nothing he depended only on himself. As soon as he loves, he depends on those to whom he is attached. In this way are forged the first links that bind him to mankind. But do not imagine that his newborn affections will embrace all men. To begin with, this attachment will be confined to his fellows, and his fellows will only be those with whom he associates, people who think and feel like himself, and have similar pains and pleasures, those in short whose obvious identity of nature with himself increases his self-love. It will only be after he has developed his native disposition in a thousand ways and reflected long on the sentiments he observes in himself and others, that he will succeed in comprehending his individual notions under the abstract idea of humanity and combining his personal affections, with those that identify him with mankind.

At last we are entering the moral sphere. We have reached the second stage of manhood. If this were the place for it, I would try to show how the first impulses of the heart give rise to the first utterances of conscience, and how from the sentiments of love and hate come the first ideas of good and evil. I would demonstrate that justice and goodness are not merely abstract terms, moral entities created by the understanding, but real affections of the soul enlightened by reason which have developed from our primitive affections. I would show too that it is impossible to establish any natural law by reason alone, independent of conscience, and that natural rights are an empty dream unless they are based on the natural needs of the human heart. But I do not think I am called on to write treatises on metaphysics and ethics or detail any courses of study whatever.

Up to the present, my Emile has thought only about himself. The first thought he gives to his fellows leads him to compare himself with them; and the first sentiment excited in him by this comparison is a desire for priority. It is at this point that self-love changes into self-esteem and that all the passions pertaining to the latter begin to be active. But to determine whether the passions which will dominate his character are to be humane and kindly, or cruel and malevolent, we must know what he regards as his proper place among men and what kind of obstacles he thinks he will have to overcome to reach it. We have already let him see the chances of life which are common to all mankind. We must now for his guidance in this quest show him the differences among men and give him a picture of the whole social order.

Here it is important to take the opposite course from the one we have been following so far, and let the young man learn from other people's experience rather than his own. I would have you choose a young man's associates so that he may think well of those who live with him, and at the same time I would have you teach him to know the world so well that he may think ill of all that goes on in it. You want him to know and feel that man is naturally good, and to judge his neighbour by himself: equally, you want him to see how society corrupts men and to find in their prejudices the source of all their vices. This method, I have to admit, has its drawbacks and it is not easy to put into practice. If a young man is set to observe men too early and too close up, he will take a hateful pleasure in interpreting everything as badness and fail to see anything good in what is really good. Soon the general perversity will serve him as an excuse rather than as a warning, and he will say that if this is what man is, he himself has no wish to be different.

To get over this obstacle and bring him to an understanding of the human heart without risk of spoiling himself I would show him men in other times and places, in such a way that he can look on the scene as an outsider. This is the time for history. By means of it he will read the hearts of men without the lessons of philosophy, and look on them as a mere spectator without prejudice and without passion: judging them, but neither their accomplice nor their accuser.

Unfortunately this study has dangers and drawbacks of various kinds. It is difficult to put one's self at a point of view from which to judge one's fellows fairly. One of the great vices of history is the portrayal of men by what is bad in them rather than by what is good. It is from revolutions and catastrophes that it derives its interest. So long as a nation grows and prospers in the calm of peaceful government, history has nothing to say about it. It only begins to tell about nations when they are no longer self-sufficient and have got mixed up in their neighbours' affairs. It only records their story when they enter on their decline. Our historians all begin where they ought to finish. Only bad men achieve fame: the good are either forgotten or held up to ridicule. Like philosophy, history always slanders mankind.

Moreover, the facts described in history never give an exact picture of what actually happened. They change form in the historian's head. They get moulded by his interests and take on the hue of his prejudices. Who can put the reader at the precise point where an event can be seen just as it took place? Ignorance or partisanship distorts everything. Without even altering a single feature a quite different face can be put on events by a broader or a narrower view of the relevant circumstances. How often a tree more or less, a rock to the right or the left, a cloud of dust blown up by the wind, have decided the outcome of a battle without anybody being aware of it! But that does not prevent the historian telling you the causes of defeat or victory with as much assurance as if he had been everywhere himself. In any case, what do the facts matter when the reason for them is unknown? And what lessons can I draw from an event when I am ignorant of the real cause of it? The historian gives me an explanation, but it is his own invention. And is not criticism itself, of which there is so much talk, only an art of guessing, the art of choosing among various lies the one most like the truth? . . .

The defect of most history is that it only keeps record of the obvious outstanding facts which can be fixed by names, places and dates. But the slow-moving, cumulative causes of the facts which cannot be fixed in this way remain unknown. We often find in a battle lost or won the reason for a revolution which even before had become inevitable. War only makes evident events already determined by moral causes, which historians are rarely able to appreciate.

To all these considerations must be added the fact that history is more concerned with actions than with men. It takes men at certain chosen moments when they are in full dress. It only depicts the public man when he is prepared to be seen, and does not follow him into the intimacies of friendship and private life. It is the coat rather than the person that is portrayed.

I would much rather have the study of human nature begin with the reading of the life story of individual men. In these stories the historian gets on the track of the man, and there is no escape from his scrutiny. "The writers most to my mind," says Montaigne, "are biographers, because they find ideas more entertaining than events, and delight more in what comes from within than from without. That is why Plutarch is the man for me in every way."

It is true that the genius of nations, or of men in association, is very different from the character of man as an individual; and the knowledge of human nature got without examination of the form it assumes in the multitude, would be very imperfect. But it is no less true that it is necessary to begin with the study of man in order to form a judgment about men, and that one who had a complete knowledge of the dispositions of the constituent individuals might be able to forsee their joint effects in the body politic. . . .

One step more and we reach the goal. Self-esteem is a useful instrument but it has its dangers. Often it wounds the hand that employs it and rarely does good without also doing evil. Emile, comparing himself with other human beings and finding himself very fortunately situated, will be tempted to give credit to his own reason for the work of his guardian, and to attribute to his own merit the effects of his good fortune. He will say: "I am wise, and men are foolish." This is the error most to be feared, because it is the one hardest to eradicate. If choice had to be made I do not know whether I would not prefer the illusion of prejudice to the illusion of pride.

There is no remedy for vanity but experience. It is doubtful indeed if it can be cured at all; but at any rate its growth may be checked when it appears. Do not waste your time on fine arguments and try to convince an adolescent that he is a man like other men and subject to the same weaknesses. Make him feel it for himself, or he will never learn it. Once again I have to make an exception to my own rules, by deliberately exposing my pupil to the mischances which may prove to him that he is no wiser than the rest of us. I will let flatterers get the better of him. If fools were to entice him into some extravagance or other I would let him run the risk. I will allow him to be duped by card sharpers, and leave him to be swindled by them. The only snares from which I would guard him with special care would be those of prostitutes. Actually Emile would not be readily tempted in these ways. It should be kept in mind that my constant plan is to take things at their worst. I try in the first place to prevent the vice, and then I assume its existence in order to show how it can be remedied.

The time for faults is the time for fables. Censure of an offender under cover of a fiction gives instruction without offence. The young man learns in this way that the moral of the tale is not a lie, from the truth that finds application in his own case. The child who has never been deceived by flattery sees no point in the fable of *The Crow and the Fox*, but the silly person who has been gulled by a flatterer understands perfectly what a fool the crow was. From a fact he draws a moral, and the experience which would speedily have been forgotten is engraved in his mind by the fable. There is no moral knowledge which cannot be acquired either through the experience of other people or of ourselves. Where the experience is too dangerous for the young man to get it at first hand, the lesson can be drawn from history. When the test has no serious consequences it is good for him to be exposed to it and to have the particular cases known to him summed up as maxims. I do not mean, however, that these maxims should be expounded or even stated. The moral at the end of most fables is badly conceived. Before I put the inimitable fables of La Fontaine into the hands of a young man I would cut out all the conclusions in which he takes the trouble to explain what he had just said so clearly and agreeably. If your pupil does not understand the fable without the explanation, you can be sure that he will not understand it in any case. Only men can learn from fables and now is the time for Emile to begin.

When I see young people confined to the speculative studies at the most active time of life and then cast suddenly into the world of affairs without the least experience, I find it as contrary to reason as to nature and am not at all surprised that so few people manage their lives well. By some strange perversity we are taught all sorts of useless things, but nothing is done about the art of conduct. We are supposed to be getting trained for society but are taught as if each one of us were going to live a life of contemplation in a solitary cell. You think you are preparing children for life when you teach them certain bodily contortions and meaningless strings of words. I also have been a teacher of the art of conduct. I have taught my Emile to live his own life, and more than that to earn his own bread. But that is not enough. To live in the world one must get on with people and know how to get a hold on them. It is necessary also to be able to estimate the action and reaction of individual interests in civil society and so forecast events as to be rarely at fault in one's enterprises.

It is by doing good that we become good. I know of no surer way. Keep your pupil occupied with all the good deeds within his power. Let him help poor people with money and with service, and get justice for the oppressed. Active benevolence will lead him to reconcile the quarrels of his comrades and to be concerned about the sufferings of the afflicted. By putting his kindly feelings into action in this way and drawing his own conclusions from the outcome of his efforts, he will get a great deal of useful knowledge. In addition to college lore he will acquire the still more important ability of applying his knowledge to the purposes of life. . . .

Let us now look at Emile as he enters into society, not to become a leader but to become acquainted with it and to find his mate. Whatever the rank into which he may be born, whatever the society he enters, his first appearance will be simple and unpretentious. He neither has nor desires the qualities that make an immediate impression. He sets too little store by the opinions of men to be concerned about their prejudices, and is not concerned to have people esteem him till they know him. His way of presenting himself is neither modest nor conceited, but just natural and sincere. He knows neither constraint nor concealment. He is the same in company as when he is alone. He speaks little, because he has no desire to attract notice. For the same reason he only speaks about things that are of practical value, being too well informed ever to be a babbler. Far from despising the ways of other people, he conforms quite readily to them: not for the sake of appearing versed in the conventions or affecting fashionable airs, but simply to avoid notice. He is never more at his ease than when nobody is paying him any attention.

When he studies the ways of men in society as he formerly studied their passions in history, he will often have occasion to reflect on the things that gratify or offend the human heart. This will lead him to philosophise on the principles of taste, and this is the study that is most fitting for this period of life.

There is no need to go far for a definition of taste. Taste is simply the faculty of judging what pleases or displeases the greatest number of people. This does not mean that there are more people of taste than others. For though the majority judge sanely about any particular thing, there are few who possess this sanity about everything. Taste is like beauty. Though the most general tastes put together make good taste, there are not many people of taste, just as beauty is constituted by an assemblage of the most common traits and yet there are few beautiful persons.

We are not concerned here with the things we like because they are useful, or dislike because they are harmful. Taste has nothing to do with the necessities of life; it applies to things which are indifferent to us or at most have the interest that goes with our amusements. This is what makes decisions of taste so difficult and seemingly so arbitrary. I should add that taste has local rules which make it dependent in very many ways on region, custom, government and institutions, as well as other rules relating to age, sex and character. That is why there can be no disputing about tastes.

Taste is natural to all men, but all do not possess it in equal measure. The degree of taste we may have depends on native sensibility; the form it takes under cultivation depends on the social groups in which we have lived. In the first place, it is necessary to live in numerous social groups and make many comparisons. In the second place, these must be groups for amusement and leisure, for in those that have to do with practical affairs it is interest and not pleasure that has to be considered. In the third place, there must not be too great inequality in the group and the tyranny of opinion must not be excessive: otherwise fashion stifles taste and people no longer desire what pleases but what gives distinction.

This matter of taste is one to which Emile cannot be indifferent in his present enquiries. The knowledge of what may be agreeable or disagreeable to men is essential to one who has need of them, and no less to one who wants to be useful to them. It is important to please people if you want to serve them. . . .

Now is the time to read agreeable books, and to teach him to analyse speech and appreciate all the beauties of eloquence and diction. Contrary to the general belief, there is little to be gained from the study of languages for themselves; but the study of languages leads to the study of the general principles of grammar. It is necessary to know Latin to get a proper knowledge of French. To learn the rules of the art of speech we must study and compare the two languages.

There is moreover a certain simplicity of taste that goes to the heart, which is to be found only in the writings of the ancients. In oratory, in poetry, in every kind of literature, the pupil will find them, as in history, abundant in matter and sober in judgment. In contrast with this our authors talk much and say little. To be always accepting their judgment as right is not the way to acquire a judgment of our own. . . .

Generally speaking Emile will have more liking for the writings of the ancients than our own, for the good reason that coming first they are nearer nature and their genius is more distinctive. Whatever may be said to the contrary the human reason shows no advance. What is gained in one direction is lost in another. All minds start from the same point, and the time spent in learning what others think is so much time lost for learning to think for ourselves. As time goes on there is more acquired knowledge and less vigour of mind.

It is not for the study of morals but of taste that I take Emile to the theatre, for it is there above all that taste reveals itself to thinking people. "Give no thought to moral precepts," I will say to him: "it is not here that you will learn them." The theatre is not intended to give truth but to humour and amuse. Nowhere can the art of pleasing men and touching the human heart be so well learned. The study of drama leads to the study of poetry; their object is the same. If Emile has even a glimmering of taste for poetry he will cultivate Greek, Latin and Italian — the languages of the poets — with great pleasure. The study of them will give him unlimited entertainment, and will profit him all the more on that account. They will bring him delight at an age and in circumstances when the heart finds charm in every kind of beauty. Imagine on the one hand my Emile, and, on the other, some young college scamp, reading the Fourth Book of the *Aeneid*, or Tibullus, or Plato's *Banquet*. What a difference there is: the heart of the one stirred to its depth by something that does not impress the other at all. Stop the reading, young man: you are too greatly moved. I want you to find pleasure in the language of love, but not to be carried away by it. Be a man of feeling, but also a wise man. Actually, it is of no consequence whether Emile succeeds in the dead languages, in literature, in poetry or not. It would not matter greatly if he were ignorant of them all. His education is not really concerned with such diversions.

My main object in teaching him to feel and love beauty in every form is to fix his affections and his tastes on it and prevent his natural appetites from deteriorating so that he comes to look for the means of happiness in his wealth instead of finding it within himself. As I have said elsewhere, taste is simply the art of appreciating the little things, but since the pleasure of life depends on a multitude of little things such concern is not unimportant. It is by means of them that we come to enrich our lives with the good things at our disposal.

All this while we have been looking for Sophie but without finding her. It was important that she should not be found too quickly, and we have been looking for her where I was sure she would not be found. But now there is urgency. It is time to look for her in earnest, for fear Emile should mistake some one else for her and discover his mistake too late. *Adieu* then, Paris, city of fame and noise and smoke and dirt, where the women no longer believe in honour nor the men in virtue. *Adieu*, Paris. We are looking for love, happiness and innocence. We cannot get too far away from you. . . .

4

JOHN DEWEY

Commentary

Biography

John Dewey (1859-1952) was born in the town of Burlington, Vermont, situated in the rural New England region of the United States, in the same year that Charles Darwin published his *Origin of Species* and Karl Marx the *Critique of Political Economy*. Vermont of a century ago was still very much a frontier-type society, where the relatively small population was engaged basically in agricultural practices. Even in the few small towns there was a close connection with the countryside, and the daily round of most people involved them in an intimate and purposeful relationship with the processes of production based on homecraft activities — a life that contrasted strongly with that in the great urban complexes already being built up in the industrial regions of the country. Dewey's background in a homespun society was always to exert a strong although perhaps unconscious influence on him.

In due course Dewey went from school to the University of Vermont, which was only half a block away from his home, where he majored in philosophy for his liberal arts degree. After graduating from Vermont he took several short jobs, chiefly schoolteaching, and then enrolled in Johns Hopkins University in Baltimore, Maryland. This was a totally new development in American education, for Johns Hopkins, founded in 1874 by a bequest from a local Quaker, was designed purely as a graduate school, intended to provide a focus of higher learning in America itself, instead of Germany where hitherto Americans were forced to go in search of advanced qualifications and degrees. The express intention of the foundation president, Daniel Coit Gilman, was to include a "faculty of philosophy", and in so writing he used the current German term, which contrasted with the American usage of a faculty of arts. Graduating in 1884, Dewey was one of the first persons educated completely in America to the doctoral level. Again his studies were in philosophy, which throughout this period was dominated by the German school of thought.

The nineteenth century saw a tremendous surge of interest in classical antiquity — it was the time of the great archaeological expeditions to Greece, Italy and the ancient Orient (the present-day Middle East) — and this was paralleled by a wave of enthusiasm for everything classical, which became expressed in much of the century's architecture, and just as forcefully in education. There was yet another revival of classical studies (following those of the Renaissance and the Reformation); Greek and Latin dominated the curriculum to the extent that they were required by most European and American colleges and universities as matriculation subjects, and were often carried over as compulsory elements of the bachelor's degree in arts, and this degree itself was generally required as a preliminary to all other degrees. It was this intellectual climate that also led to a revival in Germany of Greek philosophy of a Platonic, idealist kind, which received its greatest exposition in the teaching of Georg Wilhelm Friedrich Hegel (1770-1831), chiefly at the University of Berlin from 1818 to his death. This is a difficult philosophy to explain in a short space, but its general principles are derived from a metaphysical argument for the priority of pure Being (rather akin to Plato's Idea of the Good) over physical existence, but with the added notion that this Being is not static but is itself developing by a dialectical process to ever higher stages. This philosophy was used to explain the progress of civilisation via the unit of the state, and it argued that the rise and fall of various states was due to the working out of an inevitable historical dialectic. Built upon the earlier monumental work of Immanuel Kant in the late eighteenth century, this Hegelian philosophy — known as absolute idealism — dominated nineteenth-century thought, particularly in religion. In England it was carried forward chiefly by F. H. Bradley and in America by a number of thinkers, of whom Josiah Royce was especially prominent. One of the more influential outcomes of this theory was its incorporation by Karl Marx into his view of history.

Dewey himself studied this philosophy for his doctorate and it influenced his thought profoundly, although he later tried to eradicate it. Indeed, in his first years of lecturing, between 1884 and 1894, first at the University of Michigan and then at Minnesota, this was the general content of his courses. In 1894 he accepted an invitation to the University of Chicago as a professor of philosophy, on the condition that he was also to be able to lecture in pedagogy: the art and science of teaching. For the next ten years he directed the study of Education at Chicago; in 1904 he moved to Teachers College, Columbia University, in New York, where he remained until retirement in 1930. For the following twenty-two years he continued to be active in education and exerted a profound influence right up to his death.

Main Features of Dewey's Educational Thought

By the time of his appointment to Chicago, Dewey's ideas had begun to change, and he became receptive to the new styles of thought that were becoming current. In reaction to the involved metaphysics of absolute idealism, there was a growing movement towards acceptance of more empirical and radical doctrines. Darwin's arguments dethroned man from his place at the centre of the universe, anthropologists such as Malinowski and Fraser showed how varied and relativistic human practices were, while G. H. Mead did the same in sociology. The new study of psychology began to give fresh insights into the nature of man, of which William James was a brilliant exponent. All of this growing movement to social relativism needed a general philosophical theory, which was provided by the incisive thinking of Charles Sanders Peirce (1839–1914), an eccentric genius, employed by the U.S. Geodetic Survey. Peirce concentrated his attention on the "act", that is, on the actions or deeds by which men effect their purposes. He went on to develop his ideas, in a tremendous corpus of work that unfortunately was only collected and edited posthumously. Again his philosophy is complex, but in general outline it argues that knowledge can only be of the consequences of actions. As early as 1878 he formulated his future elaborations in the interesting and rather tersely worded dictum:

> Consider what effects, that might conceivably have practical bearings, we conceive the object of our conception to have. Then, our conception of these effects is the whole of our conception of the object.[1]

Immediately metaphysics is ruled out, and knowledge is seen as solely of effects; truth is simply the observation of the consequences of acting. Despite the growing reaction against classical doctrines, titles for newly emerging disciplines continued to be chosen from the Greek, and just as psychology was coined from the words *psyche*, the mind, and *logos*, the study, so Peirce took the Greek word *pragma*, meaning a deed or act, and gave us the new concept of pragmatism.

Pragmatism became the fashion in the radical thought of the day and it can be seen in the early writing of Dewey while at Chicago, where he became concerned with the deadness and remoteness of so much that passed for knowledge. Now Dewey became interested in education and the institution of the school, because he believed that philosophy, in essence, is "the generalised theory of education",[2] and so, following his growing acceptance of pragmatism he saw that if such a criterion were applied to school activity, most of the latter would be seen to be more than meaningless; it was positively mis-educational in the profoundest sense of the term.

What, in fact, was going on in most schools late in the nineteenth century? Obviously this is a question that requires a very full and complex answer, but generally the principal features are clear. Despite the ideas of Rousseau and his followers, the traditional model was still dominant. Education was conceived largely as the process of formal instruction, primarily in the elements of literacy and related vocational skills, and secondarily in the acquisition of a general range of knowledge. Many educational reformers and innovators exerted a moderating influence in localised instances, but the overall picture is nonetheless quite uniform. The classical revival dominated educational aims so that beyond the level of socialisation they were seen to lead to the attainment of virtue — that classic concept, unchanged from the Greek *areté* of Plato and Aristotle, and the *virtus* of Cicero and Quintilian. The task of the school was to initiate the child into the culture of civilisation and as the mind became disciplined ethical character was formed, as so persuasively argued by Johann Friedrich Herbart (1776–1841). All of this drew from a belief in knowledge as an ordered body of information, organised into the substantive disciplines of literature, language, history, geography, mathematics and so on, and this body was believed to have an independent existence. The most usual model of the mind that was employed was Aristotle's idea of a "blank tablet" with a latent capacity for receiving and ordering knowledge (he called it an "innate faculty of discrimination".)[3] As well as this, it was believed in the nineteenth century that the mind possesses specific capacities or "faculties", such as memory, will, perseverance (some lists are immensely long), which can be strengthened by being exercised, usually by verbal drill. This concept of exercise of the faculties, known as formal discipline, guided much of the teacher's activities.

The task of the teacher was quite well understood: this is the responsibility for organising knowledge into its structure, usually employing such principles of arrangement as the simple to the complex, or the known to the unknown, and then communicating it to the children, either orally, by writing on the board, or by having them read in books or from charts. The children were expected to memorise this information, and so chanting and other mnemonic devices were employed and in time the mind was supposed to become appropriately organised into a parallel paradigm of the ordered objectivity of the external world. In brief, the purpose of teaching was to get a verbal, symbolic pattern of knowledge across into the supposedly receptive mind of the child. There was, however, always a problem with the children themselves. This method of teaching, especially as large classes were common, meant that the children had to sit quietly so as to catch the teacher's words. There was a premium on passivity; schools, as one wit has remarked, were "sit-stilleries" and the teacher had the added task of keeping order. Children, of course, will persist in talking, wriggling and letting their minds wander. So in the schools of the day the complementary practices of rewards and punishments operated, usually under the general notion of discipline. Good teaching, it was held, should engage the child positively and so "motivation" became an important pedagogical activity; by this it was understood that the teacher should arouse the child's interest in the material to be learned. Rewards, always external to the task, were given for satisfactory completion, and this practice became institutionalised in one of the great paradoxes: rewards often taking the form of a release from any further work, even to the extent of an "early mark" allowing the child to leave school before the final bell. Punishments operated in reverse, and failure to learn usually meant either an increase in the workload which the child was already not coping with, or recourse to the rod or strap. These procedures, at the same time, were believed to be building moral character and leading to the cultivation of virtue.

It was against this general practice that Dewey reacted vigorously. He was not alone, of course, although he never fulminated with the intensity of Joseph Rice, a contemporary critic of the schools whose bitter castigations stimulated a wave of reform; Dewey's reaction, which was characteristic of him, was channelled into a steady, resolute philosophically constructed argument. What was wrong with education at the beginning of the twentieth century, he argued, was its almost total meaninglessness: it was the training of slaves. The aims of virtue and moral character were imposed from above and built out of a dubious, possibly empty metaphysics; the curriculum was an overwhelming corpus of information, and a corpus in the worst possible sense: totally lifeless. The whole psychology of the child as an integral human being was violated; mind and body were separated as abstractions and the latter suppressed, violently if necessary. Everything was directed towards cramming the "mind" with vast amounts of largely verbal formula, masquerading as knowledge, devoid of any real content and imposed by a necessarily authoritarian teacher, quite apart from the experiential context within which it was originally created. Traditional education, he asserted over and over again, was authoritarian; it was based on the learner being necessarily dependent upon the mind and will of another. How, under these circumstances, could the young become participating, constructive members of a democracy committed to the goals of extending the potentialities of the good life to everyone? Dewey went on to provide an answer that took the imagination, first of America, and later of much of the Western world. The whole conception and practice of education, he said, had to be radically changed.

It was his plan for reform that constitutes Dewey's significant innovation, and this is set out in some detail in his first major educational writing, *Democracy and Education*, published in 1916. All education, he argued, should be scientific in the rigorous sense of the world. The school must become a social laboratory where children learn to subject the received tradition to the pragmatic tests of truth; the accumulated knowledge of society must be demonstrably seen to work. And, moreover, this has to be an ongoing process: the school has to develop in the child the necessary competence to solve current problems and to test future plans of action according to the experimental method. This book, in which this revolutionary doctrine was set forward, immediately became the centre of educational interest across America and stimulated tremendous discussion and some quite bitter reaction. It continued to be an influential work for the following decades and it remains in print to this day.

The basis of Dewey's theory of education is not metaphysical in the traditional sense; instead he begins his argument from an anthropological and psychological position. Life, he says, seeks its own sustenance, which is secured by man through the medium of the organised society. Education is fundamental to this process because it enables the individual to maintain continuity by learning the techniques of survival and development from the accumulated experience of the group. As life becomes more complex, education becomes more "formal" and "intentional", and largely directed towards ensuring that the young come to accept the morality of their society. At this point, two paths are possible: either to see that this morality — in the full sense of the ways of society — is closed, fixed and unchangeable, or to see that it is kept open, tentative and subject to revision in the light of continued social experience. Only the latter path should be admissible in a democracy, for such a system is based, by definition, on the assumptions of the inner worth and equal dignity of all persons.

Important educational implications flow from this assumption. Children, whose dominant characteristic is plasticity, must be kept this way; must be encouraged to follow this "natural" proclivity to seek, enquire, explore, to immerse themselves in the environment and to learn by experience. This leads, Dewey says, to growth, and in this fundamental concept he expressed the notion of the most desirable form of behaviour being the disposition always to react to new situations with concern, flexibility and curiosity. Man must seek always to respond creatively. The opposite is to respond with a set solution, a prejudice, in which a static, already held attitude or belief is imposed upon the new situation. This latter approach, he asserted, was exactly what schools fostered: they closed children's eyes by imposing upon them predetermined views of the world and previously developed solutions. This, of course, was his objection to the style of schooling, described above, that dominated the nineteenth century. Children under this scheme were taught, by virtue of a preordained curriculum, to see the world as fixed, finished and ordered. Their only possible accomplishment would be to see how much of it they could memorise.

How, then, did Dewey reconcile the two concepts of the priority of social continuity with the need for the flexibility of the individual? Chiefly by arguing that the collective experience of a democratic society should be seen as a resource for solving future problems. This is how he viewed history and all learning organised as "subject matter" — a taxonomy of previous solutions. So the child should come to school subjects as to bodies of material which may hold some possible relevance for future action; subjects should not be revered and memorised for their own sake alone. Of course, so much school learning was purely verbal, as illustrated vividly in the case of children who memorised the definition of the equator as "an imaginary line running around the earth" but who later wrote it down as "a menagerie lion running around the earth". Dewey recognised that subject matter does have the possibility, if properly used, of extending the meaning of our experience, but too often it is a dry, rote-memory form of encyclopaedic recitation, often having no meaningful connection with the individual's real life experiences.

Activity is one of Dewey's key terms; it is the dominant human characteristic. Man acts constantly to maintain the continuity of life because checks upon continuity, and hence survival, are part of the order of nature. Dewey saw life as a continued sequence of challenges and this viewpoint was heightened by the times in which he was living. Science, technology and industry were burgeoning and indeed the truths of yesteryear were being superseded rapidly by the advances of experimental enquiry. Dewey was clear in his acceptance of industry; we must affirm the machine because it is the instrument by which people can be freed from slavish routine occupations and allowed to enjoy a life of purposeful, creative activity. So he derived another of his great educational ideas: that education should be consonant with society, which at that time was a developing industrial democracy. Education should be itself a democratic process of conjoint activity, guided by the highest form of solving problems yet devised: the scientific method. So as early as the Chicago years Dewey conceived of the school as a laboratory rather than a sit-stillery, and learning as experimentation and search into the unknown rather than as passive absorption of external "facts". He unscrewed the desks from the floor and put in laboratory benches; the teacher's table disappeared and children were encouraged to stand, walk about and talk together as they studied real-life issues. Over the years a tremendous literature on "activity" learning appeared along with the associated "project" method.

The experimental approach is essential to constructive solutions and Dewey was responsible for initiating it into educational thought. When do we really think? he asked, and his answer came readily: when we are challenged. And challenges, as already pointed out, are part of our life. So came his next question: *how* do we think? And his answer in this case offered two alternatives: either by accepting the views of others or by involving ourselves in a process of critical enquiry. But the former approach is not really thinking and is characteristic of the slave: the democratic person must reach genine solutions. So, following what he believed to be the scientific method, Dewey set out a five-stage sequence of the complete act of thought. We think, in the full sense of the word, when we are challenged by a problem that stimulates us to seek a solution. Our next step is to gather data; to enquire into the conditions causing the problem. Next we think out an orderly sequence of steps towards a solution, or in the words of the scientist, construct an hypothesis, and following this, test it by application which, if it yields a confirmation, solves the problem. If the hypothesis is not confirmed then we go back to the data using the failed hypothesis as one more element, try to construct a new hypothesis taking into account our former experience and proceed as before. True laboratory science often has to reconstruct hypotheses many times before final solutions come, and this is equally true of human life in general.

Dewey was always resolutely opposed both to the dualism of traditional metaphysics (mind–body, subject–object, being–becoming, and so on) and to the constant tendency to make abstractions substantive. So he criticised such concepts as mind, intelligence, interest, attention and discipline in educational discussion. Indeed, it was the belief that these and many other terms have a substantive existence that, in his opinion, had led to the bad features of traditional education. We have no "mind" as a self-contained separate entity; we are engaged always as total, reacting persons. There are no abstract faculties of intelligence, interest, attention and discipline. Instead, as we work towards the scientific solution of problems we act intelligently; and in so acting we are engaged (or "interested", from the Latin *inter est*, that which is between the doer and the activity), we attend and we control our behaviour. So Dewey believed that if schools based their activities on scientific enquiry a great deal of compulsion and coercion would disappear, and such fake practices as motivation would be unnecessary — redundant in fact. And this too would lead to the disappearance of one of democracy's greatest enemies — the dualism, inherited from the Greeks, of leisure and labour. Nothing is intrinsically liberal or illiberal: anything that helps in the solution of problems is potentially liberating, and is not the province of any special class of studies. On the other hand, anything that hinders creative activity, as does much of the traditional humanities curriculum, is potentially illiberal.

How, then, does the individual acquire morality? How does one come to develop a set of proper values? Again Dewey found the answer within his democratic, scientific theory. His rejection of an external value system imposed from above such as that advocated by traditional metaphysics was the cause of much church opposition to him. Dewey argued that morality is learned within a social context by observing the appropriate rules. And these rules, in his theory, emerge from conjoint, shared experience. So the teacher is also a co-operative learner, but older and wiser, whose role is to help the child learn the values of democratic participation not by imparting information, but by enquiry into problematic situations.

Again, in a truly democratic society education should be controlled by the state and schools provided for all, regardless of sex, religion, race or social class. Any other system is divisive and inculcates anti-democratic principles; it has, therefore, no genuine educative function and inhibits the learning of broad democratic values.

Values are not always so widely defined, and Dewey was aware of the fact that the term "values" like so many that we use, is an abstraction. In practice, there is only the act of valuing, and this comes through the scientific method. We learn when, faced with the necessity to choose between alternative courses of action, we become involved in constructing hypotheses which, by definition, anticipate the consequences of particular ways of acting. The process of forming sound hypotheses presupposes judgment, since a complete act of thought involves us in anticipating the consequences implied for others, for the wider community and for the environment, as well as for ourselves. Not that every hypothesis will achieve this objective in every case — if we could, Dewey said, we would be living in a finished world. We must accept the fact that we may fail and that our hypotheses may be imperfect; we must always accept the limitations on our vision and the reality that solutions to problems even if they work — and so meet the pragmatic test of truth — may be only partial. We are, in effect, entitled to make mistakes. But the securing and maintaining of democracy means that we cannot be negligent. We must always be alert to the tentative nature of our conclusions and to the limitations on our understanding. Genuine morality comes from seeking constantly to become flexible, alert and creatively responsive to new challenges — to transmit this quality to the young is the highest purpose that can be given to education.

NOTES AND REFERENCES

1. C. HARTSHORNE and P. WEISS (Eds), *Collected Papers of Charles Sanders Peirce*, Harvard University Press, Cambridge (Mass.), 1960, Vols 5-6, p.1.
2. J. DEWEY, *Democracy and Education*, Macmillan, New York, 1916, p.387.
3. ARISTOTLE, *Posterior Analytics*, Book II, Ch. 19, in *Aristotle*, G. Howie (Ed.), Collier-Macmillan, London, 1968, (See p. 89 of this book.)

SELECT BIBLIOGRAPHY

Dewey wrote a large number of books, of which the following are the important titles for education. In chronological sequence, they are:

> *The School and Society*, Chicago University Press, Chicago, 1899, 2nd edition, 1915.
> *The Child and the Curriculum*, Chicago University Press, Chicago, 1902, Reprinted in one binding with *The School and Society* by Chicago University Press (Phoenix Books), 1956.
> *How We Think*, D.C.Heath, Boston, 1910; revised edition, 1933.
> *Democracy and Education*, Macmillan, New York, 1916.
> *Experience and Education*, Kappa Delta Pi Lectures, Lafayette (Indiana), 1938; published by Macmillan (Collier Books), New York, 1963.

Dewey's complete works are cited in M.H. THOMAS (Ed.), *John Dewey: A Centennial Bibliography*, University of Chicago Press, Chicago, 1962.

A definitive edition of the complete works of John Dewey are being published by Southern Illinois University Press, Carbondale, Illinois, under the editorship of J. A. Boydston. So far have appeared:

> *The Early Works of John Dewey, 1882-1898* (5 Vols), 1972.
> *The Middle Works of John Dewey, 1899-1924* (12 Vols), 1980.
> *The Later Works of John Dewey, 1925-1953* (Vol. 1, 1925), 1981.

such a place. It is all made "for listening" — because simply studying lessons out of a book is only another kind of listening; it marks the dependency of one mind upon another. The attitude of listening means, comparatively speaking, passivity, absorption; that there are certain ready-made materials which are there, which have been prepared by the school superintendent, the board, the teacher, and of which the child is to take in as much as possible in the least possible time.

There is very little place in the traditional schoolroom for the child to work. The workshop, the laboratory, the materials, the tools with which the child may construct, create, and actively enquire, and even the requisite space, have been for the most part lacking. The things that have to do with these processes have not even a definitely recognised place in education. They are what the educational authorities who write editorials in the daily papers generally term "fads" and "frills". A lady told me yesterday that she had been visiting different schools trying to find one where activity on the part of the children preceded the giving of information on the part of the teacher, or where the children had some motive for demanding the information. She visited, she said, twenty-four different schools before she found her first instance. I may add that that was not in this city.

Another thing that is suggested by these schoolrooms, with their set desks, is that everything is arranged for handling as large numbers of children as possible; for dealing with children *en masse*, as an aggregate of units; involving, again, that they be treated passively. The moment children act they individualise themselves; they cease to be a mass and become the intensely distinctive beings that we are acquainted with out of school, in the home, the family, on the playground, and in the neighborhood.

On the same basis is explicable the uniformity of method and curriculum. If everything is on a "listening" basis, you can have uniformity of material and method. The ear and the book which reflects the ear, constitute the medium which is alike for all. There is next to no opportunity for adjustment to varying capacities and demands. There is a certain amount — a fixed quantity — of ready-made results and accomplishments to be acquired by all children alike in a given time. It is in response to this demand that the curriculum has been developed from the elementary school up through the college. There is just so much desirable knowledge, and there are just so many needed technical accomplishments in the world. Then comes the mathematical problem of dividing this by the six, twelve, or sixteen years of school life. Now give the children every year just the proportionate fraction of the total, and by the time they have finished they will have mastered the whole. By covering so much ground during this hour or day or week or year, everything comes out with perfect evenness at the end — provided the children have not forgotten what they have previously learned. The outcome of all this is Matthew Arnold's report of the statement, proudly made to him by an educational authority in France, that so many thousands of children were studying at a given hour, say eleven o'clock, just such a lesson

Selections

Three of Dewey's works are represented here: School and Society, Democrac
Education *and* Experience and Education. *The brief extract from* Schoc
Society *(1899) illustrates Dewey's early concern to make the classroom into a
laboratory, and the account of his search for a new kind of school furniture has a
yet today.*

The major writing featured here is from Democracy and Education. *Firs
lished in 1916, and still in print, it is a reasonably long work of more than four h
pages, organised into twenty-six chapters. All of it bears careful study, althou
central ideas appear to be contained in the sections that follow, which describe D
basic concept of growth, the need to determine aims as a guide to the proper du
of growth, the way in which we can think intelligently (scientifically) to reac.
aims, the role of subject matter (the cultural tradition) in providing assistance, t.
in which values arise and serve to guide us, and the development of values into a
of morals.*

The third selection, Chapter 4 of Experience and Education *(1938), is in
to provide an illustration of Dewey's approach to social control, which argues (
imposition by authority and for control to issue from conjoint entering into meai
activities. Control has always been a vexed school problem and Dewey here p.
view, very widely followed, that the problem of control is minimised, if not elimi
when people are willing and conscious participants in shared enterprises.*

School and Society

Chapter II: The School and the Life of the Cl

Some few years ago I was looking about the school supply stores in the
trying to find desks and chairs which seemed thoroughly suitable fro
points of view — artistic, hygienic, and educational — to the needs
children. We had a great deal of difficulty in finding what we needed
finally one dealer, more intelligent than the rest, made this remark: "
afraid we have not what you want. You want something at which the
dren may work; these are all for listening." That tells the story of the
tional education. Just as the biologist can take a bone or two and recon:
the whole animal, so, if we put before the mind's eye the ordinary sc
room, with its rows of ugly desks placed in geometrical order, cro
together so that there shall be as little moving room as possible, desks a
all of the same size, with just space enough to hold books, pencils, and p
and add a table, some chairs, the bare walls, and possibly a few pict
we can reconstruct the only educational activity that can possibly go

From John Dewey, *School and Society*, The University of Chicago Press, Chicago and Lo
Copyright 1915 and 1943 by John Dewey. All rights reserved. Published November 189!
edition, August 1915, 21st impression, 1965.

in geography; and in one of our own Western cities this proud boast used to be repeated to successive visitors by its superintendent.

I may have exaggerated somewhat in order to make plain the typical points of the old education: its passivity of attitude, its mechanical massing of children, its uniformity of curriculum and method. It may be summed up by stating that the centre of gravity is outside the child. It is in the teacher, the textbook, anywhere and everywhere you please except in the immediate instincts and activities of the child himself. On the basis there is not much to be said about the *life* of the child. A good deal might be said about the studying of the child, but the school is not the place where the child *lives*. Now the change which is coming into our education is the shifting of the centre of gravity. It is a change, a revolution, not unlike that introduced by Copernicus when the astronomical centre shifted from the earth to the sun. In this case the child becomes the sun about which the appliances of education revolve; he is the centre about which they are organised. . . .

Democracy and Education
Chapter IV: Education as Growth

The Conditions of Growth

In directing the activities of the young, society determines its own future in determining that of the young. Since the young at a given time will at some later date compose the society of that period, the latter's nature will largely turn upon the direction children's activities were given at an earlier period. This cumulative movement of action toward a later result is what is meant by growth.

The primary condition of growth is immaturity. This may seem to be a mere truism — saying that a being can develop only in some point in which he is undeveloped. But the prefix "im" of the word immaturity means something positive, not a mere void or lack. It is noteworthy that the terms "capacity" and "potentiality" have a double meaning, one sense being negative, the other positive. Capacity may denote mere receptivity, like the capacity of a quart measure. We may mean by potentiality a merely dormant or quiescent state — a capacity to become something different under external influences. But we also mean by capacity an ability, a power; and by potentiality potency, force. Now when we say that immaturity means the possibility of growth, we are not referring to absence of powers which may exist at a later time; we express a force positively present — the *ability* to develop.

Reprinted with permission of Macmillan Publishing Co., Inc., from JOHN DEWEY *Democracy and Education*, copyright 1916 by Macmillan Publishing Co., Inc., renewed 1944 by John Dewey.

Our tendency to take immaturity as mere lack, and growth as something which fills up the gap between the immature and the mature is due to regarding childhood *comparatively*, instead of intrinsically. We treat it simply as a privation because we are measuring it by adulthood as a fixed standard. This fixes attention upon what the child has not, and will not have till he becomes a man. This comparative standpoint is legitimate enough for some purposes, but if we make it final, the question arises whether we are not guilty of an overweening presumption. Children, if they could express themselves articulately and sincerely, would tell a different tale; and there is excellent adult authority for the conviction that for certain moral and intellectual purposes adults must become as little children.

The seriousness of the assumption of the negative quality of the possibilities of immaturity is apparent when we reflect that it sets up as an ideal and standard a static end. The fulfilment of growing is taken to mean an *accomplished* growth: that is to say, an ungrowth, something which is no longer growing. The futility of the assumption is seen in the fact that every adult resents the imputation of having no further possibilities of growth; and so far as he finds that they are closed to him mourns the fact as evidence of loss, instead of falling back on the achieved as adequate manifestation of power. Why an unequal measure for child and man?

Taken absolutely, instead of comparatively, immaturity designates a positive force or ability — the *power* to grow. We do not have to draw out or educe positive activities from a child, as some educational doctrines would have it. Where there is life, there are already eager and impassioned activities. Growth is not something done to them; it is something they do. The positive and constructive aspect of possibility gives the key to understanding the two chief traits of immaturity, dependence and plasticity. (1) It sounds absurd to hear dependence spoken of as something positive, still more absurd as a power. Yet if helplessness were all there were in dependence, no development could ever take place. A merely impotent being has to be carried, forever, by others. The fact that dependence is accompanied by growth in ability, not by an ever-increasing lapse into parasitism, suggests that it is already something constructive. Being merely sheltered by others would not promote growth. For (2) it would only build a wall around impotence. With reference to the physical world, the child is helpless. He lacks at birth and for a long time thereafter power to make his way physically, to make his own living. If he had to do that by himself, he would hardly survive an hour. On this side his helplessness is almost complete. The young of the brutes are immeasurably his superiors. He is physically weak and not able to turn the strength which he possesses to coping with the physical environment.

1. The thoroughgoing character of this helplessness suggests, however, some compensating power. The relative ability of the young of brute animals to adapt themselves fairly well to physical conditions from an early period suggests the fact that their life is not intimately bound up with the life of those about them. They are compelled, so to speak, to have physical gifts because they are lacking in social gifts. Human infants, on the other hand,

can get along with physical incapacity just because of their social capacity. We sometimes talk and think as if they simply happened to be *physically* in a social environment; as if social forces exclusively existed in the adults who take care of them, they being passive recipients. If it were said that children are themselves marvellously endowed with *power* to enlist the co-operative attention of others, this would be thought to be a backhanded way of saying that others are marvellously attentive to the needs of children. But observation shows that children are gifted with an equipment of the first order for social intercourse. Few grown-up persons retain all of the flexible and sensitive ability of children to vibrate sympathetically with the attitudes and doings of those about them. Inattention to physical things (going with incapacity to control them) is accompanied by a corresponding intensification of interest and attention as to the doings of people. The native mechanism of the child and his impulses all tend to facile social responsiveness. The statement that children, before adolescence, are egotistically self-centred, even if it were true, would not contradict the truth of this statement. It would simply indicate that their social responsiveness is employed on their own behalf, not that it does not exist. But the statement is not true as matter of fact. The facts which are cited in support of the alleged pure egoism of children really show the intensity and directness with which they go to their mark. If the ends which form the mark seem narrow and selfish to adults, it is only because adults (by means of a similar engrossment in their day) have mastered these ends, which have consequently ceased to interest them. Most of the remainder of children's alleged native egoism is simply an egoism which runs counter to an adult's egoism. To a grown-up person who is too absorbed in his own affairs to take an interest in children's affairs, children doubtless seem unreasonably engrossed in *their* own affairs.

From a social standpoint, dependence denotes a power rather than a weakness; it involves interdependence. There is always a danger that increased personal independence will decrease the social capacity of an individual. In making him more self-reliant, it may make him more self-sufficient; it may lead to aloofness and indifference. It often makes an individual so insensitive in his relations to others as to develop an illusion of being really able to stand and act alone — an unnamed form of insanity which is responsible for a large part of the remediable suffering of the world.

2. The specific adaptability of an immature creature for growth constitutes his *plasticity*. This is something quite different from the plasticity of putty or wax. It is not a capacity to take on change of form in accord with external pressure. It lies near the pliable elasticity by which some persons take on the colour of their surroundings while retaining their own bent. But it is something deeper than this. It is essentially the ability to learn from experience; the power to retain from one experience something which is of avail in coping with the difficulties of a later situation. This means power to modify actions on the basis of the results of prior experiences, the power to *develop dispositions*. Without it, the acquisition of habits is impossible.

It is a familiar fact that the young of the higher animals, and especially the human young, have to *learn* to utilise their instinctive reactions. The human being is born with a greater number of instinctive tendencies than other animals. But the instincts of the lower animals perfect themselves for appropriate action at an early period after birth, while most of those of the human infant are of little account just as they stand. An original specialised power of adjustment secures immediate efficiency, but, like a railway ticket, it is good for one route only. A being who, in order to use his eyes, ears, hands, and legs, has to experiment in making varied combinations of their reactions, achieves a control that is flexible and varied. A chick, for example, pecks accurately at a bit of food in a few hours after hatching. This means that definite co-ordinations of activities of the eyes in seeing and of the body and head in striking are perfected in a few trials. An infant requires about six months to be able to gauge with approximate accuracy the action in reaching which will co-ordinate with his visual activities; to be able, that is, to tell whether he can reach a seen object and just how to execute the reaching. As a result, the chick is limited by the relative perfection of its original endowment. The infant has the advantage of the *multitude* of instinctive tentative reactions and of the experiences that accompany them, even though he is at a temporary disadvantage because they cross one another. In learning an action, instead of having it given ready-made, one of necessity learns to vary its factors, to make varied combinations of them, according to change of circumstances. A possibility of continuing progress is opened up by the fact that in learning one act, methods are developed good for use in other situations. Still more important is the fact that the human being acquires a habit of learning. He learns to learn. . . .

Habits as Expressions of Growth

We have already noted that plasticity is the capacity to retain and carry over from prior experience factors which modify subsequent activities. This signifies the capacity to acquire habits, or develop definite dispositions. We have now to consider the salient features of habits. In the first place, a habit is a form of executive skill, of efficiency in doing. A habit means an ability to use natural conditions as means to ends. It is an active control of the environment through control of the organs of action. We are perhaps apt to emphasise the control of the body at the expense of control of the environment. We think of walking, talking, playing the piano, the specialised skills characteristic of the etcher, the surgeon, the bridge builder, as if they were simply ease, deftness, and accuracy on the part of the organism. They are that, of course; but the measure of the value of these qualities lies in the economical and effective control of the environment which they secure. To be able to walk is to have certain properties of nature at our disposal — and so with all other habits.

Education is not infrequently defined as consisting in the acquisition of those habits that effect an adjustment of an individual and his environment. The definition expresses an essential phase of growth. But it is essential that adjustment be understood in its active sense of *control* of means for achieving ends. If we think of a habit simply as a change wrought in the organism, ignoring the fact that this change consists in ability to effect subsequent changes in the environment, we shall be led to think of "adjustment" as a conformity to environment as wax conforms to the seal which impresses it. The environment is thought of as something fixed, providing in its fixity the end and standard of changes taking place in the organism; adjustment is just fitting ourselves to this fixity of external conditions. Habit as *habituation* is indeed something *relatively* passive; we get used to our surroundings — to our clothing, our shoes, and gloves; to the atmosphere as long as it is fairly equable; to our daily associates, and so forth. Conformity to the environment, a change wrought in the organism without reference to ability to modify surroundings, is a marked trait of such habituations. Aside from the fact that we are not entitled to carry over the traits of such adjustments (which might well be called *accommodations*, to mark them off from active adjustments) into habits of active use of our surroundings, two features of habituations are worth notice. In the first place, we get used to things by *first* using them.

Consider getting used to a strange city. At first, there is excessive stimulation and excessive and ill-adapted response. Gradually certain stimuli are selected because of their relevancy, and others are disregarded. We can say either that we do not respond to them any longer, or more truly that we have effected a persistent response to them — an equilibrium of adjustment. This means, in the second place, that this enduring adjustment supplies the background upon which are made specific adjustments, as occasion arises. We are never interested in changing the *whole* environment; there is much that we take for granted and accept just as it already is. Upon this background our activities focus at certain points in an endeavour to introduce needed changes. Habituation is thus our adjustment to an environment which at the time we are not concerned with modifying, and which supplies a leverage to our active habits.

Adaptation, in fine, is quite as much adaptation *of* the environment to our own activities as of our activities *to* the environment. A savage tribe manages to live on a desert plain. It adapts itself. But its adaptation involves a maximum of accepting, tolerating, putting up with things as they are, a maximum of passive acquiescence, and a minimum of active control, of subjection to use. A civilised people enters upon the scene. It also adapts itself. It introduces irrigation; it searches the world for plants and animals that will flourish under such conditions; it improves, by careful selection, those which are growing there. As a consequence, the wilderness blossoms as a rose. The savage is merely habituated; the civilised man has habits which transform the environment.

The significance of habit is not exhausted, however, in its executive and motor phase. It means formation of intellectual and emotional disposition as well as an increase in ease, economy, and efficiency of action. Any habit marks an *inclination* — an active preference and choice for the conditions involved in its exercise. A habit does not wait, Micawber-like, for a stimulus to turn up so that it may get busy; it actively seeks occasions to pass into full operation. If its expression is unduly blocked, inclination shows itself in uneasiness and intense craving. A habit also marks an intellectual disposition. Where there is a habit, there is acquaintance with the materials and equipment to which action is applied. There is a definite way of understanding the situations in which the habit operates. Modes of thought, of observation and reflection, enter as forms of skill and of desire into the habits that make a man an engineer, an architect, a physician, or a merchant. In unskilled forms of labour, the intellectual factors are at minimum precisely because the habits involved are not of a high grade. But there are habits of judging and reasoning as truly as of handling a tool, painting a picture, or conducting an experiment.

Such statements are, however, understatements. The habits of mind involved in habits of the eye and hand supply the latter with their significance. Above all, the intellectual element in a habit fixes the relation of the habit to varied and elastic use, and hence to continued growth. We speak of *fixed* habits. Well, the phrase may mean powers so well established that their possessor always has them as resources when needed. But the phrase is also used to mean ruts, routine ways, with loss of freshness, open-mindedness, and originality. Fixity of habit may mean that something has a fixed hold upon us, instead of our having a free hold upon things. This fact explains two points in a common notion about habits: their identification with mechanical and external modes of action to the neglect of mental and moral attitudes and the tendency to give them a bad meaning, an identification with "bad habits". Many a person would feel surprised to have his aptitude in his chosen profession called a habit, and would naturally think of his use of tobacco, liquor, or profane language as typical of the meaning of habit. A habit is to him something which has a hold on him, something not easily thrown off even though judgment condemn it.

Habits reduce themselves to routine ways of acting, or degenerate into ways of action to which we are enslaved just in the degree in which intelligence is disconnected from them. Routine habits are unthinking habits; "bad" habits are habits so severed from reason that they are opposed to the conclusions of conscious deliberation and decision. As we have seen, the acquiring of habits is due to an original plasticity of our natures: to our ability to vary responses till we find an appropriate and efficient way of acting. Routine habits, and habits that possess us instead of our possessing them, are habits which put an end to plasticity. They mark the close of power to vary. There can be no doubt of the tendency of organic plasticity, of the physiological basis, to lessen with growing years. The instinctively mobile and eagerly varying action of childhood, the love of new stimuli and new developments, too easily passes into a "settling down", which means aversion to change and a resting on past achievements. Only an environment which secures the full use of intelligence in the process of forming habits can counteract this tendency. Of course, the same hardening of the organic conditions affects the physiological structures which are involved in thinking. But this fact only indicates the need of persistent care to see to it that the function of intelligence is invoked to its maximum possibility. The short-sighted method which falls back on mechanical routine and repetition to secure external efficiency of habit, motor skill without accompanying thought, marks a deliberate closing in of surroundings upon growth.

The Educational Bearings of the Conception of Development

We have had so far but little to say in this chapter about education. We have been occupied with the conditions and implications of growth. If our conclusions are justified, they carry with them, however, definite educational consequences. When it is said that education is development, everything depends upon *how* development is conceived. Our net conclusion is that life is development, and that developing, growing, is life. Translated into its educational equivalents, this means (i) that the educational process has no end beyond itself; it is its own end; and that (ii) the educational process is one of continual reorganising, reconstructing, transforming.

1. Development when it is interpreted in *comparative* terms, that is, with respect to the special traits of child and adult life, means the direction of power into special channels: the formation of habits involving executive skill, definiteness of interest, and specific objects of observation and thought. But the comparative view is not final. The child has specific powers; to ignore that fact is to stunt or distort the organs upon which his growth depends. The adult uses his powers to transform his environment, thereby occasioning new stimuli which redirect his powers and keep them developing. Ignoring this fact means arrested development, a passive accommodation. Normal child and normal adult alike, in other words, are engaged in growing. The difference between them is not the difference between growth and no growth, but between the modes of growth appropriate to different conditions. With respect to the development of powers devoted to coping with specific scientific and economic problems we may say the child should be growing in man-hood. With respect to sympathetic curiosity, unbiased responsiveness, and openness of mind, we may say that the adult should be growing in child-likeness. One statement is as true as the other.

Three ideas which have been criticised, namely, the merely privative nature of immaturity, static adjustment to a fixed environment, and rigidity of habit, are all connected with a false idea of growth or development — that it is a movement toward a fixed goal. Growth is regarded as *having* an end, instead of *being* an end. The educational counterparts of the three fallacious ideas are first, failure to take account of the instinctive or native powers of the young; secondly, failure to develop initiative in coping with novel situations; thirdly, an undue emphasis upon drill and other devices which secure automatic skill at the expense of personal perception. In all cases, the adult environment is accepted as a standard for the child. He is to be brought up *to* it.

Natural instincts are either disregarded or treated as nuisances — as obnoxious traits to be suppressed, or at all events to be brought into conformity with external standards. Since conformity is the aim, what is distinctively individual in a young person is brushed aside, or regarded as a source of mischief or anarchy. Conformity is made equivalent to uniformity. Consequently, there are induced lack of interest in the novel, aversion to progress, and dread of the uncertain and the unknown. Since the end of growth is outside of and beyond the process of growing, external agents have to be resorted to to induce movement towards it. Whenever a method of education is stigmatised as mechanical, we may be sure that external pressure is brought to bear to reach an external end.

2. Since in reality there is nothing to which growth is relative save more growth, there is nothing to which education is subordinate save more education. It is a commonplace to say that education should not cease when one leaves school. The point of this commonplace is that the purpose of school education is to ensure the continuance of education by organising the powers that ensure growth. The inclination to learn from life itself and to make the conditions of life such that all will learn in the process of living is the finest product of schooling.

When we abandon the attempt to define immaturity by means of fixed comparison with adult accomplishments, we are compelled to give up thinking of it as denoting lack of desired traits. Abandoning this notion, we are also forced to surrender our habit of thinking of instruction as a method of supplying this lack by pouring knowledge into a mental and moral hole which awaits filling. Since life means growth, a living creature lives as truly and positively at one stage as at another, with the same intrinsic fullness and the same absolute claims. Hence education means the enterprise of supplying the conditions which ensure growth, or adequacy of life, irrespective of age. We first look with impatience upon immaturity, regarding it as something to be got over as rapidly as possible. Then the adult formed by such educative methods looks back with impatient regret upon childhood and youth as a scene of lost opportunities and wasted powers. This ironical situation will endure till it is recognised that living has its own intrinsic quality and that the business of education is with that quality.

Realisation that life is growth protects us from that so-called idealising of childhood which in effect is nothing but lazy indulgence. Life is not to be identified with every superficial act and interest. Even though it is not always easy to tell whether what appears to be mere surface fooling is a sign of some nascent as yet untrained power, we must remember that manifestations are not to be accepted as ends in themselves. They are signs of possible growth. They are to be turned into means of development, of carrying power forward, not indulged or cultivated for their own sake. Excessive attention to surface phenomena (even in the way of rebuke as well as of encouragement) may lead to their fixation and thus to arrested development. What impulses are moving toward, not what they have been, is the important thing for parent and teacher. The true principle of respect for immaturity cannot be better put than in the words of Emerson: "Respect the child. Be not too much his parent. Trespass not on his solitude. But I hear the outcry which replies to this suggestion: Would you verily throw up the reins of public and private discipline; would you leave the young child to the mad career of his own passions and whimsies, and call this anarchy a respect for the child's nature? I answer — Respect the child, respect him to the end, but also respect yourself. . . . The two points in a boy's training are, to keep his *naturel* and train off all but that; to keep his *naturel*, but stop off his uproar, fooling, and horseplay; keep his nature *and arm it with knowledge in the very direction in which it points*." And as Emerson goes on to show, this reverence for childhood and youth instead of opening up an easy and easy-going path to the instructors, "involves at once, immense claims on the time, the thought, on the life of the teacher. It requires time, use, insight, event, all the great lessons and assistances of God; and only to think of using it implies character and profoundness."

Summary

Power to grow depends upon need for others and plasticity. Both of these conditions are at their height in childhood and youth. Plasticity or the power to learn from experience means the formation of habits. Habits give control over the environment, power to utilise it for human purposes. Habits take the form both of habituation, or a general and persistent balance of organic activities with the surroundings, and of active capacities to readjust activity to meet new conditions. The former furnishes the background of growth; the latter constitute growing. Active habits involve thought, invention, and initiative in applying capacities to new aims. They are opposed to routine which marks an arrest of growth. Since growth is the characteristic of life, education is all one with growing; it has no end beyond itself. The criterion of the value of school education is the extent in which it creates a desire for continued growth and supplies means for making the desire effective in fact.

Chapter VIII: Aims in Education

The Nature of an Aim

The account of education given in our earlier chapters virtually anticipated the results reached in a discussion of the purport of education in a democratic community. For it assumed that the aim of education is to enable individuals to continue their education — or that the object and reward of learning is continued capacity for growth. Now this idea cannot be applied to *all* the members of a society except where intercourse of man with man is mutual, and except where there is adequate provision for the reconstruction of social habits and institutions by means of wide stimulation arising from equitably distributed interests. And this means a democratic society. In our search for aims in education, we are not concerned, therefore, with finding an end outside of the educative process to which education is subordinate. Our whole conception forbids. We are rather concerned with the contrast which exists when aims belong within the process in which they operate and when they are set up from without. And the latter state of affairs must obtain when social relationships are not equitably balanced. For in that case, some portions of the whole social group will find their aims determined by an external dictation; their aims will not arise from the free growth of their own experience, and their nominal aims will be means to more ulterior ends of others rather than truly their own. . . .

In contrast with fulfilling some process in order that activity may go on, stands the static character of an end which is imposed from without the activity. It is always conceived of as fixed; it is *something* to be attained and possessed. When one has such a notion, activity is a mere unavoidable means to something else; it is not significant or important on its own account. As compared with the end it is but a necessary evil; something which must be gone through before one can reach the object which is alone worthwhile. In other words, the external idea of the aim leads to a separation of means from end, while an end which grows up within an activity as plan for its direction is always both ends and means, the distinction being only one of convenience. Every means is a temporary end until we have attained it. Every end becomes a means of carrying activity further as soon as it is achieved. We call it end when it marks off the future direction of the activity in which we are engaged; means when it marks off the present direction. Every divorce of end from means diminishes by that much the significance of the activity and tends to reduce it to a drudgery from which one would escape if he could. A farmer has to use plants and animals to carry on his farming activities. It certainly makes a great difference to his life whether he is fond of them, or whether he regards them merely as means which he has to employ to get something else in which alone he is interested. In the former case, his entire course of activity is significant; each phase of it has its own value. He has the experience of realising his end at every stage; the postponed aim, or end in view, being merely a sight ahead by which to keep his activity going fully and freely. For if he does not look ahead, he is more likely to find himself blocked. The aim is as definitely a *means* of action as is any other portion of an activity.

Applications in Education

There is nothing peculiar about educational aims. They are just like aims in any directed occupation. The educator, like the farmer, has certain things to do, certain resources with which to do, and certain obstacles with which to contend. The conditions with which the farmer deals, whether as obstacles or resources, have their own structure and operation independently of any purpose of his. Seeds sprout, rain falls, the sun shines, insects devour, blight comes, the seasons change. His aim is simply to utilise these various conditions; to make his activities and their energies work together, instead of against one another. It would be absurd if the farmer set up a purpose of farming, without any reference to these conditions of soil, climate, characteristic of plant growth, etc. His purpose is simply a foresight of the consequences of his energies connected with those of the things about him, a foresight used to direct his movements from day to day. Foresight of possible consequences leads to more careful and extensive observation of the nature and performances of the things he had to do with, and to laying out a plan — that is, of a certain order in the acts to be performed.

It is the same with the educator, whether parent or teacher. It is as absurd for the latter to set up their "own" aims as the proper objects of the growth of the children as it would be for the farmer to set up an ideal of farming irrespective of conditions. Aims mean acceptance of responsibility for the observations, anticipations, and arrangements required in carrying on a function — whether farming or educating. Any aim is of value so far as it assists observation, choice, and planning in carrying on activity from moment to moment and hour to hour; if it gets in the way of the individual's own commonsense (as it will surely do if imposed from without or accepted on authority) it does harm.

And it is well to remind ourselves that education as such has no aims. Only persons, parents, teachers, and so on, have aims, not an abstract idea like education. And consequently their purposes are indefinitely varied, differing with different children, changing as children grow and with the growth of experience on the part of the one who teaches. Even the most valid aims which can be put in words will, as words, do more harm than good unless one recognises that they are not aims, but rather suggestions to educators as to how to observe, how to look ahead, and how to choose in liberating and directing the energies of the concrete situations in which they find themselves. As a recent writer has said: "To lead this boy to read Scott's novel instead of old Sleuth's stories; to teach this girl to sew; to root out the habit of bullying from John's make-up; to prepare this class to study medicine — these are samples of the millions of aims we have actually before us in the concrete work of education."

Bearing these qualifications in mind, we shall proceed to state some of the characteristics found in all good educational aims. (1) An educational aim must be founded upon the intrinsic activities and needs (including original instincts and acquired habits) of the given individual to be educated. The tendency of such an aim as preparation is, as we have seen, to omit existing powers, and find the aim in some remote accomplishment or responsibility. In general, there is a disposition to take considerations which are dear to the heart of adults and set them up as ends irrespective of the capacities of those educated. There is also an inclination to propound aims which are so uniform as to neglect the specific powers and requirements of an individual, forgetting that all learning is something which happens to an individual at a given time and place. The larger range of perception of the adult is of great value in observing the abilities and weaknesses of the young, in deciding what they may amount to. Thus the artistic capacities of the adult exhibit what certain tendencies of the child are capable of; if we did not have the adult achievements we should be without assurance as to the significance of the drawing, reproducing, modelling, colouring activities of childhood. So if it were not for adult language, we should not be able to see the import of the babbling impulses of infancy. But it is one thing to use adult accomplishments as a context in which to place and survey the doings of childhood and youth; it is quite another to set them up as a fixed aim without regard to the concrete activities of those educated.

(2) An aim must be capable of translation into a method of co-operating with the activities of those undergoing instruction. It must suggest the kind of environment needed to liberate and to organise *their* capacities. Unless it lends itself to the construction of specific procedures, and unless these procedures test, correct, and amplify the aim, the latter is worthless. Instead of helping the specific task of teaching, it prevents the use of ordinary judgment in observing and sizing up the situation. It operates to exclude recognition of everything except what squares up with the fixed end in view. Every rigid aim just because it is rigidly given seems to render it unnecessary to give careful attention to concrete conditions. Since it *must* apply anyhow, what is the use of noting details which do not count?

The vice of externally imposed ends has deep roots. Teachers receive them from superior authorities; these authorities accept them from what is current in the community. The teachers impose them upon children. As a first consequence, the intelligence of the teacher is not free; it is confined to receiving the aims laid down from above. Too rarely is the individual teacher so free from the dictation of authoritative supervisor, textbook on methods, prescribed course of study, and so forth, that he can let his mind come to close quarters with the pupil's mind and the subject matter. This distrust of the teacher's experience is then reflected in lack of confidence in the responses of pupils. The latter receive their aims through a double or treble external imposition, and are constantly confused by the conflict between the aims which are natural to their own experience at the time and those in which they are taught to acqiesce. Until the democratic criterion of the intrinsic significance of every growing experience is recognised, we shall be intellectually confused by the demand for adaptation to external aims.

(3) Educators have to be on their guard against ends that are alleged to be general and ultimate. Every activity, however specific, is, of course, general in its ramified connections, for it leads out indefinitely into other things. So far as a general idea makes us more alive to these connections, it cannot be too general. But "general" also means "abstract", or detached from all specific context. And such abstractness means remoteness, and throws us back, once more, upon teaching and learning as mere means of getting ready for an end disconnected from the means. That education is literally and all the time its own reward means that no alleged study or discipline is educative unless it is worth while in its own immediate having.

A truly general aim broadens the outlook; it stimulates one to take more consequences (connections) into account. This means a wider and more flexible observation of means. The more interacting forces, for example, that the farmer takes into account, the more varied will be his immediate resources. He will see a greater number of possible starting places, and a greater number of ways of getting at what he wants to do. The fuller one's conception of possible future achievements, the less his present activity is tied down to a small number of alternatives. If one knew enough, one could start almost anywhere and sustain activities continuously and fruitfully.

Understanding, then, the term general or comprehensive aim simply in the sense of a broad survey of the field of present activities, we shall take up some of the larger ends which have currency in the educational theories of the day, and consider what light they throw upon the immediate concrete and diversified aims which are always the educator's real concern. We premise (as indeed immediately follows from what has been said) that there is no need to make a choice among them or regard them as competitors. When we come to act in a tangible way we have to select or choose a particular act at a particular time, but any number of comprehensive ends may exist without competition, since they mean simply different ways of looking at the same scene. One cannot climb a number of different mountains simultaneously, but the views had when different mountains are ascended supplement one another: they do not set up incompatible, competing worlds. Or, putting the matter in a slightly different way, one statement of an end may suggest certain questions and observations, and another statement another set of questions, calling for other observations. Then the more general ends we have, the better. One statement will emphasise what another slurs over. What a plurality of hypotheses does for the scientific investigator, a plurality of stated aims may do for the instructor.

Summary

An aim denotes the result of any natural process brought to consciousness and made a factor in determining present observation and choice of ways of acting. It signifies that an activity has become intelligent. Specifically it means foresight of the alternative consequences attendant upon acting in a given situation in different ways, and the use of what is anticipated to direct observation and experiment. A true aim is thus opposed at every point to an aim in which is imposed upon a process of action from without. The latter is fixed and rigid; it is not a stimulus to intelligence in the given situation, but is an externally dictated order to do such and such things. Instead of connecting directly with present activities, it is remote, divorced from the means by which it is to be reached. Instead of suggesting a freer and better balanced activity, it is a limit set to activity. In education, the currency of these externally imposed aims is resposible for the emphasis put upon the notion of preparation for a remote future and for rendering the work of both teacher and pupil mechanical and slavish.

Chapter XII: Thinking in Education

The Essentials of Method

No one doubts, theoretically, the importance of fostering in school good habits of thinking. But apart from the fact that the acknowledgment is not so great in practice as in theory, there is not adequate theoretical recognition that all which the school can or need do for pupils, so far as their *minds* are concerned (that is, leaving out certain specialised muscular abilities), is to develop their ability to think. The parcelling out of instruction among various ends such as acquisition of skill (in reading, spelling, writing, drawing, reciting); acquiring information (in history and geography), *and* training of thinking is a measure of the ineffective way in which we accomplish all three. Thinking which is not connected with increase of efficiency in action, and with learning more about ourselves and the world in which we live, has something the matter with it just as thought. And skill obtained apart from thinking is not connected with any sense of the purposes for which it is to be used. It consequently leaves a man at the mercy of his routine habits and of the authoritative control of others, who know what they are about and who are not especially scrupulous as to their means of achievement. And information severed from thoughtful action is dead, a mind-crushing load. Since it simulates knowledge and thereby develops the poison of conceit, it is a most powerful obstacle to further growth in the grace of intelligence. The sole direct path to enduring improvement in the methods of instruction and learning consists in centring upon the conditions which exact, promote, and test thinking. Thinking *is* the method of intelligent learning that employs and rewards the mind. We speak, legitimately enough, about the methods of thinking, but the important thing to bear in mind about method is that thinking is method, the method of intelligent experience in the course which it takes.

I. The initial stage of that developing experience which is called thinking is *experience*. This remark may sound like a silly truism. It ought to be one; but unfortunately it is not. On the contrary, thinking is often regarded both in philosophic theory and in educational practice as something cut off from experience, and capable of being cultivated in isolation. In fact, the inherent limitations of experience are often urged as the sufficient ground for attention to thinking. Experience is then thought to be confined to the senses and appetites; to a mere material world, while thinking proceeds from a higher faculty (of reason), and is occupied with spiritual or at least literary things. So, sometimes, a sharp distinction is made between pure mathematics as a peculiarly fit subject matter of thought (since it has nothing to do with physical existences) and applied mathematics, which has utilitarian but not mental value.

Speaking generally, the fundamental fallacy in methods of instruction lies in supposing that experience on the part of pupils may be assumed. What is here insisted upon is the necessity of an actual empirical situation as the initiating phase of thought. Experience is here taken as previously defined: trying to do something and having the thing perceptibly do something to one in return. The fallacy consists in supposing that we can begin with ready-made subject matter of arithmetic, or geography, or whatever, irrespective of some direct personal experience of a situation. Even the kindergarten and Montessori techniques are so anxious to get at intellectual distinctions, without "waste of time", that they tend to ignore — or reduce — the immediate crude handling of the familiar material of experience, and to introduce pupils at once to material which expresses the intellectual distinctions which adults have made. But the first stage of contact with any new material, at whatever age of maturity, must inevitably be of the trial and error sort. An individual must actually try, in play or work, to do something with material in carrying out his own impulsive activity, and then note the interaction of his energy and that of the material employed. This is what happens when a child at first begins to build with blocks, and it is equally what happens when a scientific man in his laboratory begins to experiment with unfamiliar objects.

Hence the first approach to any subject in school, if thought is to be aroused and not words acquired, should be as unscholastic as possible. To realise what an experience, or empirical situation, means, we have to call to mind the sort of situation that presents itself outside of school; the sort of occupations that interest and engage activity in ordinary life. And careful inspection of methods which are permanently successful in formal education, whether in arithmetic or learning to read, or studying geography, or learning physics or a foreign language, will reveal that they depend for their efficiency upon the fact that they go back to the type of the situation which causes reflection out of school in ordinary life. They give the pupils something to do, not something to learn, and the doing is of such a nature as to demand thinking, or the intentional noting of connections; learning naturally results.

That the situation should be of such a nature as to arouse thinking means of course that it should suggest something to do which is not either routine or capricious — something, in other words, presenting what is new (and hence uncertain or problematic) and yet sufficiently connected with existing habits to call out an effective response. An effective response means one which accomplishes a perceptible result, in distinction from a purely haphazard activity, where the consequences cannot be mentally connected with what is done. The most significant question which can be asked, accordingly, about any situation or experience proposed to induce learning is what quality of problem it involves.

At first thought, it might seem as if usual school methods measured well up to the standard here set. The giving of problems, the putting of questions, the assigning of tasks, the magnifying of difficulties, is a large part of schoolwork. But it is indispensible to discriminate between genuine and simulated or mock problems. The following questions may aid in making such discrimination. (1) Is there anything *but* a problem? Does the question naturally suggest itself within some situation of personal experience? Or is it an aloof thing, a problem only for the purposes of conveying instruction in some school topic? Is it the sort of trying that would arouse observation and engage experimentation outside of school? (2) Is it the pupil's own problem, or is it the teacher's or textbook's problem, made a problem for the pupil only because he cannot get the required mark or be promoted or win the teacher's approval, unless he deals with it? Obviously, these two questions overlap. They are two ways of getting at the same point: Is the experience a personal thing of such a nature as inherently to stimulate and direct observation of the connections involved, and to lead to inference and its testing? Or is it imposed from without, and is the pupil's problem simply to meet the external requirement?

Such questions may give us pause in deciding upon the extent to which current practices are adapted to develop reflective habits. The physical equipment and arrangements of the average schoolroom are hostile to the existence of real situations of experience. What is there similar to the conditions of everyday life which will generate difficulties? Almost everything testifies to the great premium put upon listening, reading, and the reproduction of what is told and read. It is hardly possible to overstate the contrast between such conditions and the situations of active contact with things and persons in the home, on the playground, in fulfilling of ordinary responsibilities of life. Much of it is not even comparable with the questions which may arise in the mind of a boy or girl in conversing with others or in reading books outside of the school. No one has ever explained why children are so full of questions outside of the school (so that they pester grown-up persons if they get any encouragement), and the conspicuous absence of display of curiosity about the subject matter of school lessons. Reflection on this striking contrast will throw light upon the question of how far customary school conditions supply a context of experience in which problems naturally suggest themselves. No amount of improvement in the personal technique of the instructor will wholly remedy this state of things. There must be more actual material, more *stuff*, more appliances, and more opportunities for doing things, before the gap can be overcome. And where children are engaged in doing things and in discussing what arises in the course of their doing, it is found, even with comparatively indifferent modes of instruction, that children's inquiries are spontaneous and numerous, and the proposals of solution advanced, varied, and ingenious.

As a consequence of the absence of the materials and occupations which generate real problems, the pupil's problems are not his; or, rather, they are his *only as* a pupil, not as a human being. Hence the lamentable waste in carrying over such expertness as is achieved in dealing with them to the affairs of life beyond the schoolroom. A pupil has a problem, but it is the problem of meeting the peculiar requirements set by the teacher. His problem becomes that of finding out what the teacher wants, what will satisfy the teacher in recitation and examination and outward deportment. Relationship to subject matter is no longer direct. The occasions and material of thought are not found in the arithmetic or the history or geography itself, but in skilfully adapting that material to the teacher's requirements. The pupil studies, but unconsciously to himself the objects of his study are the conventions and standards of the school system and school authority, not the nominal "studies". The thinking thus evoked is artificially onesided at the best. At its worst, the problem of the pupil is not how to meet the requirements of school life, but how to *seem* to meet them — or, how to come near enough to meeting them to slide along without an undue amount of friction. The type of judgment formed by these devices is not a desirable addition to character. If these statements give too highly coloured a picture of usual school methods, the exaggeration may at least serve to illustrate the point: the need of active pursuits, involving the use of material to accomplish purposes, if there are to be situations which normally generate problems occasioning thoughtful inquiry.

II. There must be *data* at command to supply the considerations required in dealing with the specific difficulty which has presented itself. Teachers following a "developing" method sometimes tell children to think things out for themselves as if they could spin them out of their own heads. The material of thinking is not thoughts, but actions, facts, events, and the relations of things. In other words, to think effectively one must have had, or now have, experiences which will furnish him resources for coping with the difficulty at hand. A difficulty is an indispensable stimulus to thinking, but not all difficulties call out thinking. Sometimes they overwhelm and submerge and discourage. The perplexing situation must be sufficiently like situations which have already been dealt with so that pupils will have some control of the means of handling it. A large part of the art of instruction lies in making the difficulty of new problems large enough to challenge thought, and small enough so that, in addition to the confusion naturally attending the novel elements, there shall be luminous familiar spots from which helpful suggestions may spring.

In one sense, it is a matter of indifference by what psychological means the subject matter for reflection is provided. Memory, observation, reading, communication, are all avenues for supplying data. The relative proportion to be obtained from each is a matter of the specific features of the particular problem in hand. It is foolish to insist upon observation of objects presented to the senses if the student is so familiar with the objects that he could just as well recall the facts independently. It is possible to induce undue and crippling dependence upon sense presentations. No one can carry around with him a museum of all the things whose properties will assist the conduct of thought. A well-trained mind is one that has a maximum of resources behind it, so to speak, and that is accustomed to go over its past experience to see what they yield. On the other hand, a quality or relation of even a familiar object may previously have been passed over, and be just the fact that is helpful in dealing with the question. In this case direct observation is called for. The same principle applies to the use to be made of observation on one hand and of reading and "telling" on the other. Direct observation is naturally more vivid and vital. But it has its limitations; and in any case it is a necessary part of education that one should acquire the ability to supplement the narrowness of his immediately personal experiences by utilising the experiences of others. Excessive reliance upon others for data (whether got from reading or listening) is to be depreciated. Most objectionable of all is the probability that others, the book or the teacher, will supply solutions ready-made, instead of giving material that the student has to adapt and apply to the question in hand for himself.

There is no inconsistency in saying that in schools there is usually both too much and too little information supplied by others. The accumulation and acquisition of information for purposes of reproduction in recitation and examination is made too much of. "Knowledge", in the sense of information, means the working capital, the indispensable resources, of further enquiry; of finding out, or learning, more things. Frequently it is treated as an end itself, and then the goal becomes to heap it up and display it when called for. The static, cold-storage ideal of knowledge is inimical to educative development. It not only lets occasions for thinking go unused, but it swamps thinking. No one could construct a house on ground cluttered with miscellaneous junk. Pupils who have stored their "minds" with all kinds of material which they have never put to intellectual uses are sure to be hampered when they try to think. They have no practice in selecting what is appropriate, and no criterion to go by; everything is on the same dead static level. On the other hand, it is quite open to question whether, if information actually functioned in experience through use in application to the student's own purposes, there would not be need of more varied resources in books, pictures, and talks than are usually at command.

III. The correlate in thinking of facts, data, knowledge already acquired, is suggestions, inferences, conjectured meanings, suppositions, tentative explanations — *ideas*, in short. Careful observation and recollection determine what is given, what is already there, and hence assured. They cannot furnish what is lacking. They define, clarify, and locate the question, they cannot supply its answer. Projection, invention, ingenuity, devising come in for that purpose. The data *arouse* suggestions, and only by reference to the specific data can we pass upon the appropriateness of the suggestions. But the suggestions run beyond what is, as yet, actually *given* in experience. They forecast possible results, things *to* do, not facts (things already done). Inference is always an invasion of the unknown, a leap from the known.

In this sense, a thought (what a thing suggests but is not as it is presented) is creative — an incursion into the novel. It involves some inventiveness. What is suggested must, indeed, be familiar in *some* context; the novelty, the inventive devising, clings to the new light in which it is seen, the different use to which it is put. When Newton thought of his theory of gravitation, the creative aspect of his thought was not found in its materials. They were familiar; many of them commonplaces — sun, moon, planets, weight, distance, mass, square of numbers. These were not original ideas; they were established facts. His originality lay in the *use* to which these familiar acquaintances were put by introduction into an unfamiliar context. The same is true of every striking scientific discovery, every great invention, every admirable artistic production. Only silly folk identify creative originality with the extraordinary and fanciful; others recognise that its measure lies in putting everyday things to uses which had not occurred to others. The operation is novel, not the materials out of which it is constructed.

The educational conclusion which follows is that *all* thinking is original in a projection of considerations which have not been previously apprehended. The child of three who discovers what can be done with blocks, or of six who finds out what he can make by putting five cents and five cents together, is really a discoverer, even though everybody else in the world knows it. There is a genuine increment of experience; not another item mechanically added on, but enrichment by a new quality. The charm which the spontaneity of little children has for sympathetic observers is due to perception of this intellectual originality. The joy which children themselves experience is the joy of intellectual constructiveness — of creativeness, if the word may be used without misunderstanding.

The educational moral I am chiefly concerned to draw is not, however, that teachers would find their own work less of a grind and strain if school conditions favoured learning in the sense of discovery and not in that of storing away what others pour into them; nor that it would be possible to give even children and youth the delights of personal intellectual productiveness — true and important as are these things. It is that no thought, no idea, can possibly be conveyed as an idea from one person to another. When it is told, it is, to the one to whom it is told, another given fact, not an idea. The communication may stimulate the other person to realise the question for himself and to think out a like idea, or it may smother his intellectual interest and suppress his dawning effort at thought. But what he *directly* gets cannot be an idea. Only by wrestling with the conditions of the problem at first hand, seeking and finding his own way out, does he think. When the parent or teacher has provided the conditions which stimulate thinking and has taken a sympathetic attitude toward the activities of the learner by entering into a common or conjoint experience, all has been done which a second party can do to instigate learning. The rest lies with the one directly concerned. If he cannot devise his own solution (not of course in isolation, but in correspondence with the teacher and other pupils) and find his own way out he will not learn, not even if he can recite some correct answer with one hundred per cent accuracy. We can and do supply ready-made "ideas" by the thousand; we do not usually take many pains to see that the one learning engages in significant situations where his own activities generate, support, and clinch ideas — that is, perceived meanings or connections. This does not mean that the teacher is to stand off and look on; the alternative to furnishing ready-made subject matter and listening to the accuracy with which it is reproduced is not quiescence, but participation, sharing, in an activity. In such shared activity, the teacher is a learner, and the learner is, without knowing it, a teacher — and upon the whole, the less consciousness there is, on either side, of either giving or receiving instruction, the better.

IV. Ideas, as we have seen, whether they be humble guesses or dignified theories, are anticipations of possible solutions. They are anticipations of some continuity or connection of an activity and a consequence which has not as yet shown itself. They are therefore tested by the operation of acting upon them. They are to guide and organise further observations, recollections, and experiments. They are intermediate in learning, not final. All educational reformers, as we have had occasion to remark, are given to attacking the passivity of traditional education. They have opposed pouring in from without, and absorbing like a sponge; they have attacked drilling in material as into hard and resisting rock. But it is not easy to secure conditions which will make the getting of an idea identical with having an experience which widens and makes more precise our contact with the environment. Activity, even self-activity, is too easily thought of as something merely mental, cooped up within the head, or finding expression only through the vocal organs.

While the need for application of ideas gained in study is acknowledged by all the more successful methods of instruction, the exercises in application are sometimes treated as devices for *fixing* what has already been learned and for getting greater practical skill in its manipulation. These results are genuine and not to be despised. But practice in applying what has been gained in study ought primarily to have an intellectual quality. As we have already seen, thoughts just as thoughts are incomplete. At best they are tentative; they are suggestions, indications. They are standpoints and methods for dealing with situations of experience. Till they are applied in these situations they lack full point and reality. Only application tests them, and only testing confers full meaning and a sense of their reality. Short of use made of them, they tend to segregate into a peculiar world of their own. It may be seriously questioned whether the philosophies which isolate mind and set it over against the world did not have their origin in the fact that the reflective or theoretical class of men elaborated a large stock of ideas which social conditions did not allow them to act upon and test. Consequently men were thrown back into their own thoughts as ends in themselves.

However this may be, there can be no doubt that a peculiar artificiality attaches to much of what is learned in schools. It can hardly be said that many students consciously think of the subject matter as unreal; but it assuredly does not possess for them the kind of reality which the subject matter of their vital experiences possesses. They learn not to expect that sort of reality of it; they become habituated to treating it as having reality for the purposes of recitations, lessons, and examinations. That it should remain inert for the experiences of daily life is more or less a matter of course. The bad effects are twofold. Ordinary experience does not receive the enrichment which it should; it is not fertilised by school learning. And the attitudes which spring from getting used to and accepting half-understood and ill-digested material weaken vigour and efficiency of thought.

If we have dwelt especially on the negative side, it is for the sake of suggesting positive measures adapted to the effectual development of thought. Where schools are equipped with laboratories, shops, and gardens, where dramatisations, plays, and games are freely used, opportunities exist for reproducing situations of life, and for acquiring and applying information and ideas in the carrying forward of progressive experience. Ideas are not segregated, they do not form an isolated island. They animate and enrich the ordinary course of life. Information is vitalised by its function; by the place it occupies in direction of action.

The phrase "opportunities exist" is used purposely. They may not be taken advantage of; it is possible to employ manual and constructive activities in a physical way, as means of getting just bodily skill; or they may be used almost exclusively for "utilitarian", that is, pecuniary, ends. But the disposition on the part of upholders of "cultural" education to assume that such activities are merely physical or professional in quality, is itself a product of the philosophies which isolate mind from direction of the course of experience and hence from action upon and with things. When the "mental" is regarded as a self-contained separate realm, a counterpart fate befalls bodily activity and movements. They are regarded as at the best mere external annexes to mind. They may be necessary for the satisfaction of bodily needs and the attainment of external decency and comfort, but they do not occupy a necessary place in mind nor enact an indispensable role in the completion of thought. Hence they have no place in a liberal education — that is, one which is concerned with the interests of intelligence. If they come in at all, it is as a concession to the material needs of the masses. That they should be allowed to invade the education of the élite is unspeakable. This conclusion follows irresistibly from the isolated conception of mind, but by the same logic it disappears when we perceive what mind really is — namely, the purposive and directive factor in the development of experience.

While it is desirable that all educational institutions should be equipped so as to give students an opportunity for acquiring and testing ideas and information in active pursuits typifying important social situations, it will, doubtless, be a long time before all of them are thus furnished. But this state of affairs does not afford instructors an excuse for folding their hands and persisting in methods which segregate school knowledge. Every recitation in every subject gives an opportunity for establishing cross connections between the subject matter of the lesson and the wider and more direct experiences of everyday life. Classroom instruction falls into three kinds. The least desirable treats each lesson as an independent whole. It does not put upon the student the responsibility of finding points of contact between it and other lessons in the same subject, or other subjects of study. Wiser teachers see to it that the student is systematically led to utilise his earlier lessons to help understand the present one, and also to use the present to throw additional light upon what has already been acquired. Results are better, but school subject matter is still isolated. Save by accident, out-of-school experience is left in its crude and comparatively irreflective state. It is not subject to the refining and expanding influences of the more accurate and comprehensive material of direct instruction. The latter is not motivated and impregnated with a sense of reality by being intermingled with the realities of everyday life. The best type of teaching bears in mind the desirability of affecting this inter-connection. It puts the student in the habitual attitude of finding points of contact and mutual bearings.

Summary

Processes of instruction are unified in the degree in which they centre in the production of good habits of thinking. While we may speak, without error, of the method of thought, the important thing is that thinking is the method of an educative experience. The essentials of method are therefore identical with the essentials of reflection. They are, first, that the pupil have a genuine situation or experience — that there be a continuous activity in which he is interested for its own sake; secondly, that a genuine problem develop within this situation as a stimulus to thought; third, that he possess the information and make the observations needed to deal with it; fourth, that suggested solutions occur to him which he shall be responsible for developing in an orderly way; fifth that he have opportunity and occasion to test his ideas by application, to make their meaning clear and to discover for himself their validity.

Chapter XIV: The Nature of Subject Matter

Subject Matter of Educator and of Learner

So far as the nature of subject matter in principle is concerned, there is nothing to add to what has been said. It consists of the facts observed, recalled, read, and talked about, and the ideas suggested, in course of the development of a situation having a purpose. This statement needs to be rendered more specific by connecting it with the materials of school instruction, the studies which make up the curriculum. What is the significance of our definition in application to reading, writing, mathematics, history, nature study, drawing, singing, physics, chemistry, modern and foreign languages, and so on?

Let us recur to two of the points made earlier in our discussion. The educator's part in the enterprise of education is to furnish the environment which stimulates responses and directs the learner's course. In the last analysis, *all* that the educator can do is modify stimuli so that response will as surely as is possible result in the formation of desirable intellectual and emotional dispositions. Obviously studies or the subject matter of the curriculum have intimately to do with this business of supplying an environment. The other point is the necessity for a social environment to give meaning to habits formed. In what we have termed informal education, subject matter is carried directly in the matrix of social intercourse. It is what the persons with whom an individual associates do and say. This fact gives a clue to the understanding of the subject matter of formal or deliberate instruction.

A connecting link is found in the stories, traditions, songs, and liturgies which accompany the doings and rites of a primitive social group. They represent the stock of meanings which have been precipitated out of previous experience, which are so prized by the group as to be identified with their conception of their own collective life. Not being obviously a part of the skill exhibited in the daily occupations of eating, hunting, making war and peace, constructing rugs, pottery, baskets, and so forth, they are consciously impressed upon the young; often, as in the initiation ceremonies, with intense emotional fervour. Even more pains are consciously taken to perpetuate the myths, legends, and sacred verbal formulae of the group than to transmit the directly useful customs of the group just because they cannot be picked up, as the latter can be in the ordinary processes of association.

As the social group grows more complex, involving a greater number of acquired skills which are dependent, either in fact or in the belief of the group, upon standard ideas deposited from past experience, the content of social life gets more definitely formulated for purposes of instruction. As we have previously noted, probably the chief motive for consciously dwelling upon the group life, extracting the meanings which are regarded as most important and systematising them in a coherent arrangement, is just the need of instructing the young so as to perpetuate group life. Once started on this road of selection, formulation, and organisation, no definite limit exists. The invention of writing and of printing gives the operation an immense impetus. Finally, the bonds which connect the subject matter of school study with the habits and ideas of the social group are disguised and covered up. The ties are so loosened that it often appears as if there were none; as if subject matter existed simply as knowledge on its own independent behalf, and as if study were the mere act of mastering it for its own sake, irrespective of any social values. Since it is highly important for practical reasons to counteract this tendency, the chief purposes of our theoretical discussion are to make clear the connection which is so readily lost from sight, and to show in some detail the social content and function of the chief constituents of the course of study.

The points need to be considered from the standpoint of instructor and of student. To the former, the significance of a knowledge of subject matter, going far beyond the present knowledge of pupils, is to supply definite standards and to reveal to him the possibilities of the crude activities of the immature. *(i)* The material of school studies translates into concrete and detailed terms the meanings of current social life which it is desirable to transmit. It puts clearly before the instructor the essential ingredients of the culture to be perpetuated, in such an organised form as to protect him from the haphazard efforts he would be likely to indulge in if the meanings had not been standardised. *(ii)* A knowledge of the ideas which have been achieved in the past as the outcome of activity places the educator in a position to perceive the meaning of the seeming impulsive and aimless reactions of the young, and to provide the stimuli needed to direct them so that they will amount to something. The more the educator knows of music the more he can perceive the possibilities of the inchoate musical impulses of a child. Organised subject matter represents the ripe fruitage of experiences like theirs, experiences involving the same world and powers and needs similar to theirs. It does not represent perfection or infallible wisdom; but it is the best at command to further new experiences which may, in some respects at least, surpass the achievements embodied in existing knowledge and works of art.

From the standpoint of the educator, in other words, the various studies represent working resources, available capital. Their remoteness from the experience of the young is not, however, seeming; it is real. The subject matter of the learner is not, therefore, it cannot be, identical with the formulated, the crystallised, and systematised subject matter of the adult; the material as found in books and in works of art, and so forth. The latter represents the *possibilities* of the former; not its existing state. It enters directly into the activities of the expert and the educator, not into that of the beginner, the learner. Failure to bear in mind the difference in subject matter from the respective standpoints of teacher and student is responsible for most of the mistakes made in the use of texts and other expressions of pre-existent knowledge.

The need for a knowledge of the constitution and functions, in the concrete, of human nature is great just because the teacher's attitude to subject matter is so different from that of the pupil. The teacher presents in actuality what the pupil represents only in *posse*. That is, the teacher already knows the things which the student is only learning. Hence the problem of the two is radically unlike. When engaged in the direct act of teaching, the instructor needs to have subject matter at his fingers' ends; his attention should be upon the attitude and response of the pupil. To understand the latter in its interplay with subject matter is his task, while the pupil's mind, naturally, should be not on itself but on the topic in hand. Or to state the same point in a somewhat different manner: the teacher should be occupied not with subject matter in itself but in its interaction with the pupil's present needs and capacities. Hence simple scholarship is not enough. In fact, there are certain features of scholarship or mastered subject matter — taken by itself — which get in the way of effective teaching *unless* the instructor's habitual attitude is one of concern with its interplay in the pupil's own experience. In the first place, his knowledge extends indefinitely beyond the range of the pupil's acquaintance. It involves principles which are beyond the immature pupil's understanding and interest. In and of itself, it may no more represent the living world of the pupil's experience than the astronomer's knowledge of Mars represents a baby's acquaintance with the room in which he stays. In the second place, the method of organisation of the material of achieved scholarship differs from that of the beginner. It is not true that the experience of the young is unorganised — that it consists of isolated scraps. But it is organised in connection with direct practical centres of interest. The child's home is, for example, the organising centre of his geographical knowledge. His own movements about the locality, his journeys abroad, the tales of his friends, give the ties which hold his items of information together. But the geography of the geographer, of the one who has already developed the implications of these smaller experiences, is organised on the basis of the relationship which the various facts bear to one another — not the relations which they bear to his house, bodily movements, and friends. To the one who is learned, subject matter is extensive, accurately defined, and logically interrelated. To the one who is learning, it is fluid, partial, and connected through his personal occupations. The problem of teaching is to keep the experience of the student moving in the direction of what the expert already knows. Hence the need that the teacher know both subject matter and the characteristic needs and capacities of the student. . . .

Summary

The subject matter of education consists primarily of the meanings which supply content to existing social life. The continuity of social life means that many of these meanings are contributed to present activity by past collective experience. As social life grows more complex, these factors increase in number and import. There is need for special selection, formulation, and organisation in order that they may be adequately transmitted to the new generation. But this very process tends to set up subject matter as something of value just by itself, apart from its function in promoting the realisation of the meanings implied in the present experience of the immature. Especially is the educator exposed to the temptation to conceive his task in terms of the pupil's ability to appropriate and reproduce the subject matter in set statements, irrespective of its organisation into his activities as a developing social member. The positive principle is maintained when the young begin with active occupations having a social origin and use, and proceed to a scientific insight in the materials and laws involved, through assimilating into their more direct experience the ideas and facts communicated by others who have had a larger experience.

Chapter XVIII: Educational Values

The Valuation of Studies

The theory of educational values involves not only an account of the nature of appreciation as fixing the measure of subsequent valuations, but an account of the specific directions in which these valuations occur. To value means primarily to prize, to esteem; but secondarily it means to apprise, to estimate. It means, that is, the act of cherishing something, holding it dear, and also the act of passing judgment upon the nature and amount of its value as compared with something else. To value in the latter sense is to valuate or evaluate. The distinction coincides with that sometimes made between intrinsic and instrumental values. Intrinsic values are not objects of judgment, they cannot (as intrinsic) be compared, or regarded as greater and less, better or worse. They are invaluable; and if a thing is invaluable, it is neither more nor less so than any other invaluable. But occasions present themselves when it is necessary to choose, when we must let one thing go in order to take another. This establishes an order of preference, a greater and less, better and worse. Things judged or passed upon have to be estimated in relation to some third thing, some further end. With respect to that, they are means, or instrumental values.

We may imagine a man who at one time thoroughly enjoys converse with his friends, at another the hearing of a symphony; at another the eating of his meals; at another the reading of a book; at another the earning of money, and so on. As an appreciative realisation, each of these is an intrinsic value. It occupies a particular place in life; it serves its own end, which cannot be supplied by a substitute. There is no question of comparative value, and hence none of valuation. Each is the specific good which it is, and that is all that can be said. In its own place, none is a means to anything beyond itself. But there may arise a situation in which they compete or conflict, in which a choice has to be made. Now comparison comes in. Since a choice has to be made, we want to know the respective claims of each competitor. What is to be said for it? What does it offer in comparison with, as balanced over against, some other possibility? Raising these questions means that a particular good is no longer an end in itself, an intrinsic good. For if it were, its claims would be incomparable, imperative. The question is now as to its status as a means of realising something else, which is then the invaluable of *that* situation. If a man has just eaten, or if he is well fed generally and the opportunity to hear music is a rarity, he will probably prefer the music to eating. In the given situation that will render the greater contribution. If he is starving, or if he is satiated with music for the time being, he will naturally judge food to have the greater worth. In the abstract or at large, apart from the needs of a particular situation in which choice has to be made there is no such thing as degrees or order of value.

Certain conclusions follow with respect to educational values. We cannot establish a hierarchy of values among studies. It is futile to attempt to arrange them in an order, beginning with one having least worth and going on to that of maximum value. In so far as any study has a unique or irreplaceable function in experience, in so far as it marks a characteristic enrichment of life, its worth is intrinsic or incomparable. Since education is not a means to living, but is identical with the operation of living a life which is fruitful and inherently significant, the only ultimate value which can be set up is just the process of living itself. And this is not an end to which studies and activities are subordinate means; it is the whole of which they are ingredients. And what has been said about appreciation means that every study in one of its aspects ought to have just such ultimate significance. It is as true of arithmetic as it is of poetry that in some place and at some time it ought to be a good to be appreciated on its own account — just as an enjoyable experience, in short. If it is not, then when the time and place come for it to be used as a means of instrumentality, it will be in just that much handicapped. Never having been realised or appreciated for itself, one will miss something of its capacity as a resource for other ends.

It equally follows that when we compare studies as to their values, that is, treat them as means to something beyond themselves, that which controls their proper valuation is found in the specific situation, in which they are to be used. The way to enable a student to apprehend the instrumental value of arithmetic is not to lecture him upon the benefit it will be to him in some remote and uncertain future, but to let him discover that success in something he is interested in doing depends upon ability to use number.

It also follows that the attempt to distribute distinct sorts of value among different studies is a misguided one, in spite of the amount of time recently devoted to the undertaking. Science for example may have *any* kind of value, depending upon the situation into which it enters as a means. To some the value of science may be military; it may be an instrument in strengthening means of offence or defence; it may be technological, a tool for engineering; or it may be commercial — an aid in the successful conduct of business; under other conditions, its worth may be philanthropic — the service it renders in relieving human suffering; or again it may be quite conventional — of value in establishing one's social status as an "educated" person. As a matter of fact, science serves all these purposes, and it would be an arbitrary task to try to fix upon one of them as its "real" end. All that we can be sure of educationally is that science should be taught so as to be an end in itself in the lives of students — something worth while on account of its own unique intrinsic contribution to the experience of life. Primarily it must have "appreciation value". If we take something which seems to be at the opposite pole, like poetry, the same sort of statement applies. It may be that, at the present time, its chief value is the contribution it makes to the enjoyment of leisure. But that may represent a degenerate condition rather than anything necessary. Poetry has historically been allied with religion and morals; it has served the purpose of penetrating the mysterious depths of things. It has had an enormous patriotic value. Homer to the Greeks was a Bible, a textbook of morals, a history, and a national inspiration. In any case, it may be said that education which does not succeed in making poetry a resource in the business of life as well as in its leisure, has something the matter with it — or else the poetry is artificial poetry.

The same considerations apply to the value of a study or a topic of a study with reference to its motivating force. Those responsible for planning and teaching the course of study should have grounds for thinking that the studies and topics included furnish both direct increments to the enriching of lives of the pupils and also materials which they can put to use in other concerns of direct interest. Since the curriculum is always getting loaded down with purely inherited traditional matter and with subjects which represent mainly the energy of some influential person or group of persons in behalf of something dear to them, it requires constant inspection, criticism, and revision to make sure it is accomplishing its purpose. Then there is always the probability that it represents the values of adults rather than those of children and youth, or those of pupils a generation ago rather than those of the present day. Hence a further need for a critical outlook and survey. But these considerations do not mean that for a subject to have motivating value to a pupil (whether intrinsic or instrumental) is the same thing as for him to be aware of the value, or to be able to tell what the study is good for.

In the first place, as long as any topic makes an immediate appeal, it is not necessary to ask what it is good for. This is a question which can be asked only about instrumental values. Some goods are not good *for* anything; they are just goods. Any other notion leads to an absurdity. For we cannot stop asking the question about an instrumental good, one whose value lies in its being good *for* something, unless there is at some point something intrinsically good, good for itself. To a hungry, healthy child, food is a good of the situation; we do not have to bring him to consciousness of the ends subserved by food in order to supply a motive to eat. The food in connection with his appetite *is* a motive. The same thing holds of mentally eager pupils with respect to many topics. Neither they nor the teacher could possibly foretell with any exactness the purposes learning is to accomplish in the future; nor as long as the eagerness continues is it advisable to try to specify particular goods which are to come of it. The proof of a good is found in the fact that the pupil responds; his response *is* use. His response to the material shows that the subject functions in his life. It is unsound to urge that, say, Latin has a value *per se* in the abstract, just as a study, as a sufficient justification for teaching it. But it is equally absurd to argue that unless teacher or pupil can point out some definite assignable future use to which it is to be put, it lacks justifying value. When pupils are genuinely concerned in learning Latin, that is of itself proof that it possesses value. The most which one is entitled to ask in such cases is whether in view of the shortness of time, there are not other things of intrinsic value which in addition have greater instrumental value.

This brings us to the matter of instrumental values — topics studied because of some end beyond themselves. If a child is ill and his appetite does not lead him to eat when food is presented, or if his appetite is perverted so that he prefers candy to meat and vegetables, conscious reference to results is indicated. He needs to be made conscious of consequences as a justification of the positive or negative value of certain objects. Or the state of things may be normal enough, and yet an individual not be moved by some matter because he does not grasp how his attainment of some intrinsic good depends upon active concern with what is presented. In such cases, it is obviously the part of wisdom to establish consciousness of connection. In general what is desirable is that a topic be presented in such a way that it either have an immediate value, and require no justification, or else be perceived to be a means of achieving something of intrinsic value. An instrumental value then has the intrinsic value of being a means to an end.

It may be questioned whether some of the present pedagogical interest in the matter of values of studies is not either excessive or else too narrow. Sometimes it appears to be a laboured effort to furnish an apologetic for topics which no longer operate to any purpose, direct or indirect, in the lives of pupils. At other times, the reaction against useless lumber seems to have gone to the extent to supposing that no subject or topic should be taught unless some quite definite future utility can be pointed out by those making the course of study or by the pupil himself, unmindful of the fact that life is its own excuse for being; and that definite utilities which can be pointed out are themselves justified only because they increase the experienced content of life itself. . . .

Chapter XXVI: Theories of Morals

Intelligence and Character

A noteworthy paradox often accompanies discussion of morals. On the one hand, there is an identification of the moral with the rational. Reason is set up as a faculty from which proceed ultimate moral intuitions, and sometimes, as in the Kantian theory, it is said to supply the only proper moral motive. On the other hand, the value of concrete, everyday intelligence is constantly underestimated, and even deliberately depreciated. Morals are often thought to be an affair with which ordinary knowledge has nothing to do. Moral knowledge is thought to be a thing apart, and conscience is thought of as something radically different from consciousness. This separation, if valid, is of especial significance for education. Moral education in school is practically hopeless when we set up the development of character as a supreme end, and at the same time treat the acquiring of knowledge and the development of understanding, which of necessity occupy the chief part of school time, as having nothing to do with character. On such a basis, moral education is inevitably reduced to some kind of catechetical instruction, or lessons about morals. Lessons "about morals" signify as matter of course lessons in what other people think about virtues and duties. It amounts to something only in the degree in which pupils happen to be already animated by a sympathetic and dignified regard for the sentiments of others. Without such a regard, it has no more influence on character than information about the mountains of Asia; with a servile regard, it increases dependence upon others, and throws upon those in authority the responsibility for conduct. As a matter of fact, direct instruction in morals has been effective only in social groups where it was a part of the authoritative control of the many by the few. Not the teaching as such but the reinforcement of it by the whole regime of which it was an incident made it effective. To attempt to get similar results from lessons about morals in a democratic society is to rely upon sentimental magic.

At the other end of the scale stands the Socratic-Platonic teaching which identifies knowledge and virtue — which holds that no man does evil knowingly but only because of ignorance of the good. This doctrine is commonly attacked on the ground that nothing is more common than for a man to know the good and yet do the bad: not knowledge, but habituation or practice, and motive are what is required. Aristotle, in fact, at once attacked the Platonic teaching on the ground that moral virtue is like an art, such as medicine; the experienced practitioner is better than a man who has theoretical knowledge but no practical experience of disease and remedies. The issue turns, however, upon what is meant by knowledge. Aristotle's objection ignored the gist of Plato's teaching to the effect that man could not attain a theoretical insight into the good except as he had passed through years of practical habituation and strenuous discipline. Knowledge of the good was not a thing to be got either from books or from others, but was achieved through a prolonged education. It was the final and culminating grace of a mature experience of life. Irrespective of Plato's position, it is easy to perceive that the term knowledge is used to denote things as far apart as intimate and vital personal realisation — a conviction gained and tested in experience — and a second-handed, largely symbolic, recognition that persons in general believe so and so — a devitalised remote information. That the latter does not guarantee conduct, that it does not profoundly affect character, goes without saying. But if knowledge means something of the same sort as our conviction gained by trying and testing that sugar is sweet and quinine bitter, the case stands otherwise. Every time a man sits on a chair rather than on a stove, carries an umbrella when it rains, consults a doctor when ill — or in short performs any of the thousand acts which make up his daily life, he proves that knowledge of a certain kind finds issue in conduct. There is every reason to suppose that the same sort of knowledge of good has a like expression; in fact "good" is an empty term unless it includes the satisfactions experienced in such situations as those mentioned. Knowledge that other persons are supposed to know something might lead one to act so as to win the approbation others attach to certain actions, or at least so as to give others the impression that one agrees with them; there is no reason why it should lead to personal initiative and loyalty on behalf of the beliefs attributed to them.

It is not necessary, accordingly, to dispute about the proper meaning of the term knowledge. It is enough for educational purposes to note the different qualities covered by the one name, to realise that it is knowledge gained at first hand through the exigencies of experience which affects conduct in significant ways. If a pupil learns things from books simply in connection with school lessons and for the sake of reciting what he has learned when called upon, then knowledge will have effect upon *some* conduct — namely upon that of reproducing statements at the demand of others. There is nothing surprising that such "knowledge" should not have much influence in the life out of school. But this is not a reason for making a divorce between knowledge and conduct, but for holding in low esteem this kind of knowledge. The same thing may be said of knowledge which relates merely to an isolated and technical speciality; it modifies action but only in its own narrow line. In truth, the problem of moral education in the schools is one with the problem of securing knowledge — the knowledge connected with the system of impulses and habits. For the use to which any known fact is put depends upon its connections. The knowledge of dynamite of a safe-cracker may be identical in verbal form with that of a chemist; in fact, it is different, for it is knit into connection with different aims and habits, and thus has a different import.

Our prior discussion of subject matter as proceeding from direct activity having an immediate aim, to the enlargement of meaning found in geography and history, and then to scientifically organised knowledge, was based upon the idea of maintaining a vital connection between knowledge and activity. What is learned and employed in an occupation having an aim and involving co-operation with others is moral knowledge, whether conciously so regarded or not. For it builds up a social interest and confers the intelligence needed to make that interest effective in practice. Just because the studies of the curriculum represent standard factors in social life, they are organs of initiation into social values. As mere school studies, their acquistion has only a technical worth. Acquired under conditions where their social significance is realised, they feed moral interest and develop moral insight. Moreover, the qualities of mind discussed under the topic of method of learning are all of them intrinsically moral qualities. Open-mindedness, singlemindedness, sincerity, breadth of outlook, thoroughness, assumption of responsibility for developing the consequences of ideas which are accepted, are moral traits. The habit of identifying moral characteristics with external conformity to authoritative prescriptions may lead us to ignore the ethical value of these intellectual attitudes, but the same habit tends to reduce morals to a dead and machine-like routine. Consequently while such an attitude has moral results, the results are morally undesirable — above all in a democratic society where so much depends upon personal disposition.

The Social and the Moral

All of the separations which we have been criticising — and which the idea of education set forth in the previous chapters is designed to avoid — spring from taking morals too narrowly — giving them, on one side, a sentimental goody-goody turn without reference to effective ability to do what is socially needed, and, on the other side, overemphasising convention so as to limit morals to a list of definitely stated acts. As a matter of fact, morals are as broad as acts which concern our relationships with others. And potentially this includes all our acts, even though their social bearing may not be thought of at the time of performance. For every act, by the principle of habit, modifies disposition — it sets up a certain kind of inclination and desire. And it is impossible to tell when the habit thus strengthened may have a direct and perceptible influence on our association with others. Certain traits of character have such an obvious connection with our social relationships that we call them "moral" in an emphatic sense — truthfulness, honesty, chastity, amiability, etc. But this only means that they are, as compared with some other attitudes, central — that they carry other attitudes with them. They are moral in an emphatic sense not because they are isolated and exclusive, but because they are so intimately connected with thousands of other attitudes which we do not explicitly recognise — which perhaps we have not even names for. To call them virtues in their isolation is like taking the skeleton for the living body. The bones are certainly important, but their importance lies in the fact that they support other organs of the body in such a way as to make them capable of integrated effective activity. And the same is true of the qualities of character which we specifically designate virtues. Morals concern nothing less than the whole character, and the whole character is identical with the man in all his concrete make-up and manifestations. To possess virtue does not signify to have cultivated a few nameable and exclusive traits; it means to be fully and adequately what one is capable of becoming through association with others in all the offices of life.

The moral and the social quality of conduct are, in the last analysis, identical with each other. It is then but to restate explicitly the import of our earlier chapters regarding the social function of education to say that the measure of the worth of the administration, curriculum, and methods of instruction of the school is the extent to which they are animated by a social spirit. And the great danger which threatens schoolwork is the absence of conditions which make possible a permeating social spirit; this is the great enemy of effective moral training. For this spirit can be actively present only when certain conditions are met.

(*i*) In the first place, the school must itself be a community life in all that that implies. Social perceptions and interests can be developed only in a genuinely social medium — one where there is give and take in the building up of a common experience. Informational statements about things can be acquired in relative isolation by any one who previously has had enough intercourse with others to have learned language. But realisation of the *meaning* of the linguistic signs is quite another matter. That involves a context of work and play in association with others. The plea which has been made for education through continued constructive activities in this book rests upon the fact they afford an opportunity for a social atmosphere. In place of a school set apart from life as a place for learning lessons, we have a miniature social group in which study and growth are incidents of present shared experience. Playground, shops, workrooms, laboratories not only direct the natural active tendencies of youth, but they involve intercourse, communication, and co-operation — all extending the perception of connections.

(*ii*) The learning in school should be continuous with that out of school. There should be a free interplay between the two. This is possible only when there are numerous points of contact between the social interests of the one and of the other. A school is conceivable in which there should be a spirit of companionship and shared activity, but where its social life would no more represent or typify that of the world beyond the school walls than that of a monastery. Social concern and understanding would be developed, but they would not be available outside; they would not carry over. The proverbial separation of town and gown, the cultivation of academic seclusion, operate in this direction. So does such adherence to the culture of the past as generates a reminiscent social spirit, for this makes an individual feel more at home in the life of other days than in his own. A professedly cultural education is peculiarly exposed to this danger. An idealised past becomes the refuge and solace of the spirit; present day concerns are found sordid, and unworthy of attention. But as a rule, the absence of a social environment in connection with which learning is a need and a reward is the chief reason for the isolation of the school; and this isolation renders school knowledge inapplicable to life and so infertile in character.

A narrow and moralistic view of morals is responsible for the failure to recognise that all the aims and values which are desirable in education are themselves moral. Discipline, natural development, culture, social efficiency, are moral traits — marks of a person who is a worthy member of that society which it is the business of education to further. There is an old saying to the effect that it is not enough for a man to be good; he must be good for something. The something for which a man must be good is capacity to live as a social member so that what he gets from living with others balances with what he contributes. What he gets and gives as a human being, a being with desires, emotions, and ideas, is not external possessions, but a widening and deepening of conscious life — a more intense, disciplined, and expanding realisation of meanings. What he *materially* receives and gives is at most opportunities and means for the evolution of conscious life. Otherwise, it is neither giving nor taking, but a shifting about of the position of things in space, like the stirring of water and sand with a stick. Discipline, culture, social efficiency, personal refinement, improvement of character are but phases of the growth of capacity nobly to share in such a balanced experience. And education is not a mere means to such a life. Education is such a life. To maintain capacity for such education is the essence of morals. For conscious life is a continual beginning afresh. . . .

Experience and Education

Chapter IV: Social Control

I have said that educational plans and projects, seeing education in terms of life experience, are thereby committed to framing and adopting an intelligent theory or, if you please, philosophy of experience. Otherwise they are at the mercy of every intellectual breeze that happens to blow. I have tried to illustrate the need for such a theory by calling attention to two principles which are fundamental in the constitution of experience: the principles of interaction and of continuity. If, then, I am asked why I have spent so much time on expounding a rather abstract philosophy, it is because practical attempts to develop schools based upon the idea that education is found

From JOHN DEWEY, *Experience and Education*, Kappa Delta Pi Lectures Lafayette (Indiana), © 1938. Published by Macmillian (Collier Books), 1963. Reprinted by permission of Kappa Delta Pi, An Honor Society in Education.

in life experience are bound to exhibit inconsistencies and confusions unless they are guided by some conception of what experience is, and what marks off educative experience from non-educative and mis-educative experience. I now come to a group of actual educational questions the discussion of which will, I hope, provide topics and material that are more concrete than the discussion up to this point.

The two principles of continuity and interaction as criteria of the value of experience are so intimately connected that it is not easy to tell just what special educational problem to take up first. Even the convenient division into problems of subject matter or studies and of methods of teaching and learning is likely to fail us in selection and organisation of topics to discuss. Consequently, the beginning and sequence of topics is somewhat arbitrary. I shall commence, however, with the old question of individual freedom and social control and pass on to the questions that grow naturally out of it.

It is often well in considering educational problems to get a start by temporarily ignoring the school and thinking of other human situations. I take it that no one would deny that the ordinary good citizen is as a matter of fact subject to a great deal of social control and that a considerable part of this control is not felt to involve restriction of personal freedom. Even the theoretical anarchist, whose philosophy commits him to the idea that state or government control is an unmitigated evil, believes that with abolition of the political state other forms of social control would operate: indeed, his opposition to governmental regulation springs from his belief that other and to him more normal modes of control would operate with abolition of the state.

Without taking up this extreme position, let us note some examples of social control that operate in everyday life, and then look for the principle underlying them. Let us begin with the young people themselves. Children at recess or after school play games, from tag and one-old-cat to baseball and football. The games involve rules, and these rules order their conduct. The games do not go on haphazardly or by a succession of improvisations. Without rules there is no game. If disputes arise there is an umpire to appeal to, or discussion and a kind of arbitration are means to a decision; otherwise the game is broken up and comes to an end.

There are certain fairly obvious controlling features of such situations to which I want to call attention. The first is that the rules are a part of the game. They are not outside of it. No rules, then no game; different rules, then a different game. As long as the game goes on with a reasonable smoothness, the players do not feel that they are submitting to external imposition but that they are playing the game. In the second place an individual may at times feel that a decision isn't fair and he may even get angry. But he is not objecting to a rule but to what he claims is a violation of it, to some one-sided and unfair action. In the third place, the rules, and hence the conduct of the game, are fairly standardised. There are recognised ways of counting out, of selection of sides, as well as for positions to be taken, movements to be made, and so on. These rules have the sanction of tradition and precedent. Those playing the game have seen, perhaps, professional matches and they want to emulate their elders. An element that is conventional is pretty strong. Usually, a group of youngsters change the rules by which they play only when the adult group to which they look for models have themselves made a change in the rules, while the change made by the elders is at least supposed to conduce to making the game more skilful or more interesting to spectators.

Now, the general conclusion I would draw is that control of individual actions is effected by the whole situation in which individuals are involved, in which they share and of which they are co-operative or interacting parts. For even in a competitive game there is certain kind of participation, of sharing in a common experience. Stated the other way around, those who take part do not feel that they are bossed by an individual person or are being subjected to the will of some outside superior person. When violent disputes do arise, it is usually on the alleged ground that the umpire or some person on the other side is being unfair; in other words, that in such cases some individual is trying to impose his individual will on someone else.

It may seem to be putting too heavy a load upon a single case to argue that this instance illustrates the general principle of social control of individuals without the violation of freedom. But if the matter were followed out through a number of cases, I think the conclusion that this particular instance does illustrate a general principle would be justified. Games are generally competitive. If we took instances of co-operative activities in which all members of a group take part, as for example in well-ordered family life in which there is mutual confidence, the point would be even clearer. In all such cases, it is not the will or desire of any one person which establishes order but the moving spirit of the whole group. The control is social, but individuals are parts of a community, not outside of it.

I do not mean by this that there are no occasions upon which the authority of, say the parent does not have to intervene and exercise fairly direct control. But I do say that, in the first place, the number of these occasions is slight in comparison with the number of those in which the control is exercised by situations in which all take part. And what is even more important, the authority in question when exercised in a well-regulated household or other community group is not a manifestation of merely personal will; the parent or teacher exercises it as the representative and agent of the interests of the group as a whole. With respect to the first point, in a well-ordered school the main reliance for control of this and that individual is upon the activities carried on and upon the situations in which these activities are maintained. The teacher reduces to a minimum the occasions in which he or she has to exercise authority in a personal way. When it is necessary, in the second place, to speak and act firmly, it is done in behalf of the interest of the group, not as an exhibition of personal power. This makes the difference between action which is arbitrary and that which is just and fair.

Moreover, it is not necessary that the difference should be formulated in words, by either teacher or the young, in order to be felt in experience. The number of children who do not feel the difference (even if they cannot articulate it and reduce it to an intellectual principle) between action that is motivated by personal power and desire to dictate and action that is fair, because in the interest of all, is small. I should even be willing to say that upon the whole children are more sensitive to the signs and symptoms of this difference than are adults. Children learn the difference when playing with one another. They are willing, often too willing if anything, to take suggestions from one child and let him be a leader if his conduct adds to the experienced value of what they are doing, while they resent the attempt at dictation. Then they often withdraw and when asked why, say that it is because so-and-so "is too bossy".

I do not wish to refer to the traditional school in ways which set up a caricature in lieu of a picture. But I think it is fair to say that one reason the personal commands of the teacher so often played an undue role and a reason why the order which existed was so much a matter of sheer obedience to the will of an adult was because the situation almost forced it upon the teacher. The school was not a group or community held together by participation in common activities. Consequently, the normal, proper conditions of control were lacking. Their absence was made up for, and to a considerable extent had to be made up for, by the direct intervention of the teacher, who, as the saying went, "*kept* order". He kept it because order was in the teacher's keeping, instead of residing in the shared work being done.

The conclusion is that in what are called the new schools, the primary source of social control resides in the very nature of the work done as a social enterprise in which all individuals have an opportunity to contribute and to which all feel a responsibility. Most children are naturally "sociable". Isolation is even more irksome to them than to adults. A genuine community life has its ground in this natural sociability. But community life does not organise itself in an enduring way purely spontaneously. It requires thought and planning ahead. The educator is responsible for a knowledge of individuals and for a knowledge of subject matter that will enable activities to be selected which lend themselves to social organisation, an organisation in which all individuals have an opportunity to contribute something, and in which the activities in which all participate are the chief carriers of control.

I am not romantic enough about the young to suppose that every pupil will respond or that any child of normally strong impulses will respond on every occasion. There are likely to be some who, when they come to school, are already victims of injurious conditions outside of the school and who have become so passive and unduly docile that they fail to contribute. There will be others who, because of previous experience, are bumptious and unruly and perhaps downright rebellious. But it is certain that the general principle of social control cannot be predicated upon such cases. It is also true that no general rule can be laid down for dealing with such cases. The teacher has to deal with them individually. They fall into general classes, but no two are exactly alike. The educator has to discover as best he or she can the causes for the recalcitrant attitudes. He or she cannot, if the educational process is to go on, make it a question of pitting one will against another in order to see which is strongest, nor yet allow the unruly and non-participating pupils to stand permanently in the way of the educative activities of others. Exclusion perhaps is the only available measure at a given-juncture, but it is no solution. For it may strengthen the very causes which have brought about the undesirable anti-social attitude, such as desire for attention or to show off.

Exceptions rarely prove a rule or give a clue to what the rule should be. I would not, therefore, attach too much importance to these exceptional cases, although it is true at present that progressive schools are likely often to have more than their fair share of these cases, since parents may send children to such schools as a last resort. I do not think weakness in control when it is found in progressive schools arises in any event from these exceptional cases. It is much more likely to arise from failure to arrange in advance for the kind of work (by which I mean all kinds of activities engaged in) which will create situations that of themselves tend to exercise control over what this, that, and the other pupil does and how he does it. This failure most often goes back to lack of sufficiently thoughtful planning in advance. The causes for such lack are varied. The one which is peculiarly important to mention in this connection is the idea that such advance planning is unnecessary and even that it is inherently hostile to the legitimate freedom of those being instructed.

Now, of course, it is quite possible to have preparatory planning by the teacher done in such a rigid and intellectually inflexible fashion that it does result in adult imposition, which is none the less external because executed with tact and the semblance of respect for individual freedom. But this kind of planning does not follow inherently from the principle involved. I do not know what the greater maturity of the teacher and the teacher's greater knowledge of the world, of subject matters and of individuals, is for unless the teacher can arrange conditions that are conducive to community activity and to organisation which exercises control over individual impulses by the mere fact that all are engaged in communal projects. Because the kind of advance planning heretofore engaged in has been so routine as to leave little room for the free play of individual thinking or for contributions due to distinctive individual experience, it does not follow that all planning mst be rejected. On the contrary, there is incumbent upon the educator the duty of instituting a much more intelligent, and consequently more difficult, kind of planning. He must survey the capacities and needs of the particular set of individuals with whom he is dealing and must at the same time arrange the conditions which provide the subject matter or content for experience that satisfy these needs and develop these capacities. The planning must be flexible enough to permit free play for individuality of experience and yet firm enough to give direction towards continuous development of power.

The present occasion is a suitable one to say something about the province and office of the teacher. The principle that development of experience comes about through interaction means that education is essentially a social process. This quality is realised in the degree in which individuals form a community group. It is absurd to exclude the teacher from membership in the group. As the most mature member of the group he has a peculiar responsibility for the conduct of the interactions and intercommunications which are the very life of the group as a community. That children are individuals whose freedom should be respected while the more mature person should have no freedom as an individual is an idea too absurd to require refutation. The tendency to exclude the teacher from a positive and leading share in the direction of the activities of the community of which he is a member is another instance of reaction from one extreme to another. When pupils were a class rather than a social group, the teacher necessarily acted largely from the outside, not as a director of processes of exchange in which all had a share. When education is based upon experience and educative experience is seen to be a social process, the situation changes radically. The teacher loses the position of external boss or dictator but takes on that of leader of group activities.

In discussing the conduct of games as an example of normal social control, reference was made to the presence of a standardised conventional factor. The counterpart of this factor in school life is found in the question of manners, expecially of good manners in the manifestations of politeness and courtesy. The more we know about customs in different parts of the world at different times in the history of mankind, the more we learn how much manners differ from place to place and time to time. This fact proves that there is a large conventional factor involved. But there is no group at any time or place which does not have some code of manners as, for example, with respect to proper ways of greeting other persons. The particular form a convention takes has nothing fixed and absolute about it. But the existence of some form of convention is not itself a convention. It is a uniform attendant of all social relationships. At the very least, it is the oil which prevents or reduces friction.

It is possible, of course, for these social forms to become, as we say, "mere formalities". They may become merely outward show with no meaning behind them. But the avoidance of empty ritualistic forms of social intercourse does not mean the rejection of every formal element. It rather indicates the need for development of forms of intercourse that are inherently appropriate to social situations. Visitors to some progressive schools are shocked by the lack of manners they come across. One who knows the situation better is aware that to some extent their absence is due to the eager interest of children to go on with what they are doing. In their eagerness they may, for example, bump into each other and into visitors with no word of apology. One might say that this condition is better than a display of merely external punctilio accompanying intellectual and emotional lack of interest in schoolwork. But it also represents a failure in education, a failure to learn one of the most important lessons of life, that of mutual accommodation and adaptation. Education is going on in a one-sided way, for attitudes and habits are in process of formation that stand in the way of the future learning that springs from easy and ready contact and communication with others.

PART II
Variations on the Debate

Some Recent Innovations

Part II of this book carries the debate of Part I up to the present. Having seen the main features of the two basic standpoints on education as represented by their major exponents, it is now appropriate to examine some significant variations on these that have taken place in this century. This will enable readers to deepen their understanding of these two viewpoints and better equip them to decide where they stand in respect to the debate on the nature and aims of education.

Two writers representing variations on the traditional model are presented first. One is A. S. Makarenko, the Russian communist educator who presents a model of a different type of citizen, the "new Soviet person", to be produced by education. The other is B. F. Skinner, the American psychologist and social theorist, who sees the function of education as the production of the "planned person" in the fully scientifically controlled, harmonious society of the future. Both these writers share many of the presuppositions of the traditional approach to education; in particular they both see the importance of producing the ideal society through education as outweighing the value of individual freedom.

Completely opposed to this approach is A. S. Neill, the British progressive writer and headmaster of the famous Summerhill School, who through his stress on the "free child", offers a present-day version of the progressive model.

R. S. Peters, the contemporary British analytical philosopher of education, attempts a synthesis of the two opposed models of education in his notion of "education as initiation".

Finally there is Ivan Illich, brought up in Europe but now working in Mexico, whose response to the debate on education is the most radical of all in that he rejects any standpoint on education that presupposes a school or an authoritarian teacher–pupil relationship. His ideal model is of the "deschooled society", in which education takes place on a completely informal and voluntary basis.

5

A. S. MAKARENKO

Commentary

Biography

Anton Semyonovitch Makarenko (1888–1939) was born in the small Ukrainian town of Belopole, in the province of Kharkov, the son of a painter in a railway workshop. His first schooling was gained from a neighbouring boy and only when his father was transferred to the village of Kruikov, near Kremenchug, did Makarenko go to school. Even that required some sacrifice on the part of his parents, who had to pay the tuition fees in "copper money", as it was called; that is, small change, which would nonetheless have been difficult for a day labourer to find. Then, as now, Russian schools graded children's work on a five-point scale, and Makarenko consistently scored "fives", the highest grade.

Makarenko became involved with teaching as soon as he had completed school. Always a diligent scholar, with a flair for creative writing and literature generally, he was successful in being admitted, some months after his sixteenth birthday in 1904, to a one year course of teacher training. Upon completion he was appointed back to the railway school of Kruikov, where he had commenced his own formal education. He remained in that post for six years until transferred, apparently as an attempted bureaucratic control over his openly revolutionary sympathies, to the railway town school at South Dolinsk in the Khersonski province. He was now showing himself to be a promising teacher and secured admission to an advanced course of teacher training at the Poltava Teachers' Institute, where he graduated in 1917 (after a brief period of military service cut short by his poor eyesight) with the Institute's gold medal. He was then reappointed to the railway school at Kruikov and two years later, in September 1919, became director of the school in Poltava, a position which he held until twelve months later, when he was given charge of an institution for juvenile delinquents.

This last appointment was occasioned by Makarenko's criticisms of the apparent slowness of the Bolshevik regime, which had ruled Russia since November 1917, to implement its educational reforms with sufficient speed. Makarenko had become a vocal critic of Russian education as early as 1905 when he had vigorously supported workers' rights during the period of widespread risings stimulated by the formation in 1905 of the Union of Liberation (*Soyuz Osvobozhdenia*), a popular movement seeking the constitutionalisation of the whole country. Although never a ringleader, Makarenko attracted some official attention, and his agitation for reform, which continued after the Bolshevik *coup*, brought him in 1920 to the notice of the provincial Department of Education. As a result of an interview with the head of that department, he accepted the challenge to substantiate his words with action by taking over the direction of a colony of delinquents (*malolet-nikh prestupnikov*). For seven years, until October 1927, he directed this institution (called the Maxim Gorki Colony), during which time he developed his educational methods aimed at producing the communist ideal of the "new Soviet person".

However, in that period Makarenko remained at odds with official educational policy and was increasingly criticised in official educational circles. On 20 October 1927 he accepted the directorship of a new orphans' colony, founded in Kharkov as a memorial to the assassinated chief of the secret police, Felix Dzerzhinski. This was named the Dzerzhinski Commune, and Makarenko, now secure from interference (Stalin had by this time consolidated his dictatorship) conducted its educational policies by the same methods that he had developed in the Gorki Colony. He remained in charge until 1 July 1935. Stalin was then in the middle of the great purges which reached into nearly every aspect of Russian life, establishing his own authority and eliminating opposition of every kind, and Makarenko suddenly became famous as a "genuine" Soviet educator whose methods offered a promising way of producing the "new Soviet person". He was, in effect, relieved of his directorship of the Dzerzhinski Commune so that he could travel the countryside lecturing on his methods, arousing enthusiasm, and encouraging emulation by other teachers. This he did for nearly four years, in his official capacity as Assistant Director of the Department of Labour Colonies of the People's Commissariat of Internal Affairs for the Ukraine, in the course of which he delivered, in an endless number of talks, the substance of the readings collected here, and first published in January 1938 under the title *Problems of Soviet School Education (Problemi Shkol'novo Sovetskovo Vospitaniya)*.

The strain of public appearances, however, seems to have undermined his health and he collapsed, apparently of a heart attack, and died in a railway carriage en route to Moscow in April 1939, just two months after being awarded the prestigious Order of the Red Banner of Labour, for literary achievement.

Main Features of Makarenko's Educational Thought

What is it about Makarenko's work that makes him an important educational figure? In what respects does his work provide a significant innovation in Western educational thought? This is very easily answered. By means of his practices, which extended over sixteen years, and the theory that he extracted from them and which he set out in his extensive body of writing, Makarenko provided Russia with a model for the production of the citizen of the new Utopia that communism sought to introduce. His total publications run to seven large volumes; within this vast outpouring there are three works that have been enormously influential in the Soviet Union: his epic story of the Gorki Colony, entitled in Russian *A Pedagogical Poem* (*Pedagogicheskaya Poema*) and generally known in English-speaking countries as *The Road to Life*; a second, similar account (this time in quasi-fictional form) of the Dzerzhinski Commune called in Russian *Flags on the Battlements* (*Flagi na Bashnyakh*) and known in English as *Learning to Live*; and his celebrated *Book for Parents* (*Kniga dlya Roditelei*). All of these books have had a very wide circulation indeed, and circulation of *The Road to Life* alone had reached one-and-a-quarter million copies in the Russian language by 1948. Throughout the Soviet Union his ideas have been very influential; today he is revered as the father of Soviet education. During the thirties and forties his ideas became the orthodoxies of Soviet education; today, with the world-wide concern for the problems of mass society and appropriate forms of education, his ideas continue to exert an attraction, and remain valid to many socialist educators. Present-day practice probably would make some new interpretations of his ideas, but in their essentials they appear to remain generally relevant. In China, particularly, in the period of the Cultural Revolution of the 1960s, it would seem that many of Makarenko's principles, although not expressly recognised as such, were implemented.

The essence of Makarenko's educational theory lies in his concept of the primary of the collective, and not of the individual; the major concern of education should be the subordination of individuality to the common good. Now the common good is itself the product of a classless society in which all persons contribute as fully as possible, and this implies a society in which work, particularly manual labour, is accepted — and discharged — positively by all. So education, for Makarenko, is fundamentally the process whereby every person, from the earliest years of life, comes to value both learning and labour; to see them, in fact, in intimate and inseparable connection, and to recognise that a really good society will emerge only in the degree to which this achievement is made by everyone. Makarenko, of course, never pretended to originate this position; he attributed it to the Marxist-Leninist tradition and simply claimed that he was seeking to make a correct educational application. For it is a rather astonishing fact that none of the great Communist thinkers — Marx, Engels or Lenin — wrote very much about education; nothing of sufficient bulk, that is, to serve as a theory of education. Throughout all of Makarenko's work there is a great deal that rests implicitly in Communist theory; the great problem, and need, however, is to determine just how conscious Makarenko was of this theory, and how much knowledge of it he took for granted on the part of his readers. It is possible, for example, to read into Marxism an epistemological position in which activity in productive work changes our knowledge of the world. Can we say that Makarenko knew this, and developed a practical method implementing it through education? Even more crucially, can we say that Makarenko really did evolve a genuinely Marxist theory and practice of education? To answer this, and so to assess Makarenko's contributions, we need first to look briefly at some of Marx's major ideas.

The most influential writing of Karl Marx (1812–83) has been his monumental *Capital*, published in German in three volumes in 1867, 1885 and 1894 respectively, the final volume being edited posthumously by Friedrich Engels. In this great work Marx attempted to reverse the Hegelian philosophy by assigning priority to the material world, although he retained the general notion of some kind of progressive evolution. This, however, is an evolution of man in society rather than of some divine spirit. Marx identified three forms of society — feudal, capitalist and socialist — each with its own characteristic "mode" of production. He saw the current nineteenth-century mode of production, capitalism, as a transitional form because built into it were the inherent causes of its own decline. In his view, capitalism has separated man into two classes: the capitalists, who own the means of production, and the mass of workers, the proletariat, who are forced to sell their labour to find the means of subsistence. Everything in a capitalist mode of production exists on a "commodity" basis, and the sale of these gives wealth to the producers. The proletariat do not share in this wealth; indeed, they give value to the commodities they produce but do not get all of this returned to them. Instead, the capitalists keep this "surplus-value" as their "profit" and this builds up the store of "capital". Inherent in this system is the need for the capitalist enterprises to grow bigger, to eliminate smaller competition, and to mechanise their factories increasingly. This, of course, increasingly widens the gulf between the two classes in a series of continuing crises between the frustrated, underprivileged workers and the ever-wealthier, and ever-decreasing capitalists, until the workers unite, overthrow the system and replace it with a socialist, and eventually communist mode of production.

It was *Capital*, read in conjunction with some of Marx's other economic and political writings, that guided Lenin's interpretation and the general development of Russian revolutionary thought. *Capital*, however, belongs to what is now called the late period of Marx's thought. In itself, it contains no theory of education, nor any indication of how education is related to the process of implementing the transition to the third mode of production of socialism. The joint Marx-Engels *Communist Manifesto*, published in 1848, stresses the need for the workers to make educational policy dominant in the new order, but says little more. Lenin concurred with Marx's reasoning that the workers by themselves could not effect the transition to socialism, and in fact needed intellectuals like himself; Lenin interpreted it as the rationale for the Communist Party — the party should serve as the guiding instrument of the socialist people. The whole theory, as we well know, was conceived as applicable to an industrial, capitalist society of the kind existing in the western European states. It is a tremendous irony of history that the doctrines of Marx should be first applied in industrially under-developed Russia at the end of 1917. That country, of course, had virtually lost control of its theatre of war by 1915 and for two years the nation and the government were in continual crisis. When the Tsar was deposed early in 1917 and the subsequent Provisional Government of Kerensky fell in the Bolshevik *coup*, almost no one, probably not even the Bolsheviks themselves, imagined that they could sustain for long the government of such a backward, generally illiterate, agrarian nation. For three tense years, against formidable odds, however, the Bolsheviks did so, and by 1920 they had formed an enduring government led by the political genius of Lenin. When the smoke of battle and the disorder of war had cleared, the Bolsheviks set to the task of implementing the Utopian socialist state, and it was the slow pace of this activity that so irked Makarenko.

Meanwhile, however, had Marx anything to say on the nature of man, society, or education? Here a historical problem emerges. For indeed, in his early years Marx did have something to say on the nature of man and the nature of society, which he set down in what are now called his *Economic and Philosophical Manuscripts* of 1844 — usually referred to, because of their provenance, as the *Paris Manuscripts*. In these Marx set forth his very influential doctrine of alienation, which has recently become so important in social and political thought. Very briefly, the *Paris Manuscripts* section on "Alienated Labour" argues that the more man objectifies himself in the products of his labour, the more they become external to him, and the more externalised man becomes to himself. "Nature" for Marx is not inside man, it is outside in what he terms the "sensuous exterior world". In a sense, man defines himself by engaging in creative production with the world, and as the objects of his labour become objectified (as commodities) man becomes external (*entfremdung*) to himself. This is his tragedy and is the root cause of his unhappiness under the capitalist mode of production. Unable to sustain his creative engagement with the world, cut off from the products of his labour, man is forced to fall back on his non-working hours for solace, and is reduced to the only thing he can call his own: his appetitive animal functions, chiefly eating and reproducing. It is small wonder that the proletariat is in a condition of continued barbarism. The remedy for this is communism, defined by Marx as

> . . . the complete and conscious return of man conserving all the riches of previous development for man himself as a social, that is, a human being. Communism as completed naturalism is humanism, and as completed humanism is naturalism. It is the genuine solution of the antagonism between man and nature, and between man and man. It is the true solution of the struggle between existence and essence, between objectification and self-affirmation, between individual and species. It is the solution to the riddle of history, and knows itself to be this solution.[1]

It is the existence of these *Paris Manuscripts*, with their provocative concept of alienation under a capitalist mode of production, and the solution through communism, that creates the historical problem. For these works of the young Marx appear to have become lost sometime in the second half of the nineteenth century. It would seem that they were unknown to most socialist and revolutionary thinkers. Did Lenin know of their existence, or at least of the concept of alienation? The controversy still continues,[2] and if Lenin did know the concept, it certainly seems that it was not directly through the *Manuscripts* themselves, but by means of their key ideas, expressed even in the same terminology, in subsequent writings by the mature Marx. The *Manuscripts* themselves were not rediscovered until 1932, and translations from German did not appear for a while. This has the most profound consequences for the formulation of a Marxist — that is, a genuinely communist — theory of education. Neither Makarenko nor any other Russian educator, without the *Paris Manuscripts*, had sufficient Marxist theory to build on.

Throughout the first decade of Bolshevik power, from 1918 to 1928, therefore, Soviet educators had to develop their own theory and practice of communist education. Many approaches were tried, and one of the most favoured was the project method developed by William Heard Kilpatrick out of the theories of John Dewey. Although a single Unified Workers' School was introduced, schools remained free to experiment with the curriculum, and indeed many did to the extent that in places organised education even broke down; yet we must be sceptical of stories of excesses in Soviet schools of the period, particularly since these generally came from foreign travellers who were critical of communism and perhaps went looking for evidence of failure. Soviet educational methods were borrowed widely from the United States, in addition to the Deweyan experimental theory, Russian educational psychologists made a wholesale introduction of the mental testing movement, and under the energetic Petr Pavel Blonski a programme to test all children was commenced. Throughout this decade, Soviet educationalists saw no apparent conflict between communist ideals on the one hand, and the various American theories and practices on the other. It was not until 1936 that there was a complete and thoroughgoing rejection of all foreign influences on Soviet education. In that year, a radical break with what the English socialists Sidney and Beatrice Webb called the period of "luxuriant experiment" was effected. In the famous historical decree issued in July 1936, entitled "On the Pedagogical Distortions of the Narkomprosov",[3] the project and similar methods were banned, mental testing abolished and it was decreed that the schools were to return to the formal lesson and lecture methods. It was at this point that Makarenko, who had been in opposition to these imitative approaches all along and had himself been in disfavour, suddenly became not only respectable but widely acclaimed as a true Soviet educator; his works received wide dissemination and his principles were enthusiastically implemented.

In coming, then, to the study of Makarenko's approach to education, we can usefully begin with a consideration of the actual colonies in which he developed his theories. The most superficially striking fact about both of them, for he only ever worked in two, is that they were organised on military lines. The children (about equal numbers of girls and boys) were grouped into detachments, were dressed in uniforms and generally followed a military schedule, down to such details as having the segments of the day announced by bugle calls and drum rolls. A firm martial discipline — in the specific sense — was imposed and the "colonists", as they were called, were required to walk or march smartly as the occasion demanded, to salute and return salutes and to conduct themselves at all times with something closely corresponding to a military decorum. Makarenko developed this approach slowly, by trial and error, and its obvious origins lay in the time of civil disorder, between 1917 and 1920, when many armies were still contesting Russian territory. A distinct nationalist pride was involved. When the exigencies of war had passed, Makarenko found it convenient to maintain this form of organisation.

Of course, since the chief educational institutions in which Makarenko worked were orphanages, or colonies, they were, as he freely admitted, atypical of the usual kind of educational environment. Yet they must be seen in the light of official policy at the time. Stemming from the writings of both Marx and Engels, this policy was to eliminate the family as the fundamental institution of bourgeois capitalism, and as first moves to implement that policy, the new Bolshevik government had decreed both divorce and abortion available on demand, in 1917 and 1920 respectively. Moreover, it was originally intended to collectivise all children from their earliest practicable years into communist kindergartens so as "to exempt them from the pernicious influence of the family [and to substitute] the beneficial influence of communist kindergartens and schools", as Zlata Lilina, Head of the Petrograd Education Department, said in a speech at a teachers' conference in 1918. The practical difficulties in doing this were enormous, since in 1917 there was already the staggering number of seven million homeless war orphans and waifs *(besprizorniki)* alone waiting to be housed, clothed and reared. It was children of this kind with whom Makarenko largely worked and his successes provided an idealistic vision of what might be achieved. In a sense, in view of this official policy of eventually collectivising all children, Makarenko's work was something in the nature of an experiment.

Makarenko himself denied, however, that his theory was limited simply because it had been developed in an atypical situation. He argued that the various elements of his colonies had counterparts in the outside society. Education he recognised as a pervasive process in all life, and all through life. So all of the institutions of society could be seen as having a potentially educational influence: schools, youth groups (Pioneers and Komsomols), circles, clubs and so on. In fact, as he admitted later even the family *could* have an educational influence — if it were large enough to act as a true collective. Doubtless he came around to this view, expressed in *A Book for Parents*, because of the unrealistic expectation of collectivising all children. So Makarenko argued that the various influences on the child in a normal family home, if taken together and appropriately organised, could provide the same total experience as his all-embracing colonies.

In moving on to a consideration of Makarenko's specific theory of education it is necessary to know that in the Russian language — in which

Makarenko wrote despite his Ukrainian nationality — there are three words that can be translated, according to context, as "education": *prosveshchenie*, *obrazovanie* and *vospitanie*. The first means "enlightenment"; the second (from the noun *obraz*, a shape) means "shaping" or "formation"; the third means "discipline" and also "self-discipline". It is significant in reading Makarenko that he habitually uses the last term, *vospitanie*.

The fundamental purpose of education, Makarenko asserted (and he was well aware that the process extends beyond the school into all life) is to produce the "new Soviet man"; to create a person thoroughly imbued with communist morality. The school itself must be the primary agent, particularly since the family was considered to be a pernicious influence. The aims of education, moreover, he argued, must not be determined in advance, *a priori*; instead, they must come from the social needs of the people themselves. Central to the new communist morality, and expressed as its aim, is the cultivation of a particular type of character, and Makarenko always maintained a stress upon character and morality rather than on cognitive and intellectual attainment as the purpose of education. How is this to be achieved? Through the conjoint operation of a programme of disciplining in all phases of life: formal instruction in school subjects, and guidance in social and political thinking. In his general theory Makarenko followed Marxist-Leninist orthodoxy.

In his daily methods, Makarenko showed himself to be an uncompromising behaviourist. He rejected the current psychological belief in individual differences (apart from obvious cases of congenital or accidental brain damage) and even refused to accept the cumulative record files of children when they were transferred to his care. Every child was seen as a person to be absorbed into the collective of the school. Since everything man becomes is, in his view, the product of experience, then the way in which the school is organised is of paramount importance. In fact he defined the school as a collective with a common goal — that of producing a communist morality — achieved by ensuring that the school has a definite system (which he called regimen (*rezhim*)) that conduces towards the development of discipline (*distsiplina*). Yet he was careful to distinguish discipline from the processes of reward and punishment. Discipline has a definitely moral quality. While it demands submission to the collective, it must be seen by each person as benefitting both the collective and the individual. It is his insistence on regimen, that is, a highly structured predictable school routine, that gives his work such a strongly behaviourist quality, although he preferred to use for this conditioning concept, the word "tradition". Throughout all of his writings this is a central element.

The collective tradition, or regimen (and we can easily see in the military cast to his colonies how closely related this idea is to "regimental"), acts as a positive reinforcement for children's behaviour, for indeed, the child who willingly enters into the spirit of the school finds rewards liberally built into the system. But what of punishments? Makarenko was resolutely against physical coercion and in general argued that punishment in its most effective and appropriate form consists in restructuring the relevant situation in such a way that the transgressor comes to see how he has failed to meet the collective norms. Essentially, by exerting group pressure and actually involving each child in behavioural tasks, Makarenko took very definite steps to promote moral growth.[4]

The next step in the achievement of a communist morality is for the individual to effect a transition from the primary collective to the wider Soviet society. The corresponding problem in other societies is a vexed one, and indeed it is a central preoccupation of Western educational thought today. Makarenko was incapable of any final answer here, nor should we expect this from him. The problem of moral growth, of how the transition to a wider vision and corresponding practice is achieved, is universal. Makarenko's claims for success were at the level of anecdote and individual testimony, and throughout his works he cites numerous instances of those of his students who effectively entered Soviet life as good citizens. Nor does he try to cover up his failures: these too are recorded.

In the strictest interpretation of Marx's theory of alienation given in the *Paris Manuscripts*, man does not need a programme of formal schooling; indeed, this is itself an alienating process. Man develops his nature through interaction with the environment, and it is this activity which is man's education. Since such interaction must necessarily be a constantly evolving affair, it is strictly impossible to set up a curriculum in advance. Makarenko's thinking and writing, however, show no awareness whatsoever of the concept of alienation, and his very successful attempts to make the school a productive enterprise where the children manufactured chairs, electric drills and cameras is more easily seen as a rather intuitive interpretation of more general features of the labour principle. Lenin himself complained of the lack of understanding of Marx's ideas by most Bolsheviks and indeed as early as 1914 wrote, in what certainly must be construed as having a somewhat hyperbolic tone, that "it is impossible to fully grasp Marx's *Capital* and especially the first chapter, if you have not studied or understood the whole of Hegel's *Logic*. Consequently, none of the Marxists for the past half-century has understood Marx!"[5] This does not provide sufficient and conclusive evidence against Makarenko, of course, but his own writings do show that he was not acting out of any conscious attempt to counteract the problem of alienation.

Where, then, did Makarenko come by his practices of devoting a large part of the school day to productive labour? We do not need to look past the widely distributed educational theory of the early Bolsheviks. Anatole Lunacharski, the new People's Commissar of Education, stated in his first report that the "labour character of the school [will come from] the fact that labour, pedagogical as well as, in particular, productive labour, will be made the basis of teaching",[6] and P. M. Lepeshinski in a paper read to the First All-Russian Congress of Teacher-Internationalists on 2 June, 1918, set out the fundamental principles of the new Unified Workers' School in which labour and academic instruction were to be "fused", manual labour was to become an integral part of school life and the school itself was to be organised as a productive commune, both producing and consuming, and based on the two principles of autonomy and collective self-determination. The general, comprehensive concept used by Lepeshinski was that of "all-round development for modern society, that is, polytechnical education", and this came through a continued concern with "bringing up the child as a social creature, and with developing in him an understanding of social labour in its historical evolution."[7]

The concept of polytechnisation needs explanation. One of its earliest uses was by Lepeshinski in his paper of 1918, and it certainly was given wider use by Lenin when he addressed the Eighth Congress of the Communist Party in March 1919 in a speech entitled "On Polytechnical Education",[8] and it was popularised even further by his wife Nadezhda Krupskaya who, as early as 1918 — and in many similar writings later — said, in a speech published under the title of "The Problems of the Socialist School" that "the population is interested in having a single aim in primary, secondary and higher education: that is, the training of many-sided men with conscious and organised social interests, having a well-elaborated, consistent ideology. They should be ready for any work, manual or intellectual."[9] The essence of the concept lies in the idea of the complete fusion of learning and labour, of the fact that our world view is created and recreated as we engage in productive labour. Unfortunately, the implementation of the ideal lagged, it became equated more with the level of technical and technological instruction, although it has been revived periodically as a communist ideal. There is no doubt, however, that as Lenin, Krupskaya and others used the term, they saw it as the new integrating concept of modern education; providing, as it were, a *studia humanitatis* for the age of the industrial, democratic society.

It seems that Makarenko drew his notions of productive labour in the school from this source, although his acquaintance even with this range of ideas is difficult to determine. In his writings, in fact, there are some conflicting elements. The most obvious instance is the fact that he separated his school into two apparently exclusive operations: that of formal classroom instruction, and that of social learning. Throughout all of his writing he gives only the slightest attention to formal teaching and learning, and devotes his serious interest to the procedures of developing a communist morality. Yet Makarenko was never fully secure in his own thinking and his writings have numerous instances of morally indefensible actions. In *The Road to Life* the most striking example is the faking of food orders to get rations for the Gorki Colony; in the readings given here a similar situation occurs in respect to finding the capital with which to commence the operations of the furniture factory. And this, it might be noted, proceeded like any regular capitalist enterprise. Makarenko, moreover, found no contradiction in any of his actions, or in paying wages. He appears to believe that the end justifies the means, and apparently saw no contradiction with his theory of moral discipline.

In many respects, much of Makarenko's work appears both lightweight and highly limited. Yet he has been passionately defended and in the Soviet Union a great depth of significance has been found in his thought as it is expressed in his writings. Certainly he is sufficiently comprehensive in some respects: he gives a clear aim for education, accepts a rather straightforward realist view of the world, and therefore a simple correspondence theory of truth. Were he to follow a genuinely Marxist approach, his view of the teacher's role would have to be moderated, for as learning by productive labour proceeds, then new views and outcomes are continually created and teachers cannot have so omniscient and authoritarian a role as Makarenko gives them. In fact, Makarenko's acceptance and encouragement in the commune's factory of the division of labour is a thoroughgoing means of producing alienation, and the authority of the teacher, even if it is cloaked by a seemingly non-directive strategy, appears to have nothing new about it.

We must, of course, question the highly specific nature of the colonies in which Makarenko's theories were generated, and we cannot accept at face value his assertion that his methods are transferable to outside society. Indeed he did work with a captive group, in the full sense, and expulsion — a real threat that was occasionally used — meant starvation in the early days, and in later years, being sent to a more stringent institution. The immediately superficial features of military paraphernalia should not deflect our enquiry, for the constant pressure of regimen does not necessarily involve these symbols, although military and para-military institutions find it difficult to dispense with them. Is it more than coincidence that religious orders, sporting clubs of all kinds, fraternal societies, and so on, find it necessary to maintain a certain level of external ceremonial ritual? Is it no accident that religious garb is termed a "habit"? It is, again, difficult in many European countries to see even everyday civilian clothing as anything other than a uniform, varying according to its purpose. But the question of whether Makarenko's theory really can work in a wider society must be raised and considered, and here we might do well to think of daily life and political education as it was being practised in the People's Republic of China in the 1960s.

Certainly if we wish to locate the main educational strength of Makarenko, it is to be found in his theory of the collective and his general methods of moral development by means of the conditioning process. Yet where we might express serious reservations is in respect to the generation of values. From whence do these arise? How, indeed, under Makarenko's system, can any creative criticism or growth take place? The continued preoccupation with meeting a set of rigid external goals, as expressed in daily behaviour, and with maintaining the subordination of the individual to the collective, appears to provide for no kind of innovation whatsoever. Indeed, there seems to be no provision at all for the institutionalisation of change or reform, much less for criticism. As such, Makarenko's theory of education, in the long run, is covertly coercive and maladaptive. It can of course be argued that he was preoccupied with a time of emergency — indeed that cannot be denied — but that does not stop Makarenko from claiming that he had indeed actually developed a universal method, much as he cloaked it under the guise of an artless teacher's practical experiences. Moreover, his approaches appear to fail to demonstrate that a gradual development in moral growth from the earliest stages of egocentricity and situational pressure, through those of respect for law and order, to the exhibition of respect for the rights of others and understanding of, and genuine concern for, the preeminence of justice does, or could, take place. Does Makarenko's system, in fact, provide the means for a wider moral growth beyond the primary collective? Or does the excessive maintenance of concern to conform to the collective keep moral growth arrested and at a non-generalising stage?

Yet Makarenko's work cannot be ignored. It has now achieved in the Soviet Union a "venerable founding father" status, and his works remain studied as a significant innovation in Western educational thought. Perhaps it is one of the most important yet developed since it has been seen as a means of helping man progress to the earthly beatitude of communism. Perhaps we might ask ourselves some final questions as we read these selections. What does his work have of relevance to non-Soviet educational systems? For instance, is such a society-centred approach necessary to combat the moral and social crisis in capitalist society today? Finally what does his work have in common with traditional models of education presented in Part I of this book?

NOTES AND REFERENCES

1. KARL MARX, *Early Texts*, edited and translated by D. McLellan, Basil Blackwell, Oxford, 1971, p. 141.
2. I. MESZAROS, *Marx's Theory of Alienation*, 3rd edition, Merlin Press, London, 1972, p. 93f. and Chapter 3, *passim*.
3. The Narkomprosov is an acronym made up of the first syllables of the Russian words for People's Committees for Communist Education. These were the administrative authorities.
4. In this respect compare the subsequent work of Jean Piaget in Geneva and, more recently, that of Lawrence Kohlberg at Harvard University. See L. KOHLBERG, "Moral Education in the Schools: A Developmental View", *School Review*, 1966, 74, pp. 1–30.
5. LENIN, *Aus dem philosophischen Nachlass*, 1949, p. 99, quoted and translated in K. MARX, *Early Texts*, p. xxxv.
6. A. LUNACHARSKI, "Declaration of the Principles of the Socialist School", *Naradnoe Prosveshchenie*, June 1918, X.
7. For a detailed account of the reforming programme of the Bolsheviks see SHEILA FITZPATRICK, *The Ministry of Enlightenment, 1917–1920: Soviet Organisation of Education and the Arts under Lunarcharsky, Oct. 1917–1920*, Cambridge University Press, Cambridge, 1970; and for a brief account, J. BOWEN, *Soviet Education: Anton Makarenko and the Years of Experiment*, University of Wisconsin Press, Madison, 1962, Chapter 3, *passim*.
8. LENIN, "O Politekhnicheskom Obrazovanii", in *Works*, xxv. (Russian edition).
9. NADEZHDA KRUPSKAYA, "The Problems of the Socialist School", in *Izbrannye Pedagogicheskie Proizvedeniya (Selected Writings on Pedagogy)*, Izdatel'stvo Akademii Pedagogicheskikh Nauk RSFSR, Moscow, 1955, p. 172.

SELECT BIBLIOGRAPHY

Makarenko's writings in Russian have been published in numerous editions. The standard edition of his collected works is

Sochineniya v Semi Tomakh, Izdatel'stvo Akademii Pedagogicheskikh Nauk RSFSR, Moscow 1957 (Collected Works in Seven Volumes, Academy of Pedagogical Sciences of the RSFSR, Moscow 1957).

The separate titles are:

Vol. 1 Pedagogicheskaya Poema (Epic of Education); (English title, Road to Life)
Vol. 2 Marsh 30 Goda (The March of the Year Thirty)
FD-1
Mazhor (The Major)
Vol. 3 Flagi na Bashnyakh
(Flags on the Battlements; English title: Learning to Live)
Vol. 4 Kniga dlya Roditelei (A Book for Parents)
Lektsii O Vospitanii Detei (Lectures on the Education of Children)
Vstupleniya po Voprosam Semeinovo Vospitaniya
(Speeches on the Problems of Education in the Family)
Vol. 5 Obshchie Voprosy Teorii Pedagogiki
(General Problems of Pedagogical Theory)
Vospitanie v Sovetskoi Shkole (Education in the Soviet School)
Vol. 6 Chest' (Honour)
Nastoyashchii Kharakter (The Present Character)
Komandirovka (The Mission)
Polemicheskie Stat'i (Polemical Articles)
Vol. 7 Publitsistika (Publicism)
Rasskazi i Ocherki (Stories and Sketches)
Stat'i o Literature i Retsenzii (Articles on Literature and Reviews)
Perepiska c A. M. Gorkim (Correspondence with Gorki)

Four of his works have been issued in English translations:

The Road to Life, Foreign Languages Publishing House, Moscow, 1951.
Learning to Live, Foreign Languages Publishing House, Moscow, 1953.
A Book for Parents, Foreign Languages Publishing House, Moscow, 1954.
Problems of Soviet School Education, Progress Publishers, Moscow, 1965.

There is a collected edition of talks, articles and lectures by Makarenko along with commentaries on his work by former pupils and others, published in English under the title: Makarenko, His Life and Work, Foreign Languages Publishing House, Moscow, (n.d.).

Selections

Anton Makarenko is represented here by selections taken from his four lectures delivered in January 1938, under the general title of Problems of Soviet School Education (Problemi Shkol' novo Sovetskovo Vospitaniya). *There is great difficulty in anthologising Makarenko because his writing is so prolix, with frequent digressions into illustrative examples, so that sustained passages of close argument are relatively few. None of his major works* — The Road to Life, Learning to Live *and* A Book for Parents — *lends itself easily to abridgement. After careful consideration, these lectures were chosen as representative of his major ideas on the formation of the collective and the ideal of the new Soviet person, and the correlative ways in which education should be conducted. The four lectures that follow are entitled, respectively,* Methods of Upbringing (Metodi Vospitaniya), Discipline, Regimen, Punishment and Reward (Distsiplina, Rezhim, Nakayaniya i Pooshchreniya), Methods of Individual Approach (Pedagogika Individual'novo Deistviya), *and* Work Training, Relations, Style and Tone (Trudnoe, Vospitanie, Otnosheniya, Stil', Ton, i Kollektive).

Problems of Soviet School Education

Lecture 1: Methods of Upbringing

. . . And now a few words on what can be taken as a basis of educational methods.

To begin with, I am convinced that educational methods cannot be evolved from what is suggested by adjacent sciences, no matter how far developed such sciences as psychology and biology, the latter especially after Pavlov's achievements, may be. I am convinced that deriving an educational means directly from these sciences' findings is something we have not the right to do. These sciences should play a vastly important part in educational work as control propositions for verifying our practical achievements, but by no means as prerequisites for a conclusion.

Moreover, I consider that an educational means can only be evolved from experience, and then verified and approved by such sciences as psychology and biology.

This assertion of mine is based on the following: pedagogy, and in particular the theory of education, is above all else a science of practical expediency. We cannot educate a person unless we have a clear-cut political aim in view. If we don't, we have not the right to take up educational work at all. Educational work that does not pursue a clear, far-reaching and minutely studied aim is education without a political purpose, and we find evidence

---

From A. S. MAKARENKO, *Problems of Soviet Education*, Progress Publishers, Moscow, 1965. Reprinted by permission of Mezhdunarodnaya Kniga.

proving this at every step in our Soviet public life. The Red Army is making great, an enormous success of its educational work, quite outstanding, really, in world history. This success is so great, so enormous, because the Red Army's methods are always expedient, and the Red Army educators always know what sort of people they want to bring up and what goal they want to attain. Now the best example of inexpedient pedagogical theory is the lately deceased pedology [mental testing movement]. In this sense pedology may be regarded as the exact opposite of Soviet education. It was a system not furnished with an aim.

Wherefrom can the aims of education arise? From our social needs, of course, from the aspirations of the Soviet people, from the aims and tasks of our revolution, from the aims and problems of our struggle. And so, obviously, a formula of aims cannot be derived from either biology or psychology, but only from our social history, from our social environment.

And I think that we should not make such claims on biology and psychology and seek in them a confirmation of our teaching methods. They are developing, and before the next ten years are out both psychology and biology will probably set out precise propositions on human behaviour, and then we shall be able to base our work on these sciences. The attitude of our social needs and the social aims of socialist education to the aims and findings of the theory of psychology and biology must always go on changing, and maybe the change will even involve the constant participation of psychology and biology in our educational work. But what I am convinced in firmly is that a pedagogical means cannot be derived from either psychology or biology simply by deductive logic. I have already said that pedagogical means must be originally derived from our social and political aims.

It is my belief that it was in the matter of setting an aim, in the matter of expediency, that pedagogical theory was mostly at fault. All the mistakes, all the deviations in our pedagogical work always occurred where the logic of expediency was concerned. Let us call them mistakes for reference.

I see three types of such mistakes in pedagogical theory: deductive statements, ethical fetishism and isolated means.

In my practical activity, I suffered greatly from trying to overcome these mistakes. Someone would pick on a method and assert that it would have such and such an effect. For example, take the story of the complex method [or project method], which is well known to all of you. Someone would recommend a method — in this case the complex method of teaching — and deduct speculatively, by means of logic, that this method must bring about good results.

And so the effect — the good results of the complex method — became established before experience had proved it so. But established it nevertheless was that the result would definitely be good; that the desired effect would be hiding in some secret places of the psyche.

When we, the modest practical educators, asked to be shown this good result, we were told: "How can we show you what's inside a human soul, it's there that the good result must be, it's complex harmony, the connection of parts. The connection between the separate parts of a lesson must surely leave a positive impression on a person's mentality."

In other words, even logic precluded this method from being put to the test. And a vicious circle was formed: the method was good, therefore the result must be good, and since the result was good, the method must be good.

Mistakes such as this, resulting from the prevalence of deductive logic and not experimental logic, were many.

There were also many mistakes of the so-called ethical fetishism type. For example, take labour education.

I, too, was one of those who made that mistake. The very word "labour" sounds so pleasant, it holds so much that to us is sacred and justified, that the concept "labour education" appeared to us absolutely precise, definite and correct. And then we discovered that the word "labour" as such does not contain anything like the only correct, finished logic. At first, work was regarded as ordinary work, what may be termed as self-service, and then as an aimless labour process, as unproductive labour — an exercise in the waste of muscle power. The word "labour" so illumined the logic that it appeared infallible, although it was revealed at every step that there was no genuine infallibility. But belief in the ethical power of the term itself was so strong that the logic, too, seemed sacred. And yet my own experience and the experience of my teacher friends has shown that no educative means can be evolved from the ethical colouring of a term, that labour as applicable to education can be organised in different ways and that it can bring about a different result in every separate case. At any rate, labour that does not go alongside of school education, that does not go alongside of social and political education, remains a neutral process of no educational value. You can make a person work as much as you want, but unless he receives a political and moral education at the same time, unless he takes part in public and political life, this work will be no more than a neutral process that yields no positive results.

Work can be a means of education only if it is part of a general system.

And, last but not least, the mistake of the "isolated means" type. Very often people say that such and such a means unfailingly brings about such and such a result. One particular means. Let us take an assertion which at first glance seems to be the most indisputable one and which is often voiced in pedagogical writings — the question of punishment. Punishment educates a slave — this is a precise axiom which has never been subjected to doubt. This assertion, of course, contains all three mistakes. There is the mistake of the deductive prediction type, and the ethical fetishism type. In punishment, the logic stems from the very colouring of that word. And, last but not least, there is the mistake of the "isolated means" type. And yet I am convinced that no means can be considered in isolation from a system. No means whatever can be pronounced good or bad if it is considered apart from other means, from a whole complex of influences. Punishment may educate a slave, but sometimes it may also educate a very good person, a very free and proud person. In my own experience, you will be surprised to hear, punishment was also among the means I resorted to when I was confronted with the task of inculcating dignity and self-respect in my charges.

I will tell you afterwards in what cases punishment results in the cultivation of human dignity. Obviously, this effect can be achieved only in a definite environment of other means and at a definite stage of development. No pedagogical means, not even a universally accepted means — which is what we usually call persuasion, explanation, talk, and public influence — can be termed a perfect and invariably useful means. The best of means is sure to be the worst of means sometimes. Take a means like collective influence, that is the influence of the collective on the individual. Sometimes it will be good and sometimes bad. Take individual approach, the heart-to-heart talk of teacher with pupil. Sometimes it will be beneficial and sometimes harmful. No means can be regarded from the point of view of its usefulness or harmfulness if it is considered apart from the entire system of means. And finally, no system of means can be recommended as a standing system.

I recall the history of the Dzerzhinsky Commune. This Commune, set up in 1928, grew up as a collective of boys and girls not older than eighth-form pupils (that is, fifteen or sixteen). It was a healthy, jolly collective, but it was a far cry from the collective of 1935 with its big Komsomol organisation and its veteran communards, some as old as twenty years of age. Obviously, a collective such as the latter called for an entirely different system of education.

Personally I am convinced of the following: if we took an ordinary Soviet school and placed it in the hands of good teachers, organisers and educators for twenty years, it would travel such a long and wonderful way in that time — provided it was retained in good pedagogical hands — that at the end of this road the system of education would differ greatly from what it had been at the start.

By and large, pedagogy is the most dialectical, mobile, complex and diversified of sciences. This assertion makes the credo of my pedagogical faith. I am not trying to say that I have verified everything there is to verify in practice, far from it, because I am still not clear on very many points, but I do advance it as a working hypothesis which at any rate deserves to be put to the test. I personally have the proof of my experience, but of course it needs putting to the test in extensive Soviet social practice. By the way, I am convinced that the logic of what I have said is not incompatible with the experience of our best Soviet schools nor that of very many of our best children's and adult collectives.

So much for my general preliminary observations on which I wished to dwell.

Let us now pass to the most important question, that of setting up educational goals. By whom, when and how can educational goals be set, and what exactly are educational goals?

I take the concept "educational goal" to mean the programme of a personality, the programme of a character, and what is more I put into the concept "character" all that a personality holds, that is, the nature of his outward manifestations, his inner convinctions, his political education and his knowledge — the picture of a human personality in its entirety. I maintain that we, pedagogues, should have such a programme of human personality towards which we must strive.

I could not do without a programme like that in my practical work. There's no teacher like experience. In that same Dzerzhinsky Commune I was given a few hundred people, and in every one of those people I saw deep-rooted and dangerous urges, deep-rooted habits, and I had to stop and think: what should their character be like, what must I strive for in order to mould these boys and girls into worthy citizens? And when I began to ponder over it I discovered that this question could not be answered in a brief two words. The notion — to mould a good Soviet citizen — did not yet show me the way. I had to work out a more comprehensive programme of human personality. And, as I began to tackle it, I came up against the following question: this programme now, must it be the same for everybody? Why, am I supposed to wedge every personality into a single programme, trim them to a pattern and strive for this pattern? If so, I must sacrifice the individual charm, the originality and the peculiar beauty of personality, because if I don't what sort of a pattern will I get? I could not simply go and answer this question as an abstract problem, but then it was solved for me in practice in the course of ten years.

I discovered that indeed there must be a general programme, a pattern, and also an individual amendment to it. The question did not arise for me: should my pupil grow up a courageous man or should I bring up a coward? A pattern was in order here: every one of my pupils had to grow up a brave, staunch, honest and industrious patriot. But what line to take when you have to deal with such delicate aspects of a personality as talent? And sometimes when it comes to talent, when you are confronted by it, you do have to suffer some tormenting doubts. . . .

The question of whether a person has the right to tamper with a pupil's chosen career remains unsolved for me. But I am profoundly convinced that every teacher will be confronted by this question — has he the right to interfere in the development of a character and guide it in the correct direction, or must he passively look on? To my mind, the question should be answered in the affirmative — yes, he has that right. But how to go about it? In every separate case the question has to be approached individually, because it's one thing to have the right, and another to exercise it properly. They are two different problems. And it's very possible that a time will come when teaching people how to perform this operation will play a part of paramount importance in the training of our educators. After all, a surgeon is taught how to trepan the skull. And with us, a teacher will perhaps be taught how to perform this "trepanation" — more tactfully, more successfully, than I had done, perhaps, and they'll be taught how to guide a person in the best direction by making the most of his inherent qualities, leanings and abilities.

I shall now set out those practical forms which in my experience and the experience of my colleagues were applied with the greatest success in our educational work. I regard the collective as the supremely important form of educational work. Pedagogical literature would seem to contain a great deal about the collective, but somehow the writings carry little conviction.

What is a collective and how far can we interfere with it? I am making observations of very many schools both here in Moscow and in Kiev where I often go now and have often gone in the past, and I do not always see a real collective of pupils. Occasionally I do see a *classroom* collective, but I have hardly ever seen a *school* collective.

I shall now tell you in a few simple words about my collective, reared by my friends and myself. You must remember, though, that the conditions I worked under were unlike those of an ordinary school, because in my case the pupils worked in our own factory, they lived in, and in the overwhelming majority had no parents, in other words they had no other collective. And so naturally I had more means of collective education available to me than a schoolteacher has. But I am not inclined to put it down to conditions alone. At one time I was headmaster of an ordinary school where the pupils were children of railway workers, or rather workers of a factory where railway coaches were built, and there, too, I had them knitted into a *school* collective. . . .

Correct Soviet education must be organised by forming united, strong and influential collectives. The school must be a single collective where all the educative processes are properly organised. Every separate member of the collective should feel his dependence on the collective, he should be devoted to the interests of the collective, he should uphold these interests and value them above all else. But a situation in which every separate member of a collective is free to find associates for himself after his own taste, without using his collective's help and means to do so, I consider not right. The Young Pioneer Palaces in all our towns are doing excellent work, and those in Moscow especially. We may applaud the efforts of very many of the workers and the methods of work they practise. But while they are doing such an excellent job and our society helps them in this, it gives some of our schools a chance to dodge any extra work. Many of the schools do not trouble to start hobby circles because pupils can attend them at the Palaces of Pioneers. And, certainly, excuses can always be found: either they have no suitable premises or no funds, or gain no instructors to run these circles, and so on and so forth. I am all for a collective where the entire educative process is properly organised.

Personally, I see it as a system of strong, powerful, well-equipped and fully armed collectives. But these are only the external requirements of a well-organised collective. . . .

The same Palace of Young Pioneers, or in other words the children's club, can work alongside the school, but the work should anyway be organised by the school. The school should be answerable for this work and it has got to be a joint effort. The Komsomol organiser who was against the girls attending the rhythmics circle was right. If he is responsible for the upbringing of the children in his collective, he must take an interest in and be answerable for what his charges do in the Palace of Young Pioneers. This breaking up of the educative process among different institutions and persons, bound by no mutual responsibility or authority, can serve no useful purpose.

I do realise that a single children's collective, excellently equipped and armed, would naturally cost more money to maintain, but it is very possible that in the long run it would prove to be the more economical, if efficiently organised.

All this concerns the pattern of collectives as such. In short, I am inclined to insist that the role of a single collective, guiding children in their education, must belong to the school. And all the other institutions must be subordinated to the school.

I an convinced that if a collective has no set goal, it is hopeless to try and organise it. Every collective must have a common collective goal, set not before the separate forms, but before the whole school, which is absolutely essential.

My collective numbered five hundred people. Their ages ranged from eight to eighteen, in other words, it included pupils from the first to the tenth forms. They obviously differed from one another in a great many things. The older ones were better educated, more skilled in industrial work, and more cultured. The youngest were, of course, illiterate and closer to the definition "strays". In the final count, they were simply children. Nevertheless, in the last years of my work all the five hundred made up a genuinely single-minded collective. I never permitted myself to deny any one of my charges his rights as a member of the collective or his vote, irrespective of his age or development. The general meeting of the Commune members was indeed a real governing body.

It was this idea of the general meeting functioning as the governing body that aroused the protests and doubts of my critics and chiefs. They said: You can't allow such a large general meeting to make decisions, you can't trust the management of a collective to a crowd of youngsters. They were right, of course. But then my whole point was to get those children to be not just a crowd, but a general meeting of members of a collective.

There are countless ways and means of changing a "crowd" into a general meeting. It can't be done by any artificial means, nor can it be achieved in one month. This is one of those cases when a striving for quick results invariably ends in failure. Take a school where there is no sort of collective, no co-ordination, where at best a form lives a life apart and comes together with the other forms the way we come together with the passers-by in the street. To shape a collective out of this amorphous collection of children would, naturally, be a long and difficult job (taking more than just a year or two). But then if a collective has once been shaped, if it is kept whole, well looked after and has its development closely watched, it can live for ages. And especially in school, where a child spends eight or ten years, such a collective must be treasured as the most powerful instrument of education.

A children's collective is a mighty force; in power it is practically unsurpassed, yet it can easily be broken up, of course. A sequence of errors, a series of changes in the guidance may reduce it to a "crowd". But the longer a collective lives, the stronger it grows, the keener it becomes to go on living.

And now we come to one very important condition, which I should like to stress particularly. Tradition. Nothing cements a collective so strongly as tradition. Cultivating traditions and instilling respect for them is an extremely important part of educational work. A school that lacks traditions cannot be a good school, and the best schools I have seen; in Moscow too, are those that have built some up. What is a tradition? I have met with opposition in the matter of traditions as well. Our old educationists used to say: "Every law, every rule should be sensible and logically clear. And you are bringing in tradition, the sense and logic of which have long disappeared." Quite right, I did bring in tradition. Here's an example. When I was younger and had less work to do, I used to get up at six in the morning every day and make a roll-call: that is, I went to the dormitory together with the detachment commander on duty, and my coming was saluted with the order "Attention!" I took the roll-call of the Commune members and made my morning check-up. I was the Commune's commanding officer to them then, and as such I could examine any disputes that needed settling and mete out punishments. No one in the Commune except me had the right to impose punishment, that is barring the general meeting, of course. When I was no longer able to take the roll-call personally every day I told my charges that thereafter the commander on duty would do it in my place.

Gradually this became a routine procedure. And so a tradition was established: when taking the roll-call the commander on duty had the authority of a commanding officer, and his word was law. With time, the original reason was forgotten. Newcomers to the Commune knew that the duty officer was empowered to impose punishment but they did not know why. The old ones remembered of course. The duty officer would tell them: "Two fatigues for you." And they'd answer: "Yes, sir." But if the same duty officer had tried to exercise this right at any other time of the day, they would have said to him: "And who're you to give us orders?" It became a fixed tradition, and it did much to cement the collective.

We had very many of these traditions in my collective, virtually hundreds of them. I didn't know them all, but the boys and girls did. They knew them even if they weren't recorded, they used their feelers or something to detect them. "Is this correct behaviour?" they would ask themselves. "Why? Because our elders behave this way." Copying the experience of their elders, respecting the elders' logic, respecting their endeavour to build up the Commune, and, most important, respecting the rights of the collective and its representatives — these are vastly important attitudes and they are, of course, upheld by tradition. The life of the children is made the more beautiful for these traditions. Living as they do within this pattern of traditions, they take a personal pride in these special laws peculiar to their own collective and try to perfect them.

To my mind, correct Soviet education cannot do without traditions. Nor can it be achieved unless a strong self-respecting collective of pupils has been built up with a dignity of its own. . . .

Admittedly, when creating traditions a certain instinctive conservatism must be used, laudable conservatism I mean: respecting what has been done, respecting the values created by our comrades and refusing to let them be shattered by somebody's whim. (Mine, in this case.)

Among other traditions, I value one in particular and this is the tradition of militarisation. . . . This must not be a repetition of an army unit's rules. By no manner of means must it be a copying and imitating of something.

I am against perpetual marching, which certain young educators practise to excess. Their pupils are always marching, whether they're on their way to the dining-room, to work or anywhere else. It looks bad and is quite unnecessary. But in army life, especially in the life of the Red Army, there is much that is beautiful and thrilling, and in my work I became more and more convinced in the usefulness of this beauty. Children have the knack of further beautifying this "militarisation", making it more childlike and pleasant. My collective was militarised to a certain degree. To begin with, the terminology we used was somewhat military, for instance, "detachment commander". Terminology is important. I don't agree, for instance, that it's all right to call a school an *incomplete* secondary school.* I would give this matter thought. How does it sound: I go to an incomplete secondary school? A truncated title, surely. The name itself should be attractive to the pupil. I gave thought to the question of terminology. When I suggested calling our seniors team leaders, the youngsters said it was not the thing. A team leader is the leader of a team of workers in industry, and in our detachment we had to have a commander. But, after all, he'd be doing the same thing. That's as may be, the youngsters argued, but a *commander* can give orders whereas if a *team leader* tries to do it he'll be told to mind his own business. In a children's collective they have a very nice and simple way of settling the problem of one-man management.

Take the term "report". Naturally, the boys could simply give me their account of the day, but I find that a certain formality appeals to them enormously. To make his report the commander must come dressed in his uniform and not in his overalls or the clothes he runs about in all day. He must hold his hand raised in salute while reporting, and I am not allowed to take it sitting down. All those present must also stand and salute. They are saluting the work of the detachment of the whole collective.

*Seven-year school, as distinct from the 'complete' ten-year school.

Then, there's a great deal that can be borrowed from army life and introduced into the routine and movement of the collective. For example, the Commune had a splendid tradition for opening general meetings. The privilege belonged to the commander on duty exclusively. The amazing thing was that the tradition had gained so great a significance that even when big people arrived at the Commune, even if it was the People's Commissar himself, no one was allowed to open the meeting but the commander on duty. Bugles were played to call everyone to the meeting. After that, the orchestra seated on the balcony played three marches. People could sit and talk, come and go. When they were coming to the end of the third march I knew I had to be in the hall, I felt it was my duty: if I didn't come I would be accused of violating discipline. After the music had died away I had to give the order: "Attention! The flag!" I could not see the flag, but I was sure it was near and once the order was given it would be brought in. When the flag was borne into the room everyone stood up and the orchestra played a special flag salute. The meeting was considered open as soon as the flag-bearers had taken up their positions on the stage, whereupon the officer of the day would come in and say: "The meeting is open." And for ten years no meeting was opened in any other way.

This tradition adorns the collective, it creates the framework within which life can be made beautiful, and that being so it captivates the imagination. The red flag makes a splendid content for this tradition. . . .

There has to be military smartness and trimness, but under no circumstances ordinary barracks-ground drilling. Shooting and riding are taught, and also military science. And that means efficiency and aesthetic education, which is absolutely essential in a collective of youngsters. This sort of training is especially valuable because it preserves the collective's strength, I mean it teaches the boys not to make vague, awkward gestures, slack and aimless movements. The matter of uniform is extremely important here. You know it better than I do, and on this score the People's Commissariat of Education and the Party have a definite point of view, so I shall not dwell on it. But a uniform is only good if it is handsome and comfortable. I had to go through a lot of different kinds of trouble and suffer plenty of setbacks before I was finally able to introduce a more or less comfortable and handsome uniform.

But as far as uniforms go, I am prepared to carry the matter on further. In my opinion, the clothes of children should be so beautiful and so colourful that they would evoke amazement. In past ages the troops were dressed beautifully. It was the splendour of the privileged classes. With us it is the children who should be such a privileged class of society entitled to beautiful clothes. I would not stop at anything, I would give every school a very handsome uniform. It serves as a very good glue to stick a collective together. I was more or less headed in that direction, but I had my wings clipped. I had gold and silver monograms, embroidered skull-caps, starched white pique collars, and so on. A collective which you dress well is 50 per cent easier to manage.

Lecture 2: Discipline, Regimen, Punishment and Reward

What is discipline? In our practice, some of the teachers and pedagogical thinkers are apt to regard discipline as a means of education. I hold that discipline is not a means of education but a result of education, and as a means of education it must differ from regimen. Regimen is a definite system of means and methods facilitating education. And the result of this education is discipline.

In making this assertion I suggest that discipline should be given a broader meaning than the conventionally accepted one in days before the revolution — in pre-revolutionary schools and pre-revolutionary society. Then it was a form of domination, a form of suppression of personality, individual will and individual aspirations, and even, to a certain extent, a method of domination, a method of bringing the individual into submission with respect to the elements of power. And that is how discipline was regarded by all of us who lived and went to school under the old regime, and everyone knows that we, as well as the teachers, looked upon discipline in the same way: discipline was a code of certain compulsory regulations which were essential for convenience, order, and a well-being of sorts, a purely outward well-being, a sort of bond rather than a moral state.

In our society, discipline is both a moral and a political requirement. And yet I observe certain teachers who even now cannot renounce the old view on discipline. In the old society an undisciplined person was not regarded as an immoral person, as a person who was transgressing the social moral code. You will remember that in the old school both we and our comrades looked upon this defiance of discipline as something akin to heroism, a daring feat, or at any rate a sort of witty, amusing spectacle. All mischief-making was sure to be regarded not just by the pupils but even by the teachers themselves as an expression of liveliness or quick-wittedness, or perhaps as a manifestation of a revolutionary spirit.

In our society defiance of discipline means that the person is acting against society, and we must judge his behaviour from the political and moral points of view. That is how every pedagogue should look upon discipline, provided, of course, that discipline is taken to mean a result of education.

First of all, as we already know, our discipline must always be a conscious discipline. It was precisely in the 1920s, when the theory of free education, or rather the tendency towards free education, was enjoying such wide popularity, that this formula on conscious discipline was being enlarged in the belief that discipline must stem from consciousness. Already in my early practice I saw that this formula could lead only to catastrophe. Persuading a person that he must obey and hoping that he will be persuaded into becoming disciplined means putting 50 or 60 per cent of success to the risk.

Discipline cannot be based on consciousness alone, since it is a result of the entire educational process and not of any special measures. It is a mistake to think that discipline can be instilled by means of some special methods aimed at creating it. Discipline is a product of the sum total of the educative efforts, including the teaching process, the process of political education, the process of character shaping, the process of collision — of facing and settling conflicts in the collective, the process of friendship and trust, and the whole educational process in its entirety, counting also such processes as physical education, physical development, and so on.

Expecting discipline to be built up by preachings alone means counting on extremely small returns.

It was when it came to preachings that the staunchest opposition was raised to discipline (by some of the pupils, I mean). And any attempt to convince them verbally of the need of discipline was liable to evoke as rousing a protest.

And so, trying to instil discipline by this means may only lead to endless argument. Nevertheless I emphatically insist that, as differing from prerevolutionary discipline, ours — being a moral and political requirement — should be a conscious striving, that is, it should be accompanied by a full awareness of what discipline is and what it is needed for.

How can this conscious sort of discipline be achieved?

In our school there is no theory of morals, there is no such subject, and there is no one appointed to teach this theory or obliged to communicate it to the children according to a given programme.

In the old school there was scripture. It was a subject refuted not by the pupils alone but very often by the priests themselves, who treated it as something deserving of little respect, but at the same time it did raise many moral problems which were touched upon during lessons in one way or another. Whether this theory yielded good results or not is another question, but in certain measure the problem of morals was set before the pupils in its theoretical rendering, that is, they were told: do not steal, do not kill, do not insult, obey your elders, honour your parents, and so on. These moral concepts, the concepts of Christian morals which were meant to instil faith and religion, were revealed in their theoretical rendering, and moral laws — if only in their old-fashioned religious form — were expounded to the pupils.

My practice has brought me to the conclusion that we too much render the theory of morals. No such subject is taught in our modern schools. We have a collective of educators, we have Komsomol organisers and Young Pioneer leaders who, if they wished it, could very well present to the pupils a proper theory of morals and the theory of behaviour.

I am sure that we shall inevitably arrive at this form in the future development of our school. I was forced to present the theory of morals to my pupils in a straightforward manner, as a programme subject. I had not the right to introduce such a subject as morals myself, but I had before me a programme I had drawn up for my own personal guidance, which I set out before my pupils at the general meetings under various pretexts.

In the course of my experience I worked out a programme, drafting these talks of the moral theory type. I had time and opportunity to perfect my efforts in this direction somewhat, and I saw the results — they were very good and far-reaching, incomparably better, of course, than anything that could have been achieved in the old school with the subject handled by some priest, even if an enlightened one.

Let us take the question of stealing. We have the means to develop the theory of honesty — the theory of relation to one's own things, the things belonging to the state — with infinite conviction, very strict logic and great persuasiveness. In impact and force the old preachings about the evil of stealing stand no comparison to this concrete theory of behaviour towards property, the theory of prohibiting stealing, because the old logic that a person must not steal or God will punish him hardly convinced anyone and could not act as a brake on stealing.

Self-control, respect for women, children and old men, respect for oneself, and the whole theory of actions in relation to the society as a whole or to the collective could be presented to our pupils in a most convincing and compelling form.

This theory of behaviour, Soviet behaviour I mean, is supported by so many facts in the life of our society, in our social practice, in the history of our civil war, in the history of our Soviet struggle and especially in the history of the Communist Party, that it would take little effort to present the subject beautifully and convincingly.

I have reason to assert that a collective, before whom this theory of morals has been set out, will undoubtedly take it all in, and every one of the pupils will find for himself in every separate instance some compulsory moral forms and formulas.

I recall how quickly and gladly my collective took on new life after a single talk on this moral theme. And a series, or rather a cycle, of such talks had a truly salubrious effect on the collective's philosophy of morals.

What general principles can serve as a basis here?

I have arrived at the following list of general moral principles. First of all, discipline as a form of our political and moral well-being must be exacted from the collective.

It is no use counting on discipline to appear of its own accord as a result of external measures, methods or talks given every now and again. Discipline, with a clearly defined purpose, has to be imposed on the collective in the form of a clear-cut, definite task.

These arguments, the need to exact discipline, are prompted by the following considerations. Firstly, every pupil should be convinced in his mind that discipline is a form enabling the whole collective to best attain its aim. The logic, provided it is presented clearly and fervently (I am against cool discourses on discipline), which asserts that without discipline a collective will not be able to attain its aim, will be the first brick laid in the foundation of a definite theory of action, that is, the theory of morals.

Secondly, the logic of our discipline asserts that discipline places each separate individual in a more secure and free position. This paradoxical assertion that discipline is freedom is very easily accepted by youngsters. The truth of it is confirmed for them at every step, and in their active campaigning for discipline they themselves say that it is freedom.

Discipline in a collective means perfect security for every individual, complete confidence in his right, his abilities and his future.

A great many facts in support of this principle can, of course, be found in the life of our society, in our Soviet history. Our revolution, our very society are a confirmation of this law.

Here is the second type of general moral requirements which should be set before a children's collective and which eventually will help the educator to settle any conflicts that may arise. In every separate case it is not only I but the whole collective who accuses the offender of going against the interests of the other members and depriving them of their rightful freedom.

As a matter of fact, this co-operation on the part of the pupils can perhaps be put down to the fact that a good half of the waifs and juvenile delinquents I had then had already spent some time in one of those children's collectives where discipline is lacking, and had suffered all the terrible hardships of an undisciplined life. This involved gangster law, with ringleaders from among the older and tougher boys lording it over the weaker and younger, exploiting them and forcing them to steal and commit acts of hooliganism. These once victimised children looked upon discipline as a real godsend, recognising it to be an essential condition for the full development of their personality.

If I had the time I would tell you about some very striking instances of boys being reborn almost instantaneously upon finding themselves in a disciplined environment. I shall only tell you about one such case.

One night in 1932, on orders from the NKVD I collected fifty homeless waifs off the express trains which made a stop at Kharkov. The urchins were in a very bad state. The first thing that struck me was that they all knew one another, although I took them off different trains, coming from the Caucasus and the Crimea in the main, but know each other they did. This was a "seaside resort gang" which travelled back and forth, met, crossed each other's paths and had some sort of relations among themselves.

When I brought them in, I had them washed, their hair shaved off, and so on. And the very next day they had a fight. It turned out that they had a great number of scores to settle. Someone had stolen something from someone else, someone had insulted someone, someone had broken his word, and it became clear to me at once that this group of fifty had its own ringleaders, its exploiters, its rulers and its exploited and oppressed. It was not only I who saw it but also my communards, and we realised that it was a mistake to keep those fifty together in the hopes of shaping them into a separate small collective.

The very next evening we broke up the group, taking care to put the tougher boys in the strongest detachments.

For a week we watched them trying to settle their old scores whenever they met. Under pressure of the collective an end was put to it, but several boys ran away from the Commune because they were unable to reconcile themselves to the fact that they had been forced to yield to an enemy stronger than themselves.

We gave this question a good airing at the Komsomol meeting, and brought to light many circumstances of that undisciplined life in which the individual suffered from a lack of discipline, and then, availing ourselves of the opportunity, we launched a campaign to elucidate this moral principle, to make it clear to the boys that discipline means freedom to the individual, and the ones to speak most passionately, convincingly and emotionally in support of this principle were the new boys, the street arabs I had picked up at the Kharkov Railway Station. They told the meeting how hard life was when there was no discipline, and how in that fortnight of living a new way of life they had come to understand from their own experience what discipline was.

Understanding came to them because we had launched the campaign and invited the discussion. If we had not talked to them about it they might have felt that life without discipline was hard, but they would not have apprehended it.

It was from children such as these, who had suffered from the anarchy reigning in a society of waifs and strays, that I reared the staunchest champions of discipline, its most ardent defenders and most dedicated preachers. And if I were to recall all the boys who were my right hand in the teachers' collective, you would see that they were the very people who, as children, had suffered most from the anarchy of an undisciplined society.

The third point of my moral theory, which should be set before the collective, which should always be remembered by the collective and should always guide it in its fight for discipline, is this: the interests of the collective are superior to the interests of the individual. This, it would seem, is a perfectly understandable theorem to us, Soviet citizens. And yet, in practice it is far from understandable to very many intelligent, educated, cultured and even socially cultured people.

We assert that the interests of the collective come before the interests of the individual in cases where he is opposed to the collective. . . .

This case started me thinking: how far above the interests of the individual should the interests of the collective be placed? And now I'm inclined to think that the interests of the collective should prevail to the very end, even if it is relentless — and then and only then will education really serve both the collective and the individual.

I have more to say on this subject. All I will say at this point, however, is that it need not be physically relentless, that is, the technique of relentlessness has to be organised in such a way that while the collective's interests should triumph over the individual's, the individual in question should not be placed in a grave, desperate position.

And last but not least, here is the fourth theorem which should be taught to the children as pure theory: discipline is an adornment for the collective. This aspect of discipline — its beauty and dignity — is most important. From what I know, very little is done about it in our children's collectives.

Our discipline is sometimes "a bore" — to use my strays' pet expression, it's dull, and actually boils down to nagging, pushing about, and exasperating twaddle. The question of making discipline pleasant, exciting and evocative is simply a question of pedagogical technique.

In my own experience I did not arrive at the final form of a beautiful discipline too soon. The danger to be avoided here, of course, is letting discipline become a mere outward adornment. The beauty must spring from its essence.

For my own part, at any rate, I had finally drawn up for myself a rather involved scheme to cultivate the aesthetic side of discipline. To give you an example I'll tell you about some of my methods which I used not so much to enforce discipline as to test and maintain its attractiveness. For instance, breakfast was late. The signal for breakfast was given ten minutes late. I do not know who was to blame: the kitchen staff, the commander on duty, or one of the pupils who had overslept. The question was what to do next: put off the signal for work for ten minutes, start work later, or forgo breakfast. In practice this can be a very difficult question to decide.

I had a big hired staff of engineers, foremen and instructors, about two hundred people in all, and time was precious to them too. They came to work at eight o'clock, and the factory whistle had to go at eight sharp. And there was breakfast ten minutes late, the communards were not ready to start for work, and it meant that I would have to keep the workers and engineers after hours. Many of them lived out of town, they had a train to catch, and so forth. And anyway the rules of punctuality were involved.

In my last years at the Commune I never doubted once what I had to do; nor did the pupils. Breakfast was late. I would give the order for the whistle to go at eight sharp. Some of the boys would come running out, others would only be sitting down to breakfast. I would go into the dining-room and announce that breakfast was finished. I realised perfectly well that I was making them go hungry, I knew perfectly well that it was bad for them physically, and so on. But nevertheless I never doubted my action once. If I had done this to a collective that had no feeling of the beauty of discipline, someone would have surely said: "Are we expected to go hungry, or what?"

But no one ever said such things to me. Everyone understood perfectly that this was what I had to do, and the fact that I was able to walk into the dining-room and give the order showed that I had confidence in the collective, demanding of them that they should go without breakfast. . . .

This sensitivity to beauty will be the last finishing touch to discipline, making it a thing of really fine workmanship. Not every collective will attain it, but if a collective does attain it and follows the logic that the higher you stand the more is demanded of you, if it adopts this logic as genuine, living logic, it will mean that in discipline and education the collective has reached a certain satisfactory level.

And now for the last theoretical general premise, which I thought necessary to set before my pupils as often as possible in a very simple form, easy for them to grasp: if a person has to do something he finds pleasure in doing, he will always do it, discipline or no discipline; discipline comes in when he does something he finds unpleasant to do with equal pleasure. This is a very important disciplinary thesis. It must also be made note of and stressed as often as possible at every opportunity.

Well, such is briefly the general theory of behaviour, the theory of morals, which should be set out before the children as a definite sum of knowledge, stress on which must always be laid in talks and the children's understanding of which must always be striven for. Only in this manner, by forming a general theory of it, will discipline become a conscious thing.

In all these theorems and axioms, emphasis must always be made on the main and most important thing — the political significance of discipline. In this respect our Soviet reality provides plenty of brilliant examples. The greatest achievements and the most glorious chapters of our history are associated with a splendid display of discipline. Remember our Arctic explorations, Papanin's group, all the feats of the Heroes of the Soviet Union, take the history of collectivisation, take the history of our industrialisation — and in our literature as well you will find magnificent examples which you can present to your pupils as models of Soviet discipline, based on these very principles of discipline.

Still, as I have said already, this consciousness, this theory of behaviour should be an accompaniment to discipline, it should run parallel to discipline, and not be the basis of discipline.

What then is the basis of discipline?

To put it in plain words, without delving into the depths of psychological research, the basis of discipline is exactingness without theory. If anyone were to ask me to define the essence of my pedagogical experience in the briefest of formulas, I would say: place the utmost demands upon a person and treat him with the utmost respect. I am convinced that this is the formula of Soviet discipline, the formula of our society generally. Our society differs from bourgeois society in that we place much higher demands upon a person than does bourgeois society, and our demands are more far-reaching besides. In bourgeois society a person may open a shop, he may exploit others, he may go in for speculation, or be a *rentier*. There, much fewer demands are placed upon a person than in our society.

But, on the other hand, we treat him with incomparably greater and basically different respect. This combination of the most exacting demands with the utmost respect for a person are part and parcel of the same thing — they are not two different things. By placing demands upon a person we show our respect for his strength and abilities, and by showing respect for something extraneous, something outside society, a pleasant and beautiful something. It is the respect due to a comrade who is taking part in our common endeavour, who is doing our common job with us, it is respect due to a worker.

No collective and no discipline can be formed, of course, unless demands are placed upon the individual. I am all for demands — consistent, extreme, clear-cut, without amendments or concessions. . . .

At any rate, one cannot begin to educate a collective without being sincere, frank, convinced, passionate and determined in the demands one makes. And anyone who intends to begin with vacillating, favour-currying, and pleading is making a very grave mistake.

The theory of morals should develop alongside the development of demands, but under no circumstances must the first be substituted for the second. When occasion allows you to theorise and explain to the youngsters what they must do, do so by all means. But when the occasion calls for firmness you must not indulge in any theorising, you must simply state your demands and insist on their fulfilment.

I have been to many schools, Kiev schools mostly. What really amazed me about those children was their awful shouting, the fidgeting, their lack of seriousness, their hysterical excitement, their running up and down the stairs, breaking windows, smashing noses, bruising faces, and so on.

I can't stand shouting. My nerves must have been strong enough if I was able to write my *Road to Life* while living among a crowd of youngsters. Their talking did not bother me. But shouting, screaming and dashing about are, to my mind, something children can do very well without.

And yet I have heard some pedagogues contend that a child must run about, a child must shout, it's supposed to be natural.

I object to this theory. A child needs none of it. It was everybody shouting in school that, more than anything else, frayed everyone's nerves all the time, and did nothing but harm. On the contrary, my experience has convinced me that a children's collective can easily be trained to behave in an orderly manner, to decelerate, to show consideration for others and respect property, doors, windows, and so forth. You would never hear this sort of racket going on at the Commune. I finally got the pupils to behave in a perfectly orderly manner when out in the street, on the school grounds and indoors. I demanded perfect orderliness in movement.

If I were put in charge of a school now I would begin by calling everyone together and telling them that I never wanted to see such behaviour again. No arguments, no theories. Later I would present them with a theory, but not at the very start. I would make a determined start: never let me see that again! I never want to see a yelling pupil in school again.

This emphatic demand, spoken in a tone that will brook no argument, must be made as soon as a collective is taken on. I cannot imagine how discipline could be instilled in a disorderly high-strung and uncontrolled collective unless the organiser stated his demands in this cold tone. After that, he would find things much easier.

The second stage comes when first one, then two, then three and then four pupils begin to side with you, forming a group that consciously wants to maintain discipline.

I hurried matters up. It did not worry me that my boys and girls had quite a lot of faults, I wanted to assemble a group as soon as I could so they would support my demands by making their own, voicing them at general meetings, and stating their views to the other pupils. It was imperative at the second stage of development to have a nucleus like that formed around me.

And now for the third stage when the collective begins to make the demands. It is the result and also our compensation for the nervous strain of the first stage. When the collective begins to make the demands, when stability comes to the tone and style of its activities, the educator's work becomes a thing of mathematical precision and efficiency.

I never demanded anything any more during my last five years at the Dzerzhinsky Commune. On the contrary, I acted as a sort of brake on the collective's demands, because a collective is apt to take too big a start and demand too much from an individual.

Once this stage has been reached you will be able to introduce the theory of morals on a broad scale. It will now be understandable to all that the moral and political requirements are the basic ones, and as a result each pupil will adopt an exacting attitude towards himself, taking the strongest view of his own behaviour.

I regard this line of development — from the dictatorial exactingness of the organiser to a free-will exactingness of every individual towards himself against the background of the collective's demands — the basic line in the development of a Soviet children's collective. I think there can be no fixed forms. One collective may be going through the first stage of development, and that being so it will need to have a dictator-like educator to guide it, but it must go on to the next stage — to the form of free collective demand — as soon as possible, and then on to demands made upon himself by the free individual.

Demand is not all there is, of course. It is an essential element of discipline, but not the sole one. True, in essence all the other elements also belong to the category of demands, but they are stated in a less resolute form. Attraction and compulsion are, as it were, a weaker form of demand. And last but not least comes threat — a stronger form than ordinary demand.

I maintain that all these forms must be applied in our practice.

What is attraction? It is a form subject to development as well. It is one thing if the attraction is a gift, a reward, a bonus or some other benefit to be enjoyed by individuals singly, and quite another if it is an aesthetic attraction, if the appeal lies in the inner beauty of an action.

It is the same with compulsion. At the early stage it may be expressed in a more elementary form, in the form of argument or persuasion. At a higher stage compulsion is expressed by hint, smile or joke. It is something the children value and appreciate.

Whereas at the early stages of a collective's development you may threaten the children with punishment and other trouble, later on it will no longer be necessary. In a developed collective threats are inadmissible, and at the Dzerzhinsky Commune I never permitted myself to threaten anyone, saying I'll do this and that to you! It would have been a mistake on my part. What

I did threaten my charges with was putting the matter before the general meeting, and there was nothing they feared more.

In the development of a collective, compulsion, attraction and threat may be greatly varied in form. At the Dzerzhinsky Commune in later years rewards for good work or behaviour, granted to pupils singly, were ranged in this ascending manner: gift, bonus, and gratitude endorsed by order and read before the ranks. This last, highest award, which was not accompanied by any gifts or material pleasures, was fought for by the best detachments. What was it they fought for? For the honour. All the pupils were ordered to put on their best clothes and assemble on the parade ground. Next the brass band marched in, and then all the teachers, engineers and instructors, forming a separate line. The order was given: "Attention!" The flag was borne in, the band played a flourish, and then the boy who was to be rewarded and I came out. The order: "By decision of the general meeting, gratitude is expressed to so and so", was then read out. The gratitude was entered into the detachment's and the Commune's journals, and a notice was posted on the honours board — that so and so, or detachment number so and so, had been thanked before the ranks on such and such a date.

Making this the highest award is only feasible in a collective which has noble sentiments, high moral qualities and self-respect. It is something to be striven for, but not begun with. One should begin with attraction of a more primitive kind, with material and other pleasures suited for each separate case, for instance, like going to the theatre to see a play. A good educator will, of course, find a great many nuances for the application of the different forms — attraction, compulsion, threat and demand — in each single case.

The question is — demand what? The formula I would suggest here should, rather than develop, always remain the same. First of all, the only thing that must be demanded is submission to the collective. It is the communards who taught me that. In developing their collective they arrived at a very interesting form. . . .

One has to be most exacting towards a person who goes against the collective more or less intentionally. One may be less strict when the offence can be blamed on the offender's nature, his character, his lack of self-control, or his political and moral ignorance. In such a case one may count on good influence and the gradual accumulation of good habits to have the desired effect. But in cases where a person consciously goes against the collective, refusing to recognise its power and flouting its demands, one has to be firm to the end, until this person has acknowledged the fact that the collective must be obeyed.

And now a few words about punishment. Things are not too well with us in this respect. On the one hand we have already admitted that punishment can be both necessary and useful. But on the other, although punishment is permissible, there is a line, born of our peculiar squeamishness and followed mainly by us teachers, of course, which implies that punishment is permissible but best avoided. You are free to punish, but if you do punish, you're a poor pedagogue. A pedagogue is considered good if he does not punish.

I am sure that this logic must confuse the pedagogue. And so it has to be established once and for all just what is punishment. Personally I am convinced that punishment is not so very beneficial. But I also maintain that where punishment has to be meted out the teacher has no right to suspend it. To punish is more than a right, it is a duty in cases where it is imperative to punish. In other words, I assert that a teacher may either punish or not punish, but if his conscience and his convictions dictate that he must punish, he has no right to refuse to do it. Punishment should be proclaimed an educational measure as natural, straight-forward and logically acceptable as any other.

The Christian attitude towards punishment as a necessary evil must be resolutely rejected. To my mind, the notion that punishment is an evil which for some reason is necessary does not quite agree with either logical or theoretical views. There can be no talk about evil in cases where punishment will do good, where no other measures can be adopted, and the teacher feels that it is his duty to punish. This belief that punishment is a necessary evil turns the teacher into a practising hypocrite. There must be no hypocrisy. No teacher must flirt with the notion that he is a saint since he gets along without resorting to punishment.

What is a person who knows that he ought to punish supposed to do? He broods and worries: so and so manages without punishing, and what will people say about me? They'll say I'm a second-rate pedagogue.

This sort of hypocrisy has to be done away with, I say. A teacher must apply punishment where it ought to be applied and where it can do good.

This does not at all mean, however, that we are asserting the advisability of punishment in all and every case.

What is punishment? I believe that it is in the sphere of punishment particularly that Soviet pedagogy has the opportunity of discovering much that is new. In our society we have so much respect for man, so much humaneness, that we should be able to arrive at the happiest possible norm in the matter of punishment. This is what this happy norm should be: a punishment must settle and eliminate a conflict and not create new conflicts.

The evil of the old-world punishment lay in the fact that while eliminating one conflict it created another one, the settlement of which was necessarily more involved still.

In what way does Soviet punishment differ from other punishments? In the first place, its aim must never be the infliction of suffering. According to usual logic: I shall punish you, you will suffer, and others watching you suffer will say to themselves: we can see you suffering, and we must take care not to do the same.

There must be no physical or moral suffering. What then is the meaning of punishment? Knowing that the collective condemns your action. The culprit must not feel crushed by the punishment, but it will make him think over his mistake, and ponder on his estrangement, however slight, from the collective.

And that is why punishment should be resorted to only when logic demands it and only when public opinion is for it. Punishing is wrong if the collective is not on your side, if you have not succeeded in winning it over to your side. If your decision is opposed by everyone, your punishment will do more harm than good. You are free to punish only if you feel that you have the backing of the collective.

So much for the meaning of punishment.

And now, for the form.

I am against any sort of established forms. Punishment must be entirely individual, best suited to the person in question, but nevertheless there can be certain laws and forms restricting the right to punish.

In my practical work I upheld the view that the right to punish belonged to either the whole collective, that is the general meeting, or to one person, authorised by the collective. I cannot imagine how a collective could be healthy if ten different people had the right to punish.

At the Dzerzhinsky Commune, where I had charge of the pupils in their factory work, school and everyday life, the right belonged to me alone. It is an essential requirement. It is also essential to have a single logic of punishment and not to punish often.

Lecture 3: Methods of Individual Approach

I think that in future pedagogics will pay special attention to the theory of the primary collective. How is one to understand the term — primary collective?

The term can apply to a collective the members of which are in constant business, friendly and ideological association. It is what at one time our pedagogical theory proposed calling the "contact" collective.

In our schools we do have these, of course. They are the grade or the form, and perhaps their only shortcoming is that they do not play the role of a primary collective, that is, a link between the individual and the school collective, and very often they are the final collective. I saw this in some schools, but I did not always see a school collective as such.

The conditions I had were more favourable, since my communards lived in and worked there, and thus had many logical and practical reasons for taking an interest in the affairs of the whole collective and living by its interests. But then I did not have a natural primary collective, which a school form is. I was obliged to create it. Later, we had a full ten-year school and I could have based my work on a primary collective of the school-form type. But I did not take this course. A form unites children in their everyday work and this leads to their isolating themselves from the rest of the school. The reasons for them to shut themselves in in their form interests are too many and too sound. And so in later years I gave up the idea of building up a primary collective according to a school-form pattern or even a work-team pattern. My attempts to organise a commune made up of primary collectives, united by such strong links as school-form and production work, yielded sad results. This type of primary collective always tends to withdraw from the interests of the collective generally and become isolated. If this happens, it loses its value as a primary collective, it consumes the interests of the school collective and makes transition to the higher stage rather difficult.

I came to this conclusion through my mistakes — mistakes which affected my educational work. I have the right to speak about it because I see the same thing happening in many schools where the interests of the primary collective prevail.

Collective education cannot be achieved through primary (contact) collectives only, because the unity of such a collective, where the children see each other all day long and live in friendly co-operation, engenders nepotism and leads to a type of education that cannot be called quite Soviet education. Only through a large collective, whose interests come not from simple association but from a more profound social synthesis, can the transition be made to a broad political education where the word "collective" means the whole Soviet society.

The danger of letting youngsters form a small closed collective is that theirs will be a group and not a broad political education.

I finally organised things in such a way that the primary collective was a cell which received its school and work interests from other groups. That is why, towards the end, I decided on breaking up the pupils into detachments comprised of boys and girls belonging to different forms and different work teams.

I realise perfectly that the logic of this pattern will not seem convincing enough to you. I do not have the time to go into detailed explanations, and so I will briefly set out some of the circumstances. For instance, there was the question of age grouping. I wondered how it worked, so I studied it in statistics, in action, in behaviour. At first, I too was all for building up the primary collectives from children of the same age. Partly because of their school interests.

This would seem to place the youngsters, isolated from seniors, in a more natural and correct environment. At that age (eleven or twelve) they ought to belong to one collective, with their own interests and organisations, and this I believed was the soundest pedagogical point of view. I was also influenced by pedagogical literature which maintained that age grouping was one of the most important things in education.

But then I saw that youngsters, isolated from other age groups, were in actual fact placed in an artificial environment. They were deprived of the constant influence of older boys and girls, there was no handing down of experience, they received no moral or aesthetic incentive from their older brothers, from people who were more experienced and efficient, and who, in a certain sense, were a model for the youngsters to copy.

When I tried, by way of an experiment, to unite different age groups, I found I was doing much better. And that was the form I decided on. In the last seven or eight years my detachments always included some of the oldest, most experienced, well read and politically developed Komsomol members, and some of the youngest children. A collective such as this, made up of different age groups, gave a much better educational effect, and what is more it was manoeuvrable and smart, easy for me to manage.

A collective made up of youngsters of an age always tends to shut itself up in its own shell of interests peculiar to that given age, to withdraw from me, their guide, and from the rest of the collective. Say, all of them are keen on skating; this keenness naturally shuts them in into a precinct entirely their own. But if my collective is made up of different age groups, the life it gives and the hobbies it pursues follow a more intricate pattern, requiring greater effort from both its older and younger members, making higher demands upon them, and, consequently, producing a more desirable educational effect.

In later years I practised the principle "who wants to be with whom" when forming collectives of different age groups. The boldness of this venture frightened me at first, but then I saw that it was the most natural and wholesome setup, provided that this natural primary collective included youngsters from different school forms and work teams.

Thus I reached the irrevocable decision that this was the best way. . . . .

What is a primary collective, a detachment? In our practical work at the Gorky Colony and the Dzerzhinsky Commune we arrived at the following rule: we, that is myself as head of the Commune, the bodies of self-government, the Komsomol bureau, the council of commanders, and the general meeting, tried to have no dealings with separate individuals. That is, officially. I find it very difficult to prove this logic to you. I have called it the logic of parallel educational influence. It is so difficult for me to explain because I have never written anything about it and never sought or found any formulas.

What is parallel educational influence?

We dealt only with the detachment. We had no dealings with the individual. Such was the official formula. In actual fact we dealt with the individual, but we asserted that we were not concerned with the individual.

To explain. We did not want every separate individual to feel that he was an object of education. The way I saw it was that here's a twelve- or fifteen-year-old living and enjoying life, getting some joy out of it and accumulating experience and impressions. As far as we are concerned he is an object of education, but as far as he is concerned he is a living person, and it will not serve me well to try and convince him that he is not a person, only a person in the making, that he is not a living thing but an *object* pedagogically speaking.

I tried to convince him that I was more a teacher who was teaching him to read and write than an educator; that I was helping him to learn a trade, that I appreciated his contribution to the production process, that I realised he was a citizen, and that I was an older comrade guiding his life with his help and his participation. I took care not to make him feel that he was no more than a pupil, no more than an object of education, of no social or personal worth. But actually to me he was just that.

It was the same with a detachment. We insisted that a detachment was a small Soviet cell faced with big social tasks. It was up to the detachment to try and elevate the Commune to the highest possible state. It had to help the ex-communards, help the one-time strays who came to the Commune and needed assistance.

The detachment had to be public-spirited and act as the primary cell in social work and life.

Together with my teaching staff we came to the conclusion that an individual needed very careful adjusting to his environment to make him feel himself a citizen, a person, above all else. In our subsequent work this became a tradition.

Petrenko came late to work. The matter was reported to me that same evening. I called in the commander of his detachment and said:

"One of you was late to work."

"Yes. It was Petrenko."

"See it doesn't happen again."

"It won't happen again."

But then Petrenko was late again. I summoned the detachment.

"It's the second time your Petrenko came late to work."

I ticked off the whole detachment. They promised it would not happen again. I said: "You may go."

I watched to see what would happen. I knew they would take Petrenko to task, and make enormous demands upon him as a member of their detachment, as a member of the whole collective. . . .

How did my colleagues and I organise work with the pupils, with the different personalities?

To work with a pupil one has to know him well and cultivate him. If in my imagination I had seen those personalities scattered like so many peas outside the bounds of the collective, if I had approached them without this collective yardstick, I would never have managed them.

I had five hundred different personalities. An important circumstance. The first year, I made the usual beginner's mistake. I turned my attention to personalities which were misfits in the collective. Mistakenly I directed my attention to the most dangerous characters and occupied myself with them. Naturally, it was the thieves, the hooligans, the collective's antagonists and those who wanted to run away — in other words those whom the collective would anyway cast off and drop — who engaged my attention. Naturally, I watched them particularly. I did it in the firm belief that I was a pedagogue and that I knew how to handle different personalities. I called everyone in in turn, talked, persuaded, and so on.

I changed the tone of my work in later years. I realised that the most dangerous characters were not those who made themselves conspicuous, but those who hid from me.

What made me think so? By that time I had already graduated fifteen groups, and following their careers closely I saw that many of those whom I had thought dangerous and bad were doing well, meeting life on the right terms as Soviet people should, and though they did make mistakes sometimes, as a product of education I found them quite satisfactory. Some of the boys who used to hide from me, making themselves unnoticeable in the collective, were taking a philistine attitude to life: they married too early, built a "pretty nest", squeezed themselves into soft jobs by various means, resigned from the Komsomol, severed all ties with society, and turned into small nondescript creatures, with no telling "what they are" or "how they smell". In some cases I even noticed signs of a slow but deep-seated decay. Those whose ambitions stopped at building a home and feeding up pigs, those who stopped attending meetings and reading the newspapers, were quite likely to get involved in shady deals one fine day.

I came to the profound conviction that it was the ones who hid from me and kept out of my way who made the most dangerous characters requiring my particular attention.

Incidentally, it was the communards themselves who started me thinking about it. In some cases they were quite outspoken in assuring me that the ones who kept to themselves, cramming all day (they'd probably go on cramming or fixing their radios even if a fire broke out), never speaking at meetings, never voicing an opinion, were the worst of the lot, the most dangerous, because they were clever and shrewd enough to keep out of the way, pursue their own quiet course, and go out into life intact and unconvinced.

When I had made some headway, when I had got over the shock of theft and hooliganism, I realised that the aim of my educational work was not putting two or three hooligans and thieves straight, but rearing a definite type of citizen, moulding a militant, active, efficient character, and that this positive aim could only be achieved if I trained the whole collective and not merely put straight the odd individual who needed straightening.

Some teachers make the same mistake in school, too. There are teachers who think it their duty to concentrate on difficult or backward pupils, leaving the so-called "normal" ones to carry on by themselves. But the question is: what are they carrying on and where will it carry them? . . .

We shall now deal with individual approach. The collective of tutors and teachers plays the most important role here. It is very difficult to define their task in accurate enough terms. This, perhaps, is the greatest problem in our pedagogy. In our pedagogical literature the word "tutor" appears in the singular in more cases than not: "the tutor must be this and that", "the tutor must do this and that", or "the tutor must speak in such and such a manner".

I cannot imagine how pedagogy could count on the lone tutor. Naturally we'd find things difficult without this gifted tutor, capable of managing the pupils, and possessing a keen eye, perseverance, intelligence, experience — a good tutor, in other words. But when we have thirty-five million children and teenagers to educate, can we stake everything on the chance that such tutors will be available?

Leaving this to chance means accepting that a good tutor will provide good education and a poor tutor will provide poor education. Has anyone tried to count the number of gifted and giftless tutors? And then, of course, a tutor has to be well-educated himself. What sort of upbringing must he have, what sort of person must he be, what should his aims and interests be? No one has ever counted the tutors who fail to meet these requirements. . . .

And yet we are staking everything on the tutors alone.

Since in the course of my life I have been obliged to deal mainly with the aims and problems of upbringing, I know what it means to be landed with poorly brought up tutors and how the work suffers from it. It was a waste of years and effort for me, because it is exceedingly foolish to expect such a person to do any useful upbringing for us. Later, I came to the conclusion that it is better to have no tutor at all than one who has had a poor upbringing himself. I thought it was better to have four gifted tutors than fifty giftless and ill-educated ones. I have seen how they work with my own eyes. What results could their work be expected to yield? Nothing but the disintegration of the collective. There could be no other results.

It follows that the choice of tutor is a matter of primary importance. How make that choice? For some reason little attention is paid to this matter. It is the prevalent opinion with us that any person, anyone at all, can be a tutor if he is appointed to the job and paid a tutor's salary. And yet it is a most difficult job, perhaps the most responsible job in the long run, demanding of a person not merely maximum effort, but also strength of character and uncommon ability.

No one did so much harm to my work, no one knocked out of true the structure it had taken me years to build as badly as a poor tutor. And so in later years I adopted a firm line to work without them or to use only those that were really capable. Naturally, it made extra work for me.

Then I gave up the idea of tutors altogether. I usually sought the help of schoolteachers, but I had to train them first. I am convinced that teaching a person to bring up youngsters is as easy as teaching him arithmetic, say, or reading, or operating a lathe, and so teach them I did.

How did I go about it? First of all a tutor's character, behaviour, special knowledge and his training have to be organised. Otherwise he will not make a good tutor and do useful work. He must know how to use his voice, how to speak to youngsters, and what and when to say to them. This training is essential. A tutor who cannot control his facial expression or his moods is no good. He must know how to walk, joke, appear gay or angry, and he must be able to handle the pupils. He must behave in such a way that his every movement would be educative, and he must always know exactly what he wants or does not want. If he does not know this, how can he educate others?

I am convinced that in future our teachers' colleges will introduce such compulsory subjects as voice training, posture, control of one's movements and facial expression, otherwise I cannot imagine a tutor coping with his task. Tutors need to have their voices trained not merely to sing beautifully or speak, but to express their thoughts and feelings with the utmost precision, authority and imperiousness. All these are matters of educational technique.

For instance, you must know in what tone of voice to give a scolding, how far your anger or indignation may be shown, what right you have to show it at all, and if you do — in what way. All this is, in fact, education. A pupil apprehends your feelings and your thoughts not because he knows what is going on in your heart, but because he is watching you and listening to you. Watching a play we admire the actors on the stage, and their beautiful acting gives us aesthetic pleasure. Well, here the pupil is watching too, but the actors he is watching are tutors, and the impact has to be educative.

I cannot dwell longer on this matter. The important thing is for a tutor to tackle his job consciously and actively.

Secondly, no tutor has the right to play a lone hand, to act at his own risk and on his own responsibility. There has to be a collective of educators, they have to be united, working according to a single plan, adopting the same tone and the same approach to pupils. Otherwise there can be no educational process to speak of. Therefore, it is better to have five weak tutors, united and inspired by the same thoughts, principles and style of work, than ten good educators with all of them working in any way they see fit.

There can be many different distortions here. I suppose you know what a favourite teacher is. Now, I'm a schoolteacher, and supposing I begin to imagine that I'm everyone's favourite. Without myself noticing it I begin to pursue a certain policy. I am liked, and so I want to keep the pupils' affection, I try to be well loved by them. There I am, the favourite teacher, and all the rest are no one's favourites.

What kind of educational process is this? The teacher has already divorced himself from the collective. He fancies himself so well liked that he can afford to work any way it pleases him.

I respected my helpers — some of them were absolutely brilliant in their work — but I tried to convince them that becoming the favourite teacher should be the least of their ambitions. Personally, I never tried to win the children's affection, and in my opinion this affection, encouraged by the teacher for his own pleasure, is a crime. Maybe some of the communards are attached to me, but since my main task was to make citizens and real people out of the five hundred boys and girls in my charge, I did not see why I should make it more complicated by fostering in them a hysterical sort of love for my own self.

This coquetry, this chasing after popularity, this boasting of their beloved-ness does a lot of harm to teachers and pupils both. I have persuaded myself and my comrades that there is no room for this sort of thing in our life.

Let them grow attached to you little by little, without any effort on your part. But if a teacher sees this affection as an end in itself, it can do only harm. If he does not seek this affection, he can be exacting and fair to his pupils and to himself.

Correct upbringing can be achieved only by a collective of educators united in their common views and convictions, mutually helpful, and free from jealousy, free from a craving to endear themselves personally to the pupils. That is why I warmly welcome the news, which our newspapers have published, that the People's Commissariat of Public Education is giving serious consideration to the problem of enhancing the authority and power of head-masters and directors of studies who would co-ordinate the work of the teaching staff.

A short while ago the Sovietsky Pisatel Publishers sent me a manuscript to read. The author is a Moscow teacher. The book is written in the first person, it tells about a schoolmistress, the staff, the pupils, and covers the period of a school year.

At the publishing house opinion on this book differed sharply. Some dismissed it as cheap and shoddy, while others proclaimed it wonderful: I was called in as an arbiter.

If I were to recommend the publication of this story, it would only be for a definite purpose. The schoolmistress portrayed in it is such a disgusting person that, actually, it would do people a world of good to read it and see what a schoolmistress should *not* be like. But the author is full of admiration for her.

This pedagogical fake's only care is to win the pupils' "love". All the parents are awful people, she has nothing but contempt for them, she calls all parents and families "dull, drab things", while she herself is a pedagogue with a capital P, if you please. All her fellow teachers are rotters to a man: one can't see clearly for vanity, another takes no interest in anything, a third is a schemer, and a fourth is just lazy; the headmaster is sluggish and stupid. She alone is perfect.

What's more, all this stuff is written in the nastiest tone. The book is full of tender sighing, a pining for love *à la* Verbitskaya, a chasing after affection, and the pupils are described in a most unpleasant manner. And another thing: the peculiar unwholesome attention to matters of sex.

The plot, I suppose, boils down to this: a boy looked at a girl in a special way, the girl wrote him a note, and she, the great pedagogue, brilliantly smashed these attempts at falling in love, and earned everyone's gratitude.

Her type of pedagogical fakes who flirt with themselves even when alone, who flirt with their pupils and society, cannot educate anyone. The only way to make responsible, serious educators of the schoolteachers is to unite them into a collective, rally them round the central figure — the headmaster.

This is also a very serious problem which our pedagogues should pay more attention to.

If such great demands are to be made on the educator, then even greater demands must be made on the person who unites the educators into a collective.

The length of time a collective of teachers works together is a most important condition, and I think our pedagogues do not take this matter seriously enough. If, on the average, five years is what a communard stays with us, then a tutor should also do five years' service at the Commune at the very least. It should be made a rule, because in a really close-knit collective, whose life is settled and runs a proper course, a newcomer is always a newcomer, whether he is a pupil or a tutor. And it is a mistake to imagine that a tutor who has just joined the staff will be able to give the pupils anything. The success of a tutor depends on how long he has been on the staff, how much energy and effort he has put into the shaping of the collective; if the collective of teachers is younger than that of the pupils it will be rather feeble. This does not mean at all that only old men should be taken on the staff. It is up to our pedagogues to study the peculiarities of impact made by old teachers and beginners, and strike a balance. Assembling a staff of teachers cannot be a chance or accidental thing, it has to be done intelligently. There must be a certain number of old, experienced teachers, and it is absolutely essential to include a young girl who has just graduated from college and has never yet taken an independent step. It is one of the mysteries of pedagogy: when a young girl fresh from college comes into an old collective of teachers and an old collective of pupils, an elusively subtle process, which makes education a success, is sure to begin. The girl will be learning from the old teachers and this will give them a sense of responsibility for her work.

The question of how many men and how many women should be on the staff needs serious thought. The prevalence of men creates an undesirable tone. And having too many women also results in a sort of onesided development.

I should say that the looks of the teacher are also very important. It would be best, of course, if all teachers were handsome, but at any rate there simply must be one good-looking young man and one beautiful young woman on the staff.

This is the way I did it. Let us suppose I had twenty-two teachers and one vacancy. If all the twenty-two were plain like me, I'd choose a good-looking person to fill the vacancy. The pupils should admire the staff aesthetically also. Let them be a little infatuated. This will be the best sort of infatuation, not sexual but aesthetic, pleasantly visual.

The question of how many teachers should be gay and how many glum also needs deciding. I cannot picture a collective composed of gloomy people exclusively. There must be at least one cheery person, at least one wit. Regulations governing staff composition ought to fill a volume in the pedagogics of the future. . . .

Lecture 4: Work Training, Relations, Style and Tone

And now for the concluding part of my report about the basic type and character of the individuals that ought to be shaped in our educational collective. In my opinion, we pedagogues have more thinking to do on this point. I am profoundly convinced that the traits of our Soviet personality differ fundamentally from the traits of personality in bourgeois society, and therefore our upbringing should also be fundamentally different.

In bourgeois society upbringing is limited to the individual, adapting him to the struggle for existence. And quite naturally the traits of character needed for this stuggle have to be cultivated in the individual: cunning, diplomacy, fighting one's own personal battles, fighting for oneself.

And it is quite natural that in our old school, as in any bourgeois school, this complex of dependencies, essential in a bourgeois society, was cultivated. In that society the chain of dependencies is entirely different from what it is in ours.

You will remember our schooldays. No one actually told us in so many words that we would be dependent on the wealthy class and the officialdom, but the very essence of our upbringing was permeated with the thought. And even when we were told that the rich ought to help the poor, even that beautiful-sounding, really splendid idea contained a certain indication of that dependence which exists between the rich and the poor. The idea that a rich man would help me, a poor boy, implied that he had riches, it was within his power to help me, while all I could look forward to were his help, his handouts, the help of a rich man. And I, a poor boy, was an object of his charity. In this way the system of dependencies which we would be confronted with in life was deeply impressed upon us. A dependency on position, on wealth, on charity and cruelty — such was the chain of dependencies for which a person was trained.

We also prepare our pupils for a definite chain of dependencies. It is a terrible delusion to suppose that a pupil, once having freed himself from the system of dependencies of a bourgeois society, that is, from exploitation and an inequitable distribution of material benefits, is free altogether from any chain of dependencies at all. In Soviet society there is a different chain of dependencies, the dependency of members not simply thrown together but living an organised life and striving for a definite goal. And in this organisation of ours there are processes and phenomena which determine the morals of a Soviet person and his behaviour.

All of us living in Soviet society develop and mature as members of a collective, that is as people within a definite system of dependencies. I do not know if I have probed this matter to the end in my work, but this aspect of education always interested me most of all. I have already spoken a little about it when I mentioned discipline.

To see this problem more clearly, let us look at a collective in action, I mean a collective and not a crowd, that is to say a collective which has definite common aims. The dependencies in this collective are very involved, for each separate individual has to co-ordinate his personal desires with the desires of others: first, with the collective as a whole and, second, with the primary collective of its immediate group, co-ordinating them in such a way that his personal aims would not be antagonistic to the common aims. Consequently, it is the common aims which should determine one's private aims. This harmony of common and private aims shows the character of Soviet society. For me, common aims are not simply the main and the dominating aims, they are actually linked with my personal aims. I suppose it is the only way in which to build up a children's collective. If a different pattern is followed, I assert that it will not be Soviet education.

In the practice of a collective, the contraposition of private and collective aims and the need to harmonise them are problems which arise at every step. If one senses a contradiction, it means that it is not a Soviet collective, it means that it is organised incorrectly. And only where the common and the personal aims coincide and there is no disharmony whatever, only that collective can be called a Soviet collective.

But this problem cannot be solved without contact with the routine trifling happenings of everyday life. It can be solved only in the practice of each individual communard and each separate collective. Practice is what I call the style of work. I think the question of style in educational work should be regarded as worthy of special monographs being devoted to it, that's how important I think it is.

Let us take a detail like the relations of the communards with one another, the attitude of one boy to another. The question is not new, it would seem, and yet only a feeble answer is given to it in our pedagogical theory. The problem could hardly exist in pre-revolutionary pedagogy. There, just as in pre-revolutionary society, the relations of people were treated as relations of one individual with another individual, that is to say, as relations between two free and independent worlds, and one could speak about bringing up a good person, a kind person, or this and that person.

In our pedagogy we can speak of bringing up a comrade, of the attitude of a member of one collective to a member of another collective, of members who do not revolve freely in empty space but are bound by their obligations to or their relations with the collective, by their duty to the collective, their honour as members of the collective, and their actions in regard to the collective. This organised attitude of the members of one collective to the members of another collective must play a decisive role in our educational setup.

What is a collective? It is not simply a gathering, or a group of interacting individuals, as the pedologists used to teach. It is an organised community of personalities pursuing a clear purpose and governed by its collective bodies. If a community is properly organised, it will have its collective bodies and an organisation of the collective's representatives empowered by it, and the question of a person's attitude to his comrade is not a question of friendship, affection or good neighbourliness, but a question of responsible dependence. Even if the comrades are in the same position, march shoulder to shoulder and perform practically the same functions, they are linked not simply by friendship but by their common responsibility for the job and by their joint participation in the collective's work.

Of particular interest are the relations of comrades who do not march in the same line but march in different lines, and of even greater interest are the relations of comrades who are not equally dependent on one another, with one being subordinate to the other. That's the most tricky thing in a children's collective, it is the hardest thing to create relations of subordination and not equality. It's the thing our teachers fear most of all. A pupil must be able to obey his comrade, not simply obey but know how to obey him.

And in turn his must know how to order his comrade, that is, to entrust certain functions to him and demand their execution.

This ability to obey a comrade — submitting not to force, wealth or charity, but to each other as equal members of a collective — is an extremely difficult thing to inculcate not only in a children's community but even in a society of adults. If there are any surviving vestiges of the old philosophy, it is precisely here that they cling most tenaciously. A person finds it hard to give an order to his equal just because he has been told to do so by the collective. The complex of dependencies here is extremely involved. But he will know how to give an order to a comrade, entrust him with something, rouse him to action and be answerable for him, if he feels responsible for it to the collective and knows that, by giving the order, he is carrying out the will of the collective. If he does not feel any of this, he will have scope for nothing better than the exercise of his personal vanity, his love of domination and power, and all the other inclinations alien to us. . . .

6

B. F. SKINNER

Commentary

Biography

Burrhus Frederic Skinner was born in 1904 in Susquehanna, Pennsylvania. After attending the local high school he studied for his Bachelor of Arts degree at Hamilton College, New York, where he specialised in English and classics. He graduated in 1926 and at first tried to make a career in writing fiction but found, according to his own report, that he "had nothing to say".

At this time his interest turned to psychology, with which he had made only a brief acquaintance at Hamilton College. He read the work of John B. Watson, the pioneer of the behaviourist movement, which made a strong impression on him. His growing interest in psychology induced him to return to academic work and in 1928 he enrolled for a Master of Arts degree in Psychology at Harvard University. After successfully completing his M.A. he went on to complete his Doctor of Philosophy degree in 1931. He continued to do research in experimental psychology at Harvard until 1936; he then went to the University of Minnesota to teach psychology, where he remained until the end of the Second World War.

During the war Skinner carried out work for the Office of Scientific Research and Development. This work involved an attempt to aid the war effort by applying some of his laboratory findings on the behaviour of pigeons, and he developed an ingenious scheme whereby pigeons were trained to act as pilots for bombs and torpedoes. After being conditioned to peck at the centre of a target image, the pigeons were to be placed in the nose of the missile behind a ground-glass plate that carried an electric charge. They would then guide the missile to its target by means of electrical impulses generated by their pecking. The scheme was never implemented although tests showed it to be quite feasible.

From 1945 to 1948 Skinner was Professor of Psychology at the University of Indiana. While there he again put his research to practical use by producing an automatic baby-minder or Air-Crib which was designed to cater for all the physical needs of a young baby. It consists of a large sound-proof and germ-free box, one side of which is a large pane of safety glass which can be raised like a window. The heating is electrically controlled and carefully regulated with the result that the baby does not require any blankets or clothing. Skinner used the device for his younger daughter, who spent most of her first two years inside one, and a number of other parents in America have experimented with it. It was publicised in an article by Skinner in the *Ladies Home Journal*, October 1945, but despite satisfactory reports it has not been widely adopted.

Skinner returned to Harvard in 1948 where he remained as a professor of Psychology until retirement in 1975. At Harvard he continued his experimental interests and also wrote widely in the area of education and social theory — it is these latter aspects of his work that make him of special interest to students of educational theory.

His experimental research continued to result in the production of intriguing devices such as the so-called "Skinner Box" (Skinner himself does not like the term) in which the behaviour of animals can be tested under strictly controlled conditions. Skinner has even managed to successfully teach pigeons to play a modified version of ping-pong by rewarding correct responses with a grain of corn.

His work with animals and the success he achieved in controlling their behaviour by means of regular reinforcement of desired responses eventually led Skinner to try the same principles with human subjects. This resulted in the production and popularisation of the teaching machine, the product for which Skinner is best known to the general public. Teaching machines and the method of "programmed instruction" based upon them have had enormous influence on the schools (especially in the United States) ever since.

Throughout his life Skinner has consistently championed a scientific approach to behaviour through the control of organisms by effecting changes in their immediate environment. His application of this approach to human behaviour and to social planning in general has aroused much criticism ever since he first put forward his proposals for a scientifically planned utopia in his novel *Walden II*, published in 1948. The ideas presented there were expressed systematically in his *Science and Human Behaviour* in 1953, and in his latest work, *Beyond Freedom and Dignity* (1971), he carries the idea of a planned society even further, an outlook which has generated a great deal of controversy in recent years. This debate has not been confined to academic circles and Skinner's ideas were regarded as sufficiently important to warrant his appearance on the cover of *Time* magazine along with an article inside discussing his ideas (20 September, 1971). Skinner throughout remains adamant in his view that mankind's survival requires radical changes in our approach to education, morality and government.

Main Features of Skinner's Educational Thought

As our present concern is primarily with the more theoretical aspects of Skinner's thought rather than the experimental elements, the discussion will concentrate mainly on the former. It is, however, necessary to look briefly at his laboratory studies because his educational and social theories arose largely from the results of these experiments.

His most important discovery was that known as "operant" conditioning. Until Skinner's experiments the only type of conditioning generally known was what is called "classical" conditioning, which derived from the work of the Russian physiologist Pavlov. In classical conditioning, the stimulus is presented by the experimenter and the subject responds automatically, the response being a reflex action such as the salivation of a dog when presented with food. It is similar to the eye-blink and knee-jerk in human subjects. The implications of this kind of conditioning for human learning are obviously very limited, because nearly all human learning involves some sort of conscious attention to the task in hand.

Skinner, following up the work of E. L. Thorndike on animal learning focused his interest on Thorndike's third law of learning (called the "law of effect"), which states that correct movements of an organism tend to be stamped in by the satisfaction of success and incorrect ones eradicated by the dissatisfaction of failure. (Thorndike's other two laws of learning were that movements most frequently and most recently performed tend to be repeated.) In testing this principle, Skinner would put a hungry rat in a box containing a lever at one end, which when pressed delivers a pellet of food to the animal. The rat begins with a number of random actions and eventually by chance presses the lever and receives the food. This is the first step in operant conditioning. Having been rewarded (or reinforced) once, the next time the animal is placed in the box it is more likely to press the lever than it was the first time because it has now associated receiving food with pressing the lever, and eventually, whenever it is hungry, it will go straight to the lever. The animal has then been fully conditioned.

This is called "operant" conditioning because the rat's behaviour "operates" on the environment to achieve what it wants. The behaviour is initiated by the rat, not elicited from it as in classical conditioning. Neither is there a single stimulus that produces the rat's response; there is a range of stimulus conditions which the experimenter can vary in accordance with the observed changes in the rat's behaviour.

By means of operant conditioning Skinner is able to achieve virtually complete control over the behaviour of the animal. This control is achieved not by acting directly on the animal but by carefully changing the conditions under which it acts. Skinner maintains that ultimately all behaviour, including human behaviour, can be similarly controlled and the first direct educational consequence of this was the development of teaching machines.*

The advent of teaching machines offers one way of coping with the problems of mass education while still preserving individual instruction. The machine can take over many of the more routine functions of the teacher and at the same time provide the child with a program that meets his specific needs.† Each child can work individually; when responses are correct, the

---

*He outlines this development in his article "The Science of Learning and the Art of Teaching", which is included in the readings that follow.

†It is important, however, to remember, and Skinner himself stresses the point, that strictly speaking, it is the program put into the machine that does the teaching, and not the machine itself.

next problem is attempted, if they are wrong, the next step is delayed until the right answer is obtained. The whole approach is of course based on the principle of operant conditioning, in which reinforced responses encourage further learning in the same direction. The teaching machine is ideal in this regard as it consistently and immediately reinforces the child by acknowledging each correct response.

Skinner maintains that it is a groundless fear that the teaching machine will eventually dispense with the need for the teacher. What it will do is free the teacher from many of the boring and repetitive tasks that currently have to be performed. There will always be a need for teachers to program and administer the machines and there will always be many aspects of teaching where the human relationship between teacher and learner is essential.

According to Skinner, the mechanisation of teaching is still only in its beginning stages; more complex machines will be built and these will render the learning that goes on in schools much more effective than it is at present. For further insight into Skinner's ideas on this topic see his essay "Teaching Machines".[1]

Skinner's work on operant conditioning and the mechanisation of learning has helped to provide the methodological basis for his general proposals for a science of human behaviour. It is only through such an approach to human behaviour that we can successfully institute the radical social changes that he sees as necessary for the survivial of society. What then are the changes he wants to bring about and why are they so necessary?

Society today, says Skinner, is in a crisis situation, and there seems little reason to doubt the truth of this statement; we need only consider some of the problems that are perplexing all of us: racial and religious intolerance and violence, the threat of nuclear warfare, overpopulation, pollution, exhaustion of resources, widespread poverty, drug abuse, the generation gap.

Skinner is not the first to point these problems out; what is new and what constitutes his significant innovation is his proposal on how to solve such problems. Briefly, his proposal is that we must escape from our outdated, prescientific attempts to handle these difficulties and introduce a thoroughgoing, scientifically based, planned society. For this planned society we will need to plan a new type of human being, one who is conditioned to feel and act only in socially constructive ways, in other words a man who is reasonable, co-operative, loving, sensitive, peaceful and industrious. Only if such qualities become widespread through society can it survive. If we continue along the same lines as the present we are doomed to eventual extinction by the relentless and inevitable march of events leading to the final world catastrophe, which could result from any one or more of the many problems facing us.

Now Skinner's solution seems at first sight eminently reasonable, but when it is realised exactly what is entailed, many become very critical of it. To begin with, it means the sacrifice of our traditional ideal of what Skinner calls "autonomous man". In Skinner's new society people will be programmed by those in control to act in the desired ways — development will be no longer be left to chance. Individuals are no longer to be the masters of their own destiny, no longer free to choose their own life style; autonomy is to be sacrificed for the greater good of society. Skinner does not see any harm in this, in fact he regards such notions as freedom and dignity as outdated and thus a hindrance to social progress — hence the title of his latest book: *Beyond Freedom and Dignity*. These notions, he says, were valuable when people had to struggle against tyranny or harsh social and political conditions in order to achieve fair and equal consideration. They led to the establishment of the liberal political ideology, which places great stress on the rights of the individual and remains very influential in the West today. However this set of ideals has now served its purpose; the problems of today are of a different magnitude and the philosophy of individualism only accentuates them.

The philosophy that every individual in the world has a right to an equal share of the world's goods, an equal right to educational and cultural privileges and, most important of all, the right to determine and act upon his own value system is seen by Skinner as one of the main factors accentuating the crisis situation. The tremendous acceleration in the aspirations and expectations of people in all walks of life and in all societies has led to the great pressures facing the world today. The only solution is to reverse this disastrous trend and to produce a new society in which each individual is so conditioned to desire only those things that society is able to supply without danger to itself.

From what has been said already, many people will have serious doubts about the value of Skinner's proposals. Skinner's answer would be that such doubts are a relic of a prescientific way of thinking about people and society — we have to rid ourselves of such needless fears and face up squarely to the demands of life in the society of the future. Indeed, Skinner takes his argument to its logical conclusion by suggesting that all of these inner feelings and beliefs — their hopes, desires and purposes, their whole mental life in fact — are irrelevant to a science of human behaviour. We have no way of reliably testing what goes on in our own or other people's minds; it is all purely subjective, introspective experience. The mind as such, while it may exist (Skinner has not, like some materialist philosophers, gone to the extent of denying there is such an entity as the mind), does not explain why people act as they do. Behaviour can be completely explained in terms of the nature of the environment in which a person moves. Change this and you will change the behaviour. Here Skinner draws on his experimental research and in particular his work on operant conditioning. Human beings, like all other animals, will generally act in those ways which are reinforced. If a form of behaviour results in, or is followed by, a pleasant or desired experience, it will tend to recur. Similarly, if it results in, or is followed by, the *removal* of an unpleasant or aversive experience, it will likewise tend to recur. The former case is one of positive reinforcement, the latter one of negative reinforcement.

The question that may next be raised is how to decide what values are going to guide the planned society. How can we decide scientifically that one sort of society is better than another? Skinner's answer is that values are just those ways of acting that best accomplish the survival of society. There is no need for long philosophical arguments about the derivation and justification of value judgments, because whatever conclusions are reached from such arguments, societies will in fact always choose those values they deem the most conducive to their survival. With the aid of science we can now for the first time determine what these will be with some degree of exactitude. Skinner says that "Other things being equal, I am betting on the group whose practices make for healthy, happy, secure, productive and creative people."[2]

Once accepted, values act as reinforcement to socially desired behaviour. People obey them because acting upon them is socially approved; the fact that people may also accept these values as morally binding on themselves is of secondary significance and Skinner sees no need for such inner commitments to provide reasons for action in the planned society of the future.

Education, of course, plays a crucial role in all of Skinner's thinking on this question. In fact, taking education in its broadest sense, what Skinner is recommending is a total re-education of society, a replacement of one pattern of upbringing and behaviour control by another. Taken in the narrower sense of formal education Skinner sees education as playing an essential role in the move towards a scientifically controlled society. Although he does not spell out his ideas in any detail on this point it may be assumed that the first generation of the new society would be produced mainly through the institution of the school. Programmed instruction in its broadest sense would presumably form the basis of the methods used, so that children will be programmed under controlled scientific conditions to develop the appropriate sorts of behaviour patterns.

This now raises further doubts about Skinner's scheme; it suggests very much the image of people manipulated like puppets by some omnipotent, all-knowing controller. But once again Skinner would reply that this is not as harmful as it seems. Already modern man is controlled and manipulated to a very large extent by the environment in which he lives — the requirements of the job, the restrictions of city life, the influence of advertising and the mass media all act to significantly determine behaviour. So, asks Skinner, how free are we as it is? Is not much of our supposed freedom merely an illusion? And at a deeper level, all of our behaviour is determined anyway; although we think we are exercising freedom of choice, we are really just acting out a predetermined course of behaviour dependent on the totality of our past experiences. If we knew everything there was to know about another person, we would be able to predict exactly how that person would behave in any given situation. So free will is only an illusion; we only feel we are acting freely because we have an incomplete knowledge of the causation of our own behaviour.

Skinner argues that all he is recommending is that we replace one set of controls on our behaviour with another; that we replace the present haphazard, unco-ordinated controls with controls based on a scientific examination of what is needed for mankind's survival. In the chapter "Alternatives to Punishment" from *Beyond Freedom and Dignity*, Skinner discusses what he regards as some weak forms of educational control that have been used since the time of Plato.[3] None of these, he argues, is sufficient on its own to control behaviour and all rely implicitly on other methods of control.

Furthermore, the controls Skinner wants will not take the form of coercion. By altering the environment in which we live — by redesigning of culture in fact — we will respond differently, but with no sense of unwillingness; we will simply see that one way of acting is more rewarding than another. So the methods to be used will follow broadly the principles of operant conditioning, in which the organism responds voluntarily to the changed set of circumstances arranged by the controllers.

But who are these controllers to be and how will they be selected? They are obviously going to have immense power and bearing in mind Lord Acton's well-known maxim "Power corrupts and absolute power corrupts absolutely", what safeguard have we that the controllers will not become self-seeking tyrants? Secondly, how can we be sure that the right people will be selected to do the controlling? Skinner is aware of these problems and his solution to the second difficulty is that the scientific means of selection will allow only those persons with the requisite capacities to rise to the top positions.

Skinner may have to accept that, to begin with, those already in positions of great power remain. In time, however, they will be convinced of the necessity for scientific planning of a new society. Through his writing he hopes to hasten such a conviction among the world's leaders.

Skinner's answer to the problem of the danger of corruption in the controllers is basically in terms of the fact that their behaviour will itself be partially controlled by the behaviour of those whom they are controlling. There is a reciprocal relationship between the two in which the controller has to adjust his methods to meet the needs of the subjects or else these methods will not be effective. The reader can assess the adequacy of Skinner's reply here by referring to what he says on this point in his chapter on "The Design of a Culture" in *Beyond Freedom and Dignity*.[4]

We may pause at this stage to reflect on the similarities between Skinner's proposals and those of Plato. Both want to produce a utopian society which is well ordered, happy, and changeless in its basic features; both see education as crucial in bringing this about; both see the need for a small group of leaders to institute and run the new society (Plato's guardians and Skinner's scientific controllers). The difference between them is that Plato's basic method for bringing about the new society is philosophy, in particular the philosophic vision of the world of forms (the fundamental reality which explains all experience); whereas Skinner's basic method is science, in particular the scientific principles associated with controlling behaviour by altering the environment. It is clear, then, that Skinner's significant innovation in educational thought is a new attempt to provide a contemporary variation on the traditional model, a variation that presents similar aims and goals, but uses different methods to achieve them.

Having now seen the main lines of Skinner's educational and social proposals, what assessment can we make of them? A number of possible criticisms have already been raised and the answers Skinner would give were suggested. Are these answers adequate? What other criticisms could be made? In the first place, is Skinner's behaviourist model of man acceptable? — is it true that man is simply the product of the environment and that personal ideas and purposes are irrelevant to how one lives? Skinner is perhaps assimilating man too much to the animal; having done most of his research with pigeons, rats and other animals whose inner mental processes are limited, he has tended to treat man in exactly the same way, neglecting the distinctive features of humanity of which thinkers like Aristotle were so aware. And in doing this, in reducing man to just another part of nature, has he not opened the way to treating man as merely another object to be manipulated, and thus overlooked each person's right to be respected as an individual with unique claims to consideration? What is then to stop the controllers in the planned society, having lost this distinctive sympathy for man as man, from feeling nothing but a patronising interest in him? Such an attitude would still be compatible with an acknowledged desire to act in the person's best interests and promote material welfare wherever possible.

Consider also the question of morality in the planned society. Is it really the case that moral behaviour is just a matter of acquiring socially desirable habits? Does not genuine morality require a positive commitment to principle on the part of the moral agent? While moral education may have to begin with habit training, a person is not morally mature until acting with some understanding of and commitment to the principle involved. Moreover a fully moral act would have to involve the exercise of choice, the deliberate following of one course of action rather than another, not merely adherence to a rule laid down by someone in authority.

This of course raises the question of free will. As we have seen, Skinner denies its existence and while it is not possible to prove conclusively that there is such a thing, we do however need to draw a distinction between acting merely in accordance with rules and acting because we accept the rule as providing a sufficient reason for action. In the one case we act without awareness of the reasons for so doing (it is simply the result of prior causes over which we have no control), and in the other we act deliberately and for the sake of the principle of conduct involved. Aristotle made a similar distinction in his *Nicomachean Ethics*, differentiating between the young child who has been trained to do just acts, but does not understand the concept of justice, and the adult who acts justly because he has accepted justice as a moral value. Skinner of course denies that this distinction is meaningful or significant, but is this just another instance of his reducing human behaviour to the animal model?

Further, is it really true that survival can only be ensured by accepting the values he proposes (in particular, the values implicit in the planned rather than the autonomous man), and is science the answer to all human problems? Can in fact Skinner's values be proved scientifically or do they represent a personal commitment outside of science? If the latter, why should we feel obliged to accept them?

Then there are the serious dangers implicit in the idea of the planned society itself. How can we be sure in advance exactly what sort of people will be needed for it? If we make a mistake in our planning might it not be too late to rectify it? If the new society is not right the first time, it will be very difficult to change because by then the citizens will already be programmed to behave in certain specified ways. And can we really be sure that the selection of the controllers will be adequately made? The practical problems in getting the whole enterprise started seem immense and unfortunately Skinner remains rather vague on this point.

Furthermore, does the reciprocal relationship between controller and controlled do anything more than provide the conditions under which the control will operate? In what ways does it stop the controller manipulating people towards ends which either do not conduce towards survival or which merely satisfy the controller's own desires?

Finally, we may question the efficacy of the methods by which Skinner would like to see the new person produced. Can a whole new personality type be generated just by the techniques of operant conditioning? These techniques at the moment seem inapplicable to many of the more complex aspects of human learning. And Skinner has little to say on other methods that may be used except to say they will be based on a science of human behaviour. But can any scientific method produce a whole new generation of people whose complete behaviour patterns can be laid down in advance?

There do, then, seem to be a number of serious objections that can be made to Skinner's proposals. Has he any answer to these? He, of course, believes that he has and despite the many criticisms he continues to promote enthusiastically his vision of the scientifically planned society. In general he would probably see most of the above criticisms as simply irrelevant to his scheme. They rest in the main, he would say, on an outdated, pre-scientific view of man which is no longer valid. They are likewise based on an exaggerated idea of the importance and dignity of human beings in the overall scheme of things — whether we like it or not, people are basically the same as all other living creatures, the only difference being that their brains are more highly developed and they are thus capable of a wider range of behaviour. Skinner, in this connection, makes the very telling point (originally suggested by Freud) that people's self-image has suffered three serious blows at the hands of science. "The first was cosmological and was dealt by Copernicus; the second was biological and was dealt by Darwin; the third was psychological and was dealt by Freud".[5] As a result of the first two discoveries, human beings can no longer regard themselves as living at the centre of the universe and as being a unique species, different in kind to other living species. The third blow to this self-image was more subtle, and in Skinner's words shattered "the belief that something at the centre of man knows all that goes on within him and that an instrument called willpower exercises command and control over the rest of one's personality".[6]

Human beings, Skinner says, have to realise the truth about their nature and forsake the ideal of autonomy which has been cherished for so long. If this can be done it will be seen that most of the apparent objections to the proposals for the planned person no longer apply.

There are two other replies that could be made by Skinner. In the first place, even if his behaviourist model of human beings is false, his plans for improving society nevertheless deserve detailed study. We could still go a long way in the direction of planning the perfect society on scientific lines, even if people are more complex than Skinner allows.

Secondly, even if there are philosophical and moral doubts about the way Skinner wishes to control human behaviour, are these doubts perhaps outweighed by the seriousness of the situation in which we find ourselves? Maybe they are a luxury we can no longer afford if we want society to survive. Perhaps we may have to sacrifice some of the values of human dignity and respect for the individual in order for there to be a future of any kind for humankind.

In the ultimate analysis, whether we go along with Skinner's proposals or not depends on our conception of the nature of humanity, our views about what quality of life we have a right to expect and our knowledge of the remedies that are possible for the problems that face us today. If we pin our faith on the ideal of each person as a unique personality and the determiner of personal destiny, we will resist the abolition of his autonomy that Skinner proposes. Similarly, if we see our present problems as being capable of solution by some existing form of political and social arrangement (or some modification or combination of these), we will resist the move to the fully scientifically planned and directed society that he recommends.

Skinner's theories in fact highlight one of the basic dilemmas facing us today — the conflict between technology and naturalism. Are our problems to be solved by an increase in the application of science and technology or by a return to a more natural, pre-industrial form of living? Skinner has no doubts about where he stands on this question and his work presents us with one of the most convincing and stimulating versions of the case for a fully scientific approach to human behaviour.

NOTES AND REFERENCES

1. B. F. SKINNER, "Teaching Machines", *Science*, CXXVIII, 24 October 1958. Reprinted in B. F. SKINNER, *Cumulative Record*, Appleton-Century-Crofts, New York, 1958.
2. B. F. SKINNER, "Some Issues Concerning the Control of Human Behaviour", *Science*, CXXIV, 30 November 1965. Reprinted in B. F. SKINNER, *Cumulative Record, op. cit*, p. 34.
3. See below (this volume), pp. 283–92. This chapter also provides an interesting commentary on some of the educational methods recommended by other theorists in this book, in particular, Plato, Rousseau, Dewey and Neill.
4. See below, pp. 299–301.

5. B. F. SKINNER, *Beyond Freedom and Dignity*, Alfred Knopf, New York, 1971, Chapter 9,
   p. 211.
6. *Ibid.*

SELECT BIBLIOGRAPHY

Books
Walden Two, Macmillan, New York, 1948.
Science and Human Behavior, Macmillan, New York, 1953.
Cumulative Record, Appleton-Century-Crofts, New York, 1959.
The Technology of Teaching, Appleton-Century-Crofts, New York, 1968.
Beyond Freedom and Dignity, Alfred Knopf, New York, 1971; repr. Penguin, 1973.
About Behaviorism, Random House, New York, 1974.
Walden Two Revisited, Macmillan, New York, 1976.
Autobiography in 3 Vols: I *Particulars of My Life* (1976), II *The Shaping of a Behaviorist* (1979),
   III *A Matter of Consequences* (1983), Alfred Knopf, New York.
Reflections on Behaviorism and Society, Prentice-Hall, Englewood Cliffs, N.J., 1978.
Skinner for the Classroom: Selected Papers, Ed. R. Epstein, Research Press, Champaign, Ill., 1982.

Journal Articles and Essays
"The Science of Learning and the Art of Teaching", *Harvard Educational Review*, XXIV,
   No. 2 Spring, 1954.
"The Control of Human Behaviour", *Transactions of the New York Academy of Sciences*, XVII,
   No. 7, Series II, May 1955.
"Freedom and the Control of Men", *The American Scholar*, XXV, No. 1, Winter 1955-56.
"Some Issues Concerning the Control of Human Behaviour: A Symposium" (a debate with
   Carl R. Rogers), *Science*, CXXIV, 30 November 1956.
"Teaching Machines", *Science*, CXXVIII, 24 October 1958.
"The Design of Cultures", *Daedalus*, Summer 1961. (American Academy of Arts and Sciences,
   Boston.) Reprinted in R. Ulrich *et al.* (Eds), *Control of Human Behaviour*, Scott Foresman,
   Glenview (Illinois), 1966.
"Man", *Proceedings of the American Philosophical Society*, CVIII, No. 6, December 1964.

Selections

Skinner is here represented by his essay "The Science of Learning and the Art of Teaching" and by extracts from two chapters of his book Beyond Freedom and Dignity. *The essay aroused considerable attention when it was first published in 1954 and was influential in the movement towards programmed learning. It also helps to clarify the experimental basis of Skinner's proposals for social and educational reform. The extracts from* Beyond Freedom and Dignity *show his most recent thinking on the scientific planning of society and give a clear indication of the educational implications of such planning.*

The Science of Learning and the Art of Teaching

Some promising advances have recently been made in the field of learning. Special techniques have been designed to arrange what are called "contingencies of reinforcement" — the relations which prevail between behaviour on the one hand and the consequences of that behaviour on the other — with the result that a much more effective control of behaviour has been achieved. It has long been argued that an organism learns mainly by producing changes in its environment, but it is only recently that these changes have been carefully manipulated. In traditional devices for the study of learning — in the serial maze, for example, or in the T-maze, the problem box, or the familiar discrimination apparatus — the effects produced by the organism's behaviour are left to many fluctuating circumstances. There is many a slip between the turn-to-the-right and the food-cup at the end of the alley. It is not surprising that techniques of this sort have yielded only very rough data from which the uniformities demanded by an experimental science can be extracted only by averaging many cases. In none of this work has the behaviour of the individual organism been predicted in more than a statistical sense. The learning processes which are the presumed object of such research are reached only through a series of inferences. Current preoccupation with deductive systems reflects this state of the science.

Recent improvements in the conditions which control behaviour in the field of learning are of two principal sorts. The Law of Effect has been taken seriously; we have made sure that effects *do* occur and that they occur under conditions which are optimal for producing the changes called learning. Once we have arranged the particular type of consequence called a reinforcement, our techniques permit us to shape up the behaviour of an organism almost

From B. F. SKINNER, "The Science of Learning and the Art of Teaching", *Harvard Educational Review*, 24, Spring 1954. Copyright © 1954 by President and Fellows of Harvard College. Reprinted by permission of the publisher.

This paper was presented at a conference on "Current Trends in Psychology and the Behavioural Sciences" at the University of Pittsburgh, March 12, 1954.

at will. It has become a routine exercise to demonstrate this in classes in elementary psychology by conditioning such an organism as a pigeon. Simply by presenting food to a hungry pigeon at the right time, it is possible to shape up three or four well-defined responses in a single demonstration period — such responses as turning around, pacing the floor in the pattern of a figure-8, standing still in a corner of the demonstration apparatus, stretching the neck, or stamping the foot. Extremely complex performances may be reached through successive stages in the shaping process, the contingencies of reinforcement being changed progressively in the direction of the required behaviour. The results are often quite dramatic. In such a demonstration one can *see* learning take place. A significant change in behaviour is often obvious as the result of a single reinforcement.

A second important advance in technique permits us to maintain behaviour in given states of strength for long periods of time. Reinforcements continue to be important, of course, long after an organism has learned *how* to do something, long after it has acquired behaviour. They are necessary to maintain the behaviour in strength. Of special interest is the effect of various schedules of intermittent reforcement. Charles B. Ferster and the author are currently preparing an extensive report of a five-year research programme, sponsored by the Office of Naval Research, in which most of the important types of schedules have been investigated and in which the effects of schedules in general have been reduced to a few principles. On the theoretical side we now have a fairly good idea of why a given schedule produces its appropriate performance. On the practical side we have learned how to maintain any given level of activity for daily periods limited only by the physical exhaustion of the organism and from day to day without substantial change throughout its life. Many of these effects would be traditionally assigned to the field of motivation, although the principal operation is simply the arrangement of contingencies of reinforcement.[1]

These new methods of shaping behaviour and of maintaining it in strength are a great improvement over the traditional practices of professional animal trainers, and it is not surprising that our laboratory results are already being applied to the production of performing animals for commercial purposes. In a more academic environment they have been used for demonstration purposes which extend far beyond an interest in learning as such. For example, it is not too difficult to arrange the complex contingencies which produce many types of social behaviour. Competition is exemplified by two pigeons playing a modified game of ping-pong. The pigeons drive the ball back and forth across a small table by pecking at it. When the ball gets by one pigeon, the other is reinforced. The task of constructing such a "social relation" is probably completely out of reach of the traditional animal trainer. It requires a carefully designed programme of gradually changing contingencies and the skilful use of schedules to maintain the behaviour in strength. Each pigeon is separately prepared for its part in the total performance, and the "social relation" is then arbitrarily constructed. The sequence of events leading up to this stable state is excellent material for the study of the factors important in nonsynthetic social behaviour. It is instructive to consider how a similar series of contingencies could arise in the case of the human organism through the evolution of cultural patterns.

Co-operation can also be set up, perhaps more easily than competition. We have trained two pigeons to co-ordinate their behaviour in a co-operative endeavour with a precision which equals that of the most skilful human dancers. In a more serious vein these techniques have permitted us to explore the complexities of the individual organism and to analyse some of the serial or co-ordinate behaviours involved in attention, problem solving, various types of self-control, and the subsidiary systems of responses within a single organism called "personalities". Some of these are exemplified in what we call multiple schedules of reinforcement. In general a given schedule has an effect upon the rate at which a response is emitted. Changes in the rate from moment to moment show a pattern typical of the schedule. The pattern may be as simple as a constant rate of responding at a given value, it may be a gradually accelerating rate between certain extremes, it may be an abrupt change from not responding at all to a given stable high rate, and so on. It has been shown that the performance characteristic of a given schedule can be brought under the control of a particular stimulus and that different performances can be brought under the control of different stimuli in the same organism. At a recent meeting of the American Psychological Association, Dr Ferster and the author demonstrated a pigeon whose behaviour showed the pattern typical of "fixed-interval" reinforcement in the presence of one stimulus and, alternatively, the pattern typical of the very different schedule called "fixed ratio" in the presence of a second stimulus. In the laboratory we have been able to obtain performances appropriate to *nine* different schedules in the presence of appropriate stimuli in random alternation. When Stimulus 1 is present, the pigeon executes the performance appropriate to Schedule 1. When Stimulus 2 is present, the pigeon executes the performance appropriate to Schedule 2. And so on. This result is important because it makes the extrapolation of our laboratory results to daily life much more plausible. We are all constantly shifting from schedule to schedule as our immediate environment changes, but the dynamics of the control exercised by reinforcement remain essentially unchanged.

It is also possible to construct very complex *sequences* of schedules. It is not easy to describe these in a few words, but two or three examples may be mentioned. In one experiment the pigeon generates a performance appropriate to Schedule A where the reinforcement is simply the production of the stimulus characteristic of Schedule B, to which the pigeon then responds appropriately. Under a third stimulus, the bird yields a performance appropriate to Schedule C where the reinforcement in this case is simply the production of the stimulus characteristic of Schedule D, to which the bird then responds appropriately. In a special case, first investigated by L. B. Wyckoff Jr, the organism responds to one stimulus where the reinforcement consists of the *clarification* of the stimulus controlling another response. The first response becomes, so to speak, an objective form of "paying attention" to the second stimulus. In one important version of this experiment, as yet unpublished, we could say that the pigeon is telling us whether it is "paying attention" to the *shape* of a spot of light or to its *colour*.

One of the most dramatic applications of these techniques has recently been made in the Harvard Psychological Laboratories by Floyd Ratliff and Donald S. Blough, who have skilfully used multiple and serial schedules of reinforcement to study complex perceptual processes in the infrahuman organism. They have achieved a sort of psychophysics without verbal instruction. In a recent experiment by Blough, for example, a pigeon draws a detailed dark-adaptation curve showing the characteristic breaks of rod and cone vision. The curve is recorded continuously in a single experimental period and is quite comparable with the curves of human subjects. The pigeon behaves in a way which, in the human case, we would not hesitate to describe by saying that it adjusts a very faint patch of light until it can just be seen.

In all this work, the species of the organism has made surprisingly little difference. It is true that the organisms studied have all been vertebrates, but they still cover a wide range. Comparable results have been obtained with pigeons, rats, dogs, monkeys, human children, and most recently, by the author in collaboration with Ogden R. Lindsley, human psychotic subjects. In spite of great phylogenetic differences, all these organisms show amazingly similar properties of the learning process. It should be emphasised that this has been achieved by analysing the effects of reinforcement and by designing techniques which manipulate reinforcement with considerable precision. Only in this way can the behaviour of the individual organism be brought under such precise control. It is also important to note that through a gradual advance to complex interrelations among responses, the same degree of rigour is being extended to behaviour which would usually be assigned to such fields as perception, thinking, and personality dynamics.

From this exciting prospect of an advancing science of learning, it is a great shock to turn to that branch of technology which is most directly concerned with the learning process — education. Let us consider, for example, the teaching of arithmetic in the lower grades. The school is concerned with imparting to the child a large number of responses of a special sort. The responses are all verbal. They consist of speaking and writing certain words, figures, and signs which, to put it roughly, refer to numbers and to arithmetic operations. The first task is to shape up these responses — to get the child to pronounce and to write responses correctly, but the principal task is to bring this behaviour under many sorts of stimulus control. This is what happens when the child learns to count, to recite tables, to count while ticking off the items in an assemblage of objects, to respond to spoken or written numbers by saying "odd", "even", "prime", and so on. Over and above this elaborate repertoire of numerical behaviour, most of which is often dismissed as the product of rote learning, the teaching of arithmetic looks forward to those complex serial arrangements of responses involved in original mathematical thinking. The child must acquire responses of transposing, clearing fractions, and so on, which modify the order or pattern of the original material so that the response called a solution is eventually made possible.

Now, how is this extremely complicated verbal repertoire set up? In the first place, what reinforcements are used? Fifty years ago the answer would have been clear. At that time educational control was still frankly aversive. The child read numbers, copied numbers, memorised tables, and performed operations upon numbers to escape the threat of the birch rod or cane. Some positive reinforcements were perhaps eventually derived from the increased efficiency of the child in the field of arithmetic and in rare cases some automatic reinforcement may have resulted from the sheer manipulation of the medium — from the solution of problems or the discovery of the intricacies of the number system. But for the immediate purposes of education the child acted to avoid or escape punishment. It was part of the reform movement known as progressive education to make the positive consequences more immediately effective, but anyone who visits the lower grades of the average school today will observe that a change has been made, not from aversive to positive control, but from one form of aversive stimulation to another. The child at his desk, filling in his workbook, is behaving primarily to escape from the threat of a series of minor aversive events — the teacher's displeasure, the criticism or ridicule of his classmates, an ignominious showing in competition, low marks, a trip to the office "to be talked to" by the principal, or a word to the parent who may still resort to the birch rod. In this welter of aversive consequences, getting the right answer is in itself an insignificant event, any effect of which is lost amid the anxieties, the boredom, and the aggressions which are the inevitable by-products of aversive control.[2]

Secondly, we have to ask how the contingencies of reinforcement are arranged. When is a numerical operation reinforced as "right"? Eventually, of course, the pupil may be able to check his own answers and achieve some sort of automatic reinforcement, but in the early stages the reinforcement of being right is usually accorded by the teacher. The contingencies she provides are far from optimal. It can easily be demonstrated that, unless explicit mediating behaviour has been set up, the lapse of only a few seconds between response and reinforcement destroys most of the effect. In a typical classroom, nevertheless, long periods of time customarily elapse. The teacher may walk up and down the aisle, for example, while the class is working on a sheet of problems, pausing here and there to say right or wrong. Many seconds or minutes intervene between the child's response and the teacher's reinforcement. In many cases — for example, when papers are taken home to be corrected — as much as twenty-four hours may intervene. It is surprising that this system has any effect whatsoever.

A third notable shortcoming is the lack of a skilful programme which moves forward through a series of progressive approximations to the final complex behaviour desired. A long series of contingencies is necessary to bring the organism into the possession of mathematical behaviour most efficiently.

But the teacher is seldom able to reinforce at each step in such a series because she cannot deal with the pupil's responses one at a time. It is usually necessary to reinforce the behaviour in blocks of responses — as in correcting a worksheet or page from a workbook. The responses within such a block must not be interrelated. The answer to one problem must not depend upon the answer to another. The number of stages through which one may progressively approach a complex pattern of behaviour is therefore small, and the task so much the more difficult. Even the most modern workbook in beginning arithmetic is far from exemplifying an efficient program for shaping up mathematical behaviour.

Perhaps the most serious criticism of the current classroom is the relative infrequency of reinforcement. Since the pupil is usually dependent upon the teacher for being right, and since many pupils are usually dependent upon the same teacher, the total number of contingencies which may be arranged during, say, the first four years, is of the order of only a few thousand. But a very rough estimate suggests that efficient mathematical behaviour at this level requires something of the order of 25 000 contingencies. We may suppose that even in the brighter student a given contingency must be arranged several times to place the behaviour well in hand. The responses to be set up are not simply the various items in tables of addition, subtraction, multiplication, and division; we have also to consider the alternative forms in which each item may be stated. To the learning of such material we should add hundreds of responses concerned with factoring, identifying primes, memorising series, using short-cut techniques of calculation, constructing and using geometric representations or number forms, and so on. Over and above all this, the whole mathematical repertoire must be brought under the control of concrete problems of considerable variety. Perhaps 50 000 contingencies is a more conservative estimate. In this frame of reference the daily assignment in arithmetic seems pitifully meagre.

The result of all this is, of course, well known. Even our best schools are under criticism for their inefficiency in the teaching of drill subjects such as arithmetic. The condition in the average school is a matter of widespread national concern. Modern children simply do not learn arithmetic quickly or well. Nor is the result simply incompetence. The very subjects in which modern techniques are weakest are those in which failure is most conspicuous, and in the wake of an ever-growing incompetence come the anxieties, uncertainties, and aggressions which in their turn present other problems to the school. Most pupils soon claim the asylum of not being "ready" for arithmetic at a given level or, eventually, of not having a mathematical mind. Such explanations are readily seized upon by defensive teachers and parents. Few pupils ever reach the stage at which automatic reinforcements follow as the natural consequences of mathematical behaviour. On the contrary, the figures and symbols of mathematics have become standard emotional stimuli. The glimpse of a column of figures, not to say an algebraic symbol or an integral sign, is likely to set off, not mathematical behaviour, but a reaction of anxiety, guilt, or fear.

The teacher is usually no happier about this than the pupil. Denied the opportunity to control via the birch rod, quite at sea as to the mode of operation of the few techniques at her disposal, she spends as little time as possible on drill subjects and eagerly subscribes to philosophies of education which emphasise material of greater inherent interest. A confession of weakness is her extraordinary concern lest the child be taught something unnecessary. The repertoire to be imparted is carefully reduced to an essential minimum. In the field of spelling, for example, a great deal of time and energy has gone into discovering just those words which the young child is going to use, as if it were a crime to waste one's educational power in teaching an unnecessary word. Eventually, weakness of technique emerges in the disguise of a reformulation of the aims of education. Skills are minimised in favour of vague achievements — educating for democracy, educating the whole child, educating for life, and so on. And there the matter ends; for, unfortunately, these philosophies do not in turn suggest improvements in techniques. They offer little or no help in the design of better classroom practices.

There would be no point in urging these objections if improvement were impossible. But the advances which have recently been made in our control of the learning process suggest a thorough revision of classroom practices and, fortunately, they tell us how the revision can be brought about. This is not, of course, the first time that the results of an experimental science have been brought to bear upon the practical problems of education. The modern classroom does not, however, offer much evidence that research in the field of learning has been respected or used. This condition is no doubt partly due to the limitations of earlier research. But it has been encouraged by a too hasty conclusion that the laboratory study of learning is inherently limited because it cannot take into account the realities of the classroom. In the light of our increasing knowledge of the learning process we should, instead, insist upon dealing with those realities and forcing a substantial change in them. Education is perhaps the most important branch of scientific technology. It deeply affects the lives of all of us. We can no longer allow the exigencies of a practical situation to suppress the tremendous improvements which are within reach. The practical situation must be changed.

There are certain questions which have to be answered in turning to the study of any new organism. What behaviour is to be set up? What reinforcers are at hand? What responses are available in embarking upon a programme of progressive approximation which will lead to the final form of the behaviour? How can reinforcements be most efficiently scheduled to maintain the behaviour in strength? These questions are all relevant in considering the problem of the child in the lower grades.

In the first place, what reinforcements are available? What does the school have in its possession which will reinforce a child? We may look first to the material to be learned, for it is possible that this will provide considerable automatic reinforcement. Children play for hours with mechanical toys, paints, scissors and paper, noise-makers, puzzles — in short, with almost anything which feeds back significant changes in the environment and is reasonably free of aversive properties. The sheer control of nature is itself reinforcing. This effect is not evident in the modern school because it is masked by the emotional responses generated by aversive control. It is true that automatic reinforcement from the manipulation of the environment is probably only a mild reinforcer and may need to be carefully husbanded, but one of the most striking principles to emerge from recent research is that the *net* amount of reinforcement is of little significance. A very slight reinforcement may be tremendously effective in controlling behaviour if it is widely used.

If the natural reinforcement inherent in the subject matter is not enough, other reinforcers must be employed. Even in school the child is occasionally permitted to do "what he wants to do", and access to reinforcements of many sorts may be made contingent upon the more immediate consequences of the behaviour to be established. Those who advocate competition as a useful social motive may wish to use the reinforcements which follow from excelling others, although there is the difficulty that in this case the reinforcement of one child is necessarily aversive to another. Next in order we might place the goodwill and affection of the teacher, and only when that has failed need we turn to the use of aversive stimulation.

In the second place, how are these reinforcements to be made contingent upon the desired behaviour? There are two considerations here — the gradual elaboration of extremely complex patterns of behaviour and the maintenance of the behaviour in strength at each stage. The whole process of becoming competent in any field must be divided into a very large number of very small steps and reinforcement must be contingent upon the accomplishment of each step. This solution to the problem of creating a complex repertoire of behaviour also solves the problem of maintaining the behaviour in strength. We could, of course, resort to the techniques of scheduling already developed in the study of other organisms but in the present state of our knowledge of educational practices, scheduling appears to be most effectively arranged through the design of the material to be learned. By making each successive step as small as possible, the frequency of reinforcement can be raised to a maximum, while the possibly aversive consequences of being wrong are reduced to a minimum. Other ways of designing material would yield other programmes of reinforcement. Any supplementary reinforcement would probably have to be scheduled in the more traditional way.

These requirements are not excessive, but they are probably incompatible with the current realities of the classroom. In the experimental study of learning it has been found that the contingencies of reinforcement which are most efficient in controlling the organism cannot be arranged through the personal mediation of the experimenter. An organism is affected by subtle details of contingencies which are beyond the capacity of the human organism to arrange. Mechanical and electrical devices must be used. Mechanical help is also demanded by the sheer number of contingencies which may be used efficiently in a single experimental session. We have recorded many millions of responses from a single organism during thousands of experimental hours. Personal arrangement of the contingencies and personal observation of the results are quite unthinkable. Now, the human organism is, if anything, more sensitive to precise contingencies than the other organisms we have studied. We have every reason to expect, therefore, that the most effective control of human learning will require instrumental aid. The simple fact is that, as a mere reinforcing mechanism, the teacher is out of date. This would be true even if a single teacher devoted all her time to a single child, but her inadequacy is multiplied manyfold when she must serve as a reinforcing device to many children at once. If the teacher is to take advantage of recent advances in the study of learning, she must have the help of mechanical devices.

The technical problem of providing the necessary instrumental aid is not particularly difficult. There are many ways in which the necessary contingencies may be arranged, either mechanically or electrically. An inexpensive device which solves most of the principal problems has already been constructed. It is still in the experimental stage, but a description will suggest the kind of instrument which seems to be required. The device consists of a small box about the size of a small record player. On the top surface is a window through which a question or problem printed on a paper tape may be seen. The child answers the question by moving one or more sliders upon which the digits zero through nine are printed. The answer appears in square holes punched in the paper upon which the question is printed. When the answer has been set, the child turns a knob. The operation is as simple as adjusting a television set. If the answer is right, the knob turns freely and can be made to ring a bell or provide some other conditioned reinforcement. If the answer is wrong the knob will not turn. A counter may be added to tally wrong answers. The knob must then be reversed slightly and a second attempt at a right answer made. (Unlike the flashcard, the device reports a wrong answer without giving the right answer.) When the answer is right, a further turn of the knob engages a clutch which moves the next problem into place in the window. This movement cannot be completed, however, until the sliders have been returned to zero.

The important features of the device are these: Reinforcement for the right answer is immediate. The mere manipulation of the device will probably be reinforcing enough to keep the average pupil at work for a suitable period each day, provided traces of earlier aversive control can be wiped out. A teacher may supervise an entire class at work on such devices at the same time, yet each child may progress at his own rate, completing as many problems as possible within the class period. If forced to be away from school, he may return to pick up where he left off. The gifted child will advance rapidly, but can be kept from getting too far ahead either by being excused from arithmetic for a time or by being given special sets of problems which take him into some of the interesting bypaths of mathematics.

The device makes it possible to present carefully designed material in which one problem can depend upon the answer to the preceding and where, therefore, the most efficient progress to an eventually complex repertoire can be made. Provision has been made for recording the commonest mistakes so that the tapes can be modified as experience dictates. Additional steps can be inserted where pupils tend to have trouble, and ultimately the material will reach a point at which the answers of the average child will almost always be right.

If the material itself proves not to be sufficiently reinforcing, other reinforcers in the possession of the teacher or school may be made contingent upon the operation of the device or upon progress through a series of problems. Supplemental reinforcement would not sacrifice the advantages gained from immediate reinforcement and from the possibility of constructing an optimal series of steps which approach the complex repertoire of mathematical behaviour most efficiently.

A similar device in which the sliders carry the letters of the alphabet has been devised to teach spelling. In addition to the advantages which can be gained from precise reinforcement and careful programming, the device will teach reading at the same time. It can also be used to establish the large and important repertoire of verbal relationships encountered in logic and science. In short, it can teach verbal thinking. As to content instruction, the device can be operated as a multiple-choice self-rater.

Some objections to the use of such devices in the classroom can easily be foreseen. The cry will be raised that the child is being treated as a mere animal and that an essentially human intellectual achievement is being analysed in unduly mechanistic terms. Mathematical behaviour is usually regarded, not as a repertoire of responses involving numbers and numerical operations, but as evidences of mathematical ability or the exercise of the power of reason. It is true that the techniques which are emerging from the experimental study of learning are not designed to "develop the mind" or to further some vague "understanding" of mathematical relationships. They are designed, on the contrary, to establish the very behaviours which are taken to be the evidences of such mental states or processes. This is only a special case of the general change which is under way in the interpretation of human affairs. An advancing science continues to offer more and more convincing alternatives to traditional formulations. The behaviour in terms of which human thinking must eventually be defined is worth treating in its own right as the substantial goal of education.

Of course the teacher has a more important function than to say right or wrong. The changes proposed would free her for the effective exercise of that function. Marking a set of papers in arithmetic — "Yes, nine and six *are* fifteen; no, nine and seven *are not* eighteen" — is beneath the dignity of any intelligent individual. There is more important work to be done — in which the teacher's relations to the pupil cannot be duplicated by a mechanical device. Instrumental help would merely improve these relations. One might say that the main trouble with education in the lower grades today is that the child is obviously not competent and *knows it* and that the teacher is unable to do anything about it and *knows that too*. If the advances which have recently been made in our control of behaviour can give the child a genuine competence in reading, writing, spelling, and arithmetic, then the teacher may begin to function, not in lieu of a cheap machine, but through intellectual, cultural, and emotional contacts of that distinctive sort which testify to her status as a human being.

Another possible objection is that mechanised instruction will mean technological unemployment. We need not worry about this until there are enough teachers to go around and until the hours and energy demanded of the teacher are comparable to those in other fields of employment. Mechanical devices will eliminate the more tiresome labours of the teacher but they will not necessarily shorten the time during which she remains in contact with the pupil.

A more practical objection: Can we afford to mechanise our schools? The answer is clearly yes. The device I have just described could be produced as cheaply as a small radio or phonograph. There would need to be far fewer devices than pupils, for they could be used in rotation. But even if we suppose that the instrument eventually found to be most effective would cost several hundred dollars and that large numbers of them would be required, our economy should be able to stand the strain. Once we have accepted the possibility and the necessity of mechanical help in the classroom, the economic problem can easily be surmounted. There is no reason why the schoolroom should be any less mechanised than, for example, the kitchen. A country which annually produces millions of refrigerators, dishwashers, automatic washing-machines, automatic clothes-driers, and automatic garbage disposers can certainly afford the equipment necessary to educate its citizens to high standards of competence in the most effective way.

There is a simple job to be done. The task can be stated in concrete terms. The necessary techniques are known. The equipment needed can easily be provided. Nothing stands in the way but cultural inertia. But what is more characteristic of America than an unwillingness to accept the traditional as inevitable? We are on the threshold of an exciting and revolutionary period, in which the scientific study of man will be put to work in man's best interests. Education must play its part. It must accept the fact that a sweeping revision of educational practices is possible and inevitable. When it has done this, we may look forward with confidence to a school system which is aware of the nature of its tasks, secure in its methods, and generously supported by the informed and effective citizens whom education itself will create.

NOTES AND REFERENCES

1. The reader may wish to review B. F. SKINNER, "Some Contributions of an Experimental Analysis of Behavior to Psychology as a Whole", *The American Psychologist*, 1953, **8**, pp. 69–78.
2. B. F. SKINNER, *Science and Human Behaviour*, Macmillan, New York, 1953.

Beyond Freedom and Dignity

Chapter 5: Alternatives to Punishment

Those who champion freedom and dignity do not, of course, confine themselves to punitive measures, but they turn to alternatives with diffidence and timidity. Their concern for autonomous man commits them to only ineffective measures, several of which we may now examine.

Permissiveness

An all-out permissiveness has been seriously advanced as an alternative to punishment. No control at all is to be exerted, and the autonomy of the individual will therefore remain unchallenged. If a person behaves well, it is because he is either innately good or self-controlled. Freedom and dignity are guaranteed. A free and virtuous man needs no government (governments only corrupt), and under anarchy he can be naturally good and admired for being so. He needs no orthodox religion; he is pious, and he behaves piously without following rules, perhaps with the help of direct mystical experience. He needs no organised economic incentives; he is naturally industrious and will exchange part of what he owns with others on fair terms under the natural conditions of supply and demand. He needs no teacher; he learns because he loves learning, and his natural curiosity dictates what he needs to know. If life becomes too complex or if his natural status is disturbed by accidents or the intrusion of would-be controllers, he may have personal problems, but he will find his own solutions without the direction of a psychotherapist.

Permissive practices have many advantages. They save the labour of supervision and the enforcement of sanctions. They do not generate counterattack. They do not expose the practitioner to the charge of restricting freedom or destroying dignity. They exonerate him when things go wrong. If men behave badly toward each other in a permissive world, it is because human nature is less than perfect. If they fight when there is no government to preserve order, it is because they have aggressive instincts. If a child becomes delinquent when his parents have made no effort to control him, it is because he has associated with the wrong people or has criminal tendencies.

Permissiveness is not, however, a policy; it is the abandonment of policy, and its apparent advantages are illusory. To refuse to control is to leave control not to the person himself, but to other parts of the social and non-social environments.

From *Beyond Freedom and Dignity*, by B. F. SKINNER. Copyright © 1971 by B. F. Skinner. Reprinted by permission of Alfred A. Knopf, Inc., New York and Jonathan Cape Ltd., London.

The Controller as Midwife

A method of modifying behaviour without appearing to exert control is represented by Socrates' metaphor of the midwife: one person helps another give birth to behaviour. Since the midwife plays no part in conception and only a small part in parturition, the person who gives birth to the behaviour may take full credit for it. Socrates demonstrated the art of midwifery, or maieutics, in education.[1] He pretended to show how an uneducated slave boy could be led to prove Pythagoras' theorem for doubling the square. The boy assented to the steps in the proof, and Socrates claimed that he did so without being told — in other words, that he "knew" the theorem in some sense all along. Socrates contended that even ordinary knowledge could be drawn out in the same way since the soul knew the truth and needed only to be shown that it knew it. The episode is often cited as if it were relevant to modern educational practice.

The metaphor appears also in theories of psychotherapy. The patient is not to be told how to behave more effectively or given directions for solving his problems; a solution is already within him and has only to be drawn out with the help of the midwife-therapist. As one writer has put it; "Freud shared with Socrates three principles: know thyself; virtue is knowledge; and the maieutic method, or the art of midwifery, which is, of course, the [psycho-] analytic process."[2] Similar practices in religion are associated with mysticism: a person does not need to follow rules, as orthodoxy would have it; right behaviour will well up from inner sources.

Intellectual, therapeutic, and moral midwifery is scarcely easier than punitive control, because it demands rather subtle skills and concentrated attention, but it has its advantages. It seems to confer a strange power on the practitioner. Like the cabalistic use of hints and allusions, it achieves results seemingly out of proportion to the measures employed. The apparent contribution of the individual is not reduced, however. He is given full credit for knowing before he learns, for having within him the seeds of good mental health, and for being able to enter into direct communication with God. An important advantage is that the practitioner avoids responsibility. Just as it is not the midwife's fault if the baby is stillborn or deformed, so the techer is exonerated when the student fails, the psychotherapist when the patient does not solve his problem, and the mystical religious leader when his disciples behave badly.

Maieutic practices have their place. Just how much help the teacher should give the student as he acquires new forms of behaviour is a delicate question. The teacher should wait for the student to respond rather than rush to tell him what he is to do or say. As Comenius put it, the more the teacher teaches, the less the student learns. The student gains in other ways. In general, we do not like to be told either what we already know or what we are unlikely ever to know well or to good effect. We do not read books if we are already familiar with the material or if it is so completely unfamiliar that it is likely to remain so. We read books which help us say things we are on the verge of saying anyway but cannot quite say without help. We understand the author, although we could not have formulated what we understand before he put it into words. There are similar advantages for the patient in psychotherapy. Maieutic practices are helpful, too, because they exert more control than is usually acknowledged and some of it may be valuable.

These advantages, however, are far short of the claims made. Socrates' slave boy learned nothing; there was no evidence whatever that he could have gone through the theorem by himself afterward. And it is as true of maieutics as of permissiveness that positive results must be credited to unacknowledged controls of other sorts. If the patient finds a solution without the help of his therapist, it is because he has been exposed to a helpful environment elsewhere.

Guidance

Another metaphor associated with weak practices is horticultural. The behaviour to which a person has given birth grows, and it may be guided or trained, as a growing plant is trained. Behaviour may be "cultivated".

The metaphor is particularly at home in education. A school for small children is a child-garden, or kindergarten. The behaviour of the child "develops" until he reaches "maturity". A teacher may accelerate the process or turn it in slightly different directions, but — in the classical phrase — he cannot teach, he can only help the student learn. The metaphor of guidance is also common in psychotherapy. Freud argued that a person must pass through several developmental stages, and that if the patient has become "fixated" at a given stage, the therapist must help him break loose and move forward. Governments engage in guidance — for example, when they encourage the "development" of industry through tax exemptions or provide a "climate" that is favourable to the improvement of race relations.

Guidance is not as easy as permissiveness, but it is usually easier than midwifery, and it has some of the same advantages. One who merely guides a natural development cannot easily be accused of trying to control it. Growth remains an achievement of the individual, testifying to his freedom and worth, his "hidden propensities", and as the gardener is not responsible for the ultimate form of what he grows, so one who merely guides is exonerated when things go wrong.

Guidance is effective, however, only to the extent that control is exerted. To guide is either to open new opportunities or to block growth in particular directions. To arrange an opportunity is not a very positive act, but it is nevertheless a form of control if it increases the likelihood that behaviour will be emitted. The teacher who merely selects the material the student is to study or the therapist who merely suggests a different job or change of scene has exerted control, though it may be hard to detect.

Control is more obvious when growth or development is *prevented*. Censorship blocks access to material needed for development in a given direction; it closes opportunities. De Tocqueville saw this in the America of his day: "The will of man is not shattered, but softened, bent, and guided. Men are seldom forced . . . to act, but they are constantly restrained from acting."[3] As Ralph Barton Perry put it, "Whoever determines what alternatives shall be made known to man controls what that man shall choose *from*. He is deprived of freedom in proportion as he is denied access to *any* ideas, or is confined to any range of ideas short of the totality of relevant possibilities."[4] For "deprived of freedom" read "controlled".

It is no doubt valuable to create an environment in which a person acquires effective behaviour rapidly and continues to behave effectively. In constructing such an environment we may eliminate distractions and open opportunities, and these are key points in the metaphor of guidance or growth or development; but it is the contingencies we arrange, rather than the unfolding of some predetermined pattern, which are responsible for the changes observed.

Building Dependence on Things

Jean-Jacques Rousseau was alert to the dangers of social control, and he thought it might be possible to avoid them by making a person dependent not on people but on things. In *Emile* he showed how children could learn about things themselves rather than from books. The practices he described are still common, largely because of John Dewey's emphasis on real life in the classroom.

One of the advantages in being dependent on things rather than on other people is that the time and energy of other people are saved. The child who must be reminded that it is time to go to school is dependent upon his parents, but the child who has learned to respond to clocks and other temporal properties of the world around him (not to a "sense of time") is dependent upon things, and he makes fewer demands on his parents. In learning to drive a car a person remains dependent on an instructor as long as he must be told when to apply the brakes, when to signal a turn, when to change speeds, and so on; when his behaviour comes under the control of the natural consequences of driving a car, he may dispense with the instructor. Among the "things" upon which a person should become dependent are other people when they are not acting specifically to change his behaviour. The child who must be told what to say and how to behave with respect to other people is dependent upon those who tell him; the child who has learned how to get along with other people can dispense with advice.

Another important advantage of being dependent on things is that the contingencies which involve things are more precise and shape more useful behaviour than contingencies arranged by other people. The temporal properties of the environment are more pervasive and more subtle than any series of reminders. A person whose behaviour in driving a car is shaped by the response of the car behaves more skilfully than one who is following instructions. Those who get along well with people as the result of direct exposure to social contingencies are more skilful than those who have merely been told what to say and do.

These are important advantages, and a world in which all behaviour is ependent on things is an attractive prospect. In such a world everyone would behave well with respect to his fellow men as he had learned to do when exposed to their approval and disapproval; he would work productively and carefully and exchange things with others because of their natural values; and he would learn things which naturally interest him and which are naturally useful. All this would be better than behaving well by obeying the law as enforced by police, working productively for the contrived reinforcers called money, and studying to get marks and grades.

But things do not easily take control. The procedures Rousseau described were not simple, and they do not often work. The complex contingencies involving things (including people who are behaving "unintentionally") can, unaided, have very little effect on an individual in his lifetime — a fact of great importance for reasons we shall note later. We must also remember that the control exercised by things may be destructive. The world of things can be tyrannical. Natural contingencies induce people to behave superstitiously, to risk greater and greater dangers, to work uselessly to exhaustion, and so on. Only the counter-control exerted by a social environment offers any protection against these consequences.

Dependence on things is not independence. The child who does not need to be told that it is time to go to school has come under the control of more subtle, and more useful, stimuli. The child who has learned what to say and how to behave in getting along with other people is under the control of social contingencies. People who get along together well under the mild contingencies of approval and disapproval are controlled as effectively as (and in many ways more effectively than) the citizens of a police state. Orthodoxy controls through the establishment of rules, but the mystic is no freer because the contingencies which have shaped his behaviour are more personal or idiosyncratic. Those who work productively because of the reinforcing value of what they produce are under the sensitive and powerful control of the products. Those who learn in the natural environment are under a form of control as powerful as any control exerted by a teacher.

A person never becomes truly self-reliant. Even though he deals effectively with things, he is necessarily dependent upon those who have taught him to do so. They have selected the things he is dependent upon and determined the kinds and degrees of dependencies. (They cannot, therefore, disclaim responsibility for the results.)

Changing Minds

It is a surprising fact that those who object most violently to the manipulation of behaviour nevertheless make the most vigorous efforts to manipulate minds. Evidently freedom and dignity are threatened only when behaviour is changed by physically changing the environment. There appears to be no threat when the states of mind said to be responsible for behaviour are changed, presumably because autonomous man possesses miraculous powers which enable him to yield or resist.

It is fortunate that those who object to the manipulation of behaviour feel free to manipulate minds, since otherwise they would have to remain silent. But no one directly changes a mind. By manipulating environmental contingencies, one makes changes which are said to indicate a change of mind, but if there is any effect, it is on behaviour. The control is inconspicuous and not very effective, and some control therefore seems to be retained by the person whose mind changes. A few characteristic ways of changing minds may be examined.

We sometimes induce a man to behave by prompting him (for example, when he is not able to solve a problem), or by suggesting a course of action (for example, when he is at a loss as to what to do). Prompts, hints, and suggestions are all stimuli, usually but not always verbal, and they have the important property of exerting only partial control.[5] No one responds to a prompt, hint, or suggestion unless he already has some tendency to behave in a given way. When the contingencies which explain the prevailing tendency are not identified, some part of the behaviour can be attributed to the mind. The inner control is particularly convincing when the external is not explicit, as when one tells an apparently irrelevant story which nevertheless serves as a prompt, hint, or suggestion. Setting an example exerts a similar kind of control, exploiting a general tendency to behave imitatively. Advertising testimonials "control the mind" in this way.

We also seem to be acting upon the mind when we *urge* a person to act or *persuade* him to act. Etymologically, to urge is to press or drive; it is to make an aversive situation more *urgent*. We urge a person to act as we might nudge him into acting. The stimuli are usually mild, but they are effective if they have been associated in the past with stronger aversive consequences. Thus, we urge on a dawdler by saying, "Look what time it is", and we succeed in inducing him to hurry if earlier delays have been punished. We urge a person not to spend money by pointing to his low bank balance, and we are effective if he has suffered when he has run out of money in the past. We *persuade* people, however, by pointing to stimuli associated with positive consequences. Etymologically, the word is related to sweeten. We persuade someone by making a situation more favourable for action, as by describing likely reinforcing consequences. Here again there is an apparent discrepancy between the strength of the stimuli we use and the magnitude of the effect. Urging and persuading are effective only if there is already some tendency to behave, and the behaviour can be attributed to an inner man so long as that tendency is unexplained.

Beliefs, preferences, perceptions, needs, purposes, and opinions are other possessions of autonomous man which are said to change when we change minds. What is changed in each case is a probability of action. A person's belief that a floor will hold him as he walks across it depends upon his past experience. If he has walked across it without incident many times, he will do so again readily, and his behaviour will not create any of the aversive stimuli felt as anxiety. He may report that he has "faith" in the solidity of the floor or "confidence" that it will hold him, but the kinds of things which are felt as faith or confidence are not states of mind; they are at best by-products of the behaviour in its relation to antecedent events, and they do not explain why a person walks as he does.

We build "belief" when we increase the probability of action by reinforcing behaviour. When we build a person's confidence that a floor will hold him by inducing him to walk on it, we might not be said to be changing a belief, but we do so in the traditional sense when we give him verbal assurances that the floor is solid, demonstrate its solidity by walking on it ourselves, or describe its structure or state. The only difference is in the conspicuous-ness of the measures. The change which occurs as a person "learns to trust a floor" by walking on it is the characteristic effect of reinforcement; the change which occurs when he is told that the floor is solid, when he sees someone else walking on it, or when he is "convinced" by assurances that the floor will hold him depends upon past experiences which no longer make a conspicuous contribution. For example, a person who walks on surfaces which are likely to vary in their solidity (for example, a frozen lake) quickly forms a discrimination[6] between surfaces on which no one is walking, or between surfaces called safe and surfaces called dangerous. He learns to walk confidently on the first and cautiously on the second. The sight of someone walking on a surface or an assurance that it is safe converts it from the second class into the first. The history during which the discrimination was formed may be forgotten, and the effect then seems to involve that inner event called a change of mind.

Changes in preference, perceptions, needs, purposes, attitudes, opinions, and other attributes of mind may be analysed in the same way. We change the way a person looks at something, as well as what he sees when he looks, by changing the contingencies; we do not change something called percep-tion. We change the relative strengths of responses by differential reinforce-ment of alternative courses of action; we do not change something called a preference. We change the probability of an act by changing a condition of deprivation or aversive stimulation; we do not change a need. We rein-force behaviour in particular ways; we do not give a person a purpose or an intention. We change behaviour toward something, not an attitude toward it. We sample and change verbal behaviour, not opinions.

Another way to change a mind is to point to reasons why a person should behave in a given way, and the reasons are almost always consequences which are likely to be contingent on behaviour. Let us say that a child is using a knife in a dangerous way. We may avoid trouble by making the environ-ment safer — by taking the knife away or giving him a safer kind — but that will not prepare him for a world with unsafe knives. Left alone, he may learn to use the knife properly by cutting himself whenever he uses it improperly. We may help by substituting a less dangerous form of punish-ment — spanking him, for example, or perhaps merely shaming him when we find him using a knife in a dangerous way. We may tell him that some uses are bad and others good if "Bad!" and "Good!" have already been con-ditioned as positive and negative reinforcers. Suppose, however, that all these methods have unwanted by-products, such as a change in his relation to us, and that we therefore decide to appeal to "reason". (This is possible, of course, only if he has reached the "age of reason".) We explain the contingencies, demonstrating what happens when one uses a knife in one way and not another. We may show him how rules may be extracted from the contingencies ("You should never cut *toward yourself*"). As a result we may induce the child to use the knife properly and will be likely to say that we have imparted a knowledge of its proper use. But we have had to take advantage of a great deal of prior conditioning with respect to instructions, directions, and other verbal stimuli, which are easily overlooked, and their contribution may then be attributed to autonomous man. A still more complex form of argument has to do with deriving new reasons from old, the process of deduction which depends upon a much longer verbal history and is particularly likely to be called changing a mind.

Ways of changing behaviour by changing minds are seldom condoned when they are clearly effective, even though it is still a mind which is apparently being changed. We do not condone the changing of minds when the contestants are unevenly matched; that is "undue influence". Nor do we condone changing minds surreptitiously. If a person cannot see what the would-be changer of minds is doing, he cannot escape or counter-attack; he is being exposed to "propaganda". "Brainwashing" is proscribed by those who otherwise condone the changing of minds simply because the control is obvious. A common technique is to build up a strong aversive condition, such as hunger or lack of sleep and, by alleviating it, to reinforce any behaviour which "shows a positive attitude" toward a political or religious system. A favourable "opinion" is built up simply by reinforcing favourable statements. The procedure may not be obvious to those upon whom it is used, but it is too obvious to others to be accepted as an allowable way of changing minds.

The illusion that freedom and dignity are respected when control seems incomplete arises in part from the probabilistic nature of operant behaviour. Seldom does any environmental condition "elicit" behaviour in the all-or-nothing fashion of a reflex; it simply makes a bit of behaviour more likely to occur. A hint will not itself suffice to evoke a response, but it adds strength to a weak response which may then appear. The hint is conspicuous, but the other events responsible for the appearance of the response are not.

Like permissiveness, maieutics, guidance, and building a dependence on things, changing a mind is condoned by the defenders of freedom and dignity because it is an ineffective way of changing behaviour, and the changer of minds can therefore escape from the charge that he is controlling people. He is also exonerated when things go wrong. Autonomous man survives to be credited with his achievements and blamed for his mistakes.

The apparent freedom respected by weak measures is merely inconspicuous control. When we seem to turn control over to a person himself, we simply shift from one mode of control to another. A news weekly, discussing the legal control of abortion, contended that "the way to deal with the problem forthrightly is on terms that permit the individual, guided by conscience and intelligence, to make a choice unhampered by archaic and hypocritical concepts and statutes".[7] What is recommended is not a shift from legal control to "choice" but to the control previously exerted by religious, ethical, governmental, and educational agencies. The individual is "permitted" to decide the issue for himself simply in the sense that he will act because of consequences to which legal punishment is no longer to be added.

A permissive government is a government that leaves control to other sources. If people behave well under it, it is because they have been brought under effective ethical control or the control of things, or have been induced by educational and other agencies to behave in loyal, patriotic, and law-abiding ways. Only when other forms of control are available is that government best which governs least. To the extent that government is defined by the power to punish, the literature of freedom has been valuable in promoting a shift to other measures, but in no other sense has it freed people from governmental control.

A free economy does not mean the absence of economic control, because no economy is free as long as goods and money remain reinforcing. When we refuse to impose control over wages, prices, and the use of natural resources in order not to interfere with individual initiative, we leave the individual under the control of unplanned economic contingencies. Nor is any school "free". If the teacher does not teach, students will learn only if less explicit but still effective contingencies prevail. The non-directive psychotherapist may free his patient from certain harmful contingencies in his daily life, but the patient will "find his own solution" only if ethical, governmental, religious, educational, or other contingencies induce him to do so.

(The contact between therapist and patient is a sensitive subject. The therapist, no matter how "nondirective", sees his patient, talks with him, and listens to him. He is professionally concerned for his welfare, and if he is sympathetic, he *cares* for him. All this is reinforcing. It has been suggested, however, that the therapist can avoid changing his patient's behaviour if he makes these reinforcers non-contingent — that is, if they are not permitted to follow any particular form of behaviour. As one writer has put it, "The therapist responds as a congruent person, with sensitive empathy and unqualified caring that, in learning theory terms, rewards the client as much for one behaviour as for any other." This is probably an impossible assignment and in any case would not have the effect claimed. Non-contingent reinforcers are not ineffective; a reinforcer always reinforces something. When a therapist shows that he cares, he reinforces any behaviour the patient has just emitted. One reinforcement, accidental though it may be, strengthens behaviour which is then more likely to occur and be reinforced again. The resulting "superstition" can be demonstrated in pigeons, and it is unlikely that men have become less sensitive to adventitious reinforcement. Being good to someone for no reason at all, treating him affectionately whether he is good or bad, does have Biblical support: grace must not be contingent upon works or it is no longer grace. But there are behavioural processes to be taken into account.)

The fundamental mistake made by all those who choose weak methods of control is to assume that the balance of control is left to the individual, when in fact it is left to other conditions. The other conditions are often hard to see, but to continue to neglect them and to attribute their effects to autonomous man is to court disaster. When practices are concealed or disguised, counter-control is made difficult; it is not clear from whom one is to escape or whom one is to attack. The literatures of freedom and dignity were once brilliant exercises in counter-control, but the measures they proposed are no longer appropriate to the task. On the contrary, they may have serious consequences. . . .

Chapter 8: The Design of a Culture

Many people are engaged in the design and redesign of cultural practices. They make changes in the things they use and the way they use them. They invent better mousetraps and computers and discover better ways of raising children, paying wages, collecting taxes, and helping people with problems. We need not spend much time on the word "better"; it is simply the comparative of "good", and goods are reinforcers. One camera is called better than another because of what happens when it is used. A manufacturer induces potential buyers to "value" his camera by guaranteeing that it will perform in satisfactory ways, by quoting what users have said about its performance, and so on. It is, of course, much harder to call one culture better than another, in part because more consequences need to be taken into account.

No one knows the *best* way of raising children, paying workers, maintaining law and order, teaching, or making people creative, but it is possible to propose better ways than we now have and to support them by predicting and eventually demonstrating more reinforcing results. This has been done in the past with the help of personal experience and folk wisdom, but a scientific analysis of human behaviour is obviously relevant. It helps in two ways: it defines what is to be done and suggests ways of doing it. How badly it is needed is indicated by a recent discussion in a news weekly about what is wrong with America. The problem was described as "a disturbed psychic condition of the young", "a recession of the spirit", "a psychic downturn", and "a spiritual crisis", which were attributed to "anxiety", "uncertainty", "malaise", "alienation", "generalised despair", and several other moods and states of mind, all interacting in the familiar intrapsychic pattern (lack of social assurance being said to lead to alienation, for example, and frustration to aggression). Most readers probably knew what the writer was talking about and may have felt that he was saying something useful, but the passage — which is not exceptional — has two characteristic defects which explain our failure to deal adequately with cultural problems: the troublesome behaviour is not actually described, and nothing that can be done to change it is mentioned.

Consider a young man whose world has suddenly changed. He has graduated from college and is going to work, let us say, or has been inducted into the armed services. Most of the behaviour he has acquired up to this point proves useless in his new environment. The behaviour he actually exhibits can be described, and the description translated, as follows: he lacks assurance or feels insecure or is unsure of himself (*his behaviour is weak and inappropriate*); he is dissatisfied or discouraged (*he is seldom reinforced, and as a result his behaviour undergoes extinction*); he is frustrated (*extinction is accompanied by emotional responses*); he feels uneasy or anxious (*his behaviour frequently has unavoidable aversive consequences which have emotional effects*); there is nothing he wants to do or enjoys doing well, he has no feeling of craftsmanship, no sense of leading a purposeful life, no sense of accomplishment (*he is rarely reinforced for doing anything*); he feels guilty or ashamed (*he has previously been punished for idleness or failure, which now evokes emotional responses*); he is disappointed in himself or disgusted with himself (*he is no longer reinforced by the admiration of others, and the extinction which follows has emotional effects*); he becomes hypochondriacal (*he concludes that he is ill*) or neurotic (*he engages in a variety of ineffective modes of escape*); and he experiences an identity crisis (*he does not recognise the person he once called "I"*).

The italicised paraphrases are too brief to be precise, but they suggest the possibility of an alternative account, which alone suggests effective action. To the young man himself the important things are no doubt the various states of his body. They are salient stimuli, and he has learned to use them in traditional ways to explain his behaviour to himself and others. What he tells us about his feelings may permit us to make some informed guesses about what is wrong with the contingencies, but we must go directly to the contingencies if we want to be sure, *and it is the contingencies which must be changed if his behaviour is to be changed.* . . .

Beyond interpretation lies practical action. Contingencies are accessible, and as we come to understand the relations between behaviour and the environment, we discover new ways of changing behaviour. The outlines of a technology are already clear. An assignment is stated as behaviour to be produced or modified, and relevant contingencies are then arranged. A programmed sequence of contingencies may be needed. The technology has been most successful where behaviour can be fairly easily specified and where appropriate contingencies can be constructed — for example, in child care, schools, and the management of retardates and institutionalised psychotics. The same principles are being applied, however, in the preparation of instructional materials at all educational levels, in psychotherapy beyond simple management, in rehabilitation, in industrial management, in urban

---

*Feelings may seem to be changed when we cheer a person up with a drink or two or when he himself "reduces the aversive features of his internal world" by drinking or by smoking marijuana. But what is changed is not the feeling but the bodily condition felt. The designer of a culture changes the feelings which accompany behaviour in its relation to the environment, and he does so by changing the environment.

design, and in many other fields of human behaviour. There are many varieties of "behaviour modification" and many different formulations, but they all agree on the essential point: behaviour can be changed by changing the conditions of which it is a function.[8]

Such a technology is ethically neutral. It can be used by villain or saint. There is nothing in a methodology which determines the values governing its use. We are concerned here, however, not merely with practices, but with the design of a whole culture, and the survival of a culture then emerges as a special kind of value. A person may design a better way of raising children primarily to escape from children who do not behave well. He may solve his problem, for example, by being a martinet. Or his new method may promote the good of the children or of parents in general. It may demand time and effort and the sacrifice of personal reinforcers, but he will propose and use it if he has been sufficiently induced to work for the good of others. If he is strongly reinforced when he sees other people enjoying themselves, for example, he will design an environment in which children are happy. If his culture has induced him to take an interest in its survival, however, he may study the contribution which people make to their culture as a result of their early history, and he may design a better method in order to increase that contribution. Those who adopt the method may suffer some loss in personal reinforcers.

The same three kinds of values may be detected in the design of other cultural practices. The classroom teacher may devise new ways of teaching which make life easier for him, or which please his students (who in turn reinforce him), or which make it likely that his students will contribute as much as possible to their culture. The industrialist may design a wage system that maximises his profits, or works for the good of his employees; or most effectively produces the goods a culture needs, with a minimal consumption of resources and minimal pollution. A party in power may act primarily to keep its power, or to reinforce those it governs (who in return keep it in power), or to promote the state, as by instituting a programme of austerity which may cost the party both power and support.

The same three levels may be detected in the design of a culture as a whole. If the designer is an individualist, he will design a world in which he will be under minimal aversive control and will accept his own goods as the ultimate values. If he has been exposed to an appropriate social environment, he will design for the good of others, possibly with a loss of personal goods. If he is concerned primarily with survival value, he will design a culture with an eye to whether it will work.

When a culture induces some of its members to work for its survival, what are they to do? They will need to foresee some of the difficulties the culture will encounter. These usually lie far in the future, and details are not always clear. Apocalyptic visions have had a long history, but only recently has much attention been paid to the prediction of the future. There is nothing to be done about completely unpredictable difficulties, but we may foresee some trouble by extrapolating current trends. It may be enough simply to observe a steady increase in the number of people on the earth, in the size and location of nuclear stockpiles, or in the pollution of the environment and the depletion of natural resources; we may then change practices to induce people to have fewer children, spend less on nuclear weapons, stop polluting the environment, and consume resources at a lower rate, respectively.

We do not need to predict the future to see some of the ways in which the strength of a culture depends upon the behaviour of its members. A culture that maintains civil order and defends itself against attack frees its members from certain kinds of threats and presumably provides more time and energy for other things (particularly if order and security are not maintained by force). A culture needs various goods for its survival, and its strength must depend in part on the economic contingencies which maintain enterprising and productive labour, on the availability of the tools of production, and on the development and conservation of resources. A culture is presumably stronger if it induces its members to maintain a safe and healthful environment, to provide medical care, and to maintain a population density appropriate to its resources and space. A culture must be transmitted from generation to generation, and its strength will presumably depend on what and how much its new members learn, either through informal instructional contingencies or in educational institutions. A culture needs the support of its members, and it must provide for the pursuit and achievement of happiness if it is to prevent disaffection or defection. A culture must be reasonably stable, but it must also change, and it will presumably be strongest if it can avoid excessive respect for tradition and fear of novelty on the one hand and excessively rapid change on the other. Lastly, a culture will have a special measure of survival value if it encourages its members to examine its practices and to experiment with new ones.

A culture is very much like the experimental space used in the analysis of behaviour. Both are sets of contingencies of reinforcement. A child is born into a culture as an organism is placed in an experimental space. Designing a culture is like designing an experiment; contingencies are arranged and effects noted. In an experiment we are interested in what happens, in designing a culture with whether it will work. This is the difference between science and technology.

A collection of cultural designs is to be found in the utopian literature.[9] Writers have described their versions of the good life and suggested ways of achieving them. Plato, in the *Republic*, chose a political solution; Saint Augustine, in *The City of God*, a religious one. Thomas More and Francis Bacon, both lawyers, turned to law and order, and the Rousseauean utopists of the eighteenth century, to a supposed natural goodness in man. The nineteenth century looked for economic solutions, and the twentieth century saw the rise of what may be called behavioural utopias in which a full range of social contingencies began to be discussed (often satirically).[10]

Utopian writers have been at pains to simplify their assignment. A utopian community is usually composed of a relatively small number of people living together in one place and in stable contact with each other. They can practise an informal ethical control and minimise the role of organised agencies. They can learn from each other rather than from the specialists called teachers. They can be kept from behaving badly toward each other through censure rather than the specialised punishments of a legal system. They can produce and exchange goods without specifying values in terms of money. They can help those who have become ill, infirm, disturbed, or aged with a minimum of institutional care. Troublesome contacts with other cultures are avoided through geographical isolation (utopias tend to be located on islands or surrounded by high mountains), and the transition to a new culture is facilitated by some formalised break with the past, such as a ritual of rebirth (utopias are often set in the distant future so that the neccessary evolution of the culture seems plausible). A utopia is a total social environment, and all its parts work together. The home does not conflict with the school or the street, religion does not conflict with government, and so on.

Perhaps the most important feature of the utopian design, however, is that the survival of a community can be made important to its members. The small size, the isolation, the internal coherence — all these give a community an identity which makes its success or failure conspicuous. The fundamental question in all utopias is "Would it really work?" The literature is worth considering just because it emphasises experimentation. A traditional culture has been examined and found wanting, and a new version has been set up to be tested and redesigned as circumstances dictate.

The simplification in utopian writing, which is nothing more than the simplification characteristic of science, is seldom feasible in the world at large, and there are many other reasons why it is difficult to put an explicit design into effect. A large fluid population cannot be brought under informal social or ethical control because social reinforcers, like praise and blame, are not exchangeable for the personal reinforcers on which they are based. Why should anyone be affected by the praise or blame of someone he will never see again? Ethical control may survive in small groups, but the control of the population as a whole must be delegated to specialists — to police, priests, owners, teachers, therapists, and so on, with their specialised reinforcers and their codified contingencies. These are probably already in conflict with each other and will almost certainly be in conflict with any new set of contingencies. Where it is not too difficult to change informal instruction, for example, it is nearly impossible to change an educational establishment. It is fairly easy to change marriage, divorce, and childbearing practices as the significance for the culture changes but nearly impossible to change the religious principles which dictate such practices. It is easy to change the extent to which various kinds of behaviour are accepted as right but difficult to change the laws of a government. The reinforcing values of goods are more flexible than the values set by economic agencies. The word of authority is more unyielding than the facts of which it speaks.

It is not surprising that, so far as the real world is concerned, the word utopian means unworkable. History seems to offer support; various utopian designs have been proposed for nearly twenty-five hundred years, and most attempts to set them up have been ignominious failures. But historical evidence is always against the probability of anything new; that is what is meant by history. Scientific discoveries and inventions are improbable; that is what is meant by discovery and invention. And if planned economies, benevolent dictatorships, perfectionistic societies, and other utopian ventures have failed, we must remember that unplanned, undictated, and unperfected cultures have failed too. A failure is not always a mistake; it may simply be the best one can do under the circumstances. The real mistake is to stop trying. Perhaps we cannot now design a successful culture as a whole, but we can design better practices in a piecemeal fashion. The behavioural processes in the world at large are the same as those in a utopian community, and practices have the same effects for the same reasons.

The same advantages are also to be found in emphasising contingencies of reinforcement in lieu of states of mind or feelings. It is no doubt a serious problem, for example, that students no longer respond in traditional ways to educational environments; they drop out of school, possibly for long periods of time, they take only courses which they enjoy or which seem to have relevance to their problems, they destroy school property and attack teachers and officials. But we shall not solve this problem by "cultivating on the part of our public a respect it does not now have for scholarship as such and for the practising scholar and teacher". (The cultivation of respect is a metaphor in the horticultural tradition.) What is wrong is the educational environment. We need to design contingencies under which students acquire behaviour useful to them and their culture — contingencies that do not have troublesome by-products and that generate the behaviour said to "show respect for learning". It is not difficult to see what is wrong in most educational environments, and much has already been done to design materials which make learning as easy as possible and to construct contingencies, in the classroom and elsewhere, which give students powerful reasons for getting an education.

A serious problem also arises when young people refuse to serve in the armed forces and desert or defect to other countries, but we shall not make an appreciable change by "inspiring greater loyalty or patriotism". What must be changed are the contingencies which induce young people to behave in given ways toward their governments. Governmental sanctions remain almost entirely punitive, and the unfortunate by-products are sufficiently indicated by the extent of domestic disorder and international conflict. It is a serious problem that we remain almost continuously at war with other nations, but we shall not get far by attacking "the tensions which lead to war", or by appeasing warlike spirits, or by changing the minds of men (in which, UNESCO tells us, wars begin). What must be changed are the circumstances under which men and nations make war.

We may also be disturbed by the fact that many young people work as little as possible, or that workers are not very productive and often absent, or that products are often of poor quality, but we shall not get far by inspiring a "sense of craftsmanship or pride in one's work", or a "sense of the dignity of labor", or, where crafts and skills are a part of the caste mores, by changing "the deep emotional resistance of the caste superego", as one writer has put it. Something is wrong with the contingencies which induce men to work industriously and carefully. (Other kinds of economic contingencies are wrong too.)

Walter Lippmann has said that "the supreme question before mankind" is how men can save themselves from the catastrophe which threatens them,[11] but to answer it we must do more than discover how men can "make themselves willing and able to save themselves". We must look to the contingencies that induce people to act to increase the chances that their cultures will survive. We have the physical, biological, and behavioural technologies needed "to save ourselves"; the problem is how to get people to use them. It may be that "utopia has only to be willed", but what does that mean? What are the principal specifications of a culture that will survive because it induces its members to work for its survival? . . .

A proposal to design a culture with the help of a scientific analysis often leads to Cassandran prophecies of disaster. The culture will not work as planned, and unforeseen consequences may be catastrophic. Proof is seldom offered, possibly because history seems to be on the side of failure: many plans have gone wrong, and possibly just because they were planned. The threat in a designed culture, said Mr Krutch, is that the unplanned "may never erupt again".[12] But it is hard to justify the trust which is placed in accident. It is true that accidents have been responsible for almost everything men have achieved to date, and they will no doubt continue to contribute to human accomplishments, but there is no virtue in an accident as such. The unplanned also goes wrong. The idiosyncrasies of a jealous ruler who regards any disturbance as an offense against him may have an accidental survival value if law and order are maintained, but the military strategies of a paranoid leader are of the same provenance and may have an entirely different effect. The industry which arises in the unrestrained pursuit of happiness may have an accidental survival value when war *matériel* is suddenly needed, but it may also exhaust natural resources and pollute the environment.

If a planned culture necessarily meant uniformity or regimentation, it might indeed work against further evolution. If men were very much alike, they would be less likely to hit upon or design new practices, and a culture which made people as much alike as possible might slip into a standard pattern from which there would be no escape. That would be bad design, but if we are looking for variety, we should not fall back upon accident. Many accidental cultures have been marked by uniformity and regimentation. The exigencies of administration in governmental, religious, and economic systems breed uniformity, because it simplifies the problem of control. Traditional educational establishments specify what the student is to learn at what age and administer tests to make sure that the specifications are met. The codes of governments and religions are usually quite explicit and allow little room for diversity or change. The only hope is *planned* diversification, in which the importance of variety is recognised. The breeding of plants and animals moves toward uniformity when uniformity is important (as in simplifying agriculture or animal husbandry), but it also requires planned diversity. . . .

There are, of course, good reasons why the control of human behaviour is resisted. The commonest techniques are aversive, and some sort of counter-control is to be expected. The controllee may move out of range (the controller will work to keep him from doing so), or he may attack, and ways of doing so have emerged as important steps in the evolution of cultures. Thus, the members of a group establish the principle that it is wrong to use force and punish those who do so with any available means. Governments codify the principle and call the use of force illegal, and religions call it sinful, and both arrange contingencies to suppress it. When controllers then turn to methods which are nonaversive but have deferred aversive consequences, additional principles emerge. The group calls it wrong to control through deception, for example, and governmental and religious sanctions follow.

We have seen that the literatures of freedom and dignity have extended these counter-controlling measures in an effort to suppress all controlling practices even when they have no aversive consequences or have offsetting reinforcing consequences. The designer of a culture comes under fire because explicit design implies control (if only the control exerted by the designer). The issue is often formulated by asking: Who is to control? And the question is usually raised as if the answer were necessarily threatening. To prevent the misuse of controlling power, however, we must look not at the controller himself but at the contingencies under which he engages in control.

We are misled by differences in the conspicuousness of controlling measures. The Egyptian slave, cutting stone in a quarry for a pyramid, worked under the supervision of a soldier with a whip, who was paid to wield the whip by a paymaster, who was paid in turn by a Pharaoh, who had been convinced of the necessity of an inviolable tomb by priests, who argued to this effect because of the sacerdotal privileges and power which then came to them, and so on. A whip is a more obvious instrument of control than wages, and wages are more conspicuous than sacerdotal privileges, and privileges are more obvious than the prospect of an affluent future life. There are related differences in the results. The slave will escape if he can, the soldier or paymaster will resign or strike if the economic contingencies are too weak, the Pharaoh will dismiss his priests and start a new religion if his treasury is unduly strained, and the priests will shift their support to a rival. We are likely to single out the conspicuous examples of control, because in their abruptness and clarity of effect, they seem to start something, but it is a great mistake to ignore the inconspicuous forms.

The relation between the controller and the controlled is reciprocal. The scientist in the laboratory, studying the behaviour of a pigeon, designs contingencies and observes their effects. His apparatus exerts a conspicuous control on the pigeon, but we must not overlook the control exerted by the pigeon. The behaviour of the pigeon has determined the design of the apparatus and the procedures in which it is used. Some such reciprocal control is characteristic of all science. As Francis Bacon put it, nature to be commanded must be obeyed. The scientist who designs a cyclotron is under the control of the particles he is studying. The behaviour with which a parent controls his child, either aversively or through positive reinforcement, is shaped and maintained by the child's responses. A psychotherapist changes the behaviour of his patient in ways which have been shaped and maintained by his success in changing that behaviour. A government or religion prescribes and imposes sanctions selected by their effectiveness in controlling citizen or communicant. An employer induces his employees to work industriously and carefully with wage systems determined by their effects on behaviour. The classroom practices of the teacher are shaped and maintained by the effects on his students. In a very real sense, then, the slave controls the slave driver, the child the parent, the patient the therapist, the citizen the government, the communicant the priest, the employee the employer, and the student the teacher.

It is true that the physicist designs a cyclotron *in order to* control the behaviour of certain subatomic particles; the particles do not behave in characteristic ways *in order to* get him to do so. The slave driver uses a whip *in order to* make the slave work; the slave does not work *in order to* induce the slave driver to use a whip. The intention or purpose implied by the phrase "in order to" is a matter of the extent to which consequences are effective in altering behaviour, and hence the extent to which they must be taken into account to explain it. The particle is not affected by the consequences of its action, and there is no reason to speak of its intention or purpose, but the slave may be affected by the consequences of his action. Reciprocal control is not necessarily intentional in either direction, but it becomes so when the consequences make themselves felt. A mother learns to take up and carry a baby in order to get it to stop crying, and she may learn to do so before the baby learns to cry in order to be taken up and carried. For a time only the mother's behaviour is intentional, but the baby's may become so. . . .

The great problem is to arrange effective counter-control and hence to bring some important consequences to bear on the behaviour of the controller. Some classical examples of a lack of balance between control and counter-control arise when control is delegated and counter-control then becomes ineffective. Hospitals for psychotics and homes for retardates, orphans, and old people are noted for weak counter-control, because those who are concerned for the welfare of such people often do not know what is happening. Prisons offer little opportunity for counter-control, as the commonest controlling measures indicate. Control and counter-control tend to become dislocated when control is taken over by organised agencies. Informal contingencies are subject to quick adjustments as their effects change, but the contingencies which organisations leave to specialists may be untouched by many of the consequences. Those who pay for education, for example, may lose touch with what is taught and with the methods used. The teacher is subject only to the counter-control exerted by the student. As a result, a school may become wholy autocratic or wholly anarchistic, and what is taught may go out of date as the world changes or be reduced to the things students will consent to study. There is a similar problem in jurisprudence when laws continue to be enforced which are no longer appropriate to the practices of the community. Rules never generate behaviour exactly appropriate to the contingencies from which they are derived, and the discrepancy grows worse if the contingencies change while the rules remain inviolate. Similarly, the values imposed on goods by economic enterprises may lose their correspondence with the reinforcing effects of the goods, as the latter change. In short, an organised agency which is insensitive to the consequences of its practices is not subject to important kinds of counter-control.

Self-government often seems to solve the problem by identifying the controller with the controlled. The principle of making the controller a member of the group he controls should apply to the designer of a culture. A person who designs a piece of equipment for his own use presumably takes the interests of the user into account, and the person who designs a social environment in which he is to live will presumably do the same. He will select goods or values which are important to him and arrange the kind of contingencies to which he can adapt. In a democracy the controller is found among the controlled, although he behaves in different ways in the two roles. We shall see later that there is a sense in which a culture controls itself, as a person controls himself, but the process calls for careful analysis.

The intentional design of a culture, with the implication that behaviour is to be controlled, is sometimes called ethically or morally wrong. Ethics and morals are particularly concerned with bringing the remoter consequences of behaviour into play. There is a morality of natural consequences. How is a person to keep from eating delicious food if it will later make him sick? Or how is he to submit to pain or exhaustion if he must do so to reach safety? Social contingencies are much more likely to raise moral and ethical issues. (As we have noted, the terms refer to the customs of groups.) How is a person to refrain from taking goods which belong to others in order to avoid the punishment which may then follow? Or how is he to submit to pain or exhaustion to gain their approval?

The practical question, which we have already considered, is how remote consequences can be made effective.[13] Without help a person acquires very little moral or ethical behaviour under either natural or social contingencies. The group supplies supporting contingencies when it describes its practices in codes or rules which tell the individual how to behave and when it enforces those rules with supplementary contingencies. Maxims, proverbs, and other forms of folk wisdom give a person reasons for obeying rules. Governments and religions formulate the contingencies they maintain somewhat more explicitly, and education imparts rules which make it possible to satisfy both natural and social contingencies without being directly exposed to them.

This is all part of the social environment called a culture, and the main effect, as we have seen, is to bring the individual under the control of the remoter consequences of his behaviour. The effect has had survival value in the process of cultural evolution, since practices evolve because those who practise them are as a result better off. There is a kind of natural morality in both biological and cultural evolution. Biological evolution has made the human species more sensitive to its environment and more skilful in dealing with it. Cultural evolution was made possible by biological evolution, and it has brought the human organism under a much more sweeping control of the environment.

We say that there is something "morally wrong" about a totalitarian state, a gambling enterprise, uncontrolled piecework wages, the sale of harmful drugs, or undue personal influence, not because of any absolute set of values, but because all these things have aversive consequences. The consequences are deferred, and a science that clarifies their relation to behaviour is in the best possible position to specify a better world in an ethical or moral sense. It is not true, therefore, that the empirical scientist must deny that there can be "any scientific concern with human and political values and goals", or that morally, justice, and order under law lie "beyond survival".

A special value in scientific practice is also relevant. The scientist works under contingencies that minimise immediate personal reinforcers. No scientist is "pure", in the sense of being out of reach of immediate reinforcers but other consequences of his behaviour play an important role.[14] If he designs an experiment in a particular way, or stops an experiment at a particular point, because the result will then confirm a theory bearing his name, or will have industrial uses from which he will profit, or will impress the agencies that support his research, he will almost certainly run into trouble. The published results of scientists are subject to rapid check by others, and the scientist who allows himself to be swayed by consequences that are not part of his subject matter is likely to find himself in difficulties. To say that scientists are therefore more moral or ethical than other people, or that they have a more finely developed ethical sense, is to make the mistake of attributing to the scientist what is actually a feature of the environment in which he works.

Almost everyone makes ethical and moral judgments, but this does not mean that the human species has "an inborn need or demand for ethical standards".[15] (We could say as well that it has an inborn need or demand for unethical behaviour, since almost everyone behaves unethically at some time or other.) Man has not evolved as an ethical or moral animal. He has evolved to the point at which he has constructed an ethical or moral culture. He differs from the other animals not in possessing a moral or ethical sense but in having been able to generate a moral or ethical social environment. . . .

What is needed is more "intentional" control, not less, and this is an important engineering problem. The good of a culture cannot function as the source of genuine reinforcers for the individual, and the reinforcers contrived by cultures to induce their members to work for their survival are often in conflict with personal reinforcers. The number of people explicitly engaged in improving the design of automobiles, for example, must greatly exceed the number of those concerned with improving life in city ghettos. It is not that the automobile is more important than a way of life, but rather that the economic contingencies which induce people to improve automobiles are very powerful. They arise from the personal reinforcers of those who manufacture automobiles. No reinforcers of comparable strength encourage the engineering of the pure survival of a culture. The technology of the automobile industry is also, of course, much further advanced than a technology of behaviour. These facts simply underline the importance of the threat posed by the literatures of freedom and dignity. . . .

Leisure has long been associated with artistic, literary, and scientific productivity. One must be at leisure to engage in these activities, and only a reasonably affluent society can support them on a broad scale. But leisure itself does not necessarily lead to art, literature, or science. Special cultural conditions are needed. Those who are concerned with the survival of their culture will therefore look closely at the contingencies which remain when the exigent contingencies in daily life have been attenuated.

It is often said that an affluent culture can afford leisure, but we cannot be sure. It is easy for those who work hard to confuse a state of leisure with reinforcement, partly because it often accompanies reinforcement, and happiness, like freedom, has long been associated with doing as one pleases; yet, the actual effect upon human behaviour may threaten the survival of a culture. The enormous potential of those who have nothing to do cannot be overlooked. They may be productive or destructive, conserving or consuming. They may reach the limits of their capacities or be converted into machines. They may support the culture if they are strongly reinforced by it or defect if life is boring. They may or may not be prepared to act effectively when leisure comes to an end.

Leisure is one of the great challenges to those who are concerned with the survival of a culture because any attempt to control what a person does when he does not need to do anything is particularly likely to be attacked as unwarranted meddling. Life, liberty, and the pursuit of happiness are basic rights. But they are the rights of the individual and were listed as such at a time when the literatures of freedom and dignity were concerned with the aggrandisement of the individual. They have only a minor bearing on the survival of a culture.

The designer of a culture is not an interloper or meddler. He does not step in to disturb a natural process, he is part of a natural process. The geneticist who changes the characteristics of a species by selective breeding or by changing genes may seem to be meddling in biological evolution, but he does so because his species has evolved to the point at which it has been able to develop a science of genetics and a culture which induces its members to take the future of the species into account.

Those who have been induced by their culture to act to further its survival through design must accept the fact that they are altering the conditions under which men live and, hence, engaging in the control of human behaviour. Good government is as much a matter of the control of human behaviour as bad, good incentive conditions as much as exploitation, good teaching as much as punitive drill. Nothing is to be gained by using a softer word. If we are content merely to "influence" people, we shall not get far from the original meaning of that word — "an ethereal fluid thought to flow from the stars and to affect the actions of men".

Attacking controlling practices, is, of course, a form of counter-control. It may have immeasurable benefits if better controlling practices are thereby selected. But the literatures of freedom and dignity have made the mistake of supposing that they are suppressing control rather than correcting it. The reciprocal control through which a culture evolves is then disturbed. To refuse to exercise available control because in some sense all control is wrong is to withhold possibly important forms of counter-control. We have seen some of the consequences. Punitive measures, which the literatures of freedom and dignity have otherwise helped to eliminate, are instead promoted. A preference for methods which make control inconspicuous or allow it to be disguised has condemned those who are in a position to exert constructive counter-control to the use of weak measures.

This could be a lethal cultural mutation. Our culture has produced the science and technology it needs to save itself. It has the wealth needed for effective action. It has, to a considerable extent, a concern for its own future. But if it continues to take freedom or dignity, rather than its own survival, as its principal value, then it is possible that some other culture will make a greater contribution to the future. The defender of freedom and dignity may then, like Milton's Satan, continue to tell himself that he has "a mind not to be changed by place or time"[16] and an all-sufficient personal identity ("What matter where, if I be still the same?"), but he will nevertheless find himself in hell with no other consolation than the illusion that "here at least we shall be free".

NOTES AND REFERENCES

1. PLATO, *Meno*.
2. Quoted from W. A. Kaufmann in D. SHAKOW, "Ethics for a Scientific Age: Some Moral Aspects of Psychoanalysis", *the Psychoanalytic Review*, Fall 1965, 52, No. 3.
3. A. DE TOCQUEVILLE, *Democracy in America*, translated by Henry Reeve, Sever & Francis, Cambridge, 1863.
4. R. B. PERRY, *Pacific Spectator*, Spring, 1953.
5. See B. F. SKINNER, *Verbal Behavior*, Appleton-Century-Crofts, New York, 1957, Chapter 10.
6. See B. F. SKINNER, *Science and Human Behavior*, Macmillan, New York, 1953, Chapter 7.
7. *Time*, 13 October 1967.
8. For a convenient collection of reports on contingency management, see R. Ulrich, T. Stachnik and J. Mabry (Eds), *Control of Human Behaviour*, Vols 1 and 2, Scott Foresman, Glenview, Illinois, 1966 and 1970.
9. For a discussion of utopias as experimental cultures, see B. F. SKINNER, *Contingencies of Reinforcement: A Theoretical Analysis*. Appleton-Century-Crofts, New York, 1969.
10. Aldous Huxley's *Brave New World* (1932) is no doubt the best known. It was a satire, but Huxley recanted and tried his hand at a serious version in *Island* (1962). The dominant psychology of the twentieth century, psychoanalysis, spawned no utopias. The author's *Walden Two* describes a community designed essentially on the principles which appear in the present book.
11. W. LIPPMAN in *The New York Times*, 14 September 1969.
12. J. W. KRUTCH, *The Measure of Man*, Bobbs-Merrill, Indianapolis, 1954.
13. See M. HOLROYD, *Lytton Strachey: The Unknown Years*, William Heinemann, London, 1967. According to Holroyd, G. E. Moore's concept of moral conduct may be summarised as the intelligent prediction of practical consequences. The important thing, however, is not to predict the consequences but to bring them to bear on the behaviour of the individual.
14. See P. W. BRIDGMAN, "The Struggle for Intellectual Integrity", *Harper's Magazine*, December 1933.
15. See G. G. SIMPSON, *The Meaning of Evolution*, Yale University Press, New Haven, 1960.
16. John MILTON, *Paradise Lost*, Book I.

7

A. S. NEILL

Commentary

Biography

Alexander Sutherland Neill (1883–1973) was born in the small Scottish town of Forfar, some fifteen miles north of Dundee. His father, George Neill, was a schoolmaster and since 1876 had been in charge of a one-room school in the neighbouring village of Kingsmuir, and it was there that Neill, along with his three sisters, received his own schooling. Yet Neill was not a competent scholar and at the age of fourteen he left for city work, first in Edinburgh, seventy miles to the south, and then back in Forfar, for barely two years. In 1899, at the age of sixteen, he became an apprentice schoolmaster, and for the following four years drudged away with no apparent enthusiasm. Having failed in his apprenticeship to qualify for further training in a normal school (the current term for a teachers' college) he drifted around as an uncertified teacher in Dundee. It was there that he first felt the pressure to meet society's demands and after a period of cramming passed the matriculation examination for Edinburgh University. He graduated in1905 with a degree in Arts (Edinburgh like the other Scottish universities calls it a master's degree, although it is equivalent to a bachelor's), with a major in English literature, although he was unmoved by much of this, since it seems to have been aridly scholastic. He then taught for twelve years in Scottish state schools.

By then the Great War (1914–18) was in its bloodiest phase and in 1917 Neill joined the British Army. After his discharge, Neill's life began to take a more purposive character. He taught for two years at the new, experimental King Alfred School, and then in 1921 became assistant editor to Mrs Ensor, the founder of the New Education Fellowship, publishing the associated quarterly journal, *Education for the New Era*. However, Neill was sacked later the same year for his divergent views. By this time he was confirmed in his intention to have a career in education, but not the kind of education that was currently being given. Neill had been raised, and was himself teaching, in the very system of formal discipline and abstract verbal memorising of subject matter in a repressively harsh atmosphere Dewey had been attacking for more than twenty years. Neill too wanted to work for the improvement of schooling and the liberation of the child. The chance came in 1921 when he left his assistant editorship. In Dresden, Germany, a progressive school had been established on the principles of the Eurhythmic movement founded by Jacques Dalcroze, which sought to educate through the medium of expressive action. One of the chief supporters of the school, Frau Neustatter, invited Neill to the school in Hellerau, a suburb of Dresden, to participate in this educational venture based upon arts, crafts, music, dance; upon, that is, the principle of making education a development of the self, springing from a creative engagement with meaningful activities. Germany, however, was undergoing serious political and social difficulties in the aftermath of the Great War and the school closed in 1923 and moved to what seemed a quieter, seemingly ideal location near Vienna, in an abandoned monastery atop the mountain of Sonntagberg. But within a year friction developed with the local residents who, because of their strict social attitudes, found the activities of a progressive school unacceptable.

So Neill moved back to England in 1924 to Lyme Regis, on the south coast some thirty miles east of Exeter, accompanied by Frau Neustatter, whom he married in 1927. They opened a progressive school there which they called Summerhill after the name of the property. The school prospered, although its enrolment remained small, usually around forty. In 1927 it was moved to Leiston in Suffolk, about a hundred miles north of London, where, since Neill's death in 1973, it has been conducted by his widow Ena.

Main Features of Neill's Educational Thought

The outstanding characteristic of Neill's approach to education was his concern for what he called the freedom of the child; it was his lifelong adherence to this belief, and his attempt over half a century to implement and proselytise it in practice, that constitutes his significant innovation. In brief, Neill believed, in some ways rather like Rousseau, that the child must never be compelled to learn. The child should be allowed to find its own way and seek learning only on the basis of inner needs and drives. As a consequence of maintaining and practising this belief, chiefly in Summerhill School, Neill attracted a considerable amount of publicity, a tremendous opposition and a number of dedicated disciples. Although his ideas generally resist being brought together into a coherent, rational theory that might have a general application, they have always fascinated educational thinkers and progressive teachers and Neill's ideas are very well known and frequently discussed. Against Neill, it is often alleged that his approach only worked because of his own powerful personality; without his charisma, the freedom approach, most thinkers believe, would fail. Neill himself most strenuously denies this and argues in his enormous output of books (some twenty in all, although he kept reworking the same material) that his indeed *is* a general theory, independent of his own person.

Why is it that Neill deliberately embarked on, and maintained without wavering, a lifelong career in total opposition to the established educational pattern? Why did he endure insults, harassment and violent antagonism for fifty years in defence of his ideal of freedom for the child? And in England, at least, apart from his few devoted followers, virtually alone? The answer lies in large part in his personal philosophy.

Neill himself has written about his stern Calvinistic upbringing in which the fear of God was thrashed into him (as indeed into most children in nineteenth century Scotland) with a leather strap (called a tawse). He also reveals that he was particularly disturbed by the excessively morbid suppression of childhood interest in sexual matters. Having also gained a strong intuitive aversion to formal education in a period when children were ruthlessly driven to study for public examinations, and himself having failed in these examinations, Neill came to the conclusion during World War I that civilisation itself was decadent and perhaps finished. Something totally new was needed.

Out of the Great War promising signs of a new era ahead appeared and *avant-garde* movements of all kinds began to spring up, perhaps most vividly illustrated by the art of the time. The new school of painters abandoned formal realistic compositions covered in layers of treacly varnish, and instead splashed bright colours onto their canvasses with such intensity and apparent lack of restraint that in France they were even called "wild beasts" (*les Fauves*). Sculptors stopped making copies of human figures, a practice that was seen as imposing their own conceptions on the stone, and instead tried to help the stone become more expressive of its latent "self". New criteria of art arose: fitness for purpose, form determined by function, economy of design, personal expression, and so on. This influenced architecture, where the classical ornament of the nineteenth-century revival was replaced by austere, simple shapes made up of glass and steel surfaces. These ideas were developed in other social movements as well and at this time psychoanalysis became very prominent. Following the pioneer work of Freud, Adler and Jung, the psychoanalytic movement gathered momentum after the war and became well established in *avant-garde* intellectual circles. Neill was immediately attracted to its theories and remained so throughout his life.

Psychoanalysis is not a single school of psychological thought; on the contrary, it is characterised by various and often competing theories too complex to enter into here. In broad outline, however, it has as its central doctrine the concept of the self: the unique personality of each individual. This self is genetically laid down at conception; it is endowed with a "nature" containing its own built-in patterns of future growth and development. In fact, some theorists of the psychoanalytic movement have relied upon a language of organic metaphor to explain their ideas, and so use the words "growth", "unfolding", and "development" quite freely. If the self is regarded from this viewpoint, then life should be seen as an organic sequence, as the progressive unfolding of inner latencies towards a full "blooming" of the mature form. Following this, education should be a "nurturing", the providing of optimum conditions for growth, the careful tending to ensure that this unfolding is neither hindered nor repressed.

Quite a few "new era" educators attempted to develop educational theories and practices on this basis, especially in Europe, and for all of them the key concept was freedom. Neill took up the idea very quickly, at least by the early 1920s. Freedom as he sees it is an absence of restraints on the child; it is a condition in which the latent personality is allowed to develop in whatever way it chooses, although with the underlying assumption that the inherent "self" is good and, under such conditions, will grow therefore in a "good" way. For Neill, the "good" is defined by the results of growth; process determines product, and in this he is diametrically opposed to Plato, and in full agreement with Rousseau.

If Neill's theory is correct, of course, then almost all of the educational procedures of Western civilisation are wrong, and indeed this is Neill's claim. In advancing his own theory he also attacked, head-on, the prevailing conceptions of education and most practices of the school. His objections are similar to those of Rousseau and Dewey, and need not be set out again here.

Yet Neill's theory is not quite as naive and shallow as is often alleged by its critics. For he argues that the processes of growth and development are guided by some kind of regulating mechanism. Neill himself is unable to say what this is (his own awareness seems to be very largely intuitive), but points out that our knowledge of human psychology is still very imperfect. And in the years that Neill was implementing his ideas, he was ahead of much psychological research that has subsequently supported some of his theory. In particular, Neill relied upon some kind of implicit "stage" theory of moral development that is being made more explicit in the recent enquiries of Piaget, Bronfenbrenner and Kohlberg, among others. Neill claims that if we genuinely seek to let each human being reach full stature as a person, we must allow the forces of inner growth and development to operate naturally, and for this, freedom, in the sense of absence of restraints, is essential.

If the idea of growth and development is to be employed, however, some kind of aim or end in view is necessary, as Dewey so clearly argued. What does Neill say here? He certainly is far less explicit than many expect; Neill simply appeals again to the concept of nature, suggesting that the goal is the achievement of selfhood, and that this achievement is characterised by happiness. In this respect he is not far from Aristotle's position, for Neill sees happiness as a condition in which the individual engaged in society is in complete balance, with latent capacities so cultivated as to allow meaningful participation with a satisfying sense of working optimally. Happiness is hard to define exactly, though it has a largely aesthetic quality: it arises from a daily sense of ease and satisfaction with one's engagement with life.

The implications for education are in radical contrast to the usual practices, for education itself, in Neill's view, is seen chiefly as the provision of an environment that supports the child's need to develop its potentialities. Ideally there should be no fixed curriculum at all, and the collective culture of civilisation should be an exciting realm in which the child can explore and become engaged in those features that are relevant to personal needs. Life is really a voyage of the self. Subject matter, in the formally organised sense, is not enormously important, although Neill's theories do not deal with the philosophical basis of knowledge. In this kind of learning situation, the teacher must act psychoanalytically; the task is one of helping the child, as non-directively as possible, to pursue its enquiries and search for selfhood. Emphatically, the teacher's own will or personality must not be imposed on the child, and it is therefore a canon of procedure that all punishment and coercion are banned. The child must not be compelled to do anything, and for two good reasons: because compulsion vitiates the principle of freedom, which is necessary to the proper growth of the self; and because things learned under compulsion are not fully integrated into the self.

It is in the area of the development of morality that Neill's theory has engendered most of its opposition and criticism. Neill holds that the moral realm has no absolute character, in contrast to the view that was forced upon him in his own childhood. Morality is fundamentally a social process and if it has any absolutes these are all developed from the one cardinal principle of respect for the individual. So private property is justified because it belongs to, and helps support the individual. What happens though, when there is a conflict of interests? How does Neill resolve this? What does he say of the rule of law? Unfortunately, this is where he is extremely vague. In Summerhill School it is clear that he did at times make authoritarian decisions and acted *deus ex machina*. Yet generally he let group processes work wherever possible and allowed decisions to come from the children themselves. And the instances he cites of their decisions, occasionally written down as formal rules, show that the moral concepts evolved are quite consonant with those of children elsewhere.

How has this theory worked out in practice? For a start, Neill always had a small school, varying in enrolment from ten to seventy with a stable mean of about forty, helped by up to half a dozen assistants. Summerhill also has always been fully residential, and the clientele have never been a typical cross-section. Neill freely admitted that the children have been atypical, especially in the early years of the school; disturbed, from broken or eccentric homes, and so on. So, indeed, some of the acts of irresponsible behaviour by these children would have occurred whatever school they had attended. Regardless, Neill persevered with his beliefs, and claimed never to have required any child to learn: only as the child seeks is instruction given. Yet his approach has never been fully tested. In England the education authorities exercise some control, and Neill frequently claimed that this imposes constraints upon the full flowering of his theory. A normal school subject curriculum is provided — for those children who freely present themselves in classes — because it is the only way children can gain the necessary credentials for employment or whatever in the outside world.

In so many ways it would be fair to say that Neill's theory — his innovation — has never been given an adequate trial because of the pressures of society. Yet it would also be fair to say that Neill's theory would not work in its entirety because it is not systematically argued through to a philosophical basis. It is fundamentally limited because it has no clear concept of existence or of knowledge, and its ethics are really that of a small social group without much extension to a wider society. Indeed, Neill consistently fails to show any deep understanding of the function of the higher levels of culture. The whole approach to education through freedom, in fact, can be construed as perhaps a clever pedagogical method that disguises an abdication of responsibility by the teacher. For Neill's system puts such a premium on self-motivation and sustained drive in securing knowledge by personal ability that it really leads to the survival of the strongest, in this case the most highly motivated and intelligent students. It is the consideration of these issues and the many questions that they inevitably generate that gives so much excitement and continuing interest to the educational ideas of A. S. Neill. Doubtless, as our world continues to become more complex and so less free, Neill's thought will become of even greater interest.

In examining Neill's ideas, there are many controversial issues to be considered. Central, though, is his idea of freedom. What does this freedom mean? He suggests the absence of restraints on the individual but there is also the notion of freedom as opportunity to act in one's best interest which may involve restraints on conflicting desires. Can these two approaches to freedom be reconciled? And does Neill satisfactorily distinguish freedom from licence? Also, the whole question of the relationship between philosophy and educational theory must be looked at in respect to Neill. Does a general educational theory need to include specific theories of existence, knowledge and values, or can it ignore them? Is, in effect, a psychoanalytic belief sufficient basis on which to posit a general theory of education? And can this belief provide for moral growth? Even further, is a moral realm necessary to society, and if so, how do we enter it? If not, how can society operate? And how do individuals come to relate to such a society? These are but a few of the questions his work raises and they are all of major importance in any attempt to rethink the nature and aims of education. Neill's own contribution to this attempted revision, which is his significant innovation, may be expressed as an attempt to follow through consistently and relentlessly the educational implications of a philosophical belief in freedom combined with a psychological commitment to psychoanalysis within the institution of the school.

SELECT BIBLIOGRAPHY

A. S. Neill wrote some twenty books, many containing parts of earlier works. He has published most with Herbert Jenkins in London. In the following list, those published otherwise are so indicated.

A Dominie's Log, 1915
A Dominie Dismissed, 1916
Booming of Bunkie, 1919
A Dominie in Doubt, 1920
Carroty Broon, 1920
A Dominie Abroad, 1922
A Dominie's Five, 1924
The Problem Child, 1926
The Problem Parent, 1932
Is Scotland Educated? Routledge and Kegal Paul, London, 1936.
That Dreadful School, 1937

Last Man Alive, 1938
The Problem Teacher, 1940
Hearts Not Heads in the School, 1944
The Problem Family, 1949
The Free Child, 1953
Summerhill: A Radical Approach to Education, Gollancz, London, 1962;
    Penguin, 1968
Freedom — Not License! Hart Publishing Co., New York, 1966
Talking of Summerhill, Gollancz, London, 1967

Selections

These selections from A. S. Neill deal with the critical aspects of his educational theory, and have been taken from three of his books: Hearts Not Heads in the School, Summerhill *and* Talking of Summerhill.

Neill's psychoanalytic approach to schooling is illustrated by two chapters from Hearts Not Heads in the School. *These set out his belief that we know so little about the psychology of human growth that it is dangerous to interfere by imposing our preconceived notions. Instead, teachers should be extremely cautious and act merely as careful observers of children, without projecting their own psychological attitudes and problems into the classroom.*

The second selection, taken from the 1968 compilation of earlier works, gives Neill's own succinct definition of education. In arguing that the end of education is happiness, he elaborates on this theme to urge that self-expression, feeling and play are far more important to the growing child than formal lessons and cognitive attainment. And this has the most profound consequences for his approach to rewards and punishments, as the reading shows.

Neill has always been subjected to a barrage of objections, and he answers many of these in his books. A selection of questions and answers illustrating his reaction to these objections, taken from both Summerhill *and* Talking of Summerhill, *make up the third and fourth selections from Neill.*

Hearts Not Heads in the School
Chapter 8: Freedom in Education

I recall a newspaper photographer coming to my school with his camera. I met him in the drive, and he asked if he could take a few snaps. I assented and led him to the house. Suddenly he stopped and stared at the house.

"Have I come to the right place?" he asked.

"I don't know," I said, "but this is Summerhill School."

"The freedom school?" he asked, and I nodded. He still stood staring at the building in a perplexed way.

"Here," he said, "if this is a free school why aren't all these windows broken?"

A cynic might say that after all he was only a pressman, but he expressed an attitude that many people have to freedom. One sees this attitude in the fond mother who avers that she has brought up her child in complete freedom . . . and then one turns to look at the product and finds an impudent, spoiled brat. Few seem to realise where freedom ends and licence begins.

From A. S. NEILL, *Hearts not Heads in the School*, Herbert Jenkins, London, 1944. Reprinted by permission of A. S. Neill.

Others again talk of giving freedom to children. No one can give another freedom; freedom is a natural state and all one can do is to refrain from setting up barbed-wire fences, so that the teacher's position in regard to freedom should be a negative one. His motto should be: "Let me keep out", that is, if he values freedom. If he believes that a teacher is a gardener who must train and prune the young shoots, there is no point in discussing freedom with him, and the only answer that can be given him is that the gardener knows what sort of roses or apples he wants, whereas the teacher does not know what sort of human being should be produced, and, indeed, should not know, so that when a disciple of Rudolf Steiner once claimed that Steiner knew exactly what kind of human education should produce, the disciple was surely misinterpreting a master who was undoubtedly a genius not only in education but in agriculture. No man is great enough or wise enough to say what education should produce.

We can, of course, decide what standard of learning we shall aim at, but as learning is only a minor part of education our standards cannot do very much harm. When we make a standard of behaviour, of character, we are doing something full of danger, and the logical thing to do is to refuse to influence either behaviour or character, obvious because the coming generation must be different from our one if life is to be progressive. As education is today, both in home and school, youth has to squander great weights of energy in resisting the father-mother ideal, which seeks what is static when youth is thirsting for what is dynamic. Much neurosis is simply the outward sign of an internal battle between youth's urge and parental ideals, and freedom seems to be the only solution.

But what is freedom? I am not free to drive on the right side of the road, not free to drive a car at all today. Clearly there is always a limit to freedom, and the term should mean simply living your own life in such a way that you do not interfere with the lives of others. Yet here one meets difficulty. It is right to say that I should not be free to play a blaring radiogram in my garden if the man next door wants to sleep, but what about the deacons of North Wales protesting against my pupils profaning the Lord's Day by playing hockey? Which comes first, the health and joy of children or the Sabbatarianism of chapel-goers? My own answer to this question would be a prejudiced one. I left it to the children who decided unanimously to stop playing hockey on Sundays so as not to offend their neighbours.

Freedom in a school is simply doing what you like so long as you do not spoil the peace of others, and in practice it works wonderfully. It is comparatively easy to have this kind of freedom, especially when it is accompanied by self-government by the whole community, and is free from all adult attempts to guide and suggest and rule, is free from all fear of adults. Many would go thus far. Where many would stop would be at freedom of the individual. Is Peter to be free to refuse mathematics or music or whatnot? This is the stumbling block. The cry is that the child has not the knowledge to decide, and one is asked if one would allow a baby to choose its own food and its own bedtime — the stock argument in education, just as the stock question to the vegetarian is why does he wear leather boots? The answer is that there are certain things we must impose on a child — food, warm clothing, bedtime, indeed, all things connected with bodily health. In psychic health we should impose nothing, and in learning we should demand nothing. The child should be completely free to learn or not learn. In practice, of course, every child learns, for it is his nature to do so, although, under compulsion, much learning is a disagreeable task that prohibits the child from learning what to him is more attractive and of more value. As to the critic who argues that in a free state the child will shirk all the unpleasant tasks of life, I can only refer him to the fact that Summerhill children pass entrance exams, children who were free to play all day for years if they had wanted to.

The learning side is, as I have claimed, a minor matter. What is of importance is that under freedom children acquire something that no compulsory system can give them, a sincerity that stands out bravely, an attitude to life that is independent and fluid, an interest in people and things that all the discipline and textbooks in the world cannot give; rather they inhibit it. A free child is a personality, but a disciplined child is a torn creature compelled to be insincere because he is a dual personality — self and an imposed model. For many years I have seen children from unfree schools come to freedom, poor timid souls with artificial manners, artificial voices, artificial interests. Most of them had a splurge of rebellion and cheek as their first reaction to freedom; most of them stopped washing, and their manners dropped off like discarded mantles; in short, they went in off the deep end, and anyone seeing them at this stage would have been appalled at the idea of freedom, just as a stranger from Mars seeing a dog just released from months on a chain would get a queer impression of caninity. The mere phenomenon of outburst is proof enough that discipline is wrong and dangerous. In practice the average child never has occasion for a violent reaction, for he leaves a disciplined system of education for a similarly disciplined system of work, and if our aim is an uneducated servile proletariat, well and good; but if we want to see a happy, cultured, sincere population we shall have to demand that the child will be free.

But we cannot have free children if we adults are bound. I could not run my school if my own complexes demanded that the children should respect me and call me "Sir", if my personality introduced any fear in a child's life. I can only deal with free children if I am as it were on their level — one of the gang; more than that, if I do not approve of their behaviour, not by saying so, but by acting so. Lately I have been dealing with a new girl who has been stealing small sums from her mates. Each time she stole I gave her threepence reward, and after the first reward she said: "What a fool you are, Neill. I'll steal every day so as to get the threepence." And for three days she came and told me of her thefts, and she got her threepence . . . I made it fourpence on the third occasion because the theft was a bigger one than usual. For the last few lessons she has had no theft to report, and is on the way to be cured of stealing. I give this as an instance of approving of the child, not by empty words but by deeds. Words never cured anyone of anything. I give the instance to show that, unless one has this attitude to the child, freedom will be at best what is described as "ordered freedom", a fine contradiction in terms indeed. Freedom can order itself but it cannot be ordered by an external authority.

I know that to stand by and watch children working out their freedom is not easy. It needs much patience, infinite faith. I think of Homer Lane seeing his delinquents, after hours of labour, knock down their badly built brick walls in an orgy of destruction. Lane's section was a professional job, straight and true, but he laughed with the others and kicked his wall to bits. Lane, more than any man I have known, realised what true freedom was, and his faith in child nature was supreme and infinite. He knew that inner freedom must precede true outer freedom, and could wait patiently for its triumph.

One must have not only faith in the child's nature, but one must have faith in the child's intelligence and wisdom. My own instinct was to tell the deacons to go to hell, but the children chose the surer way, the wiser way, for to stand well with one's neighbours seemed to them of greater value than the enjoyment of a game. Free children show a wisdom that almost startles. When they try an offender who has broken the community laws their judgment is invariably good, and there is never a harsh sentence, so that even the youngest stand before a jury of their peers without any fear. The cause of this is primarily that they do not live under suppression. Boys flogged by masters naturally take it out on smaller boys, and most boyish cruelty is the direct result of cruelty and hate shown to them. I suspect that those of my companions in a Scots village many years ago who used to kill young birds and toads cruelly were those who got the tawse most often in the school, for I recall them as being for the most part dunces. Punishment is hate and it must produce hate, and when I hear, as I do so often, of prefects beating up small boys with the school's consent I almost despair for education and sanity. Freedom from fear should be the first demand in the education of tomorrow . . . and today, and the beating of boys by prefects or masters or mistresses is a crying sore that brings shame to every honest teacher in the land.

I mentioned licence. Some teachers who have tried what they call freedom have only managed to achieve licence. Licence leaves out the rights of the other fellow, and its effect on character is a damning one. The spoiled child is only a nuisance to society and a failure in himself. Yet in practice it is often difficult to decide what is freedom and what is licence. If I allowed a normal child to burn holes with a red-hot poker in my radiogram I should be tolerating and encouraging licence. If he wanted to do so I should yell at him to get out − if he were a normal child (but of course he wouldn't be a normal child, although he might be one reacting to a suddenly found freedom). But if the child had been severely punished by his father for burning holes in furniture I should have to stand by and see him damage my radiogram, knowing that if I were to help him to be cured I must not take up the attitude of a father who had made the child a problem. In other words, licence should only be allowed in curative work, allowed as a means to an end. With normal children licence is automatically curbed by the feeling of the community — a most potent force in any collection either of children or adults, so that the defence against licence is self-government, or perhaps self-determination is a better term, in the school. A deep herd instinct makes us want to be approved of by our herd, and it is significant that the criminal is nearly always the one who has lost the desire to be approved of by society. Systems like the Borstal system realise this and attempt to make the young crook a good citizen by making him conscious of community life, and they have much success, although if they were modelled on The Little Commonwealth their successes would be much greater and more enduring. Their freedom is still too much "ordered freedom"; they are not applying what we know of modern child psychology fully and fearlessly enough. They still believe with the public schools that character shoud be formed from without.

Freedom in the school postulates a knowledge of child psychology in the teacher. The teacher should know what not to do rather than know what to do, which means that the teacher must not butt in and do the wrong thing. The teacher should know "more than somewhat" of cause and effect. He should know the psychological history of each child, so that he will not act wrongly and stupidly when Willie ill-uses a kitten with the name Polly, because he knows that Willie's dear little baby sister has the name Polly. When Mary returns from a vacation in a destructive mood he should know that she has had four weeks of violent quarrels between her parents. Sometimes a jury will say: "This is a psychological affair, and we leave it to Neill to deal with." But children have a flair for psychology themselves, and they love to try bold experiments like appointing a notorious destroyer of books chief librarian, often succeeding in such experiments. Freedom must be accompanied by psychology, for if it isn't all sorts of moral teachings, prejudiced suggestions, veiled threats will creep in, and the result will be the kind of self-government that one meets with sometimes, where children sit round in silence and vote for what the head proposes.

No, it must be Brand's All or Nothing. No halfway house is a healthy resting place. No ersatz freedom will do. The "strong" teacher can never succeed in a free school; the staff must be children at heart and have neither dignity nor authority. Above all they must be sincere in word and life, never lying to a child and never dissembling, never claiming the privilege of age and experience. They must never ask for obedience unless obedience is mutual. I tell a boy to buzz off because I am busy and he goes, but when I walked into a birthday party of a child of five or so he said: "Here, you weren't invited. Get out!" And I went out. (But I discovered later that his only motive was the fear that my appetite would be commensurate with my size.) Frankly, I don't know why I am writing about freedom; it all seems so natural and delightful to me, after twenty-three years of life in a community of free children.

Chapter 9: Danger Zones in Freedom Schools

There is no doubt that man is a moralist; why, I do not know; but there is in everyone a wish to teach someone, and all arguments, whether in books or lectures or the village local, aim at teaching someone something. I can refrain from moralising in my school but cannot refrain from doing it in writing. That isn't so bad, for adults can take a moral or leave it, whereas children are very amenable to adult moralising. Their docility is a real thing — if they are unfree; free children haven't much docility about them.

The danger in a pioneer school is that moralising will creep in, that expectation will raise its unwelcome head. The teacher is apt to find what he expects, and is disappointed when he doesn't find it. He may have an idea that a child of six should be able to share its tuckbox with its mates, forgetting that a child of six is a bundle of egocentricity (we all are similar bundles), and by word or gesture or expression may convey to the child that it is a selfish little brat. He (or she) may think that making a noise at table is not very nice, or that children should always say "Please" and "Thank You", and beg people's pardons. The other day I heard a new teacher say to a boy of four when he asked: "Can I have a bit of that cake?" "You forgot the last word, Philip." The boy protested that he hadn't; that he had said cake. The teacher suddenly laughed and said: "Gosh, I forgot that I am in Summerhill!" When he is seventeen, and if I am still alive, someone will tell me of Philip's good manners; I know that they will be genuine manners, at least. I have never been able to make up my mind whether psychology is a science or an art, but in one aspect it is the art of having infinite patience, the art of being able to wait and wait and wait. Psychology has no space for forcing hot-houses. The foundation of child psychology must be observation. If a teacher has any preconceived notions about child behaviour he should drop them quickly. There are no oughts in psychology: we dare not say that, at such and such an age, Tommy should be unselfish or fond of soap or polite to indifferent people.

The noise of a gang of children is tiresome to adults. I can stand it because it is part of my life, and I hear it no more than the factory worker hears the machines. Bernard Shaw would hold his ears in despair in any free school — I am told he did so once at Bertrand Russell's school. Any Montessori school I have entered was a hive of buzzless bees; but I haven't been in one for nearly thirty years, and they may be noisy now. Noise is a natural phenomenon in childhood, and the desk school, by suppressing it, is working straight against child nature. Even in the progressive school noise is too often suppressed, because teachers hate noise.

One danger is having a sentimental attitude to the child. It isn't easy to define sentimentality, and possibly the nearest definition is: attaching a big emotion to something quite small. Teachers with no sex life are very apt to project their unfulfilled emotions on to the child, either in love disguised as sentimentality or hate disguised as irritation. Most working-class women when they take up a baby say: "The poor wee lamb!" when the baby is quite busy and happy. Sentimentality is often a substitute for real love, and one sees parents who do not love their children gush over them in a very sentimental way. Teachers should guard against any tendency in themselves to be sentimental about children. They should be aware when they are trying to work on a child's emotions, striving to buy love by gushing and favouritism. It is easy to slip into a possessive attitude, easy to point to a child and say: "Lord, you should have seen that kid when he came here!" as if one were a gardener at a flower show, proudly indicating with his thumb his prize onion. Tearful sentimentality is all right when one deals with onions, but it is dangerous when one deals with humans. The school is so narrow, so isolated, that the teacher comes to believe that his geese are swans — which suggests another definition: sentimentality is a giving of a swan emotion to a goose. It is very human to make our geese swans and we project our emotions even into animals, so that we feel that our pet pig or pet lamb feels the butcher's knife more agonisingly than the rank and file of pigs and sheep. So in school the teacher is inclined to see in Betty, who acts well, a future Duse; in Bill, who loves geometry, a coming Einstein. That is why I once wrote suggesting that all teachers be compelled to take every second year off, and go to the Continent after giving a solemn and stamped promise not to enter a school there nor meet any teachers. You cannot have any perspective in a school: you cannot see the wood for desks. People envy the teacher his long holidays. They aren't nearly long enough if we are going to have staffs that have a broad outlook, and see at hearts some of the millions of children who are not in their little village or private schools.

Another danger in a pioneer school is that of the teacher's identifying himself with the children, and living out his own complexes as the children do theirs. It is astonishing how few adults can really work under freedom. I am sure that this is primarily due to bad education, one in which the play instinct was never allowed to have full scope. Unfortunately, I have not much chance of discovering how my old pupils react to teaching in a free school, because one proof of the success of the school is that no old pupil wants to be a teacher.

One danger is almost unavoidable. I don't know how many reviewers have said of my books: "Our Neill is the only man in the regiment in step." I lend myself to the gibe, and every man who is not going the same way as the herd can have this divot shied at him. Yet there is a truth behind the gibe. We do tend to forget the world outside, are apt to dismiss schools in general as out of date. We see all the bad things in the other fellow — his sadism, his stupid dignity, his dangerous authority — and we shut our eyes to the good work that is being done in many a school. We lose perspective, but that is largely due to the fact that for every letter we get telling of a good school we get fifty complaining of bad schools. In any case the good schools look after themselves, and their work inspires other teachers. Still in each of us is the infantile notion that we alone are in step. This is evident in all professions, as anyone knows who has associated with rival doctors and lawyers and psychologists — especially psychologists. There is fear that the other fellow may get in first (a fear that many inventors have — that someone else will patent the invention first). I have known scientists who hated hearing that another man had made a big discovery. Every man is a baby, and all the learning and university degrees in the world do nothing to make him grow up. Thus it comes that usually a man's work is greater than himself, and that is why we should never meet our favourite authors, for they nearly always disappoint us.

The educational pioneer must guard against the temptation to thank God that he is not like other men — disciplinarians, beaters of children, apostles of learning. No man is very far in advance of his fellows. The neighbouring Welsh village dominie who leathers his pupils is only doing and believing what I did and believed in 1916. The woman teacher who, the other day, said: "I never go to psychology lectures, because psychology is just rubbish," is not so far behind the woman who says she believes in psychology and acts as if she didn't. On the other hand when a teacher from a church school told me that the head is always leathering, especially for dirty hands, I had to conclude that he is a hell of a long way behind the founder of his church. Christianity does not dispose of hate, nor for that matter does educational pioneering. I have had teachers, idealists who fondly imagined that they could rule out the hate side of life, the aggressive side: they were determined to give out love even when a child kicked them or punctured their cycles. The first requisite of a pioneer is that he should be human and have no illusions about himself, and no tendency to consider himself a plaster saint. I find so many pacifist teachers so unrealistic about freedom. They want to substitute idealism for psychology, and to bring spirituality into the school. What people mean by spirituality I don't know. A local clergyman asked me the other day: "If you school has no religion, what is there to bring out their spirituality?" I had to say that I was damned if I knew, for he was using a term that was meaningless to me.

Among the dangers of a free school one might include the smugness of self-sacrifice. Living with children one must sacrifice much — quietness, possession of things (which get broken or taken); worst of all, one must sacrifice much privacy, a sacrifice that tortures every sensitive man in the army or navy. The temptation is to say smugly that you are giving all so that children can be happy. This is the "Christ Crucified" motif, the saviour of mankind with his hair shirt of martyrdom. Of course one does sacrifice a lot, but let us be honest about it. On the material side one has poor pay, a barren room, but on the other hand a free life with spare time and a pleasant atmosphere; on the psychic side one has enormous interest, absence of fear of authority, freedom to carry out one's own ideas in teaching and in life. The pros easily outweigh the cons, and if any teacher in a pioneer school considers himself a martyr, he is being neurotic about his job. I cannot honestly say that I enjoy the hundred of little things demanded of me daily. . . . "Can you give me some nails? I forgot to get my pocket-money on Monday: can I have it now?" I walk up to my room many a time daily to get something for a child, but if I am cutting hay I refuse to go to the house to fulfil the request. The martyr type possibly would. All these little incidents are part of the day's work. I am no martyr in the big things because the work is so fascinating that in itself it is a reward and a pleasure. Beware of the pioneer who is a Christian martyr.

The pioneer is generally termed a crank, and too often pioneer schools have specialised in sandals and short-haired women and long-haired men; they have loved to revive old-time dances in the manner of the Wander-vögel (pre-Hitler variety), and to inspire the pupils with highbrow litera-ture and art. Such pioneering leads into a cul-de-sac; it separates children from the real world of lowbrow books and cinemas and vulgar jokes. My own staff may sometimes wear sandals, but they are all known at the local tobacconist. In short, they are in touch with the larger crowd we call humanity. Anything that tends to segregate a school is bad. The pioneer may think that he is in the van of educational theory, but if he thinks that he is above his fellow citizen he is likely to find that his theories won't work. A man can't be a good pioneer if he cannot put his bob on a favourite now and again (but the converse does not hold). I don't want to see pioneer schools get into the hands of antilife people, people who love isms and who try to be examples of perfect behaviour: who play Bach to children who are longing to hear Duke Ellington. There is some justification for the frequent ques-tion: "How will crank-school kids fit into life later on?" The question does not bother me, for a self-governing school carries its civics out into life. But if the crank school is to produce children who are cranky about food and literature and art and politics and pacificism, it will not prepare them for society. Moreover no pioneer should try consciously to influence children, whether to make them communists or pacifists, vegetarians or baptists, loyalists or rebels. This is a point that cannot be overemphasised, because the moulding of children is one of the evils in — say — public schools that all progressives attack, and to force vegetarianism or pacifism on a child is just as bad as to force imperialism or toryism.

On the other hand it is almost impossible to rule out what might be called negative suggestion. In Summerhill we compel no opinions, no beliefs, no tastes, no politics, no religion. The children must realise that neither my staff nor I have any religion, even though we never mention the word: unconsciously they must feel that we live without an external God, and, as a clerical friend puts it, "they miss something that a religious staff would give them." So that we can be accused of moulding character by negation. We give them art and science, self-government and playtime, lessons and cinema because we feel that these things are important, but because we con-sider religion unimportant we withhold it. Rather should I say that we con-sider religion dangerous and antilife, just as we should not think of introducing children to sadism or anti-Semitism or fascism or sexual per-version, because they, in another form, are anti-life. We do, therefore, select and choose according to our own make-up, and we have to be honest and own up to it. Frankly I cannot see how we can do otherwise; I cannot grant facilities to encourage children to be Baptists and Mohammedans, socialists and tories, Oxford Groupers and spiritualists. And there is the parental question to consider. My parents want a school in which there is no religion, and if we are to grant leave to parents to select a line of life for their children, I do not see how we can insist on a school's being limited in its choice of a line of life. One can claim that one seeks to eradicate what is merely local, and certainly religion is local in this way that Tommy Brown would have been a Mohammedan had he been born in Cairo. Education should concentrate chiefly on what is common to all mankind, that is, it should have internationalism as an objective. Japanese boys differ from English boys in religion, manners, customs, social outlook, yet the fundamentals they have in common — love, hate, hunger and sex appetites, ambition, peace, work: these live forever while religions and politics and customs change and decay and die. Nationalism, by valuing the things that decay and die, is an evil. After Hitler and all he stands for have departed the scene Germans will be happy and loving and working. Vansittartism is an evil that perpetuates nationalism while claiming that its aim is to destroy it: it ignores the fundamentals of life and is so short-sighted that it can see only tomorrow, not next week.

Children must be given the opportunity to be tolerant of other races and alien customs: they should be ready for that World State that Wells and others advocate. Our insularity has limited our education greatly, and every schoolmaster's daydream is that he can take his school round the world in a big ship. When one is adult it is often too late to benefit from travel. I recall a midlander I got into conversation with while we looked at Cologne Cathedral — he said that he preferred his chapel; and when I took my old mother to Nuremberg she began to rhapsodise about the beauty of Edinburgh. Nationalism is dangerous because it fixes forever early infantile memories, and there is little hope for humanity until it finds a way to live without being influenced by its childhood past.

So again I must repeat, *ad nauseam* if necessary, that the pioneer must put emotion first. When we educate, our schools should be such that any child can fit in — British, German, Chinese, Negro, Jew or Gentile. They all have the same emotions, the same loves and fears and hopes. Religion differs with geography, but all nationals have the same sex problems and the same economic difficulties, so that world education should be secular and wide as the seven seas. Hearts, not heads, will make the ultimate World State.

A great danger in pioneering is that one is apt to keep oneself separate from the crowd. Contact with other teachers is vitally necessary. Sometimes when I lecture to bodies of teachers I feel humble and ashamed when I am reminded of their difficulties — large classes, barrack rooms, inspectors, codes, curricula; I feel a little mean talking to them, knowing that I have none of their difficulties myself. On the other hand they do not have mine. They are free from children's noise from Friday night to Monday morning; they have fixed salaries while I have to worry about finance, and they know that their old age will be covered by a pension. Yet in essentials I am free and they are not, and I hope that I shall never feel that I am outside the profession, one of the peculiar people who form their own caste. There is a definite danger of segregation. I recall a big teachers' conference where I was to lecture one weekend. I listened to the speeches of other teachers and was frankly bored; I could not raise any interest in methods of teaching subjects, and when an inspector talked I felt that nothing he said touched fundamentals. If one is interested primarily in child psychology the average educational conference or educational journal is dull, and teachers, by allowing the older members of the profession to monopolise the speechifying, do themselves a disservice. Talks on methods of teaching geography or long division should hardly be termed educational talks at all: they have as much to do with real education as the colour of an aeroplane has to do with flying. The preoccupation with subjects and methods so common to teachers makes contact with them difficult. They are apt to go on the defensive, especially the heads — the least interested in education of the lot. The honest, progressive teachers welcome approach and ideas, but even they have to say: "All very well for you, but I have fifty kids to teach in a classroom. I can't study each individually, can't know their home and psychological history and complexes. I must keep them quiet, for the maths man is next door, and he won't have noise. Besides the parents expect their children to learn and pass exams." The resentment many teachers have against the pioneer school is founded on envy — "Take away my desks and inspectors and local authorities and I also will pioneer. Today I am chained." It is true, and the man or woman who carries on bravely struggling against authority and conventional education in a state school is more worthy of admiration than any of the state-free pioneers. They are the real hopes for the future. They remain in the regiment even although they keep step unwillingly, whereas the pioneer who ploughs a lonely furrow in fields which the public are not invited to view is like the kind of conscientious objector who is indifferent if the world goes to chaos.

It looks as if the education of tomorrow will need a new type of teacher, one who subordinates interest in teaching to interest in living. The staff meeting of tomorrow will discuss Johnny's tendency to daydream or Mary's bad temper, rather than, as today, the children's accomplishments in subjects. It will put the child first — and it must be confessed that it often requires an effort to do so. Almost every handwork teacher would rather make something himself than stand around watching small boys using planes and saws clumsily and wrongly. True that shop assistants and bank clerks would rather garden in their allotments than stand at counters or sit at desks, yet the difficulty of the teacher is more acute, because his work is watching work, and he is constantly in an atmosphere that tempts one to create, while the shop assistant and the clerk are far away from creation. For peace of mind I would rather teach history or maths than handwork or art.

"He who can does: he who cannot teaches." But every man can do something, and school life should be such that every teacher can be creative. As one grows older one finds it more and more difficult to teach all the time, and it seems likely that the most successful teacher is he or she who is a child that has not lived out childish interests. That is all very well when the job is merely implanting knowledge; it is not enough when the job is living with children and understanding them psychologically. More than that, it is dangerous. Neurotic teachers are useless in a free school. They live out their complexes as the children do, and cannot acquire that objective approach that is essential. I had a teacher who loved to see children destroy things, unaware that they were doing vicariously what she had longed to do as a child. Another always sided with any malcontents who had a grouse against the matron, because her youthful (and adult) protest against her own mother was full of frustration and hate. Crank schools are magnets to teachers with complexes that they want to live out, and a large part of a head's time is taken up in sorting out the real teachers from the seekers after personal freedom. In a civilisation with a good education there would be fewer neurotics knocking about, and the ones I write of are really a proof of the badness of schooling, for, had they had full play for their emotions at school, they would have been past the stage of identifying themselves with children. Today a pioneer school should be judged by its children and never by its staff, a remark that does not gainsay the fact that in pioneer schools there are many excellent teachers who are grown up.

Summerhill

Summerhill Education versus Standard Education

I hold that the aim of life is to find happiness, which means to find interest. Education should be a preparation for life. Our culture has not been very successful. Our education, politics, and economics lead to war. Our medicines have not done away with disease. Our religion has not abolished usury and robbery. Our boasted humanitarianism still allows public opinion to approve of the barbaric sport of hunting. The advances of the age are advances in mechanism — in radio and television, in electronics, in jet planes. New world wars threaten, for the world's social conscience is still primitive.

If we feel like questioning today, we can pose a few awkward questions. Why does man seem to have many more diseases than animals have? Why does man hate and kill in war when animals do not? Why does cancer increase? Why are there so many suicides? So many insane sex crimes? Why the hate that is anti-Semitism? Why Negro hating and lynching? Why backbiting and spite? Why is sex obscene and a leering joke? Why is being a bastard a social disgrace? Why the continuance of religions that have long

From *Summerhill: A Radical Approach to Child Rearing*, by A. S. NEILL, copyright 1960 Hart Publishing Company, New York, Reprinted by permission of the publisher.

ago lost their love and hope and charity? Why, a thousand whys about our vaunted state of civilised eminence!

I ask these questions because I am by profession a teacher, one who deals with the young. I ask these questions because those so often asked by teachers are the unimportant ones, the ones about school subjects. I ask what earthly good can come out of discussions about French or ancient history or whatnot when these subjects don't matter a jot compared to the larger question of life's natural fulfilment — of man's inner happiness.

How much of our education is real doing, real self-expression? Handwork is too often the making of a pin tray under the eye of an expert. Even the Montessori system, well known as a system of directed play, is an artificial way of making the child learn by doing. It has nothing creative about it.

In the home, the child is always being taught. In almost every home, there is always at least one ungrownup who rushes to show Tommy how his new engine works. There is always someone to lift the baby up on a chair when baby wants to examine something on the wall. Every time we show Tommy how his engine works we are stealing from that child the joy of life — the joy of discovery — the joy of overcoming an obstacle. Worse! We make that child come to believe that he is inferior, and must depend on help.

Parents are slow in realising how unimportant the learning side of school is. Children, like adults, learn what they want to learn. All prizegiving and marks and exams sidetrack proper personality development. Only pedants claim that learning from books is education.

Books are the least important apparatus in a school. All that any child needs is the three Rs; the rest should be tools and clay and sports and theatre and paint and freedom.

Most of the schoolwork that adolescents do is simply a waste of time, of energy, of patience. It robs youth of its right to play and play and play; it puts old heads on young shoulders.

When I lecture to students at teacher training colleges and universities, I am often shocked at the ungrownupness of these lads and lasses stuffed with useless knowledge. They know a lot; they shine in dialects; they can quote the classics — but in their outlook on life many of them are infants. For they have been taught *to know* but have not been allowed *to feel*. These students are friendly, pleasant, eager, but something is lacking — the emotional factor, the power to subordinate thinking to feeling. I talk to these of a world they have missed and go on missing. Their textbooks do not deal with human character, or with love, or with freedom, or with self-determination. And so the system goes on, aiming only at standards of book learning — goes on separating the head from the heart.

It is time that we were challenging the school's notion of work. It is taken for granted that every child should learn mathematics, history, geography, some science, a little art, and certainly literature. It is time we realised that the average young child is not much interested in any of these subjects.

I prove this with every new pupil. When told that the school is free, every new pupil cries, "Hurrah! You won't catch me doing dull arithmetic and things!"

I am not decrying learning. But learning should come after play. And learning should not be deliberately seasoned with play to make it palatable.

Learning is important — but not to everyone. Nijinsky could not pass his school exams in St Petersburg, and he could not enter the state ballet without passing those exams. He simply could not learn school subjects — his mind was elsewhere. They faked an exam for him, giving him the answers with the papers — so a biography says. What a loss to the world if Nijinsky had had really to pass those exams!

Creators learn what they want to learn in order to have the tools that their originality and genius demand. We do not know how much creation is killed in the classroom with its emphasis on learning.

I have seen a girl weep nightly over her geometry. Her mother wanted her to go to the university, but the girl's whole soul was artistic. I was delighted when I heard that she had failed her college entrance exams for the seventh time. Possibly, the mother would now allow her to go on the stage as she longed to do.

Some time ago, I met a girl of fourteen in Copenhagen who had spent three years in Summerhill and had spoken perfect English here. "I suppose you are at the top of your class in English," I said.

She grimaced ruefully. "No, I'm at the bottom of my class, because I don't know English grammar," she said. I think that disclosure is about the best commentary on what adults consider education.

Indifferent scholars who, under discipline, scrape through college or university and become unimaginative teachers, mediocre doctors, and imcompetent lawyers would possibly be good mechanics or excellent brick-layers or first-rate policemen.

We have found that the boy who cannot or will not learn to read until he is, say, fifteen is always a boy with a mechanical bent who later on becomes a good engineer or electrician. I should not dare dogmatise about girls who never go to lessons, especially to mathematics and physics. Often such girls spend much time with needlework, and some, later on in life, take up dress-making and designing. It is an absurd curriculum that makes a prospective dressmaker study quadratic equations or Boyle's Law.

Caldwell Cook wrote a book called *The Play Way*, in which he told how he taught English by means of play. It was a fascinating book, full of good things, yet I think it was only a new way of bolstering the theory that learning is of the utmost importance. Cook held that learning was so important that the pill should be sugared with play. This notion that unless a child is learning something the child is wasting his time is nothing less than a curse — a curse that blinds thousands of teachers and most school inspectors. Fifty years ago the watchword was "Learn through doing." Today the watchword is "Learn through playing." Play is thus used only as a means to an end, but to what good end I do not really know.

If a teacher sees children playing with mud, and he thereupon improves the shining moment by holding forth about river-bank erosion, what end has he in view? What child cares about river erosion? Many so-called educators believe that it does not matter what a child learns as long as he is *taught* something. And, of course, with schools as they are — just mass-production factories — what can a teacher do but teach something and come to believe that teaching, in itself, matters most of all?

When I lecture to a group of teachers, I commence by saying that I am not going to speak about school subjects or discipline or classes. For an hour my audience listens in rapt silence; and after the sincere applause, the chairman announces that I am ready to answer questions. At least three-quarters of the questions deal with subjects and teaching.

I do not tell this in any superior way. I tell it sadly to show how the classroom walls and the prison-like buildings narrow the teacher's outlook, and prevent him from seeing the true essentials of education. His work deals with the part of a child that is above the neck; and perforce, the emotional, vital part of the child is foreign territory to him.

I wish I could see a bigger movement of rebellion among our younger teachers. Higher education and university degrees do not make a scrap of difference in confronting the evils of society. A learned neurotic is not any different than an unlearned neurotic.

In all countries, capitalist, socialist, or communist, elaborate schools are built to educate the young. But all the wonderful labs and workshops do nothing to help John or Peter or Ivan surmount the emotional damage and the social evils bred by the pressure on him from his parents, his schoolteachers, and the pressure of the coercive quality of our civilisation. . . .

Rewards and Punishment

The danger in rewarding a child is not as extreme as that of punishing him, but the undermining of the child's morale through the giving of rewards is more subtle. Rewards are superfluous and negative. To offer a prize for doing a deed is tantamount to declaring that the deed is not worth doing for its own sake.

No artist ever works for a monetary reward only. One of his rewards is the joy of creating. Moreover, rewards support the worst feature of the competitive system. To get the better of the other man is a damnable objective.

Giving rewards has a bad psychological effect on children because it arouses jealousies. A boy's dislike of a younger brother often dates from mother's remark, "Your little brother can do it better than you can." To the child, mother's remark is a reward given to brother for being better than he is.

When we consider a child's natural interest in things, we begin to realise the dangers of both rewards and punishment. Rewards and punishment tend to pressure a child into interest. But true interest is the life force of the whole personality, and such interest is completely spontaneous. It is possible to compel attention, for attention is an act of consciousness. It is possible to be attentive to an outline on the blackboard and at the same time to be interested in pirates. Though one can compel attention, one cannot compel interest. No man can force me to be interested in, say, collecting stamps; nor can I compel myself to be interested in stamps. Yet both rewards and punishment attempt to compel interest. . . .

Interest is, at root, always egoistic. Maud, aged fourteen, often helps me in the garden, although she declares that she hates gardening. But she does not hate *me*. She weeds because she wants to be with me. This serves her self-interest for the moment. . . .

A reward should, for the most part, be subjective: self-satisfaction in the work accomplished. One thinks of the ungratifying jobs of the world: digging coal, fitting nut No. 50 to bolt No. 51, digging drains, adding figures. The world is full of jobs that hold no intrinsic interest or pleasure. We seem to be adapting our schools to this dullness in life. By compelling our students' attention to subjects which hold no interest for them, we, in effect, condition them for jobs they will not enjoy.

If Mary learns to read or count, it should be because of her interest in these subjects — not because of the new bicycle she will get for excellence in study or because mother will be pleased.

One mother told her son that if he stopped sucking his thumb, she would give him a radio set. What an unfair conflict to give any child! Thumb-sucking is an unconscious act, beyond the control of will. The child may make a brave, conscious effort to stop the habit. But like the compulsive masturbater, he will fail again and again, and thereby acquire a mounting load of guilt and misery.

Parental fear of the future is dangerous when such fear expresses itself in suggestions that approach bribery: "When you learn to read, darling, daddy will buy you a scooter." That way leads to a ready acceptance of our greedy, profit-seeking civilisation. I am glad to say that I have seen more than one child prefer illiteracy to a shiny, new bicycle.

A variant of this form of bribery is the declaration that seeks to touch off the child's emotions: "Mummy will be very unhappy if you are always at the bottom of the class." Both methods of bribery bypass the child's genuine interests.

I have equally strong feelings about getting children to do our jobs. If we want a child to work for us, we ought to pay him according to his ability. No child wants to collect bricks for me just because I've decided to rebuild a broken wall. But if I offer threepence a barrow load, a boy may help willingly, for then I've enlisted his self-interest. But I do not like the idea of making a child's weekly pocket-money depend on his doing certain chores. Parents should give without seeking anything in return.

Punishment can never be dealt out with justice, for no man can be just. Justice implies complete understanding. Judges are no more moral than garbage collectors, nor are they less free of prejudice. A judge who is a strong conservative and a militarist could find it difficult to be just to an antimilitarist arrested for crying "Down with the Army".

Consciously or unconsciously, the teacher who is cruel to a child who has committed a sexual offence is almost certain to have deep feelings of guilt toward sex. In a law court, a judge with unconscious homosexual leanings would likely be very severe in sentencing a prisoner charged with homosexual practices.

We cannot be just because we do not know ourselves, and do not recognise our own repressed strivings. This is tragically unfair to the children. An adult can never educate beyond his own complexes. If we ourselves are bound by repressed fears, we cannot make our children free. All we do is bestow upon our children our own complexes.

If we try to understand ourselves, we find it difficult to punish a child on whom we are venting the anger that belongs to something else. Years ago, in the old days, I whacked boys again and again because I was worried — the inspector was coming, or I had had a quarrel with a friend. Or any other old excuse would serve me in place of self-understanding, of knowing what I was really angry about. Today, I know from experience that punishment is unnecessary. I never punish a child, never have any temptation to punish a child.

Recently I said to a new pupil, a boy who was being antisocial, "You are pulling all these silly tricks merely to get me to whack you, for your life has been one long whacking. But you are wasting your time. I won't punish you, whatever you do." He gave up being destructive. He no longer needed to feel hateful.

Punishment is always an act of hate. In the act of punishing, the teacher or parent is hating the child and the child realises it. The apparent remorse or tender love that a spanked child shows toward his parent is not real love. What the spanked child really feels is hatred which he must disguise in order not to feel guilty. For the spanking has driven the child into fantasy! *I wish my father would drop dead.* The fantasy immediately brings guilt — *I wanted my father to die! What a sinner I am.* And the remorse drives the child to father's knee in seeming tenderness. But underneath, the hatred is already there — and to stay.

What is worse, punishment always forms a vicious circle. Spanking is vented hatred, and each spanking is bound to arouse more and more hatred in the child. Then as his increased hatred is expressed in still worse behaviour, more spankings are applied. And these second-round spankings reap added dividends of hatred in the child. The result is a bad-mannered, sulky, destructive little hater, so inured to punishment that he sins in order to trigger some sort of emotional response from his parents. For even a hateful emotional response will do where there is no love emotion. And so the child is beaten — and he repents. But the next morning he begins the same old cycle again.

So far as I have observed, the self-regulated child does not need any punishment and he does not go through this hate cycle. He is never punished and he does not need to behave badly. He has no use for lying and for breaking things. His body has never been called filthy or wicked. He has not needed to rebel against authority or to fear his parents. Tantrums he will usually have, but they will be short-lived and not tend toward neurosis.

True, there is difficulty in deciding what is and what is not punishment. One day, a boy borrowed my best saw. The next day I found it lying in the rain. I told him that I should not lend him that saw again. That was not punishment, for punishment always involves the idea of morality. Leaving the saw out in the rain was bad for the saw, but the act was not an immoral one. It is important for a child to learn that one cannot borrow someone else's tools and spoil them, or damage someone else's property or someone else's person. For to let a child have his own way, or do what he wants to *at another's expense*, is bad for the child. It creates a spoiled child, and the spoiled child is a bad citizen.

Some time ago, a little boy came to us from a school where he had terrorised everyone by throwing things about and even threatening murder. He tried the same game with me. I soon concluded that he was using his temper for the purpose of alarming people and thus getting attention.

One day, on entering the playroom I found the children all clustered together at one end of the room. At the other end stood the little terror with a hammer in his hand. He was threatening to hit anyone who approached him.

"Cut it out, my boy," I said sharply. "We aren't afraid of you."

He dropped the hammer and rushed at me. He bit and kicked me.

"Every time you hit or bite me," I said quietly, "I'll hit you back." And I did. Very soon he gave up the contest and rushed from the room.

This was not punishment. It was a necessary lesson: learning that one cannot go about hurting others for one's own gratification.

Punishment in most homes is punishment for disobedience. In schools, too, disobedience and insolence are looked upon as bad crimes. When I was a young teacher and in the habit of spanking children, as most teachers in Britain were allowed to do, I always was most angry at the boy who had disobeyed me. My little dignity was wounded. I was the tin god of the classroom, just as daddy is the tin god of the home. To punish for disobedience is to identify oneself with the omnipotent Almighty: *Thou shalt have no other Gods*.

Later on, when I taught in Germany and Austria, I was always ashamed when teachers asked me if corporal punishment was used in Britain. In Germany, a teacher who strikes a pupil is tried for assault, and generally punished. The flogging and strapping in British schools is one of our greatest disgraces.

A doctor in one of our large cities said to me once, "There is a brute of a teacher at the head of one of our schools here, who beats the children cruelly. I often have nervous children brought to me because of him, but I can do nothing. He has public opinion and the law on his side."

Not too long ago, the papers carried the story of a case in which a judge told two erring brothers that if they had only had a few good hidings, they would never have appeared in court. As the evidence unfolded, it developed that the two boys had been beaten almost nightly by their father.

Solomon with his rod theory has done more harm than his proverbs have done good. No man with any power of introspection could beat a child, or could even have the wish to beat a child.

To repeat: hitting a child gives him fear *only when it is associated with a moral idea, with the idea of wrong*. If a street urchin knocked off my hat with a lump of clay and I caught him and gave him a swat on the ear, my reaction would be considered by the boy to be a natural one. No harm would have been done to the boy's soul. But if I went to the principal of his school and demanded punishment for the culprit, the fear introduced by the punishment would be a bad thing for the child. The affair would at once become an affair of morals and of punishment. The child would feel that he had committed a crime.

The ensuing scene can easily be imagined! I stand there with my muddy hat. The principal sits and fixes the boy with a baleful eye. The boy stands with lowered head. He is overawed by the dignity of his accusers. Running him down on the street, I had been his equal. I had no dignity after my hat had been knocked off. I was just another guy. The boy had learned a necessary lesson of life — the lesson that if you hit a guy he'll get angry and sock you back.

Punishment has nothing to do with hot temper. Punishment is cold and judicial. Punishment is highly moral. Punishment avows that it is wholly for the culprit's good. (In the case of capital punishment, it is for society's good.) Punishment is an act in which man identifies himself with God and sits in moral judgment.

Many parents live up to the idea that since God rewards and punishes they too should reward and punish their children. These parents honestly try to be just, and they often convince themselves that they are punishing the child for his own good. *This hurts me more than it hurts you* is not so much a lie as it is a pious self-deception.

One must remember that religion and morality make *punishment* a quasi-attractive institution. For punishment salves the conscience. "I have paid the price!" says the sinner.

At question time in my lectures, an old-timer often stands up and says, "My father used his slipper on me, and I don't regret it, sir! I would not have been what I am today if I had not been beaten." I never have the temerity to ask, "By the way, what exactly *are* you today?"

To say that punishment does not *always* cause psychic damage is to evade the issue, for we do not know what reaction the punishment will cause in the individual in later years. Many an exhibitionist, arrested for indecent exposure, is the victim of early punishment for childish sexual habits.

If punishment were ever successful, there might be some argument in its favour. True, it can inhibit through fear, as any ex-soldier can tell you.

If a parent is content with a child who has had his spirit completely broken by fear, then, for such a parent, punishment succeeds.

What proportion of chastised children remain broken in spirit and castrated for life, and what proportion rebel and become even more antisocial, no one can say. In fifty years of teaching in schools, I have never heard a parent say, "I have beaten my child and now he is a good boy." On the contrary, scores of times, I have heard the mournful story, "I have beaten him, reasoned with him, helped him in every way, and he has grown worse and worse."

The punished child *does* grow worse and worse. What's more, he grows into a punishing father or a punishing mother, and the cycle of hate goes on through the years.

I have often asked myself, "Why is it that parents who are otherwise kind tolerate cruel schools for their children?" These parents seem, primarily, to be concerned about a good education for their children. What they overlook is that a punishing teacher will compel interest, but the interest he compels is in the punishment and not in the sums on the blackboard. As a matter of fact, the majority of our top students in schools and colleges sink into mediocrity later on. Their interest in making good was born, for the most part, of the parental pushing, and they had little real interest in the subject.

Fear of teachers and fear of the punishments they deal out is bound to affect the relationship between the parent and the child. For symbolically, every adult is a father or a mother to the child. And every time a teacher punishes, the child acquires a fear and a hate of the adult behind the symbol — a hate of his father or a hate of his mother. This is a disturbing thought. Though children are not conscious of the feeling, I have heard a boy of thirteen say, "My last principal used to flog me a log, and I can't understand why my father and mother kept me at that school. They knew he was a cruel brute, but they didn't do anything about it."

The punishment that takes the form of a lecture is even more dangerous than a whipping. How awful those lectures can be! "But didn't you *know* you were doing wrong?" A sobbing nod. "Say you are sorry for doing it."

As a training for humbugs and hypocrites, the lecture form of punishment has no rival. Worse still is praying for the erring soul of the child in his presence. That is unpardonable, for such an act is bound to arouse a deep feeling of guilt in the child.

Another type of punishment — noncorporal but just as injurious to a child's development — is nagging. How many times have I heard a mother nag her ten-year old daughter all day long: *Don't go in the sun, darling . . . Dearest, please keep away from that railing . . . No, love, you can't go into the swimming pool today; you will catch your death of cold!* The nagging is certainly not a love token: it is a token of the mother's fear that covers an unconscious hate.

I wish that the advocates of punishment could all see and digest the delightful French film telling the life story of a crook. When the crook was a boy, he was punished for some misdeed by being forbidden to partake of the Sunday evening meal of poisoned mushrooms. Afterwards, as he watched all the family coffins being carried out, he decided that it didn't pay to be good. An immoral story with a moral, which many a punishing parent cannot see.

Questions and Answers

Under the Summerhill system, how does a child's willpower develop? If he is allowed to do what he pleases, how can he develop self-control?
In Summerhill, a child is *not* allowed to do as he pleases. His own laws hedge him in on all sides. He is allowed to do as he pleases only in things that affect *him* — and only him. He can play all day if he wants to, because work and study are matters that concern him alone. But he is not allowed to play a cornet in the schoolroom because his playing would interfere with others.

What, after all, is willpower? I can will myself to give up tobacco, but I cannot will myself to fall in love, nor can I will myself to like botany. No man can will himself to be good, or for that matter to be bad.

You cannot train a person to have a strong will. If you educate children in freedom, they will be more conscious of themselves, for freedom allows more and more of the unconscious to become conscious. That is why most Summerhill children have few doubts about life. They *know* what they want. And I guess they will get it, too.

Remember that what is called a weak will is usually a sign of lack of interest. The weak person who is easily persuaded to play tennis when he has no desire to play tennis is a person who has no idea of what his interests really are. A slave discipline system encourages such a person to remain weakwilled and futile.

If a child is doing something dangerous at Summerhill, do you allow him to do it?
Of course not. People so often fail to understand that freedom for children does not mean being a fool. We do not allow our little children to decide when they shall go to bed. We guard them against dangers from machinery, automobiles, broken glass, or deep water.

You should never give a child responsibility that he is not ready for. But remember that half the dangers that children encounter are due to bad education. The child who is dangerous with fire is one who was forbidden to know the truth about fire.

Do you accept backward children at Summerhill?
Sure. It all depends on what you mean by backward. We do not take mentally defective children, but a child who is backward at school is a different story. Many children are backward at school because the school is too dull for them.

Summerhill's criterion of backwardness has nothing to do with tests and sums and marks. In many cases, backwardness simply means that the child has an unconscious conflict and a guilty conscience. How can he take an interest in arithmetic or history if his unconscious problem is, "Am I wicked or not?"

I speak with personal feeling about this question of backwardness, for as a boy I simply couldn't learn. My pockets were full of bits of scrap iron and brass; and when my eyes were on my textbook, my thoughts wandered to my gadgets.

I have seldom seen a backward boy or girl who has not the potentialities of creative work; and to judge any child by his or her progress in school subjects is futile and fatal.

You say that the children in Summerhill have clean minds. What do you mean?
A clean mind is one that cannot be shocked. To be shocked is to show that you have repressions that make you interested in what shocks you.

Victorian women were shocked at the word *leg* because they had an abnormal interest in things leggy. Leggy things were sexual things, repressed things. So that in an atmosphere like Summerhill, where there is no taboo about sex and no connecting of sex with sin, children have no need to make sex unclean by whispering and leering. They are sincere about sex just as they are sincere about everything else.

Do you think that every parent who reads your books or hears you lecture will treat her child differently and better — once she knows? Does the cure for damaged children lie in getting knowledge to the parents?
A possessive mother, reading this book may get a very bad conscience and cry in defence, "I can't help myself. I don't want to ruin my child. It's all very well for you to diagnose, but what is the remedy?"

She is right. What *is* the remedy? Or, indeed, *is* there a remedy? The question asks so much.

What cure is there for a woman whose life is dull and full of fears? What cure is there for a man who thinks that his cheeky son is the cat's whiskers? Worst of all, what remedy is there when the parents are ignorant of what they are doing and become indignant at even the slightest suggestion that they are doing the wrong thing?

No, knowledge in itself won't help unless a parent is *emotionally ready* to receive the knowledge and has the inner capacity to act on what new knowledge comes his way.

Why do you say so much about the necessity of a child's being happy? Is anybody happy?
Not an easy question to answer because words confuse. Of course none of us is happy all the time; we have toothaches, unfortunate love affairs, boring work.

If the word happiness means anything, it means an inner feeling of well-being, a sense of balance, a feeling of being contented with life. These can exist only when one feels free.

Free children have open, fearless faces; disciplined children look cowed, miserable, fearful.

Happiness might be defined as the state of having minimal repression. The happy family lives in a home where love abides; the unhappy family, in a tense home.

I place happiness first because I place growth first. It is better to be free and contented and be ignorant of what a decimal fraction is, than to pass school exams and have your face covered with acne. I have never seen acne on the face of a happy and free adolescent.

Do you honestly think it is right to allow a boy, naturally lazy, to go his own easy way doing as he chooses, wasting time? How do you set him to work when work is distasteful to him?

Laziness doesn't exist. The lazy boy is either physically ill or he has no interest in the things that adults think he ought to do.

I have never seen a child who came to Summerhill before the age of twelve who was lazy. Many a "lazy" lad has been sent to Summerhill from a strict school. Such a boy remains "lazy" for quite a long time; that is, until he recovers from his education. I do not set him to do work that is distasteful to him, because he isn't ready for it. Like you and me, he will have many things to do later that he will hate doing; but if he is left free to live through his play period now, he will be able, later on, to face any difficulty. To my knowledge, no ex-Summerhillian has ever been accused of laziness.

Talking of Summerhill

Questions and Answers

How can Summerhill principles be applied to a state school?

Hundreds of teachers have asked me that one. I have already spoken of Michael Duane of Rising Hill School. He was headmaster and could do something about freedom. Usually the question is asked by young teachers. The answer, sadly enough, is that an assistant cannot introduce more freedom than the head will allow. I speak from experience. Long ago I was an assistant in King Alfred School, Hampstead. I had just come under the influence of Homer Lane and was enthusiastic about self-government. In staff meetings I pleaded for it, and finally dear old John Russell said: "Good, Neill can have self-government in his classes." Being a young fool I agreed. The sequel of course was that one class came from − say − a maths class with discipline to my geography class . . . and played merry hell, naturally. Teachers in near rooms protested and the experiment failed, and so did I; I left, or was I thrown out? I am not quite sure.

Any young teacher in a big school would find that it is impossible to vary from the school tradition and custom, but that is not to say that a teacher cannot use as much freedom as he dare. He can be on the side of the child; he can dispense with punishment; he can be human and jolly. Yet he will find himself in all sorts of difficulties. One of our old boys became a teacher

From A. S. NEILL, *Talking of Summerhill*, Gollancz, London, 1967. Reprinted by permission of A. S. Neill and Victor Gollancz.

in a school in which were many tough boys. He said to me: "I began with Summerhill ideas but had to drop them. If I were nice to a kid he thought I was a softy, and my classroom became a bedlam." His class had over fifty children in it.

One drawback about giving freedom in a big state school is that most of the parents do not believe in freedom: too many of them look on a school as a place in which their erring offspring can be disciplined. I experienced this in a Scottish village school fifty years ago. I had a succession of angry parents . . . "I send my laddie to the schule to lairn lessons, no' to play a' day." Freedom is easy in Summerhill because all the parents are with us.

In a state school the main work is learning school subjects. Attendance at classes is compulsory; duffers at maths have to sit there and do their best. There has to be discipline and absence of noise, but free children make a lot of noise. Everything is against the teacher — the buildings, the lack of space for real play, the marshalling, indeed the whole system of education. The teacher who has no religion has in some schools to take the religious instruction period, but in most big schools a non-believer can opt out. I used to opt out by making the religious period the singing period . . . I shoved in "Onward Christian Soldiers" to save my face, or maybe to salve my conscience.

It is sad to say it, but there can be no real freedom in a state school if the head is not on your side. Hundreds of young teachers would be delighted to have more freedom in their classes but they cannot get it and some tend to become cynical and resigned to their fate. There can be no freedom so long as the educational establishment rules that there must not be.

Have you modified your views since you started Summerhill?
Not in the essentials. I have never doubted self-government, the freedom of a child to learn when he wants to learn; I have never been tempted to mould a child's character. But children have changed in some indefinable way. Thirty years ago I could begin the cure of a young thief by giving him sixpence every time he stole, but I doubt if that method would work today. The new children appear to have a sophistication that is intangible. Maybe they have heard too many glib psychological terms . . . as too many American children have done. Perhaps new material values have changed them, giving them a false orientation. Life was simpler thirty years ago. Children did not get expensive gadgets then. Children demand more now; the old rag doll has been replaced by the talking doll, but I rejoice to notice that most girls still prefer the lower-class model. The question is so complicated, so overdetermined. I have a vague feeling that it has a lot to do with money. When I started to drive forty years ago I might meet two cars in a mile. Today I seem to meet two in ten yards. Then one seldom heard of cars being stolen by delinquents, but today gangs of get-rich-quick youths not only steal many cars, they use violence to rob people. Why work for a living when you can get all the luxury by letting the other fellow earn the dough and then cosh him as he comes out of the bank?

I am not implying that gangs have anything to do with my pupils, who are a law-abiding lot; I am trying to figure out whether the affluent society that tempts gangs has a milder but positive effect on social children. In any school, Summerhill included, it is not always the poor pupil who pinches his neighbour's five-shilling postal order. It is often the boy who feels he is not loved at home: he steals symbolic love, and I make the guess that our young gangsters never had much love at home.

However, money alone cannot be the whole story of the new shallow sophistication. So many factors may come in. Two wars that destroyed so much of ancient taboos and hypocrisies and paternalism. The young have come to see through the pretences and morals of their elders. They realise that they have been lied to, cheated. Youth today challenges more loudly than the past generation did. It was not youth that made the H-bomb: it was age. But youth knows that it is powerless. Most of the antibomb marchers are young; many feel that their lives are in the hands of the old men — the politicians, the military, the nationalists, the rich and powerful. Events and fear have made youth adult before its time, and that may be one explanation of the new sophistication. A generation ago youth accepted its lower status, accepted the directions of the fathers and their symbols. Today youth rebels but in a futile way. Its Beatle hair, its leather jackets, its blue jeans, its motorbikes are all symbols of rebellion but symbols that remain symbols. Nearly every child hates school subjects but every child knows that it can do nothing to change the system. In essentials youth is still docile, obedient, inferior; it challenges the things that do not matter — clothes, manners, hairdos, and negatively, so to speak, it challenges religion, for it does not go to church unless under compulsion.

All the talk about teenage wickedness is rubbish. Homer Lane used to say that an evil deed always had a good, if perverted motive behind it. Teenagers are no more wicked than you or I. They seek the joy of life in an era that does not know joy: all it knows are bingo and TV and football and the sensational press. Its ideals are wealth and big cars and expensive restaurants; its glamour is attached to film and radio stars and ephemeral pop music and belly-waggling singers. Youth sees mostly an acquisitive Society, a *Weltanschauung* that is trite and cheap and tawdry, and the schools, by separating themselves from after-school life do nothing for the young. Their culture of books is rejected, and if any reader says bosh, I ask him or her to compare the circulation of the *New Statesman* and the *Observer* with that of the pictorial and sensational Sunday press. Youth does not want our culture. How many young teenagers know even the names of Ibsen, Proust, Strindberg, Dante?

I am not saying this is a bad thing. Our culture was static, absorbing books and plays and ideas, but today youth's culture tends towards doing, movement, relaxation, so that one has to ask: Which is better, to sit and read D. H. Lawrence or to go to a dance hall and twist all night? I think that the love of sheer movement today is a compensation for the lack of movement forged by the patriarchal bonds that cannot be cut because of an early conditioning that was psychological castration. We smile when hundreds of girls scream hysterically at the sight of the Beatles, lads who physically do not look like he-men. Why do they scream? Someone wrote recently that it was a form of masturbation. Maybe it would be truer to say that the screaming is a sudden release of pent-up hate of all the dull schooling, all the character-moulding, all the suppression of their young lives. Rhythm is a wonderful release of emotion. Recently on TV a Nigerian psychoanalyst said that in his country there is no sex crime and no suicide. When asked why this was, he replied that he thought the natives got so much pent-up release in their tribal dances. The pop musicians stand for rhythm and if the screamers are releasing sexual emotions I fancy they do so for the most part unconsciously.

I have not given a satisfactory answer to the fact that the modern thief is unlikely to react to a psychological trick; I do not know the answer, and indeed there may not be any simple answer. One may be that modern youth has discovered that psychology is at the stone age, and that much of psychological writing is just words. In my pessimistic moments I sometimes wonder if psychological therapy ever cured anything. Therapy is beginning at the wrong end. Thousands of psychotherapists have private practices, treating for the most part people who can afford the time and money. If every therapist in the world were to do nothing but educate parents about child psychology, telling them primarily what not to do to their children, I wonder how much need there would be for adult therapy of any kind. How many psychoanalysts have said "Patching up adults isn't good enough; I'll devote my life to prophylaxis; I'll begin with mothers and babies"? Very few.

Are you an optimist or a pessimist?
I think the best definition of a pessimist is: a man who lives with an optimist. I certainly am not an optimist about the immediate future. Our lives are in the hands of men over whom we have no control. Cuba could have begun World War III and killed us all, had not Khrushchev had the courage to lose face. I am pessimistic because politicians are not usually great or wise men; no wise or great man seeks power; I am pessimistic because of the amount of hate in the world, race hate, nationalism hate, religious hate, indeed I wonder how anyone can be an optimist in this sick world. Age of course may have much to do with pessimism. H. G. Wells in his *Mind at the End of its Tether* despaired of man's future. Old men are apt to look back sadly to find their dreams of youth unfulfilled.

But I am always an optimist about children. I never despair over any child, however much he may be making no apparent progress. What makes me despair is that children never get a chance to live; their love for life is killed by an adult world that "trains", that is, castrates, youth. True, freedom is growing, but oh, so slowly. The bitter truth is that man's thinking and invention have gone far ahead of his inhibited emotions, and that is the real danger of the bomb, for wars are not caused by thinking; they are caused by emotion. A crowd goes mad if its national flag is insulted. Think of the cold war in Ireland, the Orangemen and the Catholics. There are what you might call greed factors — the German *Lebensraum*, our colonial grabbings, territorial ambitions. These do not come from the masses but the masses follow the leaders emotionally. Did the men who died in the Boer War die for patriotism or the profiteers in gold and diamonds? They never knew. They died for Queen and Country.

I am pessimistic about the slow growth of freedom. Have we time to bring up children who will be free emotionally? Free from hate and aggression, free to live and let others live? The bomb is in the hands of men who were made antilife in their cradles: men who had been left free to live happily would not require the bomb. So that the question resolves itself into this one: can humanity evolve in such a way that all people will feel free inside, free from the fatal wish to mould other people?

Who can answer?

8

R. S. PETERS

Commentary

Biography

Richard Stanley Peters was born in 1919 and educated at Clifton College, Bristol, an English public school of the traditional type, and at Oxford University, which he entered in 1938. He studied classics for his Arts degree and became very interested in religious and philosophical questions in which he also read widely while at Oxford.

When World War II came he joined the Friends Ambulance Unit*, was drafted to London during the Blitz and, after a period with the Ambulance Unit, he was sent to do social relief work. He ran a youth centre at Toynbee Hall, Whitechapel, and then started one himself, almost from nothing, at Walthamstow.

In the meantime he had been continuing with his philosophical interests and had enrolled at Birkbeck College, University of London, to work in his spare time for a degree in philosophy. He then moved from social relief work into teaching and took a position as Classics Master at Sidcot School, Somerset, a coeducational boarding school. However he resigned after a couple of years there to work fulltime for his final examinations at the University of London and was successful in gaining a university studentship and part-time lectureship at Birkbeck College. He later became a lecturer and reader in philosophy there, at the same time being active in adult education.

Because of his early youth-centre work and his teaching experience, he had maintained an interest in education, but he moved into philosophy of education in a rather unusual way. He had begun to give a number of broadcast talks on topics such as authority and responsibility, and searching around for another subject to discuss he hit upon that of the aims of education. He was prompted to this by the fact that in youth work he was continually confronted with the question of what were his aims and goals.

Peters was also attracted to philosophy of education because it draws together a number of branches of philosophy as well as psychology, in all of which he was interested. His work at Birkbeck was mainly in philosophical

---

*The Society of Friends (better known as the Quakers) who organised this Unit, is dedicated to pacifism but has always been very ready to help the victims of war in whatever way it can, as well as being active in other humanitarian endeavours.

psychology, in particular the logical status of psychological enquiry. He wrote a book on Hobbes, who appealed to Peters because his work was a mixture of psychology, philosophy and politics. He then wrote a book examining the concept of motivation. These mixed interests, he came to find, were best satisfied in the philosophy of education where, as far as he was concerned, everything came together.

Meanwhile his broadcast talks on education and related topics were published in *The Listener* and attracted the attention of Israel Scheffler, Professor of Education and Philosophy at the Graduate School of Education of Harvard University. Scheffler invited Peters to Harvard as visiting professor in 1961. Then, in 1962, he was appointed Professor of Philosophy of Education at the University of London Institute of Education, a position he held until his retirement in 1983. He has also held the position of Dean of the Faculty of Education at the Institute, and in 1966 was elected to the American National Academy of Education.

Peters has travelled widely, holding various visiting positions and guest lectureships in the USA, Canada, Australia and New Zealand. In so doing he has assisted the development of the discipline of philosophy of education in each of the countries visited.

Since his appointment, Peters developed at the University of London Institute of Education one of the largest and most influential departments of philosophy of education in the world. It offers courses in the subject from diploma right through to doctoral level and attracts students from all parts of the English-speaking world.

In philosophical circles in Great Britain, Peters is generally credited with having established a new and respectable branch of philosophy. The Royal Institute of Philosophy organised a conference on Philosophy of Education at Exeter in September 1973 — an event virtually unthinkable a decade earlier when philosophy of education was still held in low repute as an academic discipline by many philosophers. Philosophers are now at last prepared to treat philosophy of education as an important and significant aspect of philosophical enquiry. At the same time the teaching profession is on the whole now ready to regard philosophy of education as an indispensable part of educational theory. Both of these achievements for the discipline have been due in large part to the work of R. S. Peters.

Main Features of Peters' Educational Thought

The first important point to make about the work of Peters is that it represents a new approach to philosophising about education, and it is impossible to grasp the full implications of his writings without some appreciation of the nature of this new approach. Peters belongs to the school of philosophical analysis, which has been a very influential approach to the subject over recent years. According to this school of thought, the distinctive function of philosophy is analysis, covering both the analysis of concepts and of arguments, which may be called respectively linguistic and logical analysis. There has, in fact, been a so-called "revolution in philosophy" this century which led to this radically changed outlook on the nature of the subject. What, then, is this revolution, and how did it come about?

At the beginning of the century the dominant philosophical theory in the West was idealism, the founder of which was Plato, although the main contemporary influence was the German philosopher, Hegel. The important thing however is not so much the fact that this particular school of philosophy happened to dominate, but that its supremacy rested on a metaphysical conception of philosophy. It was also significant that in all the time between Plato and Hegel, no single metaphysical theory had ever achieved complete acceptance, although a very large number of conflicting theories had been put forward and had held sway for a time. Now the wheel had turned full circle and idealism was again in favour.

Metaphysics is an attempt to explain the ultimate nature of reality and relies heavily on intuitive and speculative methods of thought. The main problem with all traditional metaphysical theories is that there seems to be no way of conclusively establishing their basic premises. These have to be taken largely on faith, but once accepted, everything generally follows logically from them and a large-scale, well-integrated philosophical theory may result. However the problem remains of providing publicly acceptable evidence for the initial assumptions on which the whole system rests. Similarly, traditional moral or ethical theories that aim to set out the nature of the good life for man are, in the last analysis, based on the personal value judgments of the philosopher, and so again cannot be conclusively proved.

In striking contrast to metaphysics and theories of the good life, science had, for some centuries, been achieving a growing body of accepted conclusions and whenever a scientific theory was opposed to a metaphysical one, it won the day because its hypotheses could be publicly verified. Gradually science came to usurp many of the domains of enquiry previously reserved for philosophy. Physics, chemistry, biology, psychology and sociology came of age as distinct, empirically based studies, and the scope of philosophy became correspondingly narrowed, many of its theories being very abstruse and beyond the ken of the ordinary layman.

It was largely this contrast between the manifest success of science in developing a growing body of generally accepted and proven conclusions and the equally manifest failure of philosophy to do so, that led some philosophers to question the very nature of what they were trying to do. They came to the conclusion that many of the traditional philosophical questions were unanswerable, at least by purely philosophical methods. Metaphysics, for example, they saw as a pointless endeavour because they claimed that it is just not possible to discover new facts about the world (even facts of the most general kind) purely by philosophical speculation and reflection. Similarly, they claimed, those moral philosophers who attempt to prescribe the best way to live are basically just giving us their personal value judgments on what constitutes right and wrong. Why then should we take more notice of these than the judgments of anyone else?

Philosophers who rejected these speculative and normative aspects of philosophy set up analysis as its distinctive function. Analysis, of course, had always been part of philosophy as far back as Plato (many of his dialogues include analysis of basic concepts such as truth, justice and virtue) but the claim now was that this was not just part, but the whole of philosophy, or at least the essence of it. It was here, they said, that philosophers do have something positive to contribute. Instead of trying to answer questions that are outside their competence, they can perform the valuable analytic functions of clarifying the language we use in discussing any basic issue, pointing out logical confusions in our thinking and showing the sorts of assumptions on which our various beliefs rest.

This new approach to philosophy gradually grew in popularity from its beginnings in the early decades of this century and by the time of the Second World War had become very influential. Since then it has undergone various modifications, but it still remains an influential approach to the study of philosophy in the English-speaking world. This approach took longer to achieve widespread acceptance in philosophy of education and it is only since the early sixties that it has really become a significant component in the academic study of educational philosophy.

Perhaps the main result of this new viewpoint has been a much closer attention to the nature of language, and a realisation of how important it is to understand its complexities when grappling with philosophical problems. In the first place, philosophers today are much more aware of the many different ways in which language functions and how these were often confused in the past. For instance, it is very important in philosophy to be aware that not all sentences in the indicative form necessarily state facts. Consider the following two sentences:

"Punishing children inhibits their desire to learn."

"Punishing children is morally wrong."

The first asserts a fact that may or may not be true (only empirical investigation could decide this). The second expresses a value judgment and is equivalent to: "We ought not to punish children." Such a view could not be established by empirical means but only by some form of moral argument. This distinction between facts and values and the impossibility of deducing the latter from the former has been a cardinal principle of analytic philosophy.

Secondly, analytic philosophers argue that much previous philosophy is vitiated by the failure to use language precisely, especially in regard to basic concepts such as "good", "God", "the state", and "education". Metaphysical philosophers of the past often falsely assumed in their writing that there is a clear and generally known meaning for such basic concepts and that there is no need to explain exactly what they meant by them. Even worse, the meanings given to the concepts in some cases changed as the discussion progressed. All of this made it very difficult to form useful philosophical conclusions.

In analysing concepts, modern philosophers try to establish "necessary" and "sufficient" conditions for their use, the former being those conditions which must always be present for the concept to apply and the latter being those that are together sufficient to distinguish this concept from others with which it may be confused. Looking at the concept of education (which is Peters' basic concern), we may note that the fact that learning takes place would seem to be a necessary condition, but is it sufficient on its own, or does the learning have to be of a particular type, or achieved in a certain way to merit the title "education"?

The philosopher may also distinguish between the "defining" and the "accompanying" characteristics of a concept. For instance, although most education takes place in schools, it is not a defining characteristic of education that it must take place there (it may, for example, take place at home); it is only a characteristic generally accompanying education.

In analysing language, some philosophers are content just to try to discover what most people mean by a word, that is, how it is used in ordinary language. Other philosophers attempt to put forward what they consider to be the fundamental or most significant meaning of the word and then give reasons why this is so. They may thus be stipulating a meaning for the word which can be a legitimate undertaking so long as the reasons they give in support of their particular meaning are convincing.

By the use of these and similar techniques of analysis[1], valuable new insights into many long-standing philosophical problems have been achieved. Some of these problems have been solved and others made easier to solve as a result of the clarification of their concepts and the type of evidence that would be needed to establish their conclusions. Still others have been shown to be either pseudo-problems (based on a misunderstanding of the functions of language) or not really philosophical problems at all but rather scientific questions or perhaps issues that in the ultimate analysis rest on a personal value judgment.

Let us now consider Peters' place in this movement. He has been probably the most influential exponent of the analytic approach to philosophy of education. As a result of his application of the methods of analytic philosophy to a wide range of educational issues, he has aroused much attention among contemporary educational philosophers. Of course not all agree with his conclusions, but at least most today are aware of what these are and generally feel obliged to react to them in some way.

Peters' contribution to educational thought falls into two separate categories. The first is the light his work throws on any attempt to philosophise about education. By means of the techniques of analytic philosophy he has helped clarify many basic concepts in education; concepts like education itself, as well as those of teaching, training, indoctrinating and conditioning. A precise understanding of these is necessary whatever educational theory one adopts. In general, the influence of Peters and other analysts, by their stress on precision in the use of language, on the need to justify any important assumptions that are made, and on close attention to the laws of logical argument, has led to a general tightening up of the conditions of philosophical debate about education.

The second contribution has been the presentation of an original theory of education and it is this contribution in particular which constitutes Peters' significant innovation in educational thought. One way in which his theory differs from that of other contemporary educationists such as Skinner, Neill or Illich is that it is written primarily from the viewpoint of the philosopher. In this respect he has much in common with Plato and Aristotle. He argues his theory back to its basic philosophical principles, and in accordance with the analytic approach, is reticent about putting forward his own value judgments on what ought and ought not to be done in education.* He is, moreover, concerned not only with arriving at educational solutions in their own right but also with reaching conclusions to philosophical problems arising in education. To some, this strong philosophical element in his work may raise an initial difficulty to the full appreciation of his educational thought, but on closer acquaintance the necessity of entering into the study of such basic problems will, it is hoped, be realised.

Peters' educational theory centres upon his analysis of the concept of education. Apart from the obvious importance of clarifying its exact nature, Peters was influenced by two motives in attempting to arrive at an adequate definition. The first was to counter the growing tendency to take an expedient view of education, to treat it as merely a means of getting a good job, gaining prestige or some such aim which has nothing to do with its real value. In philosophical terms, he is opposed to treating education as instrumental to some extrinsic end and argues that it should be viewed as worthwhile in itself, as having intrinsic value. The tendency to which he objects is very much a part of the common materialistic approach to life today, which stresses social success in terms of power and wealth. According to this attitude, education must lead to some material or tangible benefit or else it is regarded as a waste of time.

Peters' second motive was a desire to resolve the conflict in educational debate between traditionalism and progressivism. He saw serious weaknesses in both doctrines and wanted to establish a middle-of-the-road position that avoided the faults on both sides. But he needed a new model of education to express this middle position and this he found in his idea of "education as initiation".

The concept of education that Peters developed as a result of these concerns was first set forth in his inaugural lecture at the University of London Institute of Education entitled "Education as Initiation"† and has since become widely known in contemporary educational philosophy. He begins by arguing that "education" is not the name of a process or activity, such

---

*However, readers can judge for themselves in the following discussion of Peters' analysis of education just how far Peters is able to avoid making value judgments.

†A slightly modified version of this lecture provides the first selection for Peters.

as "writing" or "swimming" (or for that matter, "teaching" or "instructing"), but rather is a normative term, that is, a word that sets up a standard which certain activities must satisfy if they are to rank as educational. This standard is expressed in terms of three conditions or criteria which have to be met for education to take place.

The first is that something of value must be learned or some desirable state of mind developed.* In other words, being educated is by definition a valuable experience. We would not call the learning of a mass of meaningless information education, nor would we say education had taken place if something potentially harmful is learned (such as how to be a more efficient burglar).

It follows that, strictly speaking, it does not make sense to ask what is the aim of education as such, because this question assumes that there is some value beyond education that has to be met for it to be worth-while. Education is a concept like reform; we do not ask what is the aim of reforming someone, because it is inherent in the meaning of the word that it makes someone better. Similarly, it is part of the meaning of being educated that a person is being improved in some way as a result.

So this first criterion of education brings out clearly its intrinsic value, one of Peters' main concerns as mentioned above. Peters does not want to deny, however, that the teaching that goes on in schools may serve useful external ends such as producing trained manpower, socialising future citizens and so forth but the point is that these are not what make such teaching activities *educationally* valuable, these ends are more like useful by-products of education. Unless those involved in education recognise this they may be led to completely misconceive their task.

Many disputes about the proper aims of education, Peters claims, are really disputes about the essential characteristics of what it means to be educated. The debate about whether the development of intellect is more important than the development of character is not about something external to education, but about what qualities are necessary to being an educated person.

Peters summarises his point about the intrinsic value of education in his statement: "To be educated is not to have arrived at a destination, it is to travel with a different view." [2] What this different view involves is made clear in his third condition for education.

Peters' second criterion of education concerns the manner in which the teaching and learning take place. Here he looks at the arguments of progressives such as Rousseau and Dewey, who stressed the importance of teaching methods that take full account of the child's interests and needs. Peters argues that these thinkers tended to make methods ends in themselves and thus

---

*The nature of this valuable or desirable element in education will be explained in his third criterion. At this stage he is only stating the formal condition that there is a conceptual connection between "education" and "being valuable". It should also be noted here that for Peters the value involved in education must be of a publicly acceptable type and cannot be such that benefits one individual at the expense of others.

overrated their importance, but that they did at least bring an important advance in thinking about education.

He therefore incorporates these insights into his second condition for education, which is that the pupil must be brought to care about what is worthwhile (that is, come to appreciate the value of what he learns) and this must be done in a way that involves awareness and voluntariness on his part. The criterion of awareness is simply that the learner must know that he is learning something or be conscious of the fact that there is some skill to be acquired. The criterion of voluntariness is left rather vague by Peters. Obviously many pupils do not learn voluntarily in the fullest sense (that is, they would rather be doing something else), but as long as they intentionally try to master what is taught, this is most likely sufficient to satisfy Peters' requirements.

These criteria are chiefly used to rule out processes such as hypnosis, conditioning, and brainwashing as being methods of education. They would not necessarily rule out the use of formal instruction and commands, or even indoctrination, says Peters, because in these cases children at least understand (even if only in a limited sense) what is being taught. "Furthermore," he adds, "there is a minimal sense in which they act as voluntary agents; for they can rebel and refuse to do what is required of them. Indeed they often do."[3]

Indoctrination may meet this second criterion of education, yet it would be ruled out by one or both of the other two. It is either learning something which is not in any way valuable (thus failing to meet condition one) or learning something without any rational basis and which cannot be logically related to other beliefs of the learner (therefore not fulfilling condition three).

The third criterion of education refers to the outcome of the educational process, and elaborates the first condition by specifying the nature of the desirable states of mind that should be developed. It is basically concerned with the achievement of knowledge and understanding.

A person who is educated has acquired a body of knowledge that is not just a collection of random facts; instead it is organised into some sort of conceptual scheme by which one is able to relate the various pieces of knowledge to each other, and also to how one sees the world and acts in it. An educated person is therefore different to one who is merely trained; training suggests the learning of some particular skill or ability rather than the general transformation of one's outlook on the world which is suggested by education. Consider, for example, the difference between "moral training" and "moral education", a distinction which was first brought out by Aristotle. "Moral training" suggests that the learner has been led to behave in certain required ways with no understanding of why these ways are right. "Moral education", on the other hand, implies that the learner has developed an understanding of moral principles and henceforth acts deliberately on the basis of these because he has become committed to them. The same sort of distinction applies to physical training and physical education, and even more obviously to sex training and sex education.

Peters uses the term "cognitive perspective" to express the essential nature of the mental abilities required by the educated person. Education should develop a broad perspective on life, not just one limited to a particular specialty. We would not call persons educated if they were very knowledgeable in, say, science but knew and cared very little about anything else. Of course a person may be very learned in one subject only and still be regarded as educated as long as there is some degree of acquaintance with and interest in other areas of knowledge. (Peters does not state exactly what depth of acquaintance would be necessary here and this must ultimately be a matter of judgment, because it is obviously impossible today to be an expert in more than one or two areas of knowledge.)

It may be concluded that for Peters, education results in the learning of something of value that involves knowledge and understanding which is organised into some kind of cognitive perspective, and this learning has been acquired by methods involving awareness and some degree of voluntariness on the learner's part.

Peters next goes on to develop his analysis of education by presenting a model of the educational process that aims to give us a proper perspective on the role of the teacher. This he does by describing education as a process of initiation into worthwhile activities and modes of thought. Together, these make up a valuable form of life that both teacher and learner can share, a form of life that is both public and interpersonal. The teacher, having been already initiated, is on the inside of this form of life and the task is now to bring the pupils to share it.

The obvious question that now suggests itself is what exactly are these worthwhile activities and modes of thought and conduct. Peters' rather conservative answer to this question is that they are comprised basically of the inherited knowledge and skills developed by Western civilisation from the time of the Greeks onwards. Such knowledge and skills are organised into distinct forms of thought or disciplines, such as science, history, literature, social studies and philosophy, which are all basic to our understanding of the world. Along with these, are the traditional liberal values of justice, freedom, respect for persons and consideration of the interests of others, which are also part of the form of life into which all pupils should be initiated.

Peters argues that his stress on the interpersonal and public nature of the content of education enables him to provide a synthesis between the traditional and progressive models.[4] The dominance of these two models has done serious harm to educational theory, maintains Peters, for both have serious weaknesses. The faults in most versions of the traditional model are obvious enough: generally there is not enough respect for pupils as individuals, there is insufficient attention paid either to motivation or to relating what is taught to the child's interests, and it is often doubtful how far the learning that takes place is properly understood.

The faults in the progressive model, though not so obvious, are also very serious, at least in the pure form of progressivism. In the first place, as Peters points out, it begs a very big question in placing such heavy stress on concepts such as development of potentialities, growth and self-realisation, because all of these can be good or bad depending on the direction that the development or growth takes. The development of our potentialities for selfishness or aggressiveness is surely not educationally valuable and neither is the development of a criminal or a sadist. The teacher must therefore make a value judgment on the nature of the growth and give it some positive direction. This direction will largely be dictated by the particular educational activities to which the pupils are introduced and these will be based on those areas of knowledge regarded as having objective value. In other words, the stress on self-realisation and related concepts as the essence of education tends to overlook the importance of passing on a body of worthwhile content or subject matter.

Similarly, the emphasis that the progressives place on the development of creativity, initiative and critical thought on the part of the pupil presupposes something to be creative or critical *about*. As Peters points out, these qualities do not exist in a vacuum but only in relation to certain problems or issues that acquire their meaning and significance from the disciplines in which they arise.

The basic fault of the progressive approach, then, is its failure to give adequate weight to the central role that content must play in education; that is, to the necessity to transmit a valuable form of life. This is perhaps understandable when it is viewed as a reaction against the traditional approach, which placed too much stress on subject matter; the progressives rightly pointed out that the procedures used to pass on this subject matter are also very important. However, they tended to make the error of seeing these procedures as an end in themselves.

How then does Peters' account of education try to avoid the errors of the two previous accounts and provide a model incorporating the best elements of both? He argues that the traditional and progressive models

> share the common defect of ignoring the central fact that education consists essentially in the initiation of others into a public world picked out by the language and concepts of a people and structured by rules governing their purposes and interactions with each other. In relation to this the teacher is not [as is suggested by the traditional view] an external operator who is trying to impose something of *his* from the outside on children, or [as is suggested by the progressive view] trying to develop something within them which is their own peculiar possession. His function is rather to act as a guide in helping them to explore and *share* a public world whose contours have been marked out by generations which have preceded both of them.[5]

In other words, it is not the teacher's experience that is central to education, neither is it the pupil's experience, but rather it is an experience belonging to a public world that both can share. This public world includes both the knowledge that has been developed over the centuries and the critical procedures by means of which this knowledge may be revised and further developed.

Peters is fond of referring to what D. H. Lawrence called the "holy ground" that stands between teacher and taught and to which both owe an allegiance. The task is to get the pupil to enter it and enjoy the public heritage. At the higher levels of education there is in fact little essential distinction between teachers and taught — both participate in the shared experience of exploring a common world.[6]

Any discussion of Peters' description of the nature of education is complicated by the fact that he modified somewhat his account during the seventies. However the change in his view as a result of this modification is not as great as appears at first sight. The details are described briefly here:

Ever since he gave his inaugural lecture ("Education as Initiation"), his analysis of the concept of education has been criticised for being too restrictive. It has been argued that there are legitimate uses of the term that do not meet his first and third criteria. For instance it is quite possible to regard education as being a waste of time or even harmful; this may be the view of a hard-headed practical man or perhaps of certain people wishing to preserve unquestioning belief in existing religious or political doctrines, which education may weaken. It is thus argued that the first condition of education being regarded as intrinsically valuable cannot be a necessary condition of all uses of the concept.

Secondly, it is argued that it is not contradictory to talk of someone having a specialised education or to speak of education in societies where all that is passed on are simple skills and folklore, or perhaps rigid training in a military discipline such as we understand Spartan education to have been. Obviously there is not the breadth of knowledge and understanding in such cases that is required by Peters' notion of cognitive perspective in the third criterion.

As a result of these criticisms, Peters has been forced to recognise that there is a second, more general sense of education that indiscriminately marks out a vast range of practices concerned with bringing up, rearing, instructing, and so forth. It is in this sense that the word "education" was originally used; Peters' more specific concept, which involves criteria of intrinsic value and cognitive perspective, goes back in part to the classical Greek era, but came into special prominence in the nineteenth century when it became customary to use the term "educated man" to refer approvingly to one who had successfully realised the ideal of a disinterested pursuit of knowledge and all-round understanding and development. Whenever we talk today of an "educated man", it is, according to Peters, his concept of education we have in mind (or at least something similar), when we talk just of "education" we may be thinking either of this or the older, more general, and neutral concept.[7]

How does all this affect the point of Peters' earlier analysis of education? As suggested above, not a great deal, for his intention remains fundamentally the same — to promote the sort of ideal expressed in his original analysis of education. He is now ready to admit that this is not the *only* meaning of education, but would say it is the meaning that is most significant for those engaged in teaching and the one by which their practice ought to be guided. He is thus going beyond purely conceptual analysis and is in fact putting forward a normative judgment about what he regards as most valuable in the sphere of education. However he can at least argue that the values he is suggesting for education are not purely personal preferences; they rest on distinctions that have developed in our language (for instance, the distinction between "education" and "training") and what he is doing is picking out what he regards as the most important and relevant of the characteristics and values mirrored in our present-day use of the word. Moreover, the rest of his educational writings are in large part an attempt to exemplify and justify his analysis of what is valuable in education.

On the whole, then, Peters' basic approach has not changed and he continues to champion the non-instrumental way of looking at education along with the model of education as initiation through which he aims to present a synthesis between the two previous dominant models.

We may at this stage pose a few questions for the reader to consider in respect to Peters' analysis. To begin with, does his account provide a genuine synthesis between the traditional and progressive models or does he lean more towards the traditional? He certainly seems more vehement in his criticism of progressive thought than of traditionalist thought, and appears to have much in common with the latter. For instance, the model of education as initiation suggests the need to instil in each child a body of subject matter, and it also implicitly stresses the authority of the teacher because of his role as the initiator. In this context Peters even refers to the child as "the barbarian outside the gates". He also emphasises the fact that the pupil does not always know what is in his own interest and that all learning cannot necessarily be made enjoyable. Further, he places much stress on theoretical and abstract knowledge and appears to exalt the life of intellect over the life of emotion. All of this, especially the last point, is very much in line with classical Greek thought about education and would of course be anathema to people like A. S. Neill.

On the other hand, Peters consciously sought to stress the strong points of the traditional view to counter the growing influence of progressivism in the mid-1960s and early 1970s. And it may be added on his behalf that he does emphasise the liberal values of freedom, equality, respect for persons and consideration of interests, thus avoiding the moral injustices sometimes present in traditional systems. He is also aware of the importance of personal relationships[8] and of paying attention to individual differences in teaching. Similarly, he is conscious of the faults in traditional methods of instruction that rely on drill and memorisation. Instead he favours methods involving explanation and the giving of reasons, teaching by example, and (at the higher levels) conversation and dialogue between teacher and pupil as joint enquirers after knowledge. Finally, he denies the dichotomy between intellect and emotion, arguing that the life of the intellect carries its own emotions such as "a love of truth, a passion for justice and a hatred of what is tasteless".[9]

The second question for consideration is whether Peters' concept of education is "elitist" in that it could only be achieved by the most intelligent and most privileged pupils. In other words, is his concept, with its stress on the all-round development of understanding in the basic disciplines of the Western intellectual tradition, appropriate in an age of mass education? Is it in fact possible for anyone to be broadly educated today in view of the tremendous "explosion" of knowledge? Can one ever expect to gain a thorough knowledge of anything more than a few basic disciplines?

Related to this question, it is worth considering whether his concept of education is only applicable in an economically and politically well-developed society that has achieved a certain level of material security and well-being for the whole community. Perhaps in many of the developing countries of the Third World, there may be other needs that are more urgent than the need for education, such as the production of trained manpower in agriculture and industry.

In thinking about these issues, you could consider whether one way of overcoming the problems caused by the knowledge explosion would be to concentrate on teaching the basic concepts and methods of thought in the different disciplines rather than trying to cover the whole range of facts in each. At least this would then provide students with some understanding of the nature and problems of each domain and give them the necessary experience and ability to acquire the relevant knowledge when there is the opportunity or interest to do so. Consider also whether it may not just be an unfortunate fact of life, as Peters suggests, that not all are capable of progressing as far in education as others. We have to accept the fact that not all people are equally intellectually gifted.

If you do decide that his concept of education, in its fullest sense, could only be possible for a minority (note however that this need not necessarily be an unfairly privileged minority but one based on equal opportunity), and that it is only fully applicable in an advanced society, should it therefore be rejected or does it still have value as an ideal to be aimed at wherever possible? But here another question may be raised: even as an ideal is it adequate or is it too static a view of education, one that over-emphasises the heritage of the past and provides insufficient scope for radical change in thought about the future role of education in society? Does it stress the need to *conserve* our culture at the expense of the need to *improve* it? This criticism, it could be argued, is especially relevant in view of the contemporary crisis in many aspects of society today.[10] Do we, in such a crisis situation, need a whole new approach to education, an approach that gives it a more positive and direct role in countering antisocial and antisurvival tendencies in modern society (and that may perhaps require a whole new set of moral and intellectual values)? Do the ideas of thinkers such as Skinner, or on the other hand, Neill, have more to offer in this regard? Or do we perhaps need a completely new institutional pattern for education as Ivan Illich and his followers recommend?

However, Peters could reply that what he is trying to promote is a form of life that is valuable under any circumstances and that contains within itself the necessary procedures for dealing with current problems. It is only through the broadness and flexibility of approach provided by education as Peters describes it that a solution to these problems is possible. What is needed he would argue is not a rejection of the intellectual models of rationality and scientific method or the traditional liberal values of justice, freedom and respect for persons, but a more rigorous and systematic application of these to the current scene.

It is up to each individual to work out where he or she stands on this crucial question facing us today.

Apart from his analysis of education, Peters has made another important contribution to educational thought in his discussion of moral and social issues that have direct relevance to education. This discussion helps to explain certain aspects of his approach to education discussed above and serves to fill out his general educational theory. His main work in this area is his book *Ethics and Education*, Part II of which examines the values of equality, consideration of interests, freedom, respect for persons and fraternity. He also discusses the notion of worthwhile activities (which he treats as roughly equivalent to the intellectual and theoretical pursuits of man) and how the basing of the curriculum on these can be justified.

Peters uses the same type of justificatory argument for all of these principles in his attempt to show why they are to be valued, and he would be one of the foremost exponents of this type of argument in current ethical theory. Before outlining its form, Peters discusses, and rejects (after pointing out their weaknesses), the three most common approaches to the explanation and justification of moral values: naturalism, intuitionism and emotivism. His own argument is partly derived from that of the great German philosopher Immanuel Kant and is based on the fact that we presuppose certain values whenever we engage in moral discourse. These are the values that give point and meaning to such discourse and anyone who engages in it seriously must be committed to them. To gain a proper understanding of this argument and how it is used for each of the above values (equality, consideration of interests, freedom, respect for persons, worthwhile activities), it would be necessary to read the relevant sections of *Ethics and Education*. Apart from the justificatory argument, Peters also includes there an interesting discussion of how these values should apply in education.

In Part III of the book Peters looks at the area of social control with regard to education and includes an analysis of the concepts of authority, punishment, and democracy with particular reference to their role in education.

In the essay "Form and Content in Moral Education"*, Peters takes up

---

* This essay constitutes the second Peters' selection following.

the issue of moral education and again tries to find a middle way, this time between the extremes of subjectivism and absolutism in morality. To do this he makes the important distinction between content and form (that is, between the actual moral beliefs we hold and the means we use to arrive at them) and also stresses the role of reason in morality. In the first part of the essay, he applies the distinction between content and form to the question of what is morality, and in the second part to how it is learned.

In the second section, he raises the problem of what methods can be used to teach morals before the child is able to reason about such matters. Like Aristotle, he concludes that non-rational methods such as habit training may have to be used but that there is nothing reprehensible in this because such methods are the only ones possible at this stage. The important thing is to not in any way inhibit or delay the child's progress to a rational understanding of moral principles. Rather, such an understanding should be encouraged as soon as it is possible.

Morality, then, is for Peters part of the valuable form of life into which each child is to be initiated, and it does have an objective basis in the fundamental liberal values discussed in *Ethics and Education* and mentioned again in this essay. Teachers should not, therefore, feel uneasy about initiating children into this form of life as long as they realise that there is scope for disagreement on many of the more specific values (for example, those to do with sexual behaviour, religion and personal life-styles) that differ among various societies and social groups. Generally these more specific values are ultimately based on the fundamental principles (which provide the form rather than the content of morality), but they also bring in social, cultural and religious differences and raise questions of the relative degree of weight that should be given to the basic values when more than one is involved.

The reader should now be in a position to make some preliminary assessment of the value of the analytic approach to education as exemplified by Peters. Is it as fruitful a way of approaching basic educational issues as the previous methods? Can it consistently avoid making any normative judgments and still lead to significant conclusions for educators? It is interesting to note in regard to these questions that Peters himself now acknowledges that he is going beyond strict analysis in promoting his concept of education. It is also true that in recent years a number of contemporary educational philosophers have expressed serious doubts about the strictly analytic approach.[11] While such an approach may be appropriate for philosophy as such, philosophy of education is inevitably bound up with value judgments about what should be taught, what methods should be used and what overall aim the teaching is designed to meet, and it is now felt by many people that some normative commitment on the part of the educational philosopher is unavoidable unless he is prepared to make only a minor contribution to educational thought.

There is also some relevant sociological evidence that in the initial heyday of the analytic movement, the late fifties and early sixties, there was not the value crisis in society that exists today, so that educational philosophers could to a large extent afford to play down or ignore value questions. Today this is no longer feasible and it seems that the movement towards a broader analytic approach which allows for the expression of a normative viewpoint, has more to offer. However it is important that philosophers who take this approach make it clear when they are making value judgments and attempt to build up some sort of case as to why we should share these values, while admitting that it is not possible to conclusively prove any such normative position. In this way the particular virtues of the analytic approach (clarity, logical rigour, etc.) can be coupled with the presentation of points of view that provide positive stimulation and guidance to teachers in developing their own philosophy of education.

As has been suggested in this commentary, Peters himself exemplifies the broader analytic approach; apart from the normative element involved in his analysis of the concept of education, his educational writings taken as a whole present a definite and consistent educational point of view, which represents his distinctive educational theory. At the same time his work exhibits the particular virtues of the analytic approach just mentioned.

It will be appropriate to conclude this discussion of Peters' work, which has attempted to indicate that his significant innovation in educational thought takes the form of an attempted synthesis between the models of traditionalism and progressivism in education, with a quotation in which he himself attempts to sum up his overall approach to education:

> . . . in educational theory my position is essentially a synthetic, middle-of-the-road position. I attempt to draw out what is of value both in the traditional formal education and in the child-centred revolt against it, to reconcile emphasis on the individual with the essentially social character of education, to see the value of authority while remaining fundamentally antagonistic to it, to defend freedom while stressing the necessity for constraints when dealing with children, to maintain that some pursuits are more worthwhile than others while, at the same time, stressing the importance of individual choice and individual interests. Anyone who takes such a position is likely to be attacked both by traditionalists and by progressives — nowadays probably more by progressives; for, being a more recent phenomenon, they find it difficult to accept the role of an antithesis in a developing dialectic. And, of course, texts can always be quoted to support either type of attack. This is something that anyone who tries to reconcile opposites must learn to live with; for the opposing voices come not just from outside but from within himself.[12]

NOTES AND REFERENCES

1. For further information on the methods of contemporary philosophical analysis, see J. WILSON, *Thinking with Concepts*, Cambridge University Press, Cambridge, 1963; J. HOSPERS, *An Introduction to Philosophical Analysis*, Routledge and Kegan Paul, London, 1956; and G. J. WARNOCK, *English Philosophy Since 1900*, Oxford University Press, London, 1958.
2. "Education as Initiation", see below, p. 376.
3. R. S. PETERS, *Ethics and Education*, Allen & Unwin, London, 1966, p. 42.
4. The main features of these opposed approaches to education were outlined in the Introduction and have been described further in the writings of their various exponents in previous chapters in this book.

5. R. S. PETERS, "Aims of Education — A Conceptual Enquiry", Seminar, 1966. Reprinted in R. S. Peters (Ed.) *The Philosophy of Education*, Oxford University Press, London, 1973, p. 26.

6. For further information on Peters' analysis of education and his model of education as initiation, see, in addition to the first selection, R. S. PETERS, *Ethics and Education*, Chapters 1 and 2; *The Concept of Education*, Routledge and Kegan Paul, London, 1958, Chapter 1; and "Aims of Education — A Conceptual Enquiry". In these he has slightly altered his description and presentation of the three criteria from that in "Education as Initiation", but his account remains basically the same.

7. The main reference for Peters' recognition of a second concept of education is his paper, "Education and the Educated Man", which appeared in the *Proceedings of the Annual Conference, Philosophy of Education Society of Great Britain*, 1970, IV, and is reprinted in R. F. DEARDEN, P. H. HIRST and R. S. PETERS (Eds), *Education and the Development of Reason*, Routledge and Kegan Paul, London, 1972. See also R. S. PETERS and P. H. HIRST, *The Logic of Education*, Routledge and Kegan Paul, London, 1970, Chapter 2.

8. See, for example, R. S. PETERS, "Teaching and Personal Relationships" in R. J. W. SELLECK (Ed.), *Melbourne Studies in Education*, Melbourne University Press, Melbourne, 1970; and R. S. PETERS and P. H. HIRST, *The Logic of Education*, Chapter 6.

9. "Education as Initiation" see below, p. 373.

10. See the above commentary on Skinner for further discussion of this crisis situation which includes problems such as overpopulation, exhaustion of resources, the threat of nuclear warfare, pollution, among others.

11. See, for example, J. F. SOLTIS, "Analysis and Anomalies in Philosophy of Education", *Educational Philosophy and Theory*, October 1971, III, No. 2; and A. EDEL, "Analytic Philosophy of Education at the Cross-Roads", *Educational Theory*, Spring 1972, XXII, No. 2.

12. "In Defence of Bingo: A Rejoinder", *British Journal of Educational Studies*, XV, No. 2, June 1967, p. 194.

SELECT BIBLIOGRAPHY

Peters' main published works of relevance to education, listed in order of their appearance, are given below.

Books:

Social Principles and the Democratic State, (written in conjunction with S. I. Benn), Allen & Unwin, London, 1959. (Peters' main work in the area of social and political philosophy.)

Authority, Responsibility and Education, Allen & Unwin, London, 1959, revised edition, 1973. (Originally based on a series of broadcast talks.)

Ethics and Education, Allen & Unwin, London, 1966. (Peters' main work in philosophy of education.)

The Logic of Education, (written in conjunction with P. H. Hirst), Routledge & Kegan Paul, London, 1970. (This book explores the implications of Peters' analysis of education for the curriculum, for teaching and for the authority structure of schools and colleges.)

Reason and Compassion, Routledge & Kegan Paul, London, 1973. (Philosophical examination of moral and religious issues and their relevance for moral education.)

Psychology and Ethical Development, Allen & Unwin, London, 1974. (Anthology of essays on psychological and philosophical issues relevant to education, especially in regard to moral development and human understanding, plus some biographical material.)

Education and the Education of Teachers, Routledge & Kegan Paul, London, 1977. (Anthology of essays on the nature of education and the education of teachers with some new development of his ideas on these topics.)

Essays on Educators, Allen & Unwin, London, 1981. (Includes essays on Plato, Rousseau, Dewey, Kohlberg and the latest statement of Peters' own views on education.)

Journal Articles and Essays:

The following is a brief selection only and does not include any essays reprinted in the books listed above:

"Mental Health as an Educational Aim", *Studies in Philosophy and Education*, III, No. 2, Spring 1964. Reprinted in T. H. B. Hollins (Ed.), *Aims of Education: The Philosophic Approach*, Manchester University Press, Manchester, 1964.

"The Philosophy of Education" in J. W. Tibble (Ed.), *The Study of Education*, Routledge & Kegan Paul, London, 1966.

"Aims of Education — A Conceptual Enquiry", Seminar, 1966. Reprinted in R. S. Peters (Ed.), *The Philosophy of Education*, Oxford University Press, London, 1973.

"Education and Human Development" in R. J. W. Selleck (Ed.) *Melbourne Studies in Education*, Melbourne University Press, Melbourne, 1970.

"Teaching and Personal Relationships", in R. J. W. Selleck, *ibid.*

"The Education of the Emotions", in M. Arnold (Ed.) *Feelings and Emotions*, Academic Press Inc., New York, 1970. Reprinted in R. F. Dearden, P. H. Hirst and R. S. Peters (Eds.), *Education and the Development of Reason*, Routledge and Kegan Paul, London, 1972.

"Education and the Educated Man", *Proceedings of the Annual Conference, Philosophy of Education Society of Great Britain*, IV, January 1970. Reprinted in R. F. Dearden *et al, ibid.*

"Philosophy of Education", in P. H. Hirst (Ed.) *Educational Theory and its Foundation Disciplines*, Routledge & Kegan Paul, London, 1983.

Selections

Peters is represented by two essays: "Education as Initiation" and "Form and Content in Moral Education", both of which were written with the general reader in mind as well as the student of philosophy of education. They have each been discussed in the preceding commentary. The first presents Peters' analysis of education and his model of education as initiation; the second gives his ideas on moral education, including a discussion of what morality is and how it is best taught.

Education as Initiation[1]

A novel feature of the 1960s is the extent to which education has become a subject for public debate and theoretical speculation. Previously it had been something that was prized or taken for granted by those few who had it, but not widely discussed. Of course there were plenty of schoolday reminiscences; but these were indicative more of narcissistic self-absorption than of a passionate interest in education.

All of this has now changed. Some politicians whose noses quiver at the scent of any sort of underprivilege have found in education a quarry that they think they may more safely run to earth than the ferocious old foxes of private ownership and disparity of income. Others, with nervous eyes on the technical achievements of the USA and USSR, gladly listen to economists who assure them that education is a commodity in which it is profitable for a community to invest. Sociologists assure teachers that they have a role of acting as a socialising agency in the community.

Teachers tend to be either bitter or gratified at this growing grasp of the obvious. Here are they, quiet men working at the job at which they have always worked — underpaid, unappreciated, under-staffed. And now all this. Confronted with such a welter of chatter by people, many of whom have no inside experience of the object of their theorising, it would be human, in one sense, for the teacher to turn a deaf ear. But in another sense it would not be human. For one of the distinguishing features of man is that he alone of all creatures has a variable conceptual framework which determines the aspects under which he acts. A man can conceive of his task as a teacher in many different ways. To shut his ears arbitrarily to such different accounts is to limit his view of the world — to take refuge in a kind of monadic myopia.

It may well be, however, that some of the descriptions given of what he is doing *qua* teacher seriously misrepresent what is distinctive of his calling by the generality of the description or by assimilating it to something else. Suppose, to take a parallel case, kissing were to be described as a movement

---

From R. S. PETERS, "Education as Initiation", in R. D. Archambault (Ed.) *Philosophical Analysis and Education*, Routledge and Kegan Paul, London, 1965. Reprinted by permission of the publisher and Humanities Press Inc., New York.

of the lips that has the function of stimulating the organism. The generality of this description would omit some essential features of kissing; furthermore, by describing it as a mere bodily movement it would be assimilated to salivation or to a knee-jerk which is, I think, dangerously misleading. Indeed I often think that a conceptual scheme such as that employed by behaviourists is not simply intellectually mistaken; it is also morally dangerous. For such men may habitually come to think of their fellows in such attenuated terms which they regard as scientifically sterile. Luckily most behaviourists to date have been humane men who have talked like kings in their laboratories but have preserved the common touch of ordinary discourse when they emerge. But succeeding generations may be more consistent.

Teachers may be afflicted by a similar conceptual blight if they think too much in terms of their socialising role, or pay too much attention to the notion that education is a commodity in which the nation should invest, or to the suggestion that their main concern should be for the mental health of children. Education is different from social work, psychiatry, and real estate. Everything is what it is and not some other thing. In all the hubbub about plant, supply of teachers, shortage of provision, streaming, and selection, too little attention is being paid to what it is that so many are deemed to be without. Education has become rather like the Kingdom of Heaven in former times. It is both within us and among us, yet it also lies ahead. The elect possess it, and hope to gather in those who are not yet saved. But what on earth it is is seldom made clear.

"Education" and Extrinsic Ends

To get clearer about the concept of "education", then, is an urgent necessity at the present time. Such conceptual clarification is pre-eminently the task of a philosopher of education. But is a philosopher who embarks on such a task committed to the suspect conviction shared by Socrates that there is some "essence" of education which conceptual analysis can explicate? In suggesting that teachers may be affected by a conceptual blight if they pay too much attention to economists, sociologists and psychologists, have I already put my foot on the primrose path that leads to essentialism?

Frankly I do not much mind if I have. What would be objectionable would be to suppose that certain characteristics could be regarded as essential irrespective of context and of the questions under discussion. In the context of the planning of resources it may be unobjectionable to think of education as something in which a community can invest; in the context of a theory of social cohesion education may be harmlessly described as a socialising process. But if one is considering it from the point of view of the teacher's task in the classroom these descriptions are both too general and too embedded in a dangerous dimension; for they encourage a conformist or instrumental way of looking at education.

Perhaps one of the reasons why these economic and sociological descriptions of education can be misleading, if taken out of context, is that they are made from the point of view of a spectator pointing to the "function" or effects or education in a social or economic system. They are not descriptions of it from the point of view of someone engaged in the enterprise. In a similar way one might say that the function of the medical art is to provide employment for the makers of medicine bottles or to increase the population. But this is not what the doctor conceives of himself as doing *qua* doctor, and it would be regrettable if he came to view what he should be doing *qua* doctor in terms of such remoter effects of his art. Furthermore a description of what he is doing in terms of these effects does little to distinguish his art from that of the chemist. What is essential to education must involve an aspect under which things are done which is both intentional and reasonably specific. Things like increasing the suicide rate or providing employment for printers should not be built into the concept of "education".

There are, of course, some intentional and specific activities falling under moral education and sex education which are forms of socialisation in an obvious sense. The teacher has to decide on the extent to which he is to concentrate more on these types of education than on the development of other forms of awareness — for example, scientific, mathematical. Such decisions about the content of education are usually decisions about priorities. Also, as I shall argue later, all education can be regarded as a form of "socialisation" in so far as it involves initiation into public traditions which are articulated in language and forms of thought. But this description is too general in that it fails to mark out the difference between education and other forms of socialisation. In the context in which the sociologist is speaking it may be quite clear what specific aspect of the teacher's role is being picked out. But the fact is that when these notions get noised abroad they are not always understood in the specific sense in which the sociologist may be using them. The teacher who hears that he is an agent of socialisation may come to think of himself as a sort of social worker striving in a very *general* sort of way to help children to fit into society. He may get the impression that the teacher's task is not to educate children, in the sense in which I will later define it, but to concentrate on helping them to get on with others and to settle down contentedly to a simple job, healthy hobbies, and a happy home life. It may well be the case that for some children, whose plight in our status-ridden society is spotlighted by the Newsom Report *Half Our Future*,[2] there is not much more that can be done. But so little is known about the conditions which are necessary for that cognitive development which education requires that it would be rash and dangerous to come to such a conclusion too soon. Such research as has been done[3] suggests that a great number of children, because of their early schooling and home life, are grossly deprived in this respect. It would be disastrous to say too soon that a large percentage of children are not capable of education before a serious and sustained attempt has been made to provide the necessary conditions without which talk of education is a pious hope. My fear is that teachers will be led by too undiscriminating talk of their socialising role to conceive of their task in terms of "gentling the masses". Clearer and more specific concepts both of "education" and of "socialisation" should help to avert this danger.

The other danger, which is encouraged more perhaps by the way in which economists rather than sociologists speak of "education", lies in the widespread tendency to assimilate it to some sort of instrumental process. It is actually easy to see how such an assimilation can be encouraged by rather cavalier handling of the concept. To bring this out I must now make the first of three conceptual points about "education" which are necessary for the explication of its essence.

"Education"[4] relates to some sorts of processes in which a desirable state of mind develops. It would be as much of a logical contradiction to say that a person had been educated and yet the change was in no way desirable as it would be to say that he had been reformed and yet had made no change for the better. Education, of course, is different from reform in that it does not suggest that a man has been lifted out of a state of turpitude into which he has lapsed. But it is similar in that it implies some change for the better. Furthermore education is usually thought of as intentional. We put ourselves or others in the relevant situations, knowing what we are doing. I know that Rousseau claimed that "education comes to us from nature, from men, and from things". There is this derivative sense of "education" in which almost anything can be regarded as part of it — visiting a brothel, perhaps. But the central uses of the term are confined to situations where we deliberately put ourselves or others in the way of something that is thought to be conducive to valuable states of mind.

Given, then, that "education" implies the intentional bringing about of a desirable state of mind, it is only too easy to assimilate it to the most familiar cases of bringing about what is desirable. First of all, there are cases where something is done of a neutral sort for the sake of something else that is thought to be worthwhile. Buses are boarded in order to listen to a concert; stamps are licked in order to communicate with a friend. So education, from the point of view of those being educated, often appears as something which has to be gone through, in order that some desirable outcome will ensue, like a well-paid job or a position of prestige in the community. If, on the other hand, it is viewed from the view of the teacher, a second type of model crops up — that of the useful arts where neutral materials are fashioned into something that is valuable. Just as clay is made into pots or rubber into golf balls, so minds are moulded into some desirable end-product, or topped up with something desirable like beer mugs. When education is viewed in either of these two ways the question "What is the use of it?" has pointed application — especially if a lot of money has to be spent on it.

There is, however, a fundamental confusion involved in these ways of thinking. This is due to applying these banal ways of conceiving of the promotion of what is valuable to education itself rather than to the processes or activities involved in it. Obviously enough activities which can form part of the content of education can be viewed as being either instrumentally or instrinsically valuable. It is possible to think of science or of carpentry, for instance, as being both valuable in themselves and valuable as means to increasing production or the provision of houses. Thus it is reasonable to ask what the purpose of instructing or of training someone in such activities might be. But it is as absurd to ask what the aim of education is as it is to ask what the aim of morality is, if what is required is something extrinsic to education. The only answer that can be given is to point to something intrinsic to education that is regarded as valuable such as the training of intellect or character. For to call something "educational" is to intimate that the processes and activities themselves contribute to or involve something that is worthwhile. Talk about "the aims of education" depends to a large extent on a misunderstanding about the sort of concept that "education" is.

To enlarge upon this point which is crucial for my thesis: "Education" is not a concept that marks out any particular type of process such as training, or activity such as lecturing; rather it suggests criteria to which processes such as training must conform. One of these is that something of value should be passed on. Thus we may be educating someone while we are training him; but we need not be. For we may be training him in the art of torture. The demand, however, that there should be something of value in what is being transmitted cannot be construed as meaning that education itself should lead on to or produce something of value. This is like saying, to revert to my previous parallel, that reform must lead up to a man being better. The point is that making a man better is not an aim extrinsic to reform; it is a criterion which anything must satisfy which is to be called "reform". In the same way a necessary feature of education is often extracted as an extrinsic end. People thus think that education must be for the sake of something extrinsic that is worthwhile, whereas the truth is that being worthwhile is part of what is meant by calling it "education". The instrumental and moulding models of education provide a caricature of this necessary feature of desirability by conceiving of what is worthwhile as an end brought about by the process or as a pattern imposed on the child's mind.

Confirmation of this thesis about "education" can be obtained by a brief examination of the concept of "aim". This term has its natural home in the context of activities like shooting and throwing. "Aiming" is associated with the concentration of attention on some object which must be hit or pierced. When the term is used more figuratively it has the same suggestion of the concentration on something within the field of an activity. It is odd to use it, like the term "purpose" or "motive", to suggest some end extrinsic to the activity. We ask people what they are aiming at when they seem rather confused about their purposes, or when they seem to be threshing around in rather an aimless way, or when they are drawing up their plan of campaign and have to formulate what they intend in a coherent way. Asking a person what he is aiming at is a way of getting him to concentrate or clear his mind about what he is trying to do. It is obvious enough, therefore, why the term "aim" is used so frequently in the context of education. For this is a sphere where people engage with great seriousness in activities without always being very clear about what they are trying to achieve. To ask questions about the aims of education is therefore a way of getting people to get clear about and focus their attention on what is worthwhile achieving. It is not to ask for the production of ends extrinsic to education.

Of course moral policies cannot be derived from definitions. A man who has been brought to see these conceptual points about "the aims of education" could reasonably reply "Well, I am against education then. I prefer to train people in science simply in order to increase productivity in the community, or to get them well-paid jobs. I cannot see any point in teaching science unless it can be shown to be obviously useful in these ways." This is an arguable position. But it should not masquerade as a view about the aims of *education*.

"Education" and "Growth"

Historically speaking, when the utilitarian or the moulding models of education have been challenged, others were substituted which likened education to a natural process in which the individual develops or "grows" like a plant towards something that is presumed to be desirable. Gradually, a positive child-centred ideology emerged which was passionately embraced by those in revolt against traditional methods still prevalent in the schools.

The word "ideology" is used advisedly to draw attention to a loose assembly of beliefs whose origin in an indeterminate matrix of psychological preoccupation is more obvious than their validity. The ideology of the "progressive" child-centred educator, who believes in "growth", cannot be attributed to any one central thinker. He or more likely, she, tends to believe that education consists in the development from within of potentialities rather than "moulding" from without, that the curriculum should arise from the needs and interests of the child rather than from the demands of the teacher, that self-expression is more important than the discipline of "subject matter", that children should not be coerced or punished, that children should be allowed to "learn from experience" rather than be told things. The difficulty is to pin down such views to any one important educational theorist. Froebel certainly stressed the importance of studying the child at his various stages and adapting what was provided to the child's interests and stage of development. But he believed very definitely in structuring the environment along desirable lines (witness his "gifts") and his conception of education was dominated by the mystical demand that in the individual that unity should be experienced which permeated the whole of Nature. Dewey, with whose name concepts such as "growth" and "experience" are closely associated, had to write a book[5] in order to disclaim responsibility for some of the doctrines and practices of the Progressive Education Movement and to rectify misunderstandings of his more moderate position. Even Rousseau himself, so some interpreters argue, did not believe that education consisted purely in aiding the enfoldment of "natural" propensities, but in guiding the boy, stage by stage, towards "moral freedom", self-reliance and self-control, and a love of truth and justice.

It would require the erudition of an historian of educational thought and practice to trace the development of the child-centred, progressive ideology in England and the USA. This would be beyond the scope of this paper and the competence of its author. But what emerged as associated with this ideology was a model of the educational situation in which the teacher was regarded as one who has studied the laws of development, and who has to provide appropriate conditions by arranging the "environment" so that the child can "realise himself" to the full or "grow" without becoming stunted or arrested. This model avoids the illiberal and instrumental intimations of the other models; but, like Icarus, it cannot remain for long romantically aloft once the glare of philosophical analysis is turned upon it. For concepts such as "self-realisation" and "growth" presuppose standards of value which determine both the sort of "self" which is worth realising and the direction of growth. Human beings are not like flowers in having a predetermined end which serves as a final cause of their development. "Growing" or "realising oneself" implies doing things which are thought to be worthwhile rather than others. The standards by reference to which they are judged to be worthwhile are grasped by men and handed on from generation to generation. The moulding model of the educator at least brings out this inescapable fact that the teacher has to choose what is worthwhile encouraging in children; but it does so, as I have already argued, by using too brutal a metaphor.[6]

In spite, however, of the lack of determinateness about standards which unanalysed uplift about "growth" and "self-realisation" often encourages, such caricatures of an educational situation are morally important in another way; for they suggest another dimension in which value judgments can enter into education, which relate to the *manner* rather than to the matter of education. They emphasise the place of *procedural* principles. By this I mean that they stress the importance of letting individuals choose themselves, learn by experience, and direct their own lives. The importance of such principles, which all stress the self-direction of the individual, was often overlooked by traditional teachers. They represent value judgments not so much about the matter of what is taught, nor about some illusory "end" for which things are taught, but about the manner in which children are to be treated. This is salutary not simply from a general moral standpoint but more specifically because it picks out one sort of way in which values can be conceived of as being intrinsic to education, rather than as extrinsic ends. Indeed I have argued elsewhere that much of the controversy about "aims" of education is in reality concerned with disagreements about such principles of procedure.[7] The problem for those who emphasise "growth" is to do this in a way which does justice to the fact that no educator can be indifferent to the way in which an individual grows. Dewey's treatment of the case of the burglar who might grow in stature as a burglar is one of the most unsatisfactory passages in his argument.[8]

Conceptually speaking, however, the "growth" model of education, like the instrumental or moulding model, is a caricature; though like all effective caricatures, it distorts a face by emphasising some of its salient features.

For just as the instrumental and moulding models erect the necessary moral feature of "education" into an extrinsic end, so also the growth model converts a necessary feature of educational processes into a procedural principle. Evidence of this is provided by the tendency of its adherents to stress the connection between "education" and "educere" rather than "educare", thereby moulding the concept towards "leading out" rather than "stamping in". This emerges as a persuasive definition of "education" which intimates that nothing is to be counted as "education" in which such procedural principles to do with "leading out" are ignored. The rationale underlying this transition from a conceptual point about "education" to specific moral principles needs further elucidation, which is my second main conceptual point about "education".

It comes about as follows: although "education" picks out no specific processes it does imply criteria which processes involved must satisfy in addition to the demand that something valuable must be passed on. It implies, first of all, that the individual who is educated shall come to care about the valuable things involved, that he shall want to achieve the relevant standards. We would not call a man "educated" who knew about science but cared nothing for truth or who regarded it merely as a means to getting hot water and hot dogs. Furthermore it implies that he is initiated into the content of the activity or forms of knowledge in a meaningful way, so that he knows what he is doing. A man might be conditioned to avoid dogs or induced to do something by hypnotic suggestion. But we could not describe this as "education" if he did not know what he was learning while he learned it. Some forms of drill might also be ruled out on these grounds, if the individual were made to repeat mindlessly a series of narrowly conceived stereotyped acts. For something to count as education a minimum of comprehension must be involved. This is quite compatible with children being told to do things in the early stages. For they do, in an embryonic way, know what they are meant to be doing and understand the standards which they are expected to attain. Furthermore there is a minimal sense in which they act as voluntary agents; for they can rebel and refuse to do what is required of them. These conditions do not apply to what has been induced by hypnosis, drugs, or brutal forms of brain-washing.

Those who believe in such authoritarian methods of education assume that, though children may not care about these performances in the early stages, once they get started on them they will eventually come to care. They will thus emerge as educated men. Growth-theorists, on the other hand, grasping that being educated implies interest in and care for what is worthwhile, assumed that this could only develop if the worthwhile things are always presented in a way which attracts the child. On psychological grounds they held that coercion and command are ineffective methods for getting children to care about what is worthwhile. Furthermore they had moral scruples about treating children in this way, which emerged as procedural principles demanding that children should be allowed to learn by experience and choose for themselves. Their concept of "education" was moulded by their consciences.

In brief my second conceptual point is that to be "educated" implies (a) caring about what is worthwhile and (b) being brought to care about it and to possess the relevant knowledge or skill in a way that involves at least a minimum of understanding and voluntariness. This point has been blown up by "growth" theorists into a persuasive definition of "education" in which "education" is equated with the observance of procedural principles to do with self-determination. The main defect of their view, however, is not that they were induced by psychological speculation and moral demands to puff up conceptual points about "education" into procedural principles. Rather it is that they evaded the other feature stressed by traditional teachers that education involves the intentional transmission of worthwhile content.

Plato's image of education as turning the eye of the soul outwards towards the light is, in these respects at least, much more apposite than either of the two models so far considered. For though he was convinced that there are truths to be grasped and standards to be achieved, which are public objects of desire, he claimed that coercing people into seeing them or trying to imprint them on waxlike minds was both psychologically unsound and morally base. Plato emphasised, quite rightly, what growth theorists evaded, the necessity for objective standards being written into the content of education. But he was not unmindful of the procedural principles stressed by "growth" theorists.

"Education" and Cognition

The emphasis on "seeing" and "grasping" for oneself which is to be found both in Plato and in the "growth" theorists suggests a third conceptual point about "education" in addition to those already made about the value of what is passed on and the manner in which it is to be assimilated. This concerns the cognitive aspect of the content of education.

We often say of a man that he is highly trained, but not educated. What lies behind this condemnation? It is not that the man has mastered a skill of which we disapprove. For we could say this of a doctor or even of a philosopher who had mastered certain ploys or moves in argument; and we might very much approve of their expertise. It is not that he goes through the moves like a mindless robot. For he may be passionately committed to the skill in question and may exercise it with intelligence and determination. It is rather that he has a very limited conception of what he is doing. He does not see its connection with anything else, its place in a coherent pattern of life. It is, for him, an activity which is cognitively adrift. The slogans of the educationalist such as "education is of the whole man" bear witness not simply to a protest against too much specialised training, but also to the conceptual connection between "education" and seeing what is being done in a perspective that is not too limited. We talk about a person as being trained as a philosopher, scientist, or cook, when we wish to draw attention to his acquired competence in a specific discipline of thought or art which has its own intrinsic standards; we do not use the phrase "education *as* a philosopher, scientist, or cook". We can, however, ask the further question whether such people are educated *men*. To ask this question is at least to probe the limitations of their professional vision.

Confirmation of this conceptual connection between "education" and cognitive perspective is provided by considering what we say about less specialised matters. We talk more naturally of "educating the emotions", than we do of training them. This is surely because the distinct emotions are differentiated by their cognitive core, by the different beliefs that go with them. The fundamental difference, for instance, between what is meant by "anger" as distinct from "jealousy" can only be brought out by reference to the different sorts of beliefs that the individual has about the people and situations with which he is confronted. A man who is jealous must think that someone else has something to which he is entitled; what comes over him when he is subject to a fit of jealousy is intimately connected with this belief. But a man who is angry need have no belief as specific as this; he may just regard someone as frustrating one of his purposes. If, therefore, we are contemplating bringing about changes in people's emotional attitudes or reactions, our main task consists in trying to get them to see the world differently in relation to themselves. The eye of the jealous man must be made less jaundiced by altering his concept of what he has a right to, or by getting him to see the actions of others in another light. We speak of "education" because of the work that has to be done on his beliefs.

If, on the other hand, we speak, as we sometimes do, of *training* the emotions, the implications are different. We think of standard situations such as those of the fighter pilot or the gentleman in the drawing room. Such moral heroes have to acquire by training or by drill a pattern of habits which will not be disrupted in emergencies; they will not be paralysed by fear or overcome by grief or jealousy in a public place. "Training" suggests the acquisition of appropriate habits of response in a limited situation. It lacks the wider cognitive implications of "education". We talk naturally of "the training of character" when we wish to ensure reliability of response in accordance with a code; for "character" is exhibited in the things which people can decide to do and can manifest itself in a very rigid and unadaptive form of behaviour.[9] But when we speak of "moral education" we immediately envisage addressing ourselves to the matter of what people believe, and to questions of justification and questions of fact connected with such beliefs. To make my point even more sharply: "sex education" is given by doctors, schoolmasters, and others who are capable of working information and value judgments about sexual matters into a complicated system of beliefs about the functioning of the body, personal relationships, and social institutions. If these oracles proceeded to try a bit of "sex-training" with their pupils no classroom could contain their activities.

I have often wondered what converted physical training into physical education. No doubt, historically speaking, this came about, as do most changes in educational institutions, through pressures of a militant group requiring fuller recognition. But the underlying rationale of the change was surely the conviction on the part of some that exercising the body must not be seen merely as a skilful and disciplined business related to a specific end such as physical fitness; rather it is to be seen as related to and contributing to other worthwhile things in life. To be asked to imagine that one is a leaf is to be given an unusual way of conceiving of what one is doing in the gym. But at least it conveys the impression that one is not just being trained in circumscribed skills.

This connection between "education" and cognitive content explains why it is that some activities rather than others seem so obviously to be of educational importance. Few skills have a wide-ranging cognitive content. There is very little to know about riding bicycles, swimming, or golf. It is largely a matter of "knowing how" rather than of "knowing that",[10] of knack rather than of understanding. Furthermore what there is to know throws very little light on much else. In history, science, or literature, on the other hand, there is an immense amount to know, and, if it is properly assimilated, it constantly throws light on, widens, and deepens one's view of countless other things. Similarly games are of limited educational value. For, even if a game requires great skill and has considerable cognitive content internal to it (for example, bridge), part of what is meant by calling it a "game" is that it is set apart from the main business of living, complete in itself, and limited to particular times and places.[11] Games can be conceived of as being of educational importance only in so far as they provide opportunities for acquiring knowledge, qualities of mind and character, and skills that have application in a wider area of life. Hence their accepted importance for moral education. That *many* games have these features in a pre-eminent degree is a myth perpetuated by schoolmasters who convert esoteric enthusiasms into educational panaceas.

It might be objected that in drawing attention to the cognitive content implied by "education" I am in danger of degrading it to the level of mere instruction. To suggest this would be to misunderstand the main lines of the analysis which is being proposed. My thesis is not that "education" refers to any special sort of process which might be equated with instruction, training, or drill; rather that it encapsulates three basic criteria which such processes must satisfy. Neither instruction alone, nor training alone, could properly be so described. For both training and instruction might be in futile things like opium-taking, thus failing to satisfy the first criterion of being worthwhile. Furthermore instruction might consist in presenting inert ideas which are incomprehensible to children, while training might approximate to mindless drill, thus failing to satisfy the second criterion of "education" already picked out.

Those, however, who have been hostile to mere instruction with its suggestion of "inert ideas" have been too prone to conceive of education as if it were merely a matter of acquiring skills. This is, perhaps, because the tendency of American pragmatism and behaviourism is to assimilate thinking to doing, to regard it as "surrogate behaviour". But an "educated" man is distinguished not so much by what he does as by what he "sees" or "grasps". If he does something very well, in which he has been trained, he must see this in perspective, as related to other things. It is difficult to conceive of a training that would result in an "educated" man in which a modicum of instruction has no place. For being educated involves "knowing that" as well as "knowing how".

It might also be objected that I am equating the concept of "education" with that of "liberal education". This is not my intention. The demand that education should be "liberal" has usually been put forward as a protest against confining what goes on to the service of some extrinsic end such as the production of material goods or the promotion of health or empire. The mind, it is argued, should be allowed to pursue its own bent untrammelled by such restrictions. Allegiance should be given only to standards such as those connected with truth which are intrinsic to the mind's functioning. This interpretation of "liberal" raises different issues about education which are more relevant to the first point I made about it when I stressed its necessary connection with the promotion of what is desirable. There is, however, another interpretation of "liberal" which is closer to the point I have just been making about cognitive perspective. This is the plea that education should not be confined to specialist training. The individual, it is argued, should be trained in more than one form of knowledge. This requires more than what is written into the concept of "education". For whereas an "educated" man can be trained in one sphere, for example, science, and yet be sufficiently cognisant of other ways of looking at the world, so that he can grasp the historical perspective, social significance, or stylistic merit of his work and of much else besides, "liberal" education requires that he should also be *trained*, to some degree at least, in such other ways of thinking. This is a much stronger requirement than that which is implied by anything that I have said about "education", though it is obviously a development of what is intimated by it.

But I must digress no further on this point. The discussion has been sufficient, I think, to exhibit the importance both of training and of instruction in education and to safeguard my thesis against the misinterpretation that I am equating education with either of these processes.

Education as Initiation

I now propose to put forward a more positive account of education which is constructed, in a truly dialectic manner, out of considerations brought forward in criticism of the discarded models, and which is consistent with the three criteria of "education" that I have made explicit. Of course this account will not itself present yet another model; for to produce such a model would be to sin against the glimmerings of light that may have so far flickered over my treatment of the concept of "education". For, I have claimed, "education" marks out no particular type of transaction between teachers and learners; it states criteria to which such transactions have to conform.

"Education" involves essentially processes which intentionally transmit what is valuable in an intelligible and voluntary manner and which create in the learner a desire to achieve it, this being seen to have its place along with other things in life. Terms like "training" and "instruction" — perhaps even "teaching" — are too specific. Education can occur without these specific transactions and they can take place in ways which fail to satisfy all the criteria implied by "education". The term "initiation", on the other hand, is general enough to cover these different types of transaction if it is also stipulated that initiation must be into worthwhile activities and modes of conduct.

No man is born with a mind; for the development of mind marks a series of individual and racial achievements. A child is born with an awareness not as yet differentiated into beliefs, wants, and feelings. All such specific modes of consciousness, which are internally related to types of object in a public world, develop later *pari passu* with the pointing out of paradigm objects. Gradually the child comes to want things which there are means of obtaining instead of threshing round beset by unruly and unrealistic wishes; he comes to fear things that may hurt him, and to believe that things will come to pass which have come to pass. He learns to name objects, to locate his experience in a spatio-temporal framework, and to impose causal and means-to-end categories to make sense of events and actions. He creates pools of predictability by making promises and stating his intentions. In the beginning it was not at all like this. Such an embryonic mind is the product of initiation into public traditions enshrined in a public language, which it took our remote ancestors centuries to develop.

With the mastery of basic skills the door is opened to a vaster and more variegated inheritance. Further differentiation develops as the boy becomes initiated more deeply into distinctive forms of knowledge such as science, history, mathematics, religious and aesthetic appreciation, and into the practical types of knowledge involved in moral, prudential, and technical forms of thought and action. Such differentiations are alien to the mind of a child and primitive man — indeed to that of a pre-seventeenth-century man. To have a mind is not to enjoy a private picture-show or to exercise some inner diaphanous organ; it is to have an awareness differentiated in accordance with the canons implicit in all these inherited traditions. "Education" marks out the processes by means of which the individual is initiated into them.

Why do I start off my positive account of "education" with this selective thumb-nail sketch of the social history of mind? Partly because I want to establish the notion of initiation in the centre of my account, and partly because I want to draw attention to the enormous importance of the *impersonal content and procedures* which are enshrined in public traditions. Initiation is always into some body of knowledge and mode of conduct which it takes time and determination to master. This association with activities which have what I called "cognitive content" satisfies the third of the three essential criteria of education that I dwelt on in my earlier discussion of inadequate models. But there are additional points to stress about the importance in education of impersonal content and procedures.

There have been many like Dewey who have attacked the notion that education consists in the transmission of a body of knowledge. Stress is placed on critical thinking, individual experimentation and problem-solving. I have witnessed lessons in American schools where this view was slavishly applied: the teacher used poems purely to encourage "critical thinking"; history was used, as it were, to provide riders for problem-solving. The notion that poetry should be listened to, or that one has to be, to a certain extent, a historian in order to understand a historical problem, was an alien one. The emphasis on "critical thinking" was salutary enough, perhaps, when bodies of knowledge were handed on without any attempt being made to hand on also the public procedures by means of which they had been accumulated, criticised, and revised. But it is equally absurd to foster an abstract skill called "critical thinking" without handing on anything concrete to be critical about. For there are as many brands of "critical thinking" as there are disciplines, and in the various disciplines such as history, science, and philosophy, there is a great deal to be known before the peculiar nature of the problem is grasped.

It is of course important that people should be initiated gradually into the procedures defining a discipline as well as into mastery of the established content, that people should learn to think historically for instance, not just know some history. But the only way to learn to think historically is to probe the past with someone who has mastered this form of thought. The procedures of a discipline can only be mastered by an exploration of its established content under the guidance of one who has already been initiated. Whitehead said that a merely well-informed man is the most useless bore on God's earth. I do not entirely agree. I always find encyclopaedias interesting. Equally boring, in my view, are those for whom being critical is a substitute for being well informed about anything. To parody Kant: content without criticism is blind, but criticism without content is empty.

The further point needs also to be made that the critical procedures by means of which established content is assessed, revised, and adapted to new discoveries, have public criteria written into them that stand as impersonal standards to which both teacher and learner must give their allegiance. The trouble with the models of education that I considered is that they fail to do justice to this essential inter-subjectivity of education which D. H. Lawrence referred to as "the holy ground". To liken education to therapy, to conceive of it as imposing a pattern on another person or as fixing the environment so that he "grows", fails to do justice to the shared impersonality both of the content that is handed on and of the criteria by reference to which it is criticised and revised. The teacher is not a detached operator who is bringing about some kind of result in another person which is external to him. His task is to try to get others on the inside of a public form of life that he shares and considers to be worthwhile. In science it is truth that matters, not what any individual believes to be true; in morals it is justice, not the pronouncements of any individual.

At the culminating stages of education there is little distinction between teacher and taught; they are both participating in the shared experience of exploring a common world. The teacher is simply more familiar with its contours and more skilled in handling the tools for laying bare its mysteries and appraising its nuances. Occasionally in a tutorial this exploration takes the form of a dialogue. But more usually it is a group experience. The great teachers are those who can conduct such a shared exploration in accordance with rigorous canons, and convey, at the same time, the contagion of a shared enterprise in which all are united by a common zeal. That is why humour is such a valuable aid to teachers; for if people can laugh together they step out of the shadows of self-reference cast by age, sex, and position. This creation of a shared experience can act as a catalyst which releases a class to unite in their common enterprise. This feeling of fraternity is part of the emotional underpinning for an enterprise conducted according to impersonal principles.

There has been too much loose talk about the dimension of the personal in teaching. Indeed one often fears that "the enjoyment of good personal relationships" with pupils is in danger of becoming a substitute for teaching them something. What is required of the teacher, in addition to the feeling of fraternity already mentioned, is respect for persons, not intimate relations with his pupils.[12] In a teaching situation love must be of a type that is appropriate to the special type of relationship in which the teacher is placed, to his concept of them as pupils rather than as sons or brothers. The teacher must always remember that he is dealing with others who are distinctive centres of consciousness, with peculiar idiosyncratic purposes and feelings that criss-cross their institutional roles. Each one is bound up with and takes pride of some sort in his own achievements; each one mirrors the world from a distinctive point of view. In the early stages of education the emphasis on individual differences must be more marked; for the enterprise is to present the basic skills, which are necessary for later exploration, in the manner which is most appropriate to minds comparatively unformed by public traditions. Hence the relevance of activity methods and of the model of individual growth; hence the appositeness of the slogan "We teach children, not subjects"; hence the need for teachers to understand what psychologists have discovered about individual differences and child development. Such a "child-centred" approach is as appropriate in dealing with the backward or difficult adolescent as it is at the infant stage. For the crucial difference is not one of age, but of the development of motivation and of cognitive structure, and of degrees of initiation into public and differentiated modes of thought.

At the other end of the enterprise of education, however, in universities, adult education classes, and the later stages of secondary education, the emphasis is more on the canons implicit in the forms of thought than on individual avenues of initiation. Respect for persons, enlivened by fraternity, here provides the warmth in which the teacher can perform his cardinal function of exhibiting the form of thought into which he is trying to initiate others. It is one thing to understand the canons of any discipline or mode of conduct; it is quite another to apply them with skill and judgment in particular circumstances. Judgment, said Quintilian, is the final flower of much experience. But such experience has to be acquired in the company of a man who already has judgment; it cannot be learned from books or formal lectures alone. Oakeshott has written so tellingly on this aspect of the personal element in education that it would be otiose for me to labour this point any further.[13] Need I add that the notion of "initiation" is a peculiarly apt description of this essential feature of education which consists in experienced persons turning the eye of others outwards to what is essentially independent of persons?

"Initiation" is an apt description, too, of that other aspect of education stressed by the "growth" theorists, the requirement that those who are being educated should want to do or master the worthwhile things which are handed on to them. This must be done in such a way that the coercion of the old formal instructor is not replaced by the cajoling of the progressive child-watcher. I am inclined to think that the value of command and direction is underestimated by modern educational theory, especially perhaps with less intelligent children. At least it indicates clearly what the educator considers to be worthwhile and is certainly preferable to bribery and the production of irrelevant incentives. At least it may awaken some rebellion in the child and generate a jet of desire in him to do what he thinks worthwhile, if he can find an avenue. Where everything is only to be done if it can be seen by the child to relate to what he wants, the coinage of wanting becomes debased because there is too little with which he may contrast it.

This brings me to my final and perhaps most fundamental point about "education". I have remarked before that "education" implies standards, not necessarily aims. It consists in initiating others into activities, modes of conduct and thought which have standards written into them by reference to which it is possible to act, think, and feel with varying degrees of skill, relevance and taste. If teachers are not convinced of this they should be otherwise employed. They may be a bit hazy about why these things are more valuable than others. This is not surprising; for the problem of justification in general is a very difficult problem with which moral philosophers since Socrates have been constantly wrestling. The relative weight to be given to these valuable things also presents acute problems; hence the importance of having a system which permits options. But *that* these things are valuable no dedicated teacher would dispute.

Now the teacher, having himself been initiated, is on the inside of these activities and modes of thought and conduct. He understands vividly, perhaps, that some created objects are beautiful and others not; he can recognise the elegance of a proof, or a paragraph, the cogency of an argument, and clarity of an exposition, the wit of a remark, the neatness of a plot and the justice and wisdom of a decision. He has perhaps a love of truth, a passion for justice, and a hatred of what is tasteless. To ask him what the aim or point of this form of life is, into which he has himself been initiated,

seems an otiose question. For, like Socrates, he senses that really to understand what is good is, *ipso facto*, to be committed to its pursuit. How can
a man who really understands what a cogent argument is, or a wise and
just decision, settle for one that is slipshod, slovenly, or haphazard? This
sort of question, he senses, can only be asked by barbarians outside the gates.
Of course he realises that science, mathematics, and even history *can* be
viewed in an instrumental way. They contribute to hospitals being built and
staffed, wars being won, the cultivation of the land, and to communication
across the face of the earth. And then what, he asks? What are men going
to do, how are they going to think, what are they going to appreciate when
their necessary appetites are satisfied? Are these hard men indifferent to all
that constitutes being civilised?

Children, to a large extent, are. They start off in the position of the barbarian outside the gates. The problem is to get them inside the citadel of
civilisation so that they will understand and love what they see when they
get there. It is no use concealing the fact that the activities and modes of
thought and conduct which define a civilised form of life are difficult to
master. That is why the educator has such an uphill task in which there
are no short cuts. The insistence, which one confronts in American schools,
that children should be happy, ignores this brutal fact. People can be happy
lying in the sun; but happiness such as this is not the concern of the educator. Most of our thinking about "welfare" is bedevilled by the confusion
of being happy with living a worthwhile life.

It may well be asked: if this is what is meant by "education", how many
people are capable of it? This is not a philosophical question; for though
a philosopher might concern himself with the general conditions necessary
for the application of a concept, it is an empirical question to determine
to what extent such conditions are actually realised. To take a parallel: a
philosopher might map out what it means to be moral and what general
conditions must be satisfied for the concept to have application — for
example, the possession of a central nervous system, the ability to feel sympathy for others. But it is not his business, *qua* philosopher, to speculate
about how many people there may be in whom such conditions are satisfied.

It is clear, however, from this analysis of "education" that there are necessary conditions to do with cognitive structure and motivation. Although it
is not a philosophers' task to speculate about the empirical facts in this matter,
it is not out of place for him to note that very little is known about them.
As has been remarked before, such evidence as there is suggests that a great
deal depends on early conditions in the home and school. Since a large
proportion of the population in Great Britain suffers from an environment
which militates against such motivation and cognitive development it would
be unwise as well as unfair to conclude too soon that education can only
be for the "elite".

Many educators, seeing both the indignity and the inefficacy of the traditional attempts to coerce children into doing difficult things for which they
had no inclination, preached the doctrine of "interest". If these difficult things

could be ingeniously harnessed to what children want, then, they said, the task and not the man will exert the discipline. Skill, judgment, and discrimination can be erected on a foundation of existing wants. There is much in this technique. In the Youth Service, for instance, we used a predictable interest in sex to develop manners, skill in dancing, and taste in clothes and personal adornment. The hope was that eventually the girls would come to value manners and skill in dancing for their own sake and not purely as a means of getting a boy, and would develop outwards from this solid centre. One technique of initiation is therefore to lure people inside the citadel by using their existing interests in the hope that, once inside, they will develop other interests which previously were never dreamed of. The danger of this technique is that, if used to the exclusion of others, it reinforces the instrumental attitude. It encourages people to think that things are only worth doing well if they are patently relevant to some extrinsic end.

This is, of course, a very limited conception of initiation. For it neglects the fluidity of wants. What people in fact want or are interested in is, to a large extent, a product of their previous initiation. The job of the educator is not simply to build on existing wants but to present what is worth wanting in such a way that it creates new wants and stimulates new interests. If teachers do not do this others will — advertisers, for instance, and other members of "the peer group". There are interesting studies emerging recently from the USA suggesting a connection between permissive methods in education and group conformity.[14] If teachers do not hold up standards of achievement to children in a way that gets them working, others will lure them along less exacting paths. Whitehead has much that it is wise to say here on the stage of "romance" in education. Any method which can create interest in what is worthwhile should not be debarred — even talk and chalk, if employed by a man who is good at it.[15] But the stage of romance must be followed by the stage of precision. The crunch of standards must come with all that it entails in blood, sweat, and tears. The "playway" may open up a vista of a Promised Land; but of itself it may provide little of the precision, skill and judgment which may be necessary for getting there. The pupil has gradually to get the grammar of the activity into his guts so that he can eventually win through to the stage of autonomy. But he cannot do this unless he has mastered the moves made by his predecessors which are enshrined in living traditions. *How* he can come best to this is an empirical question; but talk of encouraging "creativeness" is mischievous unless children are also equipped with competence; talk of "problem-solving" is cant unless children are knowledgeable enough to recognise a real problem when they see one. The only way into mastering what Oakeshott calls the "language" of any form of thought or activity is by first being initiated into its "literature".[16] This is an arduous business.

As a matter of fact there is evidence to suggest that the teacher may not have to rely purely on specific interests, or on the admiration which children have for him and their desire to please him, to provide incentives for precision. For there may well be a generalised interest in achievement and competence for its own sake.[17] To master some difficult task, to get things right, to do what is right, is a very powerful source of motivation. It can grip young children as well as absorbed adults. Perhaps it was one of the driving forces of the puritan movement which once galvanised England into activity. It can, of course, degenerate into compulsiveness; it can be harnessed to things that are both futile and wicked. But when harnessed to things that are also worthwhile, it is not to be despised. There is much to be said for the generalised puritan virtues of enterprise, orderliness, thoroughness, and perseverance — especially in education.

Education, then, can have no ends beyond itself. Its value derives from principles and standards implicit in it. To be educated is not to have arrived at a destination; it is to travel with a different view. What is required is not feverish preparation for something that lies ahead, but to work with precision, passion and taste at worthwhile things that lie to hand. These worthwhile things cannot be forced on reluctant minds, neither are they flowers towards which the seeds of mentality develop in the sun of the teacher's smile. They are acquired by contact with those who have already acquired them and who have patience, zeal, and competence enough to initiate others into them.

"There is a quality of life which lies always beyond the mere fact of life."[18] The great teacher is he who can convey this sense of quality to another, so that it haunts his every endeavour and makes him sweat and yearn to fix what he thinks and feels in a fitting form. For life has no one purpose; man imprints his purposes upon it. It presents few tidy problems; mainly predicaments that have to be endured or enjoyed. It is education that provides that touch of eternity under the aspect of which endurance can pass into dignified, wry acceptance, and animal enjoyment into a quality of living.

NOTES AND REFERENCES

1. Another version of this paper was given as an Inaugural Lecture to the Chair of the Philosophy of Education at the University of London Institute of Education, delivered in December 1963.
2. *Half Our Future*, report of the Central Advisory Council for Education, H.M. Stationery Office, London, 1963.
3. See, for instance, B. BERNSTEIN, "Social Class and Linguistic Development: A Theory of Social Learning", in A. H. HALSEY *et al* (Eds), *Education, Economy and Society*, Free Press, New York, 1961.
4. "Education" is actually both what Ryle calls a "task" term and an "achievement" term (see G. RYLE, *The Concept of Mind*, Hutchinson, London, 1949). For a more recent attempt at analysis, which meets some of the obvious objections to which this early attempt is open, see P. H. HIRST and R. S. PETERS, *The Logic of Education*, Routledge & Kegan Paul, London, 1970, Chapter 2.
5. John DEWEY, *Experience and Education*, Macmillan, New York, 1938.
6. For further comments on both "moulding" and "growth" metaphors, see I. SCHEFFLER, *The Language of Education*, Thomas, Springfield (Illinois), 1960, Chapter 3.
7. R. S. PETERS, *Authority, Responsibility and Education*, Allen and Unwin, London, 1963, Chapter 7.
8. JOHN DEWEY, *Experience and Education*, Constable, London, 1961, pp. 37–38.
9. For further complications in the concept of "character", see R. S. PETERS, "Moral Education and the Psychology of Character" in *Philosophy*, January, 1962.
10. See G. RYLE, *The Concept of Mind*, Hutchinson, London, 1949.
11. See J. HUIZINGA, *Homo Ludens*, Kegan Paul, London, 1949.

12. For further discussion of this issue, which is dealt with too cursorily here, see P. H. HIRST and R. S. PETERS, *op. cit.*, Chapter 6.
13. See M. OAKESHOTT, "Political Education" in his *Rationalism in Politics*, Methuen, London, 1962.
14. See, for example, F. KERLINGER, "The Implications of the Permissiveness Doctrine in American Education" in H. BURNS and C. BRAUNER, *Philosophy and Education*, Ronald Press, New York, 1962.
15. A. N. WHITEHEAD, *The Aims of Education*, Williams and Norgate, London, 1962, Chapter 2.
16. See M. OAKESHOTT, "The Teaching of Politics in a University" in *Rationalism in Politics*, Methuen, London, 1962.
17. See D. McCLELLAND, *The Achievement Motive*, Appleton-Century, New York, 1953, and other more recent publications, as well as R. WHITE, "Competence and the Psycho-sexual Stages of Development" in M. R. JONES (Ed.) *Nebraska Symposium on Motivation*, University of Nebraska Press, Lincoln, 1960.
18. A. N. WHITEHEAD, *Religion in the Making*, Cambridge University Press, 1926, p. 80.

Form and Content in Moral Education

Moral education, like curriculum reform, is a very with-it subject amongst educationalists these days; but it is also a very ticklish one. If words like "good" and "bad", and "wrong" are mentioned to any gathering of teachers there are two entirely predictable responses. The first is that the old view of moral absolutes is an anachronism. Morals are subjective, a matter of individual or group preference or upbringing. The second is a corollary of this — that any attempt to influence the young in respect of their morals is an exercise in indoctrination, an attempt to impose private preferences on immature minds.

Yet teachers feel uneasy; for they are generally convinced that it is absolutely wrong to discriminate against coloured children in their classes. They are not indifferent to whether their pupils smoke pot. And they do not regard teenage pregnancy as merely a failure of prudence. These convictions do not seem to them like private preferences for coffee as opposed to tea. In acting in the light of their convictions they do not seem to be carrying on quite like the Japanese brain-washing G.I. prisoners. There seems to be a discrepancy between what they think and do and what they are told by some pundit or other. Yet, they reflect, our Victorian ancestors cannot have been right after all. And so, understandably enough, they feel uneasy.

They are right to feel uneasy. For the alternatives are not just those of accepting an established code or of adopting some extreme subjectivist stance. Similarly the choice is not simply between imposing some fixed code on the young or letting them discover some morality for themselves. There is a middle way between traditionalism and some sort of romantic protest. This

From R. S. PETERS, *Authority, Responsibility and Education*, Allen and Unwin, London, revised edition, 1973. Reprinted by permission of the publisher.

middle way is closely connected with the use of reason. This enables people to adopt a critical attitude towards what has been established. They may accept it or reject it on its merits. But in so doing they need not adopt a purely subjective stance. It is significant, for instance, that young people who are very critical of what their elders do, criticise it in terms of the injustice, exploitation, or suffering brought about by adult mismanagement. They are united in assuming that this line of criticism is pertinent; they do not just voice private objections to the plight of coloured people, to the selectiveness of the educational system, or to the paternalism of their teachers.

In order to make clear what is meant by the use of reason in morality it is important to make a distinction between the form and content of the moral consciousness. This distinction is similar to that which can be made in the sphere of beliefs about the world. The content of a belief might be that the earth is round. But this belief could be held in different ways. It could be believed just because it had been read in a book or proclaimed by an authority. On the other hand it could be believed because someone had examined it, had viewed it critically and looked into the evidence for it, like a scientist. Thus a belief with the same content could be held in quite different ways, which would constitute two distinct forms which the belief might have. Similarly, in morals someone could believe that gambling was wrong simply because his parents had brought him up to believe it. On the other hand he might have reflected on the practice of gambling and might have decided that it was wrong because of the suffering brought about by the practice.

Holding beliefs rationally is to adopt one possible form for beliefs. It is possible, therefore, that people could share a certain content of beliefs, which had a different form. An unreflective peasant and a philosopher, for instance, might both believe that it is wrong to break promises. Alternatively, people might look at beliefs in the same sort of way but disagree with regard to content because they gave different weight to considerations relevant to holding them. Reflective people, for instance, after due thought, might disagree about the ethics of abortion, even though they both accepted the relevance of the considerations advanced on either side. This type of distinction is very pertinent when discussing morals or moral education. For too much weight may be given to consensus or to lack of it without considering whether the consensus relates to content or to form.

It is necessary, when talking about moral education, to get clear first of all about the structure of what has to be learned. One could not begin to discuss mathematical education sensibly without some view about the structure of mathematical thought. The same holds good for morals, though there may be more disagreement, in this sphere, about the structure of what has to be learned. In getting clearer about the "what" this distinction between form and context is crucial. Similarly in going on to discuss how learning takes place it will be found that this distinction between form and content is equally important. For what may be true of how some particular content is learned may not be true of how the form of the belief is acquired. It might be true, for instance, that instruction methods might be very effective in teaching a certain content of belief; but they might not do much for the development of a different form. Do it yourself types of methods might be much more effective in this sphere.

The plan of my approach is therefore as follows. I propose to examine, first of all, the structure of what has to be learned in moral education. I then propose to consider how it may be learned. In discussing both the "what" and the "how" the distinction between content and form will be employed; for this is a very relevant distinction to make in the attempt to bring out what is distinctive of the middle road in morals and moral education which is occupied by those who, like myself, wish to adopt a stance that is critical of tradition but not so subjective. This stance is intimately connected with the use of reason.

There is a very wide sense of what is ethical or desirable which includes how one should spend one's time or what one should do considering only oneself. In this wide sense it might be thought undesirable to spend a lot of time just picking one's nose in private. But I am not going to be concerned with this very wide notion of what is valuable in life. I am going to confine my discussion to the sphere of interpersonal rules and practices with which morality is mainly concerned.

To many "morality" in this sense usually conjures up a fixed code forbidding sex, stealing, and selfishness. The very word "code" suggests a content of rules in a traditional form — an arbitrary amalgam, perhaps, without any thought-out basis. Against this type of construction by convention there have been many forms of protest — especially since Victorian times. Those who have struck out on their own in defiance have often proclaimed, like D. H. Lawrence, that men ought to follow their authentic feelings or the "dark God within", that they ought to avoid "bad faith" by deciding things for themselves in existentialist agony, or, as in modern times, that they ought to "do their own thing".

These are understandable reactions against being encased in a conventional code. But are they not rather too extreme to do justice to how we may feel about some matters? Even Bertrand Russell, who held a subjectivist view of morality, was uneasy in saying that in condemning bull-fighting in Spain he was just giving vent to a personal dislike. He had the sense that his disapproval was in some way appropriate, that others should feel in this way about it. He was even more unhappy in maintaining that he simply did not like the Nazis. On the other hand to view morals just as an established code seems equally unsatisfactory. For it is obvious that codes change as a result of moral criticism.

Such criticism, which was pre-eminently voiced by sensitive critics of convention such as J. S. Mill and Bertrand Russell, surely springs from some kind of consensus about what is *important* in life, about what makes criticism relevant, about what there is reason for doing or being. When we say, for instance, that gambling is wrong, we are not just expressing a private preference. We are suggesting that there are important considerations which count against gambling which anyone could recognise — for instance that it leads to suffering. And this is not to appeal to an established code. For science and a more rational, universalistic type of morality gradually emerged precisely because social change, economic expansion and conquest led to a clash of codes and conflict between competing views of the world. At the level of life in which discussion was encouraged to determine which myths about the world had to be abandoned, which elements in a code had to be discarded, certain fundamental principles were presupposed without which the use of reason would be a shadow-play. It is these underlying principles which pick out what is important in life. What, then, are these principles?

To start with, for such discussion about matters of conduct to have point, there must be some concern to ameliorate the human predicament, to consider people's interest. For what kind of discussion would it be if there was deliberation about what ought to be done with no concern for the interests of those who might contribute and who might be affected? And, as one of the main features of the use of reason is the settling of issues on *relevant* grounds — that is, the banning of arbitrariness, some kind of impartiality with regard to people's claims is also required. They cannot be ignored just because of the colour of their eyes, or ruled out of court just because of the colour of their skin. People must be treated with respect as sources of arguments and claims. Without, too, the general presumption that people should tell the truth rational discussion would be impossible; for, as a general practice, systematic lying would be counter-productive in relation to any common concern to discover what ought to be done. Finally, too, there must be some presumption in favour of freedom. For without freedom of speech the community would be hamstrung in relation to its concern to arrive at an answer; for even the most offensive or simple members might have something of importance to contribute. There must also be a presumption in favour of freedom of action; for what rational man would seriously discuss what ought to be done without also demanding freedom to do it?

These fundamental principles do not, of course, lay down in detail what ought to be done. They do not, in other words, provide any detailed *content* to the moral life. Rather they supply a *form* for the moral consciousness; they sensitise us to what is relevant when we think about what is right and wrong. When, for instance, we ponder over a practice such as spitting in the street, considerations come to mind such as the harm done to others or the lack of respect for them, as well as limitations on our own freedom. By questioning such a practice by reference to principles provided by the form of our moral consciousness, we accept it or reject it as an element in the content of our code of behaviour.

Thus, on the one hand, recourse to principles provides development beyond a code-encased, traditional type of conduct; for codes have to be rejected or accepted in the light of such principles. On the other hand these principles provide criteria of relevance for the protest of the individual. His own independent line of conduct has coherence because it springs, for example, from concern for suffering or indignation at injustice. It is important to stress that acceptance of such principles does not guarantee uniform *content* to morality any more than the principles of procedure underlying science guarantee an agreed content for a science. In both cases all that is provided is a form of thought that structures experience. In the scientific case assumptions about the world are systematically submitted to discussion and to observational tests. Some are discarded and others survive as the current content of scientific knowledge. Similarly in the moral case, when current codes are reflected on in the light of such principles, as happened in the seventeenth century when reflective lawyers such as Grotius tried to agree upon laws of the sea against piracy, it comes to be seen that the content of codes are not all of equal importance. There are some types of rules — for instance concerning contracts, the care of the young, and property — which can be seen to be necessary to any continuing form of social life in which the human condition is going to be tolerable at all, man being what he is and the conditions of life on earth being what they are. But other rules are much more dependent on local economic and geographical conditions such as prohibitions on usury, birth control, and possessiveness. Stability and consensus at a basic level are quite compatible with change and experiment at other levels. And these differences in stability of content can be determined by reasons deriving from fundamental principles such as fairness and the consideration of people's interests. These sorts of distinctions are very relevant when one is confronted with the confident assertion that all moral matters are relative or expressions of private preference. Those who proclaim this usually point to disagreements over sexual morality, punishment or the war in Vietnam. But this is merely to make the point that the content of morality is not uniformly acceptable. Of course it is not; neither is the content of science.

Further questions, however, spring to mind when reflecting on such obvious cases of moral disagreement. Firstly in determining any particular content do not people accept as relevant more or less similar considerations, even though they give differing *weight* to them? In discussing sexual matters, for instance, is not the harm done to children by being fatherless thought morally relevant or the lack of respect for persons evident in some forms of prostitution both within and outside marriage? In considering the breaking of contracts is not the lack of truthfulness, as well as the unhappiness caused, thought to be relevant? In discussing the merits of gambling do we ever dwell approvingly or disapprovingly on the amount of greenness in the world brought about by the construction of card-tables? If we think a man wicked is it normally by virtue of his height? Maybe we do not always arrive at the same conclusion about what is right and wrong, about the content of morality. But is not the form of our thought about it structured in terms of shared principles which make considerations relevant?

Secondly, leaving aside the distinction between the form of moral thought provided by fundamental principles, and its content, is there actually widespread disagreement among reflective people on *all* matters of content? There is too facile a tendency to pass from the platitude that people disagree about sexual matters, crime and punishment, and the taking of drugs, to the assumption that the whole moral order is unstable. But is this true? Do not most people think that children should be cared for, that promises should in general be kept, that there should be some rules for the preservation of property? No doubt there are local differences in the implementation of such general requirements, but there is surely a massive consensus that there must be some general rules in such areas.

Thirdly, it may be said that anthropologists have revealed that there are some societies which have duties that we would not recognise as moral ones or which we would find absolutely repugnant, such as puberty rites and infanticide. But, although ingenuity can be displayed in discerning some function for such practices in their way of life, the more fundamental point must surely be made that many such societies have not a differentiated way of viewing such practices. They do not distinguish between what is a matter of morals as distinct from a matter of law, custom, or religion, any more than they distinguish between science, magic, and mythology. So, as I am concerned only with morality as a specific form of thought and conduct, such social phenomena are largely irrelevant. To attach much weight to them would be like studying the Trobriand Islanders' assumptions about nature if one was worried about the status of Newton's laws of motion. This should be sufficient to rebut the accusations of insularity and cultural relativism; for this analysis makes no claim to having any validity as a type of sociological generalisation. No assumptions are being made about how widespread this form of thinking is in the twentieth as distinct from in the seventeenth century. It may or may not, like a scientific way of thinking, have emerged under certain types of economic conditions; it may or may not be concentrated in certain classes in society. That is neither here nor there and certainly the *validity* of this form of thinking does not depend purely on consensus. If this were the case science would be in a sorry state as it is a way of thinking that is and always has been alien to most of the human race. All that is being claimed is that gradually, since about the seventeenth century, morality as a distinct way of thinking about conduct has become differentiated from religion, custom and law just as science has become differentiated from mythology and metaphysics, and that it was the expression of the determination of men to come together, whatever their country or creed, and to decide things by the use of reason. Democratic government is, in political terms, the institutionalisation of this determination.

In an open type of society such as ours, in which such differentiations are made, there are, as I have already argued, massive areas of disagreement about moral matters, as well as agreement. And both are possible because of the acceptance of the fundamental principles to which I have constantly referred — especially that of freedom which grants a *prima facie* right to nonconformity. Indeed, the existence of more than one fundamental principle makes disagreement probable because differing weight can be given to them. A person who tells a "white lie" does not do it for gain or glory. He does it because any alternative course of action will, in his view, cause great suffering. This point, incidentally, needs often to be made against those who argue that morals cannot be "absolute" because, on occasions, even fundamental principles have to be bent a bit. But fundamental principles do not provide commands at all — only considerations that make reasons relevant. And, as guides to conduct, they are always to be asserted with an "other things being equal" proviso. In cases like those of white lies other things are not equal because another fundamental principle is involved, for example, that of causing harm to others. The way in which the principle of freedom works is another obvious illustration of this point. There is not an absolute right to freedom, only a general presumption in favour of it. The right is abrogated when the exercise of freedom is likely to occasion great unfairness or suffering to others. But the fact that such fundamental principles sometimes conflict does not affect their status as general guides to conduct.

So much, then, for the structure of what has to be learned in a rational morality. I have tried to make explicit the distinction between form and content in morals. I have concentrated on the rational form of morality rather than on the traditional form of it because that is the one to which I am committed. In passing, therefore, to questions about how morality is to be learned I shall also pay particular attention to problems about passing on a rational form of morality.

In considering questions about moral development the work of Jean Piaget and his follower, Lawrence Kohlberg, are of particular relevance. For they are concerned with the development of a rational form of morality and Kohlberg particularly has views about the development of its form as distinct from the learning of its content. I shall not be concerned with the niceties of differences between these two psychologists — only with the general outline of the theory adopted by both.

Kohlberg broke down Piaget's three stages into six and also did some cross-cultural studies to support the main thesis that, though the content of morality varies from culture to culture, there is an invariant order in the development of its form. Children pass from an egocentric stage, at which they see rules as injunctions to be complied with in order to avoid punishment or to obtain rewards, to a stage of what Kohlberg calls "Good-boy morality", at which they see rules as there, as part of the order of the world, which are linked with praise and shame, approval and disapproval in their minds. Their morality at this stage is a conventional or traditional one. Rules are regarded as fixed entities emanating from the gang, or from authority figures such as parents. It is only when they pass to the third stage, that of autonomy, that they question the validity of rules. They begin to appreciate that they could be otherwise. They see their necessity for social life and can imagine what it would be like if they were not observed. They are capable of putting themselves in other people's shoes. The morality of consent and reciprocity begins to take the place of the morality of convention and constraint.

All sorts of qualifications are made, of course, to this simple picture. Being at a particular stage is not an all or nothing affair, only a matter of the predominating view of rules. Individuals differ in the rate at which they pass through these stages and so do cultures. In some cultures, too, there is very little development beyond the second stage and individuals within a culture, where there is such development, may get stuck at earlier stages. All this can be admitted and is admitted. But the general picture still stands.

What is the explanation of this cultural invariance? Both Piaget and Kohlberg strongly resist, for a variety of reasons, the suggestion that it comes about through the explicit instruction of adults. Their view is that there are a limited number of possible ways in which rules can be conceived and that these form a hierarchical order, logically speaking. One could not, for instance, have an autonomous or rational form of morality in which one adopts certain rules for oneself unless one had been through a stage at which one knew what it is to follow a rule. So the third stage pre-supposes the second. What then determines the transition from one stage to another, supposing that the stages must occur in a certain order? The answer is that children gradually come to see things differently as a result of social interaction. This process can be aided by "cognitive stimulation", but children cannot be explicitly taught to see rules differently any more than, in the scientific sphere, they can be taught to appreciate a principle like that of the conservation of volume. Given appropriate experiences the penny gradually drops. The content of particular rules can, however, be explicitly taught. Just as, once a child has, by this dawning process, got the concept of a thing he can be taught to recognise countless particular things, so also once he is at the second stage, for instance, he can be taught a great number of rules by instruction backed up by praise or approval for conformity. The content of morality, therefore, can be taught; but its form develops.

What is to be made of this very exciting account of moral development which seems so pertinent because of its emphasis on the distinction between form and content in the sphere of learning? In my view it can only be accepted with certain major qualifications. Let me discuss first the thesis about the development of the form of morality. I will then pass to that about the learning of its content.

The first point to make, surely, is that a very restricted view is taken of teaching which is more or less equated with pinning children down and telling them things. This is contrasted with cognitive stimulation exemplified, on Kohlberg's view, by Socrates leading the slave in the *Meno* to grasp geometrical truths by a sustained process of cross-questioning. But surely Socrates was teaching the slave all right even though he was not telling him anything in any explicit way. For to teach is to bring someone to learn something by indicating in some way what has to be learned in a manner that is adapted to his level of understanding. This can be done without any explicit telling. Indeed the Socratic type of teaching method is much favoured in the primary schools for the learning of mathematics and many other things.

Secondly, "cognitive stimulation" must include much more indirect influences than this structured type of probing; for Kohlberg notes that there is much more of such stimulation in some types of home than in others and that this is why some children advance so much more quickly in their normal understanding. This stimulation must include the example set by adults and older children and methods of child-raising, as well as the amount of discussion and cross-questioning that goes on. It also includes the type of language that is used, which may be more or less abstract and hence more or less conducive to the development of reasoning. There is ample evidence from sociological and anthropological studies to confirm the importance of these more all-pervasive influences on the development of reasoning. So "cognitive stimulation" must be extended to cover all these social influences, many of which could be legitimately thought of as forms of teaching.

Thirdly, this account of moral development is explicitly put forward only as an account of the development of moral judgment. But there is a danger of this very cognitive account of moral development being equated with the whole story. And this would be very misleading. Consider, for instance, the development of the reasoning of the autonomous person. If his reasoning is going to influence his behaviour he has to be able to grasp that, for instance, the effect on other people is a relevant consideration in reflecting on the ethics of keeping a promise. He may be capable of seeing that other people may be inconvenienced but he may not care over much about their predicament. How do children come to care? Does it not start very early on and is it not, in part, due to the attitudes of parents from whom it is "caught"? Piaget only shows that in their very early years, children cannot perform the cognitive feat of connecting something like harm to others with questions about the rightness of rules. But there is no reason why sympathy for others should not be strongly felt before such reasoning develops. And there must be some early sensitisation of this sort for concern for others to function later as a principle which influences action in a rational morality. But there is no developmental account of the genesis of sympathy in the Piaget-Kohlberg scheme. At least, therefore, their account needs supplementation in relation to the motivational and affective aspects of morality. For, as has been argued since Socrates, there is a close connection between moral judgment and action. A satisfactory account of the development of the form of rational morality must not only study the development of the ability to reason; it must also pay attention to early sensitisation to features such as the suffering of others which later are to function as principles that make reasons relevant. And this account must cover their potentiality for influencing behaviour.

With these reservations, however, there is much to be said for the Piaget-Kohlberg type of emphasis with regard to the factors which affect the development of the rational form of morality. Indirect influences and stimulation are probably more relevant than explicit instruction.

What, then, is to be said about the learning of the content of morality? Piaget and Kohlberg have little to say about this because they think it unimportant. Kohlberg, for instance, tends to make rather derisive remarks about the "bag of virtues" conception of morality. He is impressed by evidence which he thinks, however correctly, shows that such disconnected habits are situation specific and of little importance in the development of moral character.

There are reasons, however, for suggesting that more attention should be paid to this aspect of morality. To start with, children and unreflective people have to live with others. And without a few essential virtues in their bag, they are likely to be a social menace. Hobbes once made the remark that a sobering feature of the human condition is that even a small child can kill a man when he is asleep. Also, if I am robbed in the street, my interest in whether the thief is at stage one, two, or three, in the way in which he views the operation, is a trifle academic; the point is that he has relieved me of my wallet and I am lying in the gutter, dimly struggling back to consciousness. Also, as has already been pointed out, children have to pass through the second "Good-boy" stage of morality before they can emerge to autonomy. They have to learn from the inside, as it were, that a rule is a rule. And they learn this, presumably, by generalising their experience of picking up some particular "bag of virtues". It may also be the case, too, that there may be ways of teaching them rules which fix them at this stage or which even hinder them from entering it. It could be that permissive parents are so anxious for their children to become autonomous that they expect them to pass from early egocentricity, to autonomy without going through the rather conventional, authority-ridden, second stage. So they shrink from anything that smacks of instruction on their part or from acting as models for the children.

Suppose that the case for providing children with some "bag of virtues" in their early years could be made out along these lines. Two questions then arise. Firstly, what are these virtues to be? Secondly, how are they to be taught? The answer to the first question is obvious enough if the structure of morality previously set out is accepted. These virtues will either be those such as concern for others, truth-telling, and fairness which later, when the autonomous stage is attained, will function as fundamental principles. Or they will be rules such as not stealing and the keeping of promises which can be defended by reference to fundamental principles as being indispensable for social life under almost any conceivable social conditions. If, because of the influence of early learning, children do develop rather an inflexible attitude to such rules, at least they will have such an attitude to rules that are likely to be apposite in any form of social life that they are likely to encounter in a time of social change.

But how is such a content of rules to be taught? Surely in any way that helps them to learn rules which does not stunt their capacity to develop a more autonomous attitude to them. When children are at or near the autonomous stage obviously discussion, persuasion, learning "for themselves" in practical situations with adults and peers, taking part in group activities such as games and drama productions, all help to stimulate development, to encourage seeing the other person's point of view, and so on. But what about the earlier stages before these more rational types of technique are meaningful to children? There will have to be a certain amount of instruction as well as models provided by parents and older children of such rules being followed; for most of them presuppose the grasp of complicated social arrangements. It would be impossible, for instance, for a child to understand what it is not to steal unless he is instructed in concepts to do with property, the difference between borrowing, being given something, and just taking it.

But such instruction and example will probably not be sufficient. For although it is often claimed that at this stage children enjoy conforming to rules in the way in which they enjoy keeping to the rules in games, the fact is that there would be no point in having such rules unless there existed in human nature some contrary tendency to do what the rule forbids. Some counter-inclinations have therefore to be brought into play to strengthen any tendency that exists to conform to the rule. The obvious counter-inclinations are those connected with rewards and punishments, praise and blame, approval and disapproval. These are the usual rudders that steer children into the channels of rule-conformity.

Psychologists of the Skinnerian school have much to say at this point about the options that are open to parents and teachers. They claim that positive "reinforcements", such as rewards, praise, and approval, are much more conducive to learning than negative "reinforcements". There is a mass of evidence, too, that many of the cases, studied by psychologists of the Freudian school, of people who became fixated at this stage with extreme irrational feelings of guilt and unworthiness about their conduct, are the victims of punitive and rejecting parental techniques. Evidence suggests that if children are to develop sensibly to an autonomous form of morality they require a consistent pattern of rules in their early years, backed up by approval for conformity. Development is likely to be stunted either by inconsistency in relation to what is expected or by no determinate expectations; for the anxiety occasioned by such conflict or anomie is not conducive to learning. Also under such conditions the child has little basis for predictability in his social environment which is necessary for the development of planning and reasoning generally. Alternatively development can be stunted by the use of punitive, rejecting techniques. These create anxiety which hinders learning and also undermines the development of self-confidence and trust.

It might be thought that this type of teaching smacks of second-handedness and a lack of authenticity. Children, it might be objected, are being lured into conformity without appreciating the proper reasons for it. This is a poor preparation for an authentic rational form of life. But the question has to be faced: what else is practicable? If children in their early years cannot acquire rules because they see the proper point of them and if, for the reasons explained, they have to start off with some "bag of virtues", it is difficult to see what other alternatives are open. If they can think in no other way about rules at this early stage, it is difficult to make the charge of inauthenticity stick. For there exists no possibility of authenticity. Also for some virtues, such as fairness or concern for others, it is difficult to see what further reasons *could* be given. For sensitivity to them is a precondition of there being reasons. For it is principles such as these which determine relevance in morals.

Something, however, can be said to rebut any charge of indoctrination which might be levelled against this mixture of instruction and positive "reinforcement". Indoctrination can be distinguished as a special type of instruction that can be employed at this stage. It consists in getting children to accept a *fixed* body of rules in such a way that they are incapacitated from adopting a critical or autonomous attitude towards them. Various techniques can be used which permanently fixate people in a "Good-boy" type of morality. They are thus led permanently to associate such a fixed body of rules with loyalty to their group or with obedience to some authority figure whose disapproval they dare not incur. The shaming techniques of the traditional English public school or of a communist collective are an example of this. But the public schools did at least encourage prefects to develop towards a more autonomous form of morality. Their practices encouraged a stage three morality for the few and stage two for the many. But not all instruction need take this indoctrination form. Indeed, it must not take this form if development towards a rational type of morality is to take place. Thus the uneasiness felt by parents and teachers about indoctrinating children, to which I made reference at the beginning of this talk, can perhaps be dispelled by explaining in this way what is specific to it as a teaching technique.

The distinction between the form and content of morality has been shown to be extremely relevant to the question, "How is morality to be taught?" as well as to questions about the structure of what is to be taught. For the crucial problem of methods in early moral education can be stated in this way: given that it is thought desirable that children should develop an autonomous form of morality, and given that, if Piaget and Kohlberg are right, they cannot, in their early years, learn in a way that presupposes such a form, how can a basic content for morality be provided that gives them a firm basis for moral behaviour without impeding the development of a rational form for it? What non-rational methods of teaching aid, or at least do not impede, the development of rationality? This is the basic problem of early moral education.

It is to this more specific problem that sensitive parents and teachers should address themselves instead of withdrawing from the scene for fear of indoctrination. For by withdrawing and by refusing to act as models and instructors they are equally in danger of preventing the development towards autonomy that they so much desire. In moral education the method is not quite the message; for a rational morality has to evolve out of conventional mores. Socratic techniques of discussion and persuasion are the ideal. But Socrates operated on the dubious wisdom enshrined in traditions and authorities. Without these he would have had nothing to be critical about. But these traditions themselves were passed on by less rational techniques. Children were "brought up" by their parents. But the problem is to ensure an early upbringing unlike that of Alcibiades, which nullified the later efforts even of a gifted educator such as Socrates.

9

IVAN ILLICH

Commentary

Biography

Ivan Illich was born in 1926 in Vienna of a Croatian Catholic father and a German Jewish mother. He was educated in Vienna and took a doctorate in history at the University of Salzburg before going on to the Gregorian University of Rome where he completed theological studies and was ordained a Catholic priest. He took up his first pastoral duties in a Puerto Rican immigrant region of New York as an assistant parish rector, and for five years involved himself in the social welfare problems of this disadvantaged minority. The Catholic Church recognised his talent and achievement in 1955 by conferring on him the title of Monsignor, a rather loosely defined accolade used for recognising distinction in priests. He then went to Puerto Rico itself, which is basically an American colony, taken from Spain in 1898 and since dignified with the ambiguous status of "commonwealth". Here Illich became vice-rector (equivalent to the American position of vice-president or the British of deputy vice-chancellor) of the Catholic University of Puerto Rico, situated in the capital of Ponce. Puerto Rico, like most Caribbean states, has a precarious economy and a low standard of living, and the poverty of the agricultural and urban unskilled workers is exacerbated by the high birth-rate. Throughout the fifties and sixties the island became a major centre for research and testing on the birth-control pill. Illich's support of this activity brought him into conflict with the American-born James McManus, Bishop of Puerto Rico, who tried to influence the course of the elections in 1960 by forbidding Catholics to vote for the re-election of the retiring governor Luis Marin because of the latter's support of birth-control programmes on the island. Illich was forced to resign.

On his return to the United States, Illich was given a compensatory appointment to the faculty of the Catholic Fordham University. There he developed the idea of founding a centre for the study of the general problems of humanity, particularly as they existed in Latin America, which by now he had seen were closely related to the developing crises of resources, population and technological expertise. His proposal to Fordham University and to Cardinal Spellman and the American Bishops' Committee on Latin America was successful and consequently in 1961 he was able to establish a Center of Intercultural Information at Cuernavaca in Mexico. Its original purpose was to prepare Catholic priests and missionaries for work in Latin America through programmes in the Spanish language and Latin American studies. It had a vigorous library which published a bulletin, *CIDOC Informa* for Latin American distribution. Gradually, the library and the bulletin became so influential that the Center changed its name and Illich moved further from the Church. The Center, now known as CIDOC (Center for Intercultural Documentation) has become completely secular and its basic purposes are the identification of human problems particularly in Latin America (and, by extension, in all developing countries), the collection of relevant data and the stimulation and heightening of public awareness of these problems and possible avenues of solution.

Illich's activities continued to bring him into conflict with the Catholic church, and in 1968 he was summoned to Rome for a secret Vatican enquiry. Illich refused to testify under oath and, in January 1969, all members of Catholic religious orders were forbidden to visit CIDOC, while Illich found himself obliged to renounce irrevocably his rights and privileges as a priest, including the title of Monsignor.[1] He was not, however, either unfrocked or excommunicated as the impression is sometimes given; he remains a priest, but in limbo — with no right to say mass, preach, confess or administer the sacraments — and has himself since stated publicly that he is "a clergyman who [having renounced his privileges] remains a very faithful, entirely orthodox believer in the church and lover of the church."[2] CIDOC has since become independent of the church and self-supporting, and Illich is its director. It was from this institution that Illich developed his very radical ideas on the future of education and the school.

Main Features of Illich's Educational Thought

Illich's significant innovation in education is the most revolutionary to date: the school itself, he argues, must be abolished as the chief institution of the process of education. Ever since he began to enunciate this concept (beginning in the mid-sixties) in many journal articles and press releases, brought together in his book *Deschooling Society* (1971), Illich found a large and receptive audience, and his ideas were discussed widely. They were not being received with any equanimity, however: generally he polarised opinion into two groups, of devotees and resolute opponents. Perhaps this is inevitable at the outset of any strongly imaginative, revolutionary programme that deals with fundamental human concerns. Study and evaluation of Illich's ideas of deschooling society and of the need for the development of alternatives to the school as the means of education are necessary, particularly since so many of his criticisms of contemporary education seem to persuade us that much is indeed wrong, and that improvement, radical or otherwise, is needed. Illich's main ideas are few and simple, although they are usually presented in a heavily rhetorical style, probably because of the press-conference climate in which they often appear.

What are Illich's criticisms of education? It is probably better to begin by setting out what he believes genuine and good education to be, and then to see how this is being subverted. However it is important to point out that a distinctive characteristic of his thought is the avoidance of philosophical principles: we will search in vain through his writings for any theory of the nature of existence, or of knowledge, or of values. Even though Illich may remain loyal to the Catholic church it is not possible to impute any particular philosophy to him by virtue of this, since there is no Catholic orthodoxy in philosophy. Although it remains generally most responsive to the Aristotelian position developed by Thomas Aquinas, Catholicism still has its adherents to the Platonist position developed successively by Augustine and Duns Scotus, as well as to mysticism and even to pragmatism. In many ways Illich's position seems to be closest to a Marxist philosophy, particularly in his epistemological view that knowledge is a function of active engagements in real situations. Nonetheless he is never explicit in these matters. His view of education does not come from a philosophic position; instead he develops it from an intuitive description of man and society.

The model that he implies, particularly in his many Latin American examples, is an idealistic vision of the village where all activities proceed to further individual and social life, these two forms of life coexisting in an easy, complementary relationship with no necessary conflict. Illich then makes the assumption that by nature man is curious and concerned about his environment, which in turn challenges him to respond, and that response is made possible and effective by man's flexibility, plasticity and ingenuity. In responding to the challenge of the environment both man and society effect learning, and this, seen in its totality, is education. So Illich attempts to avoid the process-product dichotomy and to suggest a view of education as an abstract conceptualisation of continued flexible learning in real-life situations. Of course, there is no such society in existence that achieves this; all, he claims, have been degraded by the imposition of an alien conception of education and its bastard offspring of the school.

A great deal of Illich's thinking follows a Marxist interpretation of history, and he asserts that the school is so vicious and antihuman an institution that it must immediately — or as soon as practicable — be disestablished, just as the Catholic church was separated from the State last century in many countries. It would thus be reasonable to expect him to demonstrate how education and the school have become this way. Unfortunately he does not (although his former associate, Everett Reimer, has given a very brief resumé of the history of the school in his provocative book *School is Dead*). Instead, Illich simply begins with the assertion that the school has subverted education.

How, then, is this manifested? First of all, for Illich the "school" is a generic term; it encompasses all institutions from kindergartens through to colleges and universities, public and restricted, and at base all of these form part of a gigantic integrated system that has as its purpose the "processing" of people for employment in different vocations. It most emphatically, in his view, does not prepare individuals for a meaningful life. Moreover, the school, seen in this generic way, has a virtual monopoly through its control of the certification principle. Almost every vocation in modern life requires a certificate, ticket, diploma or degree of some kind before it can be practised, and behind these formal qualifications there is a required course or curriculum (and although Illich never makes this explicit, the Latin etymology of the word "curriculum" as a "race", or "course to be run", helps bring the idea out). So formalised has this certification principle become that those who fail to secure such qualifications become tagged with the pejorative epithet "dropout".

As part of this processing activity, and chiefly as a consequence of the school serving a market-place economy, knowledge itself, which once was generated in real situations, becomes processed and packaged into what Illich calls "commodities", with the consequence that it becomes remote and eventually meaningless. Illich generally uses commercial metaphors, particularly that of the schools holding a "knowledge stock" from which the curriculum is drawn; he might have added that, just as modern supermarket products are rendered as inert as possible, chiefly through added preservative drugs, to give a longer "shelf-life", so too has this happened in the curriculum. Individuals in the advanced technological societies are all compelled to take part in this ritual of schooling, and this in itself has created serious pressures. Schools are unbalanced social institutions and they share much in common with penitentiaries, armies, convents and monasteries in that they have large, relatively homogenous sub-populations held together by rigorous discipline, and if necessary, coercion. So the need for social control is very pressing, and in the case of the school, already maintained at vast expense, added costs are incurred in the form of research devoted to finding ways of improving this control. But because such control must be maintained, much effort in educational research — particularly in psychology and sociology — is directed towards sugar-coating the pill of compulsion, towards finding the best possible strategies for seeing that children keep to the relentless grind of acquiring as big a share of knowledge stock as possible with the least possible distress or complaint. Children are, Illich says, conditioned to accept these as the right and proper values of education and as the role of its institution, the school. And these pressures to conform make up what he calls the "hidden curriculum". But this is not working in the advanced societies, and in the United States particularly schooling is showing signs of considerable distress. When this approach to education is imposed upon developing societies, such as we find in Latin America, as Illich and his former associate Paulo Freire (the Brazilian educational reformer) are so acutely conscious, the problems become much more acute.

This "ritual of initiation", as Illich calls it, through the medium of the school with its "age-specific" population, into a commodity-oriented culture, is a "pedagogical invasion" of personal privacy, of man's inherent right to remain unviolated by the "do-good" educational missionaries. In its effects, he says in a classical Marxist concept, it leads to the alienation of persons from learning — and Illich is deeply aware that learning, and education as he sees it in the true sense, is vital to the development and maintenance of our humanity.

Illich remains adamant in the face of current proposals to reform the school. Indeed, he is extremely scornful of efforts to improve its operations as it is now conducted, for he sees these simply as more clever strategies to achieve the same ends of certification. Making the child more active and more participant in its learning, and making the curriculum more meaningful and more relevant, he sees as deceptive, for they disguise the intention of the school, which still remains that of processing people for alienated vocations; of producing non-people. He is equally derisive of the efforts to fill classrooms with electronic gadgetry, and he has the greatest contempt for, and fear of, those who would turn the whole world into a "global schoolhouse": that way lies complete big-brotherly totalitarianism. He doesn't use the precise concept of innocence, but behind his evocative prose there is always the implicit concept of rape, of the forceful defloration of an original wholeness. And in this, perhaps, he betrays his priestly vocation and fears.

Mankind is in crisis, and the school, with its faulty conception of education, is heightening this. What can be done? Deschooling society is only the destructive phase: what are the constructive steps that can be taken? Make learning completely non-formal, Illich says. Put it in its rightful place as the consequence of people being curious, active, alert and fluid and engaging themselves in the complementary activities (he does not, like Dewey, call them problems) of individual and social life. In the first instance this involves a radical change in public attitude; society itself must recognise the need for drastic change and act to implement the conviction that access to learning situations must be provided for, and kept open to, every person throughout life. This in turn means acceptance of the fact that people learn "real" and meaningful knowledge in any case in informal and random ways and not through the formalised ritual of schooling. So Illich puts forward, as the alternative to the school, his theory of "learning webs".

How do we learn? Illich asks. From four sources, he replies — things, models, peers and elders — and from these he spins his own theory of learning webs. He admits that the metaphor of a web is inadequate, because it suggests entanglement and snaring, but he feels restricted by the availability of words in the language. It is also a sociological concept and this is how he employs it, suggesting the complex interconnection of events in life. His is a positive meaning of the term. "Things", in the broadest sense of the word, imply the material aspect of our culture, and of course man, in a technological society, must have access to them. Illich suggests a much greater range of availability. "Models" has an intangible meaning; he suggests that we learn from them in the sense of patterns and paradigms exemplified in people, ideas and practices. "Peers" and "elders" are self-explanatory. Having set these up as sources of learning, Illich then suggests that these should be provided at maximum public availability; they already exist in varying degrees but are limited and restricted by private ownership. He wants access to be maximised and maintained that way, using all of the resources of our technology to support it. If possible, a vast computer-information storage and retrieval system should be set up.

In Illich's educational theory, then, education is a process of engagement in living. There is no room for concepts of superiority among people; there are only differences, and he never specifies where these come from. Yet these differences lead us to live our lives in different ways and to seek various forms of fulfilment. All are equally worthy — the rock group and the chamber consort — if they satisfy our needs for involvement. Questions of value are relative and personal; we have no right to impose our conceptions on others. The curriculum itself, in the traditional sense, is totally abolished; the content of learning is completely a matter of personal need drawn from life activities themselves, gained in the environment of objects, models, peers and elders. Teachers, of course, continue to exist, but their role is completely transmogrified. Illich would call them "educators" because the idea of a "teacher" is too authoritarian and subject-centred. But there is serious intent to the change of name; it implies a radical change of function to one of providing help in achieving learning tasks self-initiated by the learner. The state itself has no explicit role in providing education because there are no schools, and yet, as an expression of a freely educated population, it will provide a maximum support system. Moral growth, again, remains a totally personal achievement, but concerning this Illich is largely silent. We are forced to draw our own deductions about this, obliquely, from his work.

Illich's ideas have generated tremendous controversy, and he himself appears to enjoy being at the centre of it. So often when taxed with difficult questions at conferences, Illich disclaims the need to provide a thoroughly comprehensive theory. He takes the role of a prophet (although he does not use that word) who has given an exciting sketch of a theory intended expressly to transform human society, across the face of the earth, down to its very foundations; he claims it is a task for us all to work out the details. If we want to act on his proposals, then indeed it is our task, for we cannot allow ourselves — by nature of his theory — to be guided by any "big brother", even Big Brother Ivan.

If we do want to act on his theory, even to oppose it, we need first to assess it. This involves the procedures of philosophical scrutiny, and a good way of beginning is to look at his basic assumptions. Many reforming theories begin by suggesting an original condition of innocent nature, of which the outstanding example is Rousseau's proclamation in the eighteenth century of the natural goodness of man. All such utopian schemes need to be assessed for their correspondence with reality as we know it. So we must question Illich's ideological picture of the village, of flexible, multifaceted people pursuing learning with enthusiasm, or at least with involvement. We very quickly come up against the question of education as transcendence, for this idea includes that of value development. From whence do values — standards of all kinds — arise? Surely not just from empirical workability, for if so we remain at a crudely pragmatic level. Values come also from ideals — as Illich himself exemplifies in putting forward his theories — and these ideals themselves are constantly broadened by being lifted from the context of everyday activities and seen against a wider background. It is this broader frame of reference that constitutes our high culture, and to develop and maintain it we must accept the notion of knowledge subsisting in symbolic and vicarious form. Illich seems to have difficulty with the realm of abstract ideas; so many of his suggestions for reform portray the learner as largely if not completely involved in a range of concrete operations. Yet if values are to be generated, they must come from a context of abstract thinking, and if the institution of the school — in its generic sense — is abolished, where will such ideas be generated and how communicated? Surely not by the mass media, which Illich abhors, in the global schoolroom.

We must also question his argument that the school operates solely on the model he presents. Have his own experiences coloured his thoughts here? European education in the thirties certainly was characterised by its relentless pressure on students, and there is no doubt that much contemporary American schooling is at the same time vacuous and anxiety-inducing. It is also true to say that the American school when imposed on backward Latin America is a mixed blessing. But is that the total picture? Illich's failure to provide an adequate historical explanation for the present position of the school is unacceptable; he takes advantage of the lack of knowledge of most of his readers. Granted everything that he says about the school, does this prove that it has failed? and if so, what are his tests and where is his proof? For Illich only asserts these points. He is gripped in a love-hate relationship with modern technology; on the one hand he wants children to be engaged in meaningful tasks in "real life" and not be processed in schools for a vocation in a largely urbanised industrial society, yet on the other he wants to give the peasants of Bolivia and Peru tape recorders, motorised tricycles and a network of high-density roads so as to improve their lives. From whence do the scientists, engineers and technicians come to provide this industrial hardware? And what kind of technological infrastructure is required, say, to provide and maintain the network of roads he wants for the peasants in South America? These questions have to be answered seriously and all of their consequences thought out. If our present level of technology, which Illich sees as being potentially available to enrich life (for the four learning webs are to be computer supported), is at such a high state and comes through our present system of schools, how can it be seriously held that the school has failed entirely?

A promising line of investigation is to enquire into the history of the school and the concept of education, particularly in the nineteenth century, to determine just where the school began to become maladaptive. It is doubtful if anyone could seriously oppose Illich's diagnosis of the ills of the school, but he has no copyright on this claim: it was made as early as 2000 B.C. in a document that comments bitterly on rote learning under the teacher's coercive rod, and remains as a major theme in the history of education down to the present day. Improvements in the institution of the school should certainly be sought by us all, but are we acting rationally in arguing for its abolition? Is Illich really overreacting, playing the role of iconoclast by attempting to smash one of our sacred images? Consider his alternative of learning webs. What is new here? Surely all of these have always existed as part of the informal process of education which is recognised as being valuable? Could it be said that with the idea of the learning web of the skill exchange he has discovered the classified pages of the newspaper and the telephone directory? And what is there to guarantee that his learning webs will not themselves become formalised and organised so that they become in effect a school and so defeat the purpose they were intended to serve? In its best possible sense, the learning web theory is extremely sophisticated, but it certainly would be unusable by illiterates, the disadvantaged and the unmotivated. Indeed, as Illich develops it, the idea seems to hold the promise more than ever of reinforcing the middle class.

Again, it is characteristic of Illich, as of other "alternative" schooling theorists, to absolutise present values and needs and to take an unhistorical viewpoint. Surely there were valid reasons for the development of the school in the nineteenth century as an instrument of mass education. Industry was in its ugliest phases, child labour laws were either non-existent, or poorly enacted and ineffectively enforced. A reading of the Newgate Calendar for eighteenth- and nineteenth-century England with its records of the regular hanging of children as young as eight years for petty crimes will show how necessary it was to protect children. Compulsory mass schooling was found to be a ready means; and, we must remember, it *has* worked. The present growth of dissent against the school should be seen as a healthy sign, as a development of a mature society that is now becoming aware that the institution of the school has simply been overloaded; freighted with an ever-increasing number of peripheral tasks. But it is important to take an historical view and to realise that the school, and mass education over the past hundred years, has obviously been quite efficient in bringing us to the present level of articulate awareness. Could Illich himself protest so stridently if he had not been carefully schooled by the very processes he now denounces?

Freedom is not an absolute criterion in education and children are not, by virtue of their immaturity, totally qualified to judge their future needs. Is it realistic to ignore the fact that there are many circumstances where it is in the child's interest to learn something whose value will only be recognised and appreciated later? Further, certification in its truest sense, that is, in the sense of certifying fitness, cannot be in itself either good or bad. Illich quite rightly objects to excessive goal-attaining in the form of competition for grades and marks. But surely certification in its sense of assessment is necessary if done judiciously and with its discriminatory aspects minimised as much as possible.

The more positive aspects of Illich's recommendations gave rise to some fruitful questioning and the excessive emotionalism of the movement has been replaced by a better assessment of what schools are, and what they can most properly do. Schools in the full sense — from the beginning grades through to universities — may be seen in many ways, and of course they are frequently identified as substantive structures. This, however, is to miss their essential meaning. Of course schools need modification and improvement, and it will help if they are seen in their historically evolutionary role as communities of scholars. If we could define more effectively the activities that schools are best suited to pursue, and so prune out much of their extraneous activities (perhaps transferring these to other learning situations), would this not meet our needs? Schools perform many positive functions — even if some they do badly — of which the most important is providing a grounding in the basic disciplines and forms of thought, and these in themselves contain the techniques for advancing knowledge.

In dispensing with the school there is the real danger of dispensing with culture and civilisation. For another essential function of the school is that of maintaining our intellectual consciousness; schools sustain the high culture from which we all draw and on which the continuation of society depends. They alone of all human agencies are charged with the task of intellectual excellence, with providing the means of transcending the limited, the bigoted and the parochial. If they have been temporarily swamped by the demands of being all things to all people, and have been rather complaisant in accepting so many functions, isn't this rather our own fault? And doesn't the remedy lie in developing other educational institutions to supplement the school? Indeed, if the school has been excessively concerned with vocational and socialising roles, does this mean that it must be abolished once these roles are performed by other agencies? Should we not re-examine our ideas on, and priorities in, education? Have we any guarantee that deschooling society will effect the required solution?

Ivan Illich has done us all a signal service; he has had widespread influence and has fostered a radically new idea which if valid would have enormous consequences. Acting as a spokesman for a whole group of critics who are presently attacking the capitalist bureaucratic system under which schools are largely operated, he has made us stop and think carefully about the present wholesale proliferation of schools as a universal social instrument to effect nearly every kind of purpose. But Illich himself betrays a well-schooled background, and in his own sufficiently frequent references to the original Greek concept of *scholé*, he has pointed in a direction of education for transcendence of our personal limitations that we might reasonably continue to hold as a valid function of the schools.

NOTES AND REFERENCES

1. *Christian Century*, 16 April 1969, p. 503.
2. *Christianity in Crisis*, 4 August 1969, XXIX, No. 14, pp. 213f.

SELECT BIBLIOGRAPHY

Illich is represented in a large number of journal articles, press interviews, occasional papers and pamphlets, mostly of limited circulation. A thorough coverage of these up to 1971, and those of his associates will be found in:
JOHN OHLIGER and COLLEEN MCCARTHY (Eds), *Lifelong Learning or Lifelong Schooling? A Tentative View of the Ideas of Ivan Illich with a Quotational Bibliography*, Syracuse University Publications in Continuing Education, New York.

Illich's major writings on education are:

Books:

Deschooling Society, Calder and Boyars, London, 1971 and Harper and Row, New York, 1971.

Celebration of Awareness, Calder and Boyars, London, 1971 and Doubleday, New York, 1970.
  (This edition includes two chapters relevant to education: Chapter 8 "The Futility of Schooling"
  and Chapter 9 "School: The Sacred Cow".)

Journal Articles and Essays:

"After Deschooling, What?" *Social Policy*, Sept–Oct 1971. Reprinted in A. Gartner *et al*, (Eds.)
  After Deschooling, What?, Harper & Row, New York, 1973.

"The Alternative to Schooling", *Saturday Review*, 19 June 1971.

"The Breakdown of Schools: A Problem or a Symptom?", *Interchange*, II, No. 4, 1971.

"Imprisoned in the Global Classroom", (with E. Verne). Published along with the essay
  "Political Inversion" as *Imprisoned in the Global Classroom*, Writers and Readers Publishing
  Co-operative, London, 1976.

"Vernacular Values and Education", *Teachers College Record*, LXXXI, No. 1, Fall 1979.

"Eco-Paedagogics and the Commons", *New Education*, VI, 2, 1984.

Selections

Two selections from the writings of Ivan Illich are given here. The first is his article from the Saturday Review *entitled "The Alternative to Schooling". This presents his fundamental criticisms of the school and of education as it is currently mediated. In this article he expounds on his thesis of the school as an agent of a capitalist consumer-oriented society in which the chief outcome is the alienation of man from genuine, socially responsible learning. The second selection is "Learning Webs", from his major educational book,* Deschooling Society. *In this chapter he sets out his positive theory of organising "learning webs" throughout the community as a proper means of education.*

The Alternative to Schooling

For generations we have tried to make the world a better place by providing more and more schooling, but so far the endeavour has failed. What we have learned instead is that forcing all children to climb an open-ended education ladder cannot enhance equality but must favour the individual who starts out earlier, healthier, or better prepared; that enforced instruction deadens for most people the will for independent learning; and that knowledge treated as a commodity, delivered in packages, and accepted as private property once it is acquired, must always be scarce.

In response, critics of the educational system are now proposing strong and unorthodox remedies that range from the voucher plan, which would enable each person to buy the education of his choice on an open market, to shifting the responsibility for education from the school to the media and to apprenticeship on the job. Some individuals foresee that the school will have to be disestablished just as the church was disestablished all over the world during the last two centuries. Other reformers propose to replace the universal school with various new systems that would, they claim, better prepare everybody for life in modern society. These proposals for new educational institutions fall into three broad categories: the reformation of the classroom within the school system; the dispersal of free schools throughout society; and the transformation of all society into one huge classroom. But these three approaches — the reformed classroom, the free school, and the world-wide classroom — represent three stages in a proposed escalation of education in which each step threatens more subtle and more pervasive social control than the one it replaces.

I believe that the disestablishment of the school has become inevitable and that this end of an illusion should fill us with hope. But I also believe that the end of the "age of schooling" could usher in the epoch of the global schoolhouse that would be distinguishable only in name from a global madhouse or global prison in which education, correction, and adjustment

From I. ILLICH, "Alternative to Schooling". First appeared in *Saturday Review*, 19 June, 1971. Reprinted by permission of publisher and author. Copyright Ivan Illich.

become synonymous. I therefore believe that the breakdown of the school forces us to look beyond its imminent demise and to face fundamental alter natives in education. Either we can work for fearsome and potent new educational devices that teach about a world which progressively becomes more opaque and forbidding for man, or we can set the conditions for a new era in which technology would be used to make society more simple and transparent, so that all men can once again know the facts and use the tools that shape their lives. In short, we can disestablish schools or we can deschool culture.

In order to see clearly the alternatives we face, we must first distinguish education from schooling, which means separating the humanistic intent of the teacher from the impact of the invariant structure of the school. This hidden structure constitutes a course of instruction that stays forever beyond the control of the teacher or of his school board. It conveys indelibly the message that only through schooling can an individual prepare himself for adulthood in society, that what is not taught in schools is of little value, and that what is learned outside of school is not worth knowing. I call it the hidden curriculum of schooling, because it constitutes the unalterable framework of the system, within which all changes in the curriculum are made.

The hidden curriculum is always the same regardless of school or place. It requires all children of a certain age to assemble in groups of about thirty, under the authority of a certified teacher, for some five hundred to a thousand or more hours each year. It doesn't matter whether the curriculum is designed to teach the principles of fascism, liberalism, Catholicism, or socialism; or whether the purpose of the school is to produce Soviet or United States citizens, mechanics, or doctors. It makes no difference whether the teacher is authoritarian or permissive, whether he imposes his own creed or teaches students to think for themselves. What is important is that students learn that education is valuable when it is acquired in the school through a graded process of consumption; that the degree of success the individual will enjoy in society depends on the amount of learning he consumes; and that learning *about* the world is more valuable than learning *from* the world.

It must be clearly understood that the hidden curriculum translates learning from an activity into a commodity — for which the school monopolises the market. In all countries knowledge is regarded as the first necessity for survival, but also as a form of currency more liquid than rubles or dollars. We have become accustomed, through Karl Marx's writings, to speak about the alienation of the worker from his work in a class society. We must now recognise the estrangement of man from his learning when it becomes the product of a service profession and he becomes the consumer.

The more learning an individual consumes, the more "knowledge stock" he acquires. The hidden curriculum therefore defines a new class structure for society within which the large consumers of knowledge — those who have acquired large quantities of knowledge stock — enjoy special privileges, high income, and access to the more powerful tools of production. This kind of knowledge-capitalism has been accepted in all industrialised societies and establishes a rationale for the distribution of jobs and income. (This point is especially important in the light of the lack of correspondence between schooling and occupational competence established in studies such as Ivar Berg's *Education and Jobs: The Great Training Robbery*.)[1]

The endeavour to put all men through successive stages of enlightenment is rooted deeply in alchemy, the great art of the waning Middle Ages. John Amos Comenius, a Moravian bishop, self-styled Pansophist, and pedagogue, is rightly considered one of the founders of the modern schools. He was among the first to propose seven or twelve grades of compulsory learning. In his *Magna Didactica*,[2] he described schools as devices to "teach everybody everything" and outlined a blueprint for the assembly-line production of knowledge, which according to his method would make education cheaper and better and make growth into full humanity possible for all. But Comenius was not only an early efficiency expert, he was an alchemist who adopted the technical language of his craft to describe the art of rearing children. The alchemist sought to refine base elements by leading their distilled spirits through twelve stages of successive enlightenment, so that for their own and all the world's benefit they might be transmuted into gold. Of course, alchemists failed no matter how often they tried, but each time their "science" yielded new reasons for their failure, and they tried again.

Pedagogy opened a new chapter in the history of *ars magna*. Education became the search for an alchemic process that would bring forth a new type of man, who would fit into an environment created by scientific magic. But, no matter how much each generation spent on its schools, it always turned out that the majority of people were unfit for enlightenment by this process and had to be discarded as unprepared for life in a man-made world.

Educational reformers who accept the idea that schools have failed fall into three groups. The most respectable are certainly the great masters of alchemy who promise better schools. The most seductive are popular magicians, who promise to make every kitchen into an alchemic lab. The most sinister are the new Masons of the Universe, who want to transform the entire world into one huge temple of learning. Notable among today's masters of alchemy are certain research directors employed or sponsored by the large foundations who believe that schools, if they could somehow be improved, could also become economically more feasible than those that are now in trouble, and simultaneously could sell a larger package of services. Those who are concerned primarily with the curriculum claim that it is outdated or irrelevant. So the curriculum is filled with new packaged courses on African Culture, North American Imperialism, Women's Lib, Pollution, or the Consumer Society. Passive learning is wrong — it is indeed — so we graciously allow students to decide what and how they want to be taught. Schools are prison houses. Therefore, principals are authorised to approve teach-outs, moving the school desks to a roped-off Harlem street. Sensitivity training becomes fashionable. So, we import group therapy into the classroom. School which was supposed to teach everybody everything, now becomes all things to all children.

Other critics emphasise that schools make inefficient use of modern science. Some would administer drugs to make it easier for the instructor to change the child's behaviour. Others would transform school into a stadium for educational gaming. Still others would electrify the classroom. If they are simplistic disciples of McLuhan, they replace blackboards and textbooks with multi-media happenings; if they follow Skinner, they claim to be able to modify behaviour more efficiently than old-fashioned classroom practitioners can.

Most of these changes have, of course, some good effects. The experimental schools have fewer truants. Parents do have a greater feeling of participation in a decentralised district. Pupils, assigned by their teacher to an apprenticeship, do often turn out more competent than those who stay in the classroom. Some children do improve their knowledge of Spanish in the language lab because they prefer playing with the knobs of a tape recorder to conversation with their Puerto Rican peers. Yet all these improvements operate within predictably narrow limits, since they leave the hidden curriculum of school intact.

Some reformers would like to shake loose from the hidden curriculum, but they rarely succeed. Free schools that lead to further free schools produce a mirage of freedom, even though the chain of attendance is frequently interrupted by long stretches of loafing. Attendance through seduction inculcates the need for educational treatment more persuasively than the reluctant attendance enforced by a truant officer. Permissive teachers in a padded classroom can easily render their pupils impotent to survive once they leave.

Learning in these schools often remains nothing more than the acquisition of socially valued skills defined, in this instance, by the consensus of a commune rather than by the decree of a school board. New presbyter is but old priest writ large.

Free schools, to be truly free, must meet two conditions: First, they must be run in a way to prevent the reintroduction of the hidden curriculum of graded attendance and certified students studying at the feet of certified teachers. And, more importantly, they must provide a framework in which all participants — staff and pupils — can free themselves from the hidden foundations of a schooled society. The first condition is frequently incorporated in the stated aims of a free school. The second condition is only rarely recognised, and is difficult to state as the goal of a free school.

It is useful to distinguish between the hidden curriculum, which I have described, and the occult foundations of schooling. The hidden curriculum is a ritual that can be considered the official initiation into modern society; institutionally established through the school. It is the purpose of this ritual to hide from its participants the contradictions between the myth of an egalitarian society and the class-conscious reality it certifies. Once they are recognised as such, rituals lose their power, and this is what is now beginning to happen to schooling. But there are certain fundamental assumptions about growing up — the occult foundations — which now find their expression in the ceremonial of schooling, and which could easily be reinforced by what free schools do.

Among these assumptions is what Peter Schrag calls the "immigration syndrome", which impels us to treat all people as if they were newcomers who must go through a naturalisation process. Only certified consumers of knowledge are admitted to citizenship. Men are not born equal, but are made equal through gestation by *Alma Mater*.

The rhetoric of all schools states that they form a man for the future, but they do not release him for his task before he has developed a high level of tolerance to the ways of his elders: education *for* his life rather than *in* everyday life. Few free schools can avoid doing precisely this. Nevertheless they are among the most important centres from which a new lifestyle radiates, not because of the effect their graduates will have but, rather, because elders who choose to bring up their children without the benefit of properly ordained teachers frequently belong to a radical minority and because their preoccupation with the rearing of their children sustains them in their new style.

The most dangerous category of educational reformer is one who argues that knowledge can be produced and sold much more effectively on an open market than on one controlled by school. These people argue that most skills can be easily acquired from skill-models if the learner is truly interested in their acquisition; that individual entitlements can provide a more equal purchasing power for education. They demand a careful separation of the process by which knowledge is acquired from the process by which it is measured and certified. These seem to me obvious statements. But it would be a fallacy to believe that the establishment of a free market for knowledge would constitute a radical alternative in education.

The establishment of a free market would indeed abolish what I have previously called the hidden curriculum of present schooling — its age-specific attendance at a graded curriculum. Equally, a free market would at first give the appearance of counteracting what I have called the occult foundations of a schooled society: the "immigration syndrome", the institutional monopoly of teaching, and the ritual of linear initiation. But at the same time a free market in education would provide the alchemist with innumerable hidden hands to fit each man into the multiple, tight little niches a more complex technocracy can provide.

Many decades of reliance on schooling has turned knowledge into a commodity, a marketable staple of a special kind. Knowledge is now regarded simultaneously as a first necessity and also as society's most precious currency. (The transformation of knowledge into a commodity is reflected in a corresponding transformation of language. Words that formerly functioned as verbs are becoming nouns that designate possessions. Until recently dwelling and learning and even healing designated activities. They are now usually conceived as commodities or services to be delivered. We talk about the manufacture of housing or the delivery of medical care. Men are no longer regarded fit to house or heal themselves. In such a society people come to believe that professional services are more valuable than personal care. Instead of learning how to nurse grandmother, the teenager learns to picket the hospital that does not admit her.) This attitude could easily survive the disestablishment of school, just as affiliation with a church remained a condition for office long after the adoption of the First Amendment. It is even more evident that test batteries measuring complex knowledge-packages could easily survive the disestablishment of school — and with this would go the compulsion to obligate everybody to acquire a minimum package in the knowledge stock. The scientific measurement of each man's worth and the alchemic dream of each man's "educability to his full humanity" would finally coincide. Under the appearance of a "free" market, the global village would turn into an environmental womb where pedagogic therapists control the complex navel by which each man is nourished.

At present schools limit the teacher's competence to the classroom. They prevent him from claiming man's whole life as his domain. The demise of school will remove this restriction and give a semblance of legitimacy to the lifelong pedagogical invasion of everybody's privacy. It will open the way for a scramble for "knowledge" on a free market, which would lead us toward the paradox of a vulgar, albeit seemingly egalitarian, meritocracy. Unless the concept of knowledge is transformed, the disestablishment of school will lead to a wedding between a growing meritocratic system that separates learning from certification and a society committed to provide therapy for each man until he is ripe for the gilded age.

For those who subscribe to the technocratic ethos, whatever is technically possible must be made available at least to a few whether they want it or not. Neither the privation nor the frustration of the majority counts. If cobalt treatment is possible, then the city of Tegucigalpa needs one apparatus in each of its two major hospitals, at a cost that would free an important part of the population of Honduras from parasites. If supersonic speeds are possible, then it must speed the travel of some. If the flight to Mars can be conceived, then a rationale must be found to make it appear a necessity. In the technocratic ethos poverty is modernised: Not only are old alternatives closed off by new monopolies, but the lack of necessities is also compounded by a growing spread between those services that are technologically feasible and those that are in fact available to the majority.

A teacher turns "educator" when he adopts this technocratic ethos. He then acts as if education were a technological enterprise designed to make man fit into whatever environment the "progress" of science creates. He seems blind to the evidence that constant obsolescence of all commodities comes at a high price: the mounting cost of training people to know about them. He seems to forget that the rising cost of tools is purchased at a high price in education: They decrease the labor intensity of the economy, make learning on the job impossible or, at best, a privilege for a few. All over the world the cost of educating men for society rises faster than the productivity of the entire economy, and fewer people have a sense of intelligent participation in the commonweal.

A revolution against those forms of privilege and power, which are based on claims to professional knowledge, must start with a transformation of consciousness about the nature of learning. This means, above all, a shift of responsibility for teaching and learning. Knowledge can be defined as a commodity only as long as it is viewed as the result of institutional enterprise or as the fulfilment of institutional objectives. Only when a man recovers the sense of personal responsibility for what he learns and teaches can this spell be broken and the alienation of learning from living be overcome.

The recovery of the power to learn or to teach means that the teacher who takes the risk of interfering in somebody else's private affairs also assumes responsibility for the results. Similarly, the student who exposes himself to the influence of a teacher must take responsibility for his own education. For such purposes educational institutions — if they are at all needed — ideally take the form of facility centres where one can get a roof of the right size over his head, access to a piano or a kiln, and to records, books, or slides. Schools, TV stations, theatres, and the like are designed primarily for use by professionals. Deschooling society means above all the denial of professional status for the second-oldest profession, namely teaching. The certification of teachers now constitutes an undue restriction of the right to free speech: the corporate structure and professional pretensions of journalism an undue restriction on the right to free press. Compulsory attendance rules interfere with free assembly. The deschooling of society is nothing less than a cultural mutation by which a people recovers the effective use of its constitutional freedoms: learning and teaching by men who know that they are born free rather than treated to freedom. Most people learn most of the time when they do whatever they enjoy; most people are curious and want to give meaning to whatever they come in contact with; and most people are capable of personal intimate intercourse with others unless they are stupefied by inhuman work or turned off by schooling.

The fact that people in rich countries do not learn much on their own constitutes no proof to the contrary. Rather it is a consequence of life in an environment from which, paradoxically, they cannot learn much, precisely because it is so highly programmed. They are constantly frustrated by the structure of contemporary society in which the facts on which decisions can be made have become elusive. They live in an environment in which tools that can be used for creative purposes have become luxuries, an environment in which channels of communication serve a few to talk to many.

A modern myth would make us believe that the sense of impotence with which most life today is permeated is a consequence of technology that cannot but create huge systems. But it is not technology that makes systems huge, tools immensely powerful, channels of communication one-directional. Quite the contrary: Properly controlled, technology could provide each man with the ability to understand his environment better, to shape it powerfully with his own hands, and to permit him full intercommunication to a degree never before possible. Such an alternative use of technology constitutes the central alternative in education.

If a person is to grow up he needs, first of all, access to things, to places and to processes, to events and to records. He needs to see, to touch, to tinker with, to grasp whatever there is in a meaningful setting. This access is now largely denied. When knowledge became a commodity, it acquired the protections of private property, and thus a principle designed to guard personal intimacy became a rationale for declaring facts off limits for people without the proper credentials. In schools teachers keep knowledge to themselves unless it fits into the day's programme. The media inform, but exclude those things they regard as unfit to print. Information is locked into special languages, and specialised teachers live off its retranslation. Patents are protected by corporations, secrets are guarded by bureaucracies, and the power to keep others out of private preserves — be they cockpits, law offices, junkyards, or clinics — is jealously guarded by professions, institutions, and nations. Neither the political nor the professional structure of our societies, East and West, could withstand the elimination of the power to keep entire classes of people from facts that could serve them. The access to facts that I advocate goes far beyond truth in labelling. Access must be built into reality, while all we ask from advertising is a guarantee that it does not mislead. Access to reality constitutes a fundamental alternative in education to a system that only purports to teach *about* it.

Abolishing the right to corporate secrecy — even when professional opinion holds that this secrecy serves the common good — is, as shall presently appear, a much more radical political goal than the traditional demand for public ownership or control of the tools of production. The socialisation of tools without the effective socialisation of know-how in their use tends to put the knowledge-capitalist into the position formerly held by the financier. The technocrat's only claim to power is the stock he holds in some class of scarce and secret knowledge, and the best means to protect its value is a large and capital-intensive organisation that renders access to know-how formidable and forbidding.

It does not take much time for the interested learner to acquire almost any skill that he wants to use. We tend to forget this in a society where professional teachers monopolise entrance into all fields, and thereby stamp teaching by uncertified individuals as quackery. There are few mechanical skills used in industry or research that are as demanding, complex, and dangerous as driving cars, a skill that most people quickly acquire from a peer. Not all people are suited for advanced logic, yet those who are make rapid progress if they are challenged to play mathematical games at an early age. One out of twenty kids in Cuernavaca can beat me at Wiff 'n' Proof after a couple of weeks' training. In four months all but a small percentage of motivated adults at our CIDOC centre learn Spanish well enough to conduct academic business in the new language.

A first step toward opening up access to skills would be to provide various incentives for skilled individuals to share their knowledge. Inevitably, this would run counter to the interest of guilds and professions and unions. Yet, multiple apprenticeship is attractive: it provides everybody with an opportunity to learn something about almost anything. There is no reason why a person should not combine the ability to drive a car, repair telephones and toilets, act as a midwife, and function as an architectural draftsman. Special-interest groups and their disciplined consumers would, of course, claim that the public needs the protection of a professional guarantee. But this argument is now steadily being challenged by consumer protection associations. We have to take much more seriously the objection that economists raise to the radical socialisation of skills: that "progress" will be impeded if knowledge — patents, skills, and all the rest — is democratised. Their argument can be faced only if we demonstrate to them the growth rate of futile diseconomies generated by any existing educational system.

Access to people willing to share their skills is no guarantee of learning. Such access is restricted not only by the monopoly of educational programmes over learning and of unions over licensing but also by a technology of scarcity. The skills that count today are know-how in the use of highly specialised tools that were designed to be scarce. These tools produce goods or render services that everybody wants but only a few can enjoy, and which only a limited number of people know how to use. Only a few privileged individuals out of the total number of people who have a given disease ever benefit from the results of sophisticated medical technology, and even fewer doctors develop the skill to use it.

The same results of medical research have, however, also been employed to create a basic medical tool-kit that permits army and navy medics, with only a few months of training, to obtain results, under battlefield conditions, that would have been beyond the expectations of full-fledged doctors during World War II. On an even simpler level any peasant girl could learn how to diagnose and treat most infections if medical scientists prepared dosages and instructions specifically for a given geographic area.

All these examples illustrate the fact that educational considerations alone suffice to demand a radical reduction of the professional structure that now impedes the mutual relationship between the scientist and the majority of people who want access to science. If this demand were heeded, all men could learn to use yesterday's tools, rendered more effective and durable by modern science, to create tomorrow's world.

Unfortunately, precisely the contrary trend prevails at present. I know a coastal area in South America where most people support themselves by fishing from small boats. The outboard motor is certainly the tool that has changed most dramatically the lives of these coastal fishermen. But in the area I have surveyed, half of all outboard motors that were purchased between 1945 and 1950 are still kept running by constant tinkering, while half the motors purchased in 1965 no longer run because they were not built to be repaired. Technological progress provides the majority of people with gadgets they cannot afford and deprives them of the simpler tools they need.

Metals, plastics, and ferro cement used in building have greatly improved since the 1940s and ought to provide more people the opportunity to create their own homes. But while in the United States, in 1948, more then 30 per cent of all one-family homes were owner-built, by the end of the 1960s the percentage of those who acted as their own contractors had dropped to less than 20 per cent.

The lowering of the skill level through so-called economic development becomes even more visible in Latin America. Here most people still build their own homes from floor to roof. Often they use mud, in the form of adobe, and thatchwork of unsurpassed utility in the moist, hot, and windy climate. In other places they make their dwellings out of cardboard, oil-drums, and other industrial refuse. Instead of providing people with simple tools and highly standardised, durable, and easily repaired components, all governments have gone in for the mass production of low-cost buildings. It is clear that not one single country can afford to provide satisfactory modern dwelling units for the majority of its people. Yet, everywhere this policy makes it progressively more difficult for the majority to acquire the knowledge and skills they need to build better houses for themselves.

Educational considerations permit us to formulate a second fundamental characteristic that any post-industrial society must possess: a basic tool-kit that by its very nature counteracts technocratic control. For educational reasons we must work toward a society in which scientific knowledge is incorporated in tools and components that can be used meaningfully in units small enough to be within the reach of all. Only such tools can socialise access to skills. Only such tools favor temporary associations among those who want to use them for a specific occasion. Only such tools allow specific goals to emerge in the process of their use, as any tinkerer knows. Only the combination of guaranteed access to facts and of limited power in most tools renders it possible to envisage a subsistence economy capable of incorporating the fruits of modern science.

The development of such a scientific subsistence economy is unquestionably to the advantage of the overwhelming majority of all people in poor countries. It is also the only alternative to progressive pollution, exploitation, and opaqueness in rich countries. But, as we have seen, the dethroning of the GNP cannot be achieved without simultaneously subverting GNE (Gross National Education — usually conceived as manpower capitalisation). An egalitarian economy cannot exist in a society in which the right to produce is conferred by schools.

The feasibility of a modern subsistence economy does not depend on new scientific inventions. It depends primarily on the ability of a society to agree on fundamental, self-chosen antibureaucratic and antitechnocratic restraints.

These restraints can take many forms, but they will not work unless they touch the basic dimensions of life. (The decision of Congress against development of the supersonic transport plane is one of the most encouraging steps in the right direction.) The substance of these voluntary social restraints would be very simple matters that can be fully understood and judged by any prudent man. The issues at stake in the SST controversy provide a good example. All such restraints would be chosen to promote stable and equal enjoyment of scientific know-how. The French say that it takes a thousand years to educate a peasant to deal with a cow. It would not take two generations to help all people in Latin America or Africa to use and repair outboard motors, simple cars, pumps, medicine kits, and ferro cement machines if their design does not change every few years. And since a joyful life is one of constant meaningful intercourse with others in a meaningful environment, equal enjoyment does translate into equal education.

At present a consensus on austerity is difficult to imagine. The reason usually given for the impotence of the majority is stated in terms of political or economic class. What is not usually understood is that the new class structure of a schooled society is even more powerfully controlled by vested interests. No doubt an imperialist and capitalist organisation of society provides the social structure within which a minority can have disproportionate influence over the effective opinion of the majority. But in a technocratic society the power of a minority of knowledge-capitalists can prevent the formation of true public opinion through control of scientific know-how and the media of communication. Constitutional guarantees of free speech, free press, and free assembly were meant to ensure government by the people. Modern electronics, photo-offset presses, time-sharing computers, and telephones have in principle provided the hardware that could give an entirely new meaning to these freedoms. Unfortunately, these things are used in modern media to increase the power of knowledge-bankers to funnel their programme-packages through international chains to more people, instead of being used to increase true networks that provide equal opportunity for encounter among the members of the majority.

Deschooling the culture and social structure requires the use of technology to make participatory politics possible. Only on the basis of a majority coalition can limits to secrecy and growing power be determined without dictatorship. We need a new environment in which growing up can be classless, or we will get a brave new world in which Big Brother educates us all.

NOTES & REFERENCES

1. IVAR BERG, *Education and Jobs: The Great Training Robbery*, Beacon, Boston, 1971.
2. J. A. COMENIUS, *The Great Didactic* in W. M. KEATINGE (Ed. and tr.) *The Great Didactic of John A. Comenius*, Russell, N.Y., 1967.

Deschooling Society

Chapter 6: Learning Webs

In a previous chapter I discussed what is becoming a common complaint about schools, one that is reflected, for example, in the recent report of the Carnegie Commission: In school registered students submit to certified teachers in order to obtain certificates of their own; both are frustrated and both blame insufficient resources — money, time, or buildings — for their mutual frustration.

Such criticism leads many people to ask whether it is possible to conceive of a different style of learning. The same people, paradoxically, when pressed to specify how they acquired what they know and value, will readily admit that they have learned it more often outside than inside school. Their knowledge of facts, their understanding of life and work came to them from friendship or love, while viewing TV, or while reading, from examples of peers or the challenge of a street encounter. Or they may have learned what they know through the apprenticeship ritual for admission to a street gang or the initiation to a hospital, newspaper city room, plumber's shop, or insurance office. The alternative to dependence on schools is not the use of public resources for some new device which "makes" people learn; rather it is the creation of a new style of educational relationship between man and his environment. To foster this style, attitudes toward growing up, the tools available for learning, and the quality and structure of daily life will have to change concurrently.

Attitudes are already changing. The proud dependence on school is gone. Consumer resistance increases in the knowledge industry. Many teachers and pupils, taxpayers and employers, economists and policemen would prefer not to depend any longer on schools. What prevents their frustration from shaping new institutions is a lack not only of imagination but frequently also of appropriate language and of enlightened self-interest. They cannot visualise either a deschooled society or educational institutions in a society which has disestablished school.

In this chapter I intend to show that the inverse of school is possible: that we can depend on self-motivated learning instead of employing teachers to bribe or compel the student to find the time and the will to learn; that we can provide the learner with new links to the world instead of continuing to funnel all educational programmes through the teacher. I shall discuss some of the general characteristics which distinguish schooling from learning and outline four major categories of educational institutions which should appeal not only to many individuals but also to many existing interest groups.

From I. ILLICH, *Deschooling Society*, Calder and Boyars, London 1971. Reprinted by permission of the publisher and Harper and Row Inc., New York.

An Objection: Who Can Be Served by Bridges to Nowhere?

We are used to considering schools as a variable, dependent on the political and economic structure. If we can change the style of political leadership, or promote the interests of one class or another, or switch from private to public ownership of the means of production, we assume the school system will change as well. The educational institutions I will propose, however, are meant to serve a society which does not now exist, although the current frustration with schools is itself potentially a major force to set in motion change toward new social arrangements. An obvious objection has been raised to this approach: Why channel energy to build bridges to nowhere, instead of marshalling it first to change not the schools but the political and economic system?

This objection, however, underestimates the fundamental political and economic nature of the school system itself, as well as the political potential inherent in any effective challenge to it.

In a basic sense, schools have ceased to be dependent on the ideology professed by any government or market organisation. Other basic institutions might differ from one country to another: family, party, church, or press. But everywhere the school system has the same structure, and everywhere its hidden curriculum has the same effect. Invariably, it shapes the consumer who values institutional commodities above the non-professional ministration of a neighbour.

Everywhere the hidden curriculum of schooling initiates the citizen to the myth that bureaucracies guided by scientific knowledge are efficient and benevolent. Everywhere this same curriculum instils in the pupil the myth that increased production will provide a better life. And everywhere it develops the habit of self-defeating consumption of services and alienating production, the tolerance for institutional dependence, and the recognition of institutional rankings. The hidden curriculum of school does all this in spite of contrary efforts undertaken by teachers and no matter what ideology prevails.

In other words, schools are fundamentally alike in all countries, be they fascist, democratic or socialist, big or small, rich or poor. This identity of the school system forces us to recognise the profound world-wide identity of myth, mode of production, and method of social control, despite the great variety of mythologies in which the myth finds expression.

In view of this identity, it is illusory to claim that schools are, in any profound sense, dependent variables. This means that to hope for fundamental change in the school system as an effect of conventionally conceived social or economic change is also an illusion. Moreover, this illusion grants the school — the reproductive organ of a consumer society — almost unquestioned immunity.

It is at this point that the example of China becomes important. For three millennia, China protected higher learning through a total divorce between the process of learning and the privilege conferred by mandarin examinations. To become a world power and a modern nation-state, China had to adopt the international style of schooling. Only hindsight will allow us to discover if the Great Cultural Revolution will turn out to have been the first successful attempt at deschooling the institutions of society.

Even the piecemeal creation of new educational agencies which were the inverse of school would be an attack on the most sensitive link of a pervasive phenomenon, which is organised by the state in all countries. A political programme which does not explicitly recognise the need for deschooling is not revolutionary; it is demagoguery calling for more of the same. Any major political programme of the seventies should be evaluated by this measure: How clearly does it state the need for deschooling — and how clearly does it provide guidelines for the educational quality of the society for which it aims?

The struggle against domination by the world market and big-power politics might be beyond some poor communities or countries, but this weakness is an added reason for emphasising the importance of liberating each society through a reversal of its educational structure, a change which is not beyond any society's means.

General Characteristics of New Formal Educational Institutions

A good educational system should have three purposes: it should provide all who want to learn with access to available resources at any time in their lives; empower all who want to share what they know to find those who want to learn it from them; and, finally, furnish all who want to present an issue to the public with the opportunity to make their challenge known. Such a system would require the application of constitutional guarantees to education. Learners should not be forced to submit to an obligatory curriculum, or to discrimination based on whether they possess a certificate or a diploma. Nor should the public be forced to support, through a regressive taxation, a huge professional apparatus of educators and buildings which in fact restricts the public's chances for learning to the services the profession is willing to put on the market. It should use modern technology to make free speech, free assembly, and a free press truly universal and, therefore, fully educational.

Schools are designed on the assumption that there is a secret to everything in life; that the quality of life depends on knowing that secret; that secrets can be known only in orderly successions; and that only teachers can properly reveal these secrets. An individual with a schooled mind conceives of the world as a pyramid of classified packages accessible only to those who carry the proper tags. New educational institutions would break apart this pyramid. Their purpose must be to facilitate access for the learner: to allow him to look into the windows of the control room or the parliament, if he cannot get in by the door. Moreover, such new institutions should be channels to which the learner would have access without credentials or pedigree — public spaces in which peers and elders outside his immediate horizon would become available.

I believe that no more than four — possibly even three — distinct "channels" or learning exchanges could contain all the resources needed for real learning. The child grows up in a world of things, surrounded by people who serve as models for skills and values. He finds peers who challenge him to argue, to compete, to co-operate, and to understand; and if the child is lucky, he is exposed to confrontation or criticism by an experienced elder who really cares. Things, models, peers, and elders are four resources each of which requires a different type of arrangement to ensure that everybody has ample access to it.

I will use the words "opportunity web" for "network" to designate specific ways to provide access to each of four sets of resources. "Network" is often used, unfortunately, to designate the channels reserved to material selected by others for indoctrination, instruction, and entertainment. But it can also be used for the telephone or the postal service, which are primarily accessible to individuals who want to send messages to one another. I wish we had another word to designate such reticular structures for mutual access, a word less evocative of entrapment, less degraded by current usage and more suggestive of the fact that any such arrangement includes legal, organisational, and technical aspects. Not having found such a term, I will try to redeem the one which is available, using it as a synonym of "educational web".

What are needed are new networks, readily available to the public and designed to spread equal opportunity for learning and teaching.

To give an example: The same level of technology is used in TV and in tape recorders. All Latin American countries now have introduced TV: in Bolivia the government has financed a TV station, which was built six years ago, and there are no more than seven thousand TV sets for four million citizens. The money now tied up in TV installations throughout Latin America could have provided every fifth adult with a tape recorder. In addition, the money would have sufficed to provide an almost unlimited library of prerecorded tapes, with outlets even in remote villages, as well as an ample supply of empty tapes.

This network of tape recorders, of course, would be radically different from the present network of TV. It would provide opportunity for free expression: literate and illiterate alike could record, preserve, disseminate, and repeat their opinions. The present investment in TV, instead, provides bureaucrats, whether politicians or educators, with the power to sprinkle the continent with institutionally produced programmes which they — or their sponsors — decide are good for or in demand by the people.

Technology is available to develop either independence and learning or bureaucracy and teaching.

Four Networks

The planning of new educational institutions ought not to begin with the administrative goals of a principal or president, or with the teaching goals of a professional educator, or with the learning goals of any hypothetical class of people. It must not start with the question, "What should someone learn?" but with the question, "What kinds of things and people might learners want to be in contact with in order to learn?"

Someone who wants to learn knows that he needs both information and critical response to its use from somebody else. Information can be stored in things and in persons. In a good educational system access to things ought to be available at the sole bidding of the learner, while access to informants requires, in addition, others' consent. Criticism can also come from two directions: from peers or from elders, that is, from fellow learners whose immediate interests match mine, or from those who will grant me a share in their superior experience. Peers can be colleagues with whom to raise a question, companions for playful and enjoyable (or arduous) reading or walking, challengers at any type of game. Elders can be consultants on which skill to learn, which method to use, what company to seek at a given moment. They can be guides to the right questions to be raised among peers and to the deficiency of the answers they arrive at. Most of these resources are plentiful. But they are neither conventionally perceived as educational resources, nor is access to them for learning purposes easy, especially for the poor. We must conceive of new relational structures which are deliberately set up to facilitate access to these resources for the use of anybody who is motivated to seek them for his education. Administrative, technological, and especially legal arrangements are required to set up such web-like structures.

Educational resources are usually labelled according to educators' curricular goals. I propose to do the contrary, to label four different approaches which enable the student to gain access to any educational resource which may help him to define and achieve his own goals.

1. Reference Services to Educational Objects — which facilitate access to things or processes used for formal learning. Some of these things can be reserved for this purpose, stored in libraries, rental agencies, laboratories, and showrooms like museums and theatres; others can be in daily use in factories, airports, or on farms, but made available to students as apprentices or on off-hours.

2. Skill Exchanges — which permit persons to list their skills, the conditions under which they are willing to serve as models for others who want to learn these skills, and the addresses at which they can be reached.

3. Peer-Matching — a communications network which permits persons to describe the learning activity in which they wish to engage, in the hope of finding a partner for the enquiry.

4. Reference Services to Educator-at-Large — who can be listed in a directory giving the addresses and self-descriptions of professionals, paraprofessionals, and freelancers, along with conditions of access to their services. Such educators, as we will see, could be chosen by polling or consulting their former clients.

Reference Services to Educational Objects

Things are basic resources for learning. The quality of the environment and the relationship of a person to it will determine how much he learns incidentally. Formal learning requires special access to ordinary things, on the one hand, or, on the other, easy and dependable access to special things made for educational purposes. An example of the former is the special right to operate or dismantle a machine in a garage. An example of the latter is the general right to use an abacus, a computer, a book, a botanical garden, or a machine withdrawn from production and placed at the full disposal of students.

At present, attention is focused on the disparity between rich and poor children in their access to things and in the manner in which they can learn from them. OEO and other agencies, following this approach, concentrate on equalising chances by trying to provide more educational equipment for the poor. A more radical point of departure would be to recognise that in the city rich and poor alike are artificially kept away from most of the things that surround them. Children born into the age of plastics and efficiency experts must penetrate two barriers which obstruct their understanding: one built into things and the other around institutions. Industrial design creates a world of things that resist insight into their nature, and schools shut the learner out of the world of things in their meaningful setting.

After a short visit to New York, a woman from a Mexican village told me she was impressed by the fact that stores sold "only wares heavily made up with cosmetics". I understood her to mean that industrial products "speak" to their customers about their allurements and not about their nature. Industry has surrounded people with artefacts whose inner workings only specialists are allowed to understand. The non-specialist is discouraged from figuring out what makes a watch tick, or a telephone ring, or an electric typewriter work, by being warned that it will break if he tries. He can be told what makes a transistor radio work, but he cannot find out for himself. This type of design tends to reinforce a noninventive society in which the experts find it progressively easier to hide behind their expertise and beyond evaluation.

The man-made environment has become as inscrutable as nature is for the primitive. At the same time, educational materials have been monopolised by school. Simple educational objects have been expensively packaged by the knowledge industry. They have become specialised tools for professional educators, and their cost has been inflated by forcing them to stimulate either environments or teachers.

The teacher is jealous of the textbook he defines as his professional implement. The student may come to hate the lab because he associates it with schoolwork. The administrator rationalises his protective attitude toward the library as a defense of costly public equipment against those who would play with it rather than learn. In this atmosphere the student too often uses the map, the lab, the encyclopaedia, or the microscope only at the rare moments when the curriculum tells him to do so. Even the great classics become part of "sophomore year" instead of marking a new turn in a person's life. School removes things from everyday use by labelling them educational tools.

If we are to deschool, both tendencies must be reversed. The general physical environment must be made accessible, and those physical learning resources which have been reduced to teaching instruments must become generally available for self-directed learning. Using things only as part of a curriculum can have an even worse effect than just removing them from the general environment. It can corrupt the attitudes of pupils.

Games are a case in point. I do not mean the "games" of the physical education department (such as football and basketball), which the schools use to raise income and prestige and in which they have made a substantial capital investment. As the athletes themselves are well aware, these enterprises, which take the form of warlike tournaments, have undermined the playfulness of sports and are used to reinforce the competitive nature of schools. Rather I have in mind the educational games which can provide a unique way to penetrate formal systems. Set theory, linguistics, propositional logic, geometry, physics, and even chemistry reveal themselves with little effort to certain persons who play these games. A friend of mine went to a Mexican market with a game called "Wiff 'n' Proof", which consists of some dice on which twelve logical symbols are imprinted. He showed children which two or three combinations constituted a well-formed sentence, and inductively within the first hour some onlookers also grasped the principle. Within a few hours of playfully conducting formal logical proofs, some children are capable of introducing others to the fundamental proofs of propositional logic. The others just walk away.

In fact, for some children such games are a special form of liberating education, since they heighten their awareness of the fact that formal systems are built on changeable axioms and that conceptual operations have a game-like nature. They are also simple, cheap, and — to a large extent — can be organised by the players themselves. Used outside the curriculum such games provide an opportunity for identifying and developing unusual talent, while the school psychologist will often identify those who have such talent as in danger of becoming antisocial, sick, or unbalanced. Within school, when used in the form of tournaments, games are not only removed from the sphere of leisure: they often become tools used to translate playfulness into competition, a lack of abstract reasoning into a sign of inferiority. An exercise which is liberating for some character types becomes a straitjacket for others.

The control of school over educational equipment has still another effect. It increases enormously the cost of such cheap materials. Once their use is restricted to scheduled hours, professionals are paid to supervise their acquisition, storage, and use. Then students vent their anger against the school on the equipment, which must be purchased once again.

Paralleling the untouchability of teaching tools is the impenetrability of modern junk. In the thirties any self-respecting boy knew how to repair an automobile, but now car makers multiply wires and withhold manuals from everyone except specialised mechanics. In a former era an old radio contained enough coils and condensers to build a transmitter that would make all the neighbourhood radios scream in feedback. Transistor radios are more portable, but nobody dares to take them apart. To change this in the highly industrialised countries will be immensely difficult; but at least in the Third World we must insist on built-in educational qualities.

To illustrate my point, let me present a model: By spending ten million dollars it would be possible to connect forty thousand hamlets in a country like Peru with a spiderweb of six-foot-wide trails and maintain these, and, in addition, provide the country with 200,000 three-wheeled mechanical donkeys — five on the average for each hamlet. Few poor countries of this size spend less than this yearly on cars and roads, both of which are now restricted mainly to the rich and their employees, while poor people remain trapped in their villages. Each of these simple but durable little vehicles would cost $125 — half of which would pay for transmission and a six-horsepower motor. A "donkey" could make 15 mph, and it can carry loads of 850 pounds (that is, most things besides tree trunks and steel beams which are ordinarily moved).

The political appeal of such a transportation system to a peasantry is obvious. Equally obvious is the reason why those who hold power — and thereby automatically have a car — are not interested in spending money on trails and in clogging roads with engine-driven donkeys. The universal donkey could work only if a country's leaders were willing to impose a national speed limit of, say, 25 mph and adapt its public institutions to this. The model could not work if conceived only as a stopgap.

This is not the place to elaborate on the political, social, economic, financial, and technical feasibility of this model. I wish only to indicate that educational considerations may be of prime importance when choosing such an alternative to capital-intensive transport. By raising the unit cost per donkey by some 20 per cent it would become possible to plan the production of all its parts in such a manner that, as far as possible, each future owner would spend a month or two making and understanding his machine and would be able to repair it. With this additional cost it would also be possible to decentralise production into dispersed plants. The added benefits would result not only from including educational costs in the construction process. Even more significantly, a durable motor which practically anyone could learn to repair and which could be used as a plow and pump by somebody who understood it would provide much higher educational benefits than the inscrutable engines of the advanced countries.

Not only the junk but also the supposedly public places of the modern city have become impenetrable. In American society, children are excluded from most things and places on the grounds that they are private. But even in societies which have declared an end to private property children are kept away from the same places and things because they are considered the special domain of professionals and dangerous to the uninitiated. Since the last generation the railroad yard has become as inaccessible as the fire station. Yet with a little ingenuity it should not be difficult to provide for safety in such places. To deschool the artefacts of education will require making the artefacts and processes available — and recognising their educational value. Certainly, some workers would find it inconvenient to be accessible to learners; but this inconvenience must be balanced against the educational gains.

Private cars could be banned from Manhattan. Five years ago it was unthinkable. Now certain New York streets are closed off at odd hours, and this trend will probably continue. Indeed, most cross-streets should be closed to automotive traffic and parking should be forbidden everywhere. In a city opened up to people, teaching materials which are now locked up in storerooms and laboratories could be dispersed into independently operated storefront depots which children and adults could visit without the danger of being run over.

If the goals of learning were no longer dominated by schools and schoolteachers, the market for learners would be much more various and the definition of "educational artefacts" would be less restrictive. There could be tool shops, libraries, laboratories, and gaming rooms. Photo labs and offset presses would allow neighbourhood newspapers to flourish. Some storefront learning centres could contain viewing booths for closed-circuit television, others could feature office equipment for use and for repair. The jukebox or the record player would be commonplace, with some specialising in classical music, others in international folk tunes, others in jazz. Film clubs would compete with each other and with commercial television. Museum outlets could be networks for circulating exhibits of works of art, both old and new, originals and reproductions, perhaps administered by the various metropolitan museums.

The professional personnel needed for this network would be much more like custodians, museum guides, or reference librarians than like teachers. From the corner biology store, they could refer their clients to the shell collection in the museum or indicate the next showing of biology videotapes in a certain viewing booth. They could furnish guides for pest control, diet, and other kinds of preventive medicine. They could refer those who needed advice to "elders" who could provide it.

Two distinct approaches can be taken to financing a network of "learning objects". A community could determine a maximum budget for this purpose and arrange for all parts of the network to be open to all visitors at reasonable hours. Or the community could decide to provide citizens with limited entitlements, according to their age group, which would give them special access to certain materials which are both costly and scarce, while leaving other, simpler materials available to everyone.

Finding resources for materials made specifically for education is only one — and perhaps the least costly — aspect of building an educational world. The money now spent on the sacred paraphernalia of the school ritual could be freed to provide all citizens with greater access to the real life of the city. Special tax incentives could be granted to those who employed children between the age of eight and fourteen for a couple of hours each day if the conditions of employment were humane ones. We should return to the tradition of the barmitzvah or confirmation. By this I mean we should first restrict, and later eliminate, the disenfranchisement of the young and permit a boy of twelve to become a man fully responsible for his participation in the life of the community. Many "school-age" people know more about their neighbourhood than social workers or councilmen. Of course, they also ask more embarrassing questions and propose solutions which threaten the bureaucracy. They should be allowed to come of age so that they could put their knowledge and fact-finding ability to work in the service of a popular government.

Until recently the dangers of school were easily underestimated in comparison with the dangers of an apprenticeship in the police force, the fire department, or the entertainment industry. It was easy to justify schools at least as a means to protect youth. Often this argument no longer holds. I recently visited a Methodist church in Harlem occupied by a group of armed Young Lords in protest against the death of Julio Rodan, a Puerto Rican youth found hanged in his prison cell. I knew the leaders of the group, who had spent a semester in Cuernavaca. When I wondered why one of them, Juan, was not among them, I was told that he had "gone back on heroin and to the State University".

Planning, incentives, and legislation can be used to unlock the educational potential within our society's huge investment in plants and equipment. Full access to educational objects will not exist so long as business firms are allowed to combine the legal protections which the Bill of Rights reserves to the privacy of individuals with the economic power conferred upon them by their millions of customers and thousands of employees, stockholders, and suppliers. Much of the world's know-how and most of its productive processes and equipment are locked within the walls of business firms, away from their customers, employees, and stockholders, as well as from the general public, whose laws and facilities allow them to function. Money now spent on advertising in capitalist countries could be redirected toward education in and by General Electric, NBC-TV, or Budweiser beer. That is, the plants and offices should be reorganised so that their daily operations could be more accessible to the public in ways that would make learning possible; and, indeed, ways might be found to pay the companies for the learning people acquired from them.

An even more valuable body of scientific objects and data may be withheld from general access — and even from qualified scientists — under the guise of national security. Until recently science was the one forum which functioned like an anarchist's dream. Each man capable of doing research had more or less the same opportunity of access to its tools and to a hearing by the community of peers. Now bureaucratisation and organisation have placed much of science beyond public reach. Indeed, what used to be an international network of scientific information has been splintered into an arena of competing teams. The members as well as the artefacts of the scientific community have been locked into national and corporate programmes oriented toward practical achievement, to the radical impoverishment of the men who support these nations and corporations.

In a world which is controlled and owned by nations and corporations, only limited access to educational objects will ever be possible. But increased access to those objects which can be shared for educational purposes may enlighten us enough to help us to break through these ultimate political barriers. Public schools transfer control over the educational uses of objects from private to professional hands. The institutional inversion of schools could empower the individual to reclaim the right to use them for education. A truly public kind of ownership might begin to emerge if private or corporate control over the educational aspect of "things" were brought to the vanishing point.

Skill Exchanges

A guitar teacher, unlike a guitar, can be neither classified in a museum nor owned by the public nor rented from an educational warehouse. Teachers of skills belong to a different class of resources from objects needed to learn a skill. This is not to say that they are indispensable in every case. I can rent not only a guitar but also taped guitar lessons and illustrated chord charts, and with these things I can teach myself to play the guitar. Indeed, this arrangement may have advantages — if the available tapes are better than the available teachers, or if the only time I have for learning the guitar is late at night, or if the tunes I wish to play are unknown in my country, or if I am shy and prefer to fumble along in privacy.

Skill teachers must be listed and contacted through a different kind of channel from that of things. A thing is available at the bidding of the user — or could be — whereas a person formally becomes a skill resource only when he consents to do so, and he can also restrict time, place, and method as he chooses.

Skill teachers must be also distinguished from peers from whom one would learn. Peers who wish to pursue a common enquiry must start from common interests and abilities; they get together to exercise or improve a skill they share: basketball, dancing, constructing a camp site, or discussing the next election. The first transmission of a skill, on the other hand, involves bringing together someone who has the skill and someone who does not have it and wants to acquire it.

A "skill model" is a person who possesses a skill and is willing to demonstrate its practice. A demonstration of this kind is frequently a necessary resource for a potential learner. Modern inventions permit us to incorporate demonstration into tape, film, or chart; yet one would hope personal demonstration will remain in wide demand, especially in communication skills. Some ten thousand adults have learned Spanish at our centre in Cuernavaca — mostly highly motivated persons who wanted to acquire near-native fluency in a second language. When they are faced with a choice between carefully programmed instruction in a lab or drill sessions with two other students and a native speaker following a rigid routine, most choose the second.

For most widely shared skills, a person who demonstrates the skill is the only human resource we ever need or get. Whether in speaking or driving, in cooking or in the use of communication equipment, we are often barely conscious of formal instruction and learning, especially after our first experience of the materials in question. I see no reason why other complex skills, such as the mechanical aspects of surgery and playing the fiddle, of reading or the use of directories and catalogues, could not be learned in the same way.

A well-motivated student who does not labor under a specific handicap often needs no further human assistance than can be provided by someone who can demonstrate on demand how to do what the learner wants to learn to do. The demand made of skilled people that before demonstrating their skill they be certified as pedagogues is a result of the insistence either that people learn what they do not want to know or that all people — even those with a special handicap — learn certain things, at a given moment in their lives, and preferably under specified circumstances.

What makes skills scarce on the present educational market is the institutional requirement that those who can demonstrate them may not do so unless they are given public trust, through a certificate. We insist that those who help others acquire a skill should also know how to diagnose learning difficulties and be able to motivate people to aspire to learn skills. In short, we demand that they be pedagogues. People who can demonstrate skills will be plentiful as soon as we learn to recognise them outside the teaching profession.

Where princelings are being taught, the parents' insistence that the teacher and the person with skills be combined in one person is understandable, if no longer defensible. But for all parents to aspire to have Aristotle for their Alexander is obviously self-defeating. The person who can both inspire students and demonstrate a technique is so rare, and so hard to recognise, that even princelings more often get a sophist than a true philosopher.

A demand for scarce skills can be quickly filled even if there are only small numbers of people to demonstrate them; but such people must be easily available. During the forties radio repairmen, most of them with no schooling in their work, were no more than two years behind radios in penetrating the interior of Latin America. There they stayed until transistor radios, which are cheap to purchase and impossible to repair, put them out of business. Technical schools now fail to accomplish what repairmen of equally useful, more durable radios could do as a matter of course.

Converging self-interests now conspire to stop a man from sharing his skill. The man who has the skill profits from its scarcity and not from its reproduction. The teacher who specialises in transmitting the skill profits from the artisan's unwillingness to launch his own apprentice into the field. The public is indoctrinated to believe that skills are valuable and reliable only if they are the result of formal schooling. The job market depends on making skills scarce and on keeping them scarce, either by proscribing their unauthorised use and transmission or by making things which can be operated and repaired only by those who have access to tools or information which are kept scarce.

Schools thus produce shortages of skilled persons. A good example is the diminishing number of nurses in the United States, owing to the rapid increase of four-year B.S. programmes in nursing. Women from poorer families, who would formerly have enrolled in a two- or three-year programme, now stay out of the nursing profession altogether.

Insisting on the certification of teachers is another way of keeping skills scarce. If nurses were encouraged to train nurses, and if nurses were employed on the basis of their proven skill at giving injections, filling out charts and giving medicine, there would soon be no lack of trained nurses. Certification now tends to abridge the freedom of education by converting the civil right to share one's knowledge into the privilege of academic freedom, now conferred only on the employees of a school. To guarantee access to an effective exchange of skills, we need legislation which generalises academic freedom. The right to teach any skill should come under the protection of freedom of speech. Once restrictions on teaching are removed, they will quickly be removed from learning as well.

The teacher of skills needs some inducement to grant his services to a pupil. There are at least two simple ways to begin to channel public funds to noncertified teachers. One way would be to institutionalise the skill exchange by creating free skill centres open to the public. Such centres could and should be established in industrialised areas, at least for those skills which are fundamental prerequisites for entering certain apprenticeships — such skills as reading, typing, keeping accounts, foreign languages, computer programming and number manipulation, reading special languages such as that of electrical circuits, manipulation of certain machinery and so forth. Another approach would be to give certain groups within the population educational currency good for attendance at skill centres where other clients would have to pay commercial rates.

A much more radical approach would be to create a "bank" for skill exchange. Each citizen would be given a basic credit with which to acquire fundamental skills. Beyond that minimum, further credits would go to those who earned them by teaching, whether they served as models in organised skill centres or did so privately at home or on the playground. Only those who had taught others for an equivalent amount of time would have a claim on the time of more advanced teachers. An entirely new elite would be promoted, an elite of those who earned their education by sharing it.

Should parents have the right to earn skill credit for their children? Since such an arrangement would give further advantage to the privileged classes, it might be offset by granting a larger credit to the underprivileged. The operation of a skill exchange would depend on the existence of agencies which would facilitate the development of directory information and assure its free and inexpensive use. Such an agency might also provide supplementary services of testing and certification and might help to enforce the legislation required to break up and prevent monopolistic practices.

Fundamentally, the freedom of a universal skill exchange must be guaranteed by laws which permit discrimination only on the basis of tested skills and not on the basis of educational pedigree. Such a guarantee inevitably requires public control over tests which may be used to qualify persons for the job market. Otherwise, it would be possible to surreptitiously reintroduce complex batteries of tests at the work place itself which would serve for social selection. Much could be done to make skill-testing objective, for example, allowing only the operation of specific machines or systems to be tested. Tests of typing (measured according to speed, number of errors, and whether or not the typist can work from dictation), operation of an accounting system or of a hydraulic crane, driving, coding into COBOL and so on, can easily be made objective.

In fact, many of the true skills which are of practical importance can be so tested. And for the purposes of manpower management a test of a current skill level is much more useful than the information that twenty years ago a person satisfied his teacher in a curriculum in which typing, stenography, and accounting were taught. The very need for official skill-testing can, of course, be questioned: I personally believe that freedom from undue hurt to a man's reputation through labelling is better guaranteed by restricting than by forbidding tests of competence.

Peer-Matching

At their worst, schools gather classmates into the same room and subject them to the same sequence of treatment in maths, citizenship, and spelling. At their best, they permit each student to choose one of a limited number of courses. In any case, groups of peers form around the goals of teachers. A desirable educational system would let each person specify the activity for which he sought a peer.

School does offer children an opportunity to escape their homes and meet new friends. But, at the same time, this process indoctrinates children with the idea that they should select their friends from among those with whom they are put together. Providing the young from their earliest age with invitations to meet, evaluate, and seek out others would prepare them for a lifelong interest in seeking new partners for new endeavours.

A good chess player is always glad to find a close match, and one novice to find another. Clubs serve their purpose. People who want to discuss specific books or articles would probably pay to find discussion partners. People who want to play games, go on excursions, build fish tanks, or motorise bicycles will go to considerable lengths to find peers. The reward for their efforts is finding those peers. Good schools try to bring out the common interests of their students registered in the same programme. The inverse of school would be an institution which increased the chances that persons who at a given moment shared the same specific interest could meet — no matter what else they had in common.

Skill teaching does not provide equal benefits for both parties, as does the matching of peers. The teacher of skills, as I have pointed out, must usually be offered some incentive beyond the rewards of teaching. Skill teaching is a matter of repeating drills over and over and is, in fact, all the more dreary for those pupils who need it most. A skill exchange needs currency or credits or other tangible incentives in order to operate, even if the exchange itself were to generate a currency of its own. A peer-matching system requires no such incentives, but only a communications network.

Tapes, retrieval systems, programmed instruction, and reproduction of shapes and sounds tend to reduce the need for recourse to human teachers of many skills; they increase the efficiency of teachers and the number of skills one can pick up in a lifetime. Parallel to this runs an increased need to meet people interested in enjoying the newly acquired skill. A student who has picked up Greek before her vacation would like to discuss in Greek Cretan politics when she returns. A Mexican in New York wants to find other readers of the paper *Siempre* — or of *Los Agachados*, the most popular comic book. Somebody else wants to meet peers who, like himself, would like to increase their interest in the work of James Baldwin or of Bolivar.

The operation of a peer-matching network would be simple. The user would identify himself by name and address and describe the activity for which he sought a peer. A computer would send him back the names and addresses of all those who had inserted the same description. It is amazing that such a simple utility has never been used on a broad scale for publicly valued activity.

In its most rudimentary form, communication between client and computer could be established by return mail. In big cities typewriter terminals could provide instantaneous responses. The only way to retrieve a name and address from the computer would be to list an activity for which a peer was sought. People using the system would become known only to their potential peers.

A complement to the computer could be a network of bulletin boards and classified newspaper ads, listing the activities for which the computer could not produce a match. No names would have to be given. Interested readers would then introduce their names into the system. A publicly supported peer-match network might be the only way to guarantee the right of free assembly and to train people in the exercise of this most fundamental civic activity.

The right of free assembly has been politically recognised and culturally accepted. We should now understand that this right is curtailed by laws that make some forms of assembly obligatory. This is especially the case with institutions which conscript according to age group, class, or sex, and which are very time-consuming. The army is one example. School is an even more outrageous one.

To deschool means to abolish the power of one person to oblige another person to attend a meeting. It also means recognising the right of any person, of any age or sex, to call a meeting. This right has been drastically diminished by the institutionalisation of meetings. "Meeting" originally refers to the institutional product of some agency.

The ability of service institutions to acquire clients has far outgrown the ability of individuals to be heard independently of institutional media, which respond to individuals only if they are saleable news. Peer-matching facilities should be available for individuals who want to bring people together as easily as the village bell called the villagers to council. School buildings — of doubtful value for conversion to other uses — could often serve this purpose.

The school system, in fact, may soon face a problem which churches have faced before: what to do with surplus space emptied by the defection of the faithful. Schools are as difficult to sell as temples. One way to provide for their continued use would be to give over the space to people from the neighbourhood. Each could state what he would do in the classroom and when, and a bulletin board would bring the available programmes to the attention of the enquirers. Access to "class" would be free — or purchased with educational vouchers. The "teacher" could even be paid according to the number of pupils he could attract for any full two-hour period. I can imagine that very young leaders and great educators would be the two types most prominent in such a system. The same approach could be taken toward higher education. Students could be furnished with educational vouchers which entitled them to ten hours' yearly private consultation with the teacher of their choice — and, for the rest of their learning, depend on the library, the peer-matching network, and apprenticeships.

We must, of course, recognise the probability that such public matching devices would be abused for exploitative and immoral purposes, just as the telephone and the mails have been so abused. As with those networks, there must be some protection. I have proposed elsewhere a matching system which would allow only pertinent printed information, plus the name and address of the enquirer, to be used. Such a system would be virtually foolproof against abuse. Other arrangements could allow the addition of any book, film, TV programme, or other item quoted from a special catalogue. Concern about the dangers of the system should not make us lose sight of its far greater benefits.

Some who share my concern for free speech and assembly will argue that peer-matching is an artificial means of bringing people together and would not be used by the poor — who need it most. Some people become genuinely agitated when one suggests the setting up of *ad hoc* encounters which are not rooted in the life of a local community. Others react when one suggests using a computer to sort and match client-identified interests. People cannot be drawn together in such an impersonal manner, they say. Common enquiry must be rooted in a history of shared experience at many levels, and must grow out of this experience — the development of neighbourhood institutions, for example.

I sympathise with these objections, but I think they miss my point as well as their own. In the first place, the return to neighbourhood life as the primary centre of creative expression might actually work against the re-establishment of neighbourhoods as political units. Centring demands on the neighbourhood may, in fact, neglect an important liberating aspect of urban life — the ability of a person to participate simultaneously in several peer groups. Also, there is an important sense in which people who have never lived together in a physical community may occasionally have far more experiences to share than those who have known each other from childhood. The great religions have always recognised the importance of far-off encounters, and the faithful have always found freedom through them; pilgrimage, monasticism, the mutual support of temples and sanctuaries reflect this awareness. Peer-matching could significantly help in making explicit the many potential but suppressed communities of the city.

Local communities are valuable. They are also a vanishing reality as men progressively let service institutions define their circles of social relationship. Milton Kotler in his recent book has shown that the imperialism of "downtown" deprives the neighbourhood of its political significance. The protectionist attempt to resurrect the neighbourhood as a cultural unit only supports this bureaucratic imperialism. Far from artificially removing men from their local contexts to join abstract groupings, peer-matching should encourage the restoration of local life to cities from which it is now disappearing. A man who recovers his initiative to call his fellows into meaningful conversation may cease to settle for being separated from them by office protocol or suburban etiquette. Having once seen that doing things together depends on deciding to do so, men may even insist that their local communities become more open to creative political exchange.

We must recognise that city life tends to become immensely costly as city-dwellers must be taught to rely for every one of their needs on complex institutional services. It is extremely expensive to keep it even minimally livable. Peer-matching in the city could be a first step toward breaking down the dependence of citizens on bureaucratic civic services.

It would also be an essential step to providing new means of establishing public trust. In a schooled society we have come to rely more and more on the professional judgment of educators on the effect of their own work in order to decide whom we can or cannot trust: we go to the doctor, lawyer, or psychologist because we trust that anybody with the required amount of specialised educational treatment by other colleagues deserves our confidence.

In a deschooled society professionals could no longer claim the trust of their clients on the basis of their curricular pedigree, or ensure their standing by simply referring their clients to other professionals who approved of their schooling. Instead of placing trust in professionals, it should be possible, at any time, for any potential client to consult with other experienced clients of a professional about their satisfaction with him by means of another peer network easily set up by computer, or by a number of other means. Such networks could be seen as public utilities which permitted students to choose their teachers or patients their healers.

Professional Educators

As citizens have new choices, new chances for learning, their willingness to seek leadership should increase. We may expect that they will experience more deeply both their own independence and their need for guidance. As they are liberated from manipulation by others, they should learn to profit from the discipline others have acquired in a lifetime. Deschooling education should increase — rather than stifle — the search for men with practical wisdom who would be willing to sustain the newcomer in his educational adventure. As masters of their art abandon the claim to be superior informants or skill models, their claim to superior wisdom will begin to ring true.

With an increasing demand for masters, their supply should also increase. As the schoolmaster vanishes, conditions will arise which should bring forth the vocation of the independent educator. This may seem almost a contradiction in terms, so thoroughly have schools and teachers become complementary. Yet this is exactly what the development of the first three educational exchanges would tend to result in — and what would be required to permit their full exploitation — for parents and other "natural educators" need guidance, individual learners need assistance, and the networks need people to operate them.

Parents need guidance in directing their children on the road that leads to responsible educational independence. Learners need experienced leadership when they encounter rough terrain. These two needs are quite distinct: the first is a need for pedagogy, the second for intellectual leadership in all other fields of knowledge. The first calls for knowledge of human learning and of educational resource, the second for wisdom based on experience in any kind of exploitation. Both kinds of experience are indispensable for effective educational endeavour. Schools package these functions into one role — and render the independent exercise of any of them if not disreputable at least suspect.

Three types of special educational competence should, in fact, be distinguished: one to create and operate the kinds of educational exchanges or networks outlined here; another to guide students and parents in the use of these networks; and a third to act as *primus inter pares* in undertaking difficult intellectual exploratory journeys. Only the former two can be conceived of as branches of an independent profession: educational administrators and pedagogical counsellors. To design and operate the networks I have been describing would not require many people, but it would require people with the most profound understanding of education and administration, in a perspective quite different from and even opposed to that of schools.

While an independent educational profession of this kind would welcome many people whom the schools exclude, it would also exclude many whom the schools qualify. The establishment and operation of educational networks would require some designers and administrators, but not in the numbers or of the type required by the administration of schools. Student discipline, public relations, hiring, supervising, and firing teachers would have neither place nor counterpart in the networks I have been describing.

Neither would curriculum making, textbook purchasing, the maintenance of grounds and facilities, or the supervision of interscholastic athletic competition. Nor would child custody, lesson planning, and record keeping, which now take up so much of the time of teachers, figure in the operation of educational networks. Instead, the operation of learning webs would require some of the skills and attitudes now expected from the staff of a museum, a library, an executive employment agency, or a maître d'hôtel.

Today's educational administrators are concerned with controlling teachers and students to the satisfaction of others — trustees, legislatures, and corporate executives. Network builders and administrators would have to demonstrate genius at keeping themselves, and others, out of people's way, at facilitating encounters among students, skill models, educational leaders, and educational objects. Many persons now attracted to teaching are profoundly authoritarian and would not be able to assume this task: building educational exchanges would mean making it easy for people — especially the young — to pursue goals which might contradict the ideals of the traffic manager who makes the pursuit possible.

If the networks I have described could emerge, the educational path of each student would be his own to follow, and only in retrospect would it take on the features of a recognisable programme. The wise student would periodically seek professional advice: assistance to set a new goal, insight into difficulties encountered, choice between possible methods. Even now, most persons would admit that the important services their teachers have rendered them are such advice or counsel, given at a chance meeting or in a tutorial. Pedagogues, in an unschooled world, would also come into their own, and be able to do what frustrated teachers pretend to pursue today.

While network administrators would concentrate primarily on the building and maintenance of roads providing access to resources, the pedagogue would help the student to find the path which for him could lead fastest to his goal. If a student wanted to learn spoken Cantonese from a Chinese neighbour, the pedagogue would be available to judge his proficiency, and to help him select the textbook and methods most suitable to his talents, character, and the time available for study. He could counsel the would-be aeroplane mechanic on finding the best places for apprenticeship. He could recommend books to somebody who wanted to find challenging peers to discuss African history. Like the network administrator, the pedagogical counsellor would conceive of himself as a professional educator. Access to either could be gained by individuals through the use of educational vouchers.

The role of the educational initiator or leader, the master or "true" leader, is somewhat more elusive than that of the professional administrator or the pedagogue. This is so because leadership is itself hard to define. In practice, an individual is a leader if people follow his initiative and become apprentices in his progressive discoveries. Frequently, this involves a prophetic vision of entirely new standards — quite understandable today — in which present "wrong" will turn out to be "right". In a society which would honour the right to call assemblies through peer-matching, the ability to take educational initiative on a specific subject would be as wide as access to learning itself. But, of course, there is a vast difference between the initiative taken by someone to call a fruitful meeting to discuss this essay and the ability of someone to provide leadership in the systematic exploration of its implications.

Leadership also does not depend on being right. As Thomas Kuhn points out, in a period of constantly changing paradigms most of the very distinguished leaders are bound to be proven wrong by the test of hindsight. Intellectual leadership does depend on superior intellectual discipline and imagination and the willingness to associate with others in their exercise. A learner, for example, may think that there is an analogy between the US antislavery movement or the Cuban Revolution and what is happening in Harlem. The educator who is himself an historian can show him how to appreciate the flaws in such an analogy. He may retrace his own steps as a historian. He may invite the learner to participate in his own research. In both cases he will apprentice his pupil in a critical art — which is rare in school — and which money or other favours cannot buy.

The relationship of master and disciple is not restricted to intellectual discipline. It has its counterpart in the arts, in physics, in religion, in psychoanalysis, and in pedagogy. It fits mountain climbing, silverworking and politics, cabinetmaking and personnel administration. What is common to all true master-pupil relationships is the awareness both share that their relationship is literally priceless and in very different ways a privilege for both.

Charlatans, demagogues, proselytisers, corrupt masters, and simoniacal priests, tricksters, miracle workers, and messiahs have proven capable of assuming leadership roles and thus show the dangers of any dependence of a disciple on the master. Different societies have taken different measures to defend themselves against these counterfeit teachers. Indians relied on caste-lineage, Eastern Jews on the spiritual discipleship of rabbis, high periods of Christianity on an exemplary life of monastic virtue, other periods on hierarchical orders. Our society relies on certification by schools. It is doubtful that this procedure provides a better screening, but if it should be claimed that it does, then the counterclaim can be made that it does so at the cost of making personal discipleship almost vanish.

In practice, there will always be a fuzzy line between the teacher of skills and the educational leaders identified above, and there are no practical reasons why access to some leaders could not be gained by discovering the "master" in the drill teacher who introduces students to his discipline.

On the other hand, what characterises the true master-disciple relationship is its priceless character. Aristotle speaks of it as a "moral type of friendship, which is not on fixed terms: it makes a gift, or does whatever it does, as to a friend". Thomas Aquinas says of this kind of teaching that inevitably it is an act of love and mercy. This kind of teaching is always a luxury for the teacher and a form of leisure (in Greek, *scholé*) for him and his pupil: an activity meaningful for both, having no ulterior purpose.

To rely for true intellectual leadership on the desire of gifted people to provide it is obviously necessary even in our society, but it could not be made into a policy now. We must first construct a society in which personal acts themselves reacquire a value higher than that of making things and manipulating people. In such a society exploratory, inventive, creative teaching would logically be counted among the most desirable forms of leisurely "unemployment". But we do not have to wait until the advent of utopia. Even now one of the most important consequences of deschooling and the establishment of peer-matching facilities would be the initiative which "masters" could take to assemble congenial disciples. It would also, as we have seen, provide ample opportunity for potential disciples to share information or to select a master.

Schools are not the only institutions which pervert professions by packaging roles. Hospitals render home care increasingly impossible — and then justify hospitalisation as a benefit to the sick. At the same time, the doctor's legitimacy and ability to work come increasingly to depend on his association with a hospital, even though he is still less totally dependent on it than are teachers on schools. The same could be said about courts, which overcrowd their calendars as new transactions acquire legal solemnity, and thus delay justice. Or it could be said about churches, which succeed in making a captive profession out of a free vocation. The result in each case is scarce service at higher cost, and greater income to the less competent members of the profession.

So long as the older professions monopolise superior income and prestige it is difficult to reform them. The profession of the schoolteacher should be easier to reform, and not only because it is of more recent origin. The educational profession now claims a comprehensive monopoly; it claims the exclusive competence to apprentice not only its own novices but those of other professions as well. This overexpansion renders it vulnerable to any profession which would reclaim the right to teach its own apprentices. Schoolteachers are overwhelmingly badly paid and frustrated by the tight control of the school system. The most enterprising and gifted among them would probably find more congenial work, more independence, and even higher incomes by specialising as skill models, network administrators, or guidance specialists.

Finally, the dependence of the registered student on the certified teacher can be broken more easily than his dependence on other professionals — for instance, that of a hospitalised patient on his doctor. If schools ceased to be compulsory, teachers who find their satisfaction in the exercise of pedagogical authority in the classroom would be left only with pupils who were attracted by their style. The disestablishment of our present professional structure could begin with the dropping out of the schoolteacher.

The disestablishment of schools will inevitably happen — and it will happen surprisingly fast. It cannot be retarded very much longer, and it is hardly necessary to promote it vigorously, for this is being done now.

What is worthwhile is to try to orient it in a hopeful direction, for it could take place in either of two diametrically opposed ways.

The first would be the expansion of the mandate of the pedagogue and his increasing control over society even outside school. With the best of intentions and simply by expanding the rhetoric now used in school, the present crisis in the schools could provide educators with an excuse to use all the networks of contemporary society to funnel their messages to us — for our own good. Deschooling, which we cannot stop, could mean the advent of a "brave new world" dominated by well-intentioned administrators of programmed instruction.

On the other hand, the growing awareness on the part of governments, as well as of employers, taxpayers, enlightened pedagogues, and school administrators, that graded curricular teaching for certification has become harmful could offer large masses of people an extraordinary opportunity: that of preserving the right of equal access to the tools both of learning and of sharing with others what they know or believe. But this would require that the educational revolution be guided by certain goals:

1. to liberate access to things by abolishing the control which persons and institutions now exercise over their educational values;
2. to liberate the sharing of skills by guaranteeing freedom to teach or exercise them on request;
3. to liberate the critical and creative resources of people by returning to individual persons the ability to call and hold meetings — an ability now increasingly monopolised by institutions which claim to speak for the people;
4. to liberate the individual from the obligation to shape his expectations to the services offered by any established profession — by providing him with the opportunity to draw on the experience of his peers and to entrust himself to the teacher, guide, advisor, or healer of his choice. Inevitably the deschooling of society will blur the distinctions between economics, education, and politics on which the stability of the present world order and the stability of nations now rest.

Our review of educational institutions leads us to a review of our image of man. The creature whom schools need as a client has neither the autonomy nor the motivation to grow on his own. We can recognise universal schooling as the culmination of a Promethean enterprise, and speak about the alternatives as a world fit to live in for Epimethean man. While we can specify that the alternative to scholastic funnels is a world made transparent by true communication webs, and while we can specify very concretely how these could function, we can only expect the Epimethean nature of man to re-emerge; we can neither plan nor produce it.

General Bibliography

The following are some of the major commentaries and critical studies (listed in alphabetical order) on the writers covered in this book. In the case of journal articles the volume is always given in Roman numerals and the series number in Arabic numerals.

General Works

Books

The relevant writers specifically covered are given in brackets after each title.

R. Barrow, *Radical Education*, Martin Robertson, London, 1978. (Rousseau, Neill, Illich)

J. Bowen, *A History of Western Education*, Vol. 1 *The Ancient World: Orient and Mediterranean 2000 B.C. – A.D. 1054*, Methuen, London, 1972. (Plato, Aristotle)

J. Bowen, *A History of Western Education*, Vol. III *The Modern West: Europe and the New World*, Methuen, London, 1981. (Rousseau, Dewey, Makarenko, Illich)

J. S. Brubacher, *A History of the Problems of Education*, McGraw-Hill, New York, 1966. (Plato, Aristotle, Rousseau, Dewey)

B. Cohen, *Educational Thought: An Introduction*, Macmillan, London, 1969. (Plato, Rousseau, Dewey)

S. J. Curtis and M. E. A. Boultwood, *A Short History of Educational Ideas*, University Tutorial Press, London, 4th edition, 1965. (Plato, Aristotle, Rousseau, Dewey)

J. V. D'Cruz and W. Hannah, (Eds.) *Perceptions of Excellence: Studies in Educational Theory*, Polding Press, Melbourne, 1979. (Dewey, Skinner, Neill, Peters, Illich)

A. M. Dupuis, *Philosophy of Education in Historical Perspective*, Rand McNally, Chicago, 1966. (Plato, Aristotle, Rousseau, Dewey, Makarenko)

W. K. Frankena, *Three Historical Philosophies of Education*, Scott Foresman, Glenview (Illinois), 1965. (Aristotle, Dewey)

J. A. Laska & S. L. Goldstein, *Foundations of Teaching Method*, W. C. Brown, Dubuque, Iowa, 1973. (Plato, Rousseau, Dewey, Skinner)

M. D. Lawson & R. C. Peterson, *Progressive Education: An Introduction*, Angus & Robertson, Sydney, 1972. (Rousseau, Dewey, Neill)

A. E. Meyer, *Grandmasters of Educational Thought*, McGraw Hill, New York, 1975. (Plato, Aristotle, Rousseau, Dewey)

T. W. Moore, *Educational Theory: An Introduction*, Routledge & Kegan Paul, London, 1974. (Plato, Rousseau, Dewey)

I. Morrish, *Disciplines of Education*, Allen and Unwin, London, 1967. (Plato, Rousseau, Dewey, Skinner)

P. Nash *et al*, *The Educated Man: Studies in the History of Educational Thought*, John Wiley, New York, 1965. (Plato, Rousseau, Dewey, Skinner)

H. J. Perkinson, *Since Socrates: Studies in the History of Western Educational Thought*, Longmans, New York, 1980. (Plato, Rousseau, Dewey)

E. J. Power, *Evaluation of Educational Doctrine: Major Educational Theorists of the Western World*, Appleton-Century-Crofts, New York, 1969. (Plato, Rousseau, Dewey)

K. Price, *Education and Philosophical Thought*, Allyn and Bacon, Boston, 1962. (Plato, Rousseau, Dewey)

R. R. Rusk, *The Doctrines of the Great Educators*, Macmillan, London, 4th edition, 1969. (Plato, Rousseau, Dewey)

S. Smith, *Ideas of the Great Educators*, Barnes & Noble, New York, 1979. (Plato, Aristotle, Rousseau, Dewey)

Journal Articles

This list includes some essays that make a comparison between two or more of the theorists covered in this book.

J. J. Chambliss, "Human Development in Plato and Rousseau: 'Training from Childhood in Goodness' ", *Journal of Educational Thought*, XIII, No. 2, August 1979.

J. Darling, "Education as Horticulture: Some Growth Theorists and their Critics", *Journal of Philosophy of Education*, XVI, No. 2, 1982. (See also reply by K. Beckett, "Growth Theory Reconsidered", XIX, No. 1, 1985.)

J. Darling, "Progressive, Traditional and Radical: A Re-alignment", *Journal of Philosophy of Education*, XII, 1978.
J. Fennell, "Dewey on Rousseau: Natural Development as the Aim of Education", *Journal of Educational Thought*, XIII, No. 2, August 1979.
T. Kazepides, "Human Nature in its Educational Dimensions", *Journal of Philosophy of Education*, XIII, 1979.

Works dealing with particular writers

Items listed here are mainly those concerned specifically with the educational aspects of the work of these writers. Essays included in books, as well as individual chapters from books, are listed under the "Books" heading.

PLATO

Books
R. Barrow, *Plato, Utilitarianism and Education*, Routledge and Kegan Paul, London, 1975.
R. Barrow, *Plato and Education*, Routledge & Kegan Paul, London, 1976.
W. Boyd, *Plato's Republic For Today*, Heinemann, London, 1962.
R. C. Lodge, *Plato's Theory of Education*, Kegan Paul, London, 1947.
R. L. Nettleship, *The Theory of Education in Plato's Republic*, Oxford University Press, London, 1935.
R. S. Peters, "Was Plato Nearly Right About Education?", in R. S. Peters, *Essays on Educators*, Allen & Unwin, 1981. (Originally appeared in *Didaskalos*, V, No. 1, 1975.)

Journal Articles
T. H. Arcy, "Plato and Career Education", *College Student Journal*, XIV, No.1, Spring 1980.
R. H. Beck, "Plato's Views on Teaching", *Educational Theory*, XXXV, No. 2, Spring 1985.
J. A. Ogilvy, "Socratic Method, Platonic Method, and Authority", *Educational Theory*, XXI, No. 1, Winter 1971.

ARISTOTLE

Books
J. Burnet, *Aristotle on Education*, Cambridge University Press, Cambridge, 1903. (Extracts from the *Ethics* and *Politics* with an introduction and conclusion by Burnet.)
G. Howie (Ed.), *Aristotle*, (Educational Thinkers Series), Collier-Macmillan, London, 1968.
C. Lord, *Education and Culture in the Political Thought of Aristotle*, Cornell University Press, Ithaca, New York, 1982.
C. Winn & M. Jacks, *Aristotle*, (The Library of Educational Thought), Methuen, London, 1967.

ROUSSEAU

Books
G. H. Bantock, "Emile Reconsidered", in G. H. Bantock, *Education and Values*, Faber, London, 1965.
W. Boyd, *The Educational Theory of Jean-Jacques Rousseau*, Longmans Green, London, 1911.
W. Boyd, *Emile for Today*, Heinemann, London, 1956.
L. Claydon, (Ed.), *Rousseau*, (Educational Thinkers Series), Collier-Macmillan, London, 1969.
C. H. Dobinson, *Jean-Jacques Rousseau*, (Library of Educational Thought), Methuen, London, 1969.

Journal Articles
A. Bloom, "The Education of Democratic Man: Emile", *Daedalus*, CVII, No. 3, Summer 1978. (This whole issue is devoted to Rousseau and includes other relevant articles.)
D. C. Bricker, "Rousseau's Emile: Blueprint for School Reform?" *Teachers College Record*, LXXIV, No. 4, May 1973.
T. E. Cook, "Rousseau: Education and Politics", *Journal of Politics*, XXXVII, No. 1, February 1975.
J. Darling, "Understanding and Religion in Rousseau's 'Emile' " *British Journal of Educational Studies*, XXXIII, No. 1, February 1985.
G. John, "The Moral Education of Emile", *Journal of Moral Education*, XI, No. 1, October 1981.
J. R. Martin, "Sophie and Emile: A Case Study of Sex Bias in the History of Educational Thought", *Harvard Educational Review*, LI, No. 3, August 1981.
H. J. Perkinson, "Rousseau's Emile: Political Theory and Education", *History of Education Quarterly*, V, No. 2, June 1965.
E. Rosenow, "Rousseau's 'Emile': An Anti-Utopia", *British Journal of Educational Studies*, XXVIII, No. 3, October 1980.

B. A. Ryan, "Jean-Jacques Rousseau and Behaviour Control: The Technology of a Romantic Behaviourist", *Behaviourism*, IV, No. 2, 1976.
B. F. Skinner, "The Free and Happy Student", *Phi Delta Kappan*, LV, No. 1, September 1973.

DEWEY

Books
R. D. Archambault (Ed.), *Dewey on Education: Appraisals*, Random House, New York, 1966.
G. E. Axtelle & J. R. Burnett, "Dewey on Education and Schooling" in J. A. Boydston (Ed.), *Guide to the Works of John Dewey*, Southern Illinois University Press, Carbondale, 1970.
G. H. Bantock, "Dewey on Education", in G. H. Bantock, *Education in an Industrial Society*, Faber, London, 1963.
M. C. Baker, *Foundations of John Dewey's Educational Theory*, Columbia University Press, New York, 1955.
W. W. Brickman & S. Lehrer (Eds.), *John Dewey: Master Educator*, Atherton Press, New York, 1966.
W. F. Connell, "John Dewey and Education for Democracy", in W. F. Connell, *A History of Education in the Twentieth Century World*, Curriculum Development Centre, Canberra, 1980.
M. S. Dworkin (Ed.), *Dewey on Education*, Columbia University Press, New York, 1967. (Selections from Dewey with introduction by Dworkin.)
G. D. Dykhuizen, *The Life and Mind of John Dewey*, Southern Illinois University Press, Carbondale, 1973.
G. R. Geiger, *John Dewey in Perspective*, Oxford University Press, New York, 1958.
T. H. B. Hollins, "The Problem of Values and John Dewey" in T. H. B. Hollins (Ed.), *Aims in Education: The Philosophic Approach*, Manchester University Press, Manchester, 1964.
S. Hook, *Education and the Taming of Power*, Open Court, New York, 1973 (Part 1).
K. C. Mayhew and A. C. Edwards, *The Dewey School*, Atherton Press, New York, 1966.
R. S. Peters (Ed.), *John Dewey Reconsidered*, Routledge and Kegan Paul, London, 1977.
D. C. Phillips, "John Dewey and the Organismic Archetype", in R. J. W. Selleck (Ed.), *Melbourne Studies in Education*, Melbourne University Press, Melbourne, 1971.
I. Scheffler, *Four Pragmatists: A Critical Introduction to Peirce, James, Mead & Dewey*, Routledge & Kegan Paul, 1974, Part IV.
M. Skilbeck (Ed.) *Dewey* (Educational Thinkers Series), Collier-Macmillan, London, 1970.
A. G. Wirth, *John Dewey as Educator: His Design for Work in Education (1894–1904)*, John Wiley, New York, 1966.

Journal Articles
J. R. Burnett, "Whatever Happened to John Dewey?", *Teachers College Record* LXXXI, No. 2, Winter 1979.
E. Callan, "Dewey's Conception of Education as Growth", *Educational Theory*, XXXII, No. 1, Winter 1982. (Reply by F. S. Essiet in XXXV, 2, Spring 1985 and rejoinder by Callan, *ibid.*)
G. D. Dykhuizen, "John Dewey's Liberalism", *Educational Theory*, XII, No. 1, January 1962.
S. D'Urso, "Can Dewey be Marx's Educational-Philosophical Representative?", *Educational Philosophy and Theory*, XII, No. 2, October 1980.
G. Eastman, "John Dewey's Literary Style: Theory & Practice", *Educational Theory*, XVI, No. 2, April 1966.
G. J. Emerson & M. Ayim, "Dewey and Peirce on Curriculum and the Three R's", *Journal of Educational Thought*, XIV, No. 1, April 1980.
W. Feinberg, "The Conflict between Intelligence and Community in Dewey's Educational Theory", *Educational Theory*, XIX, No. 3, Summer 1969.
R. La Brecque, "Social Planning and the Imperium Humanum: John Dewey, circa 1960" *Educational Theory*, XIX, No. 4, Fall 1969.
R. La Brecque, "What is to be Done? Pragmatism at the Cross Roads", *Studies in Philosophy and Education*, VIII, No. 1, Winter 1974.
H. C. Lu, "The Goal of Enquiry in Dewey's Philosophy", *Educational Theory*, XX, No. 1, Winter 1970.
P. G. Min, "A comparison of Marx's and Dewey's Reactions to Industrialization", *Educational Theory*, XXIX, No. 1, Winter 1979.
A. H. Passow, "John Dewey's Influence on Education Around the World", *Teachers College Record*, LXXXIII, No. 3, Spring 1982.
D. C. Phillips, "John Dewey's Philosophy and his Writings on Education", *Educational Philosophy and Theory*, II, No. 2, October 1970.
R. H. Poole, "The Real Failure of John Dewey", *Educational Review*, XXVII, No. 2, February 1975.

R. Sanchez, "John Dewey's 'The School and Society': Perspectives 1969", *History of Education Quarterly*, X, No. 1, Spring 1970.
D. Vandenberg, "Education or Experience?", *Educational Theory*, XXX, No. 3, Summer 1980.
A. G. Wirth, "John Dewey in Transition from Religious Idealism to the Social Ethic of Democracy", *History of Education Quarterly*, V, No. 4, December 1965.
A. G. Wirth, "John Dewey's Design for American Education", *History of Education Quarterly*, IV, No. 2, June 1964.
J. Wood, "The Dewey School Revisited", *Childhood Education*, LVIII, No. 2, November-December 1981.

MAKARENKO
Books
J. Bowen, *Soviet Education: Anton Makarenko and the Years of Experiment*, University of Wisconsin Press, Madison, 1962.
U. Bronfenbrenner, *Two Worlds of Childhood: U.S. and U.S.S.R.,* Russell Sage Foundation, New York, 1970. (Includes an examination of Makarenko's methods of character education.)
W. F. Connell, "Makarenko and Education for a Collective Society", in W. F. Connell, *A History of Education in the Twentieth Century World*, Curriculum Development Centre, Canberra, 1980.
W. L. Goodman, *A. S. Makarenko: Russian Teacher*, Routledge and Kegan Paul, London, 1949.
F. Lilge, *Anton Semyonovitch Makarenko*, University of California Press, Berkeley, 1958.

Journal Articles
P. L. Alston, "Super Soviet Pedagogue", *New York University Education Quarterly*, X, Summer 1979.
B. Baker, "Review Article — Anton Makarenko and the Idea of the Collective", *Educational Theory*, XVIII, No. 3, Summer 1968.
R. Caskey, "The Pedagogical Theories of A. S. Makarenko: A Comparative Analysis", *Comparative Education*, XV, No. 3, October 1979.
A. R. Crane, "A. S. Makarenko and Russian Educational Thought", *Australian Journal of Education*, VII, No. 1, March 1963.
Soviet Education, XX, No. 12, October 1978. (Special issue on Makarenko.)

SKINNER
Books
C. Argyris, Review of 'Beyond Freedom and Dignity', *Education Yearbook, 1972–3*, Crowell-Collier, New York, 1972.
F. Carpenter, *The Skinner Primer: Behind Freedom and Dignity*, Collier and Macmillan, 1974.
R. I. Evans, *B. F. Skinner: The Man and his Ideas*, Dutton, New York, 1968, (Report on conversations with Skinner.)
J. McClellan, "B. F. Skinner's Philosophy of Human Nature: A Sympathetic Criticism", Ch. 5 in his *Toward an Effective Critique of American Education*, Lippincott, Philadelphia, 1968.
F. Milhollan & B. E. Forisha, *From Skinner to Rogers: Contrasting Approaches to Education*, Professional Educators Publications, Lincoln, Nebraska, 1972.
R. S. Peters, Review of B. F. Skinner, "Beyond Freedom and Dignity", in R. S. Peters, *Psychology & Ethical Development*, Allen & Unwin, 1974. (Originally appeared in *Times Educational Supplement*, 10 March, 1972.)
H. Wheeler (Ed.), *Beyond the Punitive Society, Operant Conditioning: Social and Political Aspects*, Wildwood House, London, 1973 (Includes chapter by Skinner, "Answers for my Critics".)

Journal Articles
B. V. Hill, Review Article: "Behaviour, Learning and Control: Some Philosophical Difficulties in the Writings of B. F. Skinner", *Educational Theory*, XXII, No. 2, Spring 1972.
"Mechanistic Man — a Dispute between A. H. Halsey and H. R. Beech Concerning Behaviourism and B. F. Skinner", *The Listener*, LXXXVII, No. 2247, 20 April 1972.
R. Nordberg & G. Zaret, "Skimming Skinner — A Skeptical Sketch", *Educational Theory*, XXIII, No. 4, Fall 1973.
K. A. Strike, Review Article: " 'Beyond Freedom and Dignity' by B. F. Skinner" *Studies in Philosophy and Education*, IX, Nos. 1, 2, Summer 1975.
R. G. Tiberius, "Freedom Within Control: An Elaboration of the Concept of Reciprocal Control in B. F. Skinner's 'Beyond Freedom and Dignity', *Interchange*, V, 1, 1974.

NEILL
Books
R. Barrow, "The Free School", in *Moral Philosophy for Education*, Allen & Unwin, London, 1975.
J. Croall, *Neill of Summerhill: The Permanent Rebel*, Routledge & Kegan Paul, London, 1983.

H. Hart (Ed.), *Summerhill, For and Against: Assessments of A. S. Neill*, Hart Publishing Co., New York 1970 and Angus & Robertson, Sydney, 1973.

R. Hemmings, *Fifty Years of Freedom: A Study of the Development of the Ideas of A. S. Neill*, Allen & Unwin, London, 1972.

B. Segefjord, *Summerhill Diary* (translated M. Michael), Gollancz, London, 1971.

R. Skidelsky, *English Progressive Schools*, Penguin, Harmondsworth, 1969 (Part III).

H. Snitzer, *Summerhill: A Loving World*, Macmillan, New York, 1964.

W. A. C. Stewart, *The Educational Innovators, Vol. II: Progressive Schools, 1881–1967*, Macmillan, London, 1968, Chapter 15.

J. Walmsley & L. Berg, *Neill and Summerhill, A Man and His Work: A Pictorial Study*, Penguin, Harmondsworth, 1969.

L. S. Waks, "Freedom and Desire in the Summerhill Philosophy of Education", in D. Nyberg (Ed.) *The Philosophy of Open Education*, Routledge & Kegan Paul, London, 1975.

Journal Articles

R. Barrett, "Freedom, License and A. S. Neill", *Oxford Review of Education*, VII, No. 2, 1981.

E. Bernstein, "Summerhill: A Follow-up Study of its Students", *Journal of Humanistic Psychology*, VIII, No. 2, Fall 1968.

J. Darling, "A. S. Neill on Knowledge and Learning", *British Journal of Educational Studies*, XXXII, No. 2, June 1984.

N. Friedman, "Education and the Transformation of the Self: An Essay on 'Neill, Neill, Orange Peel' ", *School Review*, LXXXII, May 1974.

R. L. Hopkins, "Freedom and Education: The Philosophy of Summerhill", *Educational Theory*, XXVI, No. 2, Spring 1976.

M. Keohane, "A. S. Neill: Latter day Dewey", *Elementary School Journal* (U.S.A.), LXX, May 1970.

PETERS

Books

D. Adelstein, "The Wit and Wisdom of R. S. Peters", in T. Pateman (Ed.), *Counter Course: A Handbook for Course Criticism*, Penguin, Harmondsworth, 1972. (Originally published as pamphlet by The Union Society, University of London Institute of Education, May 1971.)

D. E. Cooper, *Education, Values and Mind: Essays for R. S. Peters*, Routledge and Kegan Paul, London, 1986. (Essays by P. H. Hirst and R. K. Elliott)

B. Crittenden, "R. S. Peters: Moral Education and the Ideal of the Rational Man", in *Bearings in Moral Education*, Australian Educational Review, No. 12, Australian Council for Educational Research, Hawthorn, Victoria, 1978.

M. Smith, *The Underground and Education: A Guide to the Alternative Press*, Methuen, London, 1977 (Chapters 1, 2).

J. Woods & W. H. Dray, Commentary on R. S. Peters' 'Aims of Education — A Conceptual Enquiry', in R. S. Peters (Ed.) *The Philosophy of Education*, Oxford University Press, London, 1973.

Journal Articles

D. Arnstine, "R. S. Peters and the Cartography of Education", *Educational Theory*, XVIII, No. 2, Spring 1968.

A. W. Beck, "Does 'Ethics and Education' Rest on a Mistake?" *Educational Philosophy and Theory*, III, No. 2, October 1971.

J. Colbeck, "Criticising Critical Philosophy of Education", *Journal of Further and Higher Education*, IV, 2, Summer 1980.

B. A. Cooper, "Peters' Concept of Education", *Educational Philosophy and Theory*, V, No. 2, October 1973.

S. de Castell & H. Freeman, "Liberal Education as Socio-Practical Theory: Some Internal Contradictions", *Discourse*, II, No. 1, 1981.

F. W. Dunlop, "Education and Human Nature", *Proceedings of the Philosophy of Education Society of Great Britain*, IV, 1970.

J. Earwaker, "R. S. Peters and the Concept of Education", *Proceedings of the Philosophy of Education Society of Great Britain*, VII, No. 2, 1973.

R. E. Fitzgibbons, "Peters' Analysis of Education: The Pathology of an Argument" *British Journal of Educational Studies*, XXIII, No. 1, February 1975.

C. K. Harris, "Peters on Schooling", *Educational Philosophy and Theory*, IX, No. 1, March 1977.

E. A. Martin, "Perspectives on Peters", *Education for Teaching*, No. 81, Spring 1970. (Reply by Peters in the same issue.)

F. Murphy, "The Paradox of Freedom in R. S. Peters' Analysis of Education as Initiation", *British Journal of Educational Studies*, XXI, No. 1, February 1973.

K. Robinson, "Education and Initiation", *Educational Philosophy and Theory*, II, No. 2, October, 1970.

K. Robinson, "The Task-Achievement Analysis of Education", *ibid.*, IV, No. 2, October 1972.

R. J. Royce, "R. S. Peters and Moral Education, 1: The Justification of Procedural Principles", *Journal of Moral Education*, XII, No. 3, October 1983.

R. J. Royce, "R. S. Peters and Moral Education, 2: Moral Education in Practice", *Journal of Moral Education*, XIII, No. 1, January 1984.

A. Thompson, "Definition and Policy: R. S. Peters on 'Education' ", *Education for Teaching*, No. 81, Spring 1970. (Reply by Peters in same issue.)

A. J. Watt, "Conceptual Analysis and Educational Values", *Educational Philosophy and Theory*, V, No. 2, October 1973.

A. J. Watt, "Education and the Development of Reason", *Educational Philosophy and Theory*, VIII, No. 2, October 1976.

P. S. Wilson, "In Defence of Bingo", *British Journal of Educational Studies*, XV, No. 1, June 1967 (Reply by Peters in same issue.)

ILLICH

Books

P. Buckman (Ed.) *Education Without Schools*, Souvenir Press, London, 1973 (with contribution by Illich).

P. J. Crittenden, "Education and Society: A Critique of Ivan Illich's 'Deschooling Society' ", in J. V. D'Cruz & P. J. Sheehan (Eds.) *Concepts in Education: Philosophical Studies*, A Mercy Teachers' College-Twentieth Century Publication, Melbourne, 1973.

J. L. Elias, *Conscientization and Deschooling: Freire's and Illich's Proposals for Reshaping Society*, Westminster Press, Philadelphia, 1976.

A. Gartner, et. al., *After Deschooling, What?*, Harper & Row, New York, 1973 (with contribution by Illich).

D. U. Levine, & R. J. Havighurst, (Eds.) *Farewell to Schools?* Charles A. Jones Publishing Co., Worthington, Ohio, 1971.

I. Lister, *Deschooling: A Reader*, Cambridge University Press, London, 1974.

J. E. C. MacBeath, *A Question of Schooling*, Hodder & Stoughton, London, 1976.

M. Macklin, *When Schools are Gone: A Projection of the Thought of Ivan Illich*, University of Queensland Press, St. Lucia, 1976.

P. W. Musgrave & R. J. W. Selleck, *Alternative Schools*, Wiley, Sydney, 1975.

J. Ohliger & C. McCarthy, (Eds.) *Lifelong Learning or Lifelong Schooling? A Tentative View of the Ideas of Ivan Illich with a Quotational Bibliography*, Syracuse University Publications in Continuing Education, New York, 1971.

W. K. Richmond, *The Free School*, Methuen, London, 1973.

Journal Articles

B. Birchall, "Some Misconceptions in Ivan Illich" *Educational Theory*,, XXIV, No. 4, Fall 1974.

H. Gintis, "Toward a Political Economy of Education: A Radical Critique of Ivan Illich's 'Deschooling Society' ", *Harvard Educational Review*, XL, No. 1, February 1972.

I. L. Gotz, "On Man and his Schooling", *Educational Theory*, XXIV, No. 1, Winter 1974. (See also response by F. Schrag, in Vol. XXIV, No. 4, Fall 1974.)

S. Hook, "Illich's De-Schooled Utopia", *Encounter*, XXXVIII, January 1972.

R. B. King, "Ivan Illich on the Confusion of Schooling & Learning", *Australian Journal of Higher Education*, V, No. 1, December 1973.

R. A. Manners, "Ivan Illich: Schooling & Society", *Teachers College Record*, LXXVI, No. 4, May 1975.

H. Ozmon, "The School of Deschooling", *Phi Delta Kappan*, LV, 3, November 1973.

H. G. Petrie, "Review of Ivan Illich's 'Deschooling Society' ", *Educational Theory*, XXII, No. 4, Fall 1972.

"Pilgrims of the Obvious", Symposium on Illich and Freire, *Risk* (World Council of Churches) XI, No. 1, 1975.

J. Piveteau, "Illich: Enemy of Schools or School Systems?" *School Review*, LXXXII, May 1974.

T. Reagan, "The Foundations of Ivan Illich's Social Thought", *Educational Theory*, XXX, No. 4, Fall 1980.

A. J. Watt, "Illich and Anarchism", *Educational Philosophy and Theory*, XIII, No. 2, October 1981.

PART III
The Debate Continues

Prospects for the Future

Introduction

It is now twelve years since the first edition of this book was published and this final chapter has been added to the new edition in order to examine briefly some of the major developments in educational thought since 1974 (and where necessary to mention their antecedents in earlier years). Limitations of space allow only a broad historical and philosophical overview and the writers to be covered cannot be discussed in the same detail as the previous thinkers (nor can selections from their work be included)*. Rather, this chapter should be seen as a series of signposts with directions for interested readers to follow up for themselves.†

At the present moment it seems that no one figure stands out in this recent period as a significant innovator in the sense described in the Introduction, although this perception may change in the future with the benefit of hindsight. On the other hand, many have contributed to the ongoing debate about the nature and aims of education and a significant number of interesting new perspectives have developed. Generally the debate has become more complex, diffuse, and at times more intense. One factor that has become prominent in the last decade has been the growing awareness of the social and political context in which educational theories are produced and have application. No longer are thinkers inclined to develop a theory of education solely as a result of philosophical speculation about knowledge, human nature, learning, etc., without considering the normative assumptions which guide their ideas and what bearing their theory will have on the social and political dilemmas of the present time. This applies as well to the philosophical analysts such as R. S. Peters who, as we saw in Chapter 8, along with other analysts, originally believed in the possibility of a neutral or value-free analysis of education before coming to change his views on the subject.

This book has been structured in terms of the continuing historical debate between traditional and progressive theories of education, further divided into the classic exponents of the two approaches (Part I) and modern variations and modifications to these two fundamental ways of viewing the educational process (Part II). While this is a useful mechanism for gaining a coherent and structured understanding of the development of educational theories over the centuries, it should not (as we pointed out in the Introduction) be regarded as too rigid a dichotomy, since there is a degree of overlap

---

*Although the present authors' views will no doubt be apparent in places, limitations of space also prevent any detailed criticism and evaluation of the ideas presented.

†The major works of each of the key writers or schools of thought mentioned (and in some cases works about them by others) will be listed at the end of the chapter. Full publication details will not be given in the text for books that are mentioned but will be provided in the list at the back.

of views and also significant differences among thinkers in how strictly they represent the traditional or the progressive approach. Nevertheless it remains true that there is a set of fundamentally opposed assumptions about the various aspects of the educational process according to which thinkers can be placed into one or other of the two basic positions. This is still true at the present time and while some of the connections are looser it is still possible to categorize theorists into those whose ideas are an extension of the traditional approach and those who further develop the progressive model of education.

Recent Developments of the Traditional Approach

Consider first those developments growing out of the traditional way of thinking, broadly conceived. One fundamental axiom shared by all such thinkers is that there is an ordered body of knowledge and intellectual skills which should be passed on to each generation. There may be differences of opinion as to which aspects of this knowledge and skills are the most important, but all agree that there is an objective structure central to the content of education. Associated with this belief is a general emphasis on cognitive achievements as crucial to education, usually assuming a dualism between mind and body, or mind and emotions, with mind seen as prior, at least in terms of educational aims.

In respect of particular thinkers or movements, it is convenient to classify them into two further categories: liberals and conservatives; the latter representing a stronger or more extreme version of the traditional approach.* In the liberal category may be placed R. S. Peters, examined in Chapter 8 and who, as noted in the Commentary there, attempted a synthesis between traditional and progressive models. However, as was also suggested, his theory does seem to lean more towards the traditional view and the debate over his work during the last decade has confirmed that opinion. He is even viewed as an arch-conservative by various Marxist writers although his work is better seen as representing the "softer", liberal side of traditionalism. As mentioned in Chapter 8, there are various aspects of liberalism in his approach and his stress on education for the individual rather than for society throughout his work further confirms this.

The first major development in Peters' thought since the original edition of this book is his greater awareness of the social and political context in which his theory is located. He now sees educational aims as those aspects of a society's values deemed worthy of emphasis at a particular time. For Peters these are the values of democracy, which cover such principles as freedom, veracity, impartiality and respect for persons. As he says, these

---

*The word "liberal" is sometimes used (especially in the U.S.A.) as opposed to traditional, but, as will be seen, in the broader context of debate which includes radical and Marxist views, it appropriately belongs on the traditional side of the spectrum, albeit on what may be termed the moderate rather than more extreme wing of that spectrum.

values do not specify any particular form of ideal society but represent the procedures necessary in a community where matters of policy are decided by discussion and consultation rather than imposition from the top. Echoing a well-known earlier statement of his about what it means to be educated,* he concludes his latest essay on the nature of education with the statement: "Democracy is concerned more with principles for proceeding than with a determinate destination and aims of education in a democracy should emphasize the qualities of mind essential for such a shared journey."[1]

Peters has also further modified his views about the concept of education† and lessened his stress on the intrinsic value of the learning involved. He now argues that the concept of knowledge for its own sake is certainly still appropriate to the *advancement* of knowledge, but much less central to its *acquisition*. Consequently, the concept of liberal education is more relevant at university than school level, although there is still an important place for it in schools as well.[2]

Another aspect of Peters' fuller awareness of social and political factors is evident in his recent discussion of education and preparation for work.[3] He makes a distinction between "work" and "labour", the former involves skill and personal satisfaction, the latter designates more routine tasks promoting little or no personal involvement, the only reward being weekly wages. Preparation for work, given certain provisos, he considers a legitimate role of the school, which itself represents a certain change of emphasis in his views. In regard to labour, he is aware of the alienating aspects to which the Marxists point, but unlike them, he does not develop a political and economic theory blaming this on the capitalist mode of production and class exploitation. His response is much more guarded, restricted to pointing out the need for practical and piecemeal reform in working conditions to help lessen the worst features of modern alienating labour. He thus offers no wide-ranging solution to the issue and by implication sees it as a continuing problem. Nor does he address the topic of rising unemployment and its relationship to education as do theorists of a more strongly reformist or ideological bent. Basically he takes his stand on liberal democracy as the best of the available options of social organization, keeping well clear of any large-scale utopian models for reconstructing society. He would see that the danger of thinking in terms of such schemes is that we may end up sacrificing hard won freedoms for the sake of an unrealizable ideal model.

Peters' later work, then, develops his exposition of the liberal position in education, while providing a number of new insights and emphases. He acknowledges that he has not presented a comprehensive statement of this position on his own, preferring to concentrate on the social and ethical aspects. Paul Hirst, his former colleague at the University of London, has

---

*"To be educated is not to have arrived at a destination; it is to travel with a different view." (See p. 376, this volume.)

†See pp. 350–1 for discussion of earlier modifications of his original analysis in "Education as Initiation".

focused more on the epistemological basis of the liberal position. This he has done through his famous "forms of knowledge" thesis, according to which knowledge may be divided into seven categories each of which has its own distinctive types of concept and tests for truth. These seven are mathematics, physical sciences, human sciences, history, religion, literature and the fine arts, and philosophy.[4] For Hirst, these are "the complex ways of understanding experience which man has achieved, which are publicly specifiable and which are gained through learning."[5] The aim of liberal education he argues is the development of mind through the acquisition of such ordered knowledge. This model clearly reinforces the traditional conception of the educational process going back to Plato and Aristotle and provides a clear modern statement which has been very influential. Hirst's account of knowledge has given rise to a considerable literature,[6] for and against, and it is rightly seen by radical educators as a key argument of their opponents which they need to counter before they can make their own case. Peters' work in epistemology, while not extensive, reinforces Hirst's forms of knowledge model by attempting to provide a philosophical justification for stressing the traditional theoretical disciplines (or worthwhile activities as he calls them), since these correspond closely to Hirst's forms of knowledge.[7]

Hirst has made other important contributions to the liberal-analytical approach to philosophy of education* such as helping delineate the distinctive nature of educational theory, and of the concept of teaching, as well as producing significant work in the philosophy of moral and religious education.† Other influential representatives of this approach are Robert Dearden who has applied liberal analytical principles specifically to issues arising in primary education and has developed the idea of rational autonomy as essential to the liberal concept of education. John White has attempted to justify a compulsory core curriculum (similar to Hirst's forms of knowledge) and has examined the concept of educational aims in detail, also relying heavily on the concept of rational autonomy. Pat White has explored the area of political education, making a strong case for participatory democracy and how this can be supported by education. Robin Barrow has brought a fresh and distinctive focus to the general liberal approach by examining the implications of utilitarianism for such topics as Plato's *Republic*, the curriculum, and moral issues related to education. John Wilson has made important and influential contributions to moral education, religious education and the education of the emotions, also bringing some distinctive approaches not always shared by others in this group. Charles Bailey has recently written an important defence of liberal education.

---

*This is sometimes called the "London School" since most of its representatives either worked or studied at the University of London Institute of Education.

†The relevant references are indicated at the end of the chapter along with those of the other major writers mentioned. An up-to-date list of Peters' works is given on pages 356-7.

One liberal writer who has examined explicitly the relationship between the analytical approach to philosophy, and the values built into liberalism, is Brenda Cohen. She argues for a necessary link between the two, because the analytic approach includes "recognition of the natural authority of rationality — a value which is fundamental to the western cultural tradition in contrast to other traditions more concrete or more mystical in their nature, as well as to the sophisticated conception of philosophy represented by the analytic tradition."[8] Rationality, when put into practice in a social context involves such things as openness to argument, impartiality, rejection of authority and dogma, toleration, all of which in turn are an expression of the liberal values of individualism and freedom. Cohen's argument here has affinities with Peters' championing of the procedural values of democracy as fundamental to his philosophical approach since the values she points to are those essential to democratic society.

It is now clear to most in the liberal-analytic tradition that no philosopher of education can be fully neutral, but must make certain normative assumptions and in the case of the liberal-analysts, these will reflect the values of democracy. Such a recognition however is not (as sometimes seen) a weakness or problem — on the contrary it allows greater clarity and firmer commitment to one's underlying ideals. As Cohen says: "That only Marxists should appear to have a defined position on substantive moral matters — and this while repudiating objective morality altogether — is an unfortunate consequence of the excessive austerity and deliberate avoidance of moral commitment which has characterized the analytic tradition until recently".[9] Barrow develops this further by pointing out that the commitment brought by liberal-analysts to philosophy is of a different order to that of more ideologically or doctrinally determined belief systems such as Marxism, Catholicism and Behaviourism. While the latter tend to interpret all issues in terms of an ideal end product or specific system of human relationships, the liberal-analysts, by restricting their commitment basically to rationality and procedural democratic values, are able to make a wider range of possible responses to educational questions.[10]

It thus appears that after a period of stringent criticism of the liberal-analytic educational philosophers by Marxists and radicals*, and some internal soul-searching of its own, this approach to philosophy of education still has a significant and valuable role to play in combining an approach based on philosophical rigour and clarity with a conscious commitment to the basic values that still underlie most western societies.[11]

Let us now move to the other wing of the recent developments growing out of the traditional approach to philosophy of education, the conservative group of writers. They are not as cohesive a group as the liberals but rather

---

*These criticisms were often along the line of questioning of the supposed value neutrality of the liberal-analysts but sometimes there was a failure to distinguish adequately between liberal and conservative values in relation to the object of their attacks.

cover a variety of points of view, all of which represent a more extreme version of the traditional school of thought. Four such views will be examined, each highlighting a particular aspect of conservative thinking about education. It is an interesting fact that all of these positions have a significant body of followers (or like-minded thinkers) at the grass roots level and in the popular press, but are generally not as prominent in academic philosophy of education. There has been something of a conservative backlash in the 1970s and '80s, which is a reaction to the radical progressive flowering of the 1960s, and this will be discussed later. The general mood is also more sombre and less optimistic, with many causes and dimensions: economic, social, political and cultural. Fascinating as it would be to explore this topic in more detail, here there is only space to mention the basic educational theories that reflect this significant conservative swing in thought and practice.[12]

We shall begin with the so-called "Black Papers". These were written by a group of (mainly British) conservative authors, including politicians, novelists, school teachers and academics, who contributed articles to a series of pamphlets and booklets published in England between 1969 and 1977. Well-known figures represented are Kingsley Amis, G. H. Bantock, Jacques Barzun, Max Beloff, Rhodes Boyson, C. B. Cox, Robert Conquest, H. J. Eysenck, Richard Lynn and Iris Murdoch. The Black Papers constitute an unashamedly conservative polemic against everything progressives stand for, expressed in direct and in some cases vitriolic language.

An indication of the thinking underlying the Black Papers can be gleaned by considering the list of "Black Paper Basics" provided at the beginning of *Black Paper 1975*. Among others are the following:

> Children are not naturally good. They need firm, tactful discipline from parents and teachers with clear standards.
> Too much freedom for children breeds selfishness, vandalism and personal unhappiness.
> Schools are for schooling, not social engineering.
> Without (selective schooling) the clever working-class child in a deprived area stands little chance of a real academic education.
> External examinations are essential . . . without such checks, standards decline.
> . . . Equality will mean the holding back of the brighter children.[13]

Similar sentiments are echoed by like-minded groups in other countries, such as the Council for Basic Education in the United States and, in Australia, the Australian Council for Educational Standards. The Black Paper authors were particularly concerned about the growth of comprehensive schooling in the United Kingdom and wished to preserve the traditional English grammar school as an institution for the intellectual elite.

One Black Paper author who has argued his case in more depth than many of the others is G. H. Bantock who in *Black Paper 1977* argues for a two-track educational system — one for the academically talented and one for low achievers (who will be drawn mainly, though not exclusively, from the working class and will represent about 25% of the population).[14] The academically talented will be given the traditional liberal education while the other group will be provided with an education which is much less dependent on rationality and abstract thought. It will concentrate on physical activity (both of an aesthetic and gymnastic kind), design and craft work, twentieth century media and art forms (film, television, radio), domestic skills (mainly for girls) and technical education (mainly for boys).

One of the main factors leading to Bantock's advocating such a programme is his belief that the present academic curriculum is totally inappropriate for a significant segment of the school population who get little or no value from it and leave school feeling frustrated and alienated. While not everyone would agree with his solution to this problem, it has to be admitted that he has identified a real difficulty facing the school in contemporary society.

Another important influence on Bantock's thinking is his concern to preserve the traditional European "high" culture which he believes to be under threat in a mass society where general intellectual and artistic standards have fallen drastically. He sees literature, in particular, as central to liberal education, especially as represented by such writers as Samuel Taylor Coleridge, Matthew Arnold, D. H. Lawrence, T. S. Eliot, and all of whom, along with F. R. Leavis, he regards as significant social critics offering a more penetrating analysis of social and cultural problems than philosophers or sociologists.

The similarities between Bantock's two-track curriculum model and Plato's educational programme are strikingly apparent and indicate the permanent relevance and influence of Plato's work. Bantock's model is also clearly more extreme than anything the liberal writers advocate and would certainly be anathema to progressives. Nevertheless it is a provocative and influential model with which a considerable number of parents and teachers would have some sympathy. Bantock is at least to be admired for having the courage of his convictions and for honestly following through to their logical conclusion the sorts of assumptions about children and schooling that many conservatives hold.*

A quite different strand of conservative thinking is that which takes a strongly instrumentalist view of schooling and emphasizes efficiency in the teaching-learning process as the key issue. This view holds that the basic function of the school is to serve society and to produce the type of citizens needed by the state. Liberal education, or any reference to the intrinsic values of education, that people like Peters point to, are either ignored or rejected.

This school of thought has many sub-branches but all of them are characterised by a commitment to a positivistic approach to knowledge. According to this doctrine, all worthwhile knowledge is fundamentally of a scientific type because such knowledge can be reliably tested and verified, unlike, for example, metaphysical and ethical beliefs. The external world which we per-

*Bantock has also written widely outside of his Black Paper contributions and a list of his major works is included at the end of the chapter.

ceive through the senses is the true reality and the best way of understanding and controlling it is by precise and careful study of the general laws by which it is governed. These laws can normally best be understood by reducing them to their concrete particulars and testing these by observation and experiment. Overall then the emphasis is on accurate and painstaking measurement of what is held to be an objective ordered reality which exists independently of the human observer.

Consequently, when the positivist approach is applied to education, we have a stress on the mechanics of learning, on testing, accountability, measurement of objectives, and similar empirically verifiable aspects of education. Because this approach stresses education as a means to an end, it tends to accept without question the prevailing values and standards of the society, whether these be capitalist or socialist. It is thus equally applicable in both democratic and communist states as witnessed by its popularity in establishment circles in both the U.S.A. and the U.S.S.R. In England it is exemplified by the growth and influence of such bodies as the Assessment of Performance Unit, the Manpower Services Commission and the Further Education Curriculum Development Unit, all of which tend to encourage an instrumentalist, vocationally oriented, skills approach to education.

The economic recession in the West has added new impetus to this way of looking at education and has placed advocates of liberal education more on the defensive. Charles Bailey devotes a whole chapter entitled "The Challenge of Economic Utility" to this theme in his recent work arguing the case for liberal education.[15] He points to the assumed consensus in this approach of "continually accepted technological change and development, strangely related to nineteenth century conceptions of the undoubted good of 'progress', all taking place in the context of a competitive free market economy, and in a wider context of international competitive trade". He later argues that: "Education, in this model, becomes a commodity both for the individual person and for society as a whole, to be assessed like any other commodity in terms of its profitability or usefulness."[16]

In respect of the learning processes popular in such models, behaviourism has clearly been a major influence and the work of B. F. Skinner, discussed earlier in this book, is of central importance. One development of Skinner's views is to stress behavioural or instructional objectives rather than longer term or broader educational aims. This approach is popular with many people since, by stating educational goals precisely, it allows the behaviours required to be observed and measured exactly and also allows teachers to be held accountable for the learning they do or do not bring about. As G. F. Kneller points out, "instruction and content are related to behavioural objectives as means to ends or as input to output" and this input-output model is borrowed from business and industry and is justified in terms of measurable efficiency.[17] Critics of the approach claim it restricts the type of education that can take place in school to measurable, observable performances and devalues the more intangible but no less important aspects of education such as depth of understanding, autonomy, personal enrichment and emotional development.

Two other positivist (but not necessarily behaviourist) approaches to learning are those of cognitive science and systems engineering. Very briefly, the cognitive scientists see the human mind as an information-processing system similar to a computer and they aim to identify the basic cognitive skills involved in learning, which can then be fostered deliberately. Once the rules by which the mind works are identified correctly, the mind can then be programmed in the same way as a computer.

The systems engineer sees the school as a production process in which the system is the school, class or individual student which has to be processed to yield a certain type of output. If there is any interference to the smooth flow of the process the systems engineer is called in to specify those aspects that need to be altered. The engineer then models the system, represents it on a computer programme and simulates alternative scenarios to discover which is most satisfactory.*

It is clear that all these methods rely heavily on a mechanistic view of the mind and of the process of education and give little consideration to creativity, individual differences in interest and ability, knowledge valued for its own sake, intellectual doubt and curiosity, and they fit in very well with the instrumentally-oriented approach to the role of school in society. Other methods and educational techniques that similarly reflect in one way or another the instrumental approach, and were heavily influenced by the growth of educational psychology of a positivist kind in the fifties and sixties, are programmed learning, behaviour modification, taxonomies of objectives, classroom analysis, computer-assisted instruction, competency-based assessment and performance contracting. All of these have had their enthusiastic supporters and enjoyed varying degrees of popularity at one time or another, some of them still being very influential.

There is obviously a widespread range of techniques and methodologies open to those who take a positivist, instrumentalist approach to the role of the school. While not everyone who uses such methods would necessarily belong to the conservative school of thought about education, whenever such approaches become a central concern, the overall effect is to reinforce existing social and political structures. Rather than leading to any questioning or evaluating of the worth of such systems, the general thrust is towards more efficient ways of achieving goals set by those who control these systems, that is, by those who possess political and economic power. If any changes are considered necessary, they are to be made to the way we treat the student (and in some cases the teacher), not to the aim and structures of the institution in which the student is placed. Moreover the mechanistic model of

*For further description of these three approaches: behavioural objectives, cognitive science, systems engineering, see the useful account in G. F. Kneller, *Movements of Thought in Modern Education*, John Wiley, New York, 1984.

human nature and human learning typically involved in these approaches is quite opposed to views held by progressive educators, or for that matter by the liberal-analysts discussed previously.

The third conservative group to be considered may be termed the "free marketeers" or "libertarian" conservatives. This group traces its origins to the eighteenth-century writer Adam Smith who was the great pioneer of laissez-faire or free market economics. According to this doctrine, society as a whole benefits when individual members are free to pursue their own interests with minimal state interference. A society based on free competition and enlightened self-interest will, it is held, be more effective, productive and prosperous. Incentive to work and to be efficient will come from the free choice of the individual for his or her own betterment, rather than having to be coerced by the state.

Applying these notions to education, the natural consequence is a lessening of the power of the state to control education and giving more choice to parents regarding the education their children receive. In practice this generally means a voucher plan in which the state gives all parents a voucher which they can use to pay for their child's education at any school they choose, public or private. This, it is held, would lead to healthy competition between schools to attract sufficient students and in turn to more efficient schooling overall and less bureaucratic interference in education. Parents who send their children to private schools would no longer be paying twice, once through taxes for other children at state schools and once for their own children through private school fees. Parents who send their children to state schools would also benefit by having a wider choice of types of schools to which they can send their children and have more influence on what goes on in these schools.

One of the main advocates of a voucher plan is the well known free market economist, Milton Friedman. In the book *Free to Choose* (written jointly with Rose Friedman) published in 1979, he devotes one chapter to education where he presents strongly the case for increased parental choice. He would go even further than other voucher advocates and would abolish all state financing of schooling and end compulsory attendance laws; he realises, however, that these goals are unlikely to be achieved in the foreseeable future.

Friedman would also adopt a similar approach for higher education whereby students are lent sufficient money to cover their expenses on condition they agree to repay a specific proportion of their future earnings. The government would act in the role of an investor in the benefits of higher education who "could recoup more than his initial investment from relatively successful individuals, which would compensate for the failure to do so from the unsuccessful."[18] Such a policy, says Friedman, would make higher education more widely available and make it more just since parents of children who do not make use of higher education no longer would have to subsidise by way of their taxes those who do.

Naturally such far-reaching suggestions as these have given rise to much debate and have generated criticisms that education cannot be treated as an economic commodity, that such a policy would increase segregation of races and social classes and that it would permit the growth of schools promoting extremist or anti-democratic principles. There is not space to treat these issues here, but interested readers can assess Friedman's attempt to respond to them in his *Freedom to Choose* and also consult *Education by Choice: The Case for Family Control*, by Coons and Sugarman, which is devoted to a defence of family control of schooling. Many of these proposals also have clear political bearings and have attracted a good deal of interested debate in Western nations over recent years, naturally enough drawing most support from those on the conservative side of politics.

The final conservative group to consider are the Christian fundamentalists who have become very involved in setting up new schools over the last decade, especially in America, but also in other Western nations such as Australia.[19] By 1985 in the U.S.A. there were between 5000 and 6000 Christian day schools (affiliated mainly with Baptist Churches of a fundamentalist kind, but also with churches such as Assembly of God and Church of God) with a total of about a million pupils.[20] The unprecedented growth of such schools reflects a growing disenchantment by many Protestants with the public school system, in particular with what they see as declining academic standards, lack of discipline and the widespread influence of secular humanism. Not all those dissatisfied with public schools however have turned to fundamentalist schools as the alternative; many have tried to improve the system from within by promoting a return to the basics in public schools or by founding their own private schools with various religious or secular affiliations.*

However the fundamentalist schools are by far the biggest and fastest growing sector which rejects the public system and which offers the most clear-cut and distinctive alternative. For them education is thoroughly permeated by the Christian religion which is based on a literal interpretation of the Bible. The main aim of the school is to produce persons imbued with Christian faith who will live their life according to strict religious principles. Academic subjects are permeated with a religious orientation; science, for example, is based on a creationist rather than an evolutionist perspective. Many of these schools are rather small and teach children of different ages in a single room, often placing them in separate cubicles where they work at their own pace on special curriculum packages, one influential example being that known as Accelerated Christian Education (A.C.E.). The A.C.E. curriculum is divided into units, containing a three week programme of work with clearly specified objectives, learning activities, self-evaluations and a test; covering mainly the areas of mathematics, English, science and social studies. The content is strongly pervaded by religious teachings and reflects conservative political, economic and social viewpoints. Regular prayer and scripture study are an integral part of the whole programme.

---

*For a recent account of such developments in the U.S.A. see B. Y. Pines, *Back to Basics: The Traditionalist Movement That Is Sweeping Grass-Roots America*, William Morrow, New York, 1982

It is interesting to note that Christian fundamentalist schools share certain features of the two previous conservative viewpoints — they normally rely heavily on behaviourist techniques and clearly specified short-term objectives in the learning process as well as reflecting a strong role for parental choice in schooling. In fact many Christian fundamentalists would look with favour on a voucher scheme and one important source of support for educational vouchers can be found in such groups.

The rapid growth of fundamentalist schools also reflects the significant swing back to traditional principles in the 1970s and exemplifies one influential manifestation of conservative thinking about education. These schools offer a genuine alternative to the mainstream schools in placing heavy emphasis on such factors as absolute values, deep commitment, certainty about one's beliefs, hard work, discipline, emphasis on basics, and most significantly of all, indicate a type of educational programme that results when religion is placed at the centre of life.

We have now completed the survey of recent manifestations of traditional thinking in education, noting that these may be classified into liberal and conservative wings. It will have become clear by now that the latter groups are not necessarily supporters of the status quo, but in many cases see the present system as itself having departed too far from an historically earlier and preferable model. In the case of the Black Paper writers, the free marketeers and the Christian fundamentalists, earlier models of educational provision such as existed in the nineteenth century, which involved a more differentiated educational system, one where the state had less complete control and where Christian values were more central, would have been closer to their aspirations.

That the conservatives take a more extreme interpretation of the traditional model than the liberals will also have become evident from the way they focus very heavily on one particular aspect of this model, be it the preservation of our literary and artistic culture, efficiency in the transfer of knowledge from teacher to pupil, parental control of children's education or the importance of Christian values. This one aspect becomes the determining factor for their whole orientation to educational issues. It also means that they generally present a less comprehensive educational theory than the liberals who take a broader and more flexible approach to education. The underlying value for the latter can be seen as the promotion of rational autonomy for all children in so far as this can be achieved without endangering other important principles such as equality and justice. Such a wide-ranging value allows a choice of alternative models and processes by which it may be achieved, but it would none the less be inconsistent with some of the conservative approaches discussed, in that the opportunity to try to realize it is to be provided for *all* children, in a school which is not narrowly focussed on instrumental learning, one over which the state has an important say in ensuring that approved educational standards are met, and in which a critical attitude is fostered rather than premature acceptance of any one particular world view.

Recent Developments of the Progressive Approach

Turning now to recent developments of the progressive model, two broad approaches are distinguishable, which may be termed "confrontationist" and "corrective". The confrontationist version received considerable publicity in the turbulent decade from 1964 to 1974. This was a period of profound international troubles, marked by American involvement in the Vietnam war and the attempt by Mao in China to effect a major transformation of Chinese society in the Cultural Revolution. Virtually all of the world was affected by these events: fears of spill-over conflicts and the threat of all-out nuclear war, and consequent global devastation, were felt by many. Anti-war demonstrations and escalating violence throughout Europe, Britain, North America and Japan occurred with increasing regularity, and spread to smaller industrial nations such as Australia and New Zealand, and into the less-developed Third World.

A central element of the conflict of this period was a profound dissatisfaction by the growing numbers of dissentients with the emphasis on war, and the involvement of education as an important contributing agent. It was, moreover, a period of sustained affluence and rising expectations by many in the developed world, and this was reflected in an optimism about the future of society, especially among the young, if only they could enter a period of peace and constructive activity. It was in that decade, then, that more vigorous forms of progressive educational thought became promoted.

Yet Vietnam, and the military draft which created so much tension and bitter divisiveness on American university campuses, along with the other trend of optimism for the future, were in large part only aspects of more profound changes that were occurring in Western industrial societies. Throughout the 1950s and 1960s, the dominant social paradigm had become increasingly questioned, the philosophical origins of such questioning resting on earlier European intellectual traditions going back at least to the period of the Enlightenment and including more recent developments in the nineteenth century of such philosophical movements as existentialism and phenomenology. However the most important single influence at this time was Marxism which has provided much of the conceptual background of European dissenting thought of the twentieth century.

Marx's ideas have already been presented in this book in the commentary on the educational activity of Anton Makarenko. Here it is only necessary to reiterate the most seminal of these, chiefly those dealing with privileged ruling class ownership of private property and the means of production which enables it to accumulate capital, and the consequent alienation of the majority of people who are reduced to selling their labour in return for the minimum wages that a competitive labour market will provide. These ideas were influenced by Darwin's thoughts on natural selection made popular when Herbert Spencer reformulated them as the "survival of the fittest". In the nineteenth century such social Darwinism was promoted as "fair competition" and "equality of opportunity"; in economic terms, it had come through earlier in Adam Smith's concept of the "invisible hand" of marketplace competition. Marx was the first major political theorist of the modern period to focus attention on what he considered the enslaving character of the industrial system, and on his belief that the ruling class creates a plausible system of ideas, an ideology, to mask its political and economic domination. The ruling class controlled virtually all communication: it owned all of the media (exclusively print-media in the nineteenth century), it dominated parliament, the courts, the bureaucracy, the church, the armed forces and police, and the universities, colleges and schools. So, argued Marx, the labouring masses, until they are able to organize effective opposition, are subject to the ideological constructions of the ruling class. Ideology was already a well-known term in the period, referring to an organized structure of ideas; Marx made a signal contribution to political thought by arguing that ideologies are false systems of thought which deceive the masses by creating a "false consciousness". The investigation of educational ideologies and their social consequences increased rapidly in the 1960s.

By 1970 these investigations were producing an important body of dissenting literature and the phrase "new sociology of education" became prominent, one of the most influential works in this genre being *Knowledge and Control: New Directions for the Sociology of Education*, edited by Michael Young in 1971. Generally, this "new sociology", drawing upon Marxist and phenomenological theory, concerned itself heavily with such concepts as ideology, alienation, subjectivity of experience, class conflict, hegemony, privilege and oppression. A central concern was the recognition of the rapidly changing character of society as it became transformed by science and technology. Privileged technocratic elites were forming and amassing what was termed "cultural capital" which allowed them to dominate national economies. Simultaneously, these elites developed automation techniques and were responsible for the rapidly escalating technologisation of industry, commerce and finance which led to increasing unemployment or reduced opportunities for educational and social participation by the underprivileged. And, rather threateningly, there was a growing trend of reduced participation and opportunity into middle class ranks.

In 1972 came two very influential books in this wave of radical dissent: *Deschooling Society* by Ivan Illich and *Pedagogy of the Oppressed* by the Brazilian, Paulo Freire. Illich has already been discussed in Chapter 9. Having become widely known for his concept of "deschooling", he has since applied the same sorts of arguments of the harmful effects of institutionalisation and bureaucratisation that he saw in schools to other social institutions or agencies such as religion, law, medicine and transport.[21] His basic concern is to replace what he calls "manipulative" institutions, which take away individual choice, with "convivial" ones, in which persons are self-directing and either produce what they need for themselves or act co-operatively with others in the tasks of production. He wants, in fact, to replace large hierarchical and authoritarian institutions with small-scale, decentralised organisations in which important and socially useful knowledge is available to all. In such a system, people can be their own lawyers, doctors, mechanics, architects and so on, to a much greater extent than now where certain privileged groups have a monopoly on the knowledge and skills involved. He proposes a society based on a low-energy technology in which all would have an equal share of a larger range of simpler and more generally available goods and services.

In the sphere of education in particular he has developed his general attack on the school to a criticism of adult and vocational education as presently organised, in his 1976 article with Etienne Verne, *Imprisoned in the Global Classroom*[22]. In his 1979 essay, "Vernacular Values and Education",[23] Illich decries the modern all-encompassing tendency to eradicate local community vernacular languages and associated cultural values and the move to replace them with the national language, which by analogy with the Catholic Church as a Mother Church he describes as a mother tongue. The imposition of a national language is furthered by the state dominated school system which replaces meaningful community learning by the artificial procedures of institutional pedagogy. The sinister effect of all this in Illich's view, is that education becomes a commodity which helps destroy the important vernacular values that were once widely held.

In his latest essay, "Eco-Paedagogics and the Commons"[24], he is concerned with global environmental issues. Here he continues to attack the approach of industrialised nations whose schools, he argues, are designed to produce the genus *homo economicus*, that is, persons who spend most of their lives either consuming the products of industry or else working to find the money to pay for them. This, he argues, is a meaningless treadmill. Given the world environmental crisis of the past two decades, and the recognition that the earth is really a "container for scarce resources", the task of all people is to move from growth-oriented consumer cultures to steady-state sustainability. So, argues Illich, the primary task of education, and hence of the school, should be that of developing a new kind of co-management which he calls "eco-paedagogics". All people now must come to respect and treasure the resources and environment of the planet, and this realm he calls the "commons" in which "subsistence-oriented action transcends economic space" and people recover "the right to live in self-limiting communities"[25]. *

By the mid 1970s a new wave of more trenchantly critical works had begun appearing, based upon explicitly Marxist analyses of education in relation to society. There are many varieties of Marxism, but they may be separated into two broad categories, the "classical" Marxists, sometimes known by the labels "traditional", "structuralist" and "scientific", and the "Neo-Marxists", sometimes known as "humanist" and "critical" Marxists. Classical Marxists hold more firmly to the original argument that social conditions are wholly determined by economic structures. The Neo-Marxists, in

---

*An up-to-date list of Illich's works dealing with education is given on p. 398.

contrast, are somewhat more flexible in that while accepting the importance of economic structures, they believe that society can be altered by human intervention, leading to more liberating social forms and relations. Radical social change can be achieved by the growth of "conscientisation" as teachers and students come to recognise the pressures for conformity to the ideas and demands of the dominant classes and work to resist them.

While these two versions of Marxism are not mutually exclusive, most Marxist writers tend to have more in common with one or other of these positions and throughout the 1970s and 1980s, both groups have produced significant work relating Marxist thinking to education. We shall begin by mentioning some of the major examples of classical Marxist writing in this period.* In 1975 a significant English study entitled *Education and Social Control: A Study in Progressive Primary Education* was written by Rachel Sharp and Anthony Green. In this critical analysis of an English progressive school, the authors argue that liberal educational theorists fail to realise how thoroughly capitalist ideology penetrates such a school. Progressivism, they assert, is really a disguised form of liberalism which still serves dominant class interests. In 1980 Sharp followed this with *Knowledge, Ideology and the Politics of Schooling: Towards a Marxist Analysis of Schooling* which examines the political implications of schooling in contemporary capitalist society.

Meanwhile, in the United States an equally powerful attack upon capitalism was made in 1976 by Samuel Bowles and Herbert Gintis in *Schooling in Capitalist America*. This work analyses the processes of cultural reproduction at work, whereby the schools, as agents of capitalist society, reproduce class and economic divisions in their students. Bowles and Gintis were strongly influenced by the so-called "revisionist" historians such as Michael Katz, Clarence Karier and Joel Spring, who explicitly rejected the liberal view of history that had been predominant in American work in the history of education. They argued that theorists such as Dewey failed to appreciate the alienating effects of capitalist society and took too optimistic a view of the power of the school to reform society. They therefore aimed to "revise" history of education by taking a much more critical view of social institutions such as schools and how these were used to maintain the power of privileged groups in society.

In Australia, Kevin Harris, writing from a background in philosophy of education, produced *Education and Knowledge: The Structured Misrepresentation of Reality* in 1979. Taking a Marxist epistemological stance, Harris attacks the hegemonic function of school knowledge in a capitalist society and argues that it is, at base, political manipulation. In 1982 Harris brought out *Teachers and Classes* which argues that genuine education is inimical to capitalism, and that teachers must act collectively if they desire to assist in breaking down the power of the state. Also writing in Australia, similarly with a background in philosophy of education, and, like Harris, strongly influenced

---

*The following writers would not necessarily share exactly the same understanding of classical Marxism and would vary in their degree of adherence to some of its features.

by recent work in the philosophy of science, is Michael Matthews, author of *The Marxist Theory of Schooling* (1980).

Neo-Marxist analyses of education were also being made in the same period; in this area Michael Apple and Henry Giroux have produced significant studies. In 1979 appeared Apple's *Ideology and Curriculum* which analyses the role of the curriculum in perpetuating conditions which support ideological and cultural hegemony. In 1982 came his *Education and Power*, in which he discusses the role of the school in reproducing the social order dictated by the corporate class and thereby legitimising the process of capital accumulation by the privileged. Apple argues, however, that the school can resist some of these influences. Giroux, in the 1981 publication of *Ideology, Culture and the Process of Schooling* attacks the ideological and political character of positivist rationality. While focusing upon the curriculum he argues, like Apple, that schools can resist hegemonic influences, and he also presents the possibility of the school becoming an agent of emancipation from capitalist domination.

In a category by itself is *Learning to Labour: How Working Class Kids Get Working Class Jobs*, an earlier 1977 study by Paul Willis of a comprehensive school in an English industrial area. In this detailed work Willis examines the lives of a group of boys and reveals how their own working class culture militates against their achievement in wider society. In the same year appeared *Reproduction In Education, Society and Culture* by Bourdieu and Passeron (which was a translation from the French). This employs a similar style of argument, but is more theoretically oriented, and has been a significant influence on Anglo-American theorists.

At the same time, a secondary form of progressivism was emerging which could be termed corrective. Eschewing any directly confrontationist posture, the corrective approach sought an accommodation with the dominant social paradigm, believing that change had to be gradual, emerging out of new forms of consciousness. Paulo Freire could be interpreted as a theorist whose ideas actually bridge the gap between confrontationist and corrective approaches. While he believes in the overthrow of existing exploitative and authoritarian societies, he does not accept all of Marx's ideas and believes the prime agent for social change should be deeper cultural awareness rather than political and economic revolution. Concerned with the plight of the oppressed masses of Brazil, most of whom are illiterate, Freire, whose thought includes Christian, Marxist and Existentialist elements, promoted the term "conscientisation" to describe the need to raise popular awareness by the people of their oppression by the powerful and wealthy. Opposing teacher-dominated schools in which knowledge is organized in advance, Freire introduced the concept of "banking" in which he argued that teachers "bank" knowledge in learner's minds, allowing the best students to make considerable accumulations of cultural capital. Opposing this as pedagogically inept, and ideologically unsound, he promoted the concept of "dialogical" education whereby teachers and students become engaged in shared creative learning. Teachers should encourage students to become aware of their life situation — "conscientisation" — and through a dialectical interplay between thought and action — the Marxist concept of "praxis" — to become able to remake their world in more culturally appropriate ways.

Freire's widespread influence is partly due to the fact that he employed "praxis" in presenting his own theory — using the methods he recommended very successfully in his own teaching. Moreover, although he wrote and practised in a Third World context, his ideas have been taken by many as relevant to educational problems and issues in the West, such as the alienation of many students from their school experience, and in regard to approaches to adult education, particularly with the teaching of disadvantaged groups. He also struck a sympathetic chord with many by his stress on the fact that education cannot be neutral; it either "domesticates" or liberates. As already pointed out, this has become widely recognised in the last decade, at least to the extent of a general acceptance that an educational theory always reflects certain normative assumptions.

While Freire may have a bridging role between confrontationist and corrective prospectives, most corrective-style progressives adopted a lower profile. Many simply withdrew altogether into alternative communes and similar "sustainable life-style" communities where they conducted schools on more practical, utilitarian models. Another group which has its origins in Humanistic Psychology is generally characterised by a concern with "holistic" or whole-person approaches. These approaches, however, are not merely contemporary developments and it is necessary, therefore, to examine briefly their genesis.

During the 1950s the movement known as Humanistic Psychology was given firm academic impetus by Abraham Maslow in his study of what he described as "self-actualized" individuals. Generally, the trend of most Western science, both physical and social, had been reductionist in method and intent, the aim being to reduce the external world, by analytic methods, to its basic constituents, the goal being the mastery of nature. If ultimate structures could be understood, then intervention, control and reconstruction, on human terms ("man-made") would be feasible. Maslow, however, rejected such positivist and reductionist thinking. Working on the assumption that individuals seek to actualise their implicitly-felt potentials, Maslow, in his various works, put the proposition that once basic needs are satisfied actualisation can come from within the individual. All people have needs, starting with elemental physiological needs, from which each one progresses upwards, in what he terms a "hierarchy of needs" through basic social needs such as security, safety, love and acceptance to growth needs, which include simplicity, justice, truth and a search for meaning in life, and finally to the highest goal: self-actualization.

Simultaneously, Carl Rogers, working as a psychotherapist in the United States, produced *Client Centered Therapy* as early as 1951. Rejecting the traditional Freudian reductionist method of psychotherapy, Rogers maintained that by creating a non-threatening, non-judgmental environment, characterised by an attitude of empathy, trust and respect for the client, therapy could take place in a self-directed manner.

In similar vein to Rogers' non-directive therapy came the work of Fritz Perls, a prolific writer, who also believed that given the right conditions people could become self-directing. Using the famous concept of "gestalt", a German word meaning "form", "shape" or "figure" (developed from the pioneering work in Germany in the 1920s, variously, of Wertheimer, Kohler and Kafka on human perception of spatial relationships of objects and their context), Perls developed a psychotherapy known as Gestalt Therapy. Through an awareness of emotions and bodily sensations, individuals are encouraged to explore the various fragments of the incomplete gestalt, in order to bring them together to form a complete unit of experience. This process, by freeing the client from unfinished past experiences allows positive personal development to take place.

By the 1960s, with the Western world in profound disorder and open conflict in Vietnam, psychotherapeutic approaches became more popular, as did interest in Eastern philosophies. By this time even the physical sciences had begun to question the traditional Western view of reality, which had come through in Cartesian form, believing material existence to be the totality. At this time, Roberto Assagioli wrote about the human quest to reach an ultimate level of the "higher self" where true wisdom may be found, while Alan Watts was particularly concerned with the insights to be gained from meditation and inner peace as taught by Zen Buddhism. From these and similar ways of thinking, developed the new Transpersonal Psychology, a movement in the United States popularised by James Fadiman and others, in which psychology was presented as a means of helping persons transcend the limitations of a materialist, industrial, consumer world to reach higher levels of co-operation, self-awareness, integration and serenity.

As a result of these developments in psychology and psychotherapy,* new influences came to bear upon education: not within the traditional mainstream, dominated by liberal and conservative thought, but within an alternative "counter-culture". Writing in *Freedom to Learn* (1969), Carl Rogers argues that children are capable of managing their own significant, meaningful learning. The "teacher" as a concept was out; the new term was that of "facilitator", one who sets up a learning environment in which self-directed learning can take place. This, of course, threatens the traditional power structures in education and ultimately in society, and in 1977 Rogers wrote *On Personal Power* to explore these issues. Meanwhile, the Gestalt approach of Fritz Perls was adapted for the school by George Isaac Brown. He developed the evocative term "confluent education", to highlight the recognition that cognitive and emotional processes always flow together. In traditional education, body and mind have generally been rigidly separated,

*By 1962, such developments, from the work of Maslow onwards, had generated sufficient interest to warrant the establishment of the Association for Humanistic Psychology and the publication, *Journal of Humanistic Psychology*.

and even mind has been compartmentalised into its rational and emotional aspects. Brown rejected this; the curriculum, he argued, must be reformed from its cold, detached existence as a systematic arrangement of facts to have a human emphasis, organised, that is, to facilitate the integration of the child's thinking and feeling, into a series of unified experiences. The traditional approach, he argued, by concentrating solely on intellect, leads to individual unhappiness, social conflict and ultimately to international disorder.*

Transpersonal Education, with its emphasis on spirituality and techniques traditionally associated with Eastern religions as well as altered states of consciousness and untapped biological energy, provides at this stage a stimulating challenge of new perspectives and insights rather than a fully developed educational theory.

Initially, the Humanistic Psychologists (and related thinkers) were less influenced by social and political factors than were Marxist and radical thinkers, concentrating instead on the goal of individual self realisation without attending to the system within which this takes place. They are thus considered as belonging to the corrective rather than confrontationist stream of educational thought. However, as with the other theorists discussed in this chapter, they too have turned their attention recently to social and political issues. Rogers, for example, in *On Personal Power* examines the implications of his theory for power structures in society, while recent issues of the main journal in the area, *Journal of Humanistic Psychology*, have devoted considerable space to articles dealing with peace, conflict resolution, inequality and environmental issues.

Education and Contemporary Social Issues

We have now explored some of the major developments of the traditional and progressive approaches during the last decade or so and noted the various manifestations of these two broad ways of thinking about education. One theme that has been reiterated throughout is the necessity to take account of the social and political context in which educational thinking takes place. It is thus appropriate to conclude this chapter by considering briefly some of the major social issues that have become prominent in the recent period and which are likely to increase in importance in coming years. Some of the ways in which education has begun to respond to the various social problems will be mentioned as well as possible future approaches. Also, in assessing the relevance of the various educational theories discussed in the earlier part of this chapter (as well as in the book as a whole), one consideration could well be how far their recommendations would contribute to the solution of the major social problems facing us today.

Even though the 1960s and '70s saw a stream of progressive and radical

---

*There are clearly some important similarities between the ideas of Rogers, Brown and other writers discussed here and the approach used by A. S. Neill at Summerhill. (See Chapter 7.)

educational theory, by the early 1970s it was clear that the turbulent decade was coming to an end. In 1973 came the world energy crisis, which resulted from the Middle East War of that year; by 1974 the world economy was faltering and in 1975 Saigon fell to North Vietnamese forces and United States involvement in Vietnam was ended. All of these events exercised a direct brake upon social unrest and student militancy; accompanying this came a reaction. A conservative response, in the same period in fact, had been growing, and in 1975 appeared a manifesto for conservative educational and social policy, *The Crisis of Democracy*, edited by Michel Crozier and others.[26] In that book, a résumé of proceedings of a conference of corporation, government and trade union executives from Western Europe, Japan and the United States, progressive education and student militancy were denounced, the end of a decade of educational expansion was signalled, and the new, conservative programme of reduced expectations for the majority, and the pursuit of materialistic, technocratic objectives was promoted as the way ahead. For the ensuing decade, into the mid-1980s, that programme has become dominant.

Yet the conservative dominance of society since the middle of the seventies has not been entirely one-sided, nor has it seen the general introduction of a reactionary regime in education; in fact, some of the more moderate features of progressivism have become incorporated in educational thought and practice. However, since the 1974–75 economic collapse a number of world problems have risen to levels of international significance and awareness. The collapse demanded economy and efficiency which led to automation on a wide scale, especially made possible with the spectacular success of microprocessor ("silicon chip") development. Corporate growth through mergers and takeovers became accelerated, and workforces changed their composition as the less-skilled were retrenched while the highly skilled moved into what Barry Jones has called the quarternary sector of the economy, that is, that sector concerned with information processing.[27]

As industry became more efficient, and pursued objectives of greater growth and profits, with reduced workforces, social problems mounted; so too did resource and environment issues. The social problems emerged from increasing large scale unemployment, especially among the poor and underprivileged, while increasing conscientisation led to much wider awareness of racism, sexism and endemic poverty. Internationally, anxiety grew as a consequence of nuclear proliferation, international terrorism and religious fundamentalism. Equally distressing was a growing recognition of the fragility of the environment as a consequence of technological build-up, and resource depletion as a result of excessive industrialisation. As early as 1962 Rachel Carson had sounded environmental alarm in her startling exposé of widespread pesticide toxicity in *Silent Spring*.[28] Yet her warnings were ignored; resource extraction went ahead unchecked and environmental degradation came, inexorably, as a consequence.

By 1972 world environmental problems were so pressing that an international conference on the environment was held in Stockholm, resulting in the book *Only One Earth* by Barbara Ward and Rene Dubos.[29] Throughout the 1970s, with galloping population growth, more frequent droughts (due to increasing desertification as forests were cleared for "development") and energy crises, the world had forced upon it a recognition of the fact that the earth has indeed a fragile ecosystem. The concept of 'Spaceship Earth' and limits to growth became accepted, but not before the environment of developed and developing countries alike had become troubled by salinity, erosion, desertification, pollution, species loss, amenity and wilderness loss, and degradation of urban environments. Only slowly has there been any serious concerted effort to deal with resource depletion and environmental problems.

Yet these problems have produced a number of forward-looking responses. Throughout the world environmental groups have proliferated and in Europe and Britain political "Green" parties have contested elections; in Germany they have won seats. The old dominant social paradigm which stressed an anthropocentric view of nature, and which saw conflict between various social groups for material possessions, is increasingly becoming moderated by the more ecocentric view that mankind shares the earth with nature and that environmental issues require a new social paradigm of greater ecological awareness. Slowly, education is coming to respond and theorists of differing orientations are realising that these problems can no longer be ignored by educators. Various groups are beginning to address the issues of peace, violence, sexism, racism, overconsumption, overpopulation, unemployment, pollution and environmental degradation. These concerns are now beginning to influence education and in the late twentieth century they will necessarily assume greater prominence. The responsible study of such issues will become a major focus of the next wave of educational thought and debate on the role of the school and may produce the next significant innovation in Western educational thought. Theorists will of course differ in how far they see it as the school's responsibility to confront these problems and whether helpful responses to them are more likely to come from giving all children a broad general education, or from aiming to develop specific knowledge and attitudes with regard to these issues. For instance, as will be clear from the earlier discussion, the liberal-analysts would favour the teaching of general liberal moral and political values which they regard as providing a useful basis for approaching any of these problems. Some of the radical and Marxist thinkers on the other hand would want to see a more specific set of attitudes towards society fostered in children and the school used more directly as an agent of social reform.*

The survey of recent thinking about education provided in this chapter reveals a number of interesting developments in the period since 1974. The basic traditional and progressive orientations to education have continued

---

*See pp. 352-3 in the Peters' Commentary for an earlier discussion of this question.

but in a more flexible way, and with a wide spectrum of viewpoints within each category ranging from strong versions of the model to more muted ones. Most of the recent theorists have attempted to relate their thinking to the contemporary society in which they are writing and to indicate the relevance of their ideas for current social issues. It also remains true that the basic ideas of the earlier thinkers covered in this book continue to be influential and relevant to contemporary educational issues and that present day responses cannot be properly understood without appreciating their intellectual and cultural foundations in the formative thinkers of the Western educational heritage. It may be concluded by noting that the social and educational problems facing us now are more complex than at any other time in our history and that it is unlikely that any one theorist has all the answers. It is therefore necessary to consider a wide range of points of view before developing a personal position of one's own and it is hoped that the broad overview presented here and the accompanying list of references will assist in the pursuit of this aim.

NOTES AND REFERENCES

1. R. S. Peters, "Democratic Values and Educational Aims", Ch. 3 in R. S. Peters, *Essays on Educators*, Allen & Unwin, London, 1981, p. 49.
2. For further elaboration of these points see R. S. Peters, "Ambiguities in Liberal Education and the Problem of its Content" and "Dilemmas in Liberal Education", Chs. 3 and 4 in R. S. Peters, *Education and the Education of Teachers*, Routledge and Kegan Paul, London, 1977.
3. "Democratic Values and Educational Aims", pp. 47–8.
4. P. H. Hirst, "Liberal Education and the Nature of Knowledge" in R. D. Archambault (Ed.), *Philosophical Analysis and Education*, Routledge & Kegan Paul, London, 1965. Hirst has made a number of minor modifications to his original list of the forms of knowledge in later writing on the topic. See, for instance, P. H. Hirst & R. S. Peters, *The Logic of Education*, Routledge & Kegan Paul, 1970, Ch. 4; and P. H. Hirst, "The Forms of Knowledge Revisited" in P. H. Hirst, *Knowledge and the Curriculum*, Routledge and Kegan Paul, London, 1974.
5. "Liberal Education and the Nature of Knowledge", Ed. Archambault, *op.cit.* p. 122.
6. See, for example, R. Barrow, *Common Sense and the Curriculum*, Allen & Unwin, London, 1976, Ch. 2 (iii); M. Matthews, *The Marxist Theory of Schooling*, Harvester Press, Sussex, 1980, Ch. 9; D. C. Phillips, "The Distinguishing Features of Forms of Knowledge", *Educational Philosophy and Theory*, III, No. 2, October, 1971; J. P. White, *Towards a Compulsory Curriculum*, Routledge and Kegan Paul, London, 1973, Ch. 6.
7. *Ethics and Education*, Allen & Unwin, London, 1966, Ch. 5.
8. "Return to the Cave: New Directions for Philosophy of Education" in R. Barrow (Ed.), "Philosophy and Education", *Educational Analysis*, IV, No. 1, Falmer Press, Sussex, 1982, p. 96.
9. *Ibid.*, p. 99.
10. See R. Barrow, *The Philosophy of Schooling*, Wheatsheaf Books, Sussex, 1981, pp. 22–3; R. Barrow, "On Misunderstanding Philosophy", *Education for Teaching*, No. 92, Autumn 1973.
11. Some recent developments in liberal-analytic and other approaches to philosophy of education are surveyed in R. F. Dearden, "Philosophy of Education, 1952–82", *British Journal of Educational Studies*, XXX, No. 1, February 1982 and also in R. S. Peters, "Philosophy of Education" in P. H. Hirst (Ed.), *Educational Theory and its Foundation Disciplines*, Routledge & Kegan Paul, London, 1983.
12. Some of these broad trends of thought as represented in the last two decades are explored by Paul Nash in his article, "Humanism and Humanistic Education in the Eighties: The Lessons of Two Decades", *Journal of Education* (Boston), CLXII, No. 3, Summer 1980.
13. C. B. Cox and R. Boyson (Eds.), *Black Paper 1975*, J. M. Dent & Sons, London, 1975, p. 1.
14. G. H. Bantock, "An Alternative Curriculum", in C. B. Cox & R. Boyson (Eds.), *Black Paper 1977*, Temple Smith, London, 1977.

15. C. Bailey, *Beyond the Present and the Particular: A Theory of Liberal Education*, Routledge & Kegan Paul, London, 1984.
16. *Ibid.*, p. 177.
17. G. F. Kneller, *Movements of Thought in Modern Education*, John Wiley, New York, 1984, p. 153.
18. M. & R. Friedman, *Free to Choose*, Secker & Warburg, London, 1978, p. 184.
19. For a discussion of issues relating to Fundamentalist schools (and of Christian schools generally) in the Australian context see *Journal of Christian Education*, Papers 67 ("Deschooling Christianity?"), July 1980, and Papers 75 ("Christian Schools"), November 1982.
20. W. J. Reese, "Soldiers for Christ in the Army of God: The Christian School Movement in America", *Educational Theory*, XXXV, No. 2, Spring 1985, p. 175.
21. In chronological order, the relevant works by Illich are: *Tools for Conviviality*, Harper & Row, New York, 1973; *Energy and Equity*, Calder & Boyars, London, 1974; *Limits to Medicine*, Marion Boyars, London, 1976 (Revised version of *Medical Nemesis*, Calder & Boyars, London, 1975); "Disabling Professions — Notes for a Lecture", *Contemporary Crises*, VI, No. 4, 1977, and also in *Biosciences Communications*, III, No. 4, 1977; *The Right to Useful Unemployment*, Marion Boyars, London, 1978; *Toward a History of Needs*, Pantheon Books, New York, 1978, *Shadow Work*, Marion Boyars, London, 1981.
22. I. Illich & E. Verne, *Imprisoned in the Global Classroom*, Writers and Readers Publishing Co-operative, London, 1976.
23. "Vernacular Values and Education", *Teachers College Record*, LXXXI No. 1, Fall 1979, repr. in *Shadow Work*, Marion Boyars, London, 1981.
24. "Eco-Paedagogics and the Commons", *New Education*, VI, No.2, 1984.
25. *Ibid.*, pp. 33–4.
26. M. Crozier *et al*, *The Crisis of Democracy*. New York University Press, for the Trilateral Commission, New York, 1975.
27. B. Jones, *Sleepers Wake! Technology and the Future of Work*. Oxford University Press, Melbourne, 1982.
28. R. Carson, *Silent Spring*, Houghton Mifflin, New York, 1962; since reprinted in various editions, including Penguin, 1965.
29. B. Ward and R. Dubos, *Only One Earth: The Care and Maintenance of a Small Planet*. Andre Deutsch, London, 1972; reprinted Penguin, 1972.

Select Bibliography

Below is a list of the main works of each of the key writers or schools of thought mentioned in this chapter, along with some evaluations of them. They are grouped according to the major categories that have been distinguished and in the order these were introduced, beginning with some general works covering a range of categories.

GENERAL WORKS

S. Aronowitz and H. A. Giroux, *Education under Siege; the Conservative, Liberal and Radical Debate over Schooling*, Bergin and Garvey, South Hadley, Mass., 1985.

G. F. Kneller, *Movements of Thought in Modern Education*, John Wiley, New York, 1984.

LIBERAL-ANALYTIC WRITERS

Individual Writers:

C. Bailey, *Beyond the Present and the Particular: A Theory of Liberal Education*, Routledge & Kegan Paul, London, 1984.

R. Barrow, *Moral Philosophy for Education*, Allen & Unwin, London, 1975.

R. Barrow, *Radical Education: A Critique of Freeschooling and Deschooling*, Martin Robertson, London, 1978.

R. Barrow, *The Philosophy of Schooling*, Harvester Press, Sussex, 1981.

R. Barrow, *Giving Teaching back to Teachers: A Critical Introduction to Curriculum Theory*, Wheatsheaf Books, Sussex, 1984.

B. Cohen, *Education and the Individual*, Allen & Unwin, London, 1981.

B. Cohen, *Means and Ends in Education*, Allen & Unwin, London, 1983.

R. F. Dearden, *The Philosophy of Primary Education*, Routledge & Kegan Paul, London, 1968.

R. F. Dearden, *Problems in Primary Education*, Routledge & Kegan Paul, London, 1976.

R. F. Dearden, *Theory and Practice in Education*, Routledge & Kegan Paul, London, 1984.

P. H. Hirst, *Knowledge and the Curriculum*, Routledge & Kegan Paul, London, 1974.

P. H. Hirst, *Moral Education in a Secular Society*, University of London Press Ltd, London, 1974.

P. H. Hirst, "Theory of Education", Ch. 1 in P. H. Hirst (Ed.) *Educational Theory and its Foundation Disciplines*, Routledge & Kegan Paul, London, 1983.

R. S. Peters: For references see "Select Bibliography" at end of Chapter 8.

J. P. White, *Towards a Compulsory Curriculum*, Routledge & Kegan Paul, 1973.

J. P. White, *The Aims of Education Restated*, Routledge & Kegan Paul, London, 1982.

P. White, *Beyond Domination: An Essay in the Political Philosophy of Education*, Routledge & Kegan Paul, London, 1983.

J. Wilson, *Education in Religion and the Emotions*, Heinemann, London, 1971.

J. Wilson, *A Teacher's Guide to Moral Education*, Geoffrey Chapman, London,, 1973.

J. Wilson, *Philosophy and Practical Education*, Routledge & Kegan Paul, London, 1977.

J. Wilson, *Fantasy and Common Sense in Education*, Martin Robertson, Oxford, 1979.

J. Wilson, *Preface to the Philosophy of Education*, Routledge & Kegan Paul, London, 1979.

Anthologies

R. D. Archambault (Ed.), *Philosophical Analysis and Education*, Routledge and Kegan Paul, London, 1965.

R. F. Dearden, P. H. Hirst & R. S. Peters (Eds.) *Education and the Development of Reason*, Routledge & Kegan Paul, London, 1972. (Republished in three volumes in 1975: I, *A Critique of Current Educational Aims*; II, *Reason*; III, *Education and Reason*.)

J. F. Doyle (Ed.), *Educational Judgements*, Routledge & Kegan Paul, London, 1973.

G. Langford & D. J. O'Connor (Eds.), *New Essays in the Philosophy of Education*, Routledge and Kegan Paul, London, 1973.

R. S. Peters (Ed.), *The Philosophy of Education*, Oxford University Press, London, 1973.

K. A. Strike & K. Egan (Eds.), *Ethics and Educational Policy*, Routledge & Kegan Paul, London, 1978.

CONSERVATIVE WRITERS

Black Papers and G. H. Bantock

C. B. Cox & A. E. Dyson (Eds.), *Fight for Education: A Black Paper*, Critical Quarterly Society, London, 1969.
  Black Paper Two: The Crisis in Education, Critical Quarterly Society, London, 1969.
  Black Paper Three: Goodbye Mr. Short, Critical Quarterly Society, London, 1970.
C. B. Cox & R. Boyson (Eds.), *Black Paper 1975*, J. M. Dent, London, 1975.
C. B. Cox, *Black Paper 1977*, Temple Smith, London, 1977.
G. H. Bantock, *Culture, Industrialisation and Education*, Routledge & Kegan Paul, London, 1968.
G. H. Bantock, *Dilemmas of the Curriculum*, Martin Robertson, Oxford, 1980.
G. H. Bantock, *The Parochialism of the Present*, Routledge & Kegan Paul, London, 1981.
G. H. Bantock, *Studies in the History of Educational Theory*, Vol. II: *The Minds and the Masses, 1760–1980*, Allen & Unwin, London, 1984.

Instrumentalist, Positivist, Behaviourist and Associated Approaches

M. J. Brezin, "Cognitive Monitoring: From Learning Theory to Instructional Applications", *Educational Communication and Technology*, XXVIII, No. 4, Winter 1980.
H. Bull, "The Use of Behavioural Objectives", *Journal of Further and Higher Education*, IX, No. 3, Autumn 1985. (An opposed viewpoint.)
C. Clark, "Education and Behaviour Modification", *Journal of Philosophy of Education*, XIII, 1979. (An opposed viewpoint.)
A. Givner & P. S. Graubard, *A Handbook of Behaviour Modification for the Classroom*, Rinehart & Winston, New York, 1974.
G. Martin & J. Pear, *Behaviour Modification: What it is and how to do it*, Prentice-Hall, Englewood Cliffs, N.J., 1978.
K. D. & S. G. O'Leary, *Classroom Management: The Successful Use of Behaviour Modification*, Pergamon Press, New York, 1977.
J. A. Poteet, *Behaviour Modification: A Practical Guide for Teachers*, University of London Press, London, 1974.
L. Waks, "Re-Examining the Validity of Arguments Against Behavioural Goals", *Educational Theory*, XXIX, No. 2, Spring 1973.
W. A. Wittich & C. F. Schuller, *Instructional Technology: Its Nature and Use*, 6th ed., Harper & Row, New York, 1979.

Parental Choice in Schooling

J. E. Coons & S. D. Sugarman, *Education by Choice: The Case for Family Control*, University of California Press, Berkeley, 1978.
M. & R. Friedman, *Free to Choose*, Secker & Warburg, London, 1978.
M. E. Manley-Casimir (Ed.), *Family Choice in Schooling: Issues and Dilemmas*, Lexington Books, Lexington, Mass., 1982.
A. E. Wise & L. Darling-Hammond, "Education by Voucher: Private Choice and the Public Interest", *Educational Theory*, XXXIV, No. 1, Winter 1984.

Christian Fundamentalists

J. C. Carper, "The Christian Day School Movement", *Educational Forum*, XLVII, Winter 1983.
E. Dobson & E. Hindson, *The Fundamentalist Phenomenon: The Resurgence of Conservative Christianity*, Doubleday, Garden City, New York, 1981.
J. Falwell, *Listen America!* Bantam Books, New York, 1980.
W. J. Reese, "Soldiers for Christ in the Army of God: The Christian School Movement in America", *Educational Theory*, XXXV, No. 2, Spring 1985.

RADICAL AND MARXIST WRITERS

(The following list covers a wide range of viewpoints but all are sharply opposed to the traditional approach to education.)

M. W. Apple, *Ideology and the Curriculum*, Routledge & Kegan Paul, London, 1979.
M. W. Apple, *Education and Power*, Routledge & Kegan Paul, London, 1982.
M. W. Apple (Ed.), *Cultural and Economic Reproduction in Education: Essays on Class, Ideology and the State*, Routledge & Kegan Paul, London, 1982.
P. Berger and T. Luckmann, *The Social Construction of Reality*, Penguin, Harmondsworth, 1967.
P. Bourdieu and J. C. Passeron, *Reproduction in Education, Society and Culture*, Sage, London, 1977.

S. Bowles and H. Gintis, *Schooling in Capitalist America*, Routledge & Kegan Paul, London, 1976.

W. Feinberg & H. Rosemont, Jr., *Work, Technology and Education: Dissenting Essays in the Intellectual Foundations of American Education*, University of Illinois Press, Urbana, 1975.

H. A. Giroux, *Ideology, Culture and the Process of Schooling*, Falmer Press, Sussex, 1981.

H. A. Giroux, *Theory and Resistance in Education: A Pedagogy for the Opposition*, Bergin Press, South Hadley, Mass., 1983.

C. Greer, *The Great School Legend: A Revisionist Interpretation of American Public Education*, Penguin, Harmondsworth, 1972.

K. Harris, *Education and Knowledge: The Structured Misrepresentation of Reality*, Routledge & Kegan Paul, 1979.

K. Harris, *Teachers and Classes: A Marxist Analysis*, Routledge and Kegan Paul, London, 1982.

C. J. Karier, P. Violas & J. Spring, *Roots of Crisis: American Education in the Twentieth Century*, Rand McNally, Chicago, 1973.

D. W. Livingstone, *Class, Ideologies and Educational Futures*, Falmer Press, Sussex, 1983.

M. R. Matthews, *The Marxist Theory of Schooling: A Study of Epistemology and Education*, Harvester Press, Sussex, 1980.

M. Sarup, *Marxism and Education*, Routledge & Kegan Paul, London, 1978.

R. Sharp & A. Green, *Education and Social Control: A Study of Progressive Primary Education*, Routledge & Kegan Paul, London, 1975.

R. Sharp, *Knowledge, Ideology and the Politics of Schooling: Towards a Marxist Analysis of Education*, Routledge and Kegan Paul, 1980.

P. Willis, *Learning to Labour: How Working Class Kids Get Working Class Jobs*, Saxon House, Farnborough, 1977.

M. Young, (Ed.) *Knowledge and Control: New Directions for the Sociology of Education*, Collier-Macmillan, London, 1971.

M. Young & G. Whitty (Eds.), *Society, State and Schooling*, Falmer Press, Sussex, 1977.

PAULO FREIRE

Works by:

Cultural Action for Freedom, Harvard Educational Review: Monograph No. 1, 1970, repr. Penguin, 1972.

Pedagogy of the Oppressed, Seabury Press, New York, 1970; repr. Penguin, 1972.

Education for Critical Consciousness (including "Education as the Practice of Freedom"), Seabury Press, New York, 1973.

"By Learning they can Teach", *Convergence*, VI, 1, 1973.

"Pilgrims of the Obvious", Symposium on Illich and Freire, *Risk* (World Council of Churches), XI, 1, 1975.

Pedagogy in Process: The Letters to Guinea-Bissau, Seabury Press, New York, 1978.

The Politics of Education: Culture, Power and Liberation, Bergin and Garvey, South Hadley, Mass., 1985.

Works about:

J. L. Elias, *Conscientization and Deschooling: Freire's and Illich's Proposals for Reshaping Society*, Westminster Press, Philadelphia, 1976.

R. Mackie (Ed.), *Literacy and Revolution: The Pedagogy of Paulo Freire*, Pluto Press, London, 1980.

HUMANISTIC EDUCATION AND RELATED MOVEMENTS

Abraham Maslow

Motivation and Personality, Harper & Row, New York, 1954.

Toward a Psychology of Being, Van Nostrand, New York, 1968.

F. Goble, *The Third Force: The Psychology of Abraham Maslow*, Pocket Books, New York, 1971.

Carl Rogers

On Becoming a Person: A Therapist's View of Psychotherapy, Constable, London, 1961.

Freedom to Learn, C. E. Merrill, Columbus, Ohio, 1969.

On Personal Power, Delacorte Press, New York, 1977.

Freedom to Learn in the 80s, C. E. Merrill, Columbus, Ohio, 1983.

Confluent Education

G. I. Brown, *Human Teaching for Human Learning*, Viking Press, New York, 1971, repr. Penguin, 1977.

G. I. Brown, *The Live Classroom: Innovation Through Confluent Education and Gestalt*, Viking Press, New York, 1975.

F. S. Perls, *The Gestalt Approach and Eye Witness to Therapy*, Bantam Books, New York, 1976.

Transpersonal Education

J. Fadiman & G. Hendricks (Eds.), *Transpersonal Education: A Curriculum for Feeling and Being*, Prentice-Hall, Englewood Cliffs, N.J., 1976.

J. Fadiman & R. D. Prager, *Personality and Personal Growth*, Harper & Row, New York, 1976.

B. Samples *et al*, *The Wholeschool Book: Teaching and Learning Late in the Twentieth Century*, Addison-Wesley, Reading, Mass., 1977.

General Works

R. Assagioli, *Psychosynthesis: A Manual of Principles and Techniques*, Turnstone Books, London, 1975. (First published 1965 by Psychosynthesis Research Foundation.)

H. C. Lyon, *Learning to Feel — Feeling to Learn: Humanistic Education for the Whole Man*, C. E. Merrill, Columbus, Ohio, 1971.

C. H. Patterson, *Humanistic Education*, Prentice-Hall, Englewood Cliffs, N.J., 1973.

D. A. Read & S. B. Simon (Eds.), *Humanistic Education Sourcebook*, Prentice-Hall, Englewood Cliffs, N.J., 1975.

T. B. Roberts (Ed.), *Four Psychologies Applied to Education: Freudian, Behavioural, Humanistic, Transpersonal*, John Wiley, New York, 1975.

J. Rowan, *Ordinary Ecstacy: Humanistic Psychology in Education*, Routledge & Kegan Paul, London, 1976.

A. Watts, *Psychotherapy East and West*, Pantheon Books, New York, 1961, repr. Penguin, 1973.

Index

Russian education, *see* Soviet education

Scholé
Greek concept of, 5; and origin of schools, 21
Illich's references to, 397, 429
School
institution of the,
history of, 5-6, 21, 395
Illich's proposals for "deschooling society", 390-97, 399-431
School and Society (Dewey)
Selections, 171-73
"Science of Learning and the Art of Teaching, The" (Skinner), 272
essay in full in Skinner: *Selections*, 272-82
Scientific Knowledge
Aristotle on, 89-90
basic to Skinner's planned society, 264*ff.*
contrasted to philosophy, 342
Dewey on, 199
Scientific method, 381
Dewey's belief in as the basic method of problem solving, 168-69, 186-94
see also Discovery learning, Inductive reasoning, Pragmatism
Sharp, R., 456
Significant innovation
concept of, 12-13
in contemporary educational thought, 441, 462
of Aristotle, 87-88
of Dewey, 166
of Illich, 390
of Makarenko, 216-17
of Neill, 311
of Peters, 345, 355
of Plato, 20
of Rousseau, 130
of Skinner, 264, 268
"Silver, men of", *see* Auxiliaries
Skinner, B. F.
Biography, 261-62
Commentary, 261-71
compared with Plato, 267-68
Illich mentions, 402
influence on contemporary educational thinkers, 448
offers a new version of traditional position, 15, 214, 268
Peters mentions, 387
Select Bibliography, 271
Selections, 272-304
Smith, Adam, 450, 453
Social context
deeper awareness of social and political context in recent educational thinking, 441-63 *passim*
Social Contract, The (Rousseau)
idea of government as a social contract, 122
Social control in education
Dewey on, 166, 171, 205-11

Makarenko on, 221-23, 233-60 *passim*
Skinner on, 265-71, 276-79, 283-305
see also Discipline, Permissiveness, Punishment, Rewards
Social problems
education and contemporary social issues and problems, 226, 264-70, 292, 297-98, 303-4, 336-39, 352-53, 393, 460-463
Socialisation, *see* Society, education for
Society
education for,
Aristotle on, 86, 109
Dewey on, 167-69, 195
Makarenko on, 217-26, 228-60 *passim*
Peters on, 358*ff.*
Plato on, 26-27, 30-31, 31*ff.*
raises fundamental issues in education, 16, 352-53, 462
Rousseau on, 127, 133-34, 151-52, 155-60
Skinner on, 264-71, 292*ff.*
socialisation as one meaning of education, 1-3
see also Individual, Moral education, State
Socrates
his use of elenctic method, 29
his use of maieutic as exemplified in the questioning of the slave boy in *Meno*, 23; Peters on, 384; Skinner on, 284
influence on Plato, 20, 29-30
Peters on, as an educator, 388
Peters refers to his moral theory, 374, 385, 388
Soul
Aristotle on the, 83, 89-90, 93-95
Soviet education, 215-26, 228*ff.*
Spencer, H., 453
Stalin, J., 216
State, the
and education, issues involved, 16
Aristotle on forms of government, 85
role of in education
Aristotle on, 85-86, 106-7, 109
Dewey on, 169
Friedman on, 450-51
Rousseau on, 123, 127-28, 133
see also, Society
Studia humanitatis
Greek and Latin dominance of university curricula in 19th century, 163
Greek and Latin studies in Rousseau's scheme, 160-61
in modern communist form as polytechnisation, 224
Renaissance ideal of education, 126
seen by Dewey as potentially illiberal, 169
see also Liberal education
Subjectivism (in morals)
in Illich, 394
Peters discusses, 354, 377-82, 442-43
see also Morality, Objectivism, Pragmatism, Value judgments

Ollscoil na hÉireann, Gaillimh

3 1111 40079 0109